POLITICS IN LATIN AMERICA

POLITICS IN LATIN AMERICA
The Quests for Development, Liberty, and Governance

Charles H. Blake

HOUGHTON MIFFLIN COMPANY   Boston   New York

Publisher: Charles Hartford
Sponsoring Editor: Katherine Meisenheimer
Development Editor: Terri Wise
Editorial Assistant: Kendra Johnson
Project Editor: Reba Libby
Editorial Assistant: Rachel Zanders
Manufacturing Coordinator: Carrie Wagner
Senior Composition Buyer: Sarah Ambrose
Senior Art and Design Coordinator: Jill Haber Atkins
Executive Marketing Manager: Nicola Poser
Marketing Assistant: Kathleen Mellon

Cover image: Harold Burch Design/NYC.

Printed in the U.S.A.

Library of Congress Catalog Card Number: 2003109845

ISBN: 0-618-21552-2

1 2 3 4 5 6 7 8 9-MP-08 07 06 05 04

Contents

Chapter Four
The Quest for Development, Liberty, and Governance   79

Chapter Five
Argentina   123

Chapter Six
Brazil   165

Preface

FOR MUCH OF THE TWENTIETH CENTURY, many Latin American countries alternated between periods of democratic and authoritarian rule. In any given decade between 1900 and 1979, several countries had non-democratic political systems; at times, most people in Latin America lived under dictatorships. In response, textbooks on Latin American politics in the last third of the twentieth century tended to emphasize the fragility of democracy within an economic context characterized by greater scarcity than readers in industrialized democracies were accustomed to considering. Rather than focusing on the dynamics of democratic rule, they focused on the alternation between non-democratic and democratic political systems. In doing so, many scholars assumed that the specific dynamics of democratic politics had minimal or sporadic importance in Latin America: they believed that democratic institutions would be ignored or eliminated if they constrained the interests of the powerful. Texts provided historical narratives that illustrated the frequent collapse of democratic political systems. An analysis of recent political events typically comprised (well) under half of the content of those textbooks.

At the start of the twenty-first century, that type of approach to the study of politics in Latin America seems incomplete. The historical alternation between democracy and dictatorship forms a central part of the background against which domestic politics in Latin American countries unfolds—but it is not the fulcrum of contemporary political life. Since the 1980s, electoral politics has been in place in nearly all of Latin America. The move away from outright dictatorship in the region opens up a more complex political landscape. To understand that more complicated environment, one needs to consider the major facets of democratic politics. This calls on texts to discuss more issues and to cover their recent dynamics in more detail.

This textbook focuses on three issues that are examined in most courses on Latin American politics taught today: the quest for economic development, the quest for sufficient liberty, and the quest for effective governance. Governments in Latin America and around the world make choices regarding models of economic policy, models of rights protection, and models of executive power. This textbook provides students with a conceptual framework for evaluating both the substantive issues at stake and the political dynamics of these choices. In turn, the text also examines the relationship between development, liberty, and governance and the prospects for democratic consolidation.

Despite the more widespread resilience of electoral politics in Latin America in recent years, we should not blithely assume that democratic rule is now consolidated in the region, much less inevitable. On the contrary, contemporary elected leaders face many challenges. Nine of the eighteen Latin American democracies in place since the 1980s have had one or more presidents that did not finish their elected terms. Although none of those elected leaders was replaced by a military dictator, it is quite possible that some (perhaps many) Latin American countries may abandon electoral politics in the future if they cannot find a path toward better outcomes in the realm of development, liberty, and governance. Furthermore, even when the leaders of the executive and legislative branches are chosen via elections, elections alone do not guarantee that other features of democracy—including respect for basic civil liberties and respect for the rule of law—are fully in place.

Many recent scholarly books and articles have taken up these concerns regarding the nature and future of democracy across Latin America as a whole. However, these books tend to assume prior knowledge about Latin American countries and are usually written for a scholarly audience. In turn, most Latin American politics textbooks are written with students in mind but do not reflect political science scholarship very well. That is a shame because there is a rich analytical literature on the dynamics of democratic politics in the field of comparative politics in general as well as on Latin America, in particular.

This textbook tries to fill the gap left by these existing books through an examination of contemporary quest for development, liberty, and governance. These three themes have two central pedagogical advantages. First, the substantive importance of each issue in its own right is readily apparent to students. Second, these three issues also provide a useful bridge to the theoretical literature on political development as each is tied to most scholars' examinations of the dynamics of political legitimacy. That research links support for political systems to economic outcomes (development) and to governing procedures (liberty and governance). Because economic outcomes play a key role in cultivating popular support for political regimes, it is important to consider a regime's economic policy decisions. In turn, the role of governing procedures in building legitimacy underscores the importance of the protection of basic liberties and the manner in which government decisions are made (especially the role of the presidency).

The heart of this book examines the political dynamics of these three quests in seven countries. Argentina, Brazil, Chile, Cuba, and Mexico are included because these are among the most important countries in the region: most instructors examine them in their courses. Guatemala and Venezuela have been included due to their visibility in the debate over this text's three framing issues. Each experienced a serious debate over the nature of executive power in the 1990s. Human and civil rights have also been hotly debated in the two countries as Guatemala has wrestled with past human rights violations while the government led by Hugo Chávez in Venezuela has faced charges of restrictions on several basic rights. Inclusion of these countries also diversifies the selection of economic contexts examined in this text: Guatemala is the poorest of these seven countries, while Venezuela is the country that has stayed the closest to the state capitalist economic model during the last ten years. Without the inclusion of Venezuela, our consideration of contemporary economic choices would be incomplete. Beyond these two countries' pedagogical usefulness in exploring these guiding themes, Guatemala is one of an important minority of Latin American countries with a very sizable indigenous population and also provides a window into Central America within this text.

THE STRUCTURE OF THIS BOOK

This book examines contemporary responses to the quests for development, liberty, and governance in Latin America using a consistent conceptual framework. Chapter One provides a conversational introduction to the challenges of politics amid economic scarcity, highlighting differences in the personal (and national) experiences of two women born in 1974 in the United States and in Peru. The introduction goes on to introduce the three quests to be considered with reference to these two differing contexts. Chapter Two reviews Latin America's economic and political evolution from 1492 to 1979. This historical background focuses on the political dynamics of the quests for development, liberty, and governance over time. Chapter Three introduces several central components of contemporary political life in Latin America from 1980 to the early twenty-first century, placing today's Latin American democracies in a third wave of democratization in the region and around the world. The longevity and robustness of these democracies depends in good measure on elected governments' effectiveness in pursuing the quests for development, liberty, and governance.

Chapter Four provides a conceptual framework for analyzing these three quests. It begins with the debate over what constitutes economic development and then examines various schools of thought regarding the appropriate role of the government in the economy. Chapter Four then focuses on two major contemporary issues regarding liberty: the treatment of past human rights violations and the effort to protect civil, economic, and physical liberties today. The examination of governance focuses on the distribution of power in the political system with emphasis on the role of the chief executive in the political system.

Then, in Chapters Five through Eleven, the book examines these three issues in seven countries—Argentina, Brazil, Chile, Cuba, Guatemala, Mexico, and Venezuela. Each of these chapters begins with the historical context that forms the backdrop of today's political dynamics in the country, and then the bulk of each chapter focuses on the contemporary era. Each country chapter then presents the country's basic government institutions and major political actors.

Then, the quests for development, liberty, and governance are examined through a discussion of contemporary governments in each country. The closing portion of each country chapter highlights some future challenges facing each country in its pursuit of development, liberty, and governance.

Chapter Twelve wraps up the text by reviewing these seven countries' choices regarding the three major quests from a broader cross-national perspective within Latin America. After considering collectively the experiences of the seven countries at the heart of this book, we consider events and conditions elsewhere in Latin America. In the process, we will observe that the trends across these seven countries reflect broader political patterns visible in the rest of the region. Following this consideration of the quests for development, liberty, and governance in Latin America as a whole, we return to the question asked at the end of Chapter Four: what are the prospects for democratic consolidation? We explore the relationship between success in these three quests and the prospects for building enduring democracies.

Book Features

Several additional features enhance the usefulness of this book. Tables, figures, maps, and photos illustrate major points and convey important information throughout the book. For Chapters Two through Eleven, you will find a list of suggested readings covering issues related to each chapter in greater detail. You will also find a series of questions and suggested activities at the close of each of those chapters. In addition to analytical questions, these activities always include a recommended film and an activity that involves exploration of online resources. At the end of the text, there is a glossary of key terms (presented in boldface throughout the text) and an index.

Five series of feature boxes highlight important issues across the text. Three series appear throughout Chapters Two through Eleven:

- *Concepts in Action* boxes clarify a political or economic concept at hand in a given chapter. Concepts covered include bureaucratic-authoritarianism, clientelism, command economics, corporatism, dependency theory, electoral systems, exchange rate policy, judicial decision-making, land reform, and praetorianism.

- *Governing Strategies* boxes discuss the problems faced by major political leaders and the sorts of tactics they used in pursuit of their respective objectives. The list of leaders analyzed includes Salvador Allende, Jacobo Arbenz, Fernando Belaúnde, Rómulo Betancourt, Alberto Fujimori, Juscelino Kubitschek, and Evita Perón.

- *Global Perspectives* boxes compare the experiences of countries inside and outside of Latin America on several political and economic issues. The issues examined include the "Asian" economic crisis of 1997–1998, the debt crisis of the 1980s, indigenous movements, international human rights trials, military coups, regional economic integration, the relationship between resource wealth and democratization, the size of government, and state capitalist economic policies.

A fourth series of boxes, *The Peruvian Experience*, appears only in Chapters Two, Three, and Four. This feature series helps to humanize the regional overview in those chapters by considering some of these regional trends through the lens of concrete experiences in Peru. Peru has not been highlighted in these early chapters because it is somehow the most representative Latin American country. No single country can speak for the distinctive experiences of nineteen separate nation-states. However, Peru provides a useful entry point into each of the three major quests examined across the pages of this book.

A fifth series of feature boxes, *Research Questions*, appears in Chapters Five through Eleven. These boxes present contemporary cross-national political science research on questions relevant for each of the country chapters; each box is based on a recent study in an academic journal. These articles explore questions such as:

- Under what conditions is the public more likely to support market-oriented economic reform?
- Under what conditions are governments likely to develop civilian control of the military?
- Under what conditions are presidents likely to receive legislative support?

Online Resources

The website that accompanies this text includes teaching resources for instructors and learning and study resources for students, including chapter outlines, annotated web links that present several major online resources for the study of Latin American politics, bibliographies, and more. The issues examined in the *Research Questions* series can be explored in greater detail by using the bibliographies provided on the website. As a reader of this book, you are encouraged to make use of these bibliographies, suggested web links, and other online resources to learn more about particular issues and countries that interest you.

ACKNOWLEDGMENTS

Nobody writes a book alone. Over the years, I have benefited from many formal and informal discussions with colleagues and students at James Madison University. I have also profited from countless conversations about politics with scholars, government officials, and ordinary citizens in and out of Latin America. In particular, each of the scholars who reviewed this manuscript provided useful feedback that helped to improve the content, organization, and pedagogy of this book: Henry A. Dietz, University of Texas; Lawrence Littwin, California State University-Northridge; Cynthia McClintock, George Washington University; Jose M. Vadi, California State Polytechnic University at Pomona; Waltraud Q. Morales, University of Central Florida; David Scott Palmer, Boston University; Jeff Ryan, University of Arkansas; Bruce Wilson, University of Central Florida; Gary Mounce, University of Texas-Pan American; and Brian F. Crisp, University of Arizona. I owe a special debt of gratitude to León Bendesky for nurturing my interest in Latin American politics during my days as a college undergraduate. In the years to come, I welcome people reading this book to share your comments with me or with Houghton Mifflin. I am perhaps easiest to reach via e-mail (*blakech@jmu.edu*).

Many talented individuals at Houghton Mifflin worked to bring this book to life. Mary Daugherty and Katherine Meisenheimer served as excellent sounding boards for designing a new textbook; their counsel and enthusiasm proved central to carrying out this endeavor. Terri Wise and Julie Hassel provided essential editorial advice during the development of this book. Reba Libby ably guided me through the various stages of the production process with Rachel Zanders's help, while Nicola Poser designed a marketing plan that gave potential readers an opportunity to evaluate this book.

Ultimately, family sustains each of us in all that we attempt in life. I could not have written this book without the love and support of many people. Beyond acknowledging their help here, I hope that I am capable of providing them with similarly generous love and support in the months and years to come.

List of Features

Chapter Four
The Quest for Development, Liberty, and Governance   79

Chapter Five
Argentina   123

Chapter Six
Brazil 165

Chapter Seven
Chile 207

Chapter Eleven
Venezuela 369

Chapter Twelve
Challenges and Choices in the Twenty-First Century 411

CHAPTER 1

An Introduction to Latin American Politics

A NICE HOUSE, a livable environment, a bright financial future for subsequent generations—these are central economic components of the "American dream." Another strand of that vision focuses on liberty—freedom of expression, freedom of worship, freedom of organization, and freedom from harm. A third dimension of the dream focuses on hopes for a responsive, effective, and accountable government. People in the United States and elsewhere can and do disagree about the relative priority of these three sets of goals. People also differ in their preferred approaches to attaining them. Nonetheless, many people around the world desire these goals—economic development, sufficient liberty, and good governance. In short, the so-called American dream is one specific vision of a more universal series of quests.

Citizens everywhere hope that their government works toward the attainment of development, liberty, and governance. However, government itself is not always presented as the best path to these goals. Some people mobilize politically to induce government to launch new programs to improve their lives; others speak out against those policies in the belief that government should launch no policy at all. Politics centers on citizens' efforts to influence government decisions that they hope will improve their lives.

This book introduces the politics of the nineteen nation-states that comprise Latin America. These countries have roots in the contact between indigenous peoples of the hemisphere and the Spanish and Portuguese colonizers.[1] Latin America holds about one-twelfth of the world's population on one-sixth of the world's land mass and accounts for one-sixteenth of global economic activity. The countries that emerged from colonies established by Britain, France, and Holland in the Americas are also worthy of study, but they are not the focus of our attention in this book.

What path should we follow to try to understand how politics unfolds in these nineteen Latin American countries? This book employs an analytic framework that acknowledges some political challenges faced by all societies around the world—the quest for development, the quest for liberty, and the quest for governance. Despite the universality of these challenges, over the course of this book we will examine several facets of political life in Latin America that differ significantly from common perceptions of politics in the United States and in other wealthy democracies. In particular, we will see many instances in which the relative poverty of Latin American economies heightens political conflict over development, liberty, and governance.

A TALE OF TWO WOMEN AND TWO COUNTRIES

We will begin to explore the diverse landscape of Latin American politics by moving from things familiar to things less familiar. That journey begins with the tale of two women born in 1974 in two different countries: Jennifer from the United States and Cecilia from Peru. Two people can never represent all aspects of their respective countries, but Jennifer's and Cecilia's stories highlight several important issues.

Jennifer's Story

Jennifer was born and raised in a middle-class suburb outside Detroit, Michigan. Jennifer and her older sister Anne were far too young to remember the Watergate scandals that culminated in the resignation of President Richard Nixon in August 1974. Anne can remember gas lines caused by increases in the price of oil in 1978–1979 as well as the emergence of double-digit inflation in 1979, inflation that reached a peak of 13.5 percent in 1980. Jennifer can vaguely recall people discussing the failed attempt to assassinate President Ronald Reagan in 1981. Her family lived comfortably but not luxuriously while she was growing up. Her father was a construction supervisor and her mother was an elementary school teacher. In the 1980s, the U.S. economy grew by an average of 2.8 percent per year. Inflation averaged about 5.6 percent and the average annual unemployment rate was 7.3 percent.[2]

As Jennifer entered college in fall 1992 (supported by student loans and a part-time job), she began to follow politics a little more closely. She first voted in the 1992 election in which Ross Perot formed a new political party (the Reform Party) that received one-fifth of the presidential vote only to fizzle out over the remainder of the decade. While in college, Jennifer witnessed the 1994 congressional elections in which the Republican Party won control of the House of Representatives from the Democratic Party for the first time since her parents were in elementary school. On graduating from college with a degree in political science in 1996 amid a booming economy, Jennifer took an entry-level management trainee position with Beatrice, a multinational food company. As she began her managerial career, she watched evening news reports of partisan conflict in the legislature between Democrats and Republicans over the impeachment of President William Clinton. In the 1990s, the average annual economic growth rate was 3.0 percent. Inflation averaged about 3.0 percent and unemployment averaged 5.7 percent.[3] The gross domestic product (GDP) per person was $34,142 by 2000. According to this particular measure of national wealth, the United States was the second richest country in the world.[4]

In November 2000, Jennifer voted in one of the closest presidential elections in U.S. history. A series of legal challenges to the vote count were resolved in hotly debated decisions by state and federal courts—including the Supreme Court of the United States. Although Al Gore lost that election and disagreed publicly with several of the courts' decisions, he never questioned the authority of the courts to resolve the conflicts at issue. In 2001, Jennifer was promoted and earned $39,000, which was about 10 percent more than the median U.S. full-time wage earner received in 2001.

Cecilia's Story

Cecilia was born and raised in a lower-class suburb of Lima, Peru. Cecilia and her younger brother Raúl do not remember the August 1975 coup d'état that replaced the military government headed by General Juan Velasco with a new military government led by General Francisco Morales. Her older sisters Marisa and Victoria lived through the economic crisis of the late 1970s, which formed the backdrop of a return to democracy in 1980. Cecilia can vaguely recall people discussing the serious economic problems faced by the winner of those 1980 elections, President Fernando Belaúnde, the leader of the Popular Action (AP) party. Her family struggled amid this economic crisis. Her father worked in construction but found it difficult to find steady work in the 1980s. Cecilia's mother, a cleaning woman at the Ministry of Labor, watched her government salary fail to keep up with inflation. By 1985, her salary had only 75 percent of the purchasing power that it had held in 1980. In the 1980s, the Peruvian economy stagnated—shrinking by an average of 1.2 percent per year. Consumer prices rose by an average of 481 percent per year, and the annual average unemployment rate was 7.5 percent.[5]

Faced with these trying economic circumstances, Cecilia and her siblings left school to find work. Cecilia had been having problems in school because at home her parents spoke mostly Quechua, an indigenous language spoken by about 12 percent of Peruvians, while all of her classes were in Spanish. When Cecilia finished fifth grade in 1985, she found work as a housekeeper in downtown Lima with her oldest sister Marisa. In national elections held that year, the American Popular Revolutionary Alliance (APRA) won control of both the legislature and the presidency for the first time. Newly elected President Alan García announced that Peru would limit payments on its foreign debt. The negative reaction of investors and banks to this policy helped to produce an economic free fall in the late 1980s. The economy shrank by over 25 percent in the years

1988–1990 and inflation skyrocketed. By 1990, the annual inflation rate reached 7,650 percent and political conflict heated up as well. The Shining Path guerrilla movement increased its attacks on government officials and on potential rivals for popular support, such as candidates for local government and community organizers. Cecilia's sister Victoria was killed for helping to start a neighborhood soup kitchen.

In this troubled context, Cecilia began to follow politics more closely, and she remembers vividly the 1990 presidential elections. In a runoff election, Alberto Fujimori, an obscure university president running as the candidate of a newly formed political party, *Cambio 90* (Change 90), defeated acclaimed novelist Mario Vargas Llosa, who had run as the candidate of a coalition of several established political parties. Fujimori launched economic austerity measures designed to reduce inflation, and he employed more force in dealing with guerrilla movements. Then, on April 5, 1992, Fujimori announced that he was dissolving the existing legislature and judiciary. He stated that he would rule by decree indefinitely to combat the economic and political crisis with a freer hand. In so doing, Fujimori appeared to have the backing of much of the armed forces. International criticism of this unconstitutional closure of the legislature helped to speed the creation of a new political system for Peru. The new constitution concentrated more authority in the hands of the president and permitted the reelection of the president for the first time in over a century. During this transition process, special forces units of the Peruvian military gave a boost to Fujimori's popularity by capturing the leader of the Shining Path guerrillas, Abimael Guzmán. Cecilia first voted in the controversial October 1993 referendum in which the new constitution was approved with the support of a narrow majority—52 percent—of the voters.

Cecilia continued to live with her family on the outskirts of Lima. Every day she rode the bus for ninety minutes to the other side of the city, where she found work in 1995 in fish processing. Returning after what tended to be a physically tiring workday, during 1995 Cecilia watched Fujimori win reelection comfortably while his movement gained control of the legislature. Many new political parties formed in opposition to Fujimori, while the dominant parties of the past faded from the scene. In his second term, controversy grew over government efforts to repress the opposition and to pressure the news media. In 1997, Fujimori's movement approved a rules change of questionable constitutionality that permitted him to seek an unprecedented third consecutive term. A supreme court packed with Fujimori appointees declared that Fujimori could run for the presidency again in 2000. In the years that followed, several new opposition parties decided to back a single candidate, Alejandro Toledo, in an effort to defeat Fujimori. In the 1990s, the economy grew by 4.7 percent a year. Inflation averaged about 884 percent, although after the economic crisis of 1990–1991, the annual inflation rate dropped to 10.5 percent for the remainder of the 1990s. Unemployment averaged 8.5 percent. The GDP per person was $4,799 in 2000—making Peru the seventy-sixth wealthiest country in the world by this standard.[6]

Alberto Fujimori's controversial "self-coup" reshaped Peru's political institutions.   AP/Wide World Photos.

In the 2000 elections, Fujimori just missed winning the majority of the vote needed to avoid a runoff election. However, many foreign and domestic observers found fault with the election process and Toledo refused to accept the results as legitimate. He claimed that irregularities in the voter registration lists and in the admission of voters at the polls had produced a fraudulent victory for Fujimori. Toledo then refused to participate in the runoff presidential elections that Fujimori won with 52 percent of the vote. More street demonstrations followed. Cecilia found it difficult to get across Lima by bus once the news media aired videotape showing one of Fujimori's chief advisers, Vladimiro Montesinos, bribing a legislator to switch over to Fujimori's party. Fujimori announced on September 16, 2000, that he would call for new elections in 2001. Then in November he resigned from office while in Japan. Alejandro Toledo subsequently won the presidency in a runoff election against former president Alan García in May 2001. Cecilia decided to take additional work with another fish-processing plant. By working over ninety hours per week, she earned $9,200 annually, which was about 10 percent more than the average wage earner received in 2001.[7]

Comparing Two Lives and Two Political Environments

Jennifer and Cecilia have lived through personal experiences that are truly universal. Each has had her ups and downs growing up with her parents and siblings. As adults, each is deciding whether or not she wants to get married (and to whom). Jennifer and Cecilia both recognize that their incomes are above average within their respective economies, but each aspires to earn more money as time goes on.

Amid these similarities, many contrasts come to mind when we compare these two stories. Given stark societal contrasts, it should not surprise us that the political backdrops of their lives also differ notably. In Peru, the military has played a much more visible role in national politics—at times by holding office directly (as in the 1970s) and at other times indirectly (as in its support for President Fujimori's "self-coup" in 1992). While politically motivated violence occurs in different forms throughout the world, it has occurred more frequently in Peru than in the United States. In the United States, the same two parties have dominated national politics since the middle of the nineteenth century. Meanwhile, in Peru, the major parties of the 1980s lost power during the 1990s to an entirely new movement (*Cambio 90*), which in turn was replaced by another recently formed party (*Perú Posible*) at the dawn of the twenty-first century. While political life in the United States always has been filled with partisan conflict, as exemplified by the contentious 2000 presidential elections, no major U.S. presidential candidate in the years 1976 to 2000 rejected outright an entire electoral result, as Alejandro Toledo did in 2000.

The level of political conflict in Peru has tended to be higher than it has been in the United States. The relative poverty of Peru in comparison to the United States heightens political conflict over economic concerns. Recall that Jennifer and Cecilia both have slightly above-average incomes in their respective countries, but Jennifer earns over four times as much as Cecilia, and Cecilia works twice the hours per week that Jennifer does. In addition, Peru has experienced more conflict over the formal and informal rules of government, as the controversy surrounding the Fujimori government illustrates. In short, while people in the United States and Peru share some beliefs and some common experiences, political dynamics in the two countries over the years have exhibited more differences than similarities.

THE CHALLENGES OF DEVELOPMENT, LIBERTY, AND GOVERNANCE

Each society in Latin America and around the world pursues development, liberty, and governance. The debate over what constitutes economic development, sufficient liberty, and effective governance differs both over time and from country to country. In Latin America, this debate has been shaped by economic conditions, societal norms, and political dynamics that frequently differ from those prevailing in the United States.

The Search for Economic Development

One challenge faced by all governments emerges from citizens' desires for economic well-being. All citizens agree that government should take some actions to promote economic development. However, there is vibrant disagreement in most societies about the appropriate responses to two key questions:

- *What are the major defining elements and priorities of national economic development?* Some people focus on the growth of economic activity as the central goal of economic development. Others counter that if the fruits of national economic growth fail to reach a sufficient number of citizens, then poverty reduction and improving the equity with which income and wealth are distributed become core concerns. Still others focus on the diversification of national economic activity; they argue that excessive dependence on a few economic sectors makes a country's economy too sensitive to international market fluctuations in those sectors. In the late twentieth century, an additional stream of thought reemerged, calling for more emphasis on the sustainability of current economic activities over time. Among those who emphasize each of these aspects of economic development, opinions differ regarding how to measure progress.

- *What actions in the realm of economic policy should government take to help produce economic development?* In addition to disagreement about the definition of economic development, considerable debate usually exists over the role of government in promoting its achievement. This debate exists even among citizens, politicians, and analysts who share similar definitions of development. At one end of the spectrum, some advocate placing nearly all economic decisions in the hands of government. Over the course of the twentieth century, command economies were established in several countries around the globe—including Cuba within the Americas. At the other extreme, others argue that government should intervene rarely in economic matters—leaving most matters in the hands of market forces. Between these two extremes are several different mixed approaches to economic policy in which government exercises its power in various ways while also leaving an important role for private economic decision-making.

Around the world, political debates over development priorities and economic policies frequently link goals to policy approaches. Those whose primary goal is growth tend to favor market-oriented policies, while those favoring redistribution, diversification, or sustainability tend to call for some form of government intervention. For example, advocates of income redistribution might ask governments to tax wealthier citizens at a higher rate to ease the burden on poor citizens. They might also favor spending on welfare policies to provide income subsidies or educational benefits to the impoverished. Growth-first advocates often counter that government intervention hampers growth.

In the United States, the government debate over economic policy-making since the 1930s has tended to focus almost exclusively on the middle range of options between the two extremes of large-scale intervention and no intervention at all. Within that middle range, governments have tended to favor private economic activity unless unfavorable outcomes over time built a visible rationale and political pressure for government intervention. Skepticism regarding government intervention is sufficiently widespread among U.S. voters and government officials to motivate most advocates of increased government activity to pursue limited and incremental changes in policy.

In studying economic policy in Latin America, we will see a much more complex and shifting landscape in which nearly the entire range of policy options occupies some portion of the public debate from 1930 to the present. This debate takes place in a context defined by persistent poverty: just under half of Latin America was living on less than $2.00 per day at the start of the twenty-first century. From 1930 to the early 1980s, the prevailing view in most Latin American countries favored considerable government intervention in the economy. From 1985 to the present, there has been a sea change in the debate over economic policy: market-oriented policy ideas have become more visible both in public opinion and in the words and actions of government officials. In this book, we will analyze the political dynamics of this shift in economic policy as well as the economic outcomes associated with these changes.

The Search for Sufficient Liberty

The quest for economic development is one of several fundamental tasks common to all governments and societies. A second challenge emerges from citizens' desires for a certain freedom of action that they want government to nurture and protect. This search for liberty is also subject to debate within and across countries. The debate revolves around two key concerns:

■ *What liberties should be considered inviolable?* Advocates of inviolable liberties speak the language of rights. Others counter that no freedoms should be universal across all governments and all circumstances. Civil and political rights at issue include freedom of speech, freedom of the press, freedom of association, freedom of organization, the right to a fair and impartial trial, and the right to vote in the election of certain government officials. While in the twenty-first century there has been minimal debate over the desirability of these rights in the abstract, considerable disagreement exists over whether these rights are inviolable or subject to limitation. Possible limitations include the declaration of a state of siege that might suspend some or all civil rights in the name of a national emergency, and the assertion that some nonviolent forms of political expression are inherently dangerous. The debate over liberty also encompasses physical and economic rights, including the right to life, liberty, and security of person and the right to hold property. At times, these physical and economic rights can come into conflict with civil and political liberties. For example, amid concerns over crime, some may advocate changes in judicial procedure that modify the standards regarding what constitutes a fair trial.

■ *What steps should governments take in an effort to protect liberties?* Protection of these rights involves steps taken by governments to discourage infringements on liberty as well as actions taken to identify and to punish those who engage in such activity. Some call for highly specific laws to clarify the boundaries of liberty on various issues. Others prefer the creation of a set of general principles that can then be interpreted on a case-by-case basis by judges. In either scenario, effective protection of rights requires the creation of sufficient law enforcement capacity to identify violations of liberty and to prosecute those responsible. At times, concerns over the willingness of some governments to turn a blind eye toward certain violations of liberty have given rise to calls for the international community to intervene. Efforts to establish some human rights as inviolable within international law have produced binding agreements regarding genocide (1949), racial discrimination (1965), discrimination against women (1979), torture (1984), and children's rights (1989). Disappointment regarding enforcement of some international agreements—particularly in the wake of genocidal incidents in the former Yugoslavia and in Rwanda—helped to generate support for the creation of the International Criminal Court (ICC) in 2002 with jurisdiction over crimes against humanity. While the ICC may eventually change the historic dynamics of some human rights cases, until now liberties have been enforced primarily on a country-by-country basis.

In the realm of liberty, in the United States there has been no interruption in the principle of the right to vote. Elections have been held on schedule and the results have been respected over two centuries of U.S. history. While the principle of the right to vote has been inviolable in the United States, there has been disagreement over time regarding who is entitled to vote. At the birth of the U.S. democracy, only males with sufficient property and wealth could vote. Over the course of the nineteenth and twentieth centuries, restrictions based on wealth, gender, and racial origin were removed. Similarly, while freedom of speech and many other civil rights are entrenched in the Bill of Rights, the U.S. government has tried at times to redefine certain civil rights as conditional. Sometimes the courts have overturned those actions, while in some other situations the actions have been upheld. Debate in and out of the legal system regarding balancing the rights of those accused of criminal activity and the rights of the victims has been even more vigorous—particularly over the past half century. The 1960s and 1970s expanded legal and procedural protections for those accused of criminal acts. In subsequent decades, several decisions have limited those protections to reduce the chances that criminals could escape conviction due to procedural problems in investigative or trial processes.

In Latin America, the debate over the number of basic rights and their inviolability has been even more divisive and controversial. In quite a few countries, military governments in the 1970s trampled liberties that many people consider core civil rights, such as the freedoms of speech, assembly, organization, and association. These governments also violated several basic human rights—by detaining citizens without trial, by torturing and raping citizens under detention, and by executing citizens without trial. Outrage over these events has generated one of the most visible political issues of the late twentieth and early twenty-first centuries. Protests against human rights violations often played a role in restoring democracy in these countries during the 1980s. In turn, these democratic governments faced political and judicial demands stemming from allegations of human rights violations occurring during prior governments. While many human rights activists believe that current governments must allow the accused to be prosecuted, other citizens have claimed that these past actions were justifiable in the name of national defense and national security.

In addition to concerns over past crimes, Latin American governments face serious concerns over contemporary liberty. Debate continues over which civil rights merit further government protection and under what circumstances. For example, is freedom of the press an absolute, or should governments pass laws that impose harsh penalties for media stories that cannot be proven to be true? Physical and economic rights have become increasingly visible issues as crime rates have increased in many countries during the 1980s and 1990s. The right to life itself is threatened: homicide rates rose in most countries in Latin America toward the end of the twentieth century. In Peru, the murder rate increased exponentially between 1980 and 1995. In addition to concern over crime, judicial reform has become a central issue: many countries attempted to reform judicial systems that had been notorious for their slowness and were often questioned in terms of their impartiality. We will examine both past and present concerns over liberty in our analysis of Latin American politics.

The Search for Good Governance

The search for governance is never-ending. In every country, citizens would like their government to respond quickly and effectively to pressing national priorities. People disagree, however, about which issues are most important and about how they should be addressed. Amid this disagreement, as citizens we would like the government to address expeditiously the issues each of us considers important and to take the course of action that each of us believes is appropriate. This state of affairs creates a tension over the nature of good governance. That tension resides in the tradeoff between two key questions:

- *How important is it for government to be able to act quickly?* The more quickly one wants government to act, the more likely one prefers procedures that centralize government power in fewer hands. At the extreme end of this continuum, one can envision an absolute monarchy or a dictatorship in which all power resides in the hands of a single person. At the other end of the spectrum, one can think of the direct democracy of the town meeting, in which all citizens have an equal say in making government decisions. Between these extremes lie several ways of dividing power in nondemocratic governments and many forms of representative democracy in which power is divided differently among elected and appointed officials. In times of crisis, demands can emerge to concentrate power to respond rapidly to the

problems of the day. During the Great Depression of the 1930s, new legislation and some unilateral actions by the administration of Franklin Delano
Roosevelt (FDR) in the United States concentrated new powers in the executive branch. As we saw above, President Alberto Fujimori in Peru justified his
1992 closure of the legislature as a means to confront the twin perils of
guerrilla violence and economic crisis.

■ *How important are government procedures that permit adequate representation and debate over what constitutes the national interest?* The more one
values a search for consensus over what government should be doing, the
more likely one is to favor procedures that disperse power among many offices and individuals. While FDR's actions in the 1930s enjoyed support in
many segments of U.S. society, other groups and individuals opposed quite
a few of his New Deal policy initiatives. Part of the opposition resided in the
U.S. Supreme Court, which overturned some of his policies. In frustration,
FDR asked the legislature to expand the size of the Supreme Court so that he
could appoint new justices presumably more supportive of his ideas. While
the legislature supported many of FDR's initiatives, it ultimately did not increase the number of justices. In Peru, many citizens supported Fujimori's
1992 "self-coup." But in the years since the 1993 Peruvian constitution was
passed, many Peruvians wondered whether or not the new constitution
concentrated too much power in the hands of the presidency.

All countries debate what mix of speed and consensus building constitutes
effective governance. Throughout this book, we will see that this search for governance produces different choices and disagreements about how government
should be organized. In analyzing contemporary governance in Latin America,
we will pay particular attention to the issue of executive power. How much
power should be held by the chief executive relative to the other two branches
of government (the legislature and the judiciary) and relative to society as a
whole?

Regardless of the degree of presidential authority, what strategies can presidents pursue to realize their agendas? In the United States, we are accustomed
to seeing presidents plead with citizens to pressure Congress to support presidential policy proposals. Woodrow Wilson once described the U.S. system as
consisting of "congressional government," while others have termed the
foremost power of the presidency to be the power of persuasion. In contrast, in
Latin America, a longer list of pressing national concerns and economic crises
has been associated with demands in many corners of society for a stronger
presidency—even if that increased strength sacrifices consensus-building efforts in the search for speedier action. Peru is not alone in its search for the best
tradeoff between speed and consensus building. Almost all Latin American
countries have revised substantially the constitutional rules governing executive power since 1990. In this book, we will analyze the politics of these changes
and examine the ensuing debate over their positive and negative effects.

THE PLAN OF THIS BOOK

Over the course of this book, we will examine contemporary responses to the quests for development, liberty, and governance. We will also expand our knowledge of Latin American history and broaden our conceptual understanding of political life. Chapter Two presents a broad overview of the region's economic and political evolution from 1492 to 1979. Chapter Three introduces some major features of contemporary political life in Latin America from 1980 to the early twenty-first century. We will learn to appreciate today's democracies as part of a third wave of democratization in the region and around the world. The longevity of these democracies will depend in no small part on the ability of elected governments to respond effectively to the quests for development, liberty, and governance. Chapter Four presents a more in-depth look at these three quests. It begins with the debate over what constitutes economic development and then examines various schools of thought regarding the appropriate role of the government in the economy. It then focuses on two major contemporary issues regarding liberty: the treatment of past human rights violations and the effort to protect civil, economic, and physical liberties today. Our examination of governance focuses on the distribution of power in the political system, with a special emphasis on the role of the chief executive in the political system.

Chapters Five through Eleven, the core of this book, examine these three issues in seven countries—Argentina, Brazil, Chile, Cuba, Guatemala, Mexico, and Venezuela. Each of these country chapters begins with the historical context that forms the backdrop of the country's current political dynamics. The next chapter section presents basic government institutions and the major political actors of the contemporary era. Then the quests for development, liberty, and governance are examined with a focus on the contemporary era. Chapter Twelve reviews these seven countries' choices regarding the three major quests from a broader cross-national perspective within Latin America. In the process of examining these three challenges, we will consider their implications for the future of democracy.

Several additional features are intended to enhance the usefulness of this book. In Chapters Two through Eleven, you will find lists of suggested readings that cover in greater detail issues related to each chapter. You will also find a series of questions and suggested activities at the close of each of those chapters; the last activity always involves the exploration of online resources. At the end of the text is a glossary of key terms (which are presented in the chapters in bold) and an index. Three series of boxes appear throughout Chapters Two through Eleven. A series called *Governing Strategies* discusses the problems faced by major leaders and the tactics they used in pursuit of their respective political objectives. A second series, *Concepts in Action,* discusses major events emblematic of a political or economic concept in a given chapter. A third series, *Global Perspectives,* compares the experiences of countries outside the region on several political and economic issues. A fourth series of boxes, *The Peruvian Experience,* appears only in Chapters Two, Three, and Four. This series helps to humanize this regional overview by considering some of the regional trends through the lens of concrete experiences in Peru. Peru has *not* been highlighted in these early chapters because it is somehow the "most representative" Latin American country. No single country can speak for the distinctive experiences of nineteen separate nation-states; however, Peru provides a useful entry point into several of the major themes examined throughout this book. A fifth series of boxes, *Research Question,* appears in Chapters Five through Eleven. These boxes present contemporary cross-national political science research on questions relevant for each of the country chapters. The questions examined in these boxes can also be explored in greater detail by using the bibliographies provided on this book's website. That website also contains an annotated links page that presents several major online resources for the study of Latin American politics. Use these online bibliographies and links pages to learn more about particular issues and countries that interest you.

Politics in the United States, Peru, and elsewhere is always filled with debate over how government authority should be organized and used. We have already begun to explore those questions by considering Jennifer's and Cecilia's stories. In the next chapter, we will place these issues within the broader regional history of Latin America.

Endnotes

1. The term *Latin America* commonly refers to the nation-states that emerged out of Spanish and Portuguese America. Some controversy surrounds the term. The original terms used in the colonial era were *New World, America,* and *South America.* Spaniards tended to use the terms *Spanish America* or *Hispanic America.* In the middle of the nineteenth century, French observers began to use the phrase *Latin America* to distinguish between societies with northern European colonizers (especially Britain but also Holland) and those with Mediterranean or Latin colonizers (France, Portugal, and Spain). This term eventually gained acceptance in languages and societies throughout most of the world—with the notable exception of Spain and Portugal, where the term *Iberoamerica* is used to refer to societies with colonizers from the Iberian peninsula of Europe (Spain and Portugal). While Iberoamerica is the more precise term for our purposes, throughout this book we shall refer to the region as Latin America because that is the term most commonly used not only in the United States, but also in the Spanish- and Portuguese-speaking countries of the Americas.

2. *U.S. Statistical Abstract 1999* (Washington, D.C.: Government Printing Office, 2000).

3. *U.S. Statistical Abstract 2000* (Washington, D.C.: Government Printing Office, 2001).

4. United Nations Development Program, *Human Development Report 2002* (New York: Oxford University Press, 2002).

5. Unless otherwise noted, economic statistics presented in this text for Peru and for other Latin American countries come from the U.N. Economic Commission for Latin America and the Caribbean.

6. United Nations Development Program, *Human Development Report 2002* (New York: Oxford University Press, 2002).

7. Government of Peru (Instituto Nacional de Estadística e Informática).

Mexican painter Diego Rivera depicted contrasting visions of bad government and good government in these 1925 murals.   Top photo: Rivera, Diego (1866–1957) © Banco de Mexico Trust, Good Government (El buen gobierno), central section, 1924. Mural, 2.98 × 9.46 (total). Administrative area, 2nd floor foyer. Location: Universidad Autonoma, Chapingo, Mexico Photo Credit: Schalkwijk/ Art Resource, NY; bottom photo: Rivera, Diego (1866–1957) © Banco de Mexico Trust, Bad Government (El mal gobierno), central section, 1924. Mural, 2.99 × 9.47 m (total). Administrative area, 2nd floor foyer. Location: Universidad Autonoma, Chapingo, Mexico. Photo Credit: Schalkwijk/Art Resource, NY.

CHAPTER 2

A Bird's-Eye View
of Latin American History

THE NINETEEN COUNTRIES OF LATIN AMERICA share many characteristics in common. Many similarities have their roots in colonization by the two countries on the Iberian peninsula—Spain and Portugal. These colonizers swept across the Americas in the sixteenth century after dividing their claims to the non-European world in the Treaty of Tordesillas in 1494. Through colonization, Spain and Portugal planted their respective languages in the region. The Iberian countries also came to the Americas with a zeal for spreading the Catholic faith in the New World. As part of this legacy, the roughly 500 million Catholics in Latin America today constitute half of the world's congregation within the Roman Catholic Church. Beyond a legacy of language and religion, Spain and Portugal also brought forms of social, economic, and political organization that they imposed on the preexisting indigenous populations.

Contemporary Latin America is the product of the contact between Iberian and indigenous societies, along with the subsequent arrival of immigrants from around the world. The Iberian influence proved to be so profound that it provides much of the backdrop against which contemporary political life unfolds. While shared colonial influences and other similarities are the focus of this chapter, please remember that substantial diversity exists within Latin America. In reviewing five centuries of regional evolution, we will pause occasionally to consider some major departures from the general historical trends that most concern us in this chapter.

THE COLONIAL ERA (1492–1809)

In the United States, the victory of rebel forces in the American Revolution and the prominent role of Thomas Jefferson's writing in the founding of the new nation-state helped to entrench the image of the independent farmer as the backbone of colonial society. While Jefferson's ideal of the yeoman farmer provides an incomplete picture of British colonial life in North America, it certainly formed an important part of that larger reality. So, too, did the search for religious freedom by many Protestant colonists. This search for religious freedom did not typically include an open-ended tolerance for religious diversity within each colony. Instead, it tended to consist of a search for a new realm in which to establish a certain Protestant faith tradition as the dominant religion. This variety of faith traditions (and of occupations) across the colonies helped to construct an increasingly diverse society over the course of the seventeenth and eighteenth centuries. The British crown often dealt with diversity by permitting considerable subregional autonomy across its American territories until demands for further autonomy culminated in the Declaration of Independence in 1776.

If the Protestant farmer is the dominant image of British colonization in the Americas, the enduring image of Iberian colonization remains the *conquistador* intent on territorial conquest, mineral wealth, and the conversion of indigenous populations to the Catholic faith. Perhaps the most emblematic founder of Latin America is Hernán Cortés, a brash soldier of fortune who established the colony of New Spain in the first quarter of the sixteenth century. Cortés toppled a prosperous Aztec civilization through a ruthless combination of force of arms, luck, and political intrigue (see *Governing Strategies: Hernán Cortés*). Just as the British colonies were not filled solely by free-thinking Protestant farmers, the Spanish colonies established by Christopher Columbus in the Caribbean, by Cortés in Central and North America, and by Francisco Pizarro in South America were not the sole province of fortune seekers. Nonetheless, one-third of the initial wave of Spanish colonizers in South America consisted of men from the lower noble ranks, and almost two-thirds of the colonizers were men with no title whatsoever. While many had multiple motives, the desire for upward social and economic mobility was a trait shared by many colonizers.

Spanish America developed a colonial life distinctive from that found in the British colonies of North America and the Caribbean. The Spanish authorities differed from their British counterparts in three major ways. First, the Spanish crown under Isabel and Fernando finished driving the Moors from the Iberian peninsula in 1492, and this successful completion of the Reconquest of Spain helped to fuel a religious zeal that would later expand with the emergence of the Protestant Reformation in Europe during the sixteenth century. The crown authorities (and many of the colonizers themselves) placed great emphasis on converting indigenous populations to Catholicism. Second, the Spanish crown had greater economic expectations (and needs) than its British counterpart at the outset of colonization. The principal monarchs of the initial colonization drive, Carlos V (1516–1556) and Felipe II (1556–1598), had high hopes that colonial riches could fund their military quest to dominate Europe. Third, the Spanish colonizers confronted large indigenous populations. While estimates

GOVERNING STRATEGIES
Hernán Cortés

Hernán Cortés (Fernando to his friends) would become the archetype for the *conquistador* approach to colonization in the Americas. Groomed initially for a career in law, he joined an expedition to the Caribbean when he was nineteen. He demonstrated his valor and resourcefulness to Diego Velázquez, leader of the Spanish conquest of Cuba. After the first two expeditions to the Yucatán Peninsula failed, Velázquez asked Cortés to lead a third. Cortés seized the opportunity with so much gusto that Velázquez revoked his authority. The brash Cortés set sail in February 1519 before he could be arrested.

In Yucatán, Cortés met a shipwrecked Spaniard (Gerónimo Aguilar) who spoke Mayan and a woman (Malinche) who spoke both the Mayan common in southern Mexico and the Nahuatl language dominant in central Mexico. Cortés now had an advantage that prior expeditions (and his eventual Aztec adversaries) lacked. He used these translators to learn the complex political dynamics within the Aztec empire.

Cortés destroyed his ships to limit desertion and began a march to Tenochtitlán, the Aztec capital. In his travels north, he built alliances with indigenous peoples opposed to Aztec rule and saw that many considered him the possible second coming of the Aztec god Quetzalcoatl. Then, in a show of force, Cortés destroyed the city of Cholula. Cortés was received with fanfare in Tenochtitlán and carried out his boldest stroke: he took the Aztec emperor Moctezuma hostage and then tried to rule through Moctezuma.

In spring 1520, Cortés went to the coast to defeat a Spanish force sent to arrest him; he convinced many of those troops to join his forces. While Cortés was away, his troops killed hundreds of Aztecs—instigating a full-scale siege of Tenochtitlán shortly after Cortés returned. Moctezuma died in the struggle, and the Spanish fought their way out of the city with heavy losses on the *noche triste* ("sad night") of June 30, 1520. The Aztecs prepared for all-out war against the Spanish. In the months that followed, smallpox (carried by one of the new Spanish soldiers) killed thousands of Aztecs—including the new emperor, Cuitláhuac.

The next year Cortés amassed a force enlarged by new Spanish adventurers recruited from the Caribbean and by some indigenous enemies of the Aztecs. After a three-month siege, Tenochtitlán fell on August 13, 1521, and the Aztec empire crumbled with it. Cortés launched expeditions over most of Mexico and into northern Central America. Cortés personally led a force into modern-day Honduras, where his troops executed the last Aztec emperor, Cuauhtémoc, who had been taken along as a hostage.

Cortés's willingness to mix diplomacy with warfare aided his conquests, but his frequent disregard for authority created enemies who limited his political prospects once he conquered New Spain. Spain welcomed Cortés home as a conquering hero in 1528 and made him a marquis. However, he was not named viceroy of New Spain. The Spanish authorities preferred to name more bureaucratically inclined leaders to administer their new American colonies.

of the pre-Columbian population vary considerably, all concur that the indigenous population in Spanish America was much larger than that found in British America. In one highly regarded estimate (toward the middle of the existing range of calculations), there were approximately 54 million people living in what would become Spanish America when Columbus arrived in the Caribbean in 1492—with roughly 20 million in Mexico and another 11 million in the Andean heart of the Incan empire in South America.[1] These two vast confederations of various smaller indigenous nationalities were not merely larger populations; they were also more organized socially, politically, economically, and militarily than the indigenous populations found in the rest of North America, in the islands of the Caribbean, and in what would become Brazil. Cortés and many of his soldiers found the Aztec capital of Tenochtitlán (with its large population, massive marketplaces, and intricate irrigation system) to be the most striking city that they had seen anywhere in the world.

The combination of these three factors—an evangelistic zeal for the Catholic faith; high economic expectations; and a large, sophisticated indigenous population—came together in the creation of a colonial society built on conquest and was followed by the implantation of a strict social and racial hierarchy headed by the crown authority in Spain. To ensure greater loyalty to the crown in the centuries of colonial rule following the creation of the viceroyalties of New Spain in 1535 and Peru in 1544, the Spanish monarchs rotated the colonial authorities frequently. Typically, they sent new Spanish-born officials (*peninsulares*) to lead the colonial government. The descendants of Spanish colonizers born in the New World, the creoles, increasingly resented these *peninsulares*. The creoles (**criollos** in Spanish) saw themselves as the true citizens of the New World and rejected the *peninsulares* as foreigners whose authority was imposed on them from afar. Together, the *peninsulares* and the *criollos* formed the social and economic elite of colonial Spanish America.

The prevailing racism of the era presumed that the indigenous peoples (**indígenas**) and other non-Europeans were inferior. Indigenous peoples provided the initial workforce in the economic activities launched by the Spanish crown and by the Catholic church—principally as forced labor in mining operations and in agricultural enterprises. Exposure to new diseases and harsh working conditions took their toll on indigenous populations (particularly in the Spanish Caribbean). In response, the crown began to import African slaves. Even after a substantial reduction in the indigenous population, people of indigenous and African descent continued to outnumber those of Spanish origin. Many early Spanish colonizers were either bachelors or married men who left their families behind. This circumstance (along with socioeconomic norms that treated the indigenous and African women as property) helped give rise over time to a considerable population of mixed racial origins. Those presumed to stem from a combination of Spanish and indigenous origins were called **mestizos**, while those presumed to have Spanish and African roots were referred to as mulattos (**mulatos**).

NEW
FRANCE

Disputed by
England, Russia,
and Spain

ENGLISH COLONIES

ATLANTIC
OCEAN

Effective frontier
of Spanish settlement

FLORIDA
Ceded to England,
1763–1783

VICEROYALTY OF
NEW SPAIN
Guadalajara
Mexico City ★

HAITI
(SAINT DOMINGUE)
Ceded to France, 1697

Guatemala•

Santo
Domingo

JAMAICA
Conquered by
England, 1655

PACIFIC
OCEAN

Caracas•

VICEROYALTY OF
NEW GRANADA
Bogotá ★

GUIANA

Separated by
Viceroyalty of Peru,
1717, 1739

Quito •

VICEROYALTY
OF PERU

Lima ★
Cuzco•

VICEROYALTY
OF BRAZIL

Pernambuco •

Bahia •

Chuquisaca•
(La Plata; Sucre)

Viceroyalty of Brazil

Viceroyalty of Peru and
Audencia of Chile

Viceroyalty of La Plata

Viceroyalty of New Granada

Viceroyalty of New Spain

★   Viceregal capital

•   Audiencia seat

São Paulo •

Rio de Janeiro
(Capital, 1763)

VICEROYALTY
OF LA PLATA
Separated by
Viceroyalty
of Peru, 1776

Santiago •

AUDIENCIA OF CHILE
Retained by
Viceroyalty of Peru,
1776

Buenos Aires ★

Claimed but
not settled
by Spain

0   500   1000 Km.
0   500   1000 Mi.

Colonial Spanish America

Between the sixteenth century and the early nineteenth century, colonial Spanish America became increasingly diverse both racially and ethnically. The European population (primarily creole by then) had risen from around 2 percent of Spanish America to about 20 percent of the population. The indigenous population (initially the overwhelming majority) contracted to just over 40 percent of Spanish America. Those of mixed racial origins formed around 30 percent of the population, while Africans constituted the remaining 10 percent.

By the end of its colonial experience, Spanish America was a profoundly multiracial society, but one in which economic, social, and political power was concentrated in the hands of Spaniards and of their presumed descendants, the creoles. In addition to the colonial authorities, two other major groups wielded considerable power in Spanish America—the Catholic church and the owners of large, landed estates. The Catholic church constituted the most powerful nongovernmental institution in Spanish America with its large network of parishes, parishioners, and land. It also had nearly complete charge over education in the colonies. The Catholic religious order of the Jesuits formed an additional religious institution that developed its own businesses and means of support until its expulsion from Spanish America in 1767.

THE PERUVIAN EXPERIENCE
Large Landowners in Seventeenth-Century Arequipa

Through extensive research into colonial-era documents, Keith Davies created a detailed history of colonial Peru in the 1600s that focuses on the southwestern coastal region of Arequipa. Davies notes that mestizos were excluded from the Arequipan landowning elite. To be considered a member of the elite, in addition to holding property one needed to have married into a family associated with either the founding of the colony or its contemporary government:

> Arequipa's leading families borrowed heavily from the social practices of Hispanic contemporaries to confirm their prominent position. This led them to build substantial urban homes, which they furnished impressively with imported finery and Peruvian silver. A host of Indians and blacks served as their domestics. Parents also saw to it that young children received a rudimentary education at home or in one of the small schools, staffed by Spanish and American-born instructors, that sprang up in Arequipa. Some even managed to expose their offspring to such social graces as dancing. Those who enjoyed sufficient wealth sometimes sent sons and daughters off to Castile for further education, or to be placed in the church, or to be married well. A few wealthy Arequipans provided for their children by creating entailed estates, most of which

The owners of large estates formed the third major group of actors on the socioeconomic and political scene. The description of the landowning elite in *The Peruvian Experience: Large Landowners in Seventeenth-Century Arequipa* provides a glimpse into the lifestyle of this fundamental element of Latin American colonial society. Initially most land was held formally by the crown under the *encomienda* system, in which Spaniards (particularly those who participated directly in the conquest) were granted the right to tax indigenous residents in a certain territory in exchange for promising to serve as their protector and religious educator. This colonial practice led first to informal control of land within the *encomienda* that then gave way to an effort to establish private property rights. Over the course of the seventeenth century, large portions of the best arable land in Spanish America became the private property of a relatively small number of families. The major exceptions to this trend of large estates (**latifundios** in Spanish) took place in the territories that would later constitute Costa Rica and Paraguay. The concentration of land ownership in most of Spanish America would later be recognized as one of the most important legacies of colonization. Landowners (or *hacendados*) emerged as highly visible political power brokers during the independence movement and thereafter. The

consisted of property purchased and located in Spain. Nevertheless, the burdensome cost involved in establishing a *mayorazgo* either in the Old or the New World limited this option.

The heads of Arequipa's "better" families also insured their prominence by securing public posts. Seldom did any hold positions in the royal bureaucracy, however, since the royal government generally reserved these for immigrants to Peru or for those of the most distinguished colonial families. Political confirmation of preeminence required contacts with Spaniards in high places. When a Southwesterner managed after the mid-1500s to become a *corregidor* or to secure a post such as that of royal treasurer, it was almost invariably someone who had decided to live in Lima.[1]

Davies's analysis captures the seventeenth-century emergence of a landowning class that began to wield its economic power and social status on the local level. Landed families would use their influence to shape an expansion of private property during the late 1600s and early 1700s.[2] The local power and influence of landowners would be even more visible on the national level once colonial rule ended.

[1] Keith Davies, *Landowners in Colonial Peru* (Austin: University of Texas Press, 1984), pp. 142–143.
[2] For a discussion of this process and an analysis of working conditions for indigenous and mestizo Peruvians in the colonial era, see Ward Stavig, *The World of Tupac Amaru: Conflict, Community and Identity in Colonial Peru* (Lincoln: University of Nebraska Press, 1999).

property of the *hacienda* (ranch) consisted not just of the land itself but also included the many indentured servants tied to the land under a system of debt peonage.

These three groups—the colonial authorities, the church, and the large landowners—dominated the colonial economy. The Spanish crown established a set of economic policies driven by **mercantilism**. Mercantilist economic thought emphasized two main goals: the accumulation of precious metals (especially gold and silver during the sixteenth century) and the attainment of a positive balance of trade. The initial colonial policies pursued these goals through a rapid effort to exploit mineral wealth (mainly in Mexico and Bolivia) and by strict control of all commerce. Beyond mineral wealth, the backbone of the colonial economy proved to be the cultivation of crops and livestock for export to Europe. To control trade, until 1778 only four ports in Spanish America could legally ship goods to Europe, and all goods shipped out of the Americas were forced to travel through a single Spanish port (initially Seville but later Cadiz). These colonial ports could not trade legally with each other. Eventually, the 1778 Decree of Free Trade by Carlos III opened legal trade among all colonial ports and with all Spanish ports. These reforms reflected both the emergence of free-trade ideas in Europe (Adam Smith published *The Wealth of Nations* in 1776) and the desire to gain customs revenues lost to contraband trade that violated the mercantilist legal regime.

Mercantilism also shaped the evolution of colonial Brazil. Nevertheless, at the start of colonization, Brazil differed from Spanish America in two major respects. First, the indigenous population was smaller, less organized militarily, and often more nomadic. This situation made the contact between Portuguese colonizers and indigenous Brazilians more similar to that found in British America—a gradual expansion of the territory occupied by colonizers rather than one major military push aimed at conquering a large confederation of indigenous peoples. The second difference stemmed from the failure of the initial sixteenth-century colonizers to find mineral wealth. As a result, the Portuguese crown resorted to large land grants (or captaincies) to generate a colonial presence across Brazil. The descendants of the initial colonizers produced food exports on that land—primarily sugar in the northeast and cattle in the southeast. For centuries the vast interior of Brazil—much of it consisting of the Amazon rainforest—would remain scarcely inhabited. The discovery of gold in 1690 and of diamonds in 1729 in south-central Brazil led to a mining boom that would reach its peak in the mid-eighteenth century. Brazil's dominant export prior to the mining boom, sugar, would have the most profound impact on the Brazilian population. Labor-intensive sugar harvesting led to the purchase of thousands upon thousands of African slaves, just as it would in the Spanish Caribbean. As a result, the multiracial society that evolved in colonial Brazil contained a higher percentage of Africans and mulattos and a lower percentage of mestizos and indigenous peoples than that found in most of Spanish America beyond the Caribbean.

THE INDEPENDENCE MOVEMENT (1810s AND 1820s)

While the crown and the church had conflicts throughout the colonial era, each also served to reinforce the other's political and economic power. Both institutions believed in absolute monarchy guided by divine right. The church helped the royal authorities to disseminate this form of governance as an ideal throughout colonial society. The prevalence of this belief in an absolute monarchy within Spanish America would later play a crucial role in the evolution of the independence movement.

The late eighteenth century was not only a time of economic change but also of political change that would culminate in the independence of nearly all of Spanish America during the early 1800s. Cuba and Puerto Rico formed the crucial exceptions to this trend (they would not gain independence from Spain until the settlement of the 1898 Spanish-American War). Political change was in the air on the world scene: both the U.S. Declaration of Independence of 1776 and the French Revolution of 1789 called for the establishment of a republic, thereby ending monarchical rule. Republican ideals associated with the European Enlightenment formed one element of the political debate during the struggle for independence—particularly in the writing of Simón Bolívar.

Simón Bolívar succeeded in toppling Spanish colonialism, but his plans for a grand American republic collapsed.   Bettmann/Corbis.

However, many participants in the establishment of an independent Latin America did not want to chart a course aimed at expanding economic and political liberties. Instead they were driven by a desire to defend old economic and political patterns. These twin seeds of Latin American independence—republican idealism and conservative reaction to the end of absolute monarchy in Spain—were both visible in the Peruvian independence movement (see *The Peruvian Experience: Independence from Spain*). Three major events crystallized additional sources of support for independence. First, the eighteenth-century economic reforms created more enemies than supporters. Creoles who had profited from contraband trade opposed the reforms vigorously. Others found the reforms to be incomplete and demanded the freedom to trade with nations other than Spain. These grievances of the late eighteenth century, somewhat analogous to the struggle over taxation in British North America, formed the economic context in which the independence movements of the early nineteenth century would unfold.

Second, Napoleon Bonaparte's proclamation of his brother Joseph as ruler of Spain in 1808 ignited independence movements because many creoles refused to recognize the legitimacy of the French authority. Royalists in Mexico City

---

THE PERUVIAN EXPERIENCE
Independence from Spain

Peru's status as the center of the Spanish empire in South America was eroded by the creation of the viceroyalty of Buenos Aires in 1776 and by the decree of free trade of 1778 (which destroyed Peru's monopoly over transatlantic trade to Chile and Argentina). These reforms angered many rich and poor colonists. A wealthy mestizo, José Gabriel Condorcanqui, proclaimed himself Tupac Amaru II and tried to mobilize indigenous discontent with colonial rule in a bloody, unsuccessful revolt in 1780–1781. This revolt and the effects of the economic reforms convinced many landed creoles to reject liberal ideas. When much of Spanish America revolted against Bonapartist rule in the early nineteenth century, most of wealthy Peru remained loyal (often in hopes of regaining lost privileges in its colonial arrangement). Mateo García Pumacahua launched a separatist movement in 1814 that called for republican government, but the colonial authorities put down his rebellion by 1815.

The situation changed once Fernando VII adopted the liberal 1820 constitution. Many wealthy creoles welcomed the arrival of José de San Martín's troops in southern Peru in September 1820. Spanish troops later left Lima for the more readily defended terrain of the sierra. San Martín declared Peru's independence on July 28, 1821, and the Lima elite proclaimed him protector of Peru. As in Mexico, the balance of forces favored a new monarchy. San Martín commissioned a representative to recruit a European noble to serve as monarch of an independent Peru.

deposed the viceroy of New Spain named by Bonaparte in 1808 and declared their continuing loyalty to Fernando VII. In 1810 royalist creoles in Buenos Aires similarly declared the separation of the viceroyalty of Río de la Plata from Joseph Bonaparte's authority. The next year, Simón Bolívar and other creoles in Venezuela rebelled against Bonapartist rule, but Bolívar also proclaimed an additional goal—the eventual independence of the Americas. For the next few years, Spanish colonial authorities battled rebel forces and appeared to be gaining the upper hand in 1814, when Fernando VII regained the throne. For the rest of the decade, Simón Bolívar in the upper half of South America and Argentine leader José de San Martín in the lower half of the continent continued to fight for independence in the countryside while royalists dominated most of the major cities.

Third, the royalists' view of Spanish authority changed in 1820 when Fernando VII recognized the liberal principles of the Spanish constitution of 1812 as legitimate, thereby ending the absolute monarchy that had been central to Spanish American life. This third pivotal event set off a firestorm of criticism from many conservative creoles, who now joined Bolívar and San Martín in the quest for independence. This support from wealthy creoles proved instrumental

---

As wars raged in the Americas, some liberals in Lima emerged to support Simón Bolívar's calls for republican rule. Bolívar's army advanced from the northeast to tackle Spanish resistance in the Peruvian highlands. A meeting in mid-1822 between Bolívar and San Martín—the major military architects of South American independence—culminated in San Martín's decision to retire from politics, which gave even greater impetus to the republican movement. Two major military victories against the Spanish in Peru during 1824—at Junín and at Ayacucho—signaled the end to major Spanish and loyalist resistance (even though Spain would refuse to recognize Peru's independence until 1869).

Bolívar wanted to organize Peru, Upper Peru, and Gran Colombia (a territory comprising modern-day Peru, Bolivia, Ecuador, Panama, Colombia, and Venezuela) into a grand republic, but the plan broke down fairly quickly. Most in Upper Peru resisted integration with Peru and declared independence as Bolivia in 1825. Peru began to suffer a series of coup attempts and internal uprisings in 1828. In 1830, Ecuador and Venezuela proclaimed their independence from Gran Colombia, ending Bolívar's dream of a massive American republic. An embittered Bolívar wrote, "Those who served the Revolution have plowed the sea."[1] Simón Bolívar died of tuberculosis in late 1830. In Peru and elsewhere, the end to colonial rule left behind divisions between conservative and liberal landed elites and among various military leaders of the independence struggle.

[1]As translated and cited in John Johnson, *Simón Bolívar and Spanish American Independence: 1783–1830* (Princeton, N.J.: D. Van Nostrand, 1968), p. 112.

in the establishment of independence throughout nearly all of the Americas in the first half of the 1820s. It also helped to ensure that the aims of those victorious independence movements would not include many of the socioeconomic reforms pursued by Bolívar in South America and by José María Morelos and others in Mexico.

Brazilian independence took a slightly different path, albeit one also influenced by events in Europe. Napoleon's triumph in Portugal in 1807 led the entire Portuguese royal family to reign in exile from its largest colony, Brazil. On his arrival in 1808, João VI promptly severed the earlier mercantilist monopoly that Portugal had enjoyed over Brazilian international trade. This move enabled Brazil to expand trade rapidly with Britain. After the French were driven from Portugal with English assistance, João VI returned to Portugal in 1821, leaving his son Dom Pedro in Brazil. Portuguese economic interests pressured for a return to monopolistic control over Brazilian foreign trade. When this return to mercantilism was declared and the Portuguese constituent assembly rejected Dom Pedro's new title of prince regent of Brazil and heir to the combined kingdoms of Portugal and Brazil, Dom Pedro refused his recall to Portugal and instead led the declaration of Brazilian independence in 1822. The ensuing Brazilian war for independence was much shorter and less bloody than in Spanish America for two main reasons. First, the Portuguese crown was weaker economically and militarily. Second, the Brazilian independence movement did not suffer the visible division between republicans and royalists found in the rest of the Americas because royalists interested in independence could take solace in the retention of the monarchy under the leadership of Dom Pedro. By late 1823, Portuguese forces withdrew from Brazil after losing several conflicts over the course of the year.

THE AGE OF POLITICAL INSTABILITY (1820s TO 1870s)

The wars for independence in Latin America tended to leave the landowners and the church in their traditional places of importance. However, the independence struggle replaced the third pillar of colonial society—the colonial governmental authorities—with a new force: the military leaders (**caudillos**) of the battles for independence. Often these military leaders were mestizos who now found themselves rubbing elbows with the creole elite. Subsequent generations of mestizos would come to see entry into the military as perhaps their most feasible path to socioeconomic advancement in nineteenth-century Latin America. These "men on horseback" remained crucial political actors after the wars for independence. Disagreements based on conflicting ideologies and personal ambitions often culminated in military struggles between national armies and regional militias organized by ambitious *caudillos*. In many countries, the leadership of the national government proved unstable, as did the government's control over the national territory. To cite a blatant example of instability, in its first forty years of independence, from 1821 to 1860, Mexico had over fifty different governments, none of which lasted more than a year. Military leaders headed thirty-five of those governments.

Personality differences and the struggle for personal power and wealth fueled much of the political turmoil of early independence, but ideological conflicts also played a role. The visible division between republicans and royalists in most of the Latin American independence movements anticipated what would become the major political division during the first century after independence—the conflict between liberals and conservatives. The meaning of these nineteenth-century political labels is somewhat difficult to understand in the United States. U.S. citizens today tend to label as liberals those persons who favor a larger, more active government while often describing those who favor more individual freedom and smaller government as conservatives. In the political debate in Europe and Latin America, however, the meaning of these terms is nearly the opposite of what one thinks of today in the United States. In nineteenth-century Latin America, **liberals** pushed for free trade and aggressive pursuit of export opportunities, the rights of the individual, and a reduction of the power of the church in society. In contrast, **conservatives** favored a greater emphasis on agricultural production for the domestic economy; an organic view of society in which individual freedoms were conditioned by traditional ties to church, family, and the land; and a continuing role for the church in education and elsewhere.

The tendency toward political instability during early independence made the principal economic project of the liberals—further integration into the world economy—difficult to pursue. While trade did expand (particularly with Great Britain), the major commercial push would not occur until the last third of the nineteenth century. The principal economic change of early independence came from a consensus among liberal and conservative landowners that colonial laws protecting traditional, communal lands held by indigenous peoples should be abolished. This change worsened the already uneven distribution of land ownership because many more people became sharecroppers or day laborers on large estates.

Political disorder at the national level left the **patria chica** ("little country") of the large, self-sufficient estate at the center of everyday life. Landowners often functioned as informal local governments in dealing with landless peasants in their territory. Landowners resolved personal legal disputes, punished common criminals, and sometimes offered an economic safety net of last resort to peasants who respected their authority. Landowners also provided the major source of donations to the Catholic church beyond the revenues generated by church-owned lands.

As *caudillo* wars raged intermittently past mid-century in most countries (with the exceptions of Brazil and Chile), some *caudillos* began to justify their quests for political authority on a need for a strong hand to establish order nationwide. Efforts to establish enduring governments that truly controlled the national territory would not succeed in most countries until the last quarter of the nineteenth century. In Peru, the age of instability lasted until 1895 (see *The Peruvian Experience:* Caudillo *Politics (1824–1895)*).

THE AGE OF STATE BUILDING AND FREE TRADE (1880s TO 1920s)

We saw earlier how the Napoleonic era in Europe served as a catalyst that ignited latent desires for independence in Latin America. The Industrial Revolution of the late nineteenth century in Europe and the United States helped to settle the two ongoing Latin American political conflicts of the nineteenth century: the debate between liberals and conservatives on the one hand and the struggle among rival *caudillos* on the other. The Industrial Revolution influenced the first conflict by changing the global economic context in a way that supported liberal economic ideas. It also provided an additional rationale for ending *caudillo* wars by making political stability an even more important factor in the pursuit of foreign markets and foreign investment.

The late nineteenth and early twentieth centuries saw a rapid expansion in world trade because of increasing demand for primary commodities (minerals, fuels, and foodstuffs) in the industrializing countries of Europe and in the United States. Latin American countries held many of these commodities in

THE PERUVIAN EXPERIENCE
Caudillo Politics (1824–1895)

During the years following the definitive victories over Spain in 1824, military *caudillos* from the independence struggle challenged the prevailing political order on the basis of several ideas, including a desire to extend dominion over Bolivia, to increase local autonomy, and to extend government authority over the entire territory. Rebellions and coup attempts were frequent events and many succeeded. Between 1824 and 1845, more than twenty presidents governed the country, and no civilian served anything approaching a full term in office. Amid the rampant conflict, the mining sector central to the colonial era fell into further disrepair, and the national government accumulated a steadily increasing debt with foreign (especially British) lenders.

In 1845, another military leader, Ramón Castilla, became president. Castilla, a hero of the crucial 1824 victories at Junín and Ayacucho, attempted to build a national military. He also tried to revive Bolívar's vision of South American unity in response to U.S. expansion in the settlement of the Mexican-American War of 1846–1848. In this period, the export of fertilizer from bird guano provided the government with its first steady stream of economic abundance; some had substantial mineral wealth, while others had soil and climatic conditions propitious for the cultivation of foodstuffs. During the years 1881 to 1913, world exports tripled while exports in the seven largest Latin American economies quadrupled.[2] Rising demand for primary commodities created a series of commodity booms in most economies in the region—precious minerals and petroleum in Bolivia, Chile, Mexico, and Venezuela; cotton in Peru; beef and wheat in Argentina and Uruguay; coffee in Brazil, Colombia, and Costa Rica; sugar in the Caribbean countries; and bananas in Guatemala and Honduras—even as the principal raw materials at issue varied.

Rising demand for these commodities in Europe and the United States strengthened the hand of Latin American liberals, who had been calling for a modernization of the national infrastructure of railroads, roads, and ports. The economic expansion also motivated foreign banks and multinational enterprises to invest in the creation of transportation links to bring commodities to world markets. While companies and banks from many countries played a role in this process, British and U.S. firms made the bulk of the investments.

This effort to construct new transportation networks, along with rising tax revenues due to higher economic growth rates, stimulated the creation of national governments in Latin America with sufficient resources to extend their authority nationwide. To use the language of political science, this is the era of **state building** as governments (that is, states) increased their financial and organizational capacity. This newfound capacity also extended into the military

resources. Castilla yielded authority at the end of his first term as president but launched a coup in 1854 against his successor, whom Castilla and others accused of corruption. This time Castilla stayed in power until 1862. Castilla was the only Peruvian leader to serve two terms in the nineteenth century without falling to a military coup (although various insurrections threatened his power).

When Castilla stepped down, instability returned. A revolt toppled his successor's government. In 1872, Manuel Pardo (the founder of Peru's first political party, the *Civilistas*) won the presidency and became the first civilian to serve a full term. Pardo was assassinated in 1878 as he considered a second run for the presidency. The next year, the War of the Pacific (1879–1883) broke out. Peru (and its ally, Bolivia) battled Chile in a conflict over nitrate rights. Peru and Bolivia suffered several military defeats and ceded territory to victorious Chile in the settlement of the war. Discontent with the war fueled another successful coup in 1885, and two more military men governed Peru for the next ten years.

In its first seventy-two years as an independent nation-state, Peru experienced numerous insurrections. Military leaders (some emerging by force of arms and others via elections with limited suffrage) governed for all but five of those seventy-two years. These successive waves of armed challenges to the national government would not diminish noticeably until the formation of a new civilian-led government in 1895.

realm. National governments created standing militaries and national police forces that were better able to stop would-be *caudillos* from challenging their authority. In short, economic expansion helped to end the era of political instability that had characterized the first decades after independence.

State building took three major paths in Latin America in the late nineteenth and early twentieth centuries: personal dictatorships, oligarchic democracies, and U.S. intervention. First, in several countries, a single *caudillo* leader managed to impose a dictatorship for an extended period of time. The prolonged rule of Porfirio Díaz in Mexico (1876–1911) provides perhaps the most dramatic example of a national strongman with his roots in *caudillo* politics and warfare. The dictatorships of Ulises Heureaux in the Dominican Republic (1882–1899) and of Juan Vicente Gómez in Venezuela (1908–1935) also illustrate this pattern.

Second, several countries in South America, such as Argentina, Bolivia, Brazil, Chile, and Colombia, established enduring oligarchic democracies in which a small minority of men could vote (frequently 3 to 10 percent). In this system of limited participation, political parties dominated by landowners and mining interests competed for power. These elections were often shaped by outright fraud in vote counting and by the use of coercive tactics to influence

THE PERUVIAN EXPERIENCE
Oligarchic Democracy and Personal Dictatorship (1895–1930)

Peruvian politics had seen nearly ceaseless challenges to the authority of the national government in the decades following independence. This situation began to change with the 1895 election of a former treasury minister, Nicolás de Piérola, to the presidency. He worked to establish an oligarchic democracy by reassuring rural elites that his new electoral law would not diminish their authority. Piérola promised to serve landed interests through the creation of a steadier political and economic environment. The new electoral system increased the number of voters and elected offices while it retained an open (that is, nonsecret) ballot prone to machine politics. Because voting was not conducted by secret ballot, rural and urban political bosses could credibly promise to reward supporters and to punish those who voted against the local machine.

The Piérola reforms created an oligarchic democracy dominated by local political bosses (*gamonales* in Peruvian political slang) who were typically prominent landowners. Violent challenges to elected officials did not disappear, but they occurred less often and succeeded less frequently. During 1824–1895, only one civilian president served an entire term. From 1895 to 1919, four presidents completed their terms (and a fifth might have if he had not died of natural causes). As the 1919 presidential elections approached, the most visible potential threat in the minds of many propertied Peruvians was the newly formed Regional Peruvian Labor Federation (FORP). The FORP brought together many voting behavior. Despite their limitations, these oligarchic democracies constituted the first wave of democratization in the region. The Peruvian experience during this time period provides examples of both oligarchic democracy and prolonged dictatorship (see *The Peruvian Experience: Oligarchic Democracy and Personal Dictatorship (1895–1930)*).

U.S. military intervention in the Caribbean and in Central America visibly influenced a third path toward state building in which U.S. officials framed political regimes through a mixture of force, diplomacy, and economic assistance. The substantial U.S. influence in early twentieth-century Cuba—stemming from the U.S. victory in the Spanish-American War of 1898—provides a major example of this manner of state building. Panama's creation as a nation-state separate from Colombia in 1903 was intimately connected to ongoing U.S. efforts to construct a canal linking the Atlantic and Pacific oceans. U.S. military presence also shaped the evolution of national government in other countries in the Caribbean Basin—including El Salvador, Guatemala, Honduras, and Nicaragua—during the early twentieth century.

In all three of these paths to state building, the guiding political watchwords of the day are reflected in the motto on the Brazilian flag adopted in the

---

smaller labor unions that had organized a general strike in January 1919 to coincide with similar protests held in Argentina, Brazil, and Chile.

The victor in the 1919 presidential elections was past president Augusto Leguía. His campaign emphasized a need for order, and he exploited the perceived unrest by accusing outgoing president José Pardo of planning to annul Leguía's electoral triumph. On July 4, 1919, Leguía convinced sympathetic military officers to launch a coup that forced Pardo into exile and closed the legislature. This coup began the *oncenio*—an eleven-year period of dictatorial rule.

Leguía spearheaded the creation of a new constitution that expanded the powers of the presidency and synchronized presidential and legislative elections on a five-year term with unlimited reelection. Leguía then used the power of his office to win over some of the major personalist parties of the oligarchic democracy while marginalizing others. As Porfirio Díaz had done earlier in Mexico, Leguía used a combination of political favors, repression, electoral fraud, and export-promoting economic policies to win reelection handily in 1924 and again in 1929. He launched several massive public works projects that focused on road and rail links; many of the projects used conscripted rural laborers who were forced to work without pay.

This mantra of order and progress was difficult to sustain after the stock market crashed in the United States in October 1929. In the months following the crash, the markets for most Peruvian exports collapsed. A junior military officer, Luis M. Sánchez Cerro, launched a military revolt in August 1930 that forced Leguía out of the presidency. The *oncenio* was over, but a tense debate over Peru's political and economic future was just beginning.

1890s—Order and Progress. Latin American countries strove to escape the political instability of the past with a newfound order that would pave the way to export-led economic prosperity. In the political realm, this emphasis on order as a precondition for progress often meant that the debate over governance favored the centralization of authority rather than an extension of the political process and debate (although the Chilean legislature's power would provide a notable exception to this trend). The quest for order also conditioned liberty everywhere. Individuals and groups that challenged the existing political and economic order were often violently repressed. The vision of progress in economic development was tailored largely to the beliefs (and interests) of the economic elite in control of the region's commodity wealth. While people disagreed about which commodities should be favored by state policies in transportation links and other matters, a general consensus among the wealthy elite determined that economic development would be best served by the continuation of laissez-faire policies. They emphasized free trade rather than protection for local entrepreneurs attempting to launch industrial enterprises to compete with existing foreign imports.

These images of order and progress stress the role of political stability in support of commodity-led economic expansion, an expansion that would set into motion socioeconomic changes that would have much more visible political implications in the decades following this period. The commodity boom created new societal forces that would begin to exert more and more political influence. The imports paid for by export wealth created opportunities in retail commerce. Export wealth also increased demand for white-collar professionals in banking, law, medicine, architecture, and other fields. This expansion of the **middle sectors** of the social strata (those people between the traditional landed elite and the large mass of day laborers) spawned movements challenging the political dominance of landed interests. These middle-sector movements did not call so much for dramatic change in economic policy as for expanded access to political power that would include them as more meaningful participants.

In addition to stimulating an increase in the middle sectors, the expansion of transportation links tied to foreign trade created thousands of new jobs in the railroads and in the ports. These jobs often paid higher wages and provided better opportunities for labor organization than did jobs in agriculture. Labor unions began to form and to expand in many countries. In the early twentieth century, some unions would help to form the first socialist and communist parties in the region. Because these leftist ideologies called for government control of the economy, they potentially challenged the existing economic order. Both governments and businesses often fiercely repressed these leftist movements.

In the late nineteenth and early twentieth centuries, Latin America was a cauldron of change amid continuity. This period marked the peak of the economic and political power of the landed interests that had been central since the colonial era. At the same time, the commodity booms contained the seeds of societal transformation that would usher in a much more complex era in both economic and political terms.

THE SECOND WAVE OF DEMOCRATIZATION AND THE RISE OF STATE CAPITALISM (1930s TO 1950s)

Just as the Industrial Revolution set into motion a commodity boom throughout Latin America, the Great Depression of the 1930s marked the beginning of a new era in economic and political life in the region. As the demand for Latin American exports collapsed in the industrialized economies, the existing pattern of exporting commodities and importing finished goods fell apart. During 1930–1934, the total value of Latin American exports was roughly half of what it had been during the prior five years, from 1925 though 1929. As a result, Latin American foreign exchange earnings fell, and countries had less hard currency with which to import finished goods.

The political implications of these profound economic changes came in two stages. In the first stage, the economic effects of the October 1929 stock market crash created enormous pressure on governments as they attempted to steer a path out of the economic crisis. Differences among competing propertied interests as well as the conflicting perspectives of the middle-sector and working-class movements were difficult to resolve within limited to nonexistent electoral processes. Some frustrated contenders for power sought alliances with the military as a way to impose their desired plans for saving the nation from its economic distress. Many governments were unable to withstand the strain and fell victim to military coups. Within the first five years after the 1929 crash, military coups toppled governments in Argentina, Bolivia, Brazil, Chile, Cuba, the Dominican Republic, Ecuador, El Salvador, Guatemala, Honduras, Panama, Peru, and Uruguay.

The policy ideas implemented by the governments installed in this first stage of military coups varied widely. The experiences of Argentina and Brazil illustrate the two major tendencies visible in this choice between continuing the laissez-faire policies of the past and embarking on a new path marked by government intervention in the economy aimed at industrialization. In Argentina, the 1930 coup set into motion a 13-year period of fraudulent elections that frequently privileged the laissez-faire policy perspectives of the landed elite. This took place in the face of rising opposition from economic nationalists interested in industrialization and from leftist forces clamoring for societal transformation. Brazil's 1930 coup transferred power to a civilian politician named Getúlio Vargas. Vargas faced opposition from many landowners but forged a diverse coalition in support of industrialization that consisted of industrial entrepreneurs, military officers (interested in industrialization on national security grounds in the age of modern warfare), and workers who coveted jobs in the manufacturing sector.

During the second, longer stage of responses to the Great Depression, interventionist perspectives regarding economic policy prevailed and voting rights expanded (often controversially) throughout most of Latin America. In reaction to the Great Depression, the earlier elite consensus behind market-oriented economics gave way to much more divisive debates over the nature of development challenges and over the appropriate government responses to those challenges. In general, support for increased government intervention in economic matters began in the 1930s and took hold in most of the region in the 1940s and 1950s. In the 1930s, the crisis of the world economy protected newly formed manufacturing sectors in Latin America by limiting the region's ability to import goods from the industrialized world. After World War II ended in 1945, it became increasingly difficult for this first wave of industrial enterprises to survive without government help because most firms were not ready to face rising competition from the United States, Europe, and eventually Japan.

Advocates of government intervention argued that Latin America's path to prosperity depended on industrialization and that industrialization could not be carried out without substantial government help. The dominant model of state assistance aimed primarily at **import-substituting industrialization** (ISI)—the creation of domestic firms that would produce finished goods that had previously been imported from outside the region. Government offered several forms of assistance to would-be industrialists by providing subsidized lines of credit, tax breaks, and protective tariffs (that is, taxes on competing imported goods), and often by creating state-run firms in capital-intensive sectors such as steel and public utilities that could provide basic inputs at subsidized rates. Initially, optimism ran high in several circles in Latin America and elsewhere that this government intervention (often called state capitalism because of the mix of public and private enterprise involved) would help countries to catch up economically (see *Global Perspectives: State Capitalism in the 1940s and 1950s*). Advocates claimed that state capitalism would reduce dependence on foreign imports, expand the percentage of its citizens that could afford a host of modern conveniences, and still permit Latin America to maintain its earlier competitive edge in several primary commodities. These policies succeeded in cultivating an increase in manufacturing activity and employment, especially in the larger countries in the region.

Over time, some weaknesses in the ISI strategy became apparent. The prior dependence on imported finished goods was replaced by a new (and often costlier) dependence on importing the machinery used to make the refrigerators, automobiles, televisions, and other manufactured consumer goods that were now produced locally. Although the creation of manufacturing jobs increased the percentage of the population able to buy consumer goods, anywhere from 10 to 50 percent of the population in each country in Latin America

GLOBAL PERSPECTIVES
State Capitalism in the 1940s and 1950s

Classical and neoclassical economic theory traditionally emphasized the role of market forces in stimulating prosperity for all countries, whether they specialized in manufactured goods or primary commodities. The principle of comparative advantage called for all economies to specialize in their most competitive sectors and to import all other goods. Civilian and military leaders in agriculturally based economies sometimes argued for government intervention to stimulate industry in the name of national security, but economists historically tended to be hostile to plans for so-called hot-house industrialization.

Over the course of the 1940s and 1950s, however, a new breed of economists favored extensive government intervention in pursuit of industrialization in agrarian economies. Raúl Prebisch, an Argentine economist at the United Nations Economic Commission for Latin America, was one of the most influential members of this new breed. Prebisch argued that industrialization was crucial because, without it, agrarian economies would continue to fall further behind the industrialized economies at the center of the world economy. His analysis of the relative prices of manufactured goods and primary commodities during the first half of the twentieth century concluded that the terms of trade favored the industrialized economies over time. Prebisch recommended protective tariffs on manufactured imports, government subsidies for industrial investment, government investment in capital-intensive heavy industry, and taxes on agricultural exports as tools that could stimulate the creation of reasonably competitive industries. Similar government policies had helped to promote the industrialization of the United States in the nineteenth century and of Japan during the twentieth century. If those policies helped in the United States and Japan, they could work elsewhere.

The advice of Prebisch and other like-minded economists found a receptive audience not just in many Latin American governments but also among the leaders of new nation-states around the globe. In 1950, India established a planning commission that set goals for industrialization and put forth a series of measures to promote their achievement. Following the end of the Korean War, South Korea resumed infant-industry policies that the Syngman Rhee government had begun before the war in the late 1940s. Although by no means a new nation-state, Japan began to promote new manufacturing sectors such as home electronics and motor vehicles. These policy changes around the world in the 1950s formed the backdrop against which an even larger number of countries (including many of the new nation-states of Africa) would adopt similar policies in the 1960s. The state capitalist trend established in the 1940s and 1950s would remain in force throughout most of the developing world until the 1980s and 1990s bore witness to a visible reduction in state intervention in the economy.

still lived in absolute poverty, while another 10 to 25 percent were also too poor to buy most modern conveniences. Finally, many countries in the region were no longer able to rely on commodity exports as the generally successful path to export earnings, as they had done for most of the half century preceding the Great Depression of the 1930s. Prices of most major commodities became more volatile, and the prices of many commodities declined in real terms amid greater competition from African, Asian, and European producers. The golden age of commodity-led growth of the late nineteenth and early twentieth centuries had ended. This slower growth in many commodity sectors made it harder for governments to promote industrialization by using tax revenues produced by the agricultural and mining sectors.

These commodity owners did not recede into the background of national politics during the onset of the ISI strategy. In most countries, landed interests viewed the new wave of ISI policies as an attack on their traditional role at the center of economic and political life. From the 1880s through the 1920s, agricultural and mining interests had grown accustomed to being the dominant figures in politics, finding expression either in dictatorships or in the major political parties of the oligarchic democracies found in much of South America. Politicians and military officers interested in promoting ISI alternatives to the laissez-faire approach needed to find a way to dislodge the traditional elite from its place in the political realm.

In most countries, the means chosen to reduce the power of the agrarian elite was an expansion of personal liberty, namely, an expansion of voting rights. Opportunistic leaders realized that they could build electoral coalitions of urban and rural blue-collar workers by promising to industrialize. Scholars studying this time period use the term **populism** to refer to these efforts to build heterogeneous mass support through a mix of nationalism, ISI developmentalism, and personal appeal. Populist leaders often used everyday language to motivate the citizenry to wrest political power from the landed elite.

By expanding voting rights, populist leaders participated in what constituted the second wave of democratization in the region. Many populist leaders also aided democratization indirectly by improving the living and working conditions of a substantial number of citizens. At the same time, however, most leaders placed visible limits on the expansion of liberty. For instance, Juan Perón won perhaps the cleanest and most competitive election in Argentine history in 1946 and then adopted a system of universal suffrage. Yet, once in office, Perón placed serious restrictions on the freedom of the press and on other civil liberties. Even in countries with somewhat greater guarantees of freedom for the media, populist politicians transformed the old politics of allegiance to the rural boss to a new age of machine politics analogous to the nature of electoral competition in major U.S. cities in the late nineteenth century.

Machine politics involves a network of personal ties often referred to as **clientelism** (see *Concepts in Action: Clientelism and Voting*). In patron-client relations, each political party offers to help citizens in some tangible way: by

CONCEPTS IN ACTION
Clientelism and Voting

Clientelist voting involves trading favors for votes. Such favors include a hot meal, a basket of food, clothing, cash payments, and short-term jobs. To seal this bargain, the precinct captains working for clientelist parties need to know how each citizen voted. In the machine politics of the nineteenth century, many countries had open-ballot voting, in which people marked their ballots in plain view.

Once political reforms introduced the secret ballot, clientelist parties had to invent ways to identify voters' choices. In some countries, voting laws did not require people to mark their ballots inside the voting booth. Voters who desired favors from precinct captains could mark their ballots in public and then cast them inside the booth. This practice survived in portions of rural Mexico well into the 1990s. Another loophole permitted parties to distribute legal ballots that were marked for a straight party ticket. Often parties would color-code these ballots so that such voters could be easily identified. This practice remained legal in Colombia until 1991.

The so-called carrousel provides a more complex example of how secret ballots can lose their secrecy. A precinct captain gathers a group of voters at a given location and asks them to vote in sequence. The precinct captain obtains a single legal ballot and premarks the ballot for that party's candidates. This premarked ballot is given to the first voter, who goes to the precinct, casts her premarked ballot, and returns to the shared location with a blank official ballot (which she received from a poll worker after presenting her voting credentials). The blank ballot demonstrates that this voter did not vote for a competing party. The precinct captain could then proceed to give this voter her promised reward(s). Then the precinct captain premarks the new blank ballot and gives it to a second voter, who follows the same procedure. This process continues until all the voters have finished. In this elaborate system, each voter *is* voting in secret; accordingly, each could spite the precinct captain by throwing away the premarked ballot. By participating in the carrousel, however, one cannot vote for any other party.

If end runs around the secret ballot are not feasible, a political party in control of government might use its influence over public works projects to entice neighborhoods into voting for it. A precinct captain might say that if 65 percent of a precinct votes for the governing party, government projects will provide jobs and improve streets and sewers. If that target is not met, the precinct captain predicts that the governing party will punish the neighborhood by cutting public works programs in that locality.

When voting is conducted in secret, clientelist parties can attempt to win votes by providing favors, but voters retain the freedom to vote for the party of their choice. Old traditions die hard, though, and the practice of providing favors during political campaigns has endured into the twenty-first century. Political parties often organize social programs that provide small amounts of food throughout the year, especially in poorer neighborhoods. Precinct captains also drum up support by providing jobs for party activists and, less

frequently, for some of the party's presumed voters. In these contemporary clientelist practices, parties try to gain and retain support by being perceived as a movement willing and
able to provide direct assistance to voters.

providing public jobs, promising preferential treatment, and "thanking" citizens for their support with gifts of money, clothing, or food. To establish an enduring clientelist political party, two elements are crucial. First, the clientelist
party needs to establish personal relationships at the ground level between
party precinct captains and ordinary citizens. These relationships mimic in
some ways the relationship between landowners and peasants on the *patria
chica* of the hacienda. Indeed, in many rural areas, landowners offered their
services to political parties as local power brokers. Second, the clientelist party
needs some means of ensuring that voters are loyal to the party.

This desire for control over ordinary citizens was widespread among government leaders in the populist era. To attract support, enterprising populist leaders

THE PERUVIAN EXPERIENCE
The Slow Emergence of State Capitalism (1930–1968)

Commodity exports drove Peru's economic growth from 1900 to 1930. Growth fanned the
expectations of white- and blue-collar urban workers, who felt excluded economically, politically, and socially. The so-called forty families remained the central reference point for the
Peruvian elite.

The person who became the most visible critic of the landed elite was a university student in 1924 when he was exiled by the Leguía dictatorship. From exile, Víctor Raúl Haya de
la Torre founded the American Revolutionary Popular Alliance (APRA). Haya saw his country
dominated by a small elite beholden to foreign interests. Before the term became fashionable, Haya sought a "third way" between market capitalism and communism. He called on
Latin Americans to devise solutions based on their own experiences—not on European
political ideologies. He saw APRA as a multiclass movement aimed at true national sovereignty and recommended Latin American unity as a means of avoiding foreign domination.
His policy platform called for the expansion of political freedoms, greater government intervention in the economy, and the nationalization of key economic sectors.

After a 1930 coup ended the Leguía dictatorship, Haya ran for the presidency in 1931
and finished second to Luis Sánchez Cerro, the leader of the coup. APRA's strong showing
disturbed many landholders. Conflict worsened as APRA blamed its defeat on fraud. The
government then arrested Haya and all legislators affiliated with APRA. Some APRA activists
responded in July 1932 by launching a rebellion in Trujillo, Haya's hometown. Surrounded
by the military, the rebels killed tens of military and civilian hostages; the military then

used flowery language, painting themselves as the saviors of their countries during electoral campaigns or during speeches justifying taking power via military coup. Once in power, their model of governance typically called for a greater centralization of power in pursuit of each leader's vision of national transformation. This centralization of authority was more readily achievable *inside* the government itself and was not so easily achieved in relations between the chief executive and societal forces *outside* the three branches of government. For example, while Juan Perón created new government agencies that centralized the commercialization of beef, he could not force cattle ranchers to bring their products to market. Producers' strikes were a frequent form of protest against the policies of his government.

In summary, the middle third of the twentieth century was a time of tremendous economic and political change. Events in Peru provide additional insight into the political controversy attached to these economic changes in Latin America (see *The Peruvian Experience: The Slow Emergence of State Capitalism (1930–1968)*). The move toward increased government intervention in the

---

executed hundreds of rebels and presumed sympathizers. Many soldiers and wealthy Peruvians now hated APRA and vice versa.

The enmity forged in the early 1930s mobilized sectors of Peruvian society that wanted to maintain a focus on commodity exports with limited government intervention in the economy. When APRA was blamed for the assassination of Sánchez Cerro in 1933, the legislature outlawed the APRA party. When APRA supported the winning candidate in the 1936 elections, the military annulled the results. After the next two civilian presidents legalized APRA, expanded government intervention in the economy, and raised taxes on the sugar sector to fund industrialization, landowners convinced the military to seize power in 1948 and to restore market-oriented policies. When elections returned, APRA backed conservative Manuel Prado, who as president legalized APRA. In 1962, Haya won a hotly contested three-way race that was decided by the legislature. The military dissolved the congress and called for new elections in 1963.

The 1963 winner was Fernando Belaúnde. Belaúnde called for land reform but moved cautiously. When guerrillas pressured for more rapid change, the army suppressed them. Within two years, the movement was snuffed out, but thousands were dead and large swaths of the countryside were ruined. The fighting left a lasting impression both on rural Peruvians and on the soldiers conducting the war. With the economy slowing down in 1967–1968, the political climate became even more tense. When the military removed Belaúnde in October 1968, the coup leaders were convinced that heavily market-oriented policies lay at the center of Peru's economic and political problems. Full-scale state capitalism was about to arrive in Peru—one to three decades after its emergence in much of the rest of Latin America.

economy and the expansion of voting rights in the political sphere faced varying degrees of opposition from the owners of commodity interests throughout the region. In general, these shifts in economic policy were faster and more complete in the largest and wealthiest economies in the region (Argentina, Brazil, Chile, and Mexico). The smaller economies also adopted many of these new economic policies, but they did so unevenly and often more slowly. In large and small economies alike, the emergence of state capitalism unleashed new societal dynamics that proved increasingly difficult to manage in the decades ahead.

THE AGE OF AUTHORITARIAN REACTION (1960s AND 1970s)

As Latin America moved into the 1960s and 1970s, the limitations of the ISI economic strategy were becoming increasingly apparent. The political tension between conflicting societal forces—already in evidence during the previous decades—heated up still further. The industrialization of the 1940s and 1950s transformed societies and raised expectations in many corners that countries might break through into a new era of material prosperity. Despite increased industrialization that raised the wages of many workers, however, a new economic age had not yet fully emerged.

In addition to continuing dependence on primary commodities and persistent poverty (especially in rural areas), the late 1950s and early 1960s saw the emergence of a new economic problem in several countries: the rising and erratic inflation of consumer prices. While inflation worldwide averaged 4 percent annually in the 1960s, it averaged more than 20 percent annually in Argentina and Chile and more than 40 percent in Brazil and Uruguay.[3] Why did inflation become such a serious problem during this time period? Each of the three major potential causes of inflation was linked in part to the ISI strategy. First, the push to industrialize suffered from structural bottlenecks of supply. Some key portions of the new manufacturing sector struggled to meet demand. In response, manufacturers tended to raise their prices, and these price hikes sent inflationary pressures throughout the economy. Second, political demands for increased government subsidies tended to exceed the will of the government (and of taxpayers) to raise taxes and thus pay for this expansion in government activity. Rising government deficits in many countries tended to raise prices by increasing the money in circulation faster than the supply of goods was growing. Finally, the emphasis of the ISI strategy on high tariff barriers and other government measures created economies that were largely closed to foreign competition. This sheltered economic environment gave way in several countries to what economic sociologists call tug-of-war inflation. Limits on foreign competition tempted producers of certain goods to boost their incomes by raising prices; such producers were confident that limited competition in the home market would allow them to raise prices without losing customers.

These actions often produced an inflationary spiral because other sectors of the economy employed the same strategy. Before long, increases in the general price level ate up the gain in profits caused by the initial price hike, and the whole cycle began all over again.

Increasing tension in wage negotiations in the manufacturing sector helped to break down the populist political alliance between urban workers and industrial entrepreneurs, who had earlier pursued mutual interests (often at the expense of the owners of primary commodities). As inflation rates soared, industrialists began to seek common cause with landowners by supporting military governments that would continue industrialization efforts while also clamping down on wage demands from workers in urban and rural areas. In the prior period, from 1930 to 1959, military coups were often brief affairs. Portions of the military supported certain civilian interests, installed those civilians in power through the use of force, and then stepped out of government.

In the 1960s and 1970s, Latin American militaries took power and governed many countries directly for what was often announced as an indefinite period. These dictatorships differed from the personal dictatorships of the late nineteenth and early twentieth centuries because the military often chose to exercise power collectively, claiming that the military was an organized, professional force that could administer peace and prosperity in visibly strife-ridden societies. These military regimes emerged first in the two most industrialized countries in the region—Brazil (1964) and Argentina (1966)—and then began to appear elsewhere. Only three countries maintained competitive multiparty elections throughout the period from 1960 to 1979: Colombia (which is a special case because the two major political parties agreed to share power regardless of electoral outcomes between 1958 and 1974), Costa Rica, and Venezuela.

This authoritarian backlash went directly against the expectations of the **modernization theory** of political development. Developed by social scientists working in the 1950s and early 1960s, modernization theory asserted that the twin socioeconomic changes of urbanization and industrialization would create viable conditions for democratic government. Traditional cultural norms, economic bonds, and political ties common to rural life in agrarian economies would break down, while citizens' expectations regarding their right to participate in some form of representative democracy would rise. Nevertheless, in Latin America, the second wave of democratization was reversed in two of the most industrialized and urbanized societies: Argentina and Brazil. To explain why Latin American political life was not conforming to the tenets of modernization theory, Argentine political sociologist Guillermo O'Donnell put forward his theory of **bureaucratic-authoritarianism** (see *Concepts in Action: Modernization Theory and Bureaucratic-Authoritarianism* on pages 42–43).

While not all scholars accept O'Donnell's precise explanation of the return to prolonged military rule, most analysts use the term *bureaucratic-authoritarian regime* to refer to the military governments of this period. The bureaucratic element refers to the collective form of rule by the armed forces in many countries

CONCEPTS IN ACTION
Modernization Theory and Bureaucratic-Authoritarianism

The modernization theory of political development asserted that industrialization and urbanization would promote democracy. If modernization was the motor of democratization, why did military regimes emerge in two of the most industrialized and urbanized countries in Latin America in 1964 (Brazil) and in 1966 (Argentina)? This question inspired Guillermo O'Donnell to write *Modernization and Bureaucratic-Authoritarianism* in 1973.

Like modernization theorists, O'Donnell focused on links between economic development and political development, but he reached different conclusions. He associated the emergence of populist movements in Argentina and in Brazil with the rise of a protected manufacturing sector. In this horizontal phase of import-substituting industrialization (ISI), domestic firms produced nondurable consumer goods yet needed to import the capital goods used to make the finished goods. The need to import capital goods along with unfavorable terms of trade produced a crippling balance-of-payments crisis. In response, some policy makers proposed the vertical extension of ISI to the capital goods sector, what O'Donnell called "deepening." Deepening implied a bigger role for foreign companies, investments with longer maturation periods, and a greater need for social control to protect these long-term investments.

O'Donnell argued that this economic stress created a demands-performance gap, in which appetites whetted by the easy success of horizontal ISI fell out of line with the resources available amid rising inflation and a balance-of-payments crisis. During this crisis, the calls for social control multiplied amid a growing fear of emerging Marxist-inspired movements, which was fueled by the emergence of a revolutionary government in Cuba in 1959. A technocratic nucleus among business, the bureaucracy, and the military shared an antipolitical world view compatible with military rule. A new heterogeneous coalition formed in support of bureaucratic-authoritarianism (B-A). In B-A regimes, the military took power for an extended period of time, often justifying military rule as necessary to prevent Marxist insurgency and to create investment conditions favorable to economic prosperity. In 1964, the Brazilian military called for sweeping powers to pursue "the restoration of internal order" as well as "the economic, financial, political, and moral reconstruction of Brazil."[1]

O'Donnell's theory took on increased relevance when subsequent events appeared to support his association of economic changes with a novel type of military rule in Latin America. The 1973 collapse of long-standing democratic regimes in Chile and in Uruguay, the 1976 return to military rule in Argentina, and the continuation of military rule in Brazil all provided examples of authoritarian rule in some of the region's most prosperous societies. In examining these and other events, many subsequent researchers rejected

---

[1]As translated and cited in Thomas Skidmore, *The Politics of Military Rule in Brazil, 1964–1985* (New York: Oxford University Press, 1988), p. 20.

O'Donnell's thesis based on deepening because the coups' timing was not closely tied to this specific economic problem. Nevertheless, many scholars defend the utility of a more general reading of O'Donnell's theory: economic pressures worked to break up populist political coalitions while at the same time stimulating calls to suppress wage demands via military rule.

---

as well as the effort to administer the economy by repressing labor unions. This vision of politics as bureaucratic administration was similar to the order-and-progress ideas about governance in the late nineteenth century: leave power in the hands of a few. The authoritarian element refers not just to the prohibition of free elections but also to the repression of civil liberties to deter protests by those unhappy to see power concentrated and used in this fashion.

These military governments were shaped by the Cold War context of the day. The triumph of Fidel Castro's revolutionary movement in Cuba in 1959 inspired some people with similar sentiments in portions of Latin America, while it alarmed others. Bureaucratic-authoritarian regimes frequently used the threat of guerrilla takeover as a justification for what Brazilian military doctrine wryly termed the self-defense of democracy. Under this interpretation of national security doctrine, militaries tried to resolve a contradiction at the heart of their political activity. The armed forces defended their rule by referring to the need to establish a context suitable for democracy, yet they frequently resorted to violent repression unchecked by the rule of law. The legacy of human rights violations stemming from these years forms one of the most contentious political, legal, and humanitarian issues in contemporary Latin America. The issue of repression is common to all military regimes of the period, even though the level and nature of state-sponsored violence varied considerably from country to country.

In contrast to the trend of bureaucratic-authoritarian rule, Peru witnessed a different military intervention in 1968. The Peruvian coup leaders focused primarily on implementing state capitalist economic policies that were enacted earlier in many other countries. This was a somewhat tardy version of the so-called developmentalist coups of the 1930s and 1940s in Brazil and Argentina. The authoritarian reaction to state capitalism in Peru did not suffer a similar delay but instead emerged in the form of a new military government established in 1975 (see *The Peruvian Experience: Military Rule (1968–1980)* on pages 44–45).

In the 1960s and 1970s, military regimes employed many coercive techniques in the name of countering guerrilla violence. These tactics reduced support for a continuation of military rule in two ways. First, the often indiscriminant use of repression created a multitude of victims of arrest without charge, detention without trial, torture under detention, and execution or disappearance. The surviving victims and their families organized groups opposed to continued military rule as a result of these human rights abuses. Second, when these harsh measures did reduce the threat of guerrilla violence, they eliminated one of the two major justifications put forward for military rule—a desire to ensure public order.

With the threat of guerrilla violence receding in most countries, the remaining major justification for the bureaucratic-authoritarian regimes was their claim that they could ensure a healthier economic climate than did the civilian governments of prior decades. This assertion eventually ran headlong into a growing list of economic woes in most countries during the late 1970s and early 1980s. In the years from 1971 to 1975, the regional economy grew by 6.6 percent annually, while average annual growth slowed to 5.2 percent from 1976 to 1980. Much of that growth was limited to the two largest regional economies (Brazil and Mexico).[4] A recession in most industrialized countries in the early 1980s, combined with rising interest rates and falling commodity prices, placed tremendous strains on all Latin American economies. These economic problems formed another key element of the context in which a new wave of democratic political regimes would form across the region during the 1980s.

THE PERUVIAN EXPERIENCE
Military Rule (1968–1980)

Major participants in the 1968 coup had played a role in repressing peasant movements during the mid-1960s. The military government's first communiqué criticized "economic forces, national and foreign, which have frustrated the realization of basic structural reforms and have helped to maintain an unjust social and economic order, an order which permits the utilization of our national resources for the few while the majority suffers the consequences of their marginal position."[1] Foreigners owned 40 to 70 percent of the mining, manufacturing, and banking sectors, while roughly 700 people controlled over half of Peru's arable land.

General Juan Velasco Alvarado became the president of a government committed to rapid economic transformation. In its first month, the Velasco government nationalized the U.S.-owned International Petroleum Company. A 1969 agrarian reform law led to the redistribution of more land than had occurred in any other Latin American country, with the exception of the redistribution by the Castro government in Cuba. By 1975, the program had transferred roughly half of all privately owned land, typically granting the land to agricultural cooperatives organized by former tenant farmers and workers on large estates. The Velasco government compensated landowners with bonds that paid an extra premium if landowners invested in manufacturing. This policy measure was one of many launched to

[1] As translated and cited in Alfred Stepan, *The State and Society: Peru in Comparative Perspective* (Princeton, N.J.: Princeton University Press, 1978), p. 255.

While the regional trend as a whole involved a growing repudiation of military rule across Latin America, one can observe varied patterns of transition toward democracy. Not all military governments returned power to civilians under the same terms. In some countries, the economic and political chaos associated with military rule left the armed forces with few supporters in society. In such countries (for example, Argentina and Bolivia), discredited military governments found it difficult to shape the political institutions that followed the end to military rule. Conversely, in other settings, the military retained considerable support, especially among many middle- and upper-income citizens. As a result, in several countries (including Brazil, Chile, and Guatemala) the military played a central role in shaping the formal and informal political rules of the new democracies. In both settings, newly elected governments considered paths toward achieving civilian control of the military. In Chapter Three, we will return to this issue of civil-military relations and consider other important elements of contemporary political life during this third wave of democratization in Latin America.

promote import-substituting industrialization via investment incentives, protective tariffs, and the creation of several new state-owned companies.

The form and amount of compensation provided to landowners prevented a widespread backlash such as that faced by the Castro government in the late 1950s and by the Allende government in Chile in the early 1970s. Nevertheless, these economic changes generated considerable controversy. Opposition to these ambitious development plans mounted as the price of major exports fell on world markets and as inflation rose amid the global economic turmoil associated with the oil price hikes of 1973–1974. Visible conflict also emerged over the creation of a military-led political mass movement called the National System of Social Mobilization (SINAMOS). Some officers saw SINAMOS as the next step in an enduring societal transformation, while others disliked its revolutionary overtones. The initial consensus in much of the military began to unravel. Wealthy Peruvians became more active in calling for an end to the Velasco government. Velasco's failing health (from 1972 on he suffered from a prolonged bout with cancer) also made his government vulnerable. After confirming the support of leaders in all military branches, General Francisco Morales Bermúdez led a coup on August 29, 1975.

The Morales government suspended many state-led development initiatives in an effort to reduce inflation and to attract foreign investment. These changes met with limited success. Faced with growing civilian opposition and division within the armed forces, Morales announced a transition to electoral rule in July 1977. Elections to a constituent assembly in 1978 culminated in the 1979 constitution and a return to democratic rule in 1980. While state capitalism emerged in Peru later than in most Latin American countries, Peru's return to democracy occurred in the same troubled economic climate that framed contemporary democratization in much of the region.

Activities and Exercises

1. Review this chapter and outline how the quest for development changed over the years 1880–1980. As time passed and policies changed, did the major factors influencing economic success remain similar or did they evolve? If they evolved, what changed between the late nineteenth century and the middle of the twentieth century?

2. This chapter discusses three waves of democratization that attempted to expand liberty since independence. What factors helped to promote each of these waves of democratization? In light of the successes and failures of the first two waves of democratization in the region, what is your initial forecast regarding the prospects for democratic consolidation in the third wave launched in the 1980s? On what do you base your assessment?

3. One of the central features of colonial rule in the region was a hierarchical approach to governance. How did successive generations of Latin Americans approach governance during the post-independence era (1830–1979) examined in this chapter? Now, consider the evolution of presidential power in the United States during that same period. What similarities and differences do you observe? What factors do you believe drive the differences you have identified?

4. *La muralla verde* (*The Green Wall*) has remained one of the most critically acclaimed Peruvian films since its release in 1970. The film examines conflicting visions of human life in rural and urban Peru. See if the film is available in your library or local video store.

5. This chapter has provided a capsule summary of Peru's historical evolution from the colonial era through 1980. If you are curious about the evolution of another country that will not be examined in Chapters Five through Eleven of this book, look for an online history at the U.S. Library of Congress website [http://lcweb2.loc.gov/frd/cs/cshome.html#toc]. How has this country's evolution mirrored the trends examined in this chapter? If it has varied from these trends, what do you think has caused those differences?

Suggested Readings

Bulmer-Thomas, Victor. *The Economic History of Latin America Since Independence,* 2d ed. Cambridge, England: Cambridge University Press, 2003.

Burkholder, Mark, and Lyman Johnson. *Colonial Latin America.* 5th ed. New York: Oxford University Press, 2004.

Bushnell, David, and Neill Macaulay. *The Emergence of Latin America in the Nineteenth Century.* New York: Oxford University Press, 1988.

Chasteen, John. *Born in Blood and Fire: A Concise History of Latin America.* New York: W.W. Norton, 2001.

Chasteen, John, and Joseph Tulchin, eds. *Problems in Modern Latin American History: A Reader.* Wilmington, Del.: Scholarly Resources, 1994.

Coe, Michael, and Rex Koontz. *Mexico: From the Olmecs to the Aztecs,* 5th ed. New York: Thames and Hudson, 2002.

Collier, David, ed. *The New Authoritarianism in Latin America.* Princeton, N.J.: Princeton University Press, 1979.

Collier, Ruth Berins, and David Collier. *Shaping the Political Arena: Critical Junctures, the Labor Movement, and Regime Dynamics in Latin America.* Princeton, N.J.: Princeton University Press, 1991.

Conniff, Michael, ed. *Populism in Latin America.* Tuscaloosa: University of Alabama Press, 1999.

Davies, Nigel. *The Ancient Kingdoms of Peru.* London, England: Penguin, 1997.

DiTella, Torcuato. *History of Political Parties in Twentieth-Century Latin America.* New Brunswick, N.J.: Transaction, 2004.

Kicza, John, ed. *The Indian in Latin American History: Resistance, Resilience, and Acculturation.* Wilmington, Del.: Scholarly Resources, 1993.

Klarén, Peter. *Peru: Society and Nationhood in the Andes.* New York: Oxford University Press, 2000.

Klarén, Peter, and Thomas Bossert. *Promise of Development: Theories of Change in Latin America.* Boulder, Colo.: Westview, 1986.

Knight, Franklin. *The Caribbean: The Genesis of a Fragmented Nationalism,* 2d ed. New York: Oxford University Press, 1990.

Linz, Juan, and Alfred Stepan, eds. *The Breakdown of Democratic Regimes.* Baltimore, Md.: Johns Hopkins University Press, 1978.

Loveman, Brian, and Thomas Davies, Jr., eds. *The Politics of Anti-Politics: The Military in Latin America,* rev. ed. Wilmington, Del.: Scholarly Resources, 1997.

Navarro, Marysa, and Virginia Sánchez Korrol. *Women in Latin America and the Caribbean: Restoring Women to History.* Bloomington: Indiana University Press, 1999.

Schele, Linda, and David Freidel. *A Forest of Kings: The Untold Story of the Ancient Maya.* New York: William Morrow, 1990.

Schneider, Ben Ross. *Business Politics and the State in Twentieth-Century Latin America.* Cambridge, England: Cambridge University Press, 2004.

Sheahan, John. *Patterns of Development in Latin America: Poverty, Repression, and Economic Strategy.* Princeton, N.J.: Princeton University Press, 1987.

Skidmore, Thomas, and Peter Smith. *Modern Latin America,* 5th ed. New York: Oxford University Press, 2001.

Stepan, Alfred. *The State and Society: Peru in Comparative Perspective.* Princeton, N.J.: Princeton University Press, 1978.

Thorp, Rosemary, and Geoffrey Bertram. *Peru 1890–1977: Growth and Policy in an Open Economy.* New York: Columbia University Press, 1978.

Williamson, Edwin. *The Penguin History of Latin America.* London, England: Penguin, 1992.

Endnotes

1. William J. Denevan, ed., *The Native Population of the Americas in 1492,* 2d ed. (Madison: University of Wisconsin Press, 1992).

2. Angus Maddison, *Monitoring the World Economy 1820–1992* (Paris: OECD, 1995), pp. 236, 239.

3. John Sheahan, *Patterns of Development in Latin America* (Princeton, N.J.: Princeton University Press, 1987), p. 102.

4. Inter-American Development Bank, *Economic and Social Progress in Latin America: 1980–1981 Report* (Washington, D.C.: IDB, 1981), p. 7.

Contemporary Latin America

CHAPTER 3

The Context of Contemporary Latin American Politics (1980 to the Present)

L ATIN AMERICA RETURNED TO ELECTORAL DEMOCRACY IN THE 1980s. Rising discontent over human rights violations and worsening economic problems fueled an increase in protests against the continuation of military rule. In addition, political and professional divisions within the armed forces worsened after the military had spent years at the helm of government. In the third wave of democratization in the region, elected governments replaced the military regimes established over the prior two decades. By late 1990, the only Latin American government whose leadership was not chosen via some form of multiparty election was the revolutionary government led by Fidel Castro in Cuba.

The size of this third (and largest) wave of democratization is not necessarily a sign that democracy is a foregone conclusion. The emergence and consolidation of robust democracy faces many challenges. Perhaps the most obvious threat is the possibility that the military might launch a coup to overthrow elected officials. This possibility is taken seriously because of Latin America's history of active military involvement. As we saw in Chapter Two, most countries experienced one or more coups during the twentieth century.

Democracy also faces challenges from civilians who are willing to circumvent various elements of the democratic process in pursuit of their political aims. We have already seen how Alberto Fujimori unilaterally closed the Peruvian legislature in 1992. After winning a majority in the reorganized legislature, Fujimori later faced allegations of restrictions on civil liberties and illegal influence on the legislature. These political scandals emerged against a backdrop of disagreement over the desired course of national economic policy, over how government should treat its citizens, and over how government should be organized. Peru is not alone in its disagreement on these issues.

In addition to potential challenges from the armed forces and from hyper-presidentialist politicians who favor centralizing authority in the executive branch, the creation of a robust democracy faces several other important limitations. An increasingly globalized economic environment has made domestic and foreign investors more able and willing to move money quickly from one country to another. Uneven economic performance angers (and harms) citizens while it makes life more difficult for the government. Longstanding and more recent political cleavages are often mediated through clientelist practices that sometimes violate democratic norms and at other times make good economic performance more difficult. In many Latin American countries, respect for the rule of law has been uneven across all levels of government. The executive branch at the national and subnational levels often consists of an inefficient bureaucracy filled with a mix of political appointees and poorly paid but tenured civil servants. In the early twenty-first century, the third wave of democratization enters its third decade in most of Latin America, but the path toward a fully functioning democracy remains unclear.

This chapter introduces the contemporary context in which political life unfolds in Latin America. The return to democratic rule has been shaped by various domestic and international influences. We begin by reviewing economic conditions and the politics of market-oriented policy reform. Then we will place that process of economic reform within a broader international context. Next, we outline the societal context by discussing major social cleavages. We then discuss the political context in which political parties and the military pursue their goals. Against that background, we will consider the future of democratic consolidation by examining how the pursuit of development, liberty, and governance influences the prospects for democracy.

THE ECONOMIC CONTEXT

The newly formed democracies of the 1980s faced a difficult economic situation. Many countries suffered from rising inflation, stagnant economic growth rates, falling real wages, and a considerable foreign debt (often but not always inherited from a previous military government). These difficulties—combined with considerable pressure from various international forces—helped to spawn a reexamination of governmental reliance on state capitalist policies. This rethinking eventually produced a shift toward more market-oriented policies throughout most of Latin America.

The Economic Crisis of the 1980s

Many analysts refer to the 1980s as a "**lost decade**" of economic development in Latin America. The statistics speak for themselves. The gross domestic product (GDP) per person shrank by 0.9 percent annually; between 1980 and 1989, the region's economic activity shrank by almost 10 percent relative to its population size. Consumer prices in Latin America and the Caribbean rose by over 1,000 percent from December 1988 to December 1989, and they rose by over 1,000 percent again during 1990. (If inflation were 1,000 percent in the United States next year, a Sunday newspaper that cost $2.00 at the beginning of the year would cost $22.00 by year's end.) Foreign debt payments constituted 20 percent of export earnings in 1980 and doubled to over 40 percent by 1982; by the end of the 1980s, they had leveled off to around 30 percent. Income distribution worsened, and the percentage of the population living in poverty rose from 40 percent in 1980 to 48 percent by 1990.

These difficult economic conditions placed pressure on governments. As economic struggles continued, some policy makers, analysts, and politicians questioned the region's tendency toward protectionist trade policies and considerable government intervention in the domestic economy. Instead, they recommended increasing the role for market forces by slashing tariff barriers, reducing economic regulations, decreasing employment in the public sector, and privatizing state-owned enterprises. Private banks joined in this call for economic policy reform. These voices within Latin America found a welcome audience in the international financial community—particularly in the International Monetary Fund (IMF).

The Shift Toward More Market-Oriented Economic Policies

Throughout the early and mid-1980s, this call for reform went largely unheeded. The state capitalist economic approach established in the 1930s and 1940s had many defenders in government and in society as a whole. Many industrialists feared that their firms could not survive a surge in foreign competition. Many labor unions opposed the wholesale firing of workers via industrial restructuring and via the reform of public administration.

Nevertheless, as inflation and debt payment pressures worsened, several countries began to adopt substantial elements of the market-oriented reform package. They did so for various reasons: to negotiate loans from international financial institutions like the IMF, to attract investment, and to respond to a rethinking of economic policy by many analysts in and around the government. Bolivia underwent an economic "shock treatment" program after experiencing hyperinflation in 1985. Mexico underwent a more gradual reform process during the second half of the decade. Argentina, like Bolivia, turned to market-oriented reform as a way to escape its hyperinflationary crisis of 1989–1990. Brazil followed suit in the early 1990s.

By the mid-1990s, most Latin American governments had substantially reduced their tariff barriers and privatized many of their state-owned enterprises. They tried to reduce budget deficits and to stabilize national currencies. Public employment was cut back substantially in some countries, while in others the decrease was negligible. For the first time since the 1920s, market-oriented economic ideas dominated the halls of government in most of the region. Peru provides an interesting study in contrast during these two tumultuous decades. Peruvians elected one of the least market-oriented presidents (Alan García) in the region in the mid-1980s. Then, in 1990, Peruvians elected Alberto Fujimori, who delivered a series of vague campaign speeches on the economy and then undertook sweeping market-oriented reform. *The Peruvian Experience: Economic Policy from 1980 to 2000* discusses this shift in economic policy.

The two most visible political changes in Latin America during the 1980s and 1990s were the restoration of democratic rule and the shift toward more market-oriented economic policies. Democracy and the market have not enjoyed an easy, carefree coexistence. The opening of the economy harmed existing economic interests—particularly in the manufacturing sector. Many industrial entrepreneurs went bankrupt, and many jobs lost in those firms were not replaced by similar jobs elsewhere. This scenario should serve as food for thought when one considers the political dynamics of major economic policy change. Some people stand to gain considerably from these reforms, while others stand to lose everything they have worked for throughout their adult lives. The stakes can be extremely high.

THE PERUVIAN EXPERIENCE
Economic Policy from 1980 to 2000

Democracy returned to Peru in 1980 amid economic problems. The prices of its major exports fell amid a world recession, and the economy shrank by 12 percent in 1983. Rising interest rates made the public debt inherited from the military regime more burdensome. By 1984, debt obligations equaled 75 percent of Peruvian export earnings.

In the 1985 campaign, many criticized budget cutbacks implemented by outgoing president Fernando Belaúnde. APRA candidate Alan García advocated state capitalism and won 53 percent of the vote. He limited debt payments to 10 percent of Peru's export earnings so that the money saved could stimulate the economy. García gambled that the financial community would support Peru in acknowledgment that current debt obligations could not be met. Stimulus measures would reactivate the economy, thus attracting investment that, in time, could enable Peru to meet a higher percentage of its debt obligations.

The economy grew by 10.8 percent in 1986 and by 9.7 percent in 1987; however, major growth in investment did not follow. In July 1987, a frustrated García criticized the "financial oligarchy" for its unwillingness to invest and announced the nationalization of all Peruvian-owned banks. The move united upper- and middle-income Peruvians against García. Legal challenges stalled the bank nationalization, while leftist parties accused García of ceding to pressure by delaying nationalization. Amid the turmoil, the economy shrank by nearly 20 percent in two years. Annual inflation, which had averaged around

In light of potential political opposition to market-oriented policies, several reform-minded presidents requested special powers. Some asked the legislature to permit the executive branch to conduct reform by decree. The debate over economic policy also spilled into the debate over liberty because some reform-oriented presidents imposed new restrictions on the right to strike as a way to limit opposition to privatization. In each of the countries examined in this text, we will examine the twists and turns of the politics of the economic reform debate and its implications for the pursuit of development, liberty, and governance.

THE INTERNATIONAL CONTEXT

International influences played an important role in the shift toward market-oriented economic policies. As Chapter Two made clear, the international arena has long shaped debates unfolding in Latin America. Thus, our effort to understand the region today must also take into account international forces. Here we consider the roles played by economic globalization, international

100 percent during 1984–1987, exploded to 1,722 percent in 1988 and 2,755 percent in 1989.

The profound crisis shaped the 1990 elections. Center-right parties backed novelist Mario Vargas Llosa's call for more market-oriented policies. American Revolutionary Popular Alliance (APRA) candidate Luis Alva (who had resigned as García's economic minister a month prior to the nationalization decree) called for state capitalism, while the two major leftist candidates rejected capitalism. Little-known university president Alberto Fujimori blamed the crisis on traditional politicians of all ideological stripes but had a vague economic platform. A divided electorate gave Vargas Llosa 28 percent of the vote. Fujimori came in second with 25 percent, and Alva finished third with 19 percent. In a runoff election between the two leading vote-getters, Fujimori won with 57 percent of the vote.

Fujimori pursued an even more vigorous set of market-oriented reforms than those outlined by Vargas Llosa. In addition to reducing barriers to foreign imports, Fujimori privatized many state-owned enterprises. He began with the agricultural cooperatives established under the Velasco government and then sold off publicly owned banks, mining companies, the national airline, and the telephone company. The reforms led to a renegotiation of the foreign debt and to an increase in investment by 1993. The economy grew by an average of 7 percent annually during 1993–1997. When the economy slowed down noticeably during 1998–1999, however, many opposition candidates in the April 2000 elections charged that Fujimori's market-oriented approach had failed to improve conditions for most Peruvians. This debate would continue during the 2001 elections and the ensuing presidency of Alejandro Toledo.

CONCEPTS IN ACTION
Dependency Theory

Just as bureaucratic-authoritarianism challenged the modernization theory of political development (review *Concepts in Action: Modernization Theory and Bureaucratic Authoritarianism* in Chapter Two), the dependency theory of economic development questioned the applicability of neoclassical economic theory to Latin America (and to Third World countries more generally). Over the course of the 1960s and 1970s, dependency theorists in Latin America and elsewhere asserted that efforts to develop by following the market-oriented principle of comparative advantage would be unlikely to succeed. All dependency analysts emphasized the relevance of global economic dynamics for understanding national economic development; however, they proved less united in their economic policy recommendations.

Dependency theory has its roots in two intellectual traditions—Marxist theories of imperialism and structuralist theories of economic growth. While both focus on the dynamics of global capitalism, they differ in their respective conceptualizations of development obstacles and in their optimism that these obstacles can be overcome within the dynamics of a global capitalist economy. It is inappropriate to say that there is one dependency theory because considerable divergence of opinion exists in these two major streams of thought.

For some dependency analysts, the dynamics of the global economy make it almost impossible for Third World countries to develop economically. Andre Gunder Frank asserted that the emergence of modern capitalism had been based on the exploitation of colonial economies ("the satellites") by the major European colonizers ("the metropolis"). For Frank, the development of Europe (and later of North America) had been predicated on the systematic underdevelopment of most of the rest of the world. At the end of the colonial era in Latin America, the newly independent nation-states generally retained their prior role as the source of primary commodities essential for the ongoing industrial development of the metropolis. Frank argued that the political and economic activities of the metropolis would continue to prevent the satellites' development because this exploitation was central to the dynamics of capital accumulation already in place. By extension, Frank recommended exiting the global capitalist economy via the construction of a socialist state as the best path toward economic development.

Other dependency analysts (including Fernando Henrique Cardoso, Peter Evans, Enzo Faletto, and Osvaldo Sunkel) placed greater emphasis on Argentine economist Raúl Prebisch's terms-of-trade argument, which distinguished between the industrialized "core" and the commodity-based "periphery" (review *Global Perspectives: State Capitalism in the 1940s and 1950s* in Chapter Two). Like Frank, these analysts believed that reliance on primary commodities hampered Latin American economic development. They were somewhat less pessimistic, however, about the prospects for progress within the workings of the global economy. Instead, like Prebisch, they recommended that the government promote industrialization to change the structural dynamics of the national economy. These dependency theorists did not believe that the creation of an industrial base alone implied that Latin American economies would escape their dependence on global economic dynamics. Once industrialized, these societies would confront a new set of challenges: they would need to nurture industrial entrepreneurs with fewer ties to multinational corporations headquartered abroad. For Cardoso, Latin America's industrialization did not end its dependence on global economic forces but instead opened up a new era of "associated-dependent development."

---

organizations, and the United States in framing contemporary political choices in Latin America.

Economic Globalization

The phrase *economic globalization* has been heard so often over the past few years that the term seems cliché. Nevertheless, it refers to something real—an increase in the interconnections among economies around the world. Connections among national economies have existed for centuries. Advocates of the **dependency** approach to understanding economic development have long asserted that the global economy constrains Latin America's economic (and political) alternatives (see *Concepts in Action: Dependency Theory*).

Although global economic networks have existed for centuries, during the 1980s and 1990s the world experienced an increase in globalization in two tangible dimensions—the interconnectedness of the production process for many goods, and the size and speed of the international financial system. Prior to the second half of the twentieth century, most industrial production processes occurred within national boundaries. Countries often imported raw materials from abroad, but the assembly process took place domestically. Beginning in the 1950s and 1960s, some companies—particularly in consumer electronics and semiconductors—began to create transnational production processes in which portions of the product were manufactured in two or more countries. Over the rest of the twentieth century, this trend intensified as both the number of companies engaging in transnational manufacturing and the number of product lines involved (motor vehicles, clothing, home appliances) grew. Often, these operations took place in **special economic zones** (SEZs), in which companies receive government incentives for moving a portion of their production process into an SEZ. By the end of the 1980s, approximately 260s SEZs were situated around the world; by the late 1990s there were almost 850.[1] Many Latin American countries have SEZs; Mexico has perhaps the largest presence of partial manufacturing in the hundreds of assembly processing plants (*maquiladoras*) located primarily on its border with the United States. By the late 1980s, over

400,000 Mexicans worked at *maquiladoras*. Advocates of SEZs promote them as a source of export earnings and manufacturing jobs. Critics question both the desirability of those jobs and the practices of the multinational companies (MNCs) that provide them.

While transnational production has developed over the past few decades, international financial markets have existed for centuries. What is new about contemporary financial globalization is the increasing size of global financial markets and the speed with which they operate. The recent growth in global finance is nothing short of staggering. The total volume of world electronic financial trading in currencies, stocks, bonds, and other financial instruments on any given day in the early twenty-first century typically totals several trillion U.S. dollars. For example, the total volume of foreign exchange market transactions (that is, the buying and selling of national currencies) rose fifteen times between 1980 and 1998, to $1.5 trillion per day.[2] Like transnational production, the globalization of finance provides both opportunities and pitfalls for countries in Latin America and beyond.

Speculation about foreign exchange rates places pressure on policy makers around the globe. Concerns about the ability of the Thai government to meet its debt obligations and to maintain the value of its currency during early 1997 mushroomed into a regional financial crisis that affected currency values and stock market investments in Indonesia, Malaysia, Singapore, and South Korea. In the ensuing months, panic spread to other developing economies facing speculation that they could not defend their currencies. As the Russian ruble lost value in August 1998 and investors sold off holdings in Russian markets, panic struck stock markets around the world. During the last week of August alone, stock markets lost over 10 percent of their value in Argentina, Brazil, Mexico, Russia, South Africa, and Turkey. Throughout this text, we will examine the repercussions of the Asian crisis of 1997–1998 as well as the other financial crises in Latin America during the late twentieth and early twenty-first centuries.

International Organizations

Economic globalization has helped to increase the visibility and influence of international organizations. Latin America is no exception to this trend. Global **intergovernmental organizations** (IGOs) such as the International Monetary Fund (IMF) and the World Bank are frequently active participants in the economic policy-making process. Over the years, IMF loan decisions to stabilize national currencies have taken on an informal importance well beyond the size of the loan because the IMF frequently ties financing decisions to the economic policy of the government asking for credit. This **conditionality** of IMF credit can convince private investors and banks that the government is on the path to more market-oriented policies, thereby potentially opening the door to new investment and credit. At the same time, this conditionality principle makes the IMF's presence in the region politically controversial because many local opponents of market-oriented policies accuse the IMF of imposing the will of wealthy foreign countries on the rest of the world.

Global economic IGOs are not the only international organizations active in Latin America. Several groups of countries have entered into regional economic integration agreements in which they commit to reduce barriers to trade across their respective borders. The 1990s saw considerable economic integration among small sets of neighboring countries via accords such as the Central American Common Market, the Caribbean Community, the Andean Community, and the Southern Cone Common Market. In addition, beginning in 1994, thirty-four of the thirty-five countries in the Americas began negotiations toward a potential Free Trade Agreement of the Americas (FTAA) that could eliminate trade barriers across the entire Western Hemisphere.

Beyond these economic IGOs, the Organization of American States (OAS) is a multifunctional IGO for the nation-states of the Western Hemisphere. The OAS increased its workload at the dawn of the twenty-first century to engage in the coordination of efforts to tackle a diverse set of transborder issues, including children's rights, corruption, drug trafficking, education, the environment, gender discrimination, labor issues, indigenous rights, security, telecommunications, terrorism, trade, and transportation. One of the growing concerns of the OAS has been the promotion and defense of democracy in the hemisphere. For example, during the 2000 presidential elections in Peru, an OAS mission of electoral observers undertook the difficult task of evaluating the integrity of the voting process (see *The Peruvian Experience: The OAS Electoral Observation Mission in 2000* on pages 57–58).

An increasing variety of international **nongovernmental organizations** (NGOs) also form an important element of the Latin American political landscape. For the first half of the twentieth century, varied groups associated with Catholicism formed the most visible set of NGOs with international ties. After World War II, the major Catholic charity in the region, Caritas, began to expand not only its ties to Catholics around the globe but also to other NGOs based in the industrialized societies of North America and Europe. In the 1950s and 1960s, major charitable foundations such as the Ford and Rockefeller foundations increased their development initiatives in Latin America. In the last third of the twentieth century, newer NGOs began to focus on particular issues. Gender relations, the environment, and the conditions faced by indigenous peoples all attracted increasing attention. International NGOs based in the Northern Hemisphere can link NGOs headquartered in Latin America to sources of funds in wealthy countries.

U.S.-Latin American Relations

The other major international influence in Latin American politics has been the U.S. government. Indeed, a visible number of observers would argue that the United States constitutes the most important foreign influence on national politics in the Western Hemisphere, especially in the countries of the Caribbean Basin. U.S. foreign policy toward Latin America evolved over the nineteenth and twentieth centuries, but two major guiding principles were fairly constant throughout. First, in the name of an extended definition of U.S. national security, the U.S. government tried to keep the region relatively free from overt influence from outside the Western Hemisphere. This principle was formally enunciated in 1823 as the **Monroe Doctrine**, in response to British incursions during the early phase of independence in many Latin American countries. Since 1823, this doctrine has remained in place as a warning to nation-states from outside the hemisphere. Second, most U.S. presidencies have tended to place the protection of U.S. economic interests as a major priority in U.S.-Latin American relations.

During the twentieth century and the start of the twenty-first century, these two goals formed four distinct eras of U.S. policy toward the region. From 1904 to 1929, the United States greatly expanded its military presence in many countries in the Caribbean Basin. Theodore Roosevelt first established this presence to prevent European powers from using force to collect debts owed

THE PERUVIAN EXPERIENCE
The OAS Electoral Observation Mission in 2000

Prior to 1990, when the Organization of American States (OAS) organized electoral observation missions (EOMs), it sent a handful of observers who stayed for a few days. In 1990, this practice changed with the establishment of the new Unit for the Promotion of Democracy. This agency formed teams of technical advisers and recruited monitors to observe voting.

To boost sagging confidence in the electoral process, the Alberto Fujimori government asked the OAS to monitor the April 2000 elections. Former Guatemalan foreign minister Eduardo Stein led an EOM with over 100 members. The advance team arrived in early March as a scandal broke regarding the legality of signatures used to register Fujimori's *Perú2000* party. The EOM investigated this and other allegations, including intimidation of opposition activists and government manipulation of the media. The EOM also worried that the computer network for tallying votes was vulnerable to manipulation because a simulated test of the system indicated problems. Meanwhile, the EOM's technical advisers helped train thousands of temporary workers who would manage the voting process at over 87,000 polling places.

After the election, registration verification problems and questions about the security of ballot boxes surfaced. A three-day delay in the vote count raised eyebrows because the unofficial "quick count" (conducted by election monitors as paper ballots were certified and packaged for transport to computerized vote-tallying centers) proclaimed a close race for the presidency while the official results later gave Fujimori a 10-percentage-point lead. Allegations were made that the number of votes cast exceeded the number of registered by governments in the region. The interventionist slant associated with this **Roosevelt Corollary** to the Monroe Doctrine had some supporters in Latin America but also led to a firestorm of criticism from many who saw the U.S. presence as an unwarranted intrusion into the domestic affairs of sovereign nation-states.

The ill will generated over the years by these policies produced pressure on the United States to use less military coercion and more diplomacy. The governments led by Herbert Hoover and Franklin Delano Roosevelt from 1929 to 1945 responded to these pressures under the **Good Neighbor Policy**. The U.S. government formally recognized the principle of nonintervention in hemispheric relations within the Pan-American Union. Beyond this formal pledge, these administrations also reduced the frequency of U.S. military intervention.

The establishment of communist governments throughout most of eastern Europe framed a third era in U.S.-Latin American relations after World War II. U.S. foreign policy worldwide shifted to a focus on the **Cold War** rivalry between the United States and the Soviet Union. These Cold War concerns would shape U.S. policy toward Latin America from 1945 until the fall of the Berlin Wall in

---

voters in certain precincts. Some charged that data entry operators altered the results of the congressional elections. Presidential challenger Alejandro Toledo mobilized rallies denouncing fraud. Because no one received the majority needed to win the presidency, a runoff election was called for May 28. Toledo refused to participate unless the EOM and other observers found improvements in the process for the runoff.

The OAS mission urged postponement of the runoff until problems in the computer system and in the voter registration rolls could be resolved. When the elections board refused to postpone, Eduardo Stein announced that his mission would not observe the runoff. Nongovernmental observers followed suit. Toledo then withdrew his candidacy and urged people to boycott the election. The Peruvian government declared that it was too late for withdrawals and held the election, which Fujimori won.

The EOM's formal report in early June ignited debate over whether these events warranted invocation of standing OAS Resolution 1080 in defense of democracy. If invoked, the resolution would force consideration of hemispherewide sanctions for the first time in reaction to electoral problems. In the end, the OAS did not call this emergency meeting, but instead it sent a special delegation to Peru led by the OAS secretary general and by the president of the general assembly. That delegation recommended civil liberties enhancements and organized a multiparty working group to discuss reforms. This roundtable had just been launched when a videotape aired in September showing Fujimori's intelligence adviser bribing an opposition legislator to switch parties so that Fujimori could retain a legislative majority. Amid mounting domestic and international pressure, the bribery scandal proved to be the last straw. The OAS delegation brokered a deal in which Fujimori announced that he would resign and call new elections in 2001.

1989. U.S. policy makers mixed neglect toward countries with no visible threat of communist influence with a concern for countries viewed as being at risk for communist insurgency. Policy makers over the years used foreign aid in support of anticommunist dictatorships while employing covert military force and economic pressure to topple Latin American governments deemed unwilling or incapable of preventing the growth of communist movements within their national territories. In this book, we will examine two countries—Guatemala (1954) and Chile (1973)—where the United States used covert action in support of anticommunist coups, and we will also track the conflictual relationship between the Castro regime in Cuba and the U.S. government.

While the Castro government survived the fall of the Berlin Wall, the end to communist regimes in eastern Europe and the dissolution of the Soviet Union have given way to a more complex climate for U.S.-Latin American relations in the post–Cold War era that has prevailed from 1990 to the present. While security issues and the protection of U.S. economic interests remain important, the Cold War emphasis on counterinsurgency has been replaced by a more complex agenda that also includes the promotion of democratic rule, the pursuit of hemispheric free trade, protection of the environment, and the reduction of trafficking in illegal narcotics. In pursuit of this diversified agenda, U.S. presidents have often used multilateral negotiations combined with efforts to wield U.S. economic influence and foreign aid in bilateral relations. For example, in its effort to combat drug trafficking, the United States has organized presidential summits and pushed for regionwide agreements to combat money laundering. The United States has also worked unilaterally by threatening to withhold economic aid through the controversial "decertification" of a country's drug policies.

THE SOCIETAL CONTEXT

International factors shape political dynamics in Latin America and elsewhere in important ways. In particular, the economic vulnerability of the region constrains Latin American politicians, making some potential policy choices improbable, while also placing some issues higher on the public agenda than would otherwise be the case. Despite the clear importance of the international context, it should be no surprise that basic societal **cleavages** are often at the center of national politics. The term *cleavage* refers to a potential fault line of societal division and political conflict. In this section, we will examine briefly several politically relevant societal distinctions, including socioeconomic status, subnational regions, ethnicity, religion, ideology, and gender.

Socioeconomic Status

Socioeconomic status (SES) frames political activity in various ways. The level of economic resources enjoyed by a citizen can shape his or her political beliefs

TABLE 3.1   Income Inequality Around the World: Percentage of Income Earned by the Richest 20 Percent of the Population

Region	Average for 1960–1995	Average for 1990–1995
Latin America and the Caribbean	55.12	52.94
Sub-Saharan Africa	51.79	52.37
Middle East and North Africa	46.32	45.35
East Asia and the Pacific	45.73	44.33
South Asia	43.01	39.91
High-Income Countries	40.42	39.79
Eastern Europe	36.11	37.80

SOURCE: Klaus Deininger and Lyn Squire, "A New Data Set Measuring Income Inequality," *World Bank Economic Review* 10 (1996): 585.

and especially the ability to pursue personal goals in the political arena. Generally speaking, in societies around the world, the more economically comfortable people are, the more likely they are to take an ongoing interest in politics. Beyond its influence on political participation, differences in SES often entice politicians and private citizens to tailor their political demands to disputes between wealthier and poorer citizens.

This cleavage is particularly relevant in Latin America for two major reasons. First, from the colonial era onward, propertied classes have tended to see themselves and their interests as distinct from the rest of society. Second, compared to most parts of the globe, income distribution remains decidedly uneven. In the 1990s, Latin America continued to have the highest income inequality in the world (with only sub-Saharan Africa close to the same level). The richest 20 percent of the population earned almost 53 percent of all income (see Table 3.1). We will be attentive to the political relevance of these attitudinal and tangible distinctions in socioeconomic status throughout this text.

Subnational Regionalism

Regions within countries can develop a particular political relevance over time. Citizens can unite politically to protect regional cultural traditions, to pursue greater autonomy from the national government, and to extract greater financial resources and benefits from the national government. The separatist movement in Quebec within Canada illustrates the potential political power of subnational regionalism as a cleavage.

In Latin America, the nineteenth and early twentieth centuries were filled with regional challenges to the authority of national governments, a situation illustrated perhaps most dramatically by the separation of Panama from Colombia in 1903. From the early twentieth century onward, few major political movements have sought complete autonomy. However, many regionally framed political movements have organized to pressure for greater resources from the national government. Also, beyond the existence of regional political parties, nationwide political parties sometimes contain subnational factions that promote what they see as their respective regions' best interests.

Ethnicity

As is the case in Quebec, Canada, regional cleavages can become powerful when many members of a given ethnic group live within a single subnational political unit. Ethnicity can be defined by a (sometimes presumed) shared racial ancestry, by language, and by common cultural customs and practices. Latin America is a racially and ethnically diverse region. During the colonial era, the concentration of economic, political, and social power in the hands of the peninsular and creole elite limited the political power of people of non-Iberian ethnicities. Disease and death reduced further the cohesion, power, and size of indigenous societies. By the time of independence in the nineteenth century, racially and ethnically mixed mestizos had become the largest racial category in most countries.

In the present day, indigenous languages and cultural practices are shared by only tiny minorities of the population in much of the region. Indigenous peoples comprise roughly 10 percent of the total population of Latin America today. The indigenous population is concentrated primarily in southern Mexico, Guatemala, Bolivia, Colombia, Ecuador, and Peru. Indigenous peoples form a majority only in Bolivia; they also constitute nearly half of the population of Guatemala. Whether indigenous peoples constitute a small or a large portion of a country's population, they face problems of poverty, political underrepresentation, and social discrimination. In this book, we will observe recent organizational efforts to defend indigenous interests in our examination of politics in Guatemala and Mexico.

Gender

Gender provides another societal cleavage with potential relevance for political life. While several indigenous societies reserved a central role in economic life for women, the Iberian colonization experience brought with it a fairly strict division of gender roles. Women were assumed to be central to family life, while men were assumed to be central to life outside the home—in the economy, in society, and in politics.

This cultural tradition of **machismo** remains an important obstacle to female participation in politics. While women gained the right to vote by the 1950s, female participation in leadership positions in interest groups and in political parties remained minimal in most countries during the 1960s and 1970s. From the 1980s to the present, one can see the beginnings of an upswing in female participation in leadership roles. Women formed important new social movements that promoted the defense of human rights and that attempted to improve conditions in their neighborhoods. Beyond these new interest groups, female participation in national electoral politics also increased. Violeta Chamorro in Nicaragua (1990–1996) and Mireyra Moscoso in Panama (1999–2004) became the first two women elected directly to the presidency of Latin American countries. Despite these changes, women still form a small (albeit growing) minority of all legislatures and cabinet appointments, and women are almost absent from national leadership positions in business and labor confederations.

Religion

Iberian colonization led to the creation of a dominant religion—Roman Catholicism. Over the course of the 1980s and 1990s, evangelical Protestant movements attracted a sizable minority of the population in several cases, particularly in Brazil and in Central America. Nevertheless, to this day the majority of the population of every Latin American country formally adheres to the Roman Catholic faith (although the percentage that frequently attends church services is considerably lower).

While the societal predominance of Roman Catholicism radically reduced the potential for interfaith cleavages as a source of political conflict, the political power and influence of the Catholic church has motivated political mobilization from the nineteenth-century conflict between liberals and conservatives onward to the present day. Anticlerical interests among liberals culminated in a spiral of violence between liberal and conservative movements in several countries in the first half of the twentieth century, particularly in Colombia and Mexico. In the 1950s, Catholic social doctrine helped to inspire the creation of important Christian Democratic political parties in several countries, notably in Chile and Venezuela. During the 1960s and 1970s, further debate within the church led many priests and parishioners to advocate a form of **liberation theology**, which used the Bible as the basis for a profound criticism of the prevailing socioeconomic and political order (see *Concepts in Action: Liberation Theology* on pages 64–65). In the 1980s and 1990s, vigorous debate emerged in some countries over whether governments should legalize divorce (because it was forbidden by church doctrine) and whether to remove constitutional provisions that required presidential candidates to be adherents to the Catholic faith.

CONCEPTS IN ACTION
Liberation Theology

Liberation theology emerged from a broader reassessment of the Catholic church. For centuries, priests said mass in Latin and presented pastoral messages based on stable church doctrine. By the middle of the twentieth century, these practices came under increasing question from clergy and laity. Pope John XXIII responded by organizing the Second Vatican Council, or Vatican II. Vatican II (1962–1965) called for many changes. Rather than saying mass and other sacraments in Latin, priests were encouraged to speak the local language. Vatican II also acknowledged the vital role of lay parishioners in the church.

This call for a more active laity had already begun in Latin America in the late 1950s and early 1960s as priests considered interactive pastoral methods modeled on Paulo Freire's approach to literacy education. Working in the poorest region of Brazil, Freire rejected rote memorization. His approach began with the student, passed through a dialogue with the teacher, and then came back to the student. Freire termed this "a pedagogy of liberation," and his call for consciousness-raising struck a chord in parts of the Catholic community. Many Brazilian parishes formed so-called Christian base communities that employed this approach to studying the Bible. By the mid-1960s, the base community movement had begun in much of Latin America.

The reformist tone and actions of Vatican II gave further impetus to these winds of change. The 1968 conference of Latin American bishops in Medellín, Colombia, focused on the trying circumstances faced by millions of people. Influenced by Peruvian theologian Gustavo Gutiérrez, the Medellín conference called on the church to follow a "preferential option for the poor" and to pursue a "theology of liberation." Gutiérrez's subsequent book of the same name, *Teología de liberación* (1971), emphasized the active consciousness-raising pursued by Freire's pedagogy, but one guided by considering the teachings of the Bible through the lens of contemporary life. Solidarity with the poor became a watchword for many clergy and laity.

A rift emerged between the clergy in comfortable neighborhoods and parish priests in poor communities. Given the region's unequal income distribution, many economically comfortable Latin Americans responded hostilely to liberation theology. In several countries, clergy in wealthy parishes stridently criticized liberation theology and the base-community approach. On becoming pope in 1979, John Paul II joined these voices of criticism. Conversely, the focus on poverty often energized poorer parishes. The Vatican II vision of an active laity and the Medellín call for a church in solidarity with the poor were often realized.

El Salvador experienced this intrachurch conflict in the 1970s and 1980s. A guerrilla war raged on, and the government struck back at violent and nonviolent opponents with considerable force. In 1978, four bishops condemned base communities as Marxist in orientation. In response, Archbishop Oscar Romero spoke harshly from the pulpit about the oppressive nature of poverty, and he condemned the use of violence to repress demands for a more equitable distribution of income. A subsequent Romero sermon transmitted nationally by radio on March 23, 1980, asked soldiers to disobey orders to kill civilians. The next day he was assassinated while saying mass.

More than two decades have passed since Romero's death. The open violence of governmental repression in El Salvador (and elsewhere) has subsided. Yet the Catholic church in Latin America still remains divided—among the clergy and the laity—regarding the priority and meaning of the call by the Medellín conference for a theology of liberation.

THE POLITICAL CONTEXT

Religious norms are not the only belief structures that frame political activity. Expressly political ideologies can also become powerful forces in societies, particularly when these ideologies guide political parties. Party systems in most Latin American countries present an ideological diversity more familiar to European readers than they are to a U.S. audience. Amid this ideological diversity, many Latin American politicians have displayed the sort of personal independence from party discipline that is more in line with U.S. politics. In a democracy, the interaction between party platforms and voters' choices in elections determines the major leadership posts in government. In Latin America, however, the military's frequent intervention in the political realm has challenged the centrality of parties and elections in many instances.

Political Parties

Some contemporary political parties owe their origins to the nineteenth-century divide between liberalism and conservatism. During the first wave of democratization in the late nineteenth century, these disputes between liberals and conservatives typically occurred among the wealthy elite, who then attempted to organize others to vote in support of their ideas. Over the course of the twentieth century, the economic differences between the surviving liberal and conservative movements often became increasingly blurry because both began to advocate more government intervention than they had in the past.

The twentieth century brought new ideologies with competing beliefs regarding how political and economic systems should be organized. In the early twentieth century, socialist movements formed to pursue greater political and economic equality by expanding government control of the economy. In the middle of the twentieth century, during the second wave of democratization in Latin America, many enterprising politicians developed looser ideologies that incorporated a mix of liberal, conservative, and socialist ideals. In the 1960s and 1970s, fierce anticommunist ideologies emerged to justify restrictions on electoral competition as part of an effort to eliminate socialist-inspired insurgencies. When electoral democracy was restored during the 1980s, the first new elections were typically contested by the major political parties of the 1950s and 1960s—often with the same leaders at the helm.

The end of the Cold War and the frequent inability of governments to meet demands for economic prosperity have given rise to a new generation of

GOVERNING STRATEGIES
Alberto Fujimori

Alberto Fujimori is the son of Japanese immigrants to Lima, Peru. In the late 1980s, he directed the National Agrarian University and hosted a television show that examined agrarian issues. Amid terrorism and hyperinflation, Fujimori ran for president as the head of a new party, *Cambio 90* ("Change 90"). His campaign focused on poorer neighborhoods and featured the slogan "honesty, technology, and work." While providing few specifics regarding his own economic plan, Fujimori rejected market-oriented reforms advocated by novelist Mario Vargas Llosa. Fujimori defeated Vargas Llosa in a runoff election with 57 percent of the vote.

Fujimori then changed his economic policy stance and launched a series of market-oriented reforms. His proposals often faced opposition in a legislature dominated by the parties that Fujimori had criticized in his campaign. In April 1992, Fujimori (with military support) launched an *autogolpe* ("self-coup"), in which he declared a state of emergency, dissolved the congress, and called for a new constitution. During the state of emergency, the government apprehended the leader of the Shining Path guerrilla movement. While the self-coup was condemned abroad, Fujimori's popularity rose at home: his party won control of the constituent assembly. The new constitution expanded the powers of the presidency and permitted Fujimori to run for reelection.

Renewed economic growth and reduced inflation bolstered his support, even though scandals chipped away at the image of integrity and discipline that Fujimori had constructed. His wife accused him of corruption and she considered running in the 1995 presidential elections. Fujimori then backed a law prohibiting immediate relatives of the president from seeking the office. He won the 1995 presidential election with 64 percent of the vote. In the years that followed, more allegations of corruption and human rights abuses surfaced, as did tales of coercion used against Fujimori's critics in the media. While Fujimori continued to justify his centralization of power as a necessary response to Peru's challenges, criticism mounted, particularly as economic growth slowed in the late 1990s.

Fujimori sought a controversial third term in 2000, after dismissing judges who had found his bid in violation of the two-term limit in the 1993 constitution. His closest challenger, Alejandro Toledo, withdrew from a runoff election, alleging that Fujimori officials had committed electoral fraud. Fujimori won the runoff unopposed but faced condemnation from an increasing number of Peruvians and from the Organization of American States. When a video showed one of his main advisers bribing a legislator, Fujimori announced plans for new elections in 2001. Then, while traveling in Japan in November 2000, he faxed his immediate resignation.

Peru's legislature rejected Fujimori's resignation and voted him out of office as "morally unfit." Fujimori's centralization of power was initially popular with many people because of the profound crisis he inherited. Once that crisis passed, however, Fujimori's support diminished in the face of concerns regarding political and civil liberties as well as the uneven results of his economic policies.

ideologically vague, populist leaders in several countries. Their electoral campaigns tend to feature scathing criticisms of the major national leaders by a self-proclaimed political outsider with little or no experience in elected office at the national level. Several surge candidates have pushed to victory over the course of the 1990s in countries such as Brazil (Fernando Collor de Mello), Venezuela (Hugo Chávez), and Peru (see *Governing Strategies: Alberto Fujimori*).

In several other countries, the political party system has remained relatively stable, with the major parties of the 1960s and early 1970s consistently winning the post of chief executive. This was the pattern in Argentina, Chile, Costa Rica, Honduras, and Uruguay from 1983 through 2003. Among the seven countries we will study in detail in this book, we will discuss examples of both stable and unstable partisan and ideological conflict.

Electoral Politics and the Role of Clientelism

One of the most attention-grabbing features of party politics in Latin America is the heterogeneous nature of support for almost all major political parties. This characteristic contrasts with the experience of the industrialized countries. From the end of World War II to the 1990s, income was a useful predictor of which party citizens would vote for in the United States, Canada, and in the wealthy countries of western Europe. In these industrialized countries, party competition could be arranged along lines from parties favoring wholesale government intervention in the economy on the left to fiercely anticommunist parties on the right. Typically, the less income citizens earned, the more likely they were to vote for center-left parties. Richer citizens were more likely to support center-right political movements.

As we saw in Table 3.1, income distribution in Latin America has remained much more unequal than it has been in the industrialized countries. Given this fact, one might predict that electoral politics would be defined even more visibly by socioeconomic status than it has been in the industrialized world. Nonetheless, in most Latin American countries during the twentieth and twenty-first centuries, the exact opposite tendency has occurred: income frequently has been a *less* useful predictor of voting trends than in the industrialized world. What explains the general triumph of cross-class parties in Latin America?

One explanation stems from the diversity of Latin American society. Charles Anderson once claimed that Latin American politics is "a 'living museum' in which all the forms of political authority of the Western historic experience continue to exist and operate," from landed gentry and brash military officers to business entrepreneurs, labor unions, and political parties of all stripes.[3] This "**living museum**," with its uneven respect for electoral politics, encouraged most politicians to reach out to varied elements of society to win elections. They also did so to reduce the threat of a military coup.

A second potential explanation for the heterogeneous nature of most parties can be found in clientelist electoral politics. As we saw in Chapter Two, machine politics have played a major role in twentieth-century elections and continue to

Vicente Fox, Cuauhtémoc Cárdenas, and Francisco Labastida square off in the 2000 presidential debate in Mexico.   Getty Images.

be important in the early twenty-first century. Political parties of almost all ideologies reach out to the large group of low-income voters with an array of clientelist practices. Voters may be promised preferential treatment in the provision of public services or a potential place on the government payroll. Or voters who climb on the party's bus to travel to the polls on election day can be provided with food or clothing.

Amid the continuing role of clientelism, signs of change are on the horizon. Television provides a way to reach many more voters at once than can be reached by traditional clientelist techniques. But appeals made on television provide a much greater social distance between the party and the voter than prevails under the clientelist system of neighborhood precinct captains, who are personally acquainted with almost all voters. Voters who are more influenced by television advertising may be more fickle from election to election than voters who vote with the movement dominant in their neighborhood. Increases in the educational level of the citizenry can also make some less willing to respond to clientelist appeals for their vote. For example, younger, more educated citizens provided a key source of support for Vicente Fox's victory in the 2000 presidential elections in Mexico. As we will see in Chapter Ten, Fox defeated a party that had won elections for seven consecutive decades through various clientelist practices. In short, while clientelist politics remain important, one should not conclude that all voters' decisions are based on clientelist ties.

The Role of the Military in Politics

While political parties and electoral competition are at the center of political life in representative democracies, Latin American militaries in the twentieth century sometimes sidestepped electoral results by removing elected leaders and, in some cases, by outlawing elections altogether. The nature and form of military activity in politics have evolved over time. In the first century after independence, the dominant image was that of the ambitious *caudillo* who used military force as a path to national political power. Several *caudillos* established long-lived personal dictatorships, while other would-be dictators saw their paths blocked by rival armies and police forces. The era of state building from 1880 to 1929 brought with it the creation of better-trained and better-paid militaries. This situation fueled the perception in some circles that the age of *caudillo* politics would end.

In most of the region, the old-style politics of *caudillo* adventurism did fade away; however, it was replaced by a new pattern in which the military could be characterized as an arbiter. Portions of the armed forces engaged in military coups designed to place civilians with similar ideas at the head of new governments. Military intervention was more limited but still frequently decisive in settling political disputes from 1930 through the early 1960s.

Beginning in 1964 in Brazil (and spreading elsewhere during the rest of the 1960s and 1970s), a third pattern of political involvement emerged— bureaucratic-authoritarian rule. In contrast to the earlier pattern of arbiter coups, the military announced its attention to rule directly and for an indefinite period of time. The coup leaders tended to justify this prolonged intervention in government on a need to restore economic stability and to eliminate guerrilla insurgencies. The brutal nature of repression in several countries reduced public support for military rule while it provoked demonstrations calling for a restoration of democracy.

This history of *caudillo* politics, arbiter coups, and bureaucratic-authoritarian regimes forms the backdrop against which contemporary civil-military relations unfold. Perhaps the most important legacy of the bureaucratic-authoritarian era is the belief inside the armed forces that direct control of the government can be costly. Collective rule brought to the forefront internal divisions within the armed forces that disrupted the military's hierarchical chain of command. In turn, the violence and the economic problems associated with military rule lowered the percentage of the civilian population willing to embrace military rule as an alternative. Finally, as noted earlier, the OAS and other international actors in and out of the region have increased their efforts to deter the creation of military governments. For example, Paraguay's trading partners in the Southern Cone Common Market—Argentina, Brazil, and Uruguay—swiftly repudiated a revolt led by General Lino Oviedo in Paraguay during 1996.

Doubt within the armed forces itself provides an obstacle to military rule that had not existed throughout most of Latin America's history. In addition, open public support for military rule is on the decline. As a result, threats and rumors of military coups today are less credible than they would have been in decades past. This lower credibility of coup rumors makes it somewhat harder to convince potential conspirators that other officers and troops are already involved.

GLOBAL PERSPECTIVES
Military Coups in Spain and Beyond

On February 23, 1981, the Spanish legislature was in session on live television to select a prime minister to replace Adolfo Suárez (who had announced his intention to resign in January). Suárez and King Juan Carlos had led a transition to democracy following the death of General Francisco Franco in 1975. The decision to hold free elections in 1977 had not been easy. Many soldiers distrusted Marxist parties that had been outlawed since the resolution of the Spanish Civil War (1936–1939) established the Franco dictatorship. Some argued that Franco had intended to establish a monarchy and that King Juan Carlos should serve as chief executive.

At 6:23 P.M. on February 23, Lieutenant Colonel Antonio Tejero led over 200 men onto the floor of the legislature and yelled, "Everybody be still . . . sit down, #@&*!!!!!" A military coup attempt was under way. In seconds, troops had taken Prime Minister Suárez, his cabinet, and the entire legislature hostage. Tejero claimed to act in the name of the king and announced that a general would arrive to announce the formation of a new government. Elsewhere in Spain, General Jaime Milans del Bosch, commander of the regional garrison in Valencia, declared a state of siege and put his troops on the street.

King Juan Carlos spent the next few hours calling all regional commanders to line up their loyalty to the elected government. In hindsight, it became clear that troops in the Madrid garrison had been mobilizing to launch a state of siege in the capital until senior officers realized that the king opposed the coup. The Valencia garrison eventually stood down in response to the king's efforts. After midnight, King Juan Carlos appeared on national television to make even clearer his opposition to the coup and to reassure the Spanish public. Shortly after midday on February 24, Tejero's troops released the government officials and faced charges of rebellion. Tejero would later receive a thirty-year sentence for sedition.

Spaniards were left to ask: what might have happened if more garrisons had joined the revolt early on the evening of February 23? A previous series of government decisions had created palpable military discontent. Tejero and Milans del Bosch believed they had additional military support around the country, yet the coup failed despite surprising the civilian government. It seemed that many officers aware of the coup attempt took a wait-and-see approach. This hesitation stemmed from doubts regarding the king's support for the coup and from concerns that most citizens would also oppose the coup.

These dramatic events remind us that the decision by some soldiers to launch a coup does not ensure that the government will be overthrown. Any military is capable of mobilizing considerable force, but its ability to do so depends on the coordinated insubordination of many people who have been organizing in secret. While rumors and secrecy can make the government appear weak, they also can create uncertainty regarding the ability of the coup plotters to achieve their goal. The stakes could not be higher: if the coup instigators succeed, they may become key players in the new government. If they fail, they face prosecution for treason and possible execution. Over the course of this book, we will study examples of both failed and successful coups in the Americas.

This contextual difference is crucial because coup mongering, by its nature, can be a risky and uncertain affair, in which failure can mean the end of a military career, imprisonment, and even execution. Many coup attempts fail around the world because of a lack of trust and communication among the potential conspirators, even in countries with a history of military rule in the twentieth century (see *Global Perspectives: Military Coups in Spain and Beyond*).

Despite new doubts among many soldiers, military intervention still forms a potential threat to the continuation of representative democracy. From 1990 to 2003, failed coup attempts were launched against elected governments in five of the nineteen countries in the region (Argentina, Ecuador, Guatemala, Paraguay, and Venezuela), and a successful military coup was launched in Ecuador in January 2000. By contrast, in the fifteen member countries of the European Union, there were no outwardly visible coup attempts and few rumors of such activity during that same period.

The relatively greater ease of coup organization in Latin America does *not* doom this current third wave of democratization to failure. Apart from the coup attempts noted above, contemporary Latin American militaries generally have shifted their political activity away from the use of coercion to topple governments. Instead, the threat of coercion is one of several potential tools with which to influence decisions made by elected officials. In this sense, the military in contemporary Latin America can act as a distinctive form of pressure group. In pursuing its political aims, the military can use the personal contacts and relationships central to interest group politics around the world. In addition, however, the armed forces can use the threat of force as a way to influence government decisions.

Beyond this potential threat of force, the day-to-day political presence of the military is frequently much greater than one is accustomed to seeing in the United States and Europe. In many countries, active-duty military officers sit on the cabinet. The military often enjoys formal or informal control over its own personnel decisions. In addition to participating in decisions regarding defense policy, senior and junior military officers may have positions in other government agencies, particularly if the military considers them to be politically sensitive (such as land reform).

One of the major analysts of civil-military relations, Alfred Stepan, developed a model for thinking about civil-military relations that focuses on the frequency with which force is threatened (contestation, in Stepan's terminology) and on the degree of power already enjoyed by the military (prerogatives). Stepan's typology, shown in Table 3.2 on page 72, outlines four scenarios for civil-military relations. If military prerogatives are low and military contestation of that state of affairs is low (implying widespread acceptance of civilian authority), one would describe that scenario as civilian control of the military. Once military prerogatives are quite low, military rebellions that contest that state of affairs are difficult to maintain unless they succeed quickly. As a result, Stepan sees a scenario of low prerogatives and high contestation as unsustainable for the armed forces. In the United States, for example, the Clinton administration's

TABLE 3.2   Alfred Stepan's Framework for Analyzing Civil-Military Relations

	Low military prerogatives	High military prerogatives
High Military Contestation	Unsustainable for military leaders	Nearly untenable for civilian leaders
Low Military Contestation	Civilian control of the military	Unequal civilian accommodation

SOURCE: Adapted from Alfred Stepan, *Rethinking Military Politics* (Princeton, N.J.: Princeton University Press, 1988), 122.

end to the outright ban on homosexual participation in the military sparked widespread criticism from many members of the armed forces, but it was difficult for that single issue to spark an outright rejection of the elected government's authority to make defense policy.

On the other end of the spectrum, if a military that already enjoys considerable political influence becomes upset and mobilizes in rejection of policy decisions made by civilian governments, civilian leaders may be overwhelmed by the degree of military discontent. For example, when the new democratic regime in Argentina in the mid-1980s tried senior and junior officers accused of human rights violations, the controversy sparked three military rebellions in two years that convinced the president and the legislature to end most trials.

In many of the democracies that emerged in Latin America over the 1980s and 1990s, the initial situation could most aptly be described as one of unequal civilian accommodation, in which civilian leaders accepted the continuation of a wide range of military prerogatives in the hope of minimizing the prospects of military coups. While many examples of this phenomenon exist, it is perhaps most dramatically illustrated by the Chilean return to democracy. Civilian politicians in Chile accepted many military prerogatives, including the presence of senior officers appointed to the senate and a provision beyond congressional control that earmarked funds from the government-controlled copper company for the military budget.

Although unequal civilian accommodation was frequently employed during the initial transition to civilian rule, democratically elected governments have worked on several fronts to reduce the military's autonomy and its power. In several countries, the role of the military in the cabinet has decreased over time, and posts for civilian ministers of defense have been created. In turn, military spending as a share of the total national budget has tended to decline. Militaries have resisted many measures designed to reduce their prerogatives.

On some occasions resistance has blocked reforms; in other cases, reform proceeded in the face of objections. Latin American militaries still enjoy a level of autonomy that would seem unusual in a European context, but progress toward civilian control has taken place.

DEMOCRACY AND THE QUEST FOR DEVELOPMENT, LIBERTY, AND GOVERNANCE

Given this backdrop of past military coups and continuing tension between civilian and military authorities, will the democracies of the third wave be more long-lived and robust than the democratic regimes of prior eras? Will **democratic consolidation** take place? A *democracy* is a political regime characterized by competitive elections, various channels for citizen participation, and protection of civil and political liberties sufficient to safeguard the first two characteristics.[4] One of the more frequently used definitions of the term *consolidation* holds that a democracy is consolidated if it maintains these democratic principles without interruption for a period of thirty or more years.[5]

Most Latin American countries are not consolidated democracies. Using the thirty-year standard, one can readily rule out fifteen of the nineteen countries because each has been governed in a dictatorial manner at some point in the last thirty years—particularly via the military governments common in the 1970s. Four countries—Colombia, Costa Rica, Mexico, and Venezuela—are left. As we will see in Chapter Ten, Mexico is typically not considered a consolidated democracy because a single political party controlled all branches of government from 1929 to 1997 and used this power in ways that led many to doubt the transparency of the electoral process until a series of political reforms in the 1990s. Colombia and Venezuela are discussed as long-standing democracies because neither country has experienced a military government since the 1950s. Nevertheless, many analysts question the scope of democracy in Colombia over time due to widespread infringements on civil liberties, ongoing internal strife among leftist guerrillas, rightist paramilitary movements, and the violence employed by drug traffickers. As we shall see in Chapter Eleven, several observers question the openness of the political process in Venezuela during the 1980s and 1990s as well as the legality of the wholesale governmental changes pursued during the years 1999 and 2000. Costa Rica is the only country in Latin America whose political system clearly could be described as a consolidated democracy in the early twenty-first century.

What are the prospects for the consolidation of democratic rule elsewhere in Latin America? The prospects improve when the formal and informal guiding principles of the political system enjoy **legitimacy**. Political scientists say that a governmental system is legitimate when the vast majority of citizens and interest groups accept that current government officials have a right to govern in the name of the population as a whole. Note that acceptance of a government's legitimacy does not mean that citizens agree with all government policy decisions. A citizen may be opposed to most decisions made by a given president or legislator and yet still believe that the government has the right to pursue its chosen path. In fact, the willingness of citizens to accept government decisions that they stridently oppose is perhaps the sternest test of legitimacy. Many elected governments have fallen victim to military coups over the course of Latin American history precisely because a combination of civilian and military leaders were willing to remove governments from power immediately rather than accept their authority as legitimate until new elections could be held.

The three universal governmental challenges at the heart of this text—the quest for development, liberty, and governance—are central to democratic consolidation because achieving each can help to provide any political system with legitimacy. Scholars studying legitimacy believe that it can be instilled by generating support via favorable outcomes associated with concrete government decisions and by cultivating acceptance of government procedures as fundamentally fair.

The achievement of economic development can provide a path to outcome-based legitimacy. In this scenario, citizens accept the rules of the political system under the utilitarian principle that the political process has tended to generate material benefits for society as a whole (or at least in the eyes of the beholders). In discussing the link between economic outcomes and legitimacy here, we are concerned with more than just presidents' short-term capacity to serve their entire term. Their capacity to stimulate an economic climate that makes future governments less prone to coup attempts is also crucial. Many analysts argue that the relatively higher level of economic prosperity in Costa Rica and a greater degree of economic equality relative to other Latin American countries combined to serve as two of the factors for democratic consolidation. In most countries in the region, however, the goal of widespread economic satisfaction—or the reduction of substantial dissatisfaction, at a minimum—has not yet been achieved.

Procedure-based legitimacy has roots in the quest for liberty. If citizens believe that government procedures protect essential liberties, they are more likely to accept the entire political system as legitimate. Conversely, if they find government unwilling or unable to protect essential liberties, they are less likely to accept the legitimacy of the political process. For instance, the Uruguayan government's inability to prevent urban terrorism in the late 1960s and early 1970s eroded the legitimacy of the elected government in a country that had not witnessed a military coup since the 1930s. This erosion of legitimacy had two main sources. First, terrorist acts threatened the rights to person and to property so that several civilians and soldiers called for harsh measures. Second, the implementation of some of those harsh measures alienated other citizens who found these tactics unacceptable within a democracy. This sort of give and take over the protection of liberty continues in contemporary Latin America as citizens debate the adequacy of existing liberties as well as the potential need to restrict some freedoms in the name of others. The legacy of past human rights violations provides an additional challenge in many countries as citizens debate the legitimacy and the desirability of trials for government officials from a prior military regime. Many human rights advocates find a lack of trials to be an intolerable restriction on the rule of law, while defenders of past governments see trials as an unlawful attack on the authority of past governments.

Procedure-based legitimacy is also linked to the pursuit of governance. If most citizens accept the manner in which government decisions are made, they are more likely to respect those decisions as legitimate. In contrast, if many believe that formal and informal government procedures centralize too much power in the hands of a few (or that they diffuse too much power in the hands of a diverse mix of political movements), legitimacy is likely to suffer. The Fujimori government in Peru at first justified a considerable centralization of authority in the presidency in the early 1990s with the argument that the existing division of powers had proven incapable of governing the country effectively. Then, by the late 1990s, the tide had turned and many citizens began to question the wisdom of some of this centralization of power. This debate over the appropriate mix of executive authority and limitations on that authority has been central to political life in many countries in Latin America.

This brief review of the connection between these three objectives and democratic consolidation highlights the importance of development, liberty, and governance. But these few paragraphs are not enough to provide a firm understanding of the choices governments make in each of these three areas. In the next chapter, we turn our attention specifically to development, liberty, and governance.

Activities and Exercises

1. This chapter has introduced key elements of the economic, international, societal, and political contexts in which politics unfolds in Latin America. Which of those four contexts do you believe has the most influence over governmental decision-making in Latin America? Be sure to consider the case for the importance of each context. How would you rebut other students' claims that a context other than one you have chosen is the most important?

2. One major contextual difference between the contemporary era and life before 1980 lies in the ongoing process of economic globalization. Do you believe that economic globalization, on balance, will be beneficial for most people in Latin America over the next two decades? Why or why not? In turn, do you think that globalization will benefit most U.S. residents? Why or why not?

3. In several Latin American countries, indigenous peoples find themselves in situations similar to those confronted by Native Americans in the United States: they face several different problems but their small numbers, limited resources, and internal divisions make it difficult for them to improve their condition. In other Latin American countries, indigenous peoples find themselves in a situation more comparable to that faced by African Americans in the southeastern United States: they face many disadvantages but their considerable numbers make

them a potential force to be reckoned with in political and economic life. How would you design strategies for assisting indigenous peoples in each of these two distinct scenarios?

4. *Ojos que no ven* (*Eyes That Don't See*) became one of the most talked about Peruvian films of recent memory. This 2003 film examines varied dimensions of contemporary society. The movie tells six different stories that unfold against the backdrop of the scandal surrounding a videotape in which Fujimori adviser Vladimiro Montesinos is shown bribing a legislator (review *Governing Strategies: Alberto Fujimori*). See if you can find this film in your area and watch it.

5. *The Peruvian Experience* features in this chapter provide a glimpse into several elements of the contemporary national context, but a more complete examination would go beyond the scope and purpose of this chapter. If you would like to learn more about contemporary Peru, you could begin by reading works on Peru cited in the Suggested Readings list below. You can also familiarize yourself with contemporary Peru by looking at the thematically organized links page on the website for the Latin American Network Information Center (LANIC): http://info.lanic.utexas.edu/la/peru/. The LANIC website, maintained by the University of Texas, provides numerous links to online materials organized by country and by issue.

Suggested Readings

Abbassi, Jennifer, and Sheryl Lutjens, eds. *Rereading Women in Latin America and the Caribbean: The Political Economy of Gender.* Lanham, Md.: Rowman and Littlefield, 2002.

Alvarez, Sonia, Evelina Dagnino, and Arturo Escobar, eds. *Cultures of Politics/Politics of Culture: Re-visioning Latin American Social Movements.* Boulder, Colo.: Westview, 1998.

Atkins, G. Pope. *Latin America in the International Political System,* 4th ed. Boulder, Colo.: Westview, 1999.

Bowman, Kirk. *Militarization, Democracy, & Development: The Perils of Praetorianism in Latin America.* University Park: Pennsylvania State University, 2002.

Burt, Jo-Marie, and Philip Mauceri, eds. *Politics in the Andes: Identity, Conflict, Reform.* Pittsburgh, Pa.: University of Pittsburgh Press, 2004.

Buxton, Julia, and Nicola Phillips, eds. *Developments in Latin American Political Economy: States, Markets and Actors.* Manchester, England: Manchester University Press, 1999.

Cameron, Maxwell, and Philip Mauceri, eds. *The Peruvian Labyrinth: Polity, Society and Economy.* University Park: Pennsylvania State University, 1997.

Camp, Roderic, ed. *Citizen Views of Democracy in Latin America.* Pittsburgh, Pa.: University of Pittsburgh Press, 2001.

Camp, Roderic, ed. *Democracy in Latin America: Patterns and Cycles.* Wilmington, Del.: Scholarly Resources, 1996.

Cleary, Edward, and Hannah Stewart-Gambino. *Conflict and Competition: The Latin American Church in a Changing Environment.* Boulder, Colo.: Lynne Rienner, 1992.

Diamond, Larry, Jonathan Hartlyn, Juan Linz, and Seymour Martin Lipset, eds. *Democracy in Developing Countries: Latin America,* 2nd ed. Boulder, Colo.: Lynne Rienner, 1999.

Domínguez, Jorge, ed. *The Future of Inter-American Relations.* New York: Routledge, 2000.

Drake, Paul, ed. *Money Doctors, Foreign Debts, and Economic Reforms in Latin America from the 1890s to the Present.* Wilmington, Del.: Scholarly Resources, 1994.

Eckstein, Susan, ed. *Power and Popular Protest: Latin American Social Movements,* rev. ed. Berkeley: University of California Press, 2001.

Gibson, Edward, ed. *Federalism and Democracy in Latin America.* Baltimore, Md.: Johns Hopkins University Press, 2004.

Keck, Margaret, and Kathryn Sikkink, eds. *Activists Beyond Borders: Advocacy Networks in International Politics.* Ithaca, N.Y.: Cornell University Press, 1998.

Langer, Erick, and Elena Muñoz, eds. *Contemporary Indigenous Movements in Latin America.* Wilmington, Del.: Scholarly Resources, 2003.

Mainwaring, Scott, and Timothy Scully, eds. *Building Democratic Institutions: Party Systems in Latin America.* Stanford, Calif.: Stanford University Press, 1995.

Maybury-Lewis, David, ed. *The Politics of Ethnicity: Indigenous Peoples in Latin American States.* Cambridge, Mass.: Harvard University Press, 2002.

Moreno, Alejandro. *Political Cleavages: Issues, Parties, and the Consolidation of Democracy.* Boulder, Colo.: Westview, 1999.

O'Donnell, Guillermo, Philippe Schmitter, and Laurence Whitehead, eds. *Transitions from Authoritarian Rule: Latin America.* Baltimore, Md.: Johns Hopkins University Press, 1986.

Pion-Berlin, David, ed. *Civil-Military Relations in Latin America: New Analytical Perspectives.* Chapel Hill: University of North Carolina Press, 2001.

Salazar-Xirinachs, José, and Maryse Robert, eds. *Toward Free Trade in the Americas.* Washington, D.C.: Organization of American States and the Brookings Institution Press, 2001.

Smith, Peter. *Talons of the Eagle: Dynamics of U.S.-Latin American Relations,* 2nd ed. New York: Oxford University Press, 2000.

Zagorski, Paul. *Democracy vs. National Security: Civil-Military Relations in Latin America.* Boulder, Colo.: Lynne Rienner, 1992.

Endnotes

1. Jan Aart Schoulte, *Globalization: A Critical Introduction* (New York: St. Martin's Press, 2000), pp. 77–78.

2. Bank of International Settlements, *Triennial Central Bank Survey,* various issues.

3. Charles Anderson, *Politics and Economic Change in Latin America* (New York: Van Nostrand, 1967), pp. 104–05.

4. There are many different conceptualizations of democracy. The definition presented here is similar to what Larry Diamond has called "liberal democracy"—in contrast to a mere "electoral democracy" in which major government leaders are consistently chosen via elections but protection of fundamental liberties is uneven and enforcement of the rule of law is in doubt. For further discussion, see Diamond, *Developing Democracy: Toward Consolidation* (Baltimore, Md.: Johns Hopkins University Press, 1999), pp. 7–13.

5. Arend Lijphart, *Democracies* (New Haven, Conn.: Yale University Press, 1984), p. 38.

Human Development in the Americas (2001)

CHAPTER 4

The Quest for Development, Liberty, and Governance

OR A FEW MOMENTS, try to put yourself in Alejandro Toledo's shoes. In the controversial 2000 elections in Peru, he finished second to the incumbent president, Alberto Fujimori. Alleging fraud, Toledo rejected the election results and refused to compete against Fujimori in a runoff election. Subsequently, Fujimori resigned during a trip to Japan, new presidential elections were organized, and Toledo defeated former president Alan García in a runoff election in June 2001. On July 28, 2001, Alejandro Toledo took the oath of office to become president of Peru.

He won the presidency of an economically troubled country. During 1998–2000, economic growth slowed to a standstill; then, in the first four months of 2001, economic activity shrank by 2 percent. Investment, employment, and wages had all fallen noticeably since the prior period of rapid growth in the mid-1990s. National wealth as measured by gross domestic product (GDP) per person was, in real terms, equivalent to Peru's position in 1970. Roughly 60 percent of the workforce was either unemployed or underemployed.[1] At least half of the population lived on less than $2.00 a day. Toledo's inaugural address named poverty reduction as the major focus of his administration.

While economic issues were central elements of the 2001 presidential campaign, the search for liberty was also a high-profile issue. Various organizations urged the Toledo government to investigate allegations of human rights violations committed in pursuit of antigovernment insurgents and terrorists. Incidents of illegal detention, torture, and summary executions motivated a search for justice and closure among victims and their relatives. In addition to addressing past violations of liberty, the government faced multiple calls to improve the contemporary climate for political, civil, and economic rights. As we saw in Chapter Three, Toledo's rejection of the 2000 election results had centered on allegations of electoral fraud and illegal pressure on the freedom of the press. As president, Toledo now faced the formidable task of improving respect for civil and political liberty. He also inherited strong incentives to take action to protect physical and economic rights. Between 1980 and 1990, the murder rate had multiplied from 2.4 to 11.5 per 100,000 inhabitants; by 1995, it had declined only slightly, to 10.3.[2] Several public opinion polls in the late 1990s demonstrated that the majority of Lima residents saw crime of all types on the rise. As with the economy, Toledo faced a series of tough choices regarding how to improve the protection of civil, economic, and physical liberty.

Toledo also confronted challenges regarding the path to effective and respected governance. His party controlled forty-five of the 120 seats in the legislature. Regardless of the specifics of his preferred policy proposals, he would need to convince some political opponents in the legislature to support his program. If he could not muster the necessary support of legislators from other political parties, he might be tempted to pursue governance by decree or to sway legislature opponents via bribery. Fujimori had left office amid a high-profile scandal in which one of his closest advisers, Vladimiro Montesinos, was videotaped bribing a legislator. Toledo was in a difficult position. If he spent the time necessary to work out legislative compromises, he risked being accused of inaction. If he attempted to govern alone, however, he would betray the calls for more open government that he had spearheaded as a candidate.

The quests for development, liberty, and governance—and the potentially divisive debate over how they should be handled—are central elements of political life. Faced with these challenges, what would *you* want to do as president? In turn, how would you pursue those options politically? How would you justify your actions to other government officials and to the general public? In this chapter, we will examine the debate over these questions in Latin America. In the process, we will gain a better understanding of the political debate while we build our knowledge of conditions in the region.

THE QUEST FOR DEVELOPMENT

In Chapter One, we met Cecilia, who works in fish processing for two firms in Lima. The prosperous business executives who head these firms both earn over $100,000—placing them in the highest 1 percent of all households in Peru. Cecilia, on the other hand, earns around $9,200 per year by working two full-time jobs over a six-day workweek. If you count the nearly three hours per workday Cecilia spends commuting, she is either working or traveling roughly nineteen hours per day Monday through Saturday. Cecilia's life has not been an easy one.

Yet in some ways, Cecilia is relatively fortunate. Her two full-time jobs combine to pay her an annual income slightly above the average urban wage of $8,400; prevailing rural wages are substantially lower. Her earnings constitute an unusual achievement in comparison with most Peruvians, who—like Cecilia—did not attend school beyond the primary level. Cecilia's income is crucial to her family's survival. Her mother continues to make below-average wages in housekeeping for the Labor Ministry. Her father, now in his late fifties, does the occasional odd job as a bricklayer but cannot find steady work as a day laborer in construction because of his declining health. Cecilia lives with her parents in the brick and concrete house that her father built in the 1970s in what was then the outskirts of Lima.

Cecilia, her parents, and everyone else in Peru aspire to the same things that people want everywhere: personal happiness, sustained health, and the economic means to pursue these desires as the years roll by. When we consider individuals' lives, the quest for development has immediate human relevance. When we speak of a country's economic development, issues become somewhat more complicated and abstract. We should remember, however, that the socioeconomic issues at play are central to the lives of millions of individual people like Cecilia.

Defining Development

Has the quest for development in Peru or elsewhere in Latin America been successful? In responding to this question, you must make choices about what constitutes economic success for an entire country. In Latin America, as in the rest of the world, the debate over national goals for economic development continues.

One of the yardsticks used to evaluate economic conditions is national wealth. This concept is often expressed as gross domestic product (GDP) per person, where GDP equals the total value of all goods and services produced within a country's borders. This way of thinking about development is sometimes called the **growth first** approach. If economic activity grows faster than the population, then there are more goods and services in circulation per person. This situation indicates that the country—taken as a whole—is more prosperous.

However, using GDP per person alone as a development yardstick has limitations. The **basic needs** approach to development shifts the focus from growth alone to measuring progress in human survival and fulfillment across national populations. This approach implies not just growth (that is, increasing the availability of goods and services), but also an allocation of resources that enables people to enjoy longer and more fulfilling lives. The Human Development Index (HDI) defined by the United Nations is one approach for measuring progress in meeting basic needs. The HDI is a composite measure that takes into account three dimensions: the availability of goods and services (measured by GDP per person), educational attainment (measured by a combination of school enrollment and the adult literacy rate), and human survival prospects (measured by average life expectancy). The closer a country's HDI score is to 1, the closer it is to the best outcomes observed in the world in all three areas.

TABLE 4.1 Human Development Index (HDI) for 2001

Group of countries	Average life expectancy (in years)	Adult literacy rate	School enrollment rate	GDP per capita ($US)	LE index	ED index	GDP index	HDI
Arab States	66.0	60.8%	60%	$5,038	0.70	0.62	0.65	0.662
East Asia and Pacific	69.5	87.1%	65%	$4,233	0.74	0.80	0.63	0.722
Latin America and Caribbean	70.3	89.2%	81%	$7,050	0.75	0.86	0.71	0.777
South Asia	62.8	56.3%	54%	$2,730	0.64	0.56	0.55	0.582
Sub-Saharan Africa	46.5	62.4%	44%	$1,831	0.36	0.56	0.49	0.468
All Third World	*64.4*	*74.5%*	*60%*	*$3,850*	*0.66*	*0.70*	*0.61*	*0.655*
Eastern Europe and CIS	69.3	99.3%	79%	$6,598	0.74	0.92	0.70	0.787
High-Income OECD	78.1	99.0%	93%	$27,169	0.89	0.97	0.94	0.929
Entire World	*66.7*	*79.2%*	*64%*	*$7,376*	*0.70*	*0.75*	*0.72*	*0.722*
Selected countries								
Peru	69.4	90.2%	83%	$4,570	0.74	0.88	0.64	0.752
United States	76.9	99.0%	94%	$34,320	0.86	0.97	0.97	0.937

SOURCE: Adapted from United Nations Development Program, *Human Development Report 2003* (New York: Oxford University Press, 2003), pp. 237–240.

Table 4.1 presents recent HDI data for different groupings of countries as well as information for comparative purposes regarding the United States and Peru. In 2001, the United States had the seventh highest HDI in the world, at .937 (slightly above the average for all high-income countries). Educational attainment and GDP per person were both near the highest levels observed in the world (as indicated by index scores close to 1), while the U.S. average life expectancy of seventy-seven years constituted a life expectancy index score of .86. Peru ranked eighty-second in HDI among the 175 countries measured in 2001. Peru, like most of Latin America, was in the middle of the distribution for all countries on both the growth standard alone (GDP per person) and the HDI.

National averages like GDP per person and the HDI tell us something about how each country is doing, but the analogy between the prosperity of an individual and the prosperity of an entire country is imperfect. Think back to Cecilia's situation. If Cecilia gains enough purchasing power to buy more goods

TABLE 4.2 Poverty by Region (1987–1998): Percentage of the
Population Living on Less Than $1.08 per Day

Region	Year				
	1987	1990	1993	1996	1998
East Asia and Pacific	26.6	27.6	25.2	14.9	15.3
Europe and Central Asia	23.9	18.5	15.9	10.0	11.3
Latin America and the Caribbean	15.3	16.8	15.3	15.6	15.6
Middle East and North Africa	4.3	2.4	1.9	1.8	1.9
South Asia	44.9	44.0	42.4	42.3	40.0
Sub-Saharan Africa	46.6	47.7	49.7	48.5	46.3
Total	*28.3*	*29.0*	*28.1*	*24.5*	*24.0*

SOURCE: Adapted from World Bank, *World Development Report 2000/2001* (New York: Oxford
University Press, 2001), p. 23.

and services next year, we would describe her as more prosperous. However, a
country is made up of many individuals. When national wealth rises from one
year to the next, this increase does not necessarily mean that all (or even most)
residents gained access to more goods and services. In some instances, aggregate prosperity rises, but so does the percentage of people living in poverty.

In response to this concern, many have emphasized poverty reduction as a
major development goal. Discussions of **absolute poverty** try to determine
standards for individual residents that constitute an escape from poverty. These
standards vary from analyst to analyst and from government to government.
The World Bank analyzes countries against what most consider a standard of
extreme absolute poverty: an indigence line of $1.08 per day. Table 4.2 presents
poverty rates computed using this approach for different groups of countries.
Roughly one-sixth of residents in Latin America lived on less than $1.08 per day
in 1998. How one interprets this observation depends on one's perspective
when looking at the table. Relative to the much higher incidence of poverty in
sub-Saharan Africa and southern Asia, Latin America is comparatively better
off. However, minimal progress in poverty reduction has occurred in the contemporary era. When one examines Table 4.2 over time, one notices that Latin
America is the only developing region in which the incidence of poverty rose
between 1987 and 1998.

The World Bank's indigence line compares conditions to what most people
would describe as abject human misery. As we are aware from own lives, however, human beings tend to reflect on their own well-being relative to the
prevailing standard in their own societies. Thus, **relative poverty** exists when
people lack the resources needed to enjoy the activities and the living standards
customary in their own societies.[3] As we saw in Table 3.1 on income inequality,

much work is needed in Latin America to reduce relative poverty. The World Bank measures the incidence of relative poverty by calculating the percentage of the population that lives on less than one-third of average national consumption levels. In Latin America and the Caribbean, 51.4 percent of the population lived in relative poverty in 1998. The incidence of relative poverty in the Third World as a whole was 37 percent; sub-Saharan Africa was the only other Third World region with a relative poverty rate higher than 50 percent (50.5).

All of the development indicators we have examined thus far focus on conditions for current generations. Over the last third of the twentieth century, many analysts began to present **sustainable development** as a distinct goal. The sustainability of current patterns of economic activity over future generations of humanity lies at the heart of this concept. The report of the World Commission on Environment and Development asserted that current generations should try to "meet their needs without compromising the ability of future generations to meet their own needs."[4] Today's paths to development can pose roadblocks for tomorrow's generations. For example, open sewage lines for factories and residences can improve today's growth rates by freeing up the money that might have been used for sewage treatment. Over time, however, the resulting pollution can reduce the quality of life enjoyed by future generations. Similarly, air pollution from factory and automobile emissions can have a cumulative effect that reduces life expectancy for future generations.

We have examined growth, basic needs, poverty reduction, and sustainability as yardsticks for national development. With these different development goals in mind, refer to Table 4.3, which presents the socioeconomic conditions prevailing in Latin America. (For comparative purposes, U.S. data on these indicators are also included.) As we saw in previous paragraphs, Latin America is a middle-income region when compared to the rest of the world. Peru provides a good example of this trend because it is close to the regional average on most of these indicators. In particular, Peru's score on the HDI (0.747) and the percentage of Peruvians living in extreme poverty (16 percent) are in line with average conditions across Latin America.

Within this trend toward middle-income status, we still see considerable diversity in socioeconomic conditions. Four countries—Bolivia, Guatemala, Honduras, and Nicaragua—are visibly poorer than the rest of Latin America. In 2001, each had a GDP per person below $4,500 and a score on the HDI of 0.672 or less. Conversely, four countries—Argentina, Chile, Costa Rica, and Uruguay—all had a GDP per person of $8,400 or higher and had scores on the HDI higher than 0.830. The other eleven countries in Latin America faced economic conditions somewhere between these two distinct groups of lower-middle-income and upper-middle-income status.

Table 4.3 also illustrates the visible gap between conditions in the middle-income countries of Latin America and the nature of life in an upper-income country such as the United States. The average GDP per person in Latin America ($6,075) is less than one-fifth as high as that found in the United States

TABLE 4.3 Socioeconomic Conditions in Latin America and the United States (2001)

Country	Population (millions)	GDP per person ($US)	Average life expectancy (in years)	Adult literacy rate	HDI	Percentage living on less than $1 per day	Income share of richest 10%	CO_2 emissions (metric tons per person)
Argentina	37.5	$11,320	73.9	97%	0.849	NA	NA	3.8
Bolivia	8.5	$2,300	63.3	86%	0.672	14%	32.0%	1.4
Brazil	174.0	$7,360	67.8	87%	0.777	10%	48.0%	1.8
Chile	15.4	$9,190	75.8	96%	0.831	2%	45.4%	4.2
Colombia	42.8	$7,040	71.8	92%	0.779	14%	46.1%	1.5
Costa Rica	4.0	$9,460	77.9	96%	0.832	7%	34.6%	1.6
Cuba	11.2	$5,259	76.5	97%	0.806	2%	NA	2.3
Dominican Republic	8.5	$7,020	66.7	84%	0.737	2%	37.9%	2.8
Ecuador	12.6	$3,280	70.5	92%	0.731	20%	33.8%	1.9
El Salvador	6.3	$5,260	70.4	79%	0.719	21%	39.4%	0.9
Guatemala	11.7	$4,400	65.3	69%	0.652	16%	46.0%	0.9
Honduras	6.6	$2,830	68.8	76%	0.667	24%	44.4%	0.8
Mexico	100.5	$8,430	73.1	91%	0.800	8%	41.6%	3.9
Nicaragua	5.2	$2,450	69.1	67%	0.643	82%	48.8%	0.8
Panama	3.0	$5,750	74.4	92%	0.788	8%	35.7%	2.9
Paraguay	5.6	$5,210	70.5	94%	0.751	20%	43.8%	0.8
Peru	26.4	$4,799	68.8	90%	0.747	16%	35.4%	1.2
Uruguay	3.4	$8,400	75.0	98%	0.834	2%	33.8%	2.1
Venezuela	24.8	$5,670	73.5	93%	0.775	15%	36.5%	5.3
Latin American Average	*26.7*	*$6,075*	*71.2*	*88%*	*0.757*	*16%*	*40.2%*	*2.2*
United States	288.0	$34,320	76.9	99%	0.937	NA	30.5%	19.7

SOURCE: Adapted from United Nations Development Program, *Human Development Report 2003* (New York: Oxford University Press, 2003), pp. 237–239, 245–246, 250–252, 282–284, 300–302.

($34,320). In Latin America, life expectancy is lower, illiteracy is more prevalent, and extreme poverty is considerably more widespread.

This gap between Latin America and the United States is politically relevant for three reasons. First, all countries aspire to attain the highest level of material well-being observed in the world. Policy makers and citizens in Latin America know that their countries' quests for development have been only moderately successful when measured against the upper-income countries of the world. This gap creates political demands for substantial improvement. Second, the size of the gap is exaggerated by the uneven flow of information in the entertainment media. Movies and television series from the United States feature primarily the lifestyles of upper- and middle-income residents within these upper-income societies. These media create an image of U.S. life that makes the economic gap between the United States and Latin America seem even greater than statistics alone would indicate. Third, many upper-income residents of Latin America manage to emulate this image of the good life in the United States—even as thousands of other residents struggle to make ends meet. This income disparity within countries heightens further the level of political tension and disagreement surrounding the quest for development in Latin America.

Pursuing Development

Given the need and the desire for greater prosperity in Latin America, how should governments proceed? Three major policy approaches have dominated the political debate over the course of the twentieth century and into the twenty-first century (see Table 4.4). Market-oriented analysts argue for a small government that focuses on maintaining a stable economic climate in which market mechanisms shape most economic outcomes. A second approach calls for a mixed economy in which markets dominate some spheres of economic activity while government plays a major role in other economic sectors. A third approach calls for the emergence of a socialist government that controls most economic activity via the nationalization of private property. As we consider each of these approaches, we should think of them as areas along a larger continuum between minimum and maximum government intervention in economic matters. No national economy in Latin America (or elsewhere) has ever been purely market-driven or purely government-driven. Some government activities shape economic outcomes in every market-oriented economy, and some market mechanisms (even if they are formally illegal) influence outcomes in socialist systems. The policy choices at issue are ultimately a matter of degree: where should government take action in economic matters and how should it take action when government action is deemed desirable?

The **market capitalism** model advocates skepticism regarding the desirability of government intervention in the economy. In contemporary Latin America, this approach is often called the neoliberal model: the prefix *neo*

TABLE 4.4 Three Major Economic Policy Approaches

	Market capitalism	State capitalism	Command economy
Property ownership	Largely or entirely private	Mix of private and public ownership	Largely or entirely public
Investment policy	Low or no barriers to foreign investment	Domestic participation (and, sometimes, control) required in some economic sectors	Government control of all investment conditions
Trade policy	Low or no trade barriers	Trade barriers used to promote the entry of domestic firms into some economic sectors	Government management of all foreign trade opportunities
Agrarian policy	Promotion of large-scale commercial agriculture via infrastructure and tax incentives	Effort to avoid land underutilization via land reform that redistributes unused land to the landless	Nationalization of agriculture (at times with a role for small farmers' markets)
Employment policy	Employment opportunities created largely by private initiative	Employment opportunities created by private initiative, public firms, and by public policies to promote domestic firms	Employment opportunities promoted via full employment orientation of the managers of public firms
Social policy	Focus on educational opportunities with minimal or no use of public policy to redistribute wealth and income	Effort to redistribute income via the tax code and by the provision of health, education, and welfare programs	Provision of all basic services to all citizens (at times via rationing)

refers to the fact that market-oriented policies dominated the debate of the late nineteenth century and returned to the forefront during the late twentieth century. Market advocates believe that government should stay out of any activity in which market dynamics could conceivably function. This emphasis on markets emerges from two fundamental premises. First, neoliberals assert that government activity tends to reduce freedom by curtailing the ability of individuals to make decisions about how to employ their labor and their property (if they own any property). Second, neoliberals argue that government activity produces suboptimal results because they believe the market allocates resources more efficiently.

The market-oriented approach provides recommendations for international and domestic policy. In the international sphere, governments should eliminate barriers to trade with other countries and open up financial markets to permit a free flow of investment and other financial transactions. Domestically, the most insistent proponents of the market argue that government should provide only a few public goods that markets tend to underproduce, such as national defense, public roads, and law enforcement. The government should also create a judicial system capable of enforcing contracts.

As noted earlier, choosing among development policies is a matter of degree. Many advocates of a generally market-oriented approach call for a larger role for government than the previous paragraph implies. For example, some are concerned that public education is essential to development over time. Without a sound public education system, market dynamics would provide quality education only to the minority of Latin American households able to pay tuition to fund better schools. Others call for a vigorous government role in curative health care to protect many citizens who cannot afford private health insurance, much less pay the full cost of medical care on their own.

Advocates of the **state capitalism** model take this set of concerns still further, arguing that market dynamics alone would produce undesirable outcomes in many sectors. In response, they call for a mixed economy in which government intervenes in some areas while leaving others to market dynamics. State capitalism emerged as the dominant approach to development in Latin America during the 1940s and 1950s and remained so until the wave of market-oriented reforms of the 1980s and 1990s.

Proponents of state capitalism argue that markets produced pitfalls in both the international and the domestic sphere. (You might review *Global Perspectives: State Capitalism in the 1940s and 1950s* in Chapter Two.) In the global economy, economists such as Raúl Prebisch found that economies based on primary commodities (like wheat, coffee, and copper) were losing ground to industrialized economies with each passing decade. If markets alone framed investment decisions, wealthy individuals would continue to pour their money into export agriculture and mining because they would conclude that a start-up industry in Latin America would find it difficult to compete with an existing industrial firm in Europe or elsewhere. Over time, this series of rational market decisions would leave the country unindustrialized and thus poorer and more vulnerable to the greater price volatility observed in commodity markets. In response, the state capitalism model calls for governments to engage in protectionist policies that block free trade in strategic industrial sectors until new firms could compete on world markets. New firms would begin by conquering their domestic markets in this import-substituting industrialization (ISI) policy and then proceed to compete on world markets.

In addition to protectionism in the international realm, state capitalism calls for a much larger role in the domestic sphere. Moving beyond security, transportation, education, and health, governments provide financial incentives for investors to enter key economic sectors in which market incentives are currently low. In some situations, government creates public firms—particularly in areas involving high levels of initial investment that are deemed crucial to industrialization but risky (such as steel and energy production).

Just as the shortcomings of market-oriented capitalism sparked the rise of state capitalism in the middle of the twentieth century, problems with state capitalism stimulated both a renewed market-oriented critique and the emergence of a socialist alternative. Critics highlighted several problems. First, the planned emergence of competitive industries did not occur as often as some had hoped. Many uncompetitive industries lobbied successfully to retain trade barriers and other preferential government treatment decade after decade. Second, state capitalist economies demonstrated greater vulnerability to inflationary shocks and large government budget deficits than had been observed under the market-oriented era of the early twentieth century. The higher level of government intervention cost money, yet most Latin American governments had difficulty expanding their revenues. Latin American governments' economic resources remained relatively small in comparison with the situation in high-income countries (see *Global Perspectives: The Size of Government* on page 90). Third, importing the machines used to produce manufactured goods often proved more expensive than buying the finished goods from abroad. This situation gave state capitalist economies a greater tendency to run a balance-of-payments deficit in their international transactions. Finally, while state capitalist policies proved somewhat successful in expanding the middle-income sector of society, the percentage of the population living in poverty fell more slowly than some had hoped.

If state capitalism, like market capitalism, had its shortcomings, what should be done? Defenders of state capitalism often argued that the basic approach was sound yet systematically underfunded. Greater investments both in the institutions that support market dynamics (education and the judiciary) and in state-sponsored industrialization were required. Politicians needed to convince citizens to fund these activities. In contrast, market-oriented critics blamed overreaching government intervention as the root cause of state capitalism's problems. This critique came to be called the **Washington Consensus** for market-oriented reform because it was frequently voiced by the IMF and the

GLOBAL PERSPECTIVES
The Size of Government[1]

Governments in Latin America face a double burden compared with governments in wealthier countries. First, they are governing poorer economies. Latin American governments have less money to spend per inhabitant even if they taxed their populations in line with trends in wealthier countries. However, Latin American governments do not tax their populations at the levels observed in the United States and in western Europe. In the 1990s, the average Latin American country's tax revenues—excluding Cuba—equaled less than 20 percent of its gross domestic product (GDP). In the United States, the wealthy country with the least taxation, taxes constituted 27 percent of GDP. Among the fifteen countries in the European Union, taxes averaged more than double the amount observed in Latin America: over two-fifths of GDP.

With a wealthier population and greater taxation, governments in high-income countries can spend considerable sums of money in response to a wide variety of requests for government action. European Union governments spent an average of $9,559 per inhabitant in 2000. The United States spent $11,772 per person. In stark contrast, Latin American governments confront even greater demands for material improvements with far fewer resources. The average Latin American government (excluding Cuba) spent $758 per person in 2000. Public spending per person in Peru equaled $365 per person in the same year. In 2001, the new government of Alejandro Toledo did not find itself on the same financial footing as the new government of George W. Bush.

[1]Economic data on the United States and the European Union are taken from the Organization for Economic Cooperation and Development (*OECD in Figures 2001* and *OECD in Figures 2002*). Data on Latin America and Peru are from the Economic Commission on Latin America and the Caribbean (*Economic Survey of Latin America and the Caribbean 2000–2001*).

World Bank (both with headquarters in the Washington, D.C.). The Washington Consensus framed several changes in the region's economic policies over the course of the 1980s and 1990s.

While the choice between market capitalism and state capitalism dominated much of the development debate in the twentieth century, these two approaches were not the only options discussed. Proponents of the **command economy** model argued that government should nationalize most (or all) private property, thereby establishing a context in which government officials would make most economic decisions. Advocates of this socialist approach shared state capitalists' conviction that reliance on market dynamics alone discriminated against Latin American economies in the global economy. However, socialists argued that the mixed economy approach constituted a set of incomplete measures that was unlikely to break the cycle of underdevelopment.

Instead, socialists recommended a major break with market dynamics in both the international and the domestic spheres. In the international realm, trade should take place only if deemed nationally advantageous by government officials in charge of state-owned firms. Government control of the economy is supposed to prevent transactions that might be considered rational by private individuals or firms yet unproductive for the nation as a whole. In the domestic sphere, the changes implied by the command economy model are even more wide-ranging. By radically increasing government ownership of the economy, the government holds the potential power to pursue what it believes is the optimal division of activity across various economy sectors. Rather than depending on private decisions (as in market capitalism) or on government incentives and actions that frame private decisions (as in state capitalism), the government controls investment and prices in a command economy. In theory, this approach should permit the government to increase the provision of essential goods and services to previously impoverished sectors of the population. It should also enable socialist governments to diversify and industrialize their economies to make them more productive and less dependent on one or two sectors.

The command economy model entered the development debate in earnest with the Soviet Union's adoption of this approach in the 1930s. More countries created command economies in eastern Europe and in southeast Asia in the 1940s and 1950s. This rising tide of socialist revolution abroad combined with the increasingly visible shortcomings of state capitalism in Latin America to motivate greater consideration of the socialist alternative. When Fidel Castro's revolutionary movement took over the Cuban government in 1959 and established a command economy in the 1960s, the political visibility of the socialist option reached its high point in Latin America. Political movements in every country called for the establishment of socialist economies during the 1960s and 1970s. As we saw in Chapter Two, many military governments formed in this era justified their creation on a desire to defend the principle of private property from revolutionary challenges.

During the 1980s and 1990s, the calls for socialism became less frequent in most of the region. The declining visibility of the socialist alternative had several causes. First, the use of violent repression imposed serious costs on violent and nonviolent proponents of socialist ideas, resulting in the death, imprisonment, and exile of many leaders of the socialist movement. Second, the shortcomings of command economies in Cuba and elsewhere became difficult to defend. Command economies in practice tended to reduce the incidence of abject poverty without producing the sort of material well-being observed in the industrialized societies of western Europe and North America. In addition, this poverty reduction tended to be associated with a different style of repressive government, one that used its control over the economy and the courts to punish critics of governmental decisions. Third, the collapse of socialist governments in the late 1980s and early 1990s (along with the free-market reforms to the Chinese economy) made it more difficult for socialists to defend the viability of the command economy option. Finally, the shortcomings of state capitalism reduced many citizens' confidence that governments had the administrative and political capacity to take command of the entire economy. In the early twenty-first century, Cuba remained the only command economy in Latin America. In Chapter Eight, we will examine the evolution of this system and the current debate over the desirability of economic and political reform.

In the other six country chapters in this text, we will analyze the politics of the shift from state capitalism back toward market capitalism. In doing so, we will focus on two main tasks. First, we will try to understand the political dynamics of this policy shift. Second, we will ask the following question: are the political winds beginning to blow in the opposite direction? In other words, how might contemporary shortcomings of market capitalism play out politically in Latin America in the next few years? As Chapters Five through Eleven will demonstrate, the early twenty-first century has seen a rising tide of criticism surrounding the use of market capitalist economic policies in the region. *The Peruvian Experience: Economic Policy Under Toledo* provides a preliminary window into these issues by examining the debate over economic policy in Peru during the first year of the Toledo administration.

THE PERUVIAN EXPERIENCE
Economic Policy Under Toledo

In his inaugural address, Alejandro Toledo promised to fight poverty and to increase employment. He pledged to do so with a set of economic policies that largely embraced the market-oriented reforms enacted under Fujimori. While some analysts questioned Toledo's commitment to this path, he named as finance minister a market-oriented economist who had lived most of the past fifteen years in the United States. During his second month in office, Toledo announced plans for a major privatization: nearly all of the remaining public enterprises were to be sold over the next few years. The government cut spending to reduce its budget deficit (to meet fiscal targets in an International Monetary Fund [IMF] loan agreement signed in early 2002). Although the share of the budget spent on education and on poverty relief rose slightly, real social spending fell. Toledo argued that the privatization program would produce nearly $700 million that could increase social spending in future years without raising taxes or increasing deficit spending.

Visible segments of the population criticized Toledo's program from several angles. Many public employees argued that privatization would place control of key economic sectors in foreign hands. Others asserted that job losses planned in the privatization program ran against Toledo's stated goal of job creation. Still others criticized plans to sell additional

THE QUEST FOR LIBERTY

In her lifetime, Cecilia has witnessed various threats to many liberties that people aspire to around the world. She has seen the right to live free from violence denied in many different situations. Her sister Victoria died in 1990 at the hands of Shining Path guerrillas, who have not yet been apprehended. Cecilia followed media coverage regarding illegal detention and torture of suspected guerrillas during the Fujimori government with mixed emotions.

Cecilia has also experienced various threats to people's economic rights. She takes precautions during her daily commute on Lima buses to protect herself from pickpockets and muggers. She is particularly concerned now that her two jobs require her to leave home at 4:30 A.M. and return around 11:30 P.M. each evening. One of Cecilia's wealthy employers has become so worried about being kidnapped and held for ransom that he has hired bodyguards for himself and his wife. Her other employer still complains bitterly about the decision of the Velasco government to nationalize many sugar plantations, arguing that his father never recovered emotionally from the forced sale of his estate to the government. Toward the other end of the economic spectrum, Cecilia's brother Raúl suffered an accident on his construction job nine months ago and is still

public firms to Tractebel, a Belgian-owned firm implicated in corruption scandals surrounding Fujimori's privatization program.

When Tractebel emerged as the highest bidder for two electric companies in Peru's second largest city (Arequipa), thousands of protesters took to the streets and shut down the city in mid-June 2002. The mayor of Arequipa refused to negotiate an end to the protests and participated in a hunger strike against the privatization. As the protests continued, the Toledo government declared a state of siege in Arequipa. It set a citywide curfew and sent roughly 2,000 troops to restore public transportation and to clear the streets. The presidency then negotiated an end to the protests by pledging to abide by whatever the courts decided in Arequipa's legal challenge to the privatization. But the disturbances had left two dead, hundreds injured, and roughly $100 million in damaged property.

The Arequipa protests were the first major crisis of Toledo's presidency. He responded by reorganizing his cabinet while reaffirming his privatization plans. At the end of June 2002, the Peruvian economy completed its third consecutive quarter of modest economic growth, yet most believed that substantial economic progress was unlikely for most Peruvians. Public opinion polls showed that 70 percent of the people were dissatisfied with Toledo's performance during his first year in office. Toledo, like many presidents before him, was finding it hard to meet the expectations he had helped to create during his electoral campaign.

waiting to receive the benefits he is owed in accordance with workers' compensation legislation.

In the early twenty-first century, public debate in Peru began to focus more vigorously on violations of civil and political liberties. Cecilia's sister Marisa tried to convince her to vote for candidates pledging to protect native speakers of Quechua and other indigenous languages from discrimination. Some of Cecilia's friends were frustrated by Fujimori's tactics in pursuing a third consecutive term and became volunteers for Alejandro Toledo's campaign. They claimed that their campaign supervisor received threatening phone calls at work and at home. Cecilia also heard her parents debate whether the Fujimori government's alleged manipulation of the media constituted a typical advantage of incumbency or something beyond politics as usual. After Fujimori resigned and Toledo won the 2001 elections, Toledo's supporters and detractors in Cecilia's circle questioned his ability and his willingness to improve the protection of physical, economic, civil, and political liberty.

Defining Liberty

As with the quest for development, the search for liberty involves choosing priorities among a series of important goals. The Universal Declaration of Human Rights (UDHR), issued by the United Nations in 1948, asserts a long list of liberties reflecting the diverse topics in the debate. Some argue that certain physical rights should constitute the highest priority for government. Article 3 of the UDHR proclaims a right to life, liberty, and security of person. These rights are sometimes called negative liberties because they emphasize freedom from harm. In many contexts, individual criminals constitute the primary threat to these physical rights through their willingness to commit assault, battery, kidnapping, rape, and murder. When governments fail to reduce the threat and reality of violent crime, this failure can have visible political consequences. For instance, concerns over rising crime rates in Peru during the 1980s helped to discredit candidates from established political parties, thereby paving the way for Fujimori's successful outsider campaign in 1990.

Political uproar over physical rights is not limited to ineffective enforcement. At times, government officials are implicated in actions that violate citizens' physical rights. In some instances, these charges emerge as relatively isolated events in which few people appear to be involved. Events can reach the boiling point, however, when an entire government agency or even the executive or judiciary as a whole are accused of systematically violating physical rights. During the 1960s and 1970s, military governments across Latin America were accused of violating physical rights, sometimes by acting alone and sometimes by condoning or sponsoring extragovernmental groups engaged in violence against suspected enemies of the government. Firm estimates of the extent of the carnage are difficult to calculate because many people murdered during the repression were buried in hidden, unmarked gravesites. Somewhere between

100,000 and 250,000 people were killed under suspicion of antigovernment activities or sympathies between 1965 and 1985.[5] Tens of thousands more people experienced other violations of their physical rights via illegal detention, torture, and rape. The search for adjudication of these crimes has been one of the most visible political issues in contemporary Latin America.

Governments often defended these extreme measures as a way to protect economic rights. Article 17 of the UDHR asserts the right to hold property, a right that is rarely considered inviolable, not even by countries with a long-standing market-oriented approach to economic policy such as the United States. Under the principle of eminent domain, governments reserve the right to take ownership of private property that is needed to serve some public purpose. Invocation of eminent domain in the United States typically requires the government to defend its actions in court and to provide adequate compensation to the prior owner(s). For example, governments frequently exercise eminent domain for laying out highway and railroad networks.

The debate over nationalization of private property in Latin America goes beyond the use of eminent domain in establishing transportation systems. The political debate expanded to include calls for the nationalization of banks or of major export sectors. As with the use of eminent domain in transportation, proponents of economic nationalization claim that it serves a public purpose. The government-owned firm is supposed to provide services at a discount or to invest the profits in other public services. Property owners whose firms face calls for nationalization often claim that the threat of nationalization removes the incentive for individuals to take risks in establishing profitable businesses. Given the unequal distribution of wealth and income in Latin America, this political debate has frequently pitted politicians siding with the poor against politicians defending the property rights of the wealthy. In some situations, the wealthy manage to fend off calls for nationalization (as was the case of several banks in Peru during the García presidency), while in others the government steps in (as it did when the Velasco government established publicly owned cooperatives out of existing sugar plantations). We will see debates over the nationalization of key economic sectors in all of the country chapters in this book.

The freedom to enter into legal contracts also forms part of the debate over economic rights. As opposed to the nationalization issue, here those most vulnerable to having this right curtailed are the poor. It is difficult for poorer citizens around the world to find the legal representation needed to enforce their contracts in the judicial system. In Latin America, people face an added obstacle: the slow movement of the judicial process. The caseloads of judges greatly exceed the ability of their personnel to process court cases in inadequately computerized systems. Civil suits to enforce contracts can take as long as two to five years to make their way through the legal system. Under these constraints, workers who feel that they can prove they are owed back pay or severance pay often will settle for a fraction of what they are owed rather than face an arduous and expensive legal process. The crowded court system also constrains the ability of the government to provide adequate adjudication of crimes that violate citizens' physical rights.

The third and final major set of liberties that we will examine consists of civil and political rights, including freedom of speech, freedom of the press, freedom of association, freedom of organization, the right to a fair and impartial trial, the right to equal treatment under the law (regardless of gender, race, ethnicity, religion, or sexual orientation), and the right to vote in the election of certain government officials. As we saw in Chapter Two, civil liberties were unevenly enforced in the nineteenth century, and the right to vote, if it existed at all, was limited to a small minority. Over the first half of the twentieth century, civil and political rights were expanded—both in terms of the legal guarantees provided and, to a lesser extent, in terms of effective enforcement. In the tumultuous period of the 1960s and 1970s, military and civilian governments frequently curtailed civil liberties in the name of rooting out antigovernment insurgents. As the Cold War waned and as many of these dictatorships gave way to democratic regimes, the debate over civil and political rights returned to the forefront in Latin America.

Civil liberties advocates are concerned about governments' ability and willingness to promote an open climate for debate. As noted in Chapter Three, the

THE PERUVIAN EXPERIENCE
Freedom of the Press During the Fujimori Government

The Alberto Fujimori government (1990–2000) applied a carrot-and-stick approach in many of its dealings with the press. The carrot came from the power of the purse. The government spent millions of dollars on advertising each year but focused its spending on media outlets that agreed to support the Fujimori administration. Newspapers and television channels that were deemed too critical of Fujimori saw the government withdraw its advertising. During the 2000 election, the Toledo campaign staff claimed that the major television networks refused to air their ads (perhaps in fear of losing existing or future contracts with the government).

Manipulation of the media appears to have gone beyond the preferential use of advertising, however. Consider the case of Baruch Ivcher. He was the principal owner of Channel 2—the lone television network that had frequently criticized Fujimori. In 1998, Ivcher had his dual Peruvian-Israeli citizenship revoked by the Peruvian government. Because Peruvian law prohibits foreign ownership of television networks, control of Channel 2 passed to its minority shareholders. Under its new ownership, Channel 2 took an editorial line openly supportive of the Fujimori government. After Fujimori left the presidency in late 2000, Ivcher had his Peruvian citizenship restored. He was subsequently able to resume his position as controlling owner of Channel 2.

OAS electoral observation mission in Peru during the 2000 elections raised various concerns regarding the sanctity of the vote—a key political right. The OAS mission also supported allegations that the Fujimori government manipulated the media. *The Peruvian Experience: Freedom of the Press During the Fujimori Government* discusses concerns over freedom of the press during the 1990s.

Concerns over the protection of human liberty are not unique to Peru. Throughout Latin America, citizens question governments' ability to punish past violations of liberties and to deter future crimes. People also raise concerns regarding the partiality of the judicial process and regarding limitations on civil and political liberty. Doubts about the willingness of government officials to respect human liberty can breed considerable public cynicism and distrust in Peru and elsewhere.

Pursuing Liberty

Faced with this difficult panorama, what can governments do to ensure physical, economic, civil, and political rights? In part, present perceptions about governmental performance are interpreted through the lens of how past violations of liberty were handled. In this section, we will begin by examining options for

The Ivcher case is the most visible example of hundreds of allegations of intimidation designed to limit public expressions of disapproval with Fujimori's rule in the media. The Inter-American Commission on Human Rights (IACHR) investigated many such allegations during the years 1998–2000 and reached the following conclusion:

> The enjoyment of freedom of expression is fundamental to the full functioning of democracy as well as the exercise of other human rights. Chapter V of the Report is devoted to analyzing the restrictions on the dissemination of information and ideas regarding political dissent in Peru, including the systematic harassment of politicians of the opposition expressing ideas through the press, as well as independent journalists. The Report also addresses the role of the judiciary as a guarantor of freedom of expression and the fact that rather than protecting the enjoyment of this right according to law, Peruvian courts have been employed as a tool to harass those expressing ideas through the press. The Report also reflects the Commission's preoccupation for the personal safety of journalists and the lack of effective investigation of violent attacks of which they have been victims.[1]

[1]Inter-American Commission on Human Rights, *Second Report on the Human Rights Situation in Peru: Executive Summary*, found at http://www.cidh.org/countryrep/Peru2000en/execsummary.htm (accessed July 8, 2002).

dealing with human rights violations alleged under prior governments. We will then turn to the challenge of protecting liberty in the present day.

Many of the democracies formed over the course of the 1980s inherited a painful legacy of human rights violations committed under previous military dictatorships. Newly elected governments faced expectations from many sectors of society to hold responsible those accused of political murder, torture, rape, and other crimes. The cruel nature of the violence and its widespread use in many countries (especially Argentina, Chile, and Guatemala) created a public outcry for justice as the nature and extent of the violence became more public in the months and years following the end of military rule. In response, the armed forces—supported by some civilians—defended past actions as acts of war not subject to prosecution as criminal activity. Many of the accused also claimed that they were not criminally liable because they were bound to follow orders as members of a military hierarchy.

Contemporary Latin American democracies must navigate among these conflicting claims surrounding the legality of repression under prior governments. In choosing how to proceed, Brian Walsh has asserted that governments have four major potential goals: justice, deterrence, legitimacy, and reconciliation.[6] Demands for justice ask that those guilty of crimes be held accountable and that victims be compensated. In turn, many link the pursuit of justice to deterrence: the guilty need to be held accountable to deter future violations. If past government officials could violate liberties with impunity, what would prevent future officials from taking similar actions? Some argue that the vigorous enforcement of the law is linked not just to deterrence but also to the legitimacy of the entire political process. The central concern here is that respect for the rule of law should be consistently observed. If the government unevenly enforces the law, then it risks reducing citizens' confidence in the democratic process.

While the first three goals (justice, deterrence, and legitimacy) are potentially interconnected, the objective of national reconciliation can conflict with all three. Those who place a high priority on reconciliation frequently worry about whether prosecuting human rights violators will endanger the new democracy. They ask if human rights trials risk creating a new cycle of violence in which soldiers and civilians supportive of the use of past repression launch new acts of violence. In response to these concerns, those more committed to the pursuit of justice, deterrence, and legitimacy often counter that impunity can undermine respect for the civilian authorities in a different but equally powerful way.

With these conflicting perspectives and priorities in mind, Latin American governments have chosen among four major policy options when responding to accusations of past human rights violations: prosecution of the accused in domestic courts, amnesty for past violations, the establishment of truth commissions, and reparations for victims and their families (see Table 4.5). **Domestic prosecution** of human rights violators provides perhaps the most direct approach to achieving justice, deterrence, and legitimacy. It also has the potential to trigger the scenario feared by advocates of reconciliation: the military and its

TABLE 4.5 Four Major Policy Options for Handling Past Human Rights Violations

	Strategy	Potential risks
Domestic prosecution	Enforce the rule of law in the pursuit of deterrence, justice, legitimacy, and reconciliation	Might endanger reconciliation if security forces reject trials as unjust and/or illegitimate
Amnesty for the violators	Avoid prosecution in the pursuit of reconciliation	Might endanger reconciliation if victims and their families reject the amnesty as unjust and/or illegitimate
Truth commission	Account for violations without confronting the risk of trials or the risk of amnesty as the lone policy	The effort to find a middle ground between prosecution and amnesty might anger both the violators and the victims, and it may also not achieve its middle-ground goal because it can expand the pressure to prosecute
Victim reparations	Provide monetary compensation to victims and their families in pursuit of justice, legitimacy, and reconciliation (this strategy can be pursued in combination with any of the other options)	Does not address the goal of deterrence and might not achieve the other goals if pursued alone or if inadequately funded

SOURCE: Adapted from Brian Walsh, "Resolving the Human Rights Violations of a Previous Regime," *World Affairs* 158, no. 3 (1996): 111–120.

civilian allies could remove their support for the government. At the other end of the spectrum, granting **amnesty** favors reconciliation at the expense of the other goals. Formally speaking, amnesty provides a means of unevenly enforcing the law while paradoxically upholding the law; the amnesty legalizes the impunity. Nevertheless, amnesty risks outraging citizens who want to hold perpetrators responsible for their crimes.

In an effort to avoid this dilemma between outrage over trials and outrage over amnesty, governments can consider establishing a truth commission or providing reparations. The **truth commission** approach calls for an official investigation into human rights violations, but one that will not hold those identified as perpetrators criminally responsible. Potentially, governments have the option of making amnesty conditional on providing testimony to the truth commission, as was done in South Africa following the fall of the apartheid regime in the 1990s. The truth commission option tries to balance calls for reconciliation with the other three goals. Note that it risks being rejected, however, by those with strong feelings on both sides. Those involved in the violations may not accept the call to detail their actions, while victims and their families may see the truth commission as a half-measure that ultimately provides impunity. To respond to calls for justice, governments can decide to pay reparations to victims as well as to the families of deceased victims. The **reparations** approach attempts to provide a measure of justice (and hence legitimacy) to the handling of human rights violations without risking the meltdown scenario feared by reconciliation advocates. Even here, however, there are no easy answers: the losses suffered (the deaths of loved ones and the memories of brutal mistreatment) are difficult to put a price on. Those eligible for reparations understandably call for large amounts of compensation, yet governments' willingness and ability to provide reparations is often limited. In thinking about these objectives and policy options, notice that none of these policies can claim to

THE PERUVIAN EXPERIENCE
Human Rights Policy Under Toledo

During the 1980s and 1990s, elected governments battled two armed opposition groups. Government forces faced accusations of illegal detention, torture, and rape of imprisoned suspects and the summary execution of suspected rebels. Concern grew as the Fujimori government expanded the use of violence against those suspected of guerrilla involvement. Fujimori issued a series of controversial anti-terrorism laws by decree in the months following his self-coup in April 1992. The first of these decrees created a broad new definition of terrorism that included any act endangering human life, health, freedom, and security. As part of a terrorism investigation, suspects could be arrested without a warrant and held incommunicado for ten days. Beyond these attempts to legalize expansive police power, the government faced allegations of violating its own legislation by detaining suspects without a member of the prosecutor's office present and by torturing suspects. Several cases emerged in which security forces were charged with murdering suspects. The most visible case involved the murder of fifteen people (including one eight-year-old child) at a party in Lima in November 1991; the security forces claimed that the victims were Shining Path guerrillas.

In response to concern about human rights violations, the Fujimori government passed a sweeping amnesty law on June 14, 1995, that covered the period of civilian rule between May 1980 and June 1995. The judge in charge of investigating the 1991 massacre in Lima quickly ruled that the amnesty did not apply to her case because it contradicted other meet all four goals simultaneously in the minds of those most closely connected to these issues. Governments risk alienating segments of the population no matter what they do.

Many of the most visible cases in Latin America have involved actions implicating military governments—as we shall see later in chapters about Argentina, Chile, and Guatemala. Human rights violations committed by past administrations can also involve officials of elected governments. Such is the case, for example, in Peru. While allegations of human rights violations emerged during the period of military rule between 1968 and 1980, many more violations were alleged to have occurred as the war on counterinsurgency expanded during the 1980s and 1990s under democratic rule. The Toledo government faced many demands for action resulting from the dissatisfaction with how matters were handled by prior governments (see *The Peruvian Experience: Human Rights Policy Under Toledo*).

In addition to handling human rights violations committed during past governments, policy makers must decide how to protect basic liberties now and in the future. The legislature, the executive, and the judiciary all play a role in the

applicable legal norms. Before this case could reach Peru's supreme court, the Peruvian congress passed a second law asserting that the amnesty reigned supreme over all other legal norms, thus preventing the judiciary from ignoring the amnesty on grounds of legal conflict or inapplicability.

After Fujimori resigned in late 2000, the interim government headed by congressional leader Valentín Paniagua reopened the human rights issue. It established a truth commission charged with investigating all human rights abuses alleged between 1980 and 2000. In January 2001, the Peruvian congress reversed the Fujimori government's 1999 withdrawal from the Inter-American Court of Human Rights. This recognition of the court's jurisdiction had major legal implications because in March 2001, the court ruled that the 1995 amnesty laws violated the American Convention on Human Rights.

After taking office, Toledo expanded the charge of the truth commission by asking it to make recommendations for reparations. He also created a commission to investigate police conduct and earmarked $15 million for police reform. In addition to embracing the truth commission and reparations options, Toledo asserted that the legal framework of the truth commission did not prevent the prosecution of offenses identified by the commission. In late 2001, Fujimori and his security adviser Vladimiro Montesinos were formally charged as responsible for the 1991 massacre. It remained to be seen whether the Toledo government would expand the scope of its prosecutions after the truth commission completed its report in August 2003. In early September, the commission asked prosecutors to consider filing charges regarding twenty-two cases that implicated over fifty government officials.

protection of liberty. These three components of governmental efforts to ensure liberty are not mutually exclusive options; all three are pursued simultaneously. The political debate centers on identifying and implementing improvements when one or more branches appear to be performing poorly.

At the turn of the twenty-first century, the legislative debate in Latin America over the dimensions of liberty frequently focused on whether groups subjected to historical patterns of discrimination received adequate legal protection. Interest groups representing women and other groups representing indigenous peoples pressured for additional legal protections. Over the course of the 1980s, for instance, most Latin American legislatures enshrined in national law the 1979 United Nations Convention on the Elimination of All Forms of Discrimination Against Women. These legislative changes confirmed or in some way expanded legal protections extended to women in previous decades. Recent changes in the realm of indigenous rights have been much more striking. Prior to the 1980s, indigenous peoples enjoyed relatively few legal protections and were rarely mentioned in Latin American constitutions. By the end of the 1990s, however, eight countries granted indigenous peoples corporate personhood, six recognized the validity of customary indigenous law in civil disputes, twelve protected the right of indigenous peoples to hold property in common, and five recognized the official status of indigenous languages in territories with high percentages of native speakers.[7] As the twenty-first century began, many countries debated the creation of autonomous subnational political regimes based on ethnicity, and the Organization of American States worked on a proposed declaration on the rights of indigenous peoples.

After defining the legal boundaries of liberty, do sanctions for rights violations provide a sufficient deterrent to ensure the enjoyment of basic rights? Perhaps the most visible issue here has been recent concern that statutory sentences for many violent crimes are relatively lenient. At the same time, it is difficult to expect harsher sentences to be issued and carried out in a context dominated by rampant prison overcrowding. All nineteen countries in Latin America have prison populations in excess of their jails' intended capacities, with nearly half severely overcrowded.[8] Overcrowding and the stark conditions in many prisons draw attention to another item on the legislative agenda: when and how might legislators dedicate additional funds to expand prison capacity, to improve conditions for inmates, or to improve the enforcement of existing laws?

Many also question the judiciary's ability to work expeditiously yet carefully and impartially. Judicial reform has become a major issue in contemporary Latin America. In contrast to the legal tradition of case law in the United Kingdom and the United States, many Latin American legal systems continue to follow the code law tradition more prevalent in continental Europe (see *Concepts in Action: Case Law Versus Code Law*). In addition, Latin American judiciaries historically have relied heavily on written judicial procedures. This practice makes it difficult for people lacking education to participate in their

CONCEPTS IN ACTION
Case Law Versus Code Law

The case law (also called common law) tradition in the United States has its origins in the British colonial experience. In interpreting the law, judges consider customary practices and past judicial interpretations. The doctrine of *stare decisis* emerged: lower courts are not to overturn reasoning in past decisions by higher courts faced with similar cases. The use of precedent gives higher courts considerable authority because their reasoning applies to similar future decisions—unless or until a future higher court overturns the precedent.

The code law tradition dominant in Latin America also has its origins in the colonial past. Spain and Portugal have a code law system (also called civil law) in which the law consists of statutes created by governments. Judges are expected to apply the relevant statutes to the facts of each case. Past decisions might influence judges' thought processes, but there is no principle of *stare decisis* to bind judges to past decisions.

We can see the effects of these judicial differences in the definition and protection of many liberties. For example, consider search and seizure provisions. In most countries around the world, the right of the police to search for evidence of criminal activity is limited; these limits exist to defend citizens' right to privacy. The thorny issues are twofold. First, on what basis should judges grant search warrants and under what circumstances, if any, can police conduct searches without warrant? Second, when these conditions are not met, how should the right to privacy be enforced?

The right to privacy in one's residence and the resulting need for search warrants granted under reasonable procedures are core liberties enshrined in the constitutions of the United States (Fourth Amendment) and of Argentina (Article 18). When we examine how this right has been defended over time, we can appreciate some differences between case law and code law. One means of defending the right to privacy in both countries is the exclusionary rule: information or materials seized illegally cannot be used in evidence. In *Mapp* v. *Ohio* (1961), the U.S. Supreme Court decided that the exclusionary rule would be enforced in all situations of illegal search and seizure. Through *stare decisis*, this landmark ruling meant that all lower courts enforced the exclusionary rule. Once decided, only the Supreme Court could impose modifications to the categorical language in the *Mapp* case— as it would do in providing a "good faith" exemption to the exclusionary rule in *United States* v. *Leon* (1984). Shortly after Argentina returned to democracy in late 1983, the Argentine supreme court overturned a 1981 conviction by applying the exclusionary rule in the *Fiorentino* case (1984). Within the code law system, the Argentine supreme court's decision was not binding on future lower court decisions. Accordingly, while some lower court judges in future cases in the 1980s and 1990s chose to follow the reasoning in *Fiorentino*, others failed to apply the exclusionary rule.

own defense. This reliance on written procedures—in a context of minimal staff and uneven computerization—also makes the judiciary move notoriously slowly. Often, over half of the prison population consists of accused criminals awaiting trial; many wait for three or more years. To deal with these concerns, six countries moved toward greater reliance on oral trials between 1990 and 2001.

The code law tradition also limits the role of the judiciary in ensuring basic liberties. In the case law system familiar in the United States, the use of legal precedent implies that past decisions by higher courts are binding on lower courts. Accordingly, major U.S. Supreme Court decisions defining civil liberties and other matters can be landmark events. In code law, however, precedent is not binding on future decisions. As a result, in many Latin American countries, no central judicial authority has the power to shape future interpretations of the boundaries of liberty. Judges still perform the important task of interpreting the law for the case at hand, but their decisions have a wider impact only if they influence other judges' thinking, or if they place pressure on the legislature to change existing laws.

In addition to the speed and nature of the judicial process, the impartiality of judicial decisions has been hotly debated in contemporary Latin America. Many assert that judges are either corrupt or corruptible, that is, subject to influence from government leaders and the wealthy. While some propose expanding the number of judgeships with lifetime appointment, others counter that a lifetime appointee with minimal pay might be even more willing to take bribes because he or she might believe that removal from office would be unlikely. Beyond the corruption of certain judges, the independence of the judiciary has also been under attack by some presidents who have not tolerated decisions that go against them. For example, when the Peruvian constitutional tribunal ruled that Fujimori's pursuit of a third consecutive term violated the 1993 constitution, Fujimori had the justices removed. When a lower court judge ruled that a 1995 amnesty law did not apply to the 1991 case before her, Fujimori pushed through legislation that prohibited judges from ruling on the legality of the law before the appeal of that decision reached the higher court. Concerns over judicial corruption and over executive activism cast long shadows over the ideal of judicial independence.

Although many criticize presidential efforts to reduce the judiciary's power and independence, the executive branch clearly has a role to play in the search for liberty. Its traditional role consists of providing a police force capable of enforcing the law and identifying wrongdoers. In its larger role within the political process, the executive also shapes new legislation and budgetary decisions. As crime rates rose in Latin America during the 1980s and 1990s, presidents faced demands to spend more money on law enforcement. Calls from some in society went further and asked for tough tactics against criminals. Other groups asked for police reform in the opposite direction: changes designed to eliminate the use of strong-arm tactics to obtain confessions.

The Fujimori government found itself in the middle of these conflicting viewpoints. Its draconian tactics were applauded by some as necessary to reduce terrorism and street crime. Others criticized the increased use of violence by police and military officers, the prolonged use of preventive detention, and the trial of civilians in military tribunals. In the country chapters that follow, we will examine similar debates over the appropriate dimensions of liberty and the role of government in protecting citizens' rights.

THE QUEST FOR GOVERNANCE

Cecilia's first political memories date back to the early 1980s, when she was in elementary school. She recalls family mealtime discussions regarding the differences between the period of military rule from 1968 to 1980 and the Belaúnde government that followed. Her father defended the 1968 coup, arguing that the Velasco government had centralized control of the government to make changes to help working families. The 1975 coup and the results of the 1980 elections had produced center-right governments that he felt ignored most Peruvians' problems. His father, Cecilia's grandfather, stridently disagreed. He argued that governments needed to cater to the wealthy or they would simply take their money out of the country. This disagreement made itself felt nearly every Sunday afternoon.

In the process, however, the two men did share one point: Peru needed a strong president to implement their respective visions of what government should do. Her grandfather would often cite a quotation from Simón Bolívar that he learned in school: "What was once Spanish America needs kings that are called presidents." Without a strong ruler, nothing was possible in the minds of Cecilia's father and grandfather.

As Cecilia's sisters grew older, they challenged those views. Her oldest sister Marisa argued that compromises regarding the role of government should be worked out among the various parties in the legislature in coordination with the executive branch. Without these efforts, Marisa argued that Peru would experience more of the dramatic swings in policy that it experienced between the Velasco and Morales military governments and between the elected governments of Belaúnde and García. Her other sister, Victoria, was much more skeptical regarding politicians. She would say that most were corrupt, and those who were not were neither numerous nor powerful enough to make a difference. Shunning political parties, she spent her spare time working in a neighborhood soup kitchen until her death at the hands of Shining Path guerrillas.

Cecilia participated as a young adult in debates regarding the Fujimori government. For some, Fujimori was a savior who centralized authority to restore economic growth and to fight crime. For others, his policies favored the wealthy and largely ignored the poor. By the end of the 1990s, people with all sorts of

Well over half of the population of Peru cannot afford to shop at the Larcomar mall in the Miraflores district of Lima.   Top photo: © Gustavo Gilabert/Corbis Saba; bottom photo: © Jimmy Dorantes/Latin Focus.

economic policy preferences began to reject Fujimori as a power-hungry politician interested primarily in his ability to stay in power.

Defining Governance

In this chapter, we have examined the enormous challenges implied by the pursuit of development and liberty in Latin America. Despite the middle-income status of the region as a whole, many people lack basic necessities, and many more have seen their basic liberties threatened in various ways. A perceptible distance exists between people's aspirations and the lives they lead. This difference places governments under serious pressure to implement public policies to improve the existing state of affairs. Yet opinions differ regarding the role of government in the economy and in protecting liberty. These disagreements make themselves felt in the political system: many citizens push for the policies they prefer by lobbying, voting, and protesting.

Faced with these diverse pressures and demands, how should governments make decisions? Should power be concentrated or dispersed? Which government positions, if any, should be elected offices? How often should elections be held and how should they be organized? In the United States, the answers to these questions have focused on how to organize democratic governance. As we saw in Chapter Two, the governance debate in Latin America historically has embraced a much wider variety of alternatives.

In the nineteenth century, immediately after independence, several countries actively considered monarchy as a potential path to effective governance. In Mexico and in Brazil, the leadership of the new nation-states was placed in the hands of monarchs that would presumably pass that power down to their descendants in the decades to come. The Mexican Empire lasted less than a year. Emperor Agustín Iturbide abdicated and fled into exile rather than face a military challenge from another hero of the independence movement, Antonio López de Santa Anna. In Brazil, however, the monarchy endured for nearly seven decades before the government of Dom Pedro II fell to a bloodless military coup in 1889. While monarchy would be discussed as an alternative in some circles throughout the nineteenth century, no other countries adopted dynastic rule.

Instead, most nineteenth-century discourse presented democracy as the definition of effective governance. While people shared a notion that democracy implied some dispersion of authority among various elected offices, debate raged over how to organize those elections and over which citizens should have the right to vote. As was the case in the United States and in many European democracies, early Latin American democracies had restrictive suffrage laws that limited voting to a small minority of men who met literacy and property requirements. Amid the economic changes of the late nineteenth century, calls for universal male suffrage (and later for universal suffrage regardless of gender) were made. While many countries eased limitations on male suffrage in the late nineteenth and early twentieth centuries, women's suffrage took time to emerge. Across the nineteen countries in the region, women gained the right to vote between 1929 and 1961. Illiterate citizens of both sexes in several countries did not gain the vote until the second half of the twentieth century. In Peru, where illiterate citizens gained the right to vote in 1979, the literacy requirement blocked more than one-third of adult Peruvians from voting during the 1960s. Today in Latin America, voting rights are not just universal but also frequently obligatory. Voting laws in most countries require citizens to vote on the principle that their participation is a defining characteristic of democracy. In countries with compulsory voting, people can be fined for failing to vote.

While universal suffrage eventually became central to nearly all discussions of democracy, debate over the appropriate dispersion of power among elected offices has continued almost without interruption in Latin America. As the Bolívar quotation cited by Cecilia's grandfather illustrates, political discourse and subsequent governing institutions have frequently called for considerable centralization of authority. Latin American presidents typically have more discretion to appoint government officials and wider appointment powers in that they control many more positions than do U.S. presidents. Latin American chief executives often also have greater ability to control the legislative agenda and, in some cases, they have the ability to make laws by executive degree. For example, in the 1979 constitution, Peruvian presidents gained the ability to issue temporary decrees in economic and financial matters without congressional approval. They also received the ability to declare a state of exception (suspending all constitutional guarantees) without legislative support. The 1993 constitution that emerged after Fujimori's *autogolpe* ("self-coup") further enhanced presidential decree and emergency powers; Alejandro Toledo invoked these powers in May 2003 to declare a thirty-day national state of emergency in response to widespread strikes launched in protest of his government. The 1993 reforms also centralized authority in new ways not contemplated by the prior constitution. Local and regional governments lost their autonomy from the national executive, and the president gained the power to appoint governors. Many advocates of the centralization of power in Latin America have justified these sorts of changes by citing a need for quick decisive action.

Throughout the nineteenth and twentieth centuries, frustration with the speed and effectiveness of democratic rule was used at times to rationalize the creation of a dictatorship in which elections were either suspended or held under such severe restrictions that few would consider them meaningful. As democracies came to govern in more and more corners of the world during the twentieth century, dictatorships frequently defined their rationale for existence as a necessary expedient amid a national crisis. Many civilian and military dictators felt a need to fend off criticism from advocates of democracy by justifying the suspension of electoral politics as a temporary measure designed to restore democracy at some future date.

Not all advocates of nondemocratic rule in the twentieth century defined dictatorship as a temporary interruption in electoral politics. Following the emergence of the Soviet Union as a one-party state with a command economy in the 1930s, some advocates of socialism embraced revolutionary rule as a means to establish and maintain the nationalization of the economy. In this view, the end of competitive elections (via the creation of a one-party state) was not a temporary expedient but rather the definition of effective governance now and into the future. The establishment of a socialist dictatorship in Cuba under Castro motivated many to take up arms in pursuit of socialism. To date, no revolutionary dictatorships have emerged elsewhere in Latin America. Some thought that the triumph of FSLN (Sandinista) guerrillas over the Somoza dictatorship in 1979 would produce revolutionary rule. Over the course of the 1980s, however, the FSLN government—amid ongoing civil war and considerable economic turmoil—never fully nationalized the economy nor did it abolish electoral politics. When the FSLN lost the 1990 elections, it respected the results of the vote by ceding control of the executive and legislative branches to some of its sharpest critics. By the 1990s, guerrilla movements elsewhere in the region either had been defeated militarily or were locked in prolonged stalemates (such as those that existed in Colombia, El Salvador, and Guatemala). As Latin America began the twenty-first century, the lone example of socialist revolutionary rule remained the Castro dictatorship.

The defeat of guerrilla movements, the end to revolutionary rule in the Soviet bloc, and the retreat to the barracks of many military rulers left democracy as the most prevalent definition of effective governance at the outset of the twenty-first century. But this development does not mark the end of the governance debate for two reasons. First, despite triumphal proclamations such as Francis Fukuyama's suggestion that democracy's current acceptance represents the "end of history," no one can say with confidence that new challenges to democracy as the standard for governance might not emerge in the future.[9] This is particularly true when one considers the extent of discontent with contemporary conditions in many countries in and out of Latin America. Second, even at a time in which democracy dominates debates over the definition of governance, many disagree over how democratic rule should be pursued. In particular, the debate over the power of the presidency remains active.

Pursuing Governance

Because most contemporary Latin American political systems are presidential democracies, our analysis of the pursuit of effective governance will focus on the power of the presidency. In a **presidential system**, the chief executive is elected to a fixed term, normally four to six years. There is no guarantee that voters will choose a legislative majority that supports the president's agenda. In the United States, the term **gridlock** is used to refer to situations in which the president's party does not control a majority of seats in the legislature. Even when the president's party controls the legislature, steady support for presidential initiatives is not ensured because legislators may enjoy a durable source of electoral support that is not tied to the president's popularity.

To avoid the gridlock scenario, many nineteenth-century presidents in Latin America tried to build electoral machines designed to ensure comfortable legislative majorities. When they succeeded in building durable electoral machines (often by a mix of legal and illegal means), those with competing political platforms complained of *continuismo*—presidents who continued in office term after term via elections of questionable fairness. To prevent this scenario, many countries inserted constitutional clauses that prevented the immediate reelection of the president. By 1920, nearly all countries in the region prohibited presidents from serving consecutive terms.

The prohibition against reelection meant that most twentieth-century presidents in Latin America had four to six years to pursue their agendas. One approach to governance in this situation is to view the president's role as one of government by consensus. To build legislative support, presidents can employ various strategies, including lobbying, the mobilization of public opinion, pork barrel politics, logrolling, patronage politics, and coercion. Presidents routinely send their advisers to lobby legislators. In advance of important votes, presidents try to signal the priority they place on a bill by personally attempting to persuade legislators. In combination with this tactic, presidents engage in the mobilization of public opinion. Using their access to the national media, presidents and their cabinets attempt to sway the public toward the president's preferred policy. Sometimes presidents attract support by crafting draft legislation using pork barrel politics. In this approach, the president's collaborators in the legislature add provisions to a bill that target spending to particular geographic districts. In this way, legislators who support the bill can later take credit for bringing public spending to their constituents. For example, legislation to build a new major bridge might include a series of road and bridge projects sprinkled throughout the country. Presidents also engage in logrolling: they offer to support a legislator's future bill in exchange for his or her support on a current bill. Perhaps the most important resource directly controlled by the executive branch, however, is the power of patronage. The executive branch controls thousands and thousands of positions in the bureaucracy. To win legislative support, presidents often offer jobs to close associates of the legislator or, more broadly, to his or her constituents. In addition to all of these deal-making techniques, presidents can also engage in legal acts of coercion in which they threaten to withhold their future support, pork barrel projects, or patronage posts if a legislator refuses to vote with them.

In pursuing their agendas during the twentieth century, many Latin American presidents faced not just legislative gridlock but also a divided electorate (see *Governing Strategies: Fernando Belaúnde*). In presidential elections, the elected candidate might receive as little as 25 percent of the popular vote. Voters

GOVERNING STRATEGIES
Fernando Belaúnde

Fernando Belaúnde became a double-minority president in 1963, seven years after founding the Popular Action (AP) party. Belaúnde won with 39 percent of the vote in a tight race against former dictator General Manuel Odría and veteran American Revolutionary Popular Alliance (APRA) leader Víctor Haya de la Torre (whose even narrower victory over Belaúnde in the 1962 elections had been blocked by a military coup). Belaúnde's campaign called for democratization, land redistribution, and economic nationalism ("the conquest of Peru by Peruvians").

AP held about one-third of the seats in the legislature. Several AP leaders tried to negotiate a pact with APRA: if AP and APRA voted together, they would control a legislative majority. But both parties were internally divided. Several AP members argued that a coalition with APRA risked a military coup. Others in AP felt that APRA was no longer committed to major reform. On the APRA side, some questioned the wisdom of helping Belaúnde because, if the policies were popular, AP might gain the lion's share of the credit in the next elections. Haya de la Torre was said to resent Belaúnde's presidency. Haya de la Torre's many attempts to become president had been blocked, while Belaúnde won by running largely on APRA's historic platform. In the end, the talks aiming at a coalition failed. Instead, Haya de la Torre announced that APRA would work with the rightist *Unión Nacional Odríista* (UNO) to form a majority in Congress.

The gap between Belaúnde's campaign promises and his weak legislative support quickly became apparent. In anticipation of agrarian reform, many peasants had seized unused land before Belaúnde took office. The APRA-UNO majority in Congress blamed AP for the rural unrest and called for repression. It then delayed agrarian reform along with most of the Belaúnde platform. Several AP leaders urged Belaúnde to call a national referendum to pressure the Peruvian congress to cooperate; he decided against it.

Years of stalemate followed. The legislature refused to raise taxes to support the presidency's effort to expand many public programs. Belaúnde resorted to deficit spending to increase education and social spending. When congress finally enacted land reform, it excluded the major export sectors and provided little money with which to buy land for redistribution. Meanwhile, the president's effort to launch a new public oil refinery stalled in prolonged talks with the U.S.-owned International Petroleum Company (IPC).

In June 1968, Belaúnde appointed an economic minister with ties to APRA, Manuel Ulloa. Reversing its earlier opposition, APRA agreed to delegate sweeping authority to Ulloa for sixty days because it hoped to recruit him as its presidential candidate in the upcoming 1969 elections. Belaúnde then announced an end to the lengthy dispute with IPC. Rather than nationalizing the IPC as many had urged, the government ceded to U.S. pressure to end the dispute on terms largely favorable to the IPC. As Belaúnde reorganized his cabinet in response to the oil scandal, reformist military officers launched a successful coup on October 3, 1968. Fernando Belaúnde would have to wait twelve years for new democratic elections to be held.

could also elect legislatures in which no party held more than 30 to 40 percent of the seats. This scenario has often been dubbed the **double-minority presidency**. Double-minority presidents frequently struggled to implement the public policies they had proposed as candidates. When they did manage to create legislative majorities, they frequently did so via pork barrel spending and patronage politics. Public spending and public employment provided a path to governance in the double-minority scenario but often resulted in rising budget deficits and inflation because many governments proved reluctant to raise taxes to keep revenues in line with rising expenditures. Many of the military governments that came to power in the 1960s and 1970s blamed inflation (and economic problems more generally) on politics as usual. Once in power, many military governments nevertheless failed to control inflation better than prior elected leaders.

When democracy returned over the course of the 1980s, voices from some in society called for a stronger presidency. Several reforms constitute potential elements of this contemporary brand of **hyperpresidentialism**. One frequent change has been a move away from plurality election of the president to a two-round (**ballotage**) system. Prior to 1979, most countries employed the plurality electoral system used in U.S. legislative elections: the candidate with the most votes was declared the winner, even if no candidate received a majority of the popular vote. Beginning in 1979 with reforms in Ecuador and Peru, eight countries now have ballotage electoral systems that require a candidate to get at least 50 percent of the vote to win election (while three more have a threshold of 40 or 45 percent). If no candidate receives the necessary votes, a second runoff election is held between the two candidates who received the most votes. This ballotage reform attempts to strengthen the president's hand by increasing the percentage of the vote won by successful candidates.

In several countries, debate began over the desirability of the prevailing prohibition against reelection of sitting presidents. Proponents of the change presented two main arguments. First, they argued that supporters of the incumbent ought to have the right to extend the mandate of presidents they believe are performing well. Second, they asserted that the possibility of reelection would improve the president's ability to work with the legislature because popular presidents could more credibly claim to be able to mobilize voters against uncooperative legislators in the next elections. Alberto Fujimori in Peru was not alone in achieving this change: Argentina, Brazil, and Venezuela also removed the ban on reelection, while several other countries actively debated the possibility.

While these electoral reforms aimed at one-half of the double-minority scenario, others called for strengthening the president's powers to deal with legislative opposition. Presidential power to influence the legislative agenda was expanded in several ways. In some countries, presidents gained the exclusive ability to introduce budgetary or other economic legislation. In others, presidents acquired the authority to designate certain legislation as urgent, thereby requiring the legislature to make a decision within two to six weeks. In Argentina, Brazil, Colombia, Ecuador, and Venezuela, presidents gained broader constitutional authority to issue laws by decree. Some presidents with weak vetoes (that could be overridden by a simple majority) asked for strong vetoes that would require a special majority to override (such as the two-thirds majority required in the United States). Beyond constitutional changes, many presidents across the region pressured their respective legislatures to pass sweeping legislation in which the legislature delegated law-making authority in many economic areas to the executive branch for periods as long as one to two years.

Scott Mainwaring and Matthew Shugart developed a typology describing four different scenarios for presidential legislative power (see Table 4.6). Presidents with strong vetoes, decree powers, and exclusive rights to introduce some legislation could be termed potentially dominant. The combination of agenda-setting capabilities with the blocking power of a strong veto gives the president many tools to influence legislative behavior. Conversely, some countries' presidencies have no agenda-setting powers and either a weak veto or no veto whatsoever. These presidents' limited institutional authority makes them potentially marginal unless they can manage to win over the legislature via other means. The two midrange scenarios distinguish between the proactive and reactive nature of these presidential powers. Reactive presidents have strong vetoes and some agenda-setting powers, yet they lack the decree power needed to shape the timing of legislative activity. The U.S. presidency could be described as reactive,

TABLE 4.6 A Typology of Presidential Authority in Legislative Matters*

	Strong agenda-setting powers	Weak agenda-setting powers
Strong Veto	*Potentially dominant:* strong veto, exclusive introduction, decree power	*Reactive:* strong veto, exclusive introduction
Weak Veto	*Proactive:* weak veto, exclusive introduction, decree power	*Potentially marginal:* weak or no veto

*A weak presidential veto requires a legislative majority for override while a strong veto requires a higher majority. Exclusive introduction refers to presidential rights to initiate legislation on certain issue(s). Decree power refers to the ability to enact laws by presidential decree without legislative authorization (as opposed to executive regulation of existing legislation).

SOURCE: Adapted from Scott Mainwaring and Matthew Shugart, "Presidentialism and Democracy in Latin America: Rethinking the Debate," in Mainwaring and Shugart, eds., *Presidentialism and Democracy in Latin America* (Cambridge, England: Cambridge University Press, 1997), p. 49.

with its exclusive right to begin the budget process and its strong veto. Conversely, proactive presidents have a full range of agenda-setting powers, but they lack the blocking power of a strong veto.

Beyond executive-legislative relations, presidents also attempted to expand their authority in other ways. Some sought an enhanced role in the appointment and dismissal of judges. Others tried to increase executive discretion in the definition and enforcement of liberty. Some countries expanded the president's ability to declare a state of siege, in which constitutional guarantees could be suspended in response not just to foreign invasion but also in reaction to domestic disorder. Other countries debated legislation that would place limits on the ability of the media to criticize governmental officials.

The Fujimori government in Peru provides an extreme example of hyperpresidentialism. In several respects, the 1979 constitution already gave Peruvian presidents more authority than did the constitutions of many Latin American countries. When Fujimori launched his *autogolpe* in 1992, however, he pushed through various changes that strengthened the authority of the executive branch in general and of the president in particular. Peru already had ballotage elections for the presidency in place since 1979, and then Fujimori succeeded in removing the prohibition on reelection. Peruvian presidents, like their U.S. counterparts, enjoyed the privilege of beginning the budgetary debate with their own proposal. Under the new 1993 constitution, however, Fujimori gained the exclusive right to propose changes in the tax code and also made it illegal for the legislature to enact spending levels higher than those found in his budget proposal. He obtained greater authority over the judiciary, powers which he used to dismiss the justices on the constitutional tribunal who had ruled against his pursuit of a third consecutive term. The new constitution also expanded presidential authority to suspend constitutional guarantees by declaring a state of exception in part or all of the national territory. Finally, one of the most controversial provisions of the 1993 constitution made permanent all laws passed by decree in the months following the coup, including the sweeping anti-terrorism legislation discussed in *The Peruvian Experience: Human Rights Policy Under Toledo* on pages 100–101.

While some praise these sorts of reforms as a useful response to trying national conditions, critics of hyperpresidentialism raise concerns central to the debate over development, liberty, and governance. First, some argue that economic (and other) policies forced into law by "superpresidents" will not be as effective or as enduring as policies enacted via the consensus-building approach. Citizens may despair of their ability to influence legislation and instead may take the approach of ignoring policies that they do not support. Second, critics worry that expanding executive authority threatens liberty and the rule of law by making the presidency too powerful. Without adequate legislative oversight and an independent judiciary, violations of liberty may become more difficult to detect and punish. The crimes at issue range from undetected acts of corruption by government officials to violations of individual citizens' human rights. Finally, some question the effectiveness of hyperpresidentialism over the medium to long run. A powerful president may be better able to enact his or her program, but if one does so without building consensus (among political parties, interest groups, and the citizenry), the chances that the next president will continue along that policy path are reduced. Hyperpresidentialism thus may produce swings in policies from one term to the next that make economic continuity more limited and the enjoyment of liberty more uncertain.

In addition to viewing hyperpresidentialism as unproductive, many of its critics are concerned that it constitutes a mix of democratic and authoritarian rule that Guillermo O'Donnell dubbed **delegative democracy.**[10] These critics argue that several contemporary Latin American countries have left military rule behind, but they are not on the path to a robust democracy characterized by the meaningful rule of law and considerable participation by citizens and their representatives. Instead, competing presidential candidates present themselves as potential saviors who ask for legislators and citizens alike to delegate additional power in the name of responding to difficult economic and/or security crises. In these delegative democracies, the lack of meaningful checks and balances enables enterprising politicians (and some private citizens) to circumvent the rule of law while the political process is largely reduced to presidential elections. Disenchanted citizens become increasingly skeptical about politicians, and this skepticism raises concern that delegative democracy is a step toward a return to authoritarian rule in the Americas.

Who is correct in this debate over the costs and benefits of hyperpresidentialism? Is delegative democracy weakening the political present while poisoning its future? Or is a strong president the best approach to governance? In the country chapters that follow, you will have an opportunity to build your answer to this question by considering the experiences of seven countries.

At least one issue appears certain: political leaders and citizens throughout Latin America face a difficult task. The gaps among current aspirations for development, liberty, and governance are considerable. If you have any doubts, you might reconsider the plight of Alejandro Toledo. Taking office amid widespread concern over hyperpresidentialism as practiced by Fujimori, Toledo initially made an effort to engage in governance by consensus. During the first half of his term, however, Alejandro Toledo faced considerable criticism regarding his own approach to governance (see *The Peruvian Experience: Toledo's Search for Governance* on pages 116–117).

Peru is not the only country in Latin America facing difficult problems. Poverty is widespread, and it is rising in many cases. Crime also remains a serious concern, while the dark shadow of past human rights violations creates skepticism regarding the ability and willingness of government to protect the rule of law. Skepticism about government officials' honesty frames a difficult context for governance. While many call for governmental reforms to increase checks and balances, others call for further centralization of power in the hope that, somehow, a new national leader will make progress in the search for development, liberty, and governance.

The above paragraph depicts a gloomy horizon. As we shall see in the chapters that follow, conditions in much of Latin America worsened during the first few years of the twenty-first century. These same years bore witness to several grim events in the United States. The depressing elements of the present should not prevent us from considering the possibility of a brighter future for all of the Americas and for the world as a whole. A central step toward human progress consists of a firm understanding of the past and present upon which that brighter future can be built. In the next seven chapters, we improve our understanding of past and present events in Argentina, Brazil, Chile, Cuba, Guatemala, Mexico, and Venezuela.

As we study these countries, consider several major questions raised over the course of Chapters One through Four:

■ *What are the political dynamics of economic policy in Latin America in the early twenty-first century?* Here you should consider what factors tend to produce support for market capitalism and what conditions tend to produce

---

THE PERUVIAN EXPERIENCE
Toledo's Search for Governance

At the beginning of this chapter, we examined the difficult context in which Alejandro Toledo became president of Peru on July 28, 2001. Would he follow Fujimori's no-holds-barred approach to governance or would he bargain earnestly with opposing political parties, interest groups, and private citizens? Toledo needed the support of opposition legislators because his political party, *Perú Posible*, held only forty-five of the 120 seats in an eleven-party legislature.

During the 2001 campaign, Toledo had pledged to govern by consensus. Once in office, he organized a roundtable with leaders of seven political parties (representing 95 percent of the legislature) and seven major interest groups (two business confederations, the major labor union, two religious organizations, a confederation of regional interest groups, and an antipoverty nongovernmental organization [NGO]). Toledo asked for a national accord on public ethics, poverty reduction, and economic competitiveness. The process called for the participants to agree on goals, then to set specific objectives tied to those goals, and finally to recommend policies for realizing those objectives.

Despite broad agreement on general goals, these discussions proved extremely difficult for three major reasons. First, participants differed in their understanding of the core problems. For example, which of the following is the most important cause of poverty: inadequate

political opposition. How can elected officials and engaged citizens take action to build support for the policy option that they prefer? As a political analyst, how would you advise a politician advocating market capitalism? In turn, what political strategies would you recommend to politicians advocating state capitalism or command economics?

- *Which economic model should most Latin American countries adopt?* Consider here the evidence supporting market capitalism, state capitalism, and command economics found in the experiences of these seven countries. What is the best case in support of each option? How would you rebut counterarguments to your own view? In building your analysis, clarify which of the various development goals discussed in Chapter Four you are trying to maximize.

- *In the countries confronting human rights violations committed under prior governments, which strategies seemed most effective?* As you did when considering economic development, remember to clarify which of the goals discussed in Chapter Four you are emphasizing as essential priorities. Among the four major policy options (amnesty, domestic trials, reparations, and

---

economic activity, low educational levels, or inequitable distribution of wealth and income? Second, even when some agreement regarding the nature of the policy problem existed, serious disagreement emerged regarding the appropriate government remedy. Third, beyond these policy disagreements, discord among party leaders came out of political motivations. Toledo asked for a potentially far-reaching agreement, yet his own approval rating in polls began at 45 percent and fell below 20 percent during spring 2002. Many politicians privately questioned the wisdom of agreeing to support Toledo as his approval rating slipped.

The original May 30 deadline for the national-accord process passed with no agreement whatsoever. Only after the tense June protests in Arequipa against Toledo's privatization of government electric companies did the participants sign the National Accord on July 22, 2002. The twenty-nine-point accord listed sweeping goals, including improving economic competitiveness, reducing poverty, providing quality education and health care, protecting civil liberties, eradicating government corruption, and protecting the rule of law. On only one issue, however, did the National Accord lay out a specific policy initiative: education spending would be raised by 4 percent above its current level.

The largely unsuccessful search for a more concrete consensus during Toledo's first year in office raises several questions. What else could Toledo have done to expand legislative and public support for his presidency? Which tactics would have been useful in the tough climate he inherited and why? Finally, has his presidency succeeded in the period since the National Accord? Why or why not?

truth commissions), have any proven to be consistently successful in realizing their goals when applied? In turn, how would you build political support for the goals and the policy options that you prefer?

■ *What are the most important obstacles to securing contemporary liberties in Latin America?* Are some liberties more imperiled than others? What endangers those liberties? If some liberties are threatened more than others, how would you design a political strategy for policy reform in that area and what policy(ies) would you recommend?

■ *Do you believe that increasing presidential power has improved the prospects for effective governance in Latin America or not?* Consider potential evidence on each side of this question as you read these country chapters. If you believe that stronger presidents have been more effective, what powers seem most useful? How would you respond to critics of hyperpresidentialism? Conversely, if you believe that the delegative democracy critique is convincing, in what ways have presidents been constrained effectively and how would you justify those constraints when faced with demands for quick action?

■ *Taking all aspects of these seven countries' experiences into account, are you more optimistic about the prospects for democratic consolidation than you were before you read this book on Latin American politics?* If you are more optimistic, what trends and events provide the source of that optimism? If your reading of the country chapters has made you more pessimistic regarding democracy's future, what drives that pessimism? What strategies could be used to improve the prospects for democracy over time?

At the close of this book, we will review these countries' experiences with an eye toward these important questions. Before we can do so, we need to familiarize ourselves with each country. We will begin in Chapter Five by analyzing the dynamics of what has historically been the most prosperous Latin American country—Argentina.

Activities and Exercises

1. Review this chapter's presentation of development goals and economic strategies. If no government is likely to dedicate equal energy to the achievement of all these goals, which two goals should be given priority in Peru? How would you justify your priorities? In light of your priorities, which of the three economic policy models seems best suited to realize your priorities and why?

2. Review this chapter's discussion of the dimensions of contemporary liberty. Which two dimensions should constitute Peru's highest priorities and why? How would you try to achieve these objectives?

3. Review this chapter's discussion of presidential strategies for governance. Which of these tactics did the George W. Bush administration in the United States seem to emphasize during the years 2001–2004? Remember that Bush also faced a situation similar to that of double-minority presidents: he received less than half

of the popular vote; his party lacked a majority in the Senate during 2001–2002; and even after gaining a Senate majority in 2003, the Republicans lacked the sixty seats necessary to stop the Democrats from blocking legislation via filibusters. Would these same strategies favored by Bush seem to work equally well in Latin America? If so, why? If not, why not?

4. *La boca del lobo* (*The Wolf's Mouth*) is a 1988 film that dramatizes the counterinsurgent efforts of the Peruvian military taken against the Shining Path guerrillas in Peru. See if you can obtain a copy of this movie in your library or video store.

5. Update this chapter's treatment of Alejandro Toledo's presidency. In addition to consulting the LANIC (Latin American Network Information Center) website discussed at the end of Chapter Three, you could also consult various online news sources: the BBC world news service at http://news.bbc.co.uk/1/hi/world/, the CNN world news website at http://edition.cnn.com/world, *The Economist* at http://www.economist.com, *The Miami Herald* at http://www.herald.com, and *The New York Times* at http://www.nytimes.com. To consult Latin American newspapers on the Internet, see the news section of the LANIC website or examine the country-by-country list of newspapers available on the Yahoo website at http://dir.yahoo.com/News_and_Media/Newspapers/By_Region/Countries/.

Suggested Readings

Chilcote, Ronald, ed. *Development in Theory and Practice: Latin American Perspectives.* Lanham, Md.: Rowman and Littlefield, 2003.

Colburn, Forrest. *Latin America at the End of Politics.* Princeton, N.J.: Princeton University Press, 2002.

Crabtree, John, and J. J. Thomas, eds. *Fujimori's Peru: The Political Economy.* London: Institute of Latin American Studies, 1998.

Franko, Patrice. *The Puzzle of Latin American Economic Development,* 2d ed. Lanham, Md.: Rowman and Littlefield, 2003.

Geddes, Barbara. *Politician's Dilemma: Building State Capacity in Latin America.* Berkeley: University of California, 1994.

Grindle, Merilee. *Audacious Reforms: Institutional Invention and Democracy in Latin America.* Baltimore, Md.: Johns Hopkins University Press, 2001.

Hammergren, Linn. *The Politics of Justice and Justice Reform in Latin America: The Peruvian Case in Comparative Perspective.* Boulder, Colo.: Westview, 1998.

Hillman, Richard, John Peeler, Elsa Cardozo, eds. *Democracy and Human Rights in Latin America.* New York: Praeger, 2002.

Jelin, Elizabeth, and Eric Hershberg, eds. *Constructing Democracy: Human Rights, Citizenship, and Society in Latin America.* Boulder, Colo.: Westview, 1996.

Kenney, Charles. *Fujimori's Coup and the Breakdown of Democracy in Latin America.* South Bend, Ind.: University of Notre Dame Press, 2004.

Linz, Juan, and Arturo Valenzuela, eds. *The Failure of Presidential Democracy: The Case of Latin America.* Baltimore, Md.: Johns Hopkins University Press, 1994.

Lustig, Nora, ed. *Coping with Austerity: Poverty and Inequality in Latin America.* Washington, D.C.: Brookings Institution Press, 1995.

Lustig, Nora, ed. *Shielding the Poor: Social Protection in the Developing World.* Washington, D.C.: Brookings Institution Press, 2001.

Mainwaring, Scott, and Matthew Shugart, eds. *Presidentialism and Democracy in Latin America.* Cambridge, England: Cambridge University Press, 1997.

Méndez, Juan, Guillermo O'Donnell, and P. S. Pinheiro, eds. *The (Un)rule of Law and the Underprivileged in Latin America.* South Bend, Ind.: University of Notre Dame Press, 1999.

Morgenstern, Scott. *Patterns of Legislative Politics: Roll Call Voting in Latin America and the United States.* Cambridge, England: Cambridge University Press, 2004.

Morgenstern, Scott, and Benito Nacif, eds. *Legislative Politics in Latin America.* Cambridge, England: Cambridge University Press, 2002.

Murillo, Victoria. *Labor Unions, Partisan Coalitions and Market Reforms in Latin America.* Cambridge, England: Cambridge University Press, 2001.

Nickson, R. Andrew. *Local Government in Latin America.* Boulder, Colo.: Lynne Rienner, 1995.

Roniger, Luis. *The Legacy of Human Rights Violations in the Southern Cone.* New York: Oxford University Press, 1999.

Selbin, Eric. *Modern Latin American Revolutions,* 2d ed. Boulder, Colo.: Westview, 1999.

Smith, William, Carlos Acuña, and Eduardo Gamarra, eds. *Latin American Political Economy in the Age of Neoliberal Reform.* Miami, Fla.: North-South Center Press, 1994.

Stern, Steve. *Shining and Other Paths: War and Society in Peru, 1980–1995.* Durham, N.C.: Duke University Press, 1998.

Tulchin, Joseph, and Gary Bland, eds. *Peru in Crisis: Dictatorship or Democracy?* Boulder, Colo.: Lynne Rienner, 1994.

Wise, Carol. *Reinventing the State: Economic Strategy and Institutional Change in Peru.* Ann Arbor: University of Michigan Press, 2003.

Endnotes

1. "Toledo reaches the palace, at last," *The Economist* (June 6, 2001).

2. Irma Arriagada and Lorena Godoy, "Prevention or Repression? The False Dilemma of Citizen Security," *CEPAL Review* 70 (April 2000): 116.

3. This particular definition of relative poverty is based on Peter Townsend, "Sociological Approach to the Measurement of Poverty," *Oxford Economic Papers* 37 (1985): 659–668.

4. World Commission on Environment and Development, *Our Common Future* (Oxford, England: Oxford University Press, 1987), p. 43.

5. This estimate was calculated using official government reports for the low range and unofficial calculations by human rights groups for the upper range. Note that these totals do not include tens of thousands of deaths among combatants in ongoing civil wars of the period.

6. This discussion of goals and policy alternatives is inspired by the treatment found in Brian Walsh, "Resolving the Human Rights Violations of a Previous Regime," *World Affairs* 158, no. 3 (1996): 111–120. However, the analysis provided here (and in Table 4.5) of the implications of the policy options differs somewhat from Walsh's. One of the policy options he examined—trial in international courts—has been omitted here because it was not very viable during the period under examination (1980–2002). At the turn of the century, some have requested that individual foreign countries assert jurisdiction over particular cases in Argentina,

Chile, and Guatemala. With the launching of the International Criminal Court in 2002, international prosecution may become an option more actively discussed in the years to come.

7. Donna Lee van Cott, "Latin America: Constitutional Reform and Ethnic Rights," *Parliamentary Affairs* 53 (2000): 41–54.

8. Mark Ungar, *Elusive Reform: Democracy and the Rule of Law in Latin America* (Boulder, Colo.: Lynne Rienner, 2002), p. 35.

9. Francis Fukuyama, *The End of History and the Last Man* (New York: Avon Books, 1992).

10. Guillermo O'Donnell, "Delegative Democracy," *Journal of Democracy* 5 (1994): 55–69.

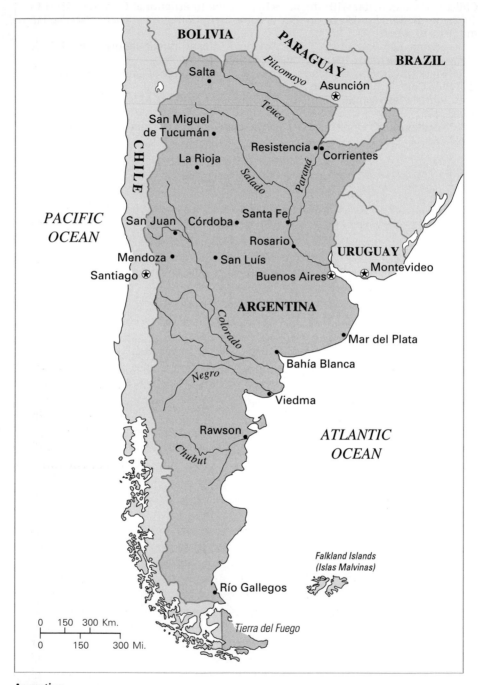

Argentina

CHAPTER 5

Argentina

O N WEDNESDAY, December 19, 2001, President Fernando de la Rúa awoke to learn that a few hundred people looted several supermarkets at dawn in greater Buenos Aires. In his first two years as president, he had already received more than his share of bad news. When he took office in December 1999, the economy had been in a recession for one year. Two years later, the recession continued—the longest economic contraction in Argentine history. People were losing faith in the financial system. On November 30, 2001, nearly $2 billion was withdrawn from Argentine banks; the next day, the government froze certificates of deposit and placed a $1,000 per month limit on bank withdrawals. Many citizens protested the moves. On December 6, the International Monetary Fund (IMF) announced that it would not furnish $1.3 billion in credit planned for year's end because the government had not balanced its budget. Although the government had cut public employees' wages by 13 percent in August, public revenues also fell as the recession deepened. The IMF's action worsened the existing crisis of confidence. The government then debated how to reduce the deficit; on December 17, it proposed spending cuts of roughly 20 percent. Now, on December 19, De la Rúa began his day with reports of looting.

Despite this backdrop of bad news, neither Fernando de la Rúa nor other Argentines could imagine the events that would follow the predawn lootings that Wednesday morning. Lootings spread throughout Buenos Aires and elsewhere as the day progressed. On Wednesday evening, De la Rúa announced a state of siege and sent security forces into the streets. This move did not calm nervous middle-class citizens who had been following the day's turmoil. Instead, thousands took to the streets to demand the resignation of the economic minister (who resigned by night's end), to criticize the government's use of force, and to express discontent over worsening economic problems. The next day, looting, protests, and clashes with security authorities continued. By Thursday evening, an expanding wave of looting, protests, and violence left over thirty people dead and hundreds injured nationwide. That same evening, President De la Rúa announced his resignation. His eventual replacement—Adolfo Rodríguez Saá—stated in his inaugural address that the government would default on its existing debt obligations; the default was the largest in world history. By the end of December, he, too, had resigned.

The new year brought a new president, Eduardo Duhalde, but most economic changes were for the worse. In 2002, the gross domestic product (GDP) shrank by 11 percent. Unemployment increased from 17 percent to 20 percent, while consumer prices rose by 41 percent. The value of the Argentine peso fell by 70 percent against the U.S. dollar over the course of the year. The number of Argentines living below the indigence line tripled: over one-fifth of the population lived on less than $1.00 per day in 2002.

Argentine political life swirls with debate over disappointments regarding development, liberty, and governance. People ask how much of the 2001–2002 crisis should be attributed to Argentina's political leaders. How much of it is the responsibility of Argentine citizens outside the government? How have international influences shaped Argentina's recent decline? This debate goes on not just within Argentina but also around the world because Argentina had been presented during the 1990s as a leading success story of the benefits of market-oriented economic reform. Today, politicians, interest group leaders, and scholars attempt to draw lessons from the Argentine experience to inform their own respective searches for a viable path toward development, liberty, and governance.

Argentina's crisis of 2001–2002 would have been a grave blow for any country. It was even harder for Argentina because it had long been one of the most prosperous countries in Latin America. In this chapter, we will study the dynamics of this country of over 37 million people on the Southern Cone of the Americas.

HISTORICAL BACKGROUND FROM 1880 TO 1983

From its independence until 1852, Argentine politics was characterized by rivalries among *caudillos* who disagreed over many issues—especially regarding the role of the port city of Buenos Aires in the political system. These disagreements frequently led to violence. From 1835 until his military defeat in 1852, Juan Manuel de Rosas of Buenos Aires led a repressive dictatorship that eventually united diverse forces in a successful military effort to drive him from power. The defeat of Rosas set into motion three decades of turbulent change. Argentina adopted a federal system and subdued various potential challenges to national authority—culminating in the so-called Indian Wars of 1874–1880. The military leader of the "conquest of the desert," Julio Argentino Roca, would become the central figure of Argentine political life in the oligarchic democracy to follow.

Oligarchic Democracy in the Age of Laissez-Faire (1880–1916)

Roca was elected president in 1880 and then later won a second nonconsecutive six-year term in 1898. He and other presidents of this period argued that laissez-faire economic policies would permit central Argentina to take advantage of its fertile land and temperate climate for grain cultivation and cattle grazing. Due to rising demand for these commodities at the time, the economy grew nearly 6 percent a year. Argentina briefly became one of the world's wealthiest countries: at the start of World War I, Argentina's GDP per person was roughly equal to that of France. In some respects, Roca's 1880 campaign slogan of "peace and administration" had been realized.

Because Argentina had been scarcely populated in the interior beyond Buenos Aires since colonial times, national policies encouraged immigration, particularly from Europe. The government paid passage for European immigrants, and the strategy bore fruit. By the 1895 census, 52 percent of the population of Buenos Aires was foreign-born. In the 1914 census, first-generation immigrants comprised 30 percent of the national population (around 12 percent of the U.S. population was foreign-born at the time). Nearly half of the immigrants came from Italy, while another 30 percent came from Spain. Argentina formed an exception to the multiracial demographics of Latin America: in the early twenty-first century, the majority of the population is presumed to be of European descent.

This sustained economic boom and mammoth immigration wave transformed Argentine society and eventually its political life. Although the largest chunk of the commodity boom fell into the hands of the landed elite, the new money led to an expansion in white-collar professions and in retail commerce. Many middle-class Argentines demanded entry into a political system that permitted less than 10 percent of males to vote. The largest of these movements, the Radical Civic Union (*Unión Cívica Radical* [UCR]), led two failed revolts and organized many protests demanding political reform. Urban blue-collar workers formed labor unions influenced by a kaleidoscope of European political ideologies spanning the spectrum from anarchism to syndicalism, to socialism.

These varied calls for change were initially repressed, but in 1912, President Roque Saenz Peña convinced a majority of legislators to grant the right to vote to all Argentine male citizens who were willing to serve one year in the military. He argued that failure to change would generate even greater turmoil, as events were demonstrating with the outbreak of violent revolution in Mexico in 1911. The measure created universal male suffrage, but it initially excluded a majority of urban blue-collar workers who, as first-generation immigrants, had not yet been granted citizenship. Despite this limitation, the reform dramatically increased the voting population. The Saenz Peña Law, as it would come to be known, ushered in a new era in Argentine politics.

From Expanded Suffrage to the Infamous Decade (1916–1943)

The immediate beneficiary of this expansion of suffrage was the most organized of the middle-class movements: the UCR led by Hipólito Yrigoyen. In the 1916 presidential campaign, Yrigoyen reached out to the middle sectors and also promised labor law reforms. Once in office, however, Yrigoyen's policies concentrated primarily on rewarding his middle-class supporters. A reduced concern for labor issues became dramatically apparent in the repression of strikes. In the "tragic week" (*semana trágica*) of January 1919, government forces and paramilitary bands killed roughly 1,000 people. In 1921, the army again employed massive force in crushing strikes in southern Argentina, resulting in over 2,000 deaths.

The UCR enjoyed considerable support from middle-class Argentines, who formed the bulk of the electorate. The Radical candidate in the 1922 presidential elections, Marcelo T. de Alvear, won handily. Having sat out a term as mandated by the constitution's prohibition of direct reelection, Yrigoyen then triumphed in the 1928 campaign.

Yrigoyen's second term did not begin with the optimism generated by his 1916 victory. He was now seventy-six years old, and some accused him of senility. These charges provided ammunition to a growing list of opponents. Within the UCR, many chafed at a second term for the man who had led the Radicals for nearly three decades without interruption. Outside the party, many conservatives disliked the seeming electoral lock of the UCR in legislative and presidential elections. Military officers complained of political favoritism accorded to Radical supporters in military promotions and assignments. Labor leaders and many in the Socialist party painted Yrigoyen as an enemy of working people who had sanctioned the crackdowns of 1919 and 1921. When the economy weakened after the 1929 U.S. stock market crash, a diverse coalition of landowners, socialists, and military officers supported the 1930 coup that removed Yrigoyen from power.

While these diverse forces united to stop the UCR, it was not easy for them to agree on how to govern. Military leaders and civilian conservatives supportive of the coup were initially divided into two main camps. One group, led by General José Uriburu, proposed to establish a fascist-style dictatorship. By 1932, however, an alternative plan (associated with General Agustín Justo) returned the conservative, landed elite to power via fraudulent elections. The frequent recourse to electoral fraud earned this period the nickname of the infamous decade.

Fraud and economic problems stimulated opposition to the continuing influence of wealthy landowners. A new generation of military officers discussed making industrialization the centerpiece of national policies. These officers had little patience for the major political parties of the day: the conservative parties, the Radicals, and the Socialists. After launching a coup on June 6, 1943, many of these officers believed that they would change Argentina. Few would have predicted, however, that Juan Domingo Perón would become the central figure of Argentine politics for the next three decades.

The Rise and Fall of Juan Perón (1943–1955)

One of the coup plotters was a forty-seven-year-old colonel who had served as military attaché to the Argentine embassy in Italy, Juan Perón. He asked for and received the little-respected job of secretary of labor. Perón used this position to transform Argentine labor relations and, in turn, to build popular support for himself. He encouraged anticommunist unions to conduct membership drives and to push for wage increases. When businesses failed to provide wage hikes, Perón often intervened on behalf of workers. In exchange, he demanded political loyalty from the unions he assisted.

Perón's strategy worked. Over the course of 1944, Perón's political star rose rapidly as he added the posts of war minister and vice president to his list of achievements. This rapid ascent bred him opponents in and out of the military. In early October 1945, these opponents convinced President Edelmiro Farrell to arrest Perón and to remove him from all his government posts. The arrest provoked a public reaction of unprecedented scope: around 200,000 Argentines mobilized on October 17, 1945, in front of the presidential mansion to demand his release. A startled government released Perón and permitted him to thank his supporters from the presidential balcony to disperse the crowd. Shortly after his release, Perón married his mistress, radio actress Eva (Evita) Duarte. Evita would become his principal partner in relations with the Argentine labor movement and with the Argentine people more generally.

Perón's opponents now pinned their hopes of defeating him on a return to free elections in February 1946. A coalition of all major political parties formed to oppose Perón. Perón used his labor-union connections to get out the working-class vote; the labor vote was now considerable because many workers were second-generation immigrants and naturalized citizens. Perón also used U.S. ambassador Spruille Braden's support of major rival José Tamborini to paint his opponents as antinationalists. In the end, Perón won with 52 percent of the vote (versus Tamborini's 42 percent).

Once in power, Perón pushed quickly to implement fully the import-substituting industrialization (ISI) economic policy that had begun under prior junta governments in the mid-1940s. He used a surplus of foreign exchange (earned mainly via food exports during World War II) to bankroll ambitious industrialization programs. This money was also used to pay off the entire national debt in 1947 and to nationalize the British-owned railroad network in 1948. His first years in office were filled with economic triumphs. The economy grew at an average annual rate of 8.8 percent per year from 1946 to 1948. Real hourly wages rose dramatically as a result of both economic growth and a re-distribution of income. Labor's share of GDP rose by 25 percent between 1946 and 1950. Various social welfare programs—some funded by the government and others by the newly formed Eva Perón Foundation—built new schools and hospitals and subsidized homes. Evita Perón became the major spokesperson for the enfranchisement of women in 1947 and the head of the new women's branch of the Peronist party. For working Argentines, Perón's presidency repre-sented a new golden age to rival the landed oligarchy's recollections of the early twentieth century. This popularity (combined with restrictions on freedom of the press) fueled Perón's successful effort to eliminate the no-reelection clause of the 1853 constitution by holding a new constitutional convention in 1949.

But storm clouds were gathering on the horizon. Prices for Argentina's major exports began to fall on world markets, while prices for capital goods imports needed for industrialization rose. A growing number of landowners protested Perón's policies by reducing production. Many military officers blocked Evita's nomination as a vice-presidential running mate; they refused to accept a woman as their potential commander-in-chief. The government put down a military coup attempt in 1951.

Despite these burgeoning problems, Perón was reelected to the presidency with 67 percent of the vote in 1951. To the dismay of many working-class Argentines, a cancer-stricken Evita voted from a hospital bed and rode in the 1952 inauguration parade in a specially made brace. Her death from ovarian cancer at age thirty-three on July 26, 1952, marked the end of an era in the po-litical dynamics of Perón's presidency (see *Governing Strategies: Evita Perón*).

The economic climate soured in the early 1950s, which made it more diffi-cult for the government to pour money into its development programs, as it had done in the late 1940s. Instead, the government pursued an economic stabiliza-tion package designed to bring inflation under control by slowing the growth of real wages and reducing government spending trends. In 1954, amid this trou-bled economic backdrop, Perón also polarized the country by taking on a former ally—the Catholic church—by legalizing divorce and asserting govern-ment control over Catholic schools. These measures and subsequent anticleri-cal demonstrations by Peronist activists in 1955 provided a new impetus to anti-Peronist factions within the military. These groups launched a successful military coup in September 1955. Perón boarded a Paraguayan gunboat and claimed political asylum rather than ordering loyal factions of the military to resist the coup.

The "Impossible Game" of Constrained Democracy (1955–1966)

Evita Perón's death had led to a myth that would help maintain the popularity of Peronism for years to come. Her power coincided with the peak of prosperity during Perón's presidency. Many later asserted that Evita would have kept the

GOVERNING STATEGIES
Evita Perón

Evita Perón entered national politics through her association with Juan Perón. Her forceful approach to politics helped to change the Argentine political landscape. Prior to the 1943 military coup, Eva María Duarte was a well-known actress in radio soap operas. She met Juan Perón in early 1944 at a fundraising drive he had organized for earthquake victims in San Juan. Evita became the widower's new live-in mistress and continued her acting career. When Perón was arrested in October 1945, Evita stood by him, despite being fired from her radio contract after his arrest. The two were married four days following his release from prison.

After Perón won the 1946 elections, Evita became a glamorous first lady and opened an office in which she fielded requests for welfare assistance. When opposition politicians and some military officers attacked her activities, a December 1946 press release described her as the government's ambassador to "the shirtless poor" (*los descamisados*). In early 1947, she organized a Peronist women's group supporting legislation to grant women the vote. In mid-1947, she went on a two-month state tour of several European countries.

Evita's high profile polarized Argentina. To many workers, her life represented a dream come true: the poor girl made good. Among the wealthy, it became fashionable to insult her. Rich women refused to refer to Evita by name: in polite society they called her "that woman"; "the whore" and other derogatory profanities were used privately.

Evita made herself synonymous with the Peronist theme of social justice. She gave numerous public speeches promoting her husband as Argentina's savior. Many analysts assert that her long-winded tributes to her husband were part of a conscious effort to make her substantive role in government more palatable in a male-dominated society. Evita's charitable foundation served as an unofficial governmental welfare system. It built hundreds of schools and hospitals; constructed thousands of homes; and distributed food, clothes, and cash to thousands of families. Evita spent many hours each week fielding requests for help and asking (many might say ordering) businesses to make donations. She also spearheaded the newly formed Peronist women's party, which had more affiliates than its male counterpart. In addition, Evita became a key broker between the president and his unionized supporters.

With Evita's death in 1952, Juan Perón lost a valuable political partner. She had given most of the speeches attacking the landed oligarchy and promoting the Peronist theme of social justice. This freed Juan Perón to be more conciliatory in private meetings with agricultural and industrial entrepreneurs. During his second term, he gave more of the firebrand speeches once delivered by Evita, but this move weakened his credibility in private discussions with businesspeople. Evita Perón had served as the bad cop to Juan Perón's good cop. After her death, Juan Perón found it increasingly difficult to maintain the delicate balance achieved during his first term.

good times coming and prevented the 1955 coup. The military junta that unseated Juan Perón in 1955 hid Evita's embalmed corpse in Europe to limit her ability to rally Peronists as a symbol of his fallen government.

The military officers leading the coup were united in their opposition to Perón, but they were divided regarding their approach to governing. One hard-line faction wanted to purge all governmental and nongovernmental organizations of Peronist influence prior to returning to democratic rule. The other major faction pressed for a quicker return to elections (albeit elections in which Peronists could not participate). In a nutshell, representative democracy was acceptable provided that people did not openly espouse Peronist themes or vote for Peronist candidates. This was a substantial limitation on political liberty because anywhere from 40 to 60 percent of the voting population was very to somewhat supportive of the Peronist movement. Argentine scholar Guillermo O'Donnell (who served as a cabinet minister during the early 1960s) would later dub this period the "impossible game" of democracy: the military would not accept any democracy that permitted the Peronists to govern, while many citizens would not accept as democratic any system that denied them the option of voting Peronist.[1]

The UCR now had its first clear chance to govern in decades. The Radicals split into two factions that presented separate candidates in the 1957 presidential elections. Arturo Frondizi (*Unión Cívica Radical Intransigente* [UCRI]) defeated Ricardo Balbín (*Unión Cívica Radical del Pueblo* [UCRP]) by a margin of 45 to 29 percent. Frondizi had made a secret deal to legalize the Peronist party if he were elected. From exile, Perón quietly urged his supporters to vote for Frondizi. Frondizi later made good on his promise in the 1962 provincial elections. When Peronist candidates won most governorships, anti-Peronists in the military removed Frondizi from office to annul the election results. The restrictions on liberty embedded in the impossible game were still in place.

When new presidential elections were held in 1963, an extremely divided citizenry elected the UCRP candidate, Arturo Illia, with a scant 25 percent of the vote (versus 16 percent for the UCRI candidate). A striking 20 percent of the electorate cast blank or soiled ballots to protest the legitimacy of an electoral process that continued to exclude Peronists eight years after the coup. Peronist-controlled labor unions then launched a campaign of strikes and factory takeovers during 1964. In response (and in line with a personal belief in civil liberties), Illia pushed through a legalization of the Peronist party prior to midterm legislative elections in 1965. The Peronist victory in those elections angered anti-Peronists while failing to satisfy those who felt that Perón should never have been pushed out of the presidency. Amid an increasingly polarized climate, the military removed Illia from office in June 1966.

From Military Rule to the Return of Perón (1966–1976)

This time, the military officers most skeptical about representative democracy unilaterally proclaimed an "Argentine Revolution" that proposed to impose order until they deemed the country ready to return to democracy. General Juan Onganía led the second bureaucratic-authoritarian military regime in the region, two years following the establishment of indefinite military rule in neighboring Brazil. Restrictions on freedom of speech, the press, organization, and assembly went beyond the repression of civil liberties under prior military and civilian regimes. As in Brazil, the military justified its harsh stance as a way to prevent the emergence of communist-inspired youth movements.

From exile, Juan Perón changed tactics. Rather than leaning on organized labor alone, Perón—who had marginalized communist labor unions during his rise to power—issued vaguely leftist public statements designed to inspire a new generation too young to remember his presidency. He wanted them to rebel against the military government. Several new organizations formed in support of Peronism as a path toward socialism, including the Shirtless Command, the Peronist Armed Forces, and the Montoneros. From this point onward, Peronism would find itself increasingly divided as conflict increased between its new socialist factions and its traditionally anticommunist sectors.

While 1968 was a major year of college student protests in France, Mexico, and the United States, 1969 proved to be a watershed year for politically active students in Argentina. Student demonstrations in one province ended in violence that sparked a nationwide series of university strikes. These strikes culminated in hundreds of injuries and mass property destruction in Córdoba, Argentina's second-largest city. The May 1969 *cordobazo* would later be seen as the first major episode in an expanding wave of violence. The next month, the country's most important labor leader, Augusto Vandor, was assassinated (perhaps by the Shirtless Command) for not being sufficiently revolutionary. In mid-1970, the Montoneros made headlines by kidnapping and assassinating General Pedro Aramburu, the retired leader of the 1955 coup that had unseated Perón. In the wake of these events, Onganía resigned and General Roberto Levingston announced that elections would be held in four to five years.

Levingston's announcement did not stem the tide of violence. The Montoneros carried out dramatic bank robberies to bring attention to their cause. In August 1970, the Shirtless Command murdered another Peronist labor leader, José Alonso. In March 1971, violent demonstrations and riots broke out again in Córdoba, and the military again occupied the city under a state of siege. In the aftermath, Alejandro Lanusse replaced Levingston and immediately began negotiating a return to electoral politics that would include Peronism.

Lanusse's formula for ending the impossible game legalized the Peronist party while preventing Perón from running in the March 1973 presidential elections. When Peronist Héctor Cámpora won with nearly 50 percent of the vote, he paved the way for Perón's return from exile in Spain. Perón returned home with his third wife, Isabel (a singer who, at age twenty-four, met Juan Perón in Panama in December 1955). Well over 1 million Argentines assembled on June 20, 1973, at Ezeiza International Airport to greet Perón, but the tensions provoked by Perón's recent leftist rhetoric erupted. Shooting broke out between conservative and leftist Peronists, forcing Perón's plane to land at a nearby military base. Cámpora resigned in favor of new September elections that Perón won with 61 percent of the vote. Isabel served as his running mate in a nod to the earlier attempt to launch Evita as a candidate (and to avoid making one of Perón's principal advisers his designated successor).

Perón changed his rhetoric again: now he emphasized national reconciliation and an end to revolutionary violence. The tumult of the prior four years would have been difficult for any leader (much less an elderly man who suffered a heart attack shortly after returning to Argentina) to rein in. At the annual Labor Day rally on May 1, 1974, the tensions within the Peronist movement were again on public display. Montoneros shouted slogans attacking various Peronist figures during Perón's speech. When Perón criticized them, they abandoned the rally, leaving the square in front of the presidential mansion half empty. Perón developed pneumonia later that month and died on July 1, 1974.

Isabel Perón assumed the presidency. Although she was involved in the Peronist movement during Juan Perón's second decade in exile, she had no governmental experience and had spent almost her entire adult life outside her native Argentina. After the death of the man both leftist and rightist Peronists saw as the country's savior, these factions' ideological differences fueled a bloodbath. José López Rega, Isabel Perón's closest adviser and a staunch anticommunist, tried to purge the labor and student movements of leftist leaders. The already struggling economy collapsed into a free fall when inflation reached 350 percent by early 1976. In March 1976, the military launched a coup in the name of restoring order and combating socialist ideas via a "Military Process" (*Proceso Militar*) of national reorganization.

The Military Process and the Dirty War on Subversion (1976–1983)

The new bureaucratic-authoritarian regime initially had numerous supporters, especially in the middle and upper classes. Over time, however, the repression of terrorists enveloped suspected leftists in a rash of violence unlike anything in the nation's history. In this so-called dirty war, detention without trial, torture, and **disappearance** (summary execution without formal burial) became the sad fate of many young Argentines. These brutal tactics snuffed out terrorism but at an enormous human cost. New human rights organizations like the Mothers of the May Plaza worked to document and to publicize the tragedies. Estimates of the total number of disappeared persons vary from 9,000 to 40,000, while tens of thousands more were victims of torture, rape, and detention without charge. The precise number of the disappeared will never be known because many were drugged, placed on military aircraft, and dropped into the Atlantic Ocean, as several officers confirmed in 1995.

While the military achieved its goal of eradicating guerrilla movements, it proved unable to restore stable economic growth. By the early 1980s, many banks were collapsing and inflation reached new heights. A beleaguered military government briefly rallied patriotic sentiments by invading the Falkland Islands (*Islas Malvinas*) in April 1982. Argentina had long disputed the United Kingdom's claim to the islands and swift military action defeated token British opposition. The military's gamble that the United Kingdom would not respond culminated in tragedy when a British task force assembled to retake the islands against an ill-equipped, inexperienced occupying force (veteran Argentine troops were stationed on the Chilean border to guard against a possible Chilean incursion in another long-standing border dispute). The military government placed so many restrictions on freedom of the press that many Argentines thought they were winning the war until Argentina unconditionally surrendered on June 14. An expanding wave of protests then demanded an end to military rule, and a new military government under Reynaldo Bignone negotiated a transition to democracy. The 1983 elections marked the first step in the establishment of Argentina's contemporary representative democracy.

CONTEMPORARY POLITICAL FRAMEWORK

Argentina's political framework has its roots in the 1853 constitution written after the end of the Rosas dictatorship. Over the following decades, many elements of that constitution remained intact, but others underwent periodic revisions. In 1994, Argentina held a constitutional convention to change several key provisions. The 1994 constitution emerged out of bargaining between the Peronist and Radical parties. The sitting president, Peronist Carlos Menem, and the prior president, Radical leader Raúl Alfonsín, brokered the Pact of Olivos (named for the presidential residence). The deal called for several changes in the executive branch desired by Menem along with modifications to the senate and to the judiciary sought by Alfonsín.

The Executive Branch

Like all other Latin American countries, Argentina has a presidential system of government. In 1994, Menem sought and achieved the removal of the prohibition on immediate reelection; presidents can now serve a maximum of two consecutive terms. In turn, the president's term was shortened from six to four years. The 1994 constitution also changed the rules for presidential elections. Previously, presidents were elected on a plurality basis: whoever got the most votes won the election (even if one received as little as one-fourth of the vote, as we saw in the 1963 election of Arturo Illia). Now, to avoid a runoff between the two candidates who receive the most votes, someone must obtain either 45 percent of the first-round vote or 40 percent of the vote with at least a 10-percentage point lead over the next closest challenger.

The Argentine presidency can be termed potentially dominant within the analytical framework developed by Mainwaring and Shugart (review Table 4.6). Like many Latin American presidents, Argentine chief executives can name and remove most ministers at will. The 1994 reforms introduced one limitation on this power: the cabinet chief can be removed by the legislature. The president has a strong veto that can be overridden by a two-thirds majority in both houses of the Argentine congress. The 1994 constitution also expanded the president's legislative decree powers. These decrees can be reversed by the legislature, but to make the reversal stick, the Argentine congress must muster the two-thirds majority needed to override a (likely) presidential veto. This restriction gives activist presidents a potential means to force Congress to act in accord with a timetable managed by the president.

The Legislature

Like most Latin American countries, Argentina has a bicameral legislature. The lower house, the Chamber of Deputies, has a membership that represents provinces in accord with their population size (like the U.S. House of Representatives). Deputies serve four-year terms, with half of the chamber up for election every two years. They are elected in **closed-list proportional representation** (PR) elections. *Concepts in Action: Plurality Versus Proportional Representation* discusses the differences between the PR electoral system and the **plurality electoral system**, which is found in the United States. In the 1994 constitution, the lower house gained the ability to call a referendum. If the voters approve the referendum, the president cannot veto it.

The upper house in Argentina's legislature, the Senate, consists of three members from each province. Senators serve six-year terms, with one-third of the chamber standing for election every two years. Prior to 1994, senators were elected indirectly by the provincial legislatures. The 1994 reform introduced a **majority-minority electoral system** in which all parties present three candidates. Two senators are chosen from the slate with the most votes, while the runner-up slate receives the third senate seat. The UCR pursued this reform in 1994 to check presidential authority. The new majority-minority electoral system made it almost impossible for any party to control two-thirds of the Senate because a party could do so only if it finished first in Senate elections in every single province. This change is significant because a two-thirds majority is needed to confirm presidential nominations for the Supreme Court and to override a presidential veto.

In the wake of visible hostility toward politicians unleashed by the December 2001 crisis, several citizens' groups demanded modifications in the legislature. The 1994 expansion of the Senate from two to three members per province has been a frequent target of critics who call for a return to two senators in an effort to cut government expenditures. Many also call for an end to the closed-list PR electoral system used in the lower house. Advocates of a move toward plurality

CONCEPTS IN ACTION
Plurality Versus Proportional Representation

Electoral systems are rules for determining the winning candidates in elections. In the United States, legislative elections use the same electoral system in place in the United Kingdom: the single-member-district plurality (SMDP) system. In plurality elections, the candidate with the most votes wins even if no candidate receives a majority. Around the world, plurality elections pull voters toward the major candidates because other candidates (and their parties nationwide) have minimal chances to gain a voice in the legislature. Plurality systems tend to keep extremist parties from gaining legislative seats, but they can also produce situations in which voters become frustrated with the major parties and find it difficult to elect any other parties' candidates to the legislature.

As an alternative to the plurality rule, most countries in Europe and in Latin America use a system of proportional representation (PR). While PR uses many specific mathematical formulas, all try to match each party's share of the vote with its share of legislative seats. To have the number of seats match the number of each party's votes, PR systems use multi-member districts in which each voter selects one party's slate of candidates for office. For example, if one party received 51 percent of the votes in a ten-seat district, it would probably win five of the ten seats. Another party with 19 percent of the votes would likely earn two seats, and so on.

You may wonder: if people vote for parties and not for individuals, who determines which candidates go to the legislature? In closed-list PR, each party controls the order of the names on the list. If a ten-candidate slate wins five seats, then the top five names on the party's list go to the legislature. If a party won only one seat, then the top name on the list would win election. Most parties place their experienced leaders at the top of the list, while inexperienced or less well-connected candidates appear at the bottom of the list. Closed-list PR is used in lower house elections in Argentina and in most of Latin America and Europe.

In the open-list PR system used in Brazil, voters choose a party's list and then vote for their favorite candidate(s) on that party's slate. As in closed-list PR, party votes are counted to determine how many seats go to each party. In determining the winning candidates, however, preference votes are then totaled for each party's list. If a party wins five seats in a ten-seat district in this system, the seats go to the five candidates on the slate who received the most preference votes.

In open-list systems, candidates tend to compete not just with other parties but also with candidates from their own parties. In contrast, in closed-list PR, legislators have a greater need to stay loyal to the party leadership to improve their chances of moving up on the list in future elections. Meanwhile, in a plurality system, candidates tend to run campaigns more finely tuned to district-level issues because they expect to face the same voters alone in the next elections. Like their colleagues in open-list PR systems, legislators elected via plurality rules tend to display less party discipline than those chosen via closed-list PR.

elections argue that individual candidacies would make deputies more accountable to their constituents, as do advocates of a shift toward an **open-list proportional representation system** (review *Concepts in Action: Plurality Versus Proportional Representation* on page 135). Over the years 2002–2003, the executive branch and the legislature had discussed both ideas (particularly in 2002) but did not make either change. In May 2004, President Nestor Kirchner proposed a reform that would elect half of the lower house via closed-list proportional representation while electing the other half of the deputies via single-member-district plurality elections.

The Judiciary

The Argentine supreme court has more power than many other Latin American high courts. Justices are appointed for life, and the Supreme Court is the highest court of appeal for all cases. The Supreme Court also exercises **judicial review**: it can rule that legislation is invalid on the grounds that it is unconstitutional. While this set of powers is familiar to a U.S. audience, many countries in and out of Latin America have term limits for justices, different high courts for specific types of cases, and a judicial review power limited to a separate constitutional court (or no judicial review at all).

The Supreme Court found itself in the center of several political battles in the contemporary era. Carlos Menem worried in the early 1990s that the five justices then on the bench might block several of his reforms. Menem convinced one justice to resign while adding four other seats to the court. At the time presidential nominations for justices required only a simple majority in the Senate, so Menem used Peronist control of the Senate to name five new justices he felt would be loyal to his agenda. His confidence was rewarded in several controversial decisions upholding his initiatives.

The 1994 constitution limited the president's judicial appointment powers. It toughened Senate confirmation procedures by requiring a two-thirds majority for Supreme Court nominees and it also limited presidential authority over lower courts. In the previous system, the president controlled the Justice Ministry, which named and supervised all lower court judges. The new system created a Council of Magistrates in charge of the lower courts; membership on this body consists of judges appointed from several sources in addition to the presidency.

The 2001–2002 crisis inflamed controversy between the judiciary and the other two branches of government. In early 2002, many legislators proposed impeachment procedures against several Menem appointees on the Supreme Court. Some justices allegedly responded by threatening to rule that existing restrictions on bank withdrawals were unconstitutional if impeachment proceedings were not dropped. As impeachment discussions continued, the court struck down the banking decree, sparking an impeachment trial of all justices. As that process dragged on, several justices again reportedly threatened to rule against the government if impeachment proceedings were not suspended.

When impeachment continued, the court ruled in August 2002 that the 2001 wage cut for public employees was illegal. After much debate, enough Peronist legislators voted against impeachment in October 2002 to prevent the two-thirds majority needed for removal of the justices.

All of this high-tension judicial politics led officials in the International Monetary Fund and in the U.S. government to cite a lack of judicial security as a major obstacle to Argentina's much-sought-after economic recovery. When Nestor Kirchner assumed the presidency in May 2003, he called on the Argentine congress to initiate a new impeachment of the Menem appointee most closely associated with the former president, Chief Justice Julio Nazareno. Nazareno denied all charges, but he resigned in June once it became clear that he would lose an impeachment vote. By resigning, he remained entitled to his government pension; had he been impeached, Nazareno would have lost his pension. Once Nazareno resigned, impeachment charges were filed against the other justice most closely associated with Carlos Menem, Eduardo Moliné O'Connor. He was impeached in December 2003; another justice resigned weeks earlier rather than face impeachment. Two additional justices faced impeachment investigations as of February 2004.

POLITICAL PARTICIPATION

For much of the twentieth century, Argentine political participation maintained various constants. Major business interests were divided mainly between the principal agribusiness organization and the principal industrial organization. Labor unions from 1945 onward were stronger than those found in most of Latin America and were largely Peronist in their political loyalties. Voters supported the two major parties, the Radicals and the Peronists, in election after election.

Today change can be felt on the political landscape. Business interests are more divided. Labor unions are weaker and less consistently Peronist. Several new social movements have become political forces. Perhaps most notably, the electoral dominance of the Radicals and Peronists is no longer a foregone conclusion.

Interest Groups and Social Movements

Large landowners founded the Argentine Rural Society (*Sociedad Rural Argentina* [SRA]) in 1866. During the oligarchic democracy of 1880–1916, SRA members held roughly half of all cabinet posts, and several presidents were also SRA members. The SRA played a controversial role in the decades that followed, when many of its leaders and members supported military coups in 1930, 1955, and 1966. In the contemporary era, the SRA publicly rejected the military revolts of the late 1980s. The SRA remains the major voice for export-oriented agriculture to this day.

Manufacturing interests have historically been more divided. The Argentine Industrial Union (*Unión Industrial Argentina* [UIA]) was founded in 1887. When Perón rose to power, the UIA's market orientation clashed with Peronist ISI policies. Perón initially tried to convince the UIA to support his program; when it refused, he organized the pro-Peronist General Economic Confederation (*Confederación General Económica* [CGE]). From the 1950s through the 1970s, the UIA stood for market capitalism and anti-Peronism, while the CGE was aligned with state capitalism and Peronism. From the 1980s onward, the UIA has been considerably more important both in terms of membership and influence. Once the tariff reductions the UIA had long championed were enacted in the 1990s, it has taken a more complex stance in which it supports government intervention under several circumstances.

Juan Perón marginalized leftist orientations within the labor movement and made the General Labor Confederation (*Confederación General del Trabajo* [CGT]) the major labor organization in the country. Peronist policies gave Argentine unions the economic resources that unions in most Latin American countries lacked. The loss of manufacturing jobs in the contemporary era has reduced the economic power and political influence of the CGT considerably. Over the years, the CGT frequently divided formally into two or three separate factions—a situation that continued into the early twenty-first century. Outside the CGT, the Congress of Argentine Workers (*Congreso de Trabajadores Argentinos* [CTA]) has ties to several leftist political parties along with more leftist Peronists. From the 1990s onward, the CTA has frequently mobilized its affiliates in the transportation and public administration unions to protest the shift toward market-oriented economic policies.

While business-labor conflicts provided much of the drama in twentieth-century Argentina, several new social movements emerged on the scene during the contemporary era. The Mothers of the May Plaza organized in the late 1970s and early 1980s to draw attention to human rights violations during the *Proceso*. With the return to democracy, the Mothers pressured for human rights trials, as we shall see in more detail shortly. The 1980s also saw the emergence of neighborhood organizations in urban areas that mixed self-help activities with public calls for more government resources to pave streets, improve sewage, and reduce crime. The December 2001 events saw a resurgence of many neighborhood organizations in downtown Buenos Aires. These groups now discussed a broader agenda that included possible political reforms.

The early twenty-first century also saw an expansion of a third movement dedicated to blocking roads and bridges; these roadblocks (called *piquetes* in Argentine slang) are used to publicize problems of poverty and unemployment. The *piquetero* movement formed over the course of the 1990s when poor citizens blocked highways in different provinces to demand resources from the government. By the end of the decade, several national associations of *piqueteros* had been formed. In mid-2001, they organized roadblocks across the country on multiple occasions. The *piqueteros* constitute one of the most controversial elements on the Argentine political scene. On the one hand, they voice concerns about economic misery that resonate in many parts of society. On the other hand, their protests disrupt people's freedom of movement and at times have ended in violence. Furthermore, the *piqueteros* have started negotiating with the government for welfare benefits that are distributed by the groups to their own members. In short, the *piqueteros* are the vanguard of a new politics for some; for others, they are organizations that block traffic illegally to extort benefits for their members.

Parties and Elections

Two political parties dominated elections during the twentieth century: the Radicals and the Peronists. As we saw in the section about Argentina's historical background, the UCR was established in 1893 as a middle-class movement dedicated to the expansion of suffrage. In the middle of the twentieth century, Radical leaders continued the party's call for civil and political rights while also advocating the state capitalist economic policies then in place across Latin America. Since the return to democracy in 1983, the various factions of the UCR continued to call for some measure of government intervention in the economy. The tumultuous endings to the presidencies of both Raúl Alfonsín and Fernando de la Rúa opened the door to the emergence of new leaders. As of this writing, it is not clear who will replace the two most visible Radical politicians of the 1980s and 1990s. In a divisive party primary in 2003 marred by mutual accusations of fraud, Leopoldo Moreau narrowly defeated Rodolfo Terragno. Moreau received just over 2 percent of the vote in the 2003 presidential election—by far the lowest total of any UCR candidate in party history. The UCR began the twenty-first century as a political party in disarray.

The other major party, the Peronists, was established during Perón's first presidency and was eventually renamed the Justicialist Party (*Partido Justicialista* [PJ]). Despite the name change, PJ members have continued to refer to themselves as Peronists to the present day. The major constituency of the PJ, from its founding through the 1980s, was the organized labor movement. After Perón's death in 1974, Peronist leaders maintained the party's emphasis on economic nationalism and prolabor policies. Carlos Menem changed all of that in his two-term presidency from 1989 to 1999 when he pursued a series of market-oriented reforms. Faced with criticism from some Peronists, Menem attempted to justify this shift by saying that he, like Perón, was a pragmatist not tied to any specific ideology. The two major Peronist leaders of the contemporary era—Carlos Menem and Eduardo Duhalde—frequently engaged in public and private battles for control over the PJ and over the Argentine government. In the months preceding the 2003 presidential elections, their rivalry led to a three-way split of the PJ, and it fielded three separate candidates: past presidents Menem and Adolfo Rodríguez Saá, along with governor Nestor Kirchner, the candidate backed by Duhalde. While Kirchner and Menem were the leading vote-getters in the April 2003 elections, the PJ and many of its leaders suffered a loss of support in public opinion polls in the early twenty-first century.

Over the decades, various leftist and center-left parties tried in vain to dislodge the Radicals and the Peronists. Their opportunity finally came in the 1990s, when a segment of voters opposed the market capitalist policies pursued by the Menem government. Several small parties joined Peronist dissidents to form the center-leftist Front for a Country in Solidarity (*Frente del País Solidario* [FREPASO]) in 1995. In 1997, the FREPASO formed an electoral coalition with the Radicals that won that year's legislative elections and then catapulted Fernando de la Rúa to the presidency in 1999. The disastrous end to the De la Rúa presidency cost the FREPASO dearly. In the 2001 elections, the rising party on the center-left was the Alternative for an Egalitarian Republic (*Alternativa por una República Igualitaria* [ARI]). Elisa Carrió, a dissident Radical legislator from rural Argentina, formed ARI in late 2000. In early 2003, Carrió's stern criticism of the major parties propelled her close to the top of many public opinion polls. While she eventually finished with 14 percent of the vote in the May 2003 presidential election, she presented this performance on a shoestring campaign as the first step toward establishing an enduring movement. After the 2003 legislative elections, ARI held 5 percent of the seats in the Chamber of Deputies, making it the third largest bloc in the legislature.

Center-right and rightist parties also struggled to defeat the Radicals and the Peronists at the ballot box. In the contemporary era, the three most prominent voices on the right were all market-oriented former economic ministers. In the 1980s and early 1990s, Alvaro Alsogaray led the Union of the Democratic Center (*Unión del Centro Democrático* [UCD]) to a position as the third largest party. The party's share of the vote then collapsed once most of its leaders—including Alsogaray and his daughter María Julia—took positions in the Menem government. In 1999, Menem's economic minister, Domingo Cavallo, launched a new market-oriented party: Action for the Republic (*Acción por la República* [AR]). AR finished third in the presidential and legislative elections in 1999 and 2001, but it did not exceed 10 percent in either year. By 2003, the new figure on the center-right was former UCR activist Ricardo López Murphy, who had resigned as economic minister in 2001 when his market-oriented program lacked support in the legislature. López Murphy finished third in the 2003 presidential election and received almost 17 percent of the vote. However, his new party, the Federal Movement for National Reconstruction (*Movimiento Federal Recrear* [MFR]), went on to win just one seat in the Chamber of Deputies in the legislative elections held later that year.

The results of all presidential elections during this period are shown in Table 5.1. Raúl Alfonsín's victory in the 1983 campaign represents the electoral high watermark for the Radicals in the contemporary era. Alfonsín became the

TABLE 5.1 Argentine Presidential Elections (1983, 1989, 1995, 1999, and 2003): Percentage of the Popular Vote

Party	Year				
	1983	1989	1995	1999	2003
PJ	40.2	47.4	49.9	38.1	60.0[†]
UCR	51.7	32.4	17.0	–	2.5
The Alliance	–	–	–	48.5*	–
FREPASO	–	–	29.2	–	–
MFR	–	–	–	–	16.7
ARI	–	–	–	–	14.4
Others	8.1	13.3	3.9	3.3	4.4

*In 1999, the UCR and the FREPASO formed the Alliance and supported a single candidate for the presidency, Fernando de la Rúa.

[†]In 2003, the PJ ran three separate candidates; the PJ listing is the sum of the votes received by all three.

SOURCE: Political Database of the Americas <http://www.georgetown.edu/pdba/Elecdata/Arg/arg.html> (accessed on November 14, 2003).

first Radical politician to defeat a Peronist candidate in open presidential elections. He emphasized traditional UCR themes of civil liberties and democracy; he also referred to some visible Peronist labor leaders' associations with the military government. This tactic cast suspicion on the willingness of his Peronist opponent, Italo Luder, to tackle alleged human rights violations because Luder had ties to many of the labor leaders accused of collaborating with the military regime. In the 1989 elections, Peronist Carlos Menem handily defeated Radical candidate Eduardo Angeloz amid a hyperinflationary spiral in May 1989. Menem's major slogans—the "productive revolution" and the "big wage hike"— reflected the long-standing Peronist call for state capitalism. As noted earlier, Menem led a constitutional reform that permitted him to run for reelection in the 1995 elections. These elections were the first held under a new ballotage system in which candidates needed to get either 45 percent of the vote or a 10-percentage-point margin with at least 40 percent. Menem won convincingly against a divided opposition vote, with many voters choosing José Octavio Bordón, candidate of the newly formed center-left FREPASO over the Radical candidate, Horacio Massaccessi. To avoid dividing the anti-Peronist vote, the UCR and the FREPASO formed a coalition called the Alliance in 1997. In 1999, the Alliance jointly supported Radical leader Fernando de la Rúa's successful campaign against the Peronist governor of Buenos Aires, Eduardo Duhalde. Finally, in the 2003 campaign, the Peronists did not agree on a common candidate, and the three major Peronist candidates ran under separate party

TABLE 5.2 Argentine Chamber of Deputies (1983–2003): Percentage of Seats Held, by Party

Party	Year										
	1983	1985	1987	1989	1991	1993	1995	1997	1999	2001	2003
PJ	45	41	42	44	46	48	51	47	39	45	52
UCR*	51	51	45	35	34	33	27	NA	NA	28	18
Alliance*	NA	NA	NA	NA	NA	NA	NA	40	49	NA	NA
FREPASO*	NA	NA	NA	NA	NA	NA	10	NA	NA	7	2
Others	4	9	13	21	21	20	12	14	13	21	28

*The Alliance of the UCR and the FREPASO put forward a joint slate of candidates in 1997 and 1999. Percentages do not always add up to 100 percent because of rounding.

SOURCE: For the years 1983–2001, data are from the Political Database of the Americas <http://www.georgetown.edu/pdba/Elecdata/Arg/arg.html> (accessed on November 14, 2003). For 2003, data are from *La Nación* <http://www.lanacion.com.ar> (accessed on December 19, 2003).

banners. While Menem outpaced the governor of Santa Cruz, Nestor Kirchner, in the first round, public opinion polls showed that Kirchner was likely to win the scheduled runoff election with somewhere between 60 and 70 percent of the vote. Faced with these polling results, Menem announced his withdrawal from the election in a controversial speech in which he refused to credit Kirchner with victory but rather blamed Eduardo Duhalde for working to prevent Menem's selection at the top of a unified Peronist ticket.

These presidents have rarely enjoyed a clear majority in the legislature. The Senate has tended to be controlled either by a Peronist majority or by a combination of the Peronists and various provincial parties. Election results in the Chamber of Deputies have been more varied (see Table 5.2). The UCR held a slim majority in the lower house during the first four years of Alfonsín's presidency. The Peronists never held a lower house majority during Menem's first term, thus forcing him to seek support from deputies tied to provincial and center-right parties. The 1995 elections gave Menem a narrow majority for two years that was lost after the Alliance's triumph in the 1997 midterm elections. Fernando de la Rúa faced a more difficult situation because his near-majority in the lower house in 1999 depended on the continued cooperation of the Radical and FREPASO parties; by late 2001, the Peronists controlled the lower house with the support of smaller provincial parties. The 2003 elections gave the Peronists a majority in both houses, but Kirchner could not depend consistently on legislative support due to continuing divisions within the Peronist movement.

THE CONTEMPORARY QUEST FOR DEVELOPMENT, LIBERTY, AND GOVERNANCE

Democracy returned in December 1983 amid serious economic crisis. The GDP was lower than it had been in 1974, when Perón died. Fixed investment was just over half of its 1974 level. The unemployment rate and the budget deficit were substantially higher than their average figures for the entire post–World War II era. The 1983 inflation rate of 434 percent was the highest in Argentine history: a product that cost 100 pesos in January 1983 cost 534 pesos by the end of the year. The debt-service ratio (interest paid on foreign debt as a percentage of total exports) also reached record levels (58 percent).

The new democratic government also faced several serious threats to liberty. The military government left behind a legacy of state violence as well as terrorism committed by groups on both extremes of the political spectrum. Many citizens had pressured for a return to democracy as a way to restore basic liberties, such as physical liberty and freedom of expression. The democratic government needed to find a way to heed societal demands for justice without provoking a military coup.

With major agendas awaiting the victor of Argentina's first democratic elections in a decade, the pursuit of governance would not be easy. Public protests toward the end of the military regime raised expectations that democracy would bring rapid improvements in development and liberty. At the same time, the governing Radical party had to try to create a working relationship with its historically cantankerous opposition party, the Peronists.

The Quest for Development in Argentina

Raúl Alfonsín took office flush with confidence from his impressive electoral victory and from Argentina's status as the lone democracy in the Southern Cone. The Alfonsín administration initially believed that it could solve Argentina's economic woes by injecting new dynamism into existing state capitalist policies. Alfonsín thought that the international and national goodwill generated by the democratic transition would help this approach succeed. When his progrowth policies saw inflation rise without the anticipated increase in investment and debt relief, he introduced a new, mixed set of policies—the Austral Plan—by decree in mid-1985. This combination of market-oriented currency reform and interventionist wage-price freezes temporarily brought annual inflation under 100 percent.

When inflation crept back up in 1987–1988, the administration and the legislature were divided about what to do next. Although some proposed market-oriented reforms, tariffs were reduced in only a few sectors, and privatization initiatives stalled in the legislature. In the end, the administration launched a new wage-price freeze, the 1988 Spring Plan, which broke inflationary

TABLE 5.3 Argentine Economic Indicators (1983–2002)*

Year	GDP growth	Inflation	Unemployment	Debt service ratio[†]
1983	2.6	434	4.7	58
1984	2.3	688	4.6	58
1985	−4.6	385	6.1	51
1986	5.8	82	5.6	51
1987	2.7	175	5.9	51
1988	−2.1	388	6.3	42
1989	−6.2	4,923	7.6	51
1990	−0.1	1,344	7.5	39
1991	10.0	84	6.5	36
1992	9.6	18	7.0	23
1993	5.9	7	9.6	23
1994	5.8	4	11.5	27
1995	−2.9	2	17.5	28
1996	5.5	0	17.2	28
1997	8.0	0	14.9	29
1998	3.8	1	12.9	35
1999	−3.4	−2	14.3	41
2000	−0.6	−1	15.1	40
2001	−4.4	−2	17.4	39
2002	−10.8	41	19.7	35

*All numbers are percentages.

[†]The debt service ratio expresses interest paid on foreign debts as a percentage of total exports.

SOURCE: For the years 1983–1987, data are from United Nations Economic Commission for Latin America and the Caribbean, *Preliminary Overview of the Economies of Latin America and the Caribbean 1989* (Santiago, Chile: United Nations Publications, 1989). For the years 1988–1992, data are from United Nations Economic Commission for Latin America and the Caribbean, *Preliminary Overview of the Economies of Latin America and the Caribbean 1994* (Santiago, Chile: United Nations Publications, 1994). For the years 1993–1997, data are from United Nations Economic Commission for Latin America and the Caribbean, *Preliminary Overview of the Economies of Latin America and the Caribbean 1999* (Santiago, Chile: United Nations Publications, 1999). For the years 1998–2002, data are from United Nations Economic Commission for Latin America and the Caribbean, *Preliminary Overview of the Economies of Latin America and the Caribbean 2003* (Santiago, Chile: United Nations Publications, 2003).

momentum for only a few months, until a run on the currency in early 1989 led to a hyperinflationary spiral that would force Alfonsín to leave office early (see Table 5.3). When prices tripled during June 1989, a dejected Alfonsín administration negotiated an early transfer of power, in which Carlos Menem's mandate began in July (rather than in December, as planned). Over the course of 1989, prices rose by nearly 5,000 percent.

Menem promptly executed one of the greatest about-faces in Argentine political history: he pushed through a decidedly market-oriented economic program. Deregulation of the domestic economy began in earnest, and the government reduced its budget deficit. Menem cut tariffs on imports and pledged to sell most state-owned enterprises. Allegations of corruption in some privatizations led several cabinet ministers to resign at the start of 1991 while also implicating Menem himself. Seeking credibility, Menem appointed a new economic minister, Domingo Cavallo. Cavallo overhauled the entire privatization framework with the assistance of the World Bank and renegotiated the highway and airline privatizations.

In his first months in his new post, Cavallo designed and helped shepherd through Congress the Convertibility Law, thereby fixing the Argentine peso at a one-to-one exchange rate with the U.S. dollar. The Convertibility Law required the Argentine government to back all currency in circulation with dollars held in reserve. This decision made it difficult (and dangerous) for the government to run budget deficits, and it reduced the prospect of inflationary devaluation scenarios that had been prevalent in the 1970s and 1980s. Faced with a fixed exchange rate and lower tariffs, firms would have to control their prices or suffer elimination via foreign competition. The success of convertibility in reducing inflation came at a price, however. The rigidity of the scheme made its continuation dependent on a combination of favorable terms of trade and investor confidence. When these conditions eroded over the second half of the 1990s, the country's economy began to suffer, as we shall see shortly.

With currency stability restored in the early 1990s, the economy experienced rapid growth and falling inflation rates. During the years 1991–1994, the economy grew by 7.4 percent annually. Annual inflation fell from 1,344 percent in 1990 to 84 percent in 1991. In turn, it fell below 20 percent in 1992 and below 10 percent in 1993–1994. Having beaten back hyperinflation, the Menem administration pursued additional market-oriented reforms. In August 1993, a controversial pension reform (similar to reforms in Chile under the Pinochet regime) replaced a government-run pension plan with privately managed mutual fund options. In a new round of privatizations, the railways, the power and gas companies, and various industrial state-owned enterprises were sold. On the trade policy front during 1993–1994, the Menem administration helped to push through a 1995 implementation of the Southern Cone Common Market integration accord with Brazil, Paraguay, and Uruguay (see *Global Perspectives: Regional Economic Integration* on pages 146–147).

After his reelection in 1995, Menem did not maintain the fiscal discipline characteristic of the early years of his first term. As public spending increased (especially in response to the 1995 Mexican peso crisis and the 1997–1998 Asian financial crisis), revenues failed to keep pace. Instead, the government borrowed more and more money. While inflation remained low, unemployment and public debt were on the rise and the GDP was shrinking when Menem left office in 1999.

GLOBAL PERSPECTIVES
Regional Economic Integration

There are three basic types of economic integration accords: free trade agreements, customs unions, and common markets. Free trade agreements (FTAs) eliminate tariffs between member countries. In a customs union, participants in an FTA hold a common trade policy toward all nonmember countries. A common market is a customs union that takes integration still further by coordinating members' domestic economic policies.

The first major regional accord of the post–World War II era was the 1957 Treaty of Rome, which called for a European common market. While a customs union formed in a few years, progress toward a common market was slow. The 1985 Single European Act pledged to create a common market by the early 1990s. This effort changed Europe and helped to spark new regional integration accords worldwide.

The European single-market drive coincided with the wave of market-oriented reforms in Latin America. Dormant regional agreements like the Central American Common Market, the Andean Pact, and the Caribbean Community were revived, while new accords took shape. In 1991, the Southern Cone Common Market (*Mercado Común del Cono Sur* [MERCOSUR]) linked Argentina, Brazil, Paraguay, and Uruguay. In 1992, the United States, Canada, and Mexico signed the North American Free Trade Agreement. Colombia, Mexico, and Venezuela formed the G-3 free trade zone in 1994. The December 1994 Summit of the Americas called for the creation of the hemispherewide Free Trade Agreement of the Americas (FTAA) by 2005.

Outside Europe and the Americas, the use of integration accords is expanding but is less widespread. In the late twentieth and early twenty-first centuries, several new agreements committed countries to enact FTAs over the years 2005–2010. As of early 2004, it is not clear which of these accords will produce enduring FTAs in Africa and in Asia.

The uncertain future of the FTAA and of regional integration elsewhere stems from the considerable political difficulties involved in putting these initiatives into practice. Many firms want to know if integration will reduce their profits. Other nongovernmental organizations are concerned about the impact of trade (and investment) liberalization on employment, the environment, indigenous peoples, and income distribution. This diverse antiglobalization movement has become increasingly visible from the 1990s onward. Government officials worry that integration will create more discontented constituents than happy ones. Free-trade advocates counter that liberalization lowers prices and promotes economic growth. Yet lower prices can be overshadowed if many people lose their jobs or see other important interests threatened.

MERCOSUR illustrates some of the political difficulties of integration. The pact called for a common market by 1995, yet negotiators barely agreed on a customs union by 1995 (and it was riddled with exempted sectors for each country). The early years of MERCOSUR coincided with economic recoveries in the two largest members—Brazil and Argentina—which fueled an expansion of trade. From the late 1990s onward, however, the accord began to unravel. Argentina and Brazil each instituted a series of new exceptions and found it difficult to coordinate their exchange rates and other economic policies. By 2002, several national figures in each country acknowledged that MERCOSUR might not survive, even though each government confirmed its commitment to the accord.

At the start of his term, Fernando de la Rúa tried to reduce one of the deficit pressures in the budget: federal assistance to provinces. He renegotiated the Coparticipation Law through which the federal government transferred money in block grants to the provinces. Gambling that economic recovery was around the corner, De la Rúa changed the formula from a guaranteed percentage of federal revenues to a guaranteed floor fixed at just under $1.4 billion (out of a federal budget of over $40 billion). If economic growth resumed, this approach would reduce the weight of these block grants in the federal budget over time.

As we saw at the start of this chapter, however, growth did not resume in 2000. The recession and the Coparticipation Law were two of several factors that increased the government's need to borrow. In early 2001, Brazil (Argentina's largest trading partner) devalued its currency by over 30 percent against the dollar (and thus against the Argentine peso). This devaluation (coming on the heels of a 25 percent devaluation in 1999) raised further doubts about Argentina's ability to ends its recession. Then, in March 2001, an outbreak of hoof-and-mouth disease apparently imported from the United Kingdom caused a suspension of livestock exports. The new economic minister, Ricardo López Murphy, proposed major spending cuts to balance the budget. The plan aimed at restoring investor confidence in Argentina's currency and its creditworthiness, but it was widely criticized by Peronist politicians, Peronist and non-Peronist labor unions, and several FREPASO cabinet members, who resigned in protest. Without political support for his proposal, López Murphy resigned in April.

Fernando de la Rúa replaced him with Domingo Cavallo. Cavallo initially tried to avoid budget cuts by restructuring the public debt. He postponed most remaining 2001 payments by accepting higher interest rates to extend the loans for one to two years. By August 2001, Argentina had the world's highest debt-to-exports ratio and paid the highest interest rates for debt financing. Cavallo then reversed course. To obtain an $8 billion credit agreement with the IMF, he agreed to balance the budget over the second half of 2001 by cutting all public employees' wages by 13 percent. Continuing budget deficits and the Peronist victory in the October 2001 legislative elections did not inspire confidence that the De la Rúa government could improve the situation, which exploded in December once the government instituted restrictions on bank withdrawals to prevent a run on the banks. Looting in mid-December set off a wave of antigovernment protests in Buenos Aires by angry middle-class citizens frustrated by the government's inability to solve the nation's problems. When Cavallo's resignation on the evening of December 19 did not stem the protests, looting, and violence, De la Rúa announced his own resignation the next evening.

Amid the crisis, several Peronist leaders wanted to be named president in December 2001. This intraparty rivalry led to a compromise in which Peronist legislators initially agreed to let the voters decide the issue. Adolfo Rodríguez Saá, a Peronist governor, was named interim president until elections in March. He gained the support of Peronist legislators by promising not to run in the upcoming elections. Then, on Christmas Eve, he gave a fiery inaugural address. He announced with smiling glee that Argentina would suspend payment by declaring a **default** on most of its debt. He also pledged to create 1 million jobs within the next few months. While the speech thrilled some desperate Argentines, it frightened investors (and many Peronist politicians). Rodríguez Saá planned to create government jobs paid for through a new third currency that would not be traded on world markets, thus giving it no value abroad and questionable value at home.

Opposition to his proposals and public protests criticizing cabinet members with checkered pasts placed Rodríguez Saá in a difficult position. Given the level of governmental and public opposition he faced, many questioned his ability to govern effectively. Rodríguez Saá argued that he would be able to develop a governing coalition only if he were given a longer time in which to work. He asked Peronist leaders to cancel the elections, thereby allowing him to serve the rest of De la Rúa's term until December 2003. When they refused, he announced his resignation on December 30.

The tumult of December motivated legislators in all three major parties to select someone to serve the remainder of De la Rúa's term (rather than holding the elections planned for March). Veteran Peronist leader Eduardo Duhalde was given that mandate provided that he not run for reelection in 2003. It was hoped that he could restore internal peace and economic stability so that elections could be held in a less chaotic climate.

Duhalde initially responded to the economic crisis by ending the fixed parity of the Argentine peso with the U.S. dollar. This devaluation aimed at increasing exports, thus reactivating the economy. Yet devaluation hurt many Argentine banks, firms, and individuals with loans and contracts denominated in dollars. An already wobbly financial system crumbled under the strain, making it difficult to remove the banking restrictions. The government faced a serious dilemma. If it removed the restrictions, it risked a run on the banks and capital flight. If it kept the restrictions, the lack of money in the financial system could stifle the economy.

The Duhalde government tried to escape this dilemma by quickly requesting a new line of credit with the IMF to prevent a potential banking run. The IMF refused, citing past breaches of promises and calling for further economic reform in advance of additional loans. The Duhalde government countered that several of the IMF's policy recommendations were not feasible. Amid the stalemate with the IMF and the conflicts within the government, the economy collapsed: the GDP shrank by 12 percent during the first nine months of 2002.

Over the second half of 2002, however, the Duhalde government managed to produce a budget surplus and to stabilize the exchange rate. The economy grew modestly during the last quarter of 2002. Eventually, in January 2003, the IMF agreed to extend $16 billion in credit to cover Argentina's debt obligations to international financial institutions (the IMF, the World Bank, and the Inter-American Development Bank) during the first eight months of 2003. During the first months of 2003, economic growth picked up even more, and the Duhalde government removed many of the remaining restrictions on bank withdrawals. By the time Duhalde left office on May 25, 2003, he claimed that the worst of the financial and socioeconomic crisis was finally over.

Like many Latin American countries, Argentina had returned to democracy amid an economic crisis that called into question the viability of the state capitalist model of development that had been in place for nearly half a century. Argentina's subsequent efforts to stabilize economic conditions and to reduce poverty illustrate many of the difficulties faced by the region. During the Alfonsín government, the effort to improve the performance of the state capitalist model in place was blocked by a mixture of tax evasion, wage-price conflict, government waste, and international pressure to adopt the so-called Washington Consensus model of market-oriented reforms. Menem gambled that a quick series of market-oriented reforms could gain the support of international and domestic investors, thereby creating a new path toward economic stability and growth. The Convertibility Law was a rigid measure designed to restore confidence in a country that had been a world leader in price and exchange rate instability. Convertibility's combination of a fixed exchange rate and free international movement of capital depended on a mixture of favorable international economic conditions and a political willingness to avoid growing budget deficits when economic conditions worsened. During the second half of Menem's presidency, both of these potential problems came home to roost: the world financial crises from 1995 onward made financial flows more erratic, and Menem responded to calls for increased government spending by borrowing. The De la Rúa government hoped that economic growth in 2000 would reverse these negative trends. Brazil's devaluation deepened the recession and investor pessimism grew, however, when divisions in the Alliance became more apparent.

The market-oriented model had brought new productive investment in several sectors of the economy in the 1990s, but it also made the economy even more vulnerable to international events. At the same time, the economic reforms changed political dynamics by worsening economic conditions for those workers who lost their jobs because of the reduction of trade barriers. The growth of the 1990s was an improvement relative to the stagnation of the 1980s, but the 1990s also saw a rise in income inequality and unemployment. In late 1990, the wealthiest 10 percent of the population earned nearly eighteen times as much as the poorest 10 percent. By late 1999, they earned twenty-one times as much, and by late 2002, they earned twenty-seven times as much as the poorest tenth of the population. By comparison, in the United States, the wealthiest tenth of the population earned ten times the amount earned by the poorest tenth in 2002. Amid this tumultuous mix of worsening economic inequality, domestic political divisions, and international economic pressures, contemporary Argentine governments have found it difficult to chart a stable course for development.

The Quest for Liberty in Argentina

In his 1983 election campaign, Raúl Alfonsín emphasized accountability for past human rights violations. During its last year in power, the military had issued an amnesty law by decree that blocked trials for human rights abuses occurring during the *Proceso*. Alfonsín's inaugural address coincided with International Human Rights Day (December 10), and he took the occasion to reiterate his critique of the amnesty law. Three days later, his government announced plans to try the leaders of the military government and the leaders of major guerrilla organizations who were responsible for various human rights violations. As a concession to the armed forces, military courts were granted jurisdiction. The first action of the new legislature was to overturn the prior amnesty law.

In 1984, the government formed the National Commission on Disappeared Persons (*Comisión Nacional Sobre la Desaparición de Personas* [CONADEP]) to investigate disappearances—the apparent summary execution and hidden burial of hundreds or thousands of Argentines. The CONADEP report confirmed 8,961 disappearances; human rights groups estimated that the total was two to four times that high. The report focused additional attention on the disappeared as well as on acts of torture and rape suffered by many detainees. The investigations conducted by CONADEP and by nongovernmental organizations demonstrated that Argentina had suffered a higher frequency of political murder than had been observed in neighboring Brazil, Chile, and Uruguay (see Table 5.4). In 1985, the government provided a small (supplemental) monthly pension for the dependents of disappeared persons.

When the military tribunal did not complete its trial of the high command within the six-month deadline set by the military code, civilian courts seized the opportunity and took jurisdiction over the matter. Five junta leaders were found guilty. Their sentences ranged from several years to life imprisonment. The verdicts rejected the principle of due obedience (which asserts that subordinate officers should not be held criminally liable when they were following orders issued by the high command). Instead, these court decisions expressly called for more trials. Human rights groups used the opening to pressure for trials regarding many senior and junior officers.

The Alfonsín government found itself at a new crossroads. It had attempted to limit fear and bitterness in the military by pledging not to try officers below

TABLE 5.4 Human Rights Abuses During Dictatorships in the 1970s and 1980s: Victims Listed per 100,000 Inhabitants

	Disappearances and political murders	Other victims	Military self-amnesty	Major trials held
Argentina*	36		Yes	Yes
Brazil	0.2	15	Yes	No
Chile	27	2,623	Yes	No
Uruguay	8	900	No	No

*Argentina did not publish an official estimate of the victims of torture or rape under detention during the dictatorship. Unofficial estimates place the incidence of these abuses at or above the level found in Chile.

SOURCE: Adapted from Paul Zagorski, *Democracy vs. National Security: Civil-Military Relations in Latin America* (Boulder, Colo.: Lynne Rienner, 1992), p. 99.

the high command. Now the judicial process had taken matters well beyond that point. The government designed the Full Stop Law (*Ley de Punto Final*), which set a sixty-day period when further charges could be lodged. When the bill became law on Christmas Eve 1986, its designers thought that few additional proceedings could be launched because January and February are the traditional summer months of vacation in Argentina. Nevertheless, many judicial employees worked during the summer holiday to keep the process alive: 400 cases had been filed when the deadline expired.

The military response to the expansion of trials came quickly. During Easter week in April 1987, junior officers of the *carapintada* ("painted face") movement seized a major garrison outside Buenos Aires and harshly criticized both civilian and military authorities. In the tense negotiations that followed, many allege that a secret pact was reached in which *carapintada* leaders agreed to stand down while the government agreed to remove some senior officers and to stop the trials. In June 1987, the administration's due obedience bill was passed by the legislature. The bill stipulated that all officers below the rank of colonel were coerced into violating the law. The Due Obedience Law reduced the number of charged officers by 75 percent. Two more military rebellions followed in 1988; the participants called for amnesty, an end to all trials, and pay increases. The Alfonsín administration ended in a bitter stalemate in which human rights groups criticized the end to most trials while many military personnel criticized the trials that had taken place.

During the last phase ending the human rights trials, the Alfonsín government held firm to its efforts to establish civilian control over the military. The government quickly created a civilian-led defense ministry and also replaced military directors of several state-owned enterprises with civilians. In 1988, new legislation formally separated the military from direct responsibility for internal security, thus narrowing its role to defense from external threats. In addition, the defense budget fell visibly during Alfonsín's term. The *Research Question* here in Chapter Five considers the political dynamics of efforts to establish civilian control over the military.

In contrast to Alfonsín's approach to past human rights violations, Menem emphasized reconciliation as his major goal (although he placed civilians in top defense ministry posts). During his first several months in office, he pardoned most officers and guerrillas—as well as many soldiers who had participated in revolts during 1987–1988. In 1990, he took the much-publicized step of pardoning the high command despite a wave of protests organized by human rights groups. Human rights groups continued to try to draw public attention to past violations and also attempted to find openings in the existing legislation. In 1991, the Menem government tried to respond to criticism from human rights activists by providing lump-sum reparation to persons imprisoned without normal judicial proceedings, that is, via military tribunal or by the actions of executive branch officials.

The dirty war again came under public scrutiny in 1995, when several military officers broke two decades of silence by detailing many violations in gripping detail. Human rights lawyers began to emphasize allegations of trafficking in the children of detainees. Existing legislation blocking trials did not apply to crimes against minors. In the late 1990s, the Menem administration modified

RESEARCH QUESTION

Under What Conditions Are Governments Likely to Develop Civilian Control of the Military?

In a 1997 article, Wendy Hunter examined the dynamics of civil-military relations amid the third wave of democratization in Latin America.[1] Under what conditions can the armed forces best defend an expansive role in political life? Conversely, what factors might help elected governments to extend civilian control over the military?

Hunter examines two competing theoretical perspectives regarding civil-military relations. On one side, the modes-of-transition theory focuses on the institutional power that the military possesses at the outset of the return to democratic rule. Where the military retained institutional autonomy, a substantial governmental role, and visible public support, one would expect it to be very difficult for elected governments to roll back those institutional prerogatives. The military's expanded role in the system would give it the capacity to repel most subsequent efforts to reduce its influence.

On the other side, the electoral dynamic theory asserts that the return to electoral competition will entice politicians to erode the military's role and to make policy decisions at

[1]Wendy Hunter, "Continuity or Change? Civil-Military Relations in Democratic Argentina, Chile, and Peru," *Political Science Quarterly* 112 (1997): 453–475. For additional research in academic journals regarding civil-military relations, see the appropriate portion of this book's website.

its policy and called for federal prosecutors to pursue these cases. Several members of the high command and other senior officers were charged with child trafficking. In addition, some of these same officers faced extradition requests from European governments investigating their potential involvement in crimes against their citizenry.

Fernando de la Rúa responded to these requests by signing an executive order that suspended review of all human rights extradition cases indefinitely. However, both his administration and Eduardo Duhalde's continued the legal proceedings for child trafficking begun under Menem. When Duhalde left office in May 2003, nearly twenty years after the return to democracy, the political visibility of past human rights violations remained high. Trials infuriated the military, and the suspension of trials and subsequent pardon angered human rights activists.

In its efforts to protect current liberties, the Alfonsín administration managed to satisfy more citizens while angering fewer. It met expectations that the end to military rule would bring a reduction in arbitrary action by security forces. In turn, appointees to the Supreme Court made a series of decisions that defended core civil liberties such as the right to privacy, freedom of speech, and freedom of the press. Although some conservatives had argued that a return to civilian rule would bring a rise in the crime rate, street crime was not a visible

odds with the military's preferences. To win elections, elected officials would likely shift spending away from defense to other causes. In addition, they may find that limiting the military's role may prove popular with many of their constituents.

Hunter examines these theories via comparative case studies of the experiences of Argentina, Chile, and Peru. Chile is a prime example of a country in which the military survived the transition to democracy with considerable political strength and institutional power. Conversely, the Argentine military ceded power during an economic collapse and after a tragic military defeat in the Malvinas. Peru constitutes an intermediate case in which the military did not leave power in disgrace, but its institutional prerogatives were more limited than were those in Chile.

How did civil-military relations unfold after the return to democracy? Hunter finds that events in these countries (and in Brazil) largely confirm the electoral dynamics theory. In all of these countries—including Chile—the military lost political ground over time. She argues that the role of electoral dynamics is mediated by the nature of the political party system. Where parties rise and fall more frequently (in Peru, for example), it will be easier for the military to defend or regain its turf. Conversely, more stable party systems make it easier for elected officials to pursue civilian control. Despite the visible role of the electoral dynamics theory in these cases, Hunter also partially confirms the modes-of-transition theory: the prospects for civilian control are greatest in the countries in which the military emerged from the transition in the weakest position.

public issue until hyperinflation in 1989 helped spark supermarket lootings, particularly in the interior of the country. On balance, the Alfonsín administration received praise in the domestic and international media for efforts to restore and protect liberties.

The Menem administration faced more criticism than its predecessor. Initial criticisms focused on corrupt activities by government officials. In its first four years in office, the Menem administration was rocked by nineteen major scandals, which resulted in the resignation of twenty ministers and senior presidential aides. Most of these scandals involved government officials soliciting bribes from businesspeople in exchange for assistance in the awarding of state contracts, in the purchase of import licenses, and in several privatization processes. One of the most publicized scandals involved the privatization of the national airline, *Aerolíneas Argentinas.* When a prosecutor tried to suspend the sale to investigate irregularities, the Menem administration appealed directly to the Supreme Court. The Supreme Court (which had been previously packed with loyal Menem appointees) used an unprecedented legal procedure to claim immediate jurisdiction over the case. It then ruled in favor of the administration and let the sale go through without further investigations. The image of a Supreme Court with an automatic majority responsive to Menem's political machine cast a shadow over the judiciary that would extend beyond his presidency.

Basic civil liberties continued to be largely respected, but concern about the climate in which the press operated over the ten years of Menem's presidency increased. Throughout the 1990s, many journalists reported acts of intimidation, including threatening phone calls, personal assaults, and attacks on media headquarters. The major case that brought attention to this environment was the brutal 1997 murder of news photographer José Luis Cabezas. Subsequent investigations implicated several police officers and a controversial entrepreneur with suspected criminal ties, Alfredo Yabrán. While eight people received life sentences in 2000 for their direct involvement in the killing, Yabrán escaped trial via an apparent suicide in May 1998. This high-profile case dramatized the larger issue of efforts to intimidate journalists. On several occasions, the Menem administration contributed to this tension by presenting draft legislation restricting press freedoms in several ways, but the Argentine congress subsequently enacted few of these provisions.

The Alliance had campaigned in the late 1990s for the enhancement of liberty and clean government. Its anticorruption stance came back to haunt it when allegations surfaced about several legislators in and out of the Alliance receiving bribes to vote for the government's labor bill in April 2000. Veteran Peronist senator Antonio Cafiero publicly confirmed the allegations in August. Vice-President Chacho Alvarez, leader of the FREPASO, supported Cafiero's calls for investigations and for the resignation of the entire Senate (to be followed by new elections). Judicial investigations during De la Rúa's presidency did not produce any formal charges, but the high-profile scandal deepened the belief for many Argentines that political corruption was widespread and that the guilty were unlikely to be held accountable. Later, in mid-December 2003, a former legislative employee came forward with direct testimony about his own involvement (and that of De la Rúa and others) in bribing senators in 2000 to assure passage of the government's labor law reforms.

Rising concern over street crime also challenged the De la Rúa government. News services frequently reported on armed robberies, muggings, and kidnappings. As the economic crisis deepened, concern over crime rose. This linkage between street crime and poverty reached its most visible point in the violent events of December 19 and 20, when bands of individuals engaged in acts of looting and property destruction.

During Duhalde's presidency, the serious economic crisis worsened fears regarding a steady wave of street crime along with the threat of future looting. In 2002, the government took officers from several agencies to form a new anti-kidnapping unit. However, with just 200 members, many wondered whether the unit had the resources to reduce the threat of so-called express kidnappings, in which criminals held people briefly for ransom.

At the same time, protesters questioned the willingness and ability of the police to protect property from potentially violent individuals while respecting the right of law-abiding citizens to hold protests. Early in Duhalde's administration, many observers had commented on a decrease in violent protest and in violence between government forces and protesters. Then, in late June 2002, cameras filmed provincial police killing a protester rushing to the aid of another wounded protester; both men died by rifle shots fired far away from a struggle between road-blocking protesters and the police. The tragedy reinforced concerns about the professionalism of many police officers.

In its quest for liberty, Argentina's position as the first Southern Cone country to return to democracy placed its human rights turmoil at center stage for the region and for the world. Alfonsín's initial strategy of holding the high command responsible did not generate sufficient consensus among judges and human rights groups who called for additional trials. As the trials expanded, an explosive series of military rebellions and private lobbying convinced the government to pass the Full Stop and Due Obedience laws to reduce military discontent. Once elected, Menem took the additional step of pardoning the high command—an action that may have helped his relations with the officer corps but one that deepened resentment from citizens who had supported the trial of the junta. The 1995 revelations by junior officers broke the code of silence and reopened the political debate. From that point onward, all presidents, from Menem through Duhalde, permitted prosecutors to pursue charges involving crimes against minors (which had been excluded from the Full Stop and Due Obedience statutes). The Argentine experience dramatizes the potential for irreconcilable differences between the two most directly involved participants in the human rights debate: the advocates for the victims and the military. In the early twenty-first century, human rights groups continue to call for the military to face the rule of law for crimes against humanity, while much of the military continues to oppose prosecution. In August 2003, the Kirchner government backed legislation that repealed both the Full Stop Law and the Due Obedience Law, thus reopening a path toward additional prosecutions.

Beyond human rights turmoil, government corruption became a more visible issue under the Menem administration as media exposés described a level of corruption greater than had been experienced under past civilian and military governments. These scandals brought more attention to corruption in many aspects of government activity—in the legislature, the courts, the bureaucracy, and the police force. Amid a climate of rising poverty, declining government services, and increased fiscal pressures, demands for clean government reached a boiling point in the street protests of late 2001 and early 2002. This demand remained among the most pressing in the Argentine political system when Nestor Kirchner took office as president in May 2003.

The Quest for Governance in Argentina

In pursuing his agendas for development and for liberty, Raúl Alfonsín at first tried to govern without cooperating with the Peronists. In fact, the government attempted to revise labor relations laws to open union elections and thus weaken Peronist control of the unions. Peronists mobilized enough allies in the Senate to block the legislation. Still, the Radicals believed they could win a majority in the Senate in the 1985 midterm elections. Alfonsín launched the Austral Plan by decree not just to break inflationary momentum but also to claim credit for stabilizing prices in the October 1985 election campaign. The Radicals won the elections, but they did not gain enough seats to control the Senate.

Economic problems and tense civil-military relations changed governing dynamics. In the October 1987 midterm elections, the Peronists gained an outright majority in the Senate and replaced the Radicals as the largest party in the Chamber of Deputies. Alfonsín responded to the new scenario by pursuing a more conciliatory approach. He sought consensus for a series of more market-oriented policies, but the bad blood of the prior four years made this decidedly difficult in 1988. Prior to the presidential elections in 1989, economic conditions deteriorated so rapidly that some Peronists seemed content to isolate Alfonsín in an effort to weaken the Radicals.

The 1989 economic crisis shaped governing dynamics when Carlos Menem took office. He enjoyed an initial honeymoon with the public and with opposition parties. Arguing that the magnitude of the crisis required immediate action, Menem persuaded a divided Congress to approve the Law of Economic Emergency and the State Reform Law. In these laws, Congress authorized the president to enact economic reforms through executive orders. Accordingly, early privatization measures and other key reforms were implemented with minimal congressional oversight. For example, the bicameral commission monitoring the privatization process could ask the executive to justify its plans but had no power to stop a sale. Beyond the discretion granted by these laws, Menem enacted more policies by decree than all past Argentine presidents put together, seemingly daring the judiciary or the legislature to stop him.

Menem also reduced the judiciary's independence. As we saw earlier, the Supreme Court was packed with loyal appointees. In 1990, Menem also removed four of the five members of the fiscal tribunal, which oversees irregularities in government accounts. In 1991, he fired the state attorney in charge of prosecuting irregularities in public administration by executive order—an unconstitutional method.

At the time, many asserted that Menem's procedural shortcuts were needed to confront the crisis. His economic reforms (and the growth with low inflation that followed) made Argentina a success story in the eyes of many foreign and national observers. Capitalizing on this acclaim, Menem pushed for and got a constitutional reform that enabled him to run for reelection in 1995.

That second term did not follow Menem's proposals as closely as his first. Although Menem won reelection, his efforts had mobilized a unification of many small parties and several Peronist dissidents into the FREPASO party that won one-fifth of the deputy seats up for election in 1995. With inflation in check and growth restored, public debate focused more closely on unresolved issues: corruption allegations, persistent unemployment, and rumors that Menem would try to run for a third term. The Alliance formed between the Radicals and FREPASO in 1997 campaigned on these issues to win the 1997 midterm elections. Menem faced an often hostile legislature in his last two years in office, just as Alfonsín had during 1988–1989. Menem then pursued a third term until he was blocked by Peronist rivals. He spent much of 1999 apparently absorbed in internal Peronist politics; some claim that he mobilized party and governmental resources to keep his Peronist rival Eduardo Duhalde from winning as the PJ's presidential candidate in 1999.

After defeating Duhalde, Alliance candidate Fernando de la Rúa inherited a situation in December 1999 that was politically and economically fragile. He faced a Peronist majority in the Senate, and Peronists governed most provinces, including the three largest ones. His near-majority in the Chamber of Deputies depended on continued cooperation with his center-left allies in FREPASO.

Fernando de la Rúa's government collapsed amid both violent and nonviolent protests. What went wrong with De la Rúa's approach to governance? Divisions within the Alliance and Peronist intransigence both hamstrung his efforts. The Alliance unraveled in disagreement over economic policy and anticorruption efforts. Chacho Alvarez resigned as vice president in October 2000. The remaining FREPASO cabinet members left in protest of López Murphy's proposed spending cuts in April 2001. The breakup of the Alliance fueled speculation among several leading Peronists that electoral victory in October 2001 would give them control over both legislative chambers. Although Peronists did not win an outright majority in the lower house, they did become the largest party

Pot-banging protests (*cacerolazos*) like this one helped prompt President De la Rúa's resignation.   AP/Wide World Photos.

in that chamber. Meanwhile, Peronist governors resisted De la Rúa's efforts to renegotiate the Coparticipation Law throughout 2001.

The corruption scandal diminished Fernando de la Rúa's popularity, and his political difficulties made it harder to restore investor confidence. The government entered a vicious cycle in which each negative outcome increased pessimism. Pessimism deepened after the administration's defeat in the October 2001 legislative elections, culminating in the dramatic and violent December events that led to De la Rúa's resignation. Many citizens in downtown Buenos Aires responded to the wave of violence by banging pots in the streets to demand first Cavallo's resignation and then President De la Rúa's. While some speculated that Peronist sympathizers organized some of the violence, to date neither judicial nor journalistic investigations have produced firm evidence to support this charge.

This speculation stems from the governance situation produced by De la Rúa's resignation. Under Argentine law, no one could be appointed to replace Vice President Alvarez when he resigned. In turn, the law of presidential succession specifies that the congressional leader next in line must hold a joint session of Congress, which must select a new president within forty-eight hours. Thus, Peronists controlled the appointment of De la Rúa's successor because the PJ—with help from provincial parties—controlled Congress. After Peronist leaders rejected interim President Adolfo Rodríguez Saá's request to serve the remainder of De la Rúa's term, his resignation culminated in the selection of Eduardo Duhalde as president.

Eduardo Duhalde had tried to govern via a coalition of like-minded Peronists augmented by support from some Radical legislators. He did so because the PJ was seriously divided; his long-standing rivalry with Carlos Menem made it difficult to govern without help from other parties. When support lagged, Duhalde tried to resolve several key issues (including banking reform and electoral reform) by decree. Through the many problems and controversies, Duhalde emphasized frequently that he intended to serve out his term rather than call early elections to permit the voters to choose a new president directly.

The June 2002 protest shootings mobilized outcry across partisan and ideological lines, which made a difficult situation even worse. Duhalde responded by moving the 2003 elections from September to April and by promising to resign six months early, on May 25, 2003. Duhalde spent the remainder of 2002 and the first part of 2003 trying to recruit a candidate to challenge Peronists Carlos Menem and Adolfo Rodríguez Saá in the upcoming presidential elections. After failing to convince the popular governor of Santa Fe, Carlos Reutemann, Duhalde turned to the governor of Santa Cruz, Nestor Kirchner. In this way, Duhalde hoped to block the aspirations of his rivals while perhaps extending his own influence beyond his planned resignation.

Why did corruption become a recurring issue in contemporary Argentina? Some analysts argue that systemic corruption emerged and worsened over time as a path toward governance. On the one hand, Argentine presidents and legislators tacitly permit corruption (rather than root it out) because anticorruption efforts might limit cooperation on other issues. On the other hand, presidential administrations have also all been implicated in scandals in which their operatives have been charged with active use of corruption in an effort to build or maintain political coalitions. For example, several observers allege that a portion of the kickbacks gathered by the Menem administration were used to supplement the salaries of legislators willing to back the government. A similar scandal disrupted the coalition that had initially backed De la Rúa's presidency.

Pessimistic observers argue that the fragmented nature of the Peronist and Radical parties—along with rampant smaller circles of corruption at the provincial level—make corruption a necessary evil. In this perspective, corruption becomes a means to political cooperation in a society with no consensus over public policy, which could help forge an enduring coalition within government and between government and society. If this view is accurate, then the path to governance will remain troubled whenever economic conditions worsen (thereby reducing the money available for corruption) or until a political party can produce a majority for change in both the path of governance and/or in the nature of public policy more generally.

Future Challenges

The winner of the 2003 presidential elections, Nestor Kirchner, faced serious challenges as Argentina attempted to escape a host of problems that have shaken this once proud country to its core. The economic collapse had been severe: the GDP per person fell from $12,377 in 2000 to $10,483 by the end of 2002. This macroeconomic collapse tripled the percentage of the population living in poverty. Like Duhalde before him, Kirchner responded initially by continuing to delay the resumption of payments on roughly half of the national debt, which had been in default since late 2001.

This economic debacle framed the search for liberty. Human rights issues from the last military regime remained unresolved, and many of the accused claimed that society should move on to confront pressing economic woes. At the same time, rising unemployment and poverty multiplied concerns over crime. Business owners feared future damage by protesters and looters, similar to what they experienced in December 2001. Wealthy and low-income citizens feared street crime from pickpockets, muggers, and kidnappers. Meanwhile, citizens' confidence in the willingness and ability of politicians to respond to these dangers was perhaps at an all-time low. This pessimism stemmed partly from the gravity of the circumstances and partly from the increasingly widespread belief that most Argentine government officials in all three branches are corrupt. Many Argentines had long held this belief, but the corruption scandals of the past few years deepened this distrust. Within this context, it was no coincidence that one of the first major anticrime initiatives of the Kirchner administration involved an effort to clean up the notoriously corrupt police force of the province of Buenos Aires.

This combination of grave economic difficulties and concerns regarding liberty did not create ideal conditions for governance. Some called for greater centralization of authority to confront the crisis. Yet the widespread cynicism regarding traditional politicians and bureaucrats motivated many to question whether expanding and centralizing public authority would be a useful response. The Menem administration's use of increased discretionary authority left a bitter legacy. The continuation of serious political conflict—both between and within the major parties—also created challenges for the new government. Kirchner would have to search for a way to mend fences with Argentine citizens as well as with the legislature, the judiciary, and the international financial community, and within the Peronist movement from which he hails. In his first three months in office, Kirchner sought the approval of Argentine citizens by pressing for political changes that perhaps could be produced more quickly than economic improvements. He publicly called for the annulment of the Full Stop Law and the Due Obedience Law, and he supported efforts to remove Supreme Court justices appointed by Carlos Menem. Time will tell whether the initial popular approval of these stances will translate into enduring support on other issues from the legislature and from the business community.

Taken together, this string of problems constitutes a legitimacy crisis for the Argentine democracy. The lack of faith in the rule of law has weakened procedure-based legitimacy, and economic collapse has lowered outcome-based legitimacy. More and more people assert that the Argentine political and economic systems are broken.

Rebuilding Argentines' faith in their political and economic future will be the crucial task in the coming years. It may be hard now to recall that confidence ran high in many circles during the 1990s. In Argentina and elsewhere in Latin America, many trumpeted market capitalism as a way to escape the lost decade of the 1980s. Development successes, in turn, would improve the prospects for the protection of liberty and the pursuit of effective governance. Observers in and out of Argentina frequently presented the country as a model for the rest of the region. Its increasingly open economy grew rapidly in the early 1990s, while inflation remained low. Major civil liberties were largely respected, and the 1994 constitution included several reforms that might increase judicial independence while checking the presidency. Although many criticized Menem's governing style, the staid Fernando de la Rúa sparked expectations that he could govern more by consensus and with fewer corruption scandals.

By 2002, that optimism had given way to despair. Critics of market capitalism had long asserted that the demise of state capitalism would bring more problems than benefits. The Argentine crisis placed the country at the center of this ongoing global debate. Advocates of state capitalism and of socialism both charged that overreliance on market mechanisms and financial orthodoxy drove the country to ruin. Defenders of market capitalism countered that the collapse was driven by an incomplete dedication to fiscal discipline in which politicians spent beyond their means until the financial bubble burst. The resolution of this debate has implications that go well beyond Argentina, as we shall see in the chapters to come.

Activities and Exercises

1. Juan Perón was the most influential and controversial figure in Argentine politics from 1944 until his death in 1974. Why was he so controversial? Do you believe that he could have pursued the policies he implemented during his presidency from 1946 through 1955 without inciting such opposition to his movement? Why or why not?

2. In the contemporary Argentine democracy, Carlos Menem has been the central figure. What do you believe has been his legacy for the pursuit of development, liberty, and governance? On balance, do you believe that Menem's impact on these issues has been positive or negative?

3. If you were a low-income resident of greater Buenos Aires, name three things that you think you could do next year to improve Argentina's prospects for development, liberty, and governance. Do you believe that you could do three similar things to improve conditions in the United States? If the two lists are not the

same, why aren't they? If the two lists are identical, in which country would they be easier to achieve and why?

4. *La historia oficial* (*The Official Story*) won an Academy Award for best foreign film. The 1985 Argentine film examines the dirty war—primarily from the perspective of an upper-middle-income family in Buenos Aires. This movie should be available in your local video store if it is not in your library.

5. As noted in this chapter, Argentina's economic collapse has sparked considerable debate in and outside Argentina. To read more about this issue (and about international political economy more generally), see the Argentina section of Professor Nouriel Roubini's website at http://www.stern.nyu.edu/globalmacro/. What approach should Argentina take toward resolving its debt problems? Why?

Suggested Readings

Auyero, Javier. *Poor People's Politics: Peronist Survival Networks and the Legacy of Evita*. Durham, N.C.: Duke University Press, 2001.

Bouvard, Marguerite. *Revolutionizing Motherhood: The Mothers of the Plaza de Mayo*. Wilmington, Del.: Scholarly Resources, 1994.

Brennan, James, ed. *Peronism and Argentina*. Wilmington, Del.: Scholarly Resources, 1998.

Brysk, Alison. *The Politics of Human Rights in Argentina: Protest, Change, and Democratization*. Stanford, Calif.: Stanford University Press, 1994.

Burdick, Michael. *For God and Fatherland: Religion and Politics in Argentina*. Albany: State University of New York Press, 1995.

Catterberg, Edgardo. *Argentina Confronts Politics: Political Culture and Public Opinion in the Argentine Transition to Democracy*. Boulder, Colo.: Lynne Rienner, 1991.

De la Balze, Felipe. *Remaking the Argentine Economy*. New York: Council on Foreign Relations, 1995.

Epstein, Edward, ed. *The New Argentine Democracy: The Search for a Successful Formula*. Westport, Conn.: Praeger, 1992.

Escude, Carlos. *Foreign Policy Theory in Menem's Argentina*. Gainesville: University of Florida Press, 1997.

Feitlowitz, Marguerite. *A Lexicon of Terror: Argentina and the Legacies of Torture*. Oxford, England: Oxford University Press, 1998.

Fraser, Nicholas, and Marysa Navarro. *Eva Perón*. New York: W.W. Norton, 1980.

Gibson, Edward. *Class and Conservative Parties: Argentina in Comparative Perspective*. Baltimore, Md.: Johns Hopkins University Press, 1996.

Hodges, Donald. *Argentina's "Dirty War."* Austin: University of Texas Press, 1991.

Levitsky, Steven. *Transforming Labor-Based Parties in Latin America: Argentine Peronism in Comparative Perspective*. New York: Cambridge University Press, 2003.

Lewis, Daniel. *The History of Argentina*. Westport, Conn.: Greenwood, 2001.

Manzetti, Luigi. *Institutions, Parties, and Coalitions in Argentine Politics*. Pittsburgh, Pa.: University of Pittsburgh Press, 1993.

McGuire, James. *Peronism Without Perón: Unions, Parties and Democracy in Argentina*. Stanford, Calif.: Stanford University Press, 1997.

Norden, Deborah. *Military Rebellion in Argentina: Between Coups and Consolidation.* Lincoln: University of Nebraska Press, 1996.

Nouzeilles, Gabriela, and Graciela Montaldo, eds. *The Argentina Reader: History, Culture, Politics.* Durham, N.C.: Duke University Press, 2002.

Pion-Berlin, David. *Through Corridors of Power: Institutions and Civil-Military Relations in Argentina.* University Park, Pa.: Penn State University Press, 1997.

Powers, Nancy. *Grassroots Expectations of Democracy and Economy: Argentina in Comparative Perspective.* Pittsburgh, Pa.: University of Pittsburgh Press, 2001.

Sawers, Larry. *The Other Argentina: The Interior and National Development.* Boulder, Colo.: Westview, 1996.

Smith, William. *Authoritarianism and the Crisis of the Argentine Political Economy,* rev. ed. Stanford, Calif.: Stanford University Press, 1991.

Tulchin, Joseph, and Allison Garland, eds. *Argentina: The Challenges of Modernization.* Wilmington, Del.: Scholarly Resources, 1998.

Ungar, Mark. *Elusive Reform: Democracy and the Rule of Law in Latin America.* Boulder, Colo.: Lynne Rienner, 2002.

Endnote

1. Guillermo O'Donnell, *Modernization and Bureaucratic-Authoritarianism* (Berkeley: University of California, 1973), pp. 167–192.

Brazil

CHAPTER 6

Brazil

L UIZ INÁCIO "LULA" DA SILVA has experienced many of the varied realities of Brazilian society over the past half century. He was born in October 1945, when the dictatorship led by Getúlio Vargas was coming to a close. He spent his early childhood in rural northeastern Brazil, the most impoverished region of the country. His mother moved the family to the outskirts of São Paulo in 1952 in search of greater economic opportunities for her eight children. After the family relocated to the megacity of São Paulo, Lula da Silva—like a majority of Brazilians—entered the workforce at an early age (twelve years old). Although he did not complete his formal education, Da Silva (unlike his parents) stayed in school long enough to become literate. He entered a steel mill at age fourteen. In his spare time, he completed a three-year technical degree that improved his job prospects.

The formative political experience of his youth was the 1964 military coup that ended two decades of democratic rule. During the dictatorship that followed, Lula da Silva and one of his older brothers joined a labor union in 1968, and over time Lula became a leader of the metalworkers union in greater São Paulo. In the late 1970s, he and other union leaders organized the first major industrial strikes in Brazil in over a decade. In the process, he was imprisoned and became a symbol of rising opposition to continued military rule.

As Brazil began a transition toward civilian rule in the early 1980s, Da Silva helped to found a leftist political party, the Workers' Party (*Partido dos Trabalhadores* [PT]). Amid discontent with continuing economic instability and worsening economic inequality in the late 1980s, Da Silva became a major contender in the 1989 presidential elections—the first direct presidential elections in three decades. In the campaign, Da Silva blamed many of the country's problems on collaboration among wealthy Brazilians, foreign corporations and banks, and the International Monetary Fund (IMF). This critique struck a chord with many working-class Brazilians. Da Silva lost in a runoff election, but he had become the primary figure on the Brazilian political left. Over the next decade, Lula da

Silva remained critical of conditions in Brazil, but he and several other leaders in the PT began to modify their policy recommendations. They spoke less of economic nationalization and repudiation of the foreign debt. Instead, they talked more frequently about the need for a state capitalist model in which considerable use of market mechanisms could be combined with government-led efforts at poverty reduction. The PT vote gradually increased in the 1990s.

As Brazil faced a series of economic difficulties in the early twenty-first century, the PT held considerable support in public opinion polls. In the 2002 presidential campaign, Da Silva made further changes in his image and his message: he began to wear business suits on the campaign trail and reassured investors in and out of Brazil that he would not pursue radical change. He handily won the elections, but his victory crystallized the public debate. Would his government reduce poverty without endangering investment and/or political stability? Or would his government tread so cautiously in pursuit of economic and political stability that long-festering problems of poverty, inequality, crime, and political discontent would continue unabated?

From an analytical perspective, it is decidedly unreasonable to place responsibility for the path of the entire country on the head of the government. From a symbolic perspective, however, Lula da Silva's election in October 2002 represented a crossroads for the political center-left in Latin America and beyond: what set of actions might constitute an economically and politically viable alternative to the market-oriented Washington Consensus that dominated the policy debate for much of the 1990s? Brazil's status as the largest country in Latin America further heightened the focus on the Da Silva government.

To understand these contemporary challenges, we will look at the past two centuries of Brazil's history as the country attempts to realize its goal of becoming a world power. While some might see that goal as unrealistic, one must note that Brazil is one of the largest countries in the world. Its immense territory (nearly half of South America) makes it the fifth largest country in terms of geographic size. Its population of 178 million inhabitants was the fifth largest in the world in 2003. Brazil also has considerable economic importance as one of the ten largest economies in the world, with a gross domestic product (GDP) of $1.3 trillion in 2002.

HISTORICAL BACKGROUND FROM 1889 TO 1985

Brazil established a monarchy after attaining its independence from Portugal in 1822. The Brazilian Empire launched by Portuguese crown prince Dom Pedro, and continued under his son Dom Pedro II, came under increasing pressure from the spread of liberal political ideals within Brazil and across Latin America. In 1889, a bloodless coup ended the Empire and gave rise to the creation of an oligarchic democracy. As in neighboring Argentina, the path toward democratic consolidation in Brazil would prove rocky.

The First Republic (1889–1930)

Landed interests were the central players in the oligarchic democracy established in the late nineteenth century. Similar to the network of regional conservative parties found in Argentina at the time, various state political parties in Brazil united under the banner of the Republican party. The electoral machines in Brazil's two largest and most prosperous states, São Paulo and Minas Gerais, led this loose alliance. In exchange for the support of politicians in smaller states, the leaders of the *paulista* and *mineiro* machines pledged not to intervene too much in state-level politics. Because of the autonomy of state governments, many refer to this period as the politics of the governors. At the national level, the two major political machines agreed to share power from one election to the next in the *cafe com leite* ("coffee with milk") coalition named after the major agricultural products in São Paulo and Minas Gerais. This so-called alternating presidency continued until 1930. From 1910 on, however, those who felt excluded from the political process increasingly demanded political change.

During this era, Brazil pursued a laissez-faire economic policy based on the export of raw materials and the import of finished goods. The motto placed on the new Brazilian flag—order and progress—summed up the government's positivist approach to development. An expansion of trade transformed society over the course of the first three decades of the twentieth century. International and domestic commerce fanned ambitions that Brazil could convert its enormous territory and considerable natural resources into expanding economic and political power on the world scene. Reform-minded politicians began to call for government-sponsored industrialization as the next economic development goal. Many landed interests greeted such calls with opposition, ranging from skepticism to outright hostility.

This debate came to a head in the 1930 presidential campaign. The *cafe com leite* coalition collapsed when the São Paulo machine refused to back the pro-industrialization candidate of the Minas Gerais machine, Getúlio Vargas. After the election, Vargas claimed that fraud kept him from defeating his *paulista* opponent. Nationalist elements of the military that shared Vargas's interest in industrialization launched a coup that placed Vargas in power.

Getúlio Vargas and the New State (1930–1945)

Like Juan Perón a decade later in Argentina, Vargas presented himself as a national savior who would transform Brazil's economy for the good of all. In every state except Minas Gerais, the Vargas government replaced the elected governors with appointees. When a non-*paulista* was named the new governor of São Paulo, the *paulista* elite launched a revolt in July 1932 with the assistance of some military officers who had been discharged for opposing the 1930 coup. The Vargas government launched a siege of São Paulo in which the city itself was not invaded; in October, the rebels ended their secession. Vargas rewarded the federal military with a substantial increase in its budget. In victory, Vargas pledged to pay half of the rebels' war debts and announced plans to build a new major university in São Paulo. This victory over the secessionists—along with Vargas's hands-on approach to combating the Great Depression and his folksy, understated public image—buttressed his popular support. Vargas's supporters dominated the Constituent Assembly, which was elected to write a new constitution.

The 1934 constitution presented a mixed set of developments regarding the democratization of politics in Brazil. On one hand, it established national electoral authority to oversee the entire process, from voter registration through vote tallying. The secret ballot was introduced and voting became compulsory. Voting rights were extended: the voting age fell to eighteen years, and Brazil became one of the first countries in Latin America to grant women voting rights on an equal footing with men. However, universal suffrage was not yet in place because Brazil retained a literacy requirement that blocked a substantial majority of its citizens from voting.

On the other hand, the 1934 constitution reflected Vargas's efforts to centralize authority. The national government gained some powers previously in the hands of the states, while the president gained some additional power relative to the legislature. The new constitution also redefined the government's relationship to the private sector by shifting from interest group **pluralism** toward **corporatism** (see *Concepts in Action: Pluralist and Corporatist Interest Group Politics*). The multitude of existing labor unions was reorganized into a single national confederation, and business associations were similarly required to join a single national business confederation. Vargas portrayed himself paternalistically as the father of the nation who would resolve conflicts between labor and business or elsewhere in society.

In 1934, the Constituent Assembly elected Vargas president to a four-year term. As in the prior constitution, the immediate reelection of the president was prohibited. Vargas continued his effort to promote state capitalism, but he faced political opposition from two distinct political parties that hated each other even more than they opposed Vargas. On the left, the Brazilian Communist Party (*Partido Comunista Brasileiro* [PCB]) organized a multiparty popular front, the National Freedom Alliance (*Aliança Nacional Libertadora* [ANL]). On the right, fascist sympathizers organized the *Partido Integralista* as a bulwark against the advance of leftist ideologies. Leftists and fascists at times clashed with each other on the streets. Vargas's government declared the ANL illegal in mid-1935. When communists launched a military revolt in three major garrisons in November, the revolt was smashed and Vargas declared martial law. These powers were used to move against Vargas's leftist opponents and also to block other rivals. The 1938 presidential campaign between Vargas's chosen standard-bearer, José Américo de Almeida, and his *paulista* opponent, Armando Salles de Oliveira, began amid government propaganda stressing Vargas's role in suppressing various disruptive elements.

CONCEPTS IN ACTION
Pluralist and Corporatist Interest Group Politics

All societies have interest groups, but the relationship between interest groups and government varies across countries. In pluralist countries (such as the United States, the United Kingdom, and Chile), interest groups organize independently and compete against one another. The government interacts with nongovernmental organizations but does not intervene in these groups' activities in a systematic fashion. The extent of an interest group's influence on the policy-making process in a pluralist system often depends on its resources, such as its ability to raise funds, its personal connections to governmental officials, its expertise, and its ability to mobilize public opinion.

In corporatist political systems, fewer interest groups participate in the political process, and the relationship between groups and the government is often institutionalized and quite explicit. Typically, in each of the major interest sectors (for example, labor, farmers, government workers, and—at times—business), one large confederation encompasses the entire sector and coordinates the demands of its member organizations and speaks authoritatively for them in negotiations with the government. These encompassing groups usually are incorporated into the official policy-making process as members of a state council or committee that is consulted when making and implementing policy.

In several northern European countries, these large, encompassing confederations emerged gradually over time. Over the first half of the twentieth century, they gained inclusion in the policy-making process based on their ability to represent most groups in their sector. In contrast, fascist-influenced governments in southern Europe used the power of government to create a single confederation in each sector by rewriting the laws framing interest group organization. Scholars use the term *societal corporatism* to refer to the gradual emergence of interest group organization; government-imposed corporatism is often called *state corporatism*.

In the middle third of the twentieth century, the three largest Latin American economies—Argentina, Brazil, and Mexico—experimented with state corporatism. Similar to such efforts in southern Europe, the rhetoric of state corporatism in Latin America emphasized the search for societal harmony—at the expense of the freedom of association. State corporatist governments claimed that an organized community could avoid the divisive debates they associated with pluralist interest group competition and also block the growth of trade unions with ties to leftist political parties.

In Brazil, Getúlio Vargas spearheaded laws that forced all existing business associations to join a newly created National Confederation of Industry. In turn, labor unions fell subject to an even more sweeping reorganization that went beyond the creation of a single national labor confederation. In addition to outlawing rival labor confederations, the government reserved the right to veto candidates for union leadership positions and to outlaw strikes. The Ministry of Labor collected mandatory union dues from all workers—regardless of whether they were union members. The ministry could then use its control over union finances to punish unions that did not support the government. Unions in the urban economy gained financial resources they had never thought possible. Similar to labor unions in Peronist Argentina, however, the union leaders lost their independence from the government.

On November 10, 1937, legislators arrived at work to find the Brazilian congress surrounded by government troops. That evening, Getúlio Vargas announced the suspension of the upcoming elections, the abolition of the legislature, and the creation of a New State (*Estado Novo*) in which he would remain president. He rationalized his actions as a response to political and economic disorder. Although Vargas presented plans to hold a plebiscite in which voters could ratify a revised constitution, this plebiscite never took place. The new constitution declared a permanent state of emergency in which the president could order searches without warrant, censor the media, and exile citizens deemed dangerous. New presidential elections were scheduled for 1943. The president gained the authority to fire unilaterally any civilian government official as well as the power to retire any military officer deemed a threat to national interests. With the Brazilian congress dissolved, executive and legislative authority was centralized in Vargas's hands.

In the New State era, Vargas emphasized two major themes: economic nationalism and national security. The *integralistas* supported the proscription of the communist movement in the name of security, but their own hopes for increased influence were not realized. Several fascists responded to this disappointment by launching a failed coup attempt in 1938. Government repression increased, and most of the remaining opposition to Vargas went into hiding or fled in exile. The outbreak of World War II allowed Vargas to supplement his previous image as savior of the nation during the 1930s depression by cultivating the look of a world statesman. He courted U.S. support by joining the Allied effort to defeat the Axis powers during World War II. Brazil was the only Latin American country to send combat troops to fight in Europe. These foreign policy decisions brought U.S. military aid designed to retain the support of the Brazilian armed forces.

Nevertheless, Vargas's prolonged stay in power created a lengthening list of civilian and military enemies, particularly among large landowners critical of government-led industrialization. Opposition increased further when Vargas, citing the emergency posed by World War II, suspended the 1943 elections. By 1944, a combination of civilian and military pressure forced him to call elections to be held after the end of the war. New political parties formed in 1945. Vargas's opponents united in the National Democratic Union (*União Democrática Nacional* [UDN]). His supporters organized two new parties. Politicians associated with Vargas's movement in the executive branch and in state politics led the Social Democratic Party (*Partido Social Democrático* [PSD]). Urban labor unions became key players in the Brazilian Labor Party

(*Partido Trabalhista Brasileiro* [PTB]). Another political movement emerged in 1945 to stage public protests urging Vargas to stay in office. Vargas neither publicly endorsed nor disassociated himself with this "we want Getúlio" (*queremos Getúlio*) movement.

The *queremistas* raised suspicions in the UDN and elsewhere that Vargas had called on some supporters in the labor movement to orchestrate this call for a continuation of the New State. The UDN's presidential candidate was one of Vargas's two key generals, Eurico Dutra. Senior officers became even more concerned when massive labor protests on October 17, 1945, in Buenos Aires embarrassed the Argentine high command into releasing Juan Perón. Later that month, the Brazilian army gave Vargas an ultimatum: resign or face a coup. Vargas stepped down (and subsequently was elected to the legislature in the December 1945 elections).

The Second Republic (1945–1964)

The 1945 bloodless coup ended the New State dictatorship but it did not significantly change the balance of forces visible during Vargas's tenure in office. Populist appeals to government-subsidized industrialization as the path to national development still proved persuasive with a majority of voters, while the parties most closely tied to landed interests controlled a minority of the legislature throughout the Second Republic. For this reason, many observers refer to this period as one of competitive populism in which various parties and political leaders (including Vargas himself) curried favor with voters using similar appeals.

The politics of the Second Republic manifested four major dynamics that would also prove important later in the Brazilian democracy of the late twentieth and early twenty-first centuries. One key element was the use of an open-list proportional representation electoral system. Most countries in Latin America use proportional representation (PR) for legislative elections, thereby permitting a wide variety of parties some presence in the legislature. Brazil's open-list variant of the PR system gives voters more freedom to choose their favorite candidates while also making the victorious candidates more independent from the party leadership (review *Concepts in Action: Plurality Versus Proportional Representation* in Chapter Five). Second, a wide variety of parties with regional strongholds won seats in the legislature, thereby reducing the weight of the political parties with a larger nationwide electoral base. Third, the combination of diverse voter preferences and an open-list PR system tended to produce decidedly divided legislatures. As many as thirteen political parties held seats in Second Republic legislatures. Fourth, rural states were overrepresented in the Chamber of Deputies, even though each state in theory should be represented by population (as in the U.S. House of Representatives and the Argentine Chamber of Deputies).

Divisions in the electorate made their presence felt in presidential elections because the Second Republic produced presidents whose parties controlled a minority of the seats in the legislature. This state of affairs frequently produced gridlock during Eurico Dutra's administration. Dutra's presidency unfolded within the context of a Cold War policy in which Brazil severed diplomatic relations with the Soviet Union and outlawed the Brazilian Communist party (which had finished third in the 1945 presidential elections with 10 percent of the vote). Economic policy was largely deadlocked under Dutra, a situation that aided a spectacular return to the presidency by Getúlio Vargas, who won nearly 49 percent of the vote in the 1950 elections.

Vargas campaigned as a man of action capable of transcending the differences among parties and personalities in the legislature. Once elected, however, Vargas—who had governed without legislative interference in his prior presidency—found it difficult to build a legislative majority in support of many of his initiatives. The major policy debate centered on his proposal to create a new petroleum company (*Petrobrás*) with a mix of public and private ownership; the proposed venture would enjoy a monopoly over oil exploration and extraction. Conservatives called the proposal an intrusion on private property that would put the country on a path toward socialism. Leftist activists claimed that government employees were on the payroll of foreign oil companies and that the administration's willingness to support a role for the private sector constituted a sellout of the nation's interest. The military was also bitterly divided: anticommunist officers sided with conservative legislators while pro-industrialization officers pushed for Vargas's proposal. For two years, debate raged in Congress and Vargas found himself caught in the middle. Much to his surprise, the UDN legislators eventually embraced the creation of a publicly owned monopoly—hoping to steal from Vargas his claim to be the foremost defender of economic nationalism. The experience drained Vargas and demonstrated that he did not have much control over the legislative process, even on the policy issue he had spent the most time promoting.

Beyond this conflict, corruption scandals, rising media attacks by anti-Vargas forces, and pressure from some within the military began to isolate and frustrate Vargas. Events reached a boiling point when his bodyguard was implicated in arranging a failed assassination attempt against Vargas's most visible critic—UDN activist and journalist Carlos Lacerda. An increasingly depressed Vargas remarked, "I feel like I am standing in a sea of mud."[1] On August 24, 1954, he held a cabinet meeting dedicated to discussing his options: should he resign or should he stay in office? If he chose to remain in office, how might he reverse the current state of affairs? After the meeting, Vargas went to his bedroom and shot himself. He left behind an open letter in which he painted himself as a well-meaning politician who had tried to make Brazil better. Through his suicide, Vargas reversed the tide of public opinion: his critics became the new targets of public outrage in the weeks that followed.

The winner of the subsequent presidential elections, Juscelino Kubitschek, was another double-minority president (see *Governing Strategies: Juscelino Kubitschek*)—Kubitschek was elected with 36 percent of the vote while his PDS

GOVERNING STRATEGIES
Juscelino Kubitschek

Juscelino Kubitschek began his professional career as a doctor but later became a government administrator. In 1950, he won election as governor of his home state of Minas Gerais and then set his sights on the presidency. In the 1955 presidential campaign, Kubitschek called for rapid state-led development. His principal slogan—50 years in 5—reflected the scope of his policy ambitions. Kubitschek won election with 36 percent of the vote; his PSD party controlled around one-third of the lower house. As a double-minority president, he confronted multiple obstacles to realizing his campaign promises.

Kubitschek worked on many fronts to build political support. When air force officers launched an unsuccessful rebellion shortly after his inauguration, Kubitschek pardoned them. He then limited military discontent by modernizing military weaponry. The centerpiece of his governance strategy, however, was his thirty-one-point Program of Goals. Kubitschek disarmed opponents on the political left and on the political right by pursuing a diverse set of objectives through a mix of public and private initiatives. Government built up the transportation infrastructure and it provided fiscal incentives for private investment in manufacturing and agriculture. New development projects crisscrossed Brazil: this use of pork-barrel politics enabled Kubitschek to build a legislative coalition. The most enduring industrialization project involved the creation of an automobile industry that would prove central to Brazil's future economic growth.

The last objective listed on Kubitschek's Program of Goals was the construction of a new federal capital, Brasilia. The transfer of the capital from Rio to the center of Brazil had languished on the political back burner in Brazil since its inclusion in the 1891 constitution. Kubitschek approved a futuristic design for the city in which the layout of the government district took the shape of an airplane when viewed from overhead. Brasilia's inauguration in April 1960 celebrated a reinvigorated Brazil. The first half of the 1950s was characterized by Brazil's upset losses in two soccer World Cups and Vargas's suicide. In contrast, the presidency of JK (Juscelino Kubitschek) witnessed rapid economic growth, a 1958 World Cup triumph, and a worldwide interest in the *bossa nova* musical movement.

Nevertheless, storm clouds were gathering. Kubitschek financed his agenda with a mix of deficit spending, foreign loans, and loose monetary policy. As prices increased and pressure rose on the Brazilian currency, Kubitschek agreed to an IMF loan program in 1958 that called for visible spending cuts. He then salvaged his domestic agenda by refusing to implement the promised budget cuts. This proved popular with many Brazilians but also ensured that inflation would be a major issue in the 1960 elections.

Kubitschek left office as perhaps the most popular president in Brazilian history. He won a Senate seat and planned another run for the presidency. The 1964 military coup ended his hopes when the military government banned Kubitschek from political activity for ten years. His political career had ended, but his legend had just begun to grow. In 2001, a new biography on Juscelino Kubitschek described his audacious approach to governance as follows: politics as the art of the impossible.[1]

[1]Cláudio Bojunga, *JK, o artista do impossível* (Rio de Janeiro, Brazil: Objetiva, 2001).

party held just over one-third of the seats in Congress. While many initially questioned his ability to govern on the heels of the stalemate under Dutra and Vargas, Kubitschek built a legislative coalition through the aggressive use of **pork-barrel politics** that funneled government money into the districts of legislators who supported his programs. He gained legislative support through this approach, but government revenues did not keep pace with the rise in expenditures. Toward the end of his term, some hailed Juscelino Kubitschek as Brazil's greatest president for pulling the country out of the mire associated with Vargas's suicide. In turn, his critics emphasized rising inflation rates and reports of corruption in bidding for public works contracts.

In the 1960 elections, Jãnio Quadros won 48 percent of the vote by promising to clean up Brazilian politics and to end inflation. Quadros capitalized on his outsider image by handing out small brooms that symbolized his campaign theme of clean government. (You might recall that Arnold Schwarzenegger used the same tactic in his successful campaign for governor of California in October 2003.) To dramatize his independent persona, during the campaign Quadros renounced his nomination as a UDN candidate and ran as the official candidate of a small party. Once in office, he quickly discovered that it would be hard to change executive-legislative relations, especially because the largest party supporting his candidacy controlled just over one-fifth of the seats in the legislature. Many of the politicians directly or indirectly attacked in Quadros's campaign speeches enjoyed the opportunity to block presidential initiatives. In response, a frustrated Quadros abruptly resigned after just seven months in office. Quadros apparently hoped that this dramatic gesture would inspire a new wave of popular and legislative support. Instead, the legislature simply accepted Quadros's resignation.

That resignation ignited a series of events that both illustrated and increased the level of political conflict in Brazil. When Quadros resigned, Vice President João Goulart was on a state visit to the People's Republic of China. Goulart had been elected vice president in 1960 because Brazilian law at the time provided for a separate election for the vice presidency (as occurs in lieutenant governorship elections in several U.S. states to this day). Goulart was a protégé of Vargas, who had resigned as vice president in the prior decade amid controversy over his proposal to double the minimum wage and to organize rural workers. Conservatives seized on the China visit to reopen the charge that Goulart was a leftist unfit to serve as president. This effort to block Goulart's inauguration took place in a tense Cold War atmosphere in which some viewed the Cuban revolutionary government formed in 1959 as a threat. After lengthy negotiations, Goulart agreed to the immediate creation of a parliamentary system in which powers normally accorded to the president would be given to a prime minister elected by and responsible to the legislature. The accord also scheduled a plebiscite for 1963 in which the Brazilian public could decide whether to maintain the new parliamentary system or to return to a presidential system in which Goulart's powers would be restored. Goulart vowed to campaign vigorously for that plebiscite and, in the end, Brazilians voted to return to presidentialism.

Goulart argued that landed interests impeded his attempts to help the poor. As tensions rose on both sides, the uncertain political situation stifled economic activity: investment fell and inflation rose. Stories about a brewing revolt by leftists and of a coup plotted by anticommunist officers circulated with increasing frequency as 1963 wore on. In March 1964, Goulart tried to seize the initiative with decrees designed to launch two controversial measures: land reform and the nationalization of privately owned oil refineries. As rumors circulated that he might form a citizens' militia to defend his administration (and perhaps try to extend his term à la the New State), a military coup begun on March 31 forced Goulart's removal on April 1, 1964.

Bureaucratic-Authoritarian Rule (1964–1985)

Unlike prior military coups in Brazil, a substantial number of military officers did not want to call new elections as quickly as possible. In the internal debate within the armed forces, these hard-liners harshly criticized so-called soft-liners who supported a quick return to electoral politics. Hard-liners argued that the contentious dynamics of civilian politics would make the country increasingly vulnerable to communist takeover. While internal divisions regarding a return to free elections would continue throughout the military government established in 1964, the hard-liner perspective would help to motivate Latin America's first bureaucratic-authoritarian regime to stay in power for over two decades. Over the course of the 1960s, the military government abolished all existing political parties, eventually replacing them with a progovernment party, the Alliance for National Renewal (*Aliança Renovadora Nacional* [ARENA]) and a single opposition party subject to considerable constraints, the Brazilian Democratic Movement (*Movimento Democrático Brasileiro* [MDB]). These parties competed for seats in a greatly weakened legislature, while the military retained the reins of power within the executive branch.

The military regime publicly justified its hold on power on two grounds. First, it claimed that the suppression of basic civil and human rights would purge society of potential communist influences. Second, the military government asserted that silencing civilian politicians would pave the way to better economic performance. During the late 1960s and early 1970s, the Brazilian

military made good on both promises—albeit through the use of exile, detention without trial, and torture. The repressive tactics wiped out both violent and
nonviolent leftist-inspired political movements. Meanwhile, a booming world
economy and aggressive use of government subsidies and tax incentives
spurred the so-called Brazilian economic miracle, in which the economy grew
by an average of 10.9 percent annually during the years 1968–1974.

Over the course of its second decade in power, the military found it increasingly difficult to defend its continuation in power on the twin pillars of its justification for the 1964 coup. On the political front, any potential danger of a
leftist takeover had passed. Critics of this justification for the coup would point
out that the guerrilla movements crushed in the late 1960s and early 1970s had
formed in rebellion against the dictatorship; no major guerrilla movements
were in place at the time of the 1964 coup. The annihilation of the left made it
even more difficult than before to justify the continued suppression of civil and
political liberties. When the Geisel administration (1974–1979) implemented
a limited restoration of civil liberties, regime opponents used the new political
space to criticize the military's unwillingness to restore free elections for the
presidency. On the economic front, the oil price hikes of the 1970s motivated
the military government to borrow increasingly large sums of money to avoid a
recession. An increasing portion of these loans was contracted at variable rates
of interest tied primarily to U.S. financial indicators. When U.S. interest rates
rose during the world recession of the early 1980s, the Brazilian foreign debt
grew from $71 billion in 1980 to $94 billion in 1982.

Spiraling economic problems and the increasing boldness of the organized
opposition to military rule set into motion negotiations for a transition to democratic rule. The leader of the civilian opposition, Tancredo Neves, brokered
several agreements designed to broaden the prodemocracy coalition while
simultaneously reassuring military officers that he would oppose the initiation
of human rights trials investigating abuses alleged during the military regime.
This negotiated transition paved the way for a return to civilian rule in 1985 via
indirect elections in which the existing legislature would choose a civilian president. Neves convinced a portion of the promilitary party to break away and
support his candidacy. In exchange, Neves chose as his vice president a leader
of the breakaway faction, José Sarney.

All of Neves's hard work helped him to win the presidency, but he never took
office. He fell seriously ill on the eve of his inauguration and had emergency
surgery performed in Brasilia, in a chaotic atmosphere in which the sterility of
the operating room was thrown into question. Sarney was sworn in as acting
president while a team of physicians struggled through a series of surgeries that
failed to restore Neves to good health. Tancredo Neves died on April 21, 1985.
People debated whether the central cause of death was cancer or whether he
died as a result of infections incurred during the initial emergency surgery. One
issue was beyond debate: Brazil was returning to civilian rule under an accidental president.

CONTEMPORARY POLITICAL FRAMEWORK

Brazil's contemporary institutions were created by the Constituent Assembly held after Brazil's return to civilian rule in 1985. After the death of Neves, many legislators seemed willing to govern under the 1967 constitution drafted during military rule. A diverse set of interest groups and opposition political parties lobbied for the election of a constituent assembly to write a new constitution. The Sarney government compromised: Congress accepted his proposal to have the next legislature serve as the Constituent Assembly during 1987–1988. After the completion of the 1988 constitution, more than twenty amendments were passed in the 1990s, and many more potential reforms have been discussed. Government officials and citizens alike tend to refer to Brazil's contemporary political system as the New Republic.

One of the major expansions of liberty associated with the 1988 constitution was the extension of suffrage to all Brazilians sixteen years of age and older. Another visible change involved the inclusion of many socioeconomic provisions that past constitutions had left to the legislature. The new constitution also called for considerable fiscal decentralization: roughly half of all government revenues came under the control of state and local governments. One central element of past constitutions initially remained intact, despite the opposition of leftist parties: the military retained a clause calling on it to defend against the possibility of invasion *and* against internal disorder. This provision raised concerns that the military could infringe on liberties with little or no civilian supervision.

Another series of debates in the Constituent Assembly concerned efforts to avoid the difficulties associated with double-minority presidencies (review *Governing Strategies: Fernando Belaúnde* in Chapter Four). Some argued that adoption of a **parliamentary system** could avoid these problems by ensuring that the chief executive held the support of a legislative majority. Others countered that a parliamentary system would produce turnstile governments in which divided legislatures would frequently remove prime ministers and their cabinets; these critics of parliamentary systems offered ballotage election of the presidency as an alternative path toward avoiding double-minority presidencies. Eventually the Constituent Assembly voted to retain the presidential system but authorized a plebiscite in which voters could call for a shift toward either parliamentary politics or toward monarchy. In 1993, voters chose to retain a presidential system.

The Executive Branch

Brazilian presidents historically have been denied the possibility of reelection, and the 1988 constitution retained that prohibition. Various presidents during the New Republic discussed the possibility of a constitutional change to permit reelection. In 1997, on the heels of similar changes in neighboring Argentina and Peru, President Fernando Henrique Cardoso successfully promoted an amendment that removed the prohibition on immediate reelection. Presidents now serve a maximum of two consecutive four-year terms. The electoral system established by the 1988 constitution was left unchanged: the ballotage system chosen to eliminate the possibility of a double-minority president was retained. If no candidate gains a majority of the votes in first-round presidential elections, a second-round runoff is held between the two candidates who received the most votes in the first round.

The Brazilian presidency can be called proactive within the analytical framework developed by Mainwaring and Shugart (review Table 4.6). The president holds several agenda-setting capabilities yet has a weak veto that can be overridden by a majority vote in a joint session of both chambers of the legislature. The 1987–1988 Constituent Assembly intentionally reduced the sweeping presidential powers created by the military government in the late 1960s. The 1988 constitution eliminated the option of legislating by decree. Instead, the president's decree powers are capable of setting the agenda because the decrees have the force of law for a maximum of thirty days (unless the legislature acts more quickly to overturn the decree). This stipulation enables presidents to launch new policy initiatives and then force the legislature to respond within a short time to these decrees. Should the president choose to take a slightly less confrontational approach to agenda-setting, the president is empowered to submit his or her own bills directly to the legislature in a procedure that forces the legislature to vote on the proposal within forty-five days. The president also enjoys the exclusive ability to propose legislation to raise revenues (either by raising tax rates or by creating new taxes). These various capabilities give the president tools to manage the legislative timetable, while the weak veto reduces the ability of the president to block legislation that he or she opposes.

The Legislature

Like most Latin American countries, Brazil has a bicameral legislature. The lower house, the Chamber of Deputies, has a membership that, in theory, represents each Brazilian state according to population size. In practice, however, the rural states have been overrepresented since the 1940s and remain so to this day. For example, in the rural state of Roraima, 186,000 voters elect eight deputies (one legislator for every 23,000 voters); in Brazil's largest state (São Paulo), roughly 24 million voters elect seventy deputies (one legislator for every 342,000 voters).[2] Deputies serve four-year terms; since 1994, the entire chamber has come up for election in terms concurrent with the president. Deputies are elected via open-list proportional representation (PR) elections (review *Concepts in Action: Plurality Versus Proportional Representation* in Chapter Five). As discussed in Chapter Five, this electoral system creates a mix of intraparty and interparty competition that tends to produce legislators who act with greater independence from the party leadership than would be found in countries with closed-list PR elections.

The upper house, the Senate, consists of three members from each state. Senators serve eight-year terms with one-third or two-thirds of each state's senators standing for election every four years. In contrast to the lower house elections, senatorial elections use a plurality system. As a result, the Senate tends to have fewer parties represented but a similar lack of party discipline because senators view their electoral chances as tied more closely to their own image and actions than to those of the parties they represent.

This electoral system has worked to produce a different set of common complaints about the Brazilian legislature than one has seen historically in Argentina. In Argentina, recent calls for reform criticize the closed-list electoral system for generating legislators more accountable to party leaders than to the voters. In Brazil, however, one observes the opposite: scholars, presidents, and citizens frequently complain that the mix of open-list PR and plurality elections makes legislators so independent of the party leaders that the process of governance becomes extremely complicated. In the historical overview section of this chapter, we observed how Juscelino Kubitschek and other presidents used pork-barrel politics to promote their legislative agendas. In the second half of this chapter, we will examine the various governance strategies used by contemporary Brazilian presidents.

The Judiciary

Unlike the Argentine judiciary, the Brazilian court system looks more like the prevailing trend in Latin America and Europe. A separate constitutional court, the Supreme Federal Court, exercises the power of judicial review, yet it is not the highest court in the land for other matters. The Supreme Federal Court consists of eleven members appointed by the president and confirmed by a majority vote in the Senate.

The Superior Court of Justice serves as the highest court on most matters. This court consists of a large panel of judges, thirty-three in all, from which a smaller subset are chosen to review each individual case. The president appoints these justices from within the existing judiciary, and these appointments must be confirmed by a majority in the Senate. These judicial posts—along with all other federal and state judgeships—enjoy lifetime tenure following an initial probationary period of two years.

POLITICAL PARTICIPATION

Brazilian political life has been in an almost constant state of evolution, fragmentation, and reorganization for most of the twentieth century. Political parties have changed in both name and in membership over the decades, partly in response to leadership struggles and partly in response to changes in the political regime (in particular, the prolonged period of military rule and the democratic regime that followed). In contrast, organized interest groups have been able to maintain a more stable organizational profile and membership.

Interest Groups and Social Movements

Large landowners formed the backbone of Brazilian society in the nineteenth century and remain important political and economic actors to this day. Roughly 2 percent of the landowners control over half of the farmland in Brazil. In many rural areas and especially in the northeast, landowners employ traditional machine politics through political bosses known as colonels (*coroneis* in Brazilian political slang). As suffrage expanded during the Second Republic and then became universal in the contemporary New Republic era, landowners have organized more explicitly to protect their interests. In response to a renewed push for agrarian reform toward the end of the military regime, several existing landowners' organizations united in 1985 to form the Rural Democratic Union (*União Democrática Ruralista* [UDR]). The UDR worked hard during the New Republic to establish a formal agricultural caucus that has tended to represent about one-third of the legislature. The UDR has been a controversial group because its members have been implicated in the use of paramilitary security forces to intimidate and at times to murder political activists who threaten their interests.

In contrast to the agricultural sector, manufacturing interests have continued to use the corporatist confederations established in each state under the government of Getúlio Vargas in 1938. Each state has an industrial confederation, and these state groups are all members of the National Confederation of Industry (*Confederação Nacional da Indústria* [CNI]). Within this confederation, the most important of voice for the industrial sector has tended to be the São Paulo State Federation of Industries (*Federação das Indústrias do Estado de São Paulo* [FIESP]). From the 1930s through the 1980s, the CNI and most of its member firms tended to support the extensive use of state capitalist economic policies to nurture industrialization. Since then, the official position of the CNI has shifted to support more market-oriented economic policies, albeit with an eye toward government assistance in various circumstances.

The Brazilian labor movement was relatively small until the Vargas era. Under Vargas, industrial promotion policies and efforts to regulate interest groups among corporatist lines changed the face of organized labor. Similar to reforms later implemented by Juan Perón in Argentina, the Vargas government required all workers to pay union dues and organized each economic sector into a single, legally recognized labor federation; these federations, in turn, all became members of the General Confederation of Workers (*Confederacão Geral dos Trabalhadores* [CGT]), which was formally established in 1945. The labor movement was repressed during the military regime and only began to rejuvenate itself in the late 1970s under a new generation of leaders on the center-left—personified most visibly by Lula da Silva. In 1983, Lula and others established the Lone Workers Central (*Central Única dos Trabalhadores* [CUT]) which would become the most important labor confederation in the New Republic. In response, the CGT reorganized itself in 1986 and developed ties with the *Partido do Movimento Democrático Brasileiro* (PMDB), which was the new name for the MDB political party that had led the democratization movement from within the legislature during the military regime.

Perhaps the most visible nontraditional social movement in contemporary Brazil is the Landless Movement (*Movimento Sem Terra* [MST]). The first wave of land reform advocates in the 1950s and early 1960s were forced underground after the 1964 military coup. The MST has its roots in a series of land occupations in the late 1970s. As the political transition advanced, agrarian activists from around the country organized in the National Encounter of the Landless in 1984 and formally launched the MST. In addition to lobbying the government for agrarian reform and rural development aid for impoverished rural Brazilians, the MST seizes unoccupied land in an effort to establish title. At times, the MST seizes unused land of high-profile Brazilians in an effort to draw government and media attention to their cause. In 2002, the MST occupied land owned by then-president Fernando Henrique Cardoso. Because of the confrontational tactics the MST has employed increasingly since the mid-1990s and because of resistance to land reform among wealthy Brazilians, the MST and its leaders have been subject over the years to a combination of arrest, criminal charges, and illegal intimidation from paramilitary organizations established by landowners.

Brazil is also home to one of the most visible environmental movements in Latin America. Air and water pollution are major concerns in urban areas around the globe, and the Brazilian megacities—Rio de Janeiro (11 million inhabitants) and São Paulo (18 million inhabitants)—are not exempt from these trends. The presence of most of the Amazon rainforest within Brazilian territory provides additional impetus for environmental activism in Brazil. Tropical rainforests play a central role in regulating existing climactic patterns: they generate oxygen, produce and absorb rainfall, and prevent soil erosion. In addition, rainforests are the primary habitat to two-fifths of all bird species, two-thirds of all plant species, and four-fifths of all insects. In the Amazon alone, roughly 1 million distinct species exist. With the construction of the Transamazon Highway during the military regime, deforestation accelerated visibly and has not slowed in the New Republic. From the late 1970s onward, the Amazon has lost roughly 6,000 square miles of rainforest each year. (For comparative purposes, the land area of Connecticut is 5,500 square miles.) A diverse group of activists came forward to protect the rainforest, calling for the creation of sustainable economic pursuits that would not destroy it. In 1992, with an eye toward the U.N.-sponsored environmental summit in Rio de Janeiro, over 500 groups formed the Amazonian Working Group (*Grupo do Trabalho Amazônico* [GTA]).

The GTA remains the most visible environmental organization in Brazil to this day and has extensive ties to international nongovernmental organizations (NGOs).

Parties and Elections

Brazil's first experience with mass democracy in the middle of the twentieth century saw the emergence of many political movements capable of winning seats in the legislature. None of those parties came close to winning a majority in the legislature. The military regime criticized this multiplicity of parties as a cause (rather than as a symptom) of political division and polarization; in 1965, the military government instituted a two-party system by decree. The promilitary ARENA party (renamed the PDS in 1980) and the opposition MDB (renamed the PMDB in 1980) were the only parties competing for seats in the weakened legislature until the military permitted the creation of a few additional political parties in the early 1980s (in an effort to divide voters opposed to military rule). As we saw earlier, the PDS split into two factions when it came time for the sitting legislature to elect a civilian president to lead the return to democracy in the mid-1980s. When new legislative elections were held in 1986, the breakaway faction led by José Sarney competed as a separate entity, the Liberal Front Party (*Partido da Frente Liberal* [PFL]). As the three major political organizations in existence, the PMDB, the PFL, and the PDS won 75 percent of the seats in the lower house in the first freely held legislative elections in over two decades. In the years to come, the PDS would fade in importance, while the PFL and the PMDB would remain two of the four largest political parties in contemporary Brazilian politics.

The PFL has been the most important center-right party in Brazil since the reestablishment of democracy. The PFL has been conservative on many social issues but has not been as stridently market-oriented as parties like the UCD, AR, and MFR have been in Argentina. In turn, the PFL has been somewhat more successful electorally than Argentine conservative parties; the PFL has been the second largest party in every lower house election during the New Republic. This result stems partly from the founding role the PFL played in the return to civilian rule. At the same time, one must also note the importance of the PFL vote in rural areas that are numerically overrepresented in the Brazilian Chamber of Deputies. Despite its niche in legislative elections, to date, the PFL has not been able to generate sufficient national support to make a serious run for the presidency.

The other major party to emerge from the military regime was the *Partido do Movimento Democrático Brasileiro* (PMDB). Given the party's position as the harshest critic of military rule from within the government, the PMDB was the central actor in negotiating the transition to democracy. Despite the tragic death in 1985 of its most visible leader, president-elect Tancredo Neves, voters in the 1986 elections supported the PMDB. The party emerged with a majority of seats in the Chamber of Deputies. This initial success would erode over the next few years for two major reasons. First, the PMDB struggled to maintain its unity once its leader (Tancredo Neves) and its common enemy (the military government) were no longer present. Several figures battled for leadership of the party, and they disagreed over the centrist to center-left elements of the party's platform. Second, the return to democracy permitted the emergence of new political parties that would compete for voters (and the candidates) who had initially supported the PMDB. The party's leadership adopted a diffuse yet centrist set of policy initiatives that would alienate most of the left-leaning voters who had once supported the party. The PMDB has held its ground as one of the two largest centrist parties in Brazilian politics, yet it has been unable to mount a successful run for the presidency.

The PMDB's major challenge for the centrist vote in contemporary Brazil comes from the Brazilian Social Democratic Party (*Partido da Social Democracia Brasileira* [PSDB]). Several politicians and academics on the center-left founded the party in 1988. These founders initially launched the party as the center-left alternative positioned between PMDB in the center and a wide variety of parties on the left. Over time, the party has moved increasingly to the center, particularly once Fernando Henrique Cardoso became economic minister during the Itamar Franco government. After his reforms reduced inflation in 1994, Cardoso ran a successful presidential campaign and then won reelection in 1998. Despite rising criticism during his second government—with concerns raised from both the right and the left—the PSDB retained one-seventh of the legislature in the 2002 elections and finished second in the presidential vote.

Lula da Silva won those 2002 presidential elections in his fourth consecutive campaign as candidate of the major center-left party—the Workers' Party (*Partido dos Trabalhadores* [PT]). Da Silva and other labor leaders founded the party clandestinely in 1980 and then legally registered the party in early 1982 as the political opening of the military regime continued. At the 1991 party congress, the PT formally rejected both state socialism and pure market capitalism, arguing instead for the creation of a more progressive form of state capitalism that would reduce the income inequality that had long persisted in Brazil. As we saw at the start of this chapter, the PT moved still further toward the center in the 2002 presidential campaign as Da Silva formally promised the IMF that, if elected president, he would meet the budgetary targets set in the August 2002 IMF loan agreement with the Cardoso administration. This promise—along with the efforts of the Da Silva presidency to meet the fiscal target in early 2003—highlighted a growing rift in the PT between those supportive of this shift in the PT platform and those loyal to the PT's traditional calls for independence from IMF conditionality agreements. One of several unfolding questions regarding this presidency will be the willingness of the PT rank and file to support Da Silva's actions as president. After four PT legislators voted against pension

TABLE 6.1 Brazilian Presidential Elections (1989, 1994, 1998, and 2002): Percentage of Popular Vote in First-Round Elections

	Year			
Party	1989	1994	1998	2002
PRN	28.5*	0.6	—	—
PSDB	10.8	54.3	53.1	23.2
PT	17.0	27.0	31.7	46.4[†]
Others	43.7	18.1	15.2	30.4

*In 1989, the PRN candidate, Fernando Collor de Mello, won the presidency with 53 percent of the vote in a runoff election against PT candidate Lula da Silva (47 percent).

[†]In 2002, the PT candidate Lula da Silva won the presidency with 61 percent of the vote in a runoff election against PSDB candidate José Serra (39 percent).

SOURCE: Political Database of the Americas <http://www.georgetown.edu/pdba/Elecdata/Brazil/brazil.html> (accessed on November 14, 2003).

changes and tax reforms supported by Da Silva, the majority of the PT legislative caucus voted in December 2003 to expel those four legislators from the PT bloc in the Chamber of Deputies. This expulsion occurred despite a petition from 22,000 PT activists supporting the independent stance taken by these legislators; it remains to be seen whether this rift will grow over the course of Da Silva's presidency.

The results of all presidential elections during this period are shown in Table 6.1. The 1989 elections constituted the first direct presidential elections in three decades. While a few candidates were veteran political figures known from the prior democratic regime, many represented a new generation of political activists. Most voters had never had the opportunity before to vote for president. The election also took place in the newly instituted ballotage electoral system. Prior to the 1989 election, forty-year-old Fernando Collor de Mello had served as governor of Alagoas, a small rural state in northeastern Brazil. In a divided first-round election, Collor ran with themes reminiscent of Quadros's 1960 campaign. Like Quadros, Collor emphasized fighting inflation and eliminating corruption. He campaigned against the existing political establishment, promising to end the privileges of so-called maharajahs in the Brazilian government. Collor's telegenic appearance helped him to finish first in the first-round presidential election, with just under 29 percent of the vote. His opponent in the runoff, Lula da Silva, was the left-of-center candidate who received the most votes. Lula had an early lead in public opinion polls taken before the runoff, but most of the undecided vote eventually went to Collor in a hard-fought runoff campaign. In the end, Collor won the presidency with 53 percent of the vote in the second-round election. Subsequent presidential elections featured politicians who had established themselves already on the national scene. In 1994, Fernando Henrique Cardoso used the success of his stint as economic minister in lowering inflation to propel him to a first-round victory over Lula da Silva. Following the modification of the constitution to permit sitting presidents to run for a second consecutive term, Cardoso defeated Da Silva again in the 1998 campaign. By 2002, however, after the PSDB held the presidency for eight years, the Brazilian electorate chose Lula da Silva over Cardoso's economic minister, José Serra, in a runoff election that Da Silva won by a substantial margin.

Brazilian presidents during the New Republic have never enjoyed a partisan majority in the legislature. No sitting president's party has ever controlled more than one-fourth of the seats in the lower house; most have held between 17 and 21 percent. As a result, each president has had to try to cobble together support from other parties' legislators in an effort to build a voting majority capable of sustaining executive branch initiatives. Although the PMDB used its status as the major opposition party in place during the military regime to win control of the lower house in 1986, the political landscape became just as varied as it had been between 1945 and 1964 once additional parties had time to establish themselves. Election results in the Chamber of Deputies have varied over time, yet the presence of multiple parties and the absence of a majority party remain central features of Brazilian politics, just as they were in the democracy that followed the Vargas dictatorship (see Table 6.2). Over the years, the PMDB has been the only party to participate formally in every legislative coalition formed between 1986 and the 2002 elections. Conversely, until the election of Lula da

TABLE 6.2 Brazilian Chamber of Deputies (1986, 1990, 1994, 1998, and 2002): Percentage of Seats Won, by Party*

| Party | Year | | | | |
	1986	1990	1994	1998	2002
PFL	24	16	17	21	16
PMDB	53	21	21	16	14
PSDB	NA	7	12	19	14
PT	3	7	10	11	18
Others	19	47	40	33	38

*Percentages do not always add up to 100 percent due to rounding.

SOURCE: Political Database of the Americas <http://www.georgetown.edu/pdba/Elecdata/Brazil/brazil.html> (accessed on November 14, 2003).

Silva, the PT was the one major political party that had never joined a legislative coalition or nominated members to serve in cabinet posts.

THE CONTEMPORARY QUEST FOR DEVELOPMENT, LIBERTY, AND GOVERNANCE

In contrast to the economic debacle of military rule in Argentina, the Brazilian experience had been mixed. On one hand, the two decades of military rule saw the emergence of several competitive export sectors in agriculture and in manufacturing. In addition, despite the economic ups and downs of the early 1980s, the military government witnessed a visible expansion in overall national wealth. The GDP per person doubled from 1965 to 1985—the fastest economic growth rate of any Latin American country during that period. On the other hand, amid overall economic growth, income inequality worsened. Brazil had always had one of the most unequal income distributions in Latin America, and this situation worsened under military rule. In addition, high inflation rates wreaked more havoc on low-income families than on those with higher incomes, as they did in Argentina. Not surprisingly, the nearly half of the Brazilian population living in absolute poverty pinned their hopes for improvement on the governments to come in the New Republic.

The debate over liberty also held a mix of similarities and differences compared to the situation in Argentina. As in Argentina, the role of the military was initially at the center of the debate over liberty. In the case of Brazil, however, the debate did not focus on the potential prosecution of military violators of human rights but rather on the military's continuing participation in the government following the transition. Active-duty military officers held six positions in the first Sarney cabinet. Many politicians and ordinary citizens wondered if the new democracy would bring civilian control of the military and an expansion of civil liberties.

The governance concerns at the outset of the New Republic also differed according to distinctive national experiences. In Argentina, people wondered if the Peronist party would participate as a potentially cooperative (or at least nondisruptive) opposition party. In Brazil, most governance concerns pointed to the historical frequency of double-minority presidencies facing divided legislatures. How would a new generation of political leaders solve this set of challenges that had frequently stymied presidents in the two decades following World War II?

The Quest for Development in Brazil

As in Argentina, the most visible economic issue after the return to democracy in Brazil was high and rising inflation. Annual inflation rose from 98 percent in 1982 to 239 percent in 1985. In response, the Sarney government launched the

Cruzado Plan in 1986. Similar to the Austral Plan launched in Argentina in mid-1985, the *Cruzado* Plan combined a market-oriented response to economic instability (currency devaluation) with a more interventionist component: a wage-price freeze in which wage levels were raised by decree prior to the freeze. This plan initially spurred an increase in growth backed by consumer spending (due to the rise in real wages), and quite a few Brazilians presented themselves to serve as citizen watchdogs who would denounce any price increases in violation of the freeze. In 1986, inflation fell to 59 percent, and the Sarney presidency enjoyed a boost in public opinion polls.

As weeks and months passed, however, the Sarney administration and the legislature could not agree on the next steps to macroeconomic health. As in Argentina, the freeze unraveled when firms began to raise prices and workers pressured for new wage hikes. By 1987, a new inflationary spiral was under way. While Brazil did not suffer the level of hyperinflation experienced in Argentina, 1989 saw a record increase of 1,864 percent in the general price level (see Table 6.3 on page 188).

After his inauguration in 1990, Fernando Collor de Mello proposed sweeping economic reforms to reduce the role of government in the economy and to reduce inflation. As Carlos Menem did in Argentina, the Collor government decided to freeze bank accounts and to confiscate some deposits for government use (returning those funds to depositors as government bonds). However, Collor found it even more difficult to build legislative and public support for reducing trade barriers and privatizing state-owned enterprises. In Collor's first year in office, the economy shrank by over 4 percent and his approval ratings sagged.

Despite opposition to many of his proposed measures, Collor began a market-oriented reform that would continue in a stop-and-go process throughout the rest of the 1990s. The Collor administration announced that the average tariff in Brazil would be cut in half over the course of Collor's presidency. As part of the economic opening, Brazil signed the Treaty of Asunción, which launched the Southern Cone Common Market (review *Global Perspectives: Regional Economic Integration* in Chapter Five). Other aspects of the state capitalist model were also dismantled. Collor's privatization program did not advance as quickly as Menem's, but it still represented a tripling of all prior privatizations during the 1980s. The sale of the massive Minas Gerais Iron and Steel Mills in October 1991 accounted for two-thirds of the assets sold during the Collor presidency. In the name of sustainable development and with an eye toward the UN-sponsored environmental summit scheduled to be held in Rio in 1992, Collor made the environmental protection agency a cabinet-level ministry. Despite this change in status, the new ministry's capacity to enforce existing environmental laws remained limited.

After Collor's resignation in late 1992 amid a corruption scandal, Vice President Itamar Franco became Brazil's second accidental president in less than a decade. Like most veteran politicians in Brazil, Franco was not as willing

TABLE 6.3 Brazilian Economic Indicators (1983–2002)*

Year	GDP growth	Inflation	Unemployment	Debt service ratio[†]
1983	−3.4	179	6.7	44
1984	5.1	203	7.1	40
1985	8.4	239	5.3	40
1986	7.5	59	3.6	42
1987	3.6	395	3.7	33
1988	−0.1	993	3.8	29
1989	3.3	1,864	3.3	29
1990	−4.4	1,585	4.3	31
1991	1.0	476	4.8	27
1992	−0.3	1,149	5.8	21
1993	4.5	2,489	5.4	22
1994	6.2	1,294	5.1	18
1995	4.2	24	4.6	22
1996	2.5	12	5.4	25
1997	3.1	4	5.7	24
1998	0.1	3	7.6	28
1999	1.0	8	7.6	32
2000	4.0	6	7.1	27
2001	1.5	8	6.2	26
2002	1.9	13	11.7	22

*All numbers are percentages.

[†]The debt service ratio expresses interest paid on foreign debts as a percentage of total exports.

SOURCE: For the years 1983–1987, data are from United Nations Economic Commission for Latin America and the Caribbean, *Preliminary Overview of the Economies of Latin America and the Caribbean 1989* (Santiago, Chile: United Nations Publications, 1989). For the years 1988–1992, data are from United Nations Economic Commission for Latin America and the Caribbean, *Preliminary Overview of the Economies of Latin America and the Caribbean 1994* (Santiago, Chile: United Nations Publications, 1994). For the years 1993–1997, data are from United Nations Economic Commission for Latin America and the Caribbean, *Preliminary Overview of the Economies of Latin America and the Caribbean 1999* (Santiago, Chile: United Nations Publications, 1999). For the years 1998–2002, data are from United Nations Economic Commission for Latin America and the Caribbean, *Preliminary Overview of the Economies of Latin America and the Caribbean 2003* (Santiago, Chile: United Nations Publications, 2003).

as Collor to jettison entirely the state capitalist model that had been in place for over half a century. Franco had just seen the political whirlwind of legislative opposition unleashed by Collor's efforts to force his program on Congress. As a result of Franco's weak legislative position and a rising budget deficit, his administration found it difficult to instill confidence in the economy. Investment slowed, the Brazilian *cruzado* lost ground against the U.S. dollar, and the economic picture grew cloudier.

When inflation reached nearly 2,500 percent in 1993, Franco changed his economic strategy. He named a new economic minister, Fernando Henrique Cardoso. Cardoso had helped to found the PSDB as a center-left party at the outset of the New Republic but had become convinced that the current international environment called for several market-oriented reforms. In contrast to the surprise wage-price freeze of the *Cruzado* Plan, Cardoso detailed his intentions to major economic actors and political leaders prior to initiating the change in economic policy. In mid-1994, Cardoso's *Real* Plan combined steps to reduce budget deficits with the adoption of a fixed exchange rate, a move that was somewhat similar to the Argentine reforms in the early 1990s. The government replaced the *cruzado* with a new monetary unit, the *real*, which the government pledged to defend at its initial value of $1.10 per *real*. The measures broke the inflationary spiral and subsequently fueled Cardoso's successful presidential campaign in 1994.

In contrast to Collor's combative style, Cardoso campaigned on a pledge to negotiate economic reforms with the legislature. Many of the privatizations blocked earlier in the decade gained legislative approval during his first four years in office. The government also took steps to reduce the potential for budget deficits by restructuring some government activities and by raising taxes slightly. Cardoso's attempts to conduct more sweeping tax reform and to restructure the deficit-producing pension system for public employees did not make it through Congress during his first three years in office. Cardoso justified his pursuit of a second term on the need to complete these and other unfinished items on his legislative agenda.

In an effort to reduce economic inequality gradually, the Cardoso government made a concerted effort to improve educational opportunities for poor citizens, especially in rural areas. Teacher salaries for rural assignments were increased in an attempt to recruit more qualified teachers. At the same time, the Cardoso government launched a school enrollment initiative to keep children from poor families from dropping out of school at an early age. Poor children received an income subsidy for attending school to supplement the family income.

Beyond its efforts in education, the Cardoso government also dedicated more attention to land reform. In Cardoso's first term, the land reform agency redistributed more land than all previous presidents of the New Republic era combined. Nearly 300,000 families received plots of land. The MST argued that far more land could be redistributed by calling in land on which property taxes went unpaid. In turn, other critics asserted that the plots of land redistributed were not economically viable; some studies showed that one in four recipients abandoned their farms and sold their land within two years. In his second term, Cardoso announced a new land reform approach (backed with World Bank funding) in which citizens could apply for loans to purchase land that they selected. The loan review process would be based on the applicant's proposal to generate income sufficient to pay back the low-interest loan. As of May 2004, it was still too soon to see whether this process would generate a higher percentage of enduring farms.

GLOBAL PERSPECTIVES
The Asian Crisis of 1997–1998

The globalization of financial markets and production processes helped to expand economic activity during the 1980s and 1990s, but it also made national economies more vulnerable to foreign events. The Asian financial crisis of 1997–1998 made this vulnerability more evident. A crisis initially centered in Thailand would have implications for economies around the world.

In February 1997, the largest Thai finance company failed to make its bond repayments. The next month, the Thai government did not fulfill its pledge to cover nearly $4 billion in bad debts held by this and other financial institutions. When Moody's credit agency estimated in April that Thai government bonds were less likely to be repaid than previously thought, investors began to sell assets denominated in the Thai currency, the *baht*. The Thai government pledged not to devalue, and its central bank spent billions of dollars trying to defend the *baht* at its current exchange rate. Yet the defensive selloff of *baht*-denominated investments had created a self-fulfilling prophecy. By late May, the Thai government announced plans to devalue the *baht* and to restructure the financial sector.

International brokerage houses and wealthy individuals reevaluated their investments in Asia and elsewhere. During 1997, stock prices fell by 30 to 50 percent in Singapore, Indonesia, the Philippines, Malaysia, and Thailand. Concerns about a global financial meltdown affected the Americas: stock markets in late October suffered their worst-ever single-day losses in Argentina, Brazil, Mexico, and the United States.

In early 1998, it seemed the worst of the Asian crisis was over. Then political unrest in Indonesia laid bare the fragility of its financial markets. A selloff in Indonesia triggered a second expanding wave of investor flight. This time, attention focused on Russian debt. Russia borrowed more and more during 1997 and 1998 to acquire hard currency with which to meet its immediate debt obligations. As the total debt ballooned, concerns about the stability of the Russian government under Boris Yeltsin ignited a new financial collapse: in August 1998, Russia suspended its debt repayments. During the last full week of August, stock markets around the world lost 5 to 23 percent of their value. In Argentina, Brazil, and Mexico, stock prices fell by over 10 percent.

Pressure on Latin American currencies forced governments to offer higher interest rates on bonds to keep attracting international investors. The Brazilian government chose to devalue its currency, the *real*, in early 1999 rather than risk losing reserves defending its exchange rate. This devaluation broke the panic but laid the foundation for future speculation against Brazilian assets. At the lower exchange rate, it now would take more Brazilian *reais* to repay bonds and loans denominated in U.S. dollars. In 2001 and 2002, a beleaguered Brazilian government would again resort to devaluation and spending cuts in response to currency speculation.

Cardoso's second term faced considerable economic pressures from the global economy. As the Asian monetary crisis of 1997–1998 spread around the world, many investors began to wonder if other emerging economies would default on their government bonds, as Russia did in 1998. Amid the panic, many people pulled financial investments out of Brazil and speculated that the *real* would fall against the dollar (see *Global Perspectives: The Asian Crisis of 1997–1998*). The turbulent atmosphere generated disagreement in Cardoso's cabinet in which Economic Minister Pedro Malan called for an orthodox mix of fiscal austerity and devaluation to restore confidence in Brazil while Development Minister Clovis Cavalho called such a policy "cowardly" in early September 1999. Cavalho advocated a more aggressive attempt to promote growth and income redistribution. The next day, Cardoso asked for Cavalho's resignation.

Rather than continuing to spend its dollar reserves to defend the *real*, the Brazilian Central Bank permitted the *real* to lose 25 percent of its value in 1999. The devaluation improved Brazil's balance of trade, but also made it more difficult for the government to pay back bonds and loans denominated in dollars. As Brazilian debt grew relative to the size of the economy, a new speculative wave led the Central Bank to allow a 30 percent devaluation in 2001.

These measures reduced Brazil's trade deficit with Argentina but also deepened the Argentine recession. When Argentina defaulted on its debt in late December 2001 and then devalued its currency in January 2002, investors again began to pull money out of Brazil. When the financial panic shook the Uruguayan financial system in mid-2002, the Cardoso government negotiated a new loan agreement with the IMF to increase confidence that Brazil had both the will and the means to meet its financial obligations. These negotiations took place during Brazil's 2002 presidential election campaign, so the Cardoso government took the unusual step of helping to broker an agreement among all major presidential candidates. If elected, each candidate (including the two leading candidates on the center-left) pledged to meet the fiscal target of a 4.25 percent primary budgetary surplus, which the government would use to meet its debt obligations in the coming year.

Brazil's economic experience over the years 1985–2002 demonstrates that even the largest economy south of the equator is not immune to the major economic problems prevalent in Latin America. Vulnerability to international conditions, exchange rate instability, environmental degradation, poverty, and economic inequality all remained visible facets of Brazil's economic challenges. Like Alfonsín in Argentina, Sarney found it difficult to place the state capitalism model on a solid footing in the face of international opposition and domestic political divisions. Collor's effort at ramrod reform developed neither the legislative nor the public support necessary to implement most of his market-oriented reforms. Instead, his efforts produced a governance crisis culminating in his resignation. From that perspective, Franco's presidency marked a regrouping in which no clear direction to economic policy emerged.

Following the turmoil of the late 1980s and early 1990s, the Cardoso govern-ment tried to reduce the prospects for economic instability and investor mistrust by pursuing many reforms via consensus. He made more limited use of decree authority than his predecessors. As a result, although market-oriented reform took longer than it did in Argentina and was less complete in Brazil, its political foundations have proven somewhat more stable. In this sense, Cardoso's strat-egy paid off. Inflation ceased to be a problem. Over the years 1995–2002, amid in-ternational financial pressures, the Brazilian GDP per person grew by 7.1 percent (albeit with most of the growth occurring before the contagion of the Asian crisis in 1997–1998). The market-oriented model seemed politically entrenched at this point—at least among the nation's political leadership. The political con-sensus around a largely market-oriented model proved robust enough to gener-ate pledges by all major presidential candidates in 2002 to an IMF agreement that committed the government to run a surplus with which to meet its debt obligations.

Despite the visible shift in economic strategy, the open question remains the same as it was at the outset of the democratic transition: how will governments work to reduce poverty and economic inequality over time? To date, despite Cardoso's efforts in welfare and education policy, progress toward a sustained reduction in poverty stalled during his presidency. Prior to Cardoso, however, there had been no progress. In 1987, 45 percent of Brazilian households lived below the poverty line and the same percentage were impoverished in 1993. Strong economic growth in the mid-1990s (along with an increase in govern-ment welfare spending and a drop in inflation rates) fueled a drop in the poverty rate, down to 36 percent by 1996. As economic growth slowed, the poverty rate inched upward again, reaching 38 percent in 1999 and staying at that level through 2001. Despite some progress toward poverty reduction in the 1990s, however, income inequality worsened over the course of the decade. The percentage of income earned by the wealthiest 10 percent of the urban popula-tion increased from 42 percent in 1990 to 44 percent in 1996, and then rose to 46 percent by 1999.[3]

The Quest for Liberty in Brazil

In contrast to Argentina, human rights abuses under the Brazilian military regime did not become a central political issue after the restoration of democ-racy. Three major reasons account for this difference. First, the incidence of human rights abuses was not as widespread as it was in the dictatorships in Argentina, Chile, and Uruguay (review Table 5.4). Second, the Brazilian military regime's self-amnesty (unlike similar actions taken in Argentina and Chile) was a mutual amnesty that also exonerated many groups that had taken up arms against the military government. Third, the leading civilian politicians (includ-ing Neves and Sarney) in all three major political parties had pledged quietly not to call for human rights trials after the return to democracy. Although the return to democracy brought several journalistic exposés regarding past abuses and human rights groups called for action, this set of issues never gained the impetus and visibility that it would in neighboring countries. Eventually, under the Cardoso government, the legislature enacted a policy that provided lump-sum reparations of between $100,000 and $150,000 to the families of persons killed in government custody or who disappeared during the military regime.

Instead, the major debate over liberty after the return to democracy unfolded under different circumstances: the Constituent Assembly was charged with writing a new constitution. From 1891 onward, all Brazilian constitutions had contained a provision calling on the military to serve as the ultimate guarantor of law and order. Additional clauses placed the federal police under military command. In addition, since the 1920s, the heads of each branch of the armed forces served on the cabinet, as did the head of the Joint Chiefs of Staff. During the military regime, two additional active-duty military officers joined the cabinet: the head of the National Security Council and the head of the intelligence service. The military had a large, constitutionally sanctioned role in Brazilian political life.

In the Constituent Assembly, leftist opposition parties and several members of the PMDB wanted to reduce the military's autonomy and to limit its participation in the cabinet. Several people called for the consolidation of the six existing military ministries into a single, civilian-led ministry of defense. Some proposed making the promotion of senior officers subject to legislative approval. Others called for placing the intelligence service and/or the federal police under civilian control. Still others wanted to modify the long-standing role of the military as the ultimate protector of law and order because it provided a constitutional rationale for the military's autonomous intervention in domestic affairs (in the name of preserving order). The initial draft constitution did not embrace most of these reforms; however, it did remove the law-and-order provision.

In the Constituent Assembly, the Sarney administration formed a coalition with center-right forces in the legislature to advocate the military's position in these matters. After reviewing the draft that eliminated the law-and-order clause, the army minister made it clear that this reform was unacceptable to him and to the rest of the military. In response, the final version of Article 142 of the 1988 constitution read: "the Armed Forces' purpose is to defend the Nation, guarantee the constitutional branches of government and, on the initiative of any of these branches, law and order."[4]

In the final analysis, José Sarney's unwillingness to support a visible reduction of the military's role in government may have helped to reduce the frequency of open conflict along the lines experienced by Raúl Alfonsín in Argentina. However, the path chosen to limit open conflict involved ceding considerable authority to the military not just in the constitutional debate but also in practice. For example, while Sarney formally headed the armed forces, his control over military promotions—and over defense policy more generally—was limited.

One of the more visible examples included Uruguayan media reports that the Brazilian military attaché to Uruguay had tortured detainees during the dictatorship. At first Sarney stated publicly that the officer in question would be removed from his post. However, after Sarney reportedly received a phone call from the army chief in support of the officer, Sarney's spokesperson issued a brief retraction the following day and the government dropped the matter. In this and other incidents, Sarney's approach to civil-military relations followed what Alfred Stepan termed "unequal civilian accommodation" (review Table 3.2).

At the outset of his presidency, Fernando Collor de Mello altered civil-military relations. Following through on a campaign promise, he placed the intelligence agency—historically controlled by the military—under civilian control. This change was designed to make the agency more responsive to long-standing calls to limit the investigative prerogatives of the intelligence community. The change also slightly reduced the number of active military officers in the cabinet from six to five.

The major dispute regarding liberty in Franco's brief presidency revolved around the continuing issues of street crime and of human rights violations in anticrime efforts—particularly in the megacities of São Paulo and Rio de Janeiro. On one hand, most violent deaths went unsolved. In one study of crime in Rio during this period, over 90 percent of cases did not result in prosecution. Rising concern over violent crime motivated the Franco government to place the army in charge of an anticrime effort in Rio from late October 1994 through early February 1995. The army set up roadblocks, armed street officers with rifles (which was unprecedented in Brazilian history), and detained hundreds of shantytown residents for questioning.

An early November public opinion poll reported that 86 percent of Rio's residents supported the army's insertion in police actions and that 52 percent would favor a military occupation of the shantytown district.[5] By the end of the month, however, a significant scandal emerged when lawyers filed complaints of illegal detention and torture under imprisonment. The general in command acknowledged that violations had occurred but called the excesses inevitable. These denunciations of human rights violations took place in the context of the ongoing trial of police officers accused of murdering eight street children in their sleep outside a Rio church in 1993. The Franco government had the army minister announce that any soldiers involved in torture would be held accountable but did not subsequently charge any of the officers deployed in Rio. Amid the scandal, the government did not extend this military operation beyond its initial three-month duration.

The Cardoso government eventually made some progress in civil-military relations, albeit with some controversy. As a candidate, Cardoso had promised to create a civilian-led defense ministry, thereby ending the practice of various branch commanders serving as stand-alone cabinet officers. During Cardoso's first term, the proposal languished, but the government made its case by emphasizing that fewer than thirty countries had defense commanders who did not report to a unified defense ministry. In his second term, Cardoso appointed a civilian defense minister in June 1999. The move disturbed many senior officers, and the controversy culminated in the dismissal of the air force commander by year's end. Over time, however, the grumbling appeared to lessen and Cardoso finished his presidency with only one active-duty officer (his national security adviser) in the cabinet.

The most visible and protracted conflict over liberty during Cardoso's presidency involved long-standing tension over land reform. The Landless Movement (MST) became increasingly active in pressuring the government to redistribute land. The MST argued that the most immediate solution to rural poverty (and, by extension, to urban overcrowding) could be found in a redistribution of underused and unused land owned by large landowners and, in some instances, by the government. Existing land reform procedures permitted people to apply for title to government land, but the amount of farmland to be redistributed could increase only via the government purchase of additional tracts from private landowners.

The MST tried to get the executive branch to use existing land reform processes to redistribute more land. The MST used various tactics to pursue this goal: it provided legal advice regarding how to work within the existing land reform procedures, it pressured the government to take a more aggressive stance through lobbying efforts and rallies, and it often occupied unused land in an attempt to draw public and government attention to these issues.

Both the MST and landholders claimed their rights were being violated in this worsening dispute. The MST pointed to incidents in which landholders hired vigilantes to intimidate, to assault, and in some instances to kill land reform activists. In turn, landholders argued that the MST seizures of private land violated the right to property. In this dispute, each side harshly criticized the Cardoso government for failing to protect its rights. In an unusual media event, in 2002 the MST occupied unused land held by Cardoso himself. It did so in an effort to dramatize Cardoso's personal situation as one more in common with the landowners than with the landless. Despite the increase in land redistribution during the Cardoso government, this conflict over land reform continued largely unabated, with new paramilitary organizations emerging to offer so-called proactive protection to landowners.

The other major area of high-profile concern regarding contemporary liberty involved corruption by government officials. As in Argentina, corruption had long been a concern, but public and governmental attention increased during the early 1990s. The controversy during the Collor administration centered on the activities of the president and of his campaign treasurer, Paulo Cesar Farias. With an executive order on the day of his inauguration, Collor froze all bank and savings accounts and overnight deposits. The freezing of

Squatter settlements serve a dual purpose: they can initiate land claims while they draw attention to the concerns of the landless. © Ricardo Azoury/Corbis.

bank accounts gave the executive branch control over the country's financial liquidity; this power was apparently used to elicit bribes from companies that wanted government permission to access their accounts to pay salaries, taxes, and other ongoing expenses. Farias appeared to have been the crucial go-between who arranged corrupt deals, collected the money, and deposited it in hidden accounts that could be accessed by the president and by other government officials. According to the legislature's subsequent investigation of these matters, Farias distributed over $32 million in these accounts, with over $6 million going to the president and his family. Farias also seemed to have elicited bribes in exchange for arranging government loans and granting government contracts.

The scandal that eventually culminated in the abrupt end to Collor's term involved a Collor-Farias venture in the media sector. Brazil's powerful media conglomerate *O Globo* was ambivalent about the president's policies. Collor and Farias bought several rival broadcasting companies and newspapers. When Farias tried to create a newspaper in direct competition with a paper run by the president's brother (Pedro Collor de Mello), the rivalry ignited the largest scandal of his presidency. When the president and his operatives showed no apparent willingness to limit their challenge to Pedro Collor's newspaper, Pedro went to the national media and spoke openly about several corruption allegations surrounding the president.

These allegations in the media led to a congressional investigation that culminated in impeachment hearings and Collor's resignation. Concerns about corruption did not evaporate, however, with this early ending to Collor's presidency. Instead, corruption would return to the center of the political debate when operatives associated with the Cardoso administration faced accusations of bribery in the drive to eliminate the no-reelection clause in the constitution.

Despite several ongoing concerns, the expansion of liberty during the New Republic has not suffered the high-profile tension generated by human rights controversies in Argentina. Instead, the continuing issues have been the reduction of the military's role in government and the pursuit of public safety in a radically unequal society. These two demands have often come into conflict as voices from inside and outside the military call for a strong hand to combat various perceived and real threats to public safety. Over time, after the initial caution of the Sarney administration, later presidents have gradually chipped away at the military's role in the cabinet and at some of its autonomy of action. Nonetheless, as controversies over the implicated role of security forces in the deaths of political activists and unidentified street children demonstrate, the pursuit of liberty needs to rest on a broad foundation of trust and security that has not yet fully emerged.

The Quest for Governance in Brazil

José Sarney was a president ruling without electoral support. When Neves fell ill and died, Sarney faced suspicion from most legislators. Many in the promilitary PDS saw Neves as a traitor; many in the PMDB saw him as an opportunist who only broke away from the PDS when it was clear that the days of military rule were ending. With this difficult beginning, Sarney became Brazil's first civilian leader in over two decades.

If Sarney could have mobilized the support of the PMDB and the PFL (the parties that had elected him vice president), he would have held a dominant position in the legislature throughout his presidency. However, his status as a president without electoral support and the distrust he faced from almost all legislators outside the PFL placed him in a defensive position from the outset. Sarney tried to reverse this situation by launching the *Cruzado* Plan by decree. If the plan succeeded, Sarney hoped to use public opinion as a tool to build legislative support and, if possible, to influence the Constituent Assembly to provide him with a five-year term (instead of the four-year mandate contained in the draft proposal).

Initially, the decrease in inflation and a boom in consumer spending in mid-1986 fueled the surge in public support that Sarney sought. However, when inflation returned in 1987 and the economy slowed down, Sarney's situation worsened. When the 1988 constitution retained the traditional prohibition on reelection, Sarney's influence weakened further still and attention turned to the 1989 presidential campaign—the first presidential election in almost thirty years.

Fernando Collor's presidency, like that of Janio Quadros, began from an extremely weak legislative base. The PRN held a minuscule 8 percent of the lower house following the 1990 legislative elections. To make matters worse, many legislators had campaigned against most of Collor's proposed economic reforms. When Collor could not build legislative support, he instituted reforms by decree. In theory, Brazilian presidential decrees in the 1988 constitution are agenda-setting tools that force the legislature to respond quickly to block measures it opposes or to validate measures it approves. Decrees that do not receive legislative support expire in thirty days because they fail to push the legislature toward supporting the president's position. However, in many instances in which Congress did not endorse the decree, Collor simply reinstated the controversial measures as slightly modified new decrees. This expedient practice set a precedent that would be imitated by future presidents (albeit less frequently).

Collor's combative political style, his weak legislative position, and his controversial economic agenda built him a list of political enemies almost immediately. The list grew when rumors spread that Collor had created a kickback scheme that generated money on a scale rarely seen in Brazilian politics. Collor's corruption scandal exploded into a governance crisis when his brother Pedro denounced his illegal activities in the Brazilian newsmagazine *Veja* in May 1992. Over the next three months, a congressional commission formed to investigate these allegations formally alleged a wide array of corrupt activities.

Collor responded to the allegations with a televised speech in which he called the congressional report a pack of lies worthy of a national day of mourning. In response to the president's call for citizens to wear black armbands protesting the report, however, citizens took to the streets wearing the national colors and chanting anti-Collor slogans. Collor then tried to pursue anti-impeachment votes in the legislature by sponsoring a series of pork-barrel spending bills, but his position was too weak. In late September, the Chamber of Deputies overwhelmingly launched an impeachment process by a vote of 441 to 38. Prior to the end of his impeachment trial, Collor resigned in December 2002.

Observers vary in their assessment of Itamar Franco's subsequent presidency. Some emphasize the lack of consensus within the legislature as the major obstacle to creating a coherent economic and political strategy after the fall of the Collor government. Others highlight Franco's limitations as a public speaker, which prevented him from rallying public opinion around the presidency and thus creating a honeymoon period in which to cultivate legislative cooperation. Still others characterize Franco's indecisiveness as a personality trait. All of these problems clearly played a role, as did a vicious cycle of continuing economic instability that kept the government on the defensive until the launching of the *Real* Plan in the final year of Franco's presidency.

Once Cardoso assumed the post of economic minister and launched the *Real* Plan, the administration tried to make a virtue out of its limitations by arguing that limited scope of the economic package constituted a welcome departure from past attempts at rapid change. Cardoso argued that incremental changes in spending and slower efforts to pursue additional opening of the economy would ensure a more stable economic climate for investors. To a certain extent, at least within the brief mandate of Itamar Franco, one could conceivably agree that an interim president who took office amid a serious political and economic crisis could not reasonably aspire to possess much influence over public events.

Fernando Henrique Cardoso used the initial success of the *Real* Plan in braking inflation to build support for his presidential candidacy. He became the first candidate since Vargas in 1934 to win over 50 percent of the vote in a multiparty presidential election. With his party controlling just one-fifth of the legislature, Cardoso promised to build a multiparty coalition and made progress toward doing so prior to taking office in early 1995.

Cardoso began his first term with a cabinet representing parties controlling less than one-third of the legislature. The major coalition partners were Cardoso's own PSDB and the PFL. Early in his term, he cobbled together a broader coalition of parties that controlled a majority of seats in both houses by attracting support from the PMDB and several other parties. He did so using several methods: making modifications to his legislative agenda so that each party would have some of its goals realized (logrolling), offering executive branch positions to party leaders, and pointing to his historic majority election and high job approval ratings to keep his coalition together in the months ahead. At times, Cardoso also used pork-barrel politics to maintain legislative support. The *Research Question* on pages 200–201 further analyzes the dynamics of executive-legislative relations in Latin America as a whole.

As legislative momentum slowed in the middle of his term, Cardoso began pushing for a constitutional amendment that would permit him to run for reelection. The amendment did not come easily. Several parties attempted to block the change to improve their own candidates' chances. Other legislators engaged in fierce horse-trading for initiatives in their own districts. In the end, the amendment narrowly gained the necessary votes in 1997, but it also created the first major scandal of Cardoso's presidency. In a taped telephone conversation, a legislator discussed with presidential operatives the bribe that he would be paid in exchange for supporting the amendment.

Despite the scandal, the reelection drive served two purposes to a certain extent. First, it increased Cardoso's influence during the latter portion of his first term. Second, despite the scandal, Cardoso won reelection in 1998. Cardoso's lame-duck position in his second term limited his influence over the legislature, but various international economic pressures increased his discretion over many government responses to these financial challenges. Nonetheless, Cardoso's second term did not produce all the reforms discussed in his second presidential campaign. In particular, the social security system was not reformed and the tax system was changed only minimally. Nevertheless, Cardoso's skill in working with legislators and governors avoided the financial meltdown that emerged in Argentina in the early twenty-first century.

The pursuit of governance in contemporary Brazil remained difficult in the face of continuing political divisions in the fragmented Brazilian legislature. The ballotage system was adopted to strengthen the hand of the president in forging coalitions within the legislature. Collor's combative style neutralized whatever advantages might have come from his election via a majority of voters in the second round. In contrast, Cardoso combined his majority electoral victories along with a more consensual style to build support for many of his proposals. Despite the criticism that he has received for goals not accomplished, Cardoso demonstrated that it is possible to work out compromises in many instances without massive injections of additional spending or other means. Although the corruption scandal surrounding the reelection amendment tarnished his image, it still must be noted that many initiatives passed without resort to corruption.

RESEARCH QUESTION
Under What Conditions Are Presidents Likely to Receive Legislative Support?

In a 2001 article, Gary Cox and Scott Morgenstern analyzed executive-legislative relations in contemporary Latin America.[1] How do presidents work to convert their agendas into active policies? What factors help us understand when the legislature is likely to play a more meaningful role in the policy process?

Cox and Morgenstern view executive-legislative relations in Latin America as distinct from patterns typically observed in the U.S. presidential system and in the parliamentary systems prevalent in Europe. Latin American legislatures lack the power to select the chief executive (found in European parliamentary systems); they also lack the financial resources and staff expertise needed to take a more proactive role in developing policy proposals (typical in the U.S. Congress). Nevertheless, Cox and Morgenstern argue that the reactive role of responding to presidential initiatives does not condemn Latin American legislatures to irrelevance. Presidential governing strategies vary according to the degree and nature of legislative opposition they face.

Three principal factors determine the legislature's position. The first factor is the most straightforward influence on executive-legislative relations: the percentage of seats held by

[1]Gary Cox and Scott Morgenstern, "Latin America's Reactive Assemblies and Proactive Presidents," *Comparative Politics* 33 (2001): 171–189. For additional research in academic journals regarding executive-legislative relations, see the appropriate portion of this book's website.

Future Challenges

This mixed political and economic legacy of the Cardoso presidency forms the backdrop against which Lula da Silva took the oath of office in early 2003. On the economic front, most of Da Silva's supporters come from the so-called other Brazil in this dualist economy. This other Brazil is below the median educational level, which in Brazil means they have no more than a primary school education. This other Brazil lives below the World Bank's poverty line of $2.00 per day. While Cardoso's emphasis on improving educational outcomes for poor children may help in the long run, it did little to alleviate poverty in the short term.

One of Da Silva's first policy statements in office called for the creation of the Zero Hunger program in which needy families would receive roughly US$17.00 in monthly subsidies to purchase foodstuffs. The hunger reduction program began in northeastern Brazil—the poorest region in the country and birthplace of President Da Silva. By August 2003, the government announced plans to expand the initiative nationwide in the hope of eventually assisting 46 million

the party or coalition of parties that supported the president's campaign. Presidents with large majorities may assume what Cox and Morgenstern call a "subservient assembly," while those with few loyal legislators face a "recalcitrant assembly," which offers little hope of cultivating a stable base of support.

What happens if the president enjoys an intermediate level of support? Here, Cox and Morgenstern emphasize two additional factors: the length of legislative careers and the ideological nature of party politics. When legislative careers are shorter and parties are less ideological, the president can expect a "venal assembly," which will demand pork-barrel spending (or perhaps kickbacks) in exchange for its support. Conversely, greater longevity and ideological coherence tend to produce a "workable assembly," which is willing to search for policy compromises between its position and the president's.

Cox and Morgenstern find that presidents base their legislative strategies on which type of assembly they face: subservient, recalcitrant, venal, or workable. Presidents act with little regard for subservient assemblies under most circumstances. In turn, presidents hamstrung by a recalcitrant assembly are more likely to emphasize the unilateral powers of their office (decrees, the ability to set the legislative agenda, and the power of regulation and patronage); their unilateral action stems from their anticipation that support is unlikely. One would expect more policy-oriented coalition building from presidents confronting workable assemblies (which have been prevalent in Chile), while pork-barrel politics are frequently used to deal with venal assemblies (which have been frequent in Brazil, where legislative careers are shorter and most parties are less ideologically consistent than they have been in Chile).

needy Brazilians (nearly one-third of the total population). It remains to be seen whether this targeted program can achieve two crucial goals. First, will it work to reduce hunger? Second, and perhaps more important, will it generate enough political support to enable the government to expand funding so that it can become an effective, sustained nationwide program?

While the new government makes decisions regarding poverty reduction, it also faces existing demands for debt repayment and for continuing recent economic policies. Many wondered if Lula da Silva would follow through on his promise to meet the IMF agreement's fiscal target of a 4.25 percent surplus during his first year in office. To the surprise of some observers (and to the outrage of others), the Da Silva government reduced public spending in its first months to meet the target. This action pleased the international financial community but it deepened the recession, thereby worsening economic conditions for many Brazilians at the outset of his presidency. These cross-pressures between demands from the impoverished and demands from the wealthy are nothing new in Brazil (or in Latin America). Da Silva's challenge is to make good on his promise to improve conditions for ordinary Brazilians without frightening away investors.

The issue of liberty is intertwined with conflict over economic resources. As we have seen, justifications for more autonomy for the security forces come from an argument that society is too unstable. Property owners often see their rights threatened by criminals and even by active protesters. Conversely, poor citizens can be pushed beyond their limits and may decide to lash out at the government, property owners, or both. In its first year in office, the Da Silva government has attempted to limit the fears of propertied Brazilians by criticizing the MST land seizure tactics and by publicly asking labor unions for restraint in wage demands and strike activity. After these actions during the early months of Lula da Silva's presidency, one wonders if landowners will trust the government to defend their property rights, or will they lash out at MST activists on their own? On the other side of the coin, will Da Silva's effort to go slow on redistribution eventually motivate another rise in crime and/or illegal protests?

Da Silva's decision to emphasize his acceptance of many propertied interests is not just an effort to prevent a financial meltdown. It is also a response to his need to build a governing coalition. Although Lula da Silva received a healthy majority in the presidential race, the PT holds just over one-sixth of the seats in the legislature. In fact, even if he could obtain the consistent cooperation of all left-of-center forces in Congress, it would not provide him with a legislative majority. In early 2004, he formally incorporated the support of the centrist PMDB in an effort to build a stable legislative majority.

The strategy of Da Silva's wing within the PT is to build support slowly for reforms that can reduce poverty. Here, too, are open questions on both sides. First, will moderation during his first months in office succeed in building alliances with other political forces and with the business community more generally? Second, will other PT activists (and PT voters more generally) stand behind a gradual approach that contrasts sharply with Da Silva's biting criticism of propertied interests during his rise to prominence? For example, when Da Silva announced plans for a major reform of the social security system, public sector unions held a general strike in July 2003, and several PT leaders grumbled about the proposal. As noted earlier, when four PT legislators voted against the pension reform, they were expelled from the party's legislative bloc in December 2003. On this and other matters, the Da Silva presidency over the next few years will be seen by many as an object lesson for future efforts to modify the market capitalist reforms of the 1990s.

Activities and Exercises

1. Tax policy is a sensitive issue in Brazil and elsewhere. If you were a Brazilian citizen who wanted to see an increase in government spending to reduce poverty, how would you try to get the government to increase taxes as a percentage of gross domestic product (GDP)? How would you want the government to spend the additional money raised?

2. Concerns over crime have motivated considerable fear in some segments of Brazilian society. Meanwhile, many police officers and soldiers have been accused of killing marginalized Brazilians without arrest or trial. How would you work to protect the rights of the accused while also reassuring citizens that criminal suspects will be apprehended and tried in a timely manner?

3. This chapter has presented several reasons why the Brazilian legislature has been fragmented during the Second Republic and during the contemporary New Republic. If you were a Brazilian politician who wanted to reduce this political fragmentation, what would you change and how would you mobilize political support to pursue these reforms?

4. *Cidade de Deus* (*City of God*) is a 2002 film named after the real-life shantytown (*favela*) in Rio de Janeiro. In a semidocumentary style, the screenplay follows the lives of several residents growing up in a tough environment characterized by poverty and crime. This gritty movie was nominated for four Academy Awards in early 2004, including best adapted screenplay and best director. Check it out.

5. In early 2004, Brazil entered the final stages of negotiations aimed at the creation of the Free Trade Agreement of the Americas (FTAA). The proposed FTAA would eliminate tariffs throughout most of the Western Hemisphere. What has happened in these negotiations since this book went to press? In addition to checking news coverage (using the sources suggested in the Activities and Exercises section of Chapter Four), browse the official FTAA website at http://www.ftaaalca.org/. To examine the perspectives of one of several NGOs critical of the FTAA, see the appropriate section of the Public Citizen website at http://www.publiccitizen.org/trade/ftaa/.

Suggested Readings

Alvarez, Sonia. *Engendering Democracy in Brazil: Women's Movements in the Transition*. Princeton, N.J.: Princeton University Press, 1990.

Ames, Barry. *The Deadlock of Democracy in Brazil*. Ann Arbor: University of Michigan Press, 2001.

Baer, Werner. *The Brazilian Economy: Growth and Development*, 5th ed. Westport, Conn.: Praeger, 2001.

Branford, Sue, and Bernardo Kucinski. *Politics Transformed: Lula and the Workers' Party in Brazil*. London: Latin America Bureau, 2003.

Font, Mauricio. *Transforming Brazil: A Reform Era in Perspective*. Lanham, Md.: Rowman and Littlefield, 2003.

Graham, Lawrence, and Robert Wilson, eds. *The Political Economy of Brazil: Public Policies in an Era of Transition*. Austin: University of Texas Press, 1990.

Guimarães, Roberto. *The Ecopolitics of Development in the Third World: Politics and Environment in Brazil*. Boulder, Colo.: Lynne Rienner, 1991.

Hagopian, Frances. *Traditional Politics and Regime Change in Brazil*. Cambridge, England: Cambridge University Press, 1996.

Hanchard, Michael. *Racial Politics in Contemporary Brazil*. Durham, N.C.: Duke University Press, 1999.

Hunter, Wendy. *Eroding Military Influence in Brazil: Politicians Against Soldiers*. Chapel Hill: University of North Carolina Press, 1997.

Ireland, Rowan. *Kingdoms Come: Religion and Politics in Brazil*. Pittsburgh, Pa.: University of Pittsburgh Press, 1991.

Keck, Margaret. *The Workers' Party and Democratization in Brazil*. New Haven, Conn.: Yale University Press, 1992.

Kingstone, Peter, and Timothy Power, eds. *Democratic Brazil: Actors, Institutions, and Processes*. Pittsburgh, Pa.: University of Pittsburgh Press, 2000.

Mainwaring, Scott. *Rethinking Party Systems in the Third Wave of Democracies: The Case of Brazil*. Stanford, Calif.: Stanford University Press, 1999.

Martínez-Lara, Javier. *Building Democracy in Brazil: The Politics of Constitutional Change, 1985–1995*. New York: St. Martin's Press, 1996.

Payne, Leigh. *Brazilian Industrialists and Democratic Change*. Baltimore, Md.: Johns Hopkins University Press, 1994.

Power, Timothy. *The Political Right in Postauthoritarian Brazil: Elites, Institutions, and Democratization*. University Park, Pa.: Penn State University Press, 2000.

Purcell, Susan Kaufmann, and Riordan Roett, eds. *Brazil Under Cardoso*. Boulder, Colo.: Lynne Rienner, 1997.

Roett, Riordan. *Brazil: Politics in a Patrimonial Society*, 5th ed. Westport, Conn.: Praeger, 1999.

Rosenn, Keith, and Richard Downs, eds. *Corruption and Political Reform in Brazil: The Impact of Collor's Impeachment*. Miami, Fla.: North-South Center, 1999.

Samuels, David. *Ambition, Federalism, and Legislative Politics in Brazil*. Cambridge, England: Cambridge University Press, 2003.

Skidmore, Thomas. *Brazil: Five Centuries of Change*. Oxford: Oxford University Press, 1999.

Stepan, Alfred, ed. *Democratizing Brazil: Problems of Transition and Consolidation*. Oxford: Oxford University Press, 1989.

Weschler, Lawrence. *A Miracle, a Universe: Settling Accounts with Torturers*. New York: Pantheon, 1990.

Weyland, Kurt. *Democracy Without Equity: Failures of Reform in Brazil*. Pittsburgh, Pa.: University of Pittsburgh Press, 1996.

Endnotes

1. Cited in Thomas Skidmore, *Brazil: Five Centuries of Change* (Oxford, England: Oxford University Press, 1999), p. 137.

2. Scott Desposato, *Institutional Theories, Social Realities, and Party Politics in Brazil* (Ph.D. dissertation, University of California at Los Angeles, 2001), p. 137.

3. United Nations Economic Commission for Latin America and the Caribbean, *Social Panorama of Latin America 2001–2002* (Santiago, Chile: United Nations Publications), p. 226.

4. Translated and cited in Jorge Zaverucha, "The 1988 Brazilian Constitution and Its Authoritarian Legacy: Formalizing Democracy While Gutting Its Essence," paper presented at the 1997 Congress of the Latin American Studies Association, p. 13.

5. "Brazil: Controversy Explodes Over Military Anti-Crime Operations in Rio Slums," *NotiSur,* December 2, 1994, http://ssdc.ucsd.edu/news/notisur/h94/notisur. 19941202.html#a10 (accessed September 9, 2003).

Chile

CHAPTER 7

Chile

I N SEVERAL CIRCLES, Chile emerged in the 1990s as a potential economic and political model for the rest of Latin America. A 1993 *Wall Street Journal* article gushed that "while the industrialized world frets about recession and Latin America worries about debt and inflation, the talk here is of leaving the Third World behind."[1] A year later, Chile's transition to democracy would receive similar praise in *Business America*: "Continued success on the economic front has been bolstered by Chile's smooth return to traditional democratic rule."[2]

These and other journalists emphasized two central features of contemporary Chile: a prolonged economic boom and the absence of polarized political conflict regarding economic policy. Does the Chilean experience since its return to democracy in 1990 constitute a model that other countries could and should emulate? In part, your answer to this question should consider whether the dynamics of the Chilean experience involve conditions that foreign political leaders and engaged citizens could construct in their respective countries.

In addition, several analysts would suggest that you ponder the incomplete nature of Chile's economic and political successes. For example, the Chilean economy grew steadily from 1984 through 2002, yet that sustained growth did not reduce income inequality. Chile had the second highest level of income inequality in Latin America in 1984 and still did in 2002. The quest for liberty has also been uneven. The return to democracy raised hopes that perpetrators of human rights violations would face criminal trials, yet few trials took place during the 1990s. At the start of the twenty-first century, criminal charges were filed against many government officials, but most of the accused had not yet been tried as of May 2004. Finally, in the realm of democratic governance, what some labeled a political consensus others termed a nondemocratic constraint on elected officials. During this third wave of democratization in Latin America, Chile is the only country in which more than one-fifth of the upper house of the legislature consists of appointees unaccountable to the voters. Consideration of Chile's desirability as a model for other countries also involves a holistic evaluation of successes and failures in Chile's contemporary quest for development, liberty, and governance.

Over the course of this chapter, we will see that talk of Chile as a potential model for Latin America is nothing new. This midsize country of nearly 16 million inhabitants has long been considered an innovator among Latin American countries. Chilean "firsts" in the region include the first stable oligarchic democracy, the first powerful legislature, the first attempt to pursue a transition to socialism via free elections, and the first shift toward market capitalism in the late twentieth century. To appreciate how and why Chile embarked on its current economic and political path, we will begin by reviewing its history.

HISTORICAL BACKGROUND FROM 1891 TO 1989

After the end of colonial rule, most Latin American countries spent several decades embroiled in disputes among regional *caudillos* who challenged the authority of the national government. After achieving its independence in 1830, Chile managed to consolidate a national government over most of its territory much more quickly, despite the outbreak of brief civil wars in 1851 and 1859. The resistance of the indigenous Mapuche nation in the south (a people who had also largely resisted Spanish domination) formed the major exception to this trend. The Mapuche would not lose control of their southernmost land until the early 1880s. The conclusion of the so-called Indian wars coincided with the War of the Pacific (1879–1883). Chile's defeat of Bolivian and Peruvian forces enabled it to expand its territory by roughly one-third.

Chilean politics during the first six decades after independence took the form of a comparatively stable oligarchic democracy that endured until 1891. President José Manuel Balmaceda proposed to raise tax rates on nitrate extraction in the resource-rich northern territory captured in the War of the Pacific. This proposal met with stiff opposition from the Chilean Congress. When Congress impeached Balmaceda's cabinet, the president refused to ask his ministers to leave office. In the seven-month civil war that followed, both sides suffered heavy losses. After several military defeats, Balmaceda surrendered and received political asylum in the Argentine embassy. He committed suicide the day after his term would have ended.

The Parliamentary Republic (1891–1924)

The resolution of the civil war produced political reforms that significantly reduced the power of the president relative to the legislature. In particular, Congress gained the ability to remove cabinet members at will by majority vote. This form of legislative control over the executive—common in parliamentary systems but rare in presidential systems—prompted many to refer to this era as the Parliamentary Republic.

This system made conflict between the executive and legislative branches more visible because Congress frequently asserted its authority by removing cabinet ministers. On average, four cabinet changes occurred per year during this period. While Congress held sufficient power to block various presidential initiatives, this was not a pure parliamentary system. The legislature did not elect the chief executive nor did it have the power to remove presidents from office when a legislative majority opposed the chief executive's agenda. Over time, critics claimed that this was the worst possible hybrid of these two systems of executive-legislative relations because of the high frequency of stalemate, or gridlock, between the two branches.

The Search for Compromise amid a Divided Electorate (1925–1958)

Rising criticism of this state of affairs culminated in a new constitution in 1925 that did not grant the legislature the power to remove ministers at will. While this institutional shift reduced the visible conflict characteristic of the Parliamentary Republic, interbranch conflict continued because Chilean elections consistently produced the sort of double-minority president common throughout much of twentieth-century Latin America. (Review *Governing Strategies: Fernando Belaúnde* in Chapter Four.) Most Chilean presidents were elected with around one-third of the vote, and their political parties typically controlled less than one-quarter of the seats in the legislature.

Thus, the search for compromise among legislators and between the legislative and executive branches was central to governance during this period. The key power broker in the legislature was the middle-class Radical party, whose core constituents were urban, white-collar workers (similar to the UCR in Argentina). While the Radicals did not dominate the legislature numerically, their typical one-fifth of the seats often constituted the key centrist swing votes between initiatives supported by rightist parties (Conservative and Liberal) or leftist parties (Socialist and Communist). In line with Cox and Morgenstern's analysis of executive-legislative relations, Chilean presidents were more prone to seek policy compromises within the legislature because many politicians became professional (that is, long-running) legislators and because many political parties focused on ideological competition based on policy-minded platforms. (Review the *Research Question* in Chapter Six on the dynamics of executive-legislative relations.)

Tension between and within these three principal legislative blocs grew with the election of conservative Carlos Ibáñez to the presidency in 1952. The subsequent government of the controversial Ibáñez, leader of a 1931 military coup, produced a schism in the Conservative party. Many moderate Conservative politicians broke ranks to form the Christian Democratic party in 1957, when the upcoming 1958 presidential elections produced talk of a possible victory by Socialist candidate Salvador Allende.

CONCEPTS IN ACTION
Land Reform

Income inequality has been a persistent problem in Latin America (review Table 3.1). Its roots lay in unequal land distribution during the colonial period. After independence, landowners remained central to economic and political life. During the late nineteenth and early twentieth centuries, the concentration of landownership often accelerated. For example, in Mexico, a select few gained title to many properties held by the Catholic church and to village land previously farmed communally. By 1910, 1 percent of the population controlled 85 percent of all farmland. Land reform—and in particular the return of land lost by peasants who had never established a written, legal title—would become one of the principal demands of the Mexican Revolution launched in late 1910.

In the early twentieth century, Latin American agriculture had a dualistic structure: massive estates (*latifundios*) comprised most farmland while peasants either held parcels of land too small to support themselves (*minifundios*) or owned no land at all. Millions of people lived as their parents and grandparents had: serving as day laborers, sharecroppers, and indentured servants on *latifundios*. By 1950, the largest 10 percent of all Latin American estates constituted 90 percent of all farmland. Land-reform demands multiplied because many people searched for a path out of poverty.

By the early 1960s, Mexico, Bolivia, and Cuba had implemented substantial land reform; all three land-reforming governments rose to power via revolution. During the Cold War climate of the 1960s and 1970s, the potential formation of guerrilla movements motivated many Latin American governments to pass legislation permitting the redistribution of land under varying circumstances. Governments in Chile, Ecuador, El Salvador, and Peru conducted considerable agrarian reform, while in other countries the amount of land redistributed proved minimal.

Land reform had three major objectives. First, governments wanted to reduce the likelihood that rural inequality and poverty might generate political discontent capable of toppling governments, be it at the ballot box or on the battlefield. Second, some hoped to lift the rural population out of poverty by providing peasants enough land to sustain themselves. Third, in several cases, governments also aimed at increasing agricultural production by putting previously unused land into cultivation. The success of land reform undertaken in Japan, South Korea, and Taiwan from the late 1940s through the 1950s buoyed hopes that agrarian reform would bring political and economic benefits.

Land reform in Latin America did not prove to be as successful, however, in realizing these objectives. The redistribution of land played a role in reducing rural conflict in some instances, while in others the agrarian reform movement sparked political violence between reform opponents and advocates. The two economic objectives have rarely been achieved. Without additional policy reforms, the redistribution of land alone did not lift most families out of poverty. The land redistributed was often only marginally arable, and small farmers had difficulty obtaining loans needed to irrigate land, control pests, diversify planting, and improve crop yields. In turn, this low productivity on many small farms meant that agricultural production typically declined despite an increase in acreage under cultivation.

Land reform remains an issue today in many Latin American countries because the problems that first motivated calls for land redistribution persist. Over half of the rural population lives on less than $2.00 per day. How might you organize a political coalition willing to help rural Latin Americans? What policy reforms would you advocate?

The "Three Thirds" of Polarized Pluralism (1958–1973)

Over the next three presidential election cycles, the search for compromise became overwhelmed by increasingly fierce differences among activists on the political right, at the political center, and on the political left. These differences were most visible in the debate over **land reform** (see *Concepts in Action: Land Reform*) and in the debate over Chile's major export, copper. The political right, spearheaded by the Conservative party, staunchly defended the status quo: a highly unequal distribution of land and a copper sector dominated by British and U.S. firms. The left, led by the Socialist party, countered with a call for massive change in both areas: substantial redistribution of land and nationalization of the copper industry. Faced with this political landscape during the Ibañez presidency (1952–1958), the Christian Democratic party attempted to build support for a middle road between these two polar alternatives.

In the 1958 presidential elections, Conservative candidate Jorge Alessandri won 31 percent of the vote—narrowly defeating Socialist Salvador Allende (29 percent). Christian Democrat Eduardo Frei finished in third place with 21 percent. From this point onward, the Christian Democrats replaced the Radicals as the key centrist party in Chile. As Alessandri blocked reform initiatives from centrist and leftist legislators, the pressure for reform continued to mount. Public opinion polls indicated that the desire for change after a decade of Conservative rule would propel Allende to victory in 1964 if the three-way race of 1958 repeated itself.

Faced with this scenario, most rightist parties agreed to support Frei's candidacy in a coalition designed to stop Allende from winning the presidency in 1964. The U.S. government supported this strategy and provided campaign funds. The strategy worked; Frei won in a two-way race with 56 percent of the vote to Allende's 39 percent. In the legislature, however, there remained sharp divisions among leftist, centrist, and rightist forces.

If Frei's so-called middle way of moderate reform were to triumph, it would need the support of legislators from outside his own party. In copper policy, the Frei government called for a path of Chileanization, in which the government would purchase a controlling 51 percent interest in the major copper companies but leave them under the original management. Politically, the Christian Democrats' proposed mixed ownership model stirred up a hornet's nest similar to Vargas's proposal for public-private management of the oil sector in Brazil during the 1950s. Leftist parties claimed that it would not reduce foreign profiteering; conservative legislators (even those sympathetic to the proposal) withheld their support in an effort to get the Frei government to push more slowly for land reform. Although legislation to permit the Chileanization of copper passed in the middle of Frei's term, the government purchased a majority in only one of the smallest companies. The major copper firms remained under the control of private, foreign ownership.

The government faced even more difficulties regarding land reform. Frei announced plans to provide land to 100,000 peasants. Rightist parties chafed at the prospect of any reform, while leftist parties pushed for more aggressive legislation. In 1967, new legislation set a limit of eighty hectares (roughly 200 acres) per farm. The government could then redistribute any land in excess of that figure, although large landholders could determine which eighty hectares they would retain. The government would purchase the excess land based on its value in tax assessments. After making a small down payment, the authorities would pay the rest of value over a twenty-five- to thirty-year period. In the last years of Frei's presidency, over 20,000 people gained access to land managed cooperatively. For Allende's supporters, these changes were not taking place fast enough; for conservatives, any redistribution proved unacceptable.

The controversy over land reform ruptured any possibility of repeating the 1964 coalition of rightist and centrist parties in the upcoming 1970 presidential elections. Rather than backing the Christian Democrats, the rightist parties once again united behind the candidacy of former president Jorge Alessandri. In turn, the leftist parties presented themselves as the only political force willing and able to address the long-standing inequality of land and income distribution. In pursuit of victory in a three-way race, leftist and center-left parties formed the Popular Unity (*Unidad Popular* [UP]) coalition and backed the candidacy of Salvador Allende and his call for a "democratic path to socialism."

In the 1970 election, Allende received 36 percent of the vote while Alessandri garnered 35 percent. In accord with the 1925 constitution, if no candidate received a majority of the popular vote, the legislature would elect the president from the two candidates receiving the most votes. By custom, the legislature had selected the candidate receiving the most votes in all prior elections, even though legislators from the party of the runner-up often voted for their candidate. Conservative legislators announced plans to vote for Alessandri, thus making the Christian Democratic bloc the deciding factor. Two days before the scheduled vote, rightist paramilitary forces attempted to kidnap the head of the military, General René Schneider. They hoped to blame leftist groups for the kidnapping. Instead, Schneider died defending himself, and conservatives' involvement became known. This incident helped to hold Christian Democratic votes in support of Allende. Allende publicly agreed to maintain constitutional principles, and Christian Democratic legislators voted for him.

Because the parties of the Popular Unity coalition held just two-fifths of the seats in Congress, the Allende government lacked the legislative support needed to forge a socialist economic system (see *Governing Strategies: Salvador Allende*). As a result, it focused on fulfilling campaign promises to improve people's lives so that it might win control of Congress in the legislative elections

GOVERNING STRATEGIES
Salvador Allende

After completing medical school, Salvador Allende helped to found the Chilean Socialist party in 1933. Four years later, he began a thirty-three-year career as a member of the national legislature. In 1942, he became the leader of the Socialist party. Allende ran unsuccessfully for the presidency in 1952, 1958, and 1964. His narrow victory in 1970 gave him the task of pursuing a gradual transition to socialism as a double-minority president.

The Popular Unity (UP) coalition strategy aimed at expanding popular support and thus winning a majority in the 1973 legislative election. The UP tried to fulfill rapidly its promises to nationalize the copper industry, redistribute land, and raise the standard of living of poor Chileans. In its first two years in office, the Allende government nationalized the entire copper industry, redistributed twice the amount of land redistributed during the six-year Frei administration, and raised the average real wage by almost 50 percent.

However, the government's strategy further polarized an already divided society. Within the UP, some activists called for a transition to socialism by any means necessary: land occupations and factory seizures occurred frequently. In turn, on the far right, several paramilitary organizations formed to attack leftists and suspected leftists. The U.S. government stopped sending foreign aid to Chile and applied economic pressure through covert measures. A reduction in the world price for copper and crop failures in 1972 further soured the economic climate.

Salvador Allende had spent most of his adult life working out legislative compromises within a divided Congress. In early 1972, the UP began negotiations with the Christian Democratic party to work out a mutually acceptable framework for nationalizing a series of firms. The first talks broke down when Socialist legislators asked Allende to reject the bill. Then, in June 1972, Allende invited the Christian Democrats back to the table. The leaders of both the UP bloc and the Christian Democratic bloc agreed to a nationalization policy, but the conservative wing of the Christian Democratic party blocked its passage in July. They argued that the UP could be defeated electorally. If the center-right opposition could gain a two-thirds majority in Congress, it could override presidential vetoes and also reduce presidential authority via constitutional amendment.

By the time those elections were held, the fulcrum of political life had left Congress and spilled out into the streets. An October 1972 truckers' strike (backed by covert funds from the U.S. Central Intelligence Agency) doubled inflation and caused shortages of many basic goods. Food shortages stimulated the expansion of well-publicized protests known at the March of the Pots, which were organized by upper-middle-income housewives. On the other end of the political spectrum, angry workers occupied many factories.

In March 1973, the UP coalition achieved its best ever electoral result—winning 44 percent of the vote. The 1973 election did not end the executive-legislative stalemate, however; the UP failed to win a majority while the opposition failed to win two-thirds of the seats. A failed coup attempt on June 29 and a new truckers' strike demanding Allende's resignation signaled the beginning of the end. On September 11, 1973, Allende refused an offer of safe passage into exile. He gave his final radio address and apparently died by his own hand as troops stormed the *Casa de la Moneda*, the presidential office building.

scheduled for March 1973. The achievement of these campaign promises came at a high price. The controversy surrounding many of these economic measures destroyed hopes of finding common cause with Christian Democratic legislators, much less with a hardened rightist opposition. Meanwhile, fissures appeared within the UP coalition itself when more radical elements pushed for an immediate shift to a socialist economy by decree rather than backing the more gradual approach outlined by Allende.

Increasingly isolated at home and abroad by 1973, the Allende government attempted to shore up support in the armed forces by naming the armed forces chief Carlos Prats as defense minister. It proved too late, however, to avert a coup. On September 11, Augusto Pinochet, the general that Prats had nominated as head of the army just weeks earlier, helped carry out a coup that ended the Allende government. To this day, some people debate whether Salvador Allende took his own life or was killed by the military (although a 1990 autopsy by his personal physician indicated a suicide). Another issue related to the coup is beyond debate: in the days that followed, the military arrested thousands of presumed UP activists and murdered hundreds of them.

The Pinochet Regime (1973–1989)

Many centrist and rightist politicians had supported the coup. They expected the junta to call elections fairly quickly once the repression of leftists and presumed leftists was finished. Instead, the military regime, headed by Pinochet from September 13 onward, launched a substantial reorganization of Chilean economics and politics in the first episode of prolonged military rule in Chilean history. The government placed its economic policy in the hands of a young generation of market-oriented economists known as the Chicago boys (because many had been trained at the University of Chicago during the 1960s). The economic reforms of the 1970s centered on the reduction of tariff barriers and the privatization of many state-owned enterprises. Despite its market-oriented actions in many areas, the military regime left the recently nationalized copper industry (*Corporación Nacional del Cobre de Chile* [CODELCO]) in government control and earmarked a healthy percentage of CODELCO's earnings to the defense budget.

In the political realm, Pinochet first centralized additional authority in the office of the president, thus marginalizing the role of his rivals in the army, air force, and navy. He then supervised the creation of the 1980 constitution that gave him a new eight-year term in office, to be followed by an additional eight years without free elections if voters approved an extension in 1988. The 1980 constitution was ratified in an extremely controversial plebiscite. The voting took place in the wake of seven years of harsh repression in which at least 2,000 Chileans were executed and roughly one in forty were imprisoned without trial and/or tortured (review Table 5.4). Opponents of the new constitution had no access to the major media and had limited ability to organize rallies and to mobilize a vote against the new constitution. Furthermore, thousands of former UP supporters had been removed from voter registration lists. In this dark context, the plebiscite generated a two-thirds vote in favor of the proposed constitution.

The Pinochet government nonetheless presented the approval of the 1980 constitution as evidence of broad public support for its economic program. It pressed forward with a market-oriented reform of government services and labor relations known as the Seven Modernizations. These policy changes transformed the role of government in seven key areas: agriculture, education, health, justice, public administration, and social security. In agriculture, previous land reform under Frei and Allende had broken down the *latifundio* system of large estates by redistributing over two-fifths of all land. Pinochet's government returned 28 percent of the expropriated land to its original owners, while 20 percent of the expropriated land was sold to the highest bidder. The remaining 52 percent of the newly created cooperative farmland was broken into smaller parcels and sold to the participating farmers. Because many of the small parcel owners lacked access to financing, nearly half of them sold their land to agribusinesses by 1981.[3] This policy change led to the reconcentration of farmland in agribusinesses that focused largely on producing out-of-season fruit for wealthy countries in the Northern Hemisphere.

Reforms in other areas had similarly profound implications. The government placed most schools under local control while cutting the national government's funding of education at the secondary level and higher. The system of universal 6 percent payroll deductions to support a nationwide medical care policy was privatized: economically comfortable individuals could now pull their contributions out of the state-run medical system and spend them on a more expensive, more comprehensive program of private insurance. This policy change left less fortunate individuals tied to a government health system that lost half its funding when middle- and upper-income Chileans entered the private system. Sweeping judicial reform expanded the number of courts by nearly one-third while also relaxing rules of evidence so that fewer legal restrictions could preclude the presentation of material in evidence. Labor law reform fragmented the labor movement by prohibiting closed (union) shop rules and outlawing nationwide collective bargaining. These changes made it difficult for smaller, plant-level unions to negotiate because they represented fewer workers and found it hard to build a strike fund with which to bankroll a walkout if negotiations went poorly. In public administration, the government expanded the authority of local governments yet kept those governments under the control of unelected officials named by the national government. Finally, in social security, Chile became the first country in the world to transform its public pension program into a private investment program. Initially, this social security reform earned publicity the world over for injecting large sums of new money into the

Chilean financial sector. Critics note, however, that the volatility of these funds has increased over time, thereby endangering future pensions. The most acerbic critiques of pension privatization focus on the military's refusal to participate in the system: the armed forces continue to use the pay-as-you-go, formula-based public pension system that was outlawed for most other Chileans.

The initial wave of economic changes in the mid-1970s led to a reduction in inflation and an upswing in growth rates. During the world recession of the early 1980s, however, the Chilean economy collapsed. The gross domestic product (GDP) shrank by almost 14 percent during 1982–1983, and unemployment topped 20 percent. As many banks and industries went bankrupt, the Pinochet government named Hernán Büchi finance minister in 1983. Büchi restored some government subsidies for economic activity, and this stimulus—combined with economic recovery in the industrialized economies and record copper prices on the world market—spurred an economic boom in 1984 that would last the rest of the 1980s. Despite this boom, by the end of the 1980s, real wages and unemployment had not yet returned to their 1970 levels.

Buoyed by strong economic growth and pressured to protect human rights by the international community, the Pinochet government decided to hold the 1988 plebiscite on the continuation of military rule under different conditions from those prevailing in 1980. It provided free television time to regime opponents mobilized in support of a no vote that would trigger new elections. In further contrast with 1980, centrist and leftist parties came together to organize a broad coalition in support of an end to military rule. In the October 5, 1988, plebiscite, voters called for an end to the Pinochet presidency by a margin of 55 to 43 percent.

CONTEMPORARY POLITICAL FRAMEWORK

The Chilean political framework stems from the 1980 constitution, which was written under military rule. Because of the constitution's controversial origins, political party leaders and interest groups have criticized various provisions since its creation. Several key elements entrenched the role of the military in politics; others extended several portions of the political system beyond the control of elected leaders.

Over the years, the constitution has remained under the political microscope. The 1980 constitution was modified in 1989 after negotiations between civilian politicians and military leaders followed Pinochet's defeat in the 1988 plebiscite. The constitution initially called for amendments to be approved by three-fifths majorities in two successive legislative terms and by the president—a difficult and time-consuming prospect. In contrast, the four-person military junta could modify the constitution if the reforms were approved by plebiscite. Following give-and-take negotiations between civilians and the military, a plebiscite ratified fifty-four changes to the 1980 constitution in July 1989, with 86 percent voting in favor of the changes. One of those changes made the amendment process easier by requiring a three-fifths vote of a single legislature and the approval of the president. Other constitutional modifications have occurred under civilian rule. In this section, we will take stock of Chile's political institutions at the start of the twenty-first century.

The Executive Branch

The 1980 constitution initially provided for a strong president with an eight-year term in office and the possibility of reelection. This centralization of authority for potentially long periods of time took place in a context in which the Chilean military regime felt confident that Pinochet would be the president from 1980 until 1996. However, Pinochet's loss in the 1988 reelection plebiscite triggered open elections that the political forces closest to Pinochet seemed likely to lose.

Prior to those elections, the military government instituted several changes in the 1980 constitution. Fearing the loss of the presidency, the government shortened the term of the transitional civilian president to four years. In addition, the negotiations led to the restoration of the traditional prohibition on reelection. Another reform reshaped civil-military relations: the president cannot make military personnel decisions without the approval of the National Security Council (a body controlled by Pinochet appointees at the outset of the new democracy).

The president is elected via a ballotage system. If no candidate wins a majority in the first round, the two candidates receiving the most votes face each other in a runoff, second-round election. In early 1994, as the transitional presidency of Patricio Aylwin ended, the legislature voted to shorten the presidential term from eight to six years. With the important exception noted above regarding civil-military relations, the Chilean presidency can be characterized as potentially dominant within the analytical framework developed by Mainwaring and Shugart (review Table 4.6). Like many Latin American presidents, Chilean chief executives can name and remove most ministers at will. The president has a strong veto that can be overridden by a two-thirds majority in both houses of Congress. The 1980 constitution expanded the president's legislative decree powers. While standard presidential decrees cannot countermand existing legislation, decrees of urgency (similar to the power of the Argentine president) have the force of law for thirty days unless Congress acts to countermand the decree. The Chilean president has the exclusive power to modify the structure of government agencies, introduce the national budget, and propose tax changes. Furthermore, Congress has only sixty days in which to review the presidential budget proposal and agree on modifications; after sixty days, the presidential proposal becomes law. The president can also set the agenda by requiring Congress to respond within three, five, or ten days.

The Legislature

The Chilean legislature is bicameral. The lower house, the Chamber of Deputies, has a membership that is elected according to population size. The sixty electoral districts of roughly equal size each choose two deputies.

Deputies serve four-year terms, with the entire chamber coming up for election every four years. They are elected via a **binomial electoral system** in which each party presents a slate of two candidates. If a single slate wins twice as many votes as the second-place list, then both seats go to the winning party. If no party achieves this difficult task, then one seat goes to the party receiving the most votes, with the other seat going to the list receiving the second most votes.

This limited variant of proportional representation was chosen by the military government in 1980 for two reasons. First, as opposed to the traditional "three thirds" constellation of Chilean politics, the binomial system forces parties to compete for centrist votes to increase their chances of gaining a seat. Second, the military remained confident that this system would enable conservative parties to win one seat in most districts, thereby decreasing the likelihood that centrist and leftist parties could gain the three-fifths of Congress needed to amend the 1980 constitution.

The upper house, the Senate, was the focus of considerable controversy at the outset of the new democracy. The 1980 constitution originally called for eight-year senatorial terms, with twenty-six senators chosen via the binomial electoral system and nine appointed senators (all chosen by the Pinochet government when democracy returned in 1989). In other words, Pinochet appointees initially would hold just over one-fourth of the seats. This configuration meant that appointed senators, along with less than a handful of elected senators, could block constitutional amendments because amendments would require a three-fifths majority. Not surprisingly, the parties opposed to the continuation of Pinochet's presidency also opposed this effort to extend his influence in the new legislature. After the 1988 plebiscite, these parties did not manage to force the outgoing Pinochet government to eliminate the appointed seats, but they did convince the government to add twelve more elected senators—somewhat reducing the power of the appointed senators. In exchange for this reform, the Pinochet government got opposition parties to support the changes in the presidential term mentioned earlier.

As a result of these changes, the Chilean Senate consists of thirty-eight senators elected by nineteen districts, plus nine designated seats. Roughly half of the elected senators come up for election every four years. In addition, past presidents who served for six or more years held the right to serve as senators for life; this provision meant that Pinochet could serve as a senator once he retired from active duty in the military. While the designated senators' role in the system was not as great as initially planned, the combination of conservative appointees and the effects of the binomial electoral system made it difficult to overcome the conservative majority that controlled the Senate after the return to democracy.

The Judiciary

As in many Latin American countries, the Chilean judiciary historically employed the **magistrate system**, in which judges preside over both the investigative and the trial phase of legal proceedings. This system created two sets of concerns shared by many people across the political spectrum. First, the dual role of the judge slowed the judicial process because trial duties slowed down investigations (and vice versa). Second, concerns grew that this combination of tasks gave judges too much influence over prosecutions—authority that could be abused. In the 1990s, rightist and leftist legislators brought impeachment allegations against several judges, including some Supreme Court justices.

After the return to democracy, President Patricio Aylwin proposed a series of reforms to the judicial system that were blocked by conservative legislators. Then, in 1997, President Eduardo Frei Ruiz-Tagle brokered several similar reforms that gained sufficient support among leftist, centrist, and rightist legislators. Two major constitutional changes gave the Chilean judiciary its current shape. First, the reforms created the Public Ministry that would serve as a prosecutorial power with investigative authority. Second, several modifications were made to the Supreme Court. The pool of Supreme Court justices was expanded from seventeen to twenty-one. While Supreme Court justices did not receive a fixed term, a mandatory retirement age of seventy-five was introduced. This last change immediately affected six Pinochet appointees. The president can nominate new justices from a list approved by the Supreme Court itself. Those nominees must then be ratified by a two-thirds vote of the Senate.

As in most of Latin America, the Constitutional Tribunal in Chile is a separate judicial body that exercises the power of judicial review. Its seven members are chosen through various mechanisms. Three are former Supreme Court justices chosen by the Supreme Court. Two are lawyers chosen by the National Security Council. The president selects one, and the final member is elected by a majority vote in the Senate. This system of appointment, like other features of the 1980 constitution, limits the role of Chile's elected officials: only two of the seven members of the constitutional court are chosen by the chief executive and the legislature.

POLITICAL PARTICIPATION

For much of the twentieth century, Chilean political participation became framed increasingly around ideological differences. Different labor unions and peasant movements were affiliated with various political parties. Business organizations also began to divide into conservative and moderate groups. Chilean voters supported parties from across the political spectrum beginning in the 1930s. By the 1960s, political loyalties were expressed in three visible factions tied to leftist, centrist, and rightist political parties. Differences between the left and the right expanded in the 1960s and 1970s, and these ideological conflicts helped lead to the fall of the Allende government in 1973.

The military government under Augusto Pinochet set out to eliminate leftist sympathies in interest groups and political parties. Repression did not succeed in wiping out all leaders and supporters of the Socialist and Communist parties, but the left began to coordinate its opposition to military rule in concert with the Christian Democrats and other centrist forces. This cooperation crystallized in the "no" campaign against the 1988 plebiscite. After that success, most centrist and leftist forces formed the Concertation coalition, which would be the most electorally successful movement during the first fifteen years of the new democratic regime.

Interest Groups and Social Movements

Large estate owners founded the National Agricultural Society (*Sociedad Nacional de Agricultura* [SNA]) in 1869. During the years 1873–1901, SNA members held between one-fourth and one-third of all legislative seats. In some sectors (particularly in a cattle sector threatened by Argentine competitors), the SNA called for protectionist policies. For the most part, however, the SNA favored a market-oriented approach. During the middle of the twentieth century, the association successfully lobbied several presidents to impede the unionization of rural workers. The SNA was a vocal opponent of the Allende government and enjoyed access to the Pinochet dictatorship that followed. After the return to democracy, the SNA threw its support behind the conservative coalition of political parties.

The most politically vocal manufacturing interest announced its formation in 1883 in a ceremony held in the facilities of the SNA. The Manufacturing Promotion Society (*Sociedad de Fomento Fabril* [SFF]) called for the creation of an industrial base through the use of protective tariffs. By the late nineteenth century, the group succeeded in convincing the government to protect several sectors and to give domestic producers favorable treatment in bidding for government contracts. From its foundation through the 1920s, roughly one-third of the SFF's governing board simultaneously held posts in the national government in either the executive branch or the legislature. Like the SNA, the SFF tried to impede unionization and later vehemently opposed the Allende government. During the recession of the early 1980s, several SFF members helped to push for the reinsertion of government assistance to some sectors.

The ideological diversity of the Chilean labor movement in the twentieth century mirrored the multitude of perspectives found among political parties. Amid this diversity, the largest labor confederation from the 1950s through the early 1970s was the Unitary Workers Federation (*Central Única de Trabajadores* [CUT]). A rival federation, the Workers' Democratic Federation (*Central Democrática de Trabajadores* [CDT]), aligned itself with the Christian Democratic party. By 1970, two-fifths of the workforce was unionized. The Pinochet dictatorship worked to atomize the labor movement. Unions and strikes were made illegal when the military junta took power. As occurred in Argentina and Brazil under military rule, many labor leaders were arrested or driven into hiding. Then, in 1979, a new labor law legalized unions but made closed shops and obligatory membership illegal. It also enabled groups as small as twenty-five employees to form rival unions. By 1981, less than 10 percent of the workforce belonged to unions. Nonetheless, leftist and centrist union leaders came together in the early 1980s to form a coordinating confederation opposed to the continuation of military rule. In 1988, many of these unions formed the Unitary Workers Confederation (*Confederación Única de Trabajadores* [CUT]). The CUT has supported the center-left Concertation coalition and succeeded in mobilizing support for some labor law reforms after the return to democracy, including an end to a sixty-day time limit on strike activity.

The Catholic church has played a diverse set of roles over the course of Chile's political evolution. As occurred elsewhere in Latin America, the nineteenth century bore witness to an ongoing battle between liberals who were critical of the church's role in society and conservatives who defended that prominence. The Catholic church retained close ties to conservative political leaders until the late 1950s, when many clergy and active laity supported the newly formed Christian Democratic party's calls for socioeconomic reform. While many Catholics celebrated the election of Eduardo Frei in 1964, the church viewed Allende's election with considerable apprehension and mistrust. Some feared that the government would promote atheism. Although the Catholic church hierarchy initially embraced the coup and participated in ceremonies entrenching the dictatorship, the brutality of the repression that followed polarized the church. Active laity in Christian base communities and several members of the hierarchy—including the archbishop of Santiago, Cardinal Raúl Silva—eventually took an open stand against human rights violations. Many churches provided a meeting place for victims of the repression and opponents of the dictatorship. Meanwhile, other bishops and churches remained supportive of the Pinochet government throughout its rule. After the return to democratic rule, the Catholic church has loosened its ties with the Christian Democratic movement and focused its political energy on a defense of traditional Catholic doctrine. Chile entered the twenty-first century as the lone Latin American country (and one of only three countries in the world) without a divorce law. The church fought off several attempts to legalize divorce during the democratic era; however, public opinion polls showing over 70-percent support for the legalization of divorce eventually swayed the legislature. In March 2004 the Chilean legislature passed a divorce law that would take effect toward the end of the year.

Parties and Elections

Chilean political life in the decades prior to the Pinochet dictatorship witnessed the emergence of three visible blocs of voters on the left, at the center, and on the right of the political spectrum. While most of the political right supported the "yes" campaign in favor of extending Pinochet's presidency in 1988, most of the surviving leadership of the centrist and leftist parties came together in support of the "no" campaign. After voters rejected Pinochet's government, that same center-left coalition campaigned together in the 1989 presidential and legislative elections as the Concertation for Democracy (*Concertación por la Democracia*).

The Concertation has its roots in two major political parties of the 1960s and 1970s: the Christian Democrats and the Socialists. The Christian Democratic party (*Partido Demócrata Cristiano* [PDC]) has been the most important centrist party since its formation in 1957. As discussed earlier, the PDC's founding leaders had formed part of the conservative movement but grew disaffected with the intransigence of the right in the face of growing demands for social change elsewhere in society. Although its primary founder, Eduardo Frei, died during the military regime in 1982, many of its veteran leaders remained active after the return to democracy. As time passed, a new generation of PDC activists—most notably, Eduardo Frei Montalva's son, Eduardo Frei Ruiz-Tagle—began to occupy leadership posts. The PDC put forth the first two presidential candidates supported by the Concertation in 1989 and 1993, but it lost in a primary election in 1999. Some analysts wonder if the PDC might break away from the coalition if one of its politicians does not emerge as presidential candidate for the Concertation in 2005.

In turn, the Socialist party (*Partido Socialista* [PS]) has a longer history. Formed in 1933, the PS frequently fell victim to factionalization as splinter groups left the party. Nevertheless, over time, the Socialists eclipsed the Communist party as the most important leftist movement in Chilean politics. After the coup against the Allende government, many Socialist politicians and supporters were killed while others were arrested or driven into exile. With the Socialist party formally outlawed during the dictatorship, the moderate wing of the PS called for cooperation with the PDC in pursuit of a return to democracy. In 1988, they formed the Party for Democracy (*Partido por la Democracia* [PPD], to serve as a vehicle for mobilizing support for a no vote in the 1988 plebiscite. Under this same label, many Socialist politicians competed in the 1989 elections with the idea that the PS would then be legalized after the return to civilian rule. After the PS was legalized, however, the party failed to reunite fully at its December 1990 party congress. Instead, the PPD and the PS emerged as separate entities (although many socialists initially became members of both parties). As the somewhat more market-oriented PPD established its separate identity, the PS decided in 1993 to put an end to shared membership. From this point onward, the PS and the PPD maintained the allegiance of roughly 11 percent of the voters. PPD founder Ricardo Lagos lost the competition to be the Concertation's presidential nominee at a convention in May 1993. Lagos later would win a primary election to serve as the center-left coalition's candidate in 1999.

Chilean conservative parties went through several organizational transformations from the 1960s through the 1980s. Prior to that period, the two major conservative parties had been the Conservative party and the Liberal party. Conservatives and Liberals agreed on most economic issues but retained some historical differences regarding the role of the Catholic church. The creation of the PDC in 1957 and the rise of the Allende vote in the 1958 and 1964 elections motivated Conservatives and Liberals to unite and form the National party in 1965. The National party fiercely criticized the Allende government and cheered the coup. The National party went into hiatus amid the absence of electoral politics. As antigovernment protests multiplied during the 1980s, however, several conservative movements began to organize openly. Many of the leaders of the National party formed the National Unity Movement (*Movimiento de Unidad Nacional* [MUN]), while a collection of participants in the military government established the Independent Democratic Union (*Unión Democrática Independiente* [UDI]). The UDI mobilized in favor of holding the 1988 plebiscite as planned, while the MUN called for either the presentation of a new presidential candidate (other than Pinochet) or an open presidential election. When the no votes triumphed in the plebiscite, the MUN competed in the 1989 elections as the National Renewal party (*Renovación Nacional* [RN]). From 1989 to the present, the RN and the UDI have maintained an often fractious electoral alliance designed to prevent the Concertation from doubling the vote share of the second-place ticket within Chile's distinctive binomial electoral system. In the early 1990s, the RN held more support in public opinion polls than did the UDI. From the late 1990s onward, however, the rising leader on the political right has been the UDI's Joaquín Lavín, a former mayor of the Santiago suburb of Los Condes who later became mayor of Santiago in 2000. The center-right coalition has undergone several name changes over time and is currently called the Alliance for Chile (*Alianza por Chile*).

The results of all presidential elections following the return to democracy are in Table 7.1 on page 224. The Concertation coalition chose veteran PDC leader Patricio Aylwin to serve as its presidential candidate in 1989. Prior to the dictatorship, the seventy-one-year-old Aylwin had spent most of his adult life in the legislature. In stark contrast, the conservative coalition backed Pinochet's thirty-nine-year-old finance minister, Hernán Büchi. Another conservative leader, Francisco Errázuriz, ran as a center-right alternative less connected to the Pinochet government. In the end, Aylwin won the election with roughly the same percentage of votes that had supported the no vote in the 1988 plebiscite. Then, in the 1993 campaign, the Concertation convention chose a figure who symbolized generational change and also held ties to past leaders: Eduardo Frei Ruiz-Tagle, whose father founded the PDC and governed Chile from 1964 to 1970. He campaigned to pursue the unfinished business of altering the 1980 constitution and reducing poverty. The Concertation increased its margin of victory over conservative challenger Arturo Alessandri Besa (himself the nephew of a past president and the grandson of another). After ten years in the presidency, cracks began to show in the Concertation's electoral support in 1999. Youthful UDI leader Joaquín Lavín criticized problems accumulated over the Concertation's decade in the presidency and presented himself as a can-do mayor of Los Condes. His opponent, veteran politician Ricardo Lagos, managed to deflect most efforts to demonize his earlier support for socialism but

TABLE 7.1 Chilean Presidential Elections (1989, 1995, 1999, 2000): Percentage of Popular Vote

Party coalition	Year			
	1989	1995	1999	2000*
Concertation for Democracy	55.2	58.0	48.0	51.3[†]
Union for Chile[†]	29.4	24.4	47.5	48.7
Others	15.4	17.6	4.5	—

*Because no presidential candidate received a majority in the 1999 election, a runoff election was held in January 2000 between the two candidates who received the most votes in the first round.

[†]The Union for Chile ran in the 1989 elections as the Democracy and Progress Coalition; in 1995, it was called the Union for Progress.

SOURCE: Political Database of the Americas <http://www.georgetown.edu/pdba/Elecdata/Chile/chile.html> (accessed on November 14, 2003).

TABLE 7.2 Chilean Chamber of Deputies (1989, 1993, 1997, 2001): Percentage of Seats Held, by Party

Party coalition	Year			
	1989	1993	1997	2001
Concertation for Democracy	58	58	58	52
Alliance for Chile*	40	42	39	48
Independents	2	0	3	1

*The 2001 Alliance for Chile coalition has undergone name changes with each legislative election: the Democracy and Progress Coalition in 1989, the Union for Progress in 1993, and Union for Chile in 1997. Percentages do not always add up to 100 because of rounding.

SOURCE: For 1989, data are from Timothy Scully, "Reconstituting Party Politics in Chile," in Scott Mainwaring and Timothy Scully, eds., *Building Democratic Institutions: Party Systems in Latin America* (Stanford, Calif.: Stanford University Press, 1995), p. 126. For the years 1993–2001, data are from the Political Database of the Americas <http://www.georgetown.edu/pdba/Elecdata/Chile/chile.html> (accessed on November 14, 2003).

had a more difficult time inspiring enthusiasm. The first-round election was a dead heat in which neither candidate won the necessary majority within the ballotage system. In the runoff, Lagos won narrowly with 51 percent of the vote.

The reforms to the selection of legislators undertaken during the military regime served their purpose during the first fifteen years of the new democracy. The binomial electoral system to the Chamber of Deputies enabled the conservative coalition to maintain just over two-fifths of the seats with roughly one-third of the vote (see Table 7.2). A similar dynamic emerged in the Senate.

Conservatives consistently have won over two-fifths of the thirty-eight elected seats. During the 1990s, most appointed senators held conservative sympathies, which prevented the Concertation from forming a majority in the upper house.

THE CONTEMPORARY QUEST FOR DEVELOPMENT, LIBERTY, AND GOVERNANCE

The return to democracy in Chile took place on the heels of a prolonged economic boom. After the deep recession of 1982–1983, the Chilean economy grew by an annual average of 6.6 percent during the years 1984–1989. While many Latin American countries were beginning a shift toward more market-oriented economic policies during the late 1980s, that policy change took place during the Pinochet dictatorship in Chile. Although many Latin American countries were debating how to stimulate economic growth during the return to democracy, the debate in Chile focused on how to reduce socioeconomic inequality.

As in Argentina, the debate over liberty focused on the violent legacy of military rule. Many of the Chileans who voted no in the 1988 plebiscite hoped that a return to democracy would set into motion a rule of law under which those who committed human rights violations would be held accountable. Many Concertation politicians had announced their intentions to prosecute perpetrators of human rights violations. How might this goal be accomplished without reigniting the politically polarized environment that characterized Chilean politics during the 1960s and 1970s?

In stark contrast to the situation in Argentina, the pursuit of governance via civilian rule in Chile faced the ongoing governmental presence of many key leaders of the military regime. Furthermore, most of the formal political rules in Chile were laid out in the 1980 constitution, which was written under military rule. While that constitution was partially modified in 1989, many key provisions continued to restrain the new civilian authorities. Nine designated senators prevented the newly elected Aylwin government from attaining a majority in the upper house. Another provision guaranteed the armed forces a share of revenues produced by the national copper firm, thereby protecting the military's budget. Perhaps most notably, the leader of the dictatorship, General Augusto Pinochet, would remain as commander of the army because the president was powerless to remove him legally.

The Quest for Development in Chile

The Aylwin government promised to promote growth with equity while retaining many key elements of the market capitalist model installed under Pinochet. After taking office, Aylwin reiterated that market forces would shape prices; domestic price controls would not be considered. In his first year in office, Aylwin cut tariffs on imports, from 15 percent down to 11 percent. In turn, his administration began to negotiate a series of new free-trade agreements (review *Global Perspectives: Regional Economic Integration* in Chapter Five). During Aylwin's term, Chile signed free-trade agreements (FTAs) with Colombia and Venezuela and became one of the few Latin American countries to join the Asian Pacific Economic Cooperation (APEC) group. These policies aimed at expanding trade opportunities and at diversifying Chile's trade partners so that it would become less dependent on its relations with the United States and the European Union.

Equity constituted the other major development goal. The Pinochet economic reforms eventually had generated growth, but poverty increased over the course of the military regime. While one-fourth of the population was poor in 1973, nearly two-fifths were poor in 1989. The Aylwin government reinstituted a minimum wage and then systematically updated it annually via a formula tied to changes in inflation and in labor productivity. In addition, spending on health, education, and welfare expanded by nearly 50 percent over the course of Aylwin's administration. Tax reform funded the increased spending. The Concertation negotiated with conservative parties (especially the RN) to gain their support in Congress. Income tax rates for individuals and businesses went up, and the sales tax also rose, from 16 to 18 percent. This reform permitted the government to expand social programs without resorting to deficit spending and borrowing.

When Aylwin left office, he could point to many economic successes (see Table 7.3). The economy grew by over 6 percent annually. Inflation was cut in half. The percentage of Chileans living in poverty fell from 39 percent down to 28 percent. Not all of the goals were met: income inequality remained considerable. The wealthiest 10 percent of the population continued to receive just under 42 percent of all earnings, as they did when Aylwin took office.

Criticism of the Concertation economic policies during the Aylwin presidency centered on what some considered to be slow and insufficient progress in promoting greater economic equity. Frei responded to these concerns by launching the National Plan to Overcome Poverty (*Plan Nacional para la Superación de la Pobreza*). To signal his commitment, Frei personally chaired the interministerial cabinet committee administering the program. He also created a volunteer corps that recruited young professionals to work toward poverty alleviation.

At the same time, Frei also established a citizens' advisory council filled with a diverse membership of entrepreneurs, labor leaders, community activists, and researchers. Following two years of study, the council's advisory report called for greater inclusion of community groups in the design and implementation of poverty reduction strategies. The executive branch largely ignored this strategy and instead shifted its focus toward the promotion of equal opportunity in the economic sphere. When the Concertation's share of the vote fell down to a slim majority in the 1997 legislative elections, Frei responded by highlighting the role of educational subsidies in reducing poverty in the short term because they added to the income received by poor families.

TABLE 7.3   Chilean Economic Indicators (1983–2002)*

Year	GDP growth	Inflation	Unemployment	Debt service ratio[†]
1983	−0.5	24	19.0	39
1984	6.0	23	18.5	48
1985	2.4	26	17.0	44
1986	5.3	17	13.1	38
1987	5.7	21	11.9	26
1988	7.5	13	10.2	22
1989	9.8	21	7.2	19
1990	2.0	27	6.5	18
1991	7.3	19	8.2	15
1992	10.9	13	6.7	11
1993	6.6	12	6.5	10
1994	5.0	9	7.8	8
1995	9.0	8	7.4	7
1996	6.9	7	6.4	7
1997	6.7	6	6.1	7
1998	3.3	5	6.4	8
1999	−0.5	2	9.8	8
2000	4.2	5	9.2	8
2001	3.2	3	9.1	8
2002	2.1	3	9.0	6

*All numbers are percentages.
[†]The debt service ratio expresses interest paid on foreign debts as a percentage of total exports.
SOURCE: For the years 1983–1987, data are from United Nations Economic Commission for Latin America and the Caribbean, *Preliminary Overview of the Economies of Latin America and the Caribbean 1989* (Santiago, Chile: United Nations Publications, 1989). For the years 1988–1992, data are from United Nations Economic Commission for Latin America and the Caribbean, *Preliminary Overview of the Economies of Latin America and the Caribbean 1994* (Santiago, Chile: United Nations Publications, 1994). For the years 1993–1997, data are from United Nations Economic Commission for Latin America and the Caribbean, *Preliminary Overview of the Economies of Latin America and the Caribbean 1999* (Santiago, Chile: United Nations Publications, 1999). For the years 1998–2002, data are from United Nations Economic Commission for Latin America and the Caribbean, *Preliminary Overview of the Economies of Latin America and the Caribbean 2003* (Santiago, Chile: United Nations Publications, 2003).

The Frei administration maintained the free-trade orientation of recent Chilean governments. In 1998, the government reduced the average tariff from 11 percent down to 8 percent. In addition to unilateral trade liberalization, the government continued to pursue various bilateral and multilateral trade agreements. As talks about entering the North American Free Trade Agreement stalled, Chile negotiated bilateral FTAs with Canada and with Mexico. In 1994, Chile became an associate member of the Southern Cone Common Market

(*Mercado Común del Cono Sur* [MERCOSUR]) by entering into an FTA with an eye toward one day becoming a full participant in the common market as a whole. Then, in 1999, Chile entered an FTA with the member states of the Central American Common Market.

Although the economy performed well in several respects, economic conditions worsened in the latter portion of Frei's term when Chile began to feel the aftereffects of the Asian crisis during 1998–1999 (review Table 7.3). The economy grew by nearly 7 percent during his first four years in office, but growth slowed in 1998 and the economy contracted slightly during the 1999 election campaign. Inflation rates continued to decline, but unemployment rose during the economic slowdown of the last eighteen months of Frei's presidency. Nonetheless, the prevalence of poverty continued to decrease: the percentage of households living in poverty fell from 28 percent down to 21 percent. The Concertation's economic strategy did not solve all economic woes, but it did well in comparison with most Latin American countries.

The Lagos administration continued the free-trade approach of prior Concertation governments while it tried to develop new initiatives to improve education, health, and poverty reduction. In trade talks, the Lagos administration advanced in its attempts to negotiate free-trade agreements with both the European Union (EU) and with the United States. In 2002, Chile signed an FTA with the EU, and in 2003 it did so with the United States. After full implementation of these accords in the coming years, Chile will have tariff-free access to the two largest and wealthiest markets in the world. Chile also signed an FTA with South Korea and began trade negotiations with the Chinese government.

At the same time, the Lagos government pushed for passage of new legislation in social policy. The Chile in Solidarity (*Chile Solidario*) welfare program aimed at extending multifaceted assistance to the 225,000 poorest households in Chile over the years 2002–2005. The adult heads of each household would receive a diminishing income subsidy over the course of a twenty-four-month period as they tried to enter the workforce in a more self-sustaining fashion. These same households were eligible to larger educational subsidies that were conditional on keeping minors in school (similar to an initiative developed during the Cardoso government in Brazil in the 1990s). As of this writing, poverty statistics for the years in question are not yet available, so one cannot observe whether poverty reduction has continued despite slower economic growth during the first half of Lagos's term.

Chile has pursued a market capitalist approach to development longer than any other Latin American country examined in this book. By the late 1970s, the Pinochet dictatorship had dismantled most of the state capitalist policies that had been in place for much of the prior half century. While many Latin American countries have worked within a market-oriented framework since the early 1990s, Chile has consistently applied these policies for over a decade longer. All three Concertation governments have continued the process of trade liberalization begun under Pinochet. In contrast to the Seven Modernizations of the Pinochet era, however, the Concertation has worked to increase the role of government in promoting individual welfare. The *Research Question* on pages 230–231 examines further the political dynamics of **social policy** spending in contemporary Latin America. Is the Chilean experience of increased social spending within a generally market-oriented approach to economic policy the exception or the rule?

In several respects, this combination of free trade, fiscal responsibility, and social spending has been successful. The Chilean economy has grown more consistently and more quickly than any other Latin American economy. From 1990 through 2002, the GDP expanded at an annual average of 3.7 percent. High growth helped to maintain fiscal balance (because government revenues grow when economic activity increases). Accordingly, inflation declined from an annual average of 20 percent in the 1980s to an average of 6 percent during the years from 1993 to 2002. While other major Latin American countries began to experience financial crises during the late twentieth and early twenty-first century, Chile's debt service ratio remained low and stable. The greater emphasis on government policies in education, health, and welfare have helped to fight poverty. Social spending expanded from $36.00 per person in 1990 to $88.00 by 1999. In turn, while 39 percent of households were impoverished in 1990, the poverty rate had declined to 21 percent by 2001.

However, progress toward additional economic objectives has been minimal. Income distribution remains as unequal as it had been during the 1980s. The richest 10 percent of the population continues to receive 40 percent of all income. Brazil is the only Latin American country home to greater income inequality. Environmental deterioration constitutes another persistent concern. The boom in seafood exports during the 1980s and 1990s raised fears that Chile's coastline could not support continued fishing at then-current levels. Similar concerns have been raised regarding the sustainability of timber production in southern Chile.

The Quest for Liberty in Chile

The quest for liberty centered initially on the issue of human rights violations under the military regime. The military government had issued an amnesty law in April 1978 that precluded prosecution for any human rights violations occurring between the coup and March 10, 1978. This law prevented the majority of allegations from being pursued because those years covered the period of the most severe repression. During the transition to democracy, a legal challenge to the 1978 Amnesty Law was launched; it claimed that the self-amnesty was an illegal action by an illegal government. In January 1990, the Supreme Court (filled with Pinochet appointees) upheld the Amnesty Law and asserted that the law prevented not just human rights trials but also judicial investigations of allegations stemming from the period covered by the statute. After taking office in March 1990, Aylwin promised to pursue justice for the victims of repression "to the extent possible"—a clear reference to the restrictions posed by the Amnesty Law, a judiciary dominated by Pinochet appointees, a military largely free from presidential control, and the continuing presence of Pinochet as commander of the army.

In April, Patricio Aylwin announced the formation of the National Commission for Truth and Reconciliation (*Comisión Nacional de Verdad y Reconciliación*). The commission was charged with documenting all deaths due to human rights violations committed during the military regime. The group would become known informally as the Rettig commission (for its chair, Raúl Rettig). During 1990, people came forward with testimony that led to the discovery of several mass graves across the country. Both sides in the human rights debate found the commission controversial. Human rights groups like the Association of Families of Disappeared Detainees (*Agrupación de Familiares de los Detenidos Desapareci-dos* [AFDD]) were disappointed that the Rettig commission would not document the individuals committing the crimes. Conversely, the armed forces wanted no part of the investigation. In December, the army expressed its discontent by

---

RESEARCH QUESTION
Under What Conditions Are Governments Likely to Spend More Money on Social Policy?

The term *social policy* refers to government programs designed to improve individual welfare in areas including education, health care, unemployment insurance, and old-age pensions. Would the move toward market capitalism decrease spending on social policy? Robert Kaufman and Alex Segura-Ubiergo examined this issue in a 2001 study.[1]

In the theoretical debate over the impact of market-oriented policies on social spending, opinions diverge. The so-called efficiency hypothesis holds that governments in open economies are likely to reduce spending to improve the competitiveness of national firms. Pensions and unemployment insurance are often funded by payroll taxes; reducing spending on these programs would reduce the total wage bill faced by businesses. To attract and to retain foreign capital, governments will be more prone to cut all forms of spending to reduce or eliminate budget deficits. On the other hand, the compensation hypothesis asserts just the opposite: the more open the economy, the more likely are governments to increase social spending. The dislocating effects of open competition will increase political pressure to provide a safety net for those adjusting to market forces. In addition, public provision of basic human services may not necessarily be inefficient for firms because it can take the burden off them to provide their own pensions and health benefits. In turn,

---

[1]Robert Kaufman and Alex Ubiergo-Segura, "Globalization, Domestic Politics, and Social Spending in Latin America: A Time-Series, Cross-Section Analysis, 1973–1997," *World Politics* 53 (2001): 553–587. For additional research in academic journals regarding the dynamics of government spending, see the appropriate portion of this book's website.

declaring a one-day strike that it euphemistically labeled a retreat. On March 4, 1991, President Aylwin presented the findings of the Rettig commission in a nationally televised address: 2,279 confirmed deaths. This number constituted nearly three victims per 10,000 inhabitants (review Table 5.4). Aylwin apologized on behalf of the Chilean government and called on the military to do the same.

Over the remainder of Aylwin's administration, tension worsened regarding human rights policy. In September 1991, a judge ordered the arrest of two senior military officers charged with ordering the 1976 murder of Orlando Letelier, an exiled Allende cabinet member. Letelier was killed in Washington, D.C. Because this crime occurred on foreign soil, it was deemed outside the jurisdiction of the 1978 Amnesty Law. However, the Amnesty Law covered most crimes committed in Chile. With no immediate path to prosecution for most other offenses, the Aylwin government formed the National Corporation for Reparation and Reconciliation (*Corporación Nacional de Reparación y Reconciliación*) to provide reparations to the families of those who died in the repression. Aylwin also challenged the earlier court ruling that had precluded judicial investigation of

---

investment in education can help to improve the competitiveness of firms by increasing the skills in the national workforce. In discussing this second hypothesis, Kaufman and Segura-Ubiergo note that this trend observed in Europe may not hold in Latin America because, in the Americas, labor unions tend to be weaker and all government decisions take place in a context of greater economic scarcity.

The authors examine this debate via a statistical analysis of social spending trends in fourteen Latin American countries from 1973 to 1997. Specifically, they seek to identify the conditions associated with annual changes in the level of government spending on pensions, education, and health care. In addition to studying the impact of market capitalism, Kaufman and Segura-Ubiergo control for several competing hypotheses. The following factors are hypothesized to lead to increased social spending: democratic political systems, governments led by leaders from labor-based political parties, higher GDP per capita, higher levels of general government spending, urbanization, a greater proportion of senior citizens, and higher economic growth in the prior year. Other control variables are held to produce decreased spending: higher public debt, volatile exchange rates, and the global economic climate associated with the 1980s debt crisis.

Kaufman and Segura-Ubiergo conclude that the dynamics of social spending vary by the type of program. In pension policy, the efficiency hypothesis was confirmed. The political realm also made a difference because newly elected labor-based governments were more likely to raise spending. Conversely, in education and health, the compensation hypothesis received partial confirmation while democratically elected governments increased spending. In these areas of social spending, the Chilean experience of increased social spending combined with a free-trade orientation is not the exception; instead, it is the prevailing trend.

human rights; he asserted that disappearances must be investigated to determine the whereabouts of victims whose graves had not been discovered.

In early 1993, the two generals accused in the Letelier case faced trial and were found guilty; Manuel Contreras and Pedro Espinoza began a lengthy appeals process that continued beyond Aylwin's term. Meanwhile, Socialist legislators presented a bill to annul the 1978 Amnesty Law. Pinochet responded to these developments, and to the investigation of corruption allegations involving his son, by placing special forces units on high alert on May 28, 1993. Machine-gun-toting soldiers were put on the streets in front of several government installations. Conservative legislators blocked efforts to annul the Amnesty Law in the Senate and instead put forward a counterproposal to extend the legislation to cover the entire period of military rule. The issue of how to deal with past human rights violations was far from resolved during Aylwin's presidency.

Amid the controversy, Aylwin tried to link scandals over judicial behavior during the dictatorship to efforts to secure liberty in the future. He proposed several judicial reforms in 1992. High court judges responded by refusing to attend his state of the union address later that year. Negotiations regarding his proposals (including a new mandatory retirement age, the creation of public prosecutors, and an expansion of the Supreme Court) broke down because of disagreements with conservative legislators.

When Frei's presidency began, the ongoing Letelier case constituted the most visible human rights issue. The two leaders of the intelligence agency during the Pinochet dictatorship had been found guilty in 1993 of ordering the 1976 assassination of Orlando Letelier in Washington, D.C. Manuel Contreras had received a seven-year sentence; Pedro Espinoza faced a six-year sentence. Both generals appealed their convictions. While the appeals worked their way through the judicial process, the Frei government entered negotiations with RN and UDI legislators to support the construction of a new military prison intended for government officials convicted of human rights violations. Conservative senators supported the legislation in exchange for a promise from Frei not to propose change in the military code through 1998. The Punto Peuco Prison was built while the Supreme Court reviewed the Letelier case. In May 1995, the court upheld the convictions. As human rights activists celebrated and some pro-Pinochet citizens' groups held counterdemonstrations, tension increased because neither general initially surrendered himself to the civilian authorities. Pedro Espinoza was still an active-duty general, and he was not discharged from the army and placed in police custody for three weeks. The imprisonment of Manuel Contreras took even longer. After the Supreme Court ruling, the retired general defiantly declared that he would never serve a day in prison. Contreras then entered a military hospital and claimed that he was too ill to serve a prison sentence. Military personnel blocked some tentative arrest attempts by civilian police. The Frei government began private consultations with many parties to the conflict, while the Supreme Court reviewed Contreras's medical records. After his medical appeal was denied, Contreras eventually entered Punto Peuco Prison in late October 1995.

The construction of the new, comfortable prison seemed like unfair treatment to some but signaled to others the possibility that additional trials might occur. To pursue prosecution of most allegations, however, the 1978 Amnesty Law would need to be overturned. Throughout Frei's presidency, this issue remained in a stalemate similar to that at the close of Aylwin's term. Several Socialist legislators supported the annulment of the Amnesty Law. Many PDC legislators called for a new conditional amnesty law that would provide amnesty only for government officials who testified about the whereabouts of the disappeared. In turn, many conservative legislators continued to back a proposal to extend the existing amnesty to cover the entire Pinochet dictatorship.

Amid this stalemate, Augusto Pinochet retired as commander of the army on March 11, 1998, as dictated by the terms of the 1980 constitution. Then, also in accordance with the constitution, Pinochet took his lifetime seat in the Senate as a former president. Pinochet's ongoing presence in the government incensed many of his opponents. Several Concertation legislators in the Chamber of Deputies introduced a proposal to impeach Pinochet based on accusations of improper behavior as army commander. The Frei government publicly opposed the initiative and lobbied Concertation legislators to vote against it. After a month of debate, the proposal was defeated (sixty-two votes against; fifty-five votes in favor) when several Concertation legislators joined the center-right minority in the lower house in voting against impeachment. Then the Frei government began negotiations with Pinochet and other conservative senators to end the practice of celebrating the September 11 anniversary of the coup as a national holiday. While the president presented this move as another step in the process of national reconciliation, many on the political left referred to the new holiday as a day of national shame. Although no longer a national holiday, the twenty-fifth anniversary of the coup on September 11, 1998, bore witness to the same pattern of demonstrations and counterdemonstrations observed in prior years.

Then, on October 16, 1998, an unforeseen development changed the dynamics of the human rights issue in Chile. While Pinochet was recovering from a hernia operation in a London hospital, British authorities arrested him at the request of a Spanish judge. Judge Baltazar Garzón used the international treaty against torture to claim jurisdiction over Pinochet (see *Global Perspectives: International Human Rights Trials* on pages 234–235). After Pinochet's arrest, the Chilean government called for his release in the name of national sovereignty, arguing that the nation's sovereignty would be damaged if a former president were tried abroad rather than in Chile. Meanwhile, many Pinochet opponents celebrated his arrest as the first potential path to prosecution following a decade of political stalemate in Chile regarding human rights.

For many, the Frei government's assertion that people accused of crimes committed on Chilean soil should be tried in Chile rang hollow. In the international news media, the Chilean government received stern criticism for asserting jurisdiction while it simultaneously blocked most potential prosecutions in light of the 1978 Amnesty Law. While Pinochet fought his potential extradition

GLOBAL PERSPECTIVES
International Human Rights Trials

Efforts to establish some human rights as inviolable within international law have roots in the period following the Holocaust. The Allied response to the detention, torture, and murder of Jews during World War II culminated in the Nuremberg tribunal. Judges from France, Russia, the United Kingdom, and the United States convicted 142 of the 177 Austrian and German officials accused of crimes against humanity, crimes against peace, and war crimes. Outrage over the Holocaust also motivated the creation of the 1948 United Nations Convention on Genocide. The international community later ratified conventions that condemned racial discrimination (1965), outlawed discrimination against women (1979), prohibited torture (1984), and protected children's rights (1989). But if a government refused to prosecute its own officials, how would the accused face trial?

In the 1990s, genocide around the world renewed interest in international trials as a response to government complicity in grave human rights violations. An international criminal tribunal (ICT) was established in 1993 regarding genocide in Yugoslavia, and in 1994 a second ICT was formed to deal with genocide in Rwanda. In Denmark and Germany, Bosnians were arrested, tried, and found guilty of war crimes in violation of the Geneva Convention. These developments stirred support for the creation of a standing international court to deal with crimes against humanity. In July 1998, 120 countries signed the Rome Statute of the International Criminal Court (ICC). The ICC's jurisdiction includes genocide, war crimes, and crimes against humanity (such as systematic torture, enslavement, rape, and persecution).

Amid this context of heightened concern over government impunity, Augusto Pinochet was arrested while visiting the United Kingdom on October 16, 1998. Spanish judge Baltazar Garzón based his arrest order on the 1984 Convention Against Torture; British authorities acted on the Interpol warrant. Pinochet's lawyers argued that he enjoyed immunity from arrest and prosecution regarding his actions as head of the Chilean state. A British lower court invalidated the arrest, but the highest appeals court in Britain, the House of Lords, later upheld the arrest. The Lords ruled that Britain's and Chile's ratification of the Convention Against Torture prevented Pinochet from claiming immunity because the convention signatories must either try those accused of torture or extradite them. Pinochet then challenged the legality of extradition. While that case moved its way through the courts, the British interior minister, Jack Straw, announced in January 2000 that Pinochet would be permitted to return to Chile for medical reasons, alleging that his poor health would prevent him from participating in the lengthy legal process implied by his potential prosecution. Pinochet returned home to Chile in March 2000.

The debate over international prosecution continued. In February 2000, Hissène Habré, former dictator of Chad, was arrested in Senegal. Senegal claimed jurisdiction under the Convention Against Torture until an appeals court ruled in 2001 that the absence of Senegalese legislation implementing the treaty prevented prosecution. Habré remained in detention pending a Belgian extradition request. Then, in 2002, the ICC statute entered into force following its ratification by sixty countries. The ICC can try crimes occurring only since its creation. Furthermore, ICC jurisdiction requires that either the accused be a national of a participating country or that the crimes occur on the soil of a participating state. This limitation is relevant because many countries remain outside the jurisdiction of the ICC. For example, the U.S. government signed the treaty in late 2000, but the Bush administration subsequently refused to pursue ratification. International human rights trials are now an option but are controversial in some circles. (You might consider examining arguments for and against joining the ICC.)

---

in British courts, the Chilean judiciary took action that changed the terms of this debate. Throughout the 1990s, inventive human rights lawyers had pursued a potential loophole in the Amnesty Law. Although many disappeared victims of repression were presumed dead, many of their bodies had not been found. Human rights lawyers asserted that those responsible for the disappearances could be charged with kidnapping because there was no definitive proof of murder. Because the kidnapping charges constituted ongoing offenses (from the date of disappearance to the present), the crimes continued past the March 1978 deadline covered by the Amnesty Law. Under this legal reasoning, many major incidents could be prosecuted. In earlier decisions during the 1990s, the Chilean Supreme Court had rejected this argument. Amid the drama of the Pinochet case, however, the court ruled in July 1999 that this form of prosecution did not violate the amnesty law. Many soldiers faced new criminal charges, as did Pinochet himself. To avoid prosecution, the accused would have to reveal the whereabouts of the disappeared, thus demonstrating that a kidnapping was not in progress.

The army publicly criticized the new judicial decision and proposed setting a deadline for filing additional criminal charges regarding human rights violations (following the example of the 1986 Full Stop legislation in Argentina). The army also reiterated its call for Pinochet's return—sarcastically labeling his arrest in Britain as a kidnapping. In this tense climate, the Frei government continued negotiations with the British government in pursuit of Pinochet's return. In January 2000, the British government announced its intention not to extradite Pinochet to Spain; he was permitted to return home in early March (just nine days before the end of Frei's presidency).

Meanwhile, the Frei government responded to military discontent over the July 1999 Supreme Court ruling by organizing a human rights forum known as the *Mesa de Diálogo* (Roundtable for Dialogue). The roundtable included government officials, military leaders, human rights groups, and representatives of the Catholic church. The group held its first meeting in August 1999 and continued discussions for the remainder of Frei's presidency. The participants found it difficult to arrive at a compromise that would satisfy both military personnel and human rights advocates.

The ongoing controversy over human rights issues sometimes overshadowed limits on contemporary liberty in Chile. For example, various laws continued to restrict freedom of expression after the transition to civilian rule. These restrictions became well known in April 1999 when journalist Alejandra Mataus tried to publish an exposé on the judiciary, *El libro negro de la justicia chilena* (*The Black Book of Chilean Justice*). Government officials enjoy special protection from criticism. Using this statute, a former head of the Supreme Court successfully asked for an injunction to pull Mataus's book from publication. Mataus fled the country, and the publishers of the book were later arrested and charged with attacking the honor of major Chilean institutions.

The Lagos presidency began amid controversy on several fronts: Pinochet's return to Chile, various human rights trials in which officials were charged with kidnapping, and the ongoing legal battle over press censorship. The Lagos government cultivated multiparty support to revise the national security legislation that made it illegal to criticize the honorable nature of Chilean public officials. By May 2000, these changes had been signed into law, and journalist Alejandra Mataus returned from her exile in the United States.

Lagos also tried to reduce tension regarding Pinochet's presence in the Senate. In his first month in office, Lagos brokered a constitutional reform that enabled past presidents serving as lifetime senators to gain full immunity from prosecution after retiring from the Senate. The measure aimed at reducing discontent about Pinochet's Senate seat by enticing him to retire. However, the reform angered human rights activists because the immunity granted would be even more difficult to overcome than the legislative immunity Pinochet currently enjoyed.

To sort out this and other human rights controversies, Lagos inherited the *Mesa de Diálogo* launched in the final months of the Frei administration. Military representatives insisted on upholding the intent of the 1978 Amnesty Law, while human rights groups voiced opposition to impunity. On June 13, 2000, the roundtable announced a compromise accord. Military officers would be given six months to provide information regarding the whereabouts of disappeared persons; such testimony would be classified as confidential (meaning that it could not be used in evidence in other judicial proceedings). If officers revealed the location of murder victims, this admission implied that those crimes could no longer be subject to the kidnapping charges used to evade the 1978 Amnesty Law. The roundtable's proposal represented a bitter half measure in the eyes of many human rights activists. For the first time, military leaders might participate actively in the recovery of victims of past repression; however, by doing so, they would improve their chances of escaping prosecution. Despite this criticism, the core recommendations of the *Mesa de Diálogo* quickly became the basis of legislation that passed through both houses of Congress in less than two weeks.

New developments in the ongoing efforts to try Augusto Pinochet quickly overshadowed the images of reconciliation trumpeted by the Lagos administration.

On September 11, 2003, supporters and opponents of the Pinochet regime took to the streets to commemorate the thirtieth anniversary of the overthrow of the Allende government.   AP/Wide World Press.

In August 2000, the Supreme Court voted to remove Pinochet's legislative immunity (as a lifetime senator) so that he could face charges of human rights violations. Pinochet's legal team responded by reiterating the claims used to justify Pinochet's release in the United Kingdom: they asserted that the elderly general was too frail to endure a lengthy legal proceeding. In contrast to British law, however, Chilean jurisprudence did not recognize ill health alone as sufficient justification for suppressing criminal trials. Instead, Pinochet's defense would have to establish that he lacked the mental capacity necessary to participate in the legal process. The judge in the Pinochet case ordered physical and psychological exams. In July 2001, an appeals court suspended charges against Pinochet indefinitely on the grounds that he suffered from moderate subcortical dementia and that he was unlikely to recover full mental capacity. Human rights lawyers appealed that ruling, but on July 1, 2002, the Supreme Court upheld the decision. This path of legal reasoning—impunity based on mental incapacity—had implications for Pinochet's ability to serve as a senator for life and thus maintain a direct role in Chilean politics. If he was deemed too mentally challenged to go to court, how could he claim sufficient capacity to function as a voting member of the Senate? In recognition of this problem, Pinochet resigned from the Senate on July 4, 2002.

Augusto Pinochet was not the only person facing prosecution during Lagos's presidency. The 1999 Supreme Court ruling paved the way for charges against more than 300 military and police officials. From November 2002 through early August 2003, ten people were found guilty of kidnapping and given sentences ranging from three to seventeen years. UDI leaders publicly called for legislation placing a time limit on kidnapping investigations while offering to support an increase in reparations paid to families of the disappeared.

On August 12, 2003, Ricardo Lagos presented a new set of human rights proposals under the slogan "There is no tomorrow without a yesterday." In a nationally televised address, Lagos reiterated his ongoing assertion that the courts retained responsibility for determining the applicability of the 1978 Amnesty Law and the guilt or innocence of those charged with human rights violations. He also proposed several new initiatives. He proposed a 50 percent increase in reparations paid to families of the disappeared and the provision of reparations to torture victims. He pledged to seek congressional support to ratify Chile's participation in the International Criminal Court. He also wanted to create lighter sentences for government officials who provided information about the location of disappeared persons as well as for those officials who could establish that they collaborated in human rights violations under duress. As of April 2004, these initiatives remained part of Lagos's legislative agenda, but they had not been approved because of differences inside and outside the Concertation coalition.

In the contemporary quest for liberty in Chile, attention has centered on the treatment of human rights concerns inherited from the Pinochet dictatorship. The intensity and incidence of repression under military rule mirrored Argentina's experience, but the political environment of the new Chilean democracy differed substantially. In Argentina, the military regime had been discredited by the Malvinas War and an economic collapse, but the armed forces in Chile maintained considerable public support when democracy returned. Military and civilian officials of the dictatorship, including Pinochet himself, held important roles in government. The political climate in Chile made it difficult for the Concertation to pursue human rights trials after the return to democracy. Argentine President Raúl Alfonsín could count on broad legislative support to abolish his country's amnesty law as the first act of his administration. In stark contrast, Patricio Aylwin and his successors confronted a Senate packed with Pinochet appointees opposed to annulling the 1978 Amnesty Law. Faced with these constraints, Aylwin began his presidency by choosing the truth commission and reparations options. While these actions made Chile an innovator in the Western Hemisphere, they did not noticeably reduce the demands for trials on the part of human rights organizations. These trials did not become viable until several Pinochet appointees on the Supreme Court retired and the Frei government gained center-right support for an extension of the pool of justices on the court. In July 1999, the reconstituted Supreme Court opened a new era by supporting kidnapping charges as an acceptable means of avoiding the Amnesty Law. The expansion of trials during the early twenty-first century has been tense, but thus far it has not threatened the stability of Chile's government institutions.

The Quest for Governance in Chile

The peculiar constraints of the Chilean democratic transition created ample political obstacles for the Aylwin government, even though his political coalition received a majority vote in presidential, Senate, and Chamber of Deputies elections. The designated senators gave the conservative forces in the Senate the power to block Concertation initiatives that they opposed. While the most advantageous reform for the Concertation would have been the outright removal of the designated senators, many conservatives viewed the 45 percent vote for Pinochet in 1988 and the 85 percent approval of the 1989 reforms to the 1980 constitution as a vindication of the Pinochet era. While supporters of military rule were discredited or disheartened in many Latin American countries after the return to democracy, this was not the case in Chile.

Rather than opening his presidency with efforts to reform national institutions, Aylwin decided to begin with an issue that both the Concertation and the two major center-right parties had supported during the 1989 electoral campaign: reform of local government. The 1980 constitution entrenched the Pinochet regime's practice of permitting the chief executive to designate local government officials. In 1990, Aylwin proposed legislation that would permit direct municipal elections and that would also create an intermediate level of regional governments. The center-right majority in the Senate blocked the legislation because conservatives feared that direct election of mayors would favor the Concertation in most localities. Prolonged negotiations ensued in which both sides put forward various electoral systems that each thought would improve its chances of victory. In 1991, they reached a compromise in which at-large elections would take place for city councils. If the candidate for council received more 35 percent of the vote and also received the most votes, he or she would automatically become the mayor and chair the council. Otherwise, the council would elect the mayor from among its members. The Senate also came to agreement on the decentralization of several national policies by putting them under the jurisdiction of thirteen new regional governments.

As the consensus emerged around local government reforms, Aylwin announced additional reform proposals in his May 1992 state of the union address. His list included crucial aspects of the 1980 constitution that entrenched the power of the military and of conservative political forces. Aylwin proposed to eliminate the designated Senate seats, increase the number of seats in both houses of Congress, replace the binominal electoral system with a proportional representation system, streamline the legislative process, give the president the authority to remove the heads of the armed forces, and add the head of the Chamber of Deputies to the National Security Council. Ultimately, Aylwin dropped his intentions to remove the designated Senate seats in the hope that he could convince some of the designated senators to support the other proposals. The RN, the UDI, and the designated senators all opposed these changes, however, and their voting majority in the Senate enabled them to block these attempts to reduce the military's autonomy and to improve the Concertation's prospects of winning majorities in both houses of Congress in the 1993 elections.

Eduardo Frei had begun his presidency with a promise to pursue the many constitutional reforms that had been blocked during Aylwin's presidency by the center-right bloc in the Senate. In 1995, Frei promised Concertation support of a human rights bill that would speed up existing judicial investigations while contemplating a time limit for launching new investigations. In exchange, he sought the RN's support for a series of constitutional amendments. In November 1995, an RN leadership vote narrowly voiced support for elimination of the designated Senate seats and for a change in the procedures for naming justices to the Constitutional Tribunal. This horse-trading provoked ruptures in both the Concertation coalition and in the RN. Several Socialist leaders criticized the human rights bill and hinted that they would block its passage. Despite the vote at the RN party congress, many RN senators publicly opposed the constitutional changes. UDI leaders stridently opposed the constitutional changes and promised to recruit disaffected RN legislators and voters. In April 1996, the proposed deal collapsed when seven of the eleven RN senators voted against the constitutional reform bill. The compromise human rights bill also did not pass during Frei's term.

In the wake of this failure, the Frei administration regrouped and focused on efforts to pursue judicial reform. As discussed earlier, the government cultivated sufficient legislative support by 1997 to create a public prosecutor post and to reform the Supreme Court. The government convinced conservative legislators to support mandatory judicial retirement at age seventy-five by retaining limits on the president's ability to nominate Supreme Court justices. The president must continue to choose from a list of potential appointees named by the court itself, and presidential nominees must be approved by a two-thirds vote in the Senate. Because the Supreme Court was still comprised largely of Pinochet appointees, these limitations on presidential appointment gave conservatives confidence that new nominees would have to be acceptable both to conservative justices and to the conservative legislators.

Changes in the designation of senators reframed the quest for governance during Ricardo Lagos's presidency. The nine Pinochet-era appointees left the scene when their eight-year terms expired in 1998. Two of the designated senators are named by the president, which gave the Concertation a chance to reduce the number of conservative appointees. In addition, Eduardo Frei took his seat as a senator for life. Many of the other designated senators still tended to side with the center-right coalition: four were military and police commanders appointed by the National Security Council; the other three were appointed by the Supreme Court (two must be former Supreme Court justices while the other is a former comptroller general). However, when one of these senators began voting with the Lagos government, the Concertation could begin to count on twenty-four of the forty-nine votes in the Senate. When Pinochet retired from the Senate in July 2002, Ricardo Lagos became the first president in the new democracy who did not face an opposition majority in the Senate.

Much to Lagos's dismay, this majority did not last long. Several corruption scandals began to emerge over the second half of 2002. The initial concerns centered on bribes recirculated into the campaign funds of five Concertation legislators. Another inquiry uncovered bribes paid to the ministry of public works and the ministry of transportation in exchange for favorable treatment in the awarding of government contracts. Later investigations also revealed irregularities in the management of the Central Bank. Although Ricardo Lagos was not personally implicated in the allegations, the scandal tainted his presidency—especially because Lagos had served as minister of public works in the 1990s. As the scandal unfolded, one of the PPD senators, Nelson Avila, left the party in December 2002 to serve the remainder of his term in the Senate as an independent. Thus, the center-right bloc of senators regained a narrow, one-seat majority. As Lagos entered the second half of his term, the Concertation still needed to cultivate some support among conservative legislators to govern. In mid-2003, the Lagos government gained UDI and RN support for administrative reforms designed to ferret out corrupt activity and to increase the penalties for engaging in corruption.

Like the human rights issue, the quest for governance has been shaped by the presence of Pinochet supporters in the executive branch and, even more crucially, in the legislature. Although the Concertation coalition won majorities in all national elections from 1990 through 2001, the binomial electoral system and the presence of designated senators made it impossible for Aylwin and Frei to gain a Senate majority. Both presidents tried to escape this situation by changing the electoral system and by eliminating the designated Senate seats. This approach constituted a dead-end, however, because conservative votes were needed to pass the reforms and those senators were unwilling to support reforms that might eliminate their Senate majority. Once the Pinochet-era appointees retired, Lagos briefly held a Senate majority but the core issue remained: he would have enjoyed a solid majority if the sought-after reforms had been enacted.

Without these constitutional reforms, all three presidents have needed to broker agreements with one or both conservative parties to get their legislative initiatives passed by the Senate. In many instances, they have succeeded by crafting compromises in which both sides receive provisions they favor. We saw this principle in action in the tax reform enacted under Aylwin and also in the path toward judicial reform during the Frei administration. Conservatives frequently were able to defend the interests of wealthy Chileans, who form their core constituency. This political dynamic helps to explain how wealthy Chileans retained their large share of national income in the face of three successive center-left governments.

Future Challenges

In March 2004, Ricardo Lagos began the last third of his six-year term. A look toward Chile's political future centered on speculation that the center-right coalition stood poised to win the 2005 presidential elections. Joaquín Lavín followed his narrow defeat in the 1999 presidential election with a victorious campaign in 2000 to become mayor of Santiago. In preliminary public opinion polls in early 2004, Lavín held considerably more support than any of the cabinet ministers and legislative leaders of the Concertation. Regardless of the outcome of the 2005 elections, the next president seems likely to inherit many of the problems from the past decade.

Much of the economic news since the return to democracy has been positive. However, slower growth in the early twenty-first century fanned concerns that the salad days of Chile's sustained economic boom may be coming to an end. The past twenty years have seen a diversification of Chile's commodity exports so that the country is not quite as dependent on copper (although copper still comprises half of all exports). Nonetheless, Chile's dependence on primary commodities (as opposed to manufacturing and services) remains considerable: primary commodities comprised four-fifths of Chilean exports in the early twenty-first century. The commodity exports at the center of the boom faced more international competition as production expanded in other countries in the Southern Hemisphere. The Concertation responded to these trends by negotiating free-trade agreements to gain tariff-free market access for Chilean producers. If other countries follow this path, how will Chile's government respond? In turn, as potentially renewable resources in fishing and forestry become depleted, will future governments take a more aggressive stance toward environmental regulation and protection? If the above issues and other factors cut into Chile's exports, how should government react?

More than three decades after the 1973 coup, human rights abuses remain a central issue in the debate over liberty. Human rights groups continue to press for trials in the name of justice and respect for the rule of law. Changes in the Supreme Court over time led to the opening of hundreds of trials in the early twenty-first century. Military personnel and pro-Pinochet citizens remain opposed to trials in the name of national reconciliation. It remains to be seen whether the legal processes under way will lead eventually to a lessening of tension over human rights issues.

The central challenge to governance throughout the first fifteen years of the new democracy has been the peculiar configuration of the Chilean Senate. The binomial electoral system makes it extremely difficult to win much more than half of the thirty-eight elected seats. After the Pinochet appointees finished their terms in 1998, the current designated senators are more evenly divided. This situation raises an interesting question about a possible Lavín victory in the 2005 presidential elections: if Lagos joins Frei as a senator for life and the Concertation retains its narrow majority among the thirty-eight elected seats, would the center-right bloc become more willing to consider eliminating the nonelected Senate seats?

The other major political question raised by a possible Lavín victory in 2005 concerns the future of the Concertation coalition. For many years, analysts have speculated that the Concertation has held together in large part because coalition unity was seen as a path toward retaining control of the executive branch. Once the Concertation loses a presidential election, will the coalition stay together? If it stays intact, will the Concertation propose a more active role for government in Chilean life?

Chile's economic triumphs and consensual policy-making style have earned considerable praise—especially beyond its borders. At the dawn of a new century, does Chile constitute a model worthy of emulation? Economic growth has alleviated poverty, but the current trends have been less positive regarding the promotion of equity and the promotion of sustainable development. Chilean politicians have often practiced a consensual political style, yet portions of that consensus have worked to retain several nondemocratic features in the Chilean political system. In the years to come, Chile's ability to maintain steady economic growth while resolving these and other long-running problems will help to determine the attractiveness of the Chilean experience for other countries.

Activities and Exercises

1. The Popular Unity (UP) coalition formed in pursuit of a democratic path toward socialism. Why did the Allende government fail in its efforts to produce an electoral majority in support of socialism? Do you think that it would be possible to

create a voting majority in support of socialism in the early twenty-first century? Why or why not?

2. Do you believe that Chilean prosecutors and judges should charge with kidnapping those accused of human rights violations during the Pinochet dictatorship? Why or why not? How would you rebut the principal arguments of those who do not agree with your view?

3. All three presidents elected after the end of military rule tried to eliminate the nine designated Senate seats. To date, all of these efforts have failed. If you believe that future presidents should accept these unelected senators, how would you convince them to do so? If you believe no senators should be appointed, how would you design a political strategy that would succeed where past efforts have failed?

4. Chilean writer Ariel Dorfman wrote a play to dramatize the issues involved in dealing with human rights violations after the dictatorship ended. His play later became an English-language motion picture, *Death and the Maiden*. The 1994 film centers on a torture victim's suspicion that an unexpected houseguest may have been one of her torturers. This movie is worth watching.

5. Chile will hold legislative elections in 2005 and presidential elections in 2006. Electionworld.org provides concise coverage of contemporary elections in Chile and around the world. This website also provides a comprehensive election timetable and details on the most recent election results for every country in the world. If you are curious about countries in Latin America or beyond, check out this site.

Suggested Readings

Argosín, Marjorie. *Tapestries of Love, Threads of Hope: The Arpillera Movement in Chile, 1974–1994.* Albuquerque: University of New Mexico Press, 1996.

Baldez, Lisa. *Why Women Protest: Women's Movements in Chile.* Cambridge, England: Cambridge University Press, 2002.

Borzutsky, Silvia. *Vital Connections: Politics, Social Security and Inequality in Chile.* Notre Dame, Ind.: Notre Dame University Press, 2002.

Bosworth, Barry, Rudiger Dornbusch, and Raúl Labán, eds. *The Chilean Economy: Policy Lessons and Challenges.* Washington, D.C.: Brookings Institution Press, 1994.

De Brito, Alexandra Barahona. *Human Rights and Democratization in Latin America: Uruguay and Chile.* Oxford, England: Oxford University Press, 1997.

Drake, Paul, and Ivan Jaksic, eds. *The Struggle for Democracy in Chile.* Lincoln: University of Nebraska Press, 1995.

Fleet, Michael, and Brian Smith. *The Catholic Church and Democracy in Chile and Peru.* Notre Dame, Ind.: Notre Dame University Press, 1997.

Ffrench-Davis, Ricardo. *Economic Reforms in Chile: From Dictatorship to Democracy.* Ann Arbor: University of Michigan Press, 2002.

Hite, Katherine. *When the Romance Ended: Leaders of the Chilean Left, 1968–1998.* New York: Columbia University Press, 2000.

Hojman, David. *Chile: The Political Economy of Development and Democracy in the 1990s.* Pittsburgh, Pa.: University of Pittsburgh Press, 1993.

Londregan, John. *Legislative Institutions and Ideology in Chile.* Cambridge, England: Cambridge University Press, 2000.

Loveman, Brian. *Chile: The Legacy of Hispanic Capitalism,* 3d ed. New York: Oxford University Press, 2001.

Martínez, Javier, and Juan Díaz. *Chile: The Great Transformation.* Miami, Fla.: North-South Center, 1996.

Oppenheim, Lois Hecht. *Politics in Chile: Democracy, Authoritarianism and the Search for Development,* 2d ed. Boulder, Colo.: Westview, 1999.

Oxhorn, Philip. *Organizing Civil Society: The Popular Sectors and the Struggle for Democracy in Chile.* University Park, Pa.: Penn State University Press, 1995.

Paley, Julia. *Marketing Democracy: Power and Social Movements in Post-Dictatorship Chile.* Berkeley: University of California Press, 2001.

Pollack, Marcelo. *The New Right in Chile, 1973–1997.* New York: St. Martin's Press, 1999.

Roberts, Kenneth. *Deepening Democracy? The Modern Left and Social Movements in Chile and Peru.* Stanford, Calif.: Stanford University Press, 1998.

Siavelis, Peter. *The President and Congress in Postauthoritarian Chile: Institutional Constraints to Democratic Consolidation.* University Park, Pa.: Penn State University Press, 2000.

Silva, Eduardo. *The State and Capital in Chile: Business Elites, Technocrats, and Market Economics.* Boulder, Colo.: Westview, 1996.

Spooner, Mary. *Soldiers in a Narrow Land: The Pinochet Regime in Chile* (updated ed.). Berkeley: University of California Press, 1999.

Valenzuela, J. Samuel, and Arturo Valenzuela, eds. *Military Rule in Chile: Dictatorship and Oppositions.* Baltimore, Md.: Johns Hopkins University Press, 1986.

Verdugo, Patricia. *Chile, Pinochet, and the Caravan of Death.* Miami, Fla.: North-South Center, 2001.

Weeks, Gregory. *The Military and Politics in Postauthoritarian Chile.* Tuscaloosa: University of Alabama Press, 2003.

Winn, Peter, ed. *Victims of the Chilean Miracle: Workers and Neoliberalism in the Pinochet Era, 1972–2002.* Durham, N.C.: Duke University Press, 2004.

Endnotes

1. Thomas Kamm, "Free-Market Model: Chile's Economy Roars as Exports Take Off in Post-Pinochet Era," *Wall Street Journal* (January 25, 1993), p. A1.

2. Roger Turner, "Chile Sets an Example for Others to Follow," *Business America* 115, no. 4 (May 1994), p. 18.

3. Joseph Collins and John Lear, *Chile's Free-Market Miracle: A Second Look* (Oakland, Calif.: Food First, 1995), pp. 191–192.

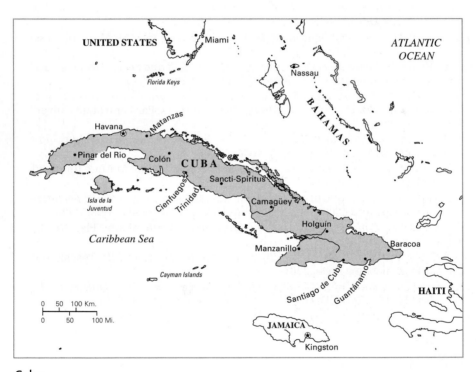

Cuba

CHAPTER 8

Cuba

DWIGHT EISENHOWER, John Kennedy, Lyndon Johnson, Richard Nixon, Gerald Ford, Jimmy Carter, Ronald Reagan, George Bush, Bill Clinton, George W. Bush—ten U.S. presidents spanning the years 1959 through 2004 expressed their opposition to the revolutionary government led by Fidel Castro in Cuba. Yet the government of this island nation, with 11 million inhabitants, frustrated various pressures from the world's most powerful country for over four decades. In the early twenty-first century, Fidel Castro spoke with the confidence of someone who had defied the odds throughout his political career.

When Fulgencio Batista's military coup prevented twenty-six-year-old Fidel Castro's 1952 candidacy for the Cuban legislature, Castro responded by leading a group of college students in an attempted takeover of the Moncada army base outside the eastern city of Santiago on July 26, 1953. The soldiers on the base quickly arrested the rebels, but Fidel Castro's speech at his trial made him a nationally known opponent of Batista's dictatorship. Castro defiantly proclaimed, "History will absolve me." After his release from prison two years later, Castro prepared a second rebellion from exile in Mexico. When the would-be rebels returned to Cuba in late 1956, most were arrested again. However, Fidel Castro, his younger brother Raúl, and a few other survivors went to the Sierra Maestra Mountains of eastern Cuba to launch a guerrilla war against the Batista government. Within two years, Castro's Rebel Army had become an opposition movement that drove Batista into exile on December 31, 1958.

Over the next three years, Castro's movement took control of all branches of government and created the first socialist state in the Americas. The United States had been Cuba's principal trading partner throughout the first half of the twentieth century, but the U.S. government rejected Cuba's shift to socialism. Fidel Castro parried numerous U.S. efforts to unseat his socialist government in the years that followed: a U.S.-sponsored invasion of Cuban exiles at the Bay of

Pigs in 1961, an embargo (in place from 1962 onward) that eliminated most economic exchange between Cuba and the United States, varied assassination ploys, pressure on other Latin American countries that convinced most to refuse to trade with Cuba from 1964 through the mid-1970s, and U.S. support for anti-Castro dissidents in and out of Cuba. In resisting these pressures from the United States, the Castro government received considerable economic assistance from the Soviet Union from 1960 through 1990. When Soviet aid ended in 1990 (and the Soviet Union itself disintegrated in 1991), Fidel Castro had to find a way to survive yet again.

How did Fidel Castro rise to the top of Cuban politics and how has his government maintained power since the end of Soviet aid? As you consider the dynamics of the Cuban political system, ask yourself: what will happen when Castro is no longer in charge? Fidel Castro has proven to be a survivor, but he turned seventy-seven in August 2003 and nobody lives forever. Will the system Fidel Castro helped to create survive his eventual death? We will return to this question at the close of this chapter. To appreciate Cuba's future political prospects, we will begin by learning about its often tumultuous past.

HISTORICAL BACKGROUND FROM 1868 TO 1990

While most Spanish-American countries gained their independence during the first three decades of the nineteenth century, the Caribbean islands of Cuba and Puerto Rico remained Spanish colonies. Cuba became the crown jewel of Spain's reduced colonial empire, and its sugar-based economy performed well in the 1830s and 1840s. Economic stagnation in the middle of the nineteenth century bubbled over into open revolt, however, in 1868.

The Struggle for Independence (1868–1901)

Creole landowners in eastern Cuba declared their independence in 1868 and launched an armed revolt (the Ten Year's War) against the colonial government. In an effort to attract support from sugar plantation owners in western Cuba, the separatists did not advocate an end to slavery. Instead, they focused on demands for reduced taxation, free trade, and representative government. However, when several separatist landowners freed their own slaves in an effort to expand their military forces, the fear of an abolitionist rebellion (and a potential for property destruction) limited western support for separatism. By 1878, negotiations led to a cessation of hostilities between Spanish troops and the Cuban rebels. Rebels received an amnesty in return for a pledge to accept Spanish authority.

The Ten Years' War damaged the Spanish economy, but even greater economic problems followed shortly thereafter. A dramatic expansion in world sugar production in the last third of the nineteenth century devastated the Cuban economy. Sugar prices tumbled, and Cuba's share of world sugar production fell from

24 percent in 1875 to 11 percent by 1888.[1] The decline in Cuba's principal export sent devastating ripples throughout the economy: many banks folded, local commerce decreased, and unemployment soared. To make matters worse for the creoles, Spanish immigration increased. Wealthy *peninsulares* tended to hire poor Spanish immigrants over struggling creoles.

Amid the economic crisis, four different currents in society competed for political support in Cuba. Many propertied creoles mobilized an autonomist movement aimed at the realization of limited self-government promised in the settlement of the Ten Years' War. In response, royalist creoles and Spaniards organized a political movement calling for more limited autonomy and continued loyalty to the Spanish crown. A third movement centered its vision for Cuba's future on annexation by the United States. The U.S. economy played an increasingly large role in Cuba's economic dynamics, and some believed that incorporation into its northern neighbor would be beneficial. Annexationists had lobbied unsuccessfully for U.S. military intervention during the Ten Years' War. The fourth major movement consisted of separatists seeking Cuban independence. José Martí was eighteen years old when he was exiled for publicly supporting the separatist rebellion. From exile, Martí would develop a sweeping vision for a free Cuba (*Cuba libre*): political sovereignty, economic independence, and full citizenship rights for all Cubans. The young writer (who spent most of his exile in the United States) became worried that Cuba might trade dependence on Spain for dependence on the United States. In 1891, the U.S. government signed a preferential trade agreement with Spain regarding Cuba; U.S. trade with Cuba thus expanded rapidly. The next year Martí helped to found the Cuban Revolutionary party (*Partido Revolucionario Cubano* [PRC]) with the goal of Cuban independence.

The double-edged sword of increasing ties to the U.S. economy revealed itself in 1894 when the 1891 trade agreement expired and the United States then levied heavy tariffs on Cuban sugar at the request of U.S. producers. The Cuban economy slowed to a halt nearly overnight. When the PRC and other separatist groups launched a rebellion in 1895, it spread across a troubled Cuba within a few months. This time, the conflict involved a total war in which insurrectionists burned the crops of royalist landowners and Spanish forces rounded peasants into so-called reconcentration camps. By early 1898, it became clear that Spanish military capacity dwindled day by day. The U.S. government chose to take action: President William McKinley requested and received authority from Congress for a military occupation of Cuba in the name of ending hostilities. Some in the United States saw this move as a first step toward annexation. However, members of Congress opposed to U.S. dominion over Cuba attached a provision requiring the U.S. government to leave Cuba's political future up to the Cuban people. What Martí had proclaimed as a war of liberation prior to his death in battle in 1895 was transformed into the 1898 Spanish-American War.

The U.S. invasion of Cuba quickly produced a settlement in which Spain ceded control over Cuba, Guam, the Philippines, and Puerto Rico to the United States. Many U.S. officials debated the potential merits of U.S. colonial rule versus U.S. statehood for Cuba. However, public opinion in Cuba leaned toward independence. When the U.S. occupying forces held municipal elections in 1900, pro-independence political parties received a substantial majority of the votes. This outcome scandalized many U.S. legislators and cabinet officials, who derisively asserted that Cubans lacked the maturity and character necessary for independence. Reflective of this disdain for Cuban self-rule, in 1901, the U.S. Congress passed several provisions collectively known as the Platt Amendment (because Senator Orville Platt shepherded the legislation through the U.S. Congress).

The Platt Amendment limited the autonomy of Cuba after its independence in various ways. The U.S. government retained the right to intervene in Cuban affairs in the name of protecting life, property, and liberty. The Cuban government could not enter into treaties without U.S. consent. The U.S. government gained claims to land and naval bases deemed necessary for security. Subsequent Cuban authorities could not overturn the prior actions of the U.S. occupying government without U.S. consent. The Cuban government also pledged to continue certain public works projects begun during the occupation. Finally, the Cuban government could not incur debts that called for funds beyond its ordinary annual revenues. The U.S. Department of State then made it clear to the delegates of the Cuban constitutional convention that the U.S. government was prepared to delay granting Cuba its independence until the Cuban authorities attached these provisions to the new constitution. Amid considerable public protest, the Platt Amendment provisions were approved by a one-vote margin in the Cuban constituent assembly.

Early Independence Under the Platt Amendment (1902–1933)

Cuba gained its independence in 1902, but the Platt Amendment constrained the Cuban government's exercise of that sovereignty. The growing role of U.S. firms in the Cuban economy further expanded U.S. influence in Cuba. The war for independence had damaged much of Cuba's productive capacity. Most Cuban entrepreneurs had mounting debts and few sources of revenue at the end of the war. As a result, many Cubans sold their sugar plantations, farms, and factories to U.S. companies. By 1905, U.S. individuals and firms owned 60 percent of all rural land, Cubans controlled around 25 percent, and Spaniards owned most of the remaining 15 percent.[2] Foreign firms from the U.S. and Europe also controlled the railroads, public utilities, and mining. The United States and Cuba entered a new trade agreement in 1903 in which Cuba gained preferential access to the U.S. sugar market and U.S. manufacturers gained special access to the Cuban market. Economic opportunities proved limited for many propertied Cubans who had been leaders of the separatist cause of independence.

Many of these leaders dedicated themselves to politics with an eye toward making money in government that had proven difficult to earn in the private sector. Separatist leaders formed the leadership of the Conservative and Liberal parties that vied for power in the new oligarchic democracy. Cuban politics became characterized by systemic political corruption in which each administration tended to view government office as a path to personal wealth. Public employment expanded rapidly because politicians placed their friends, relatives, and supporters on the government payroll. The newly created national lottery became the fiefdom of the executive branch; presidents skimmed lottery profits to supplement their incomes, legislators' incomes, and supporters' incomes. As proved the case in many oligarchic democracies during the late nineteenth and early twentieth centuries, each incumbent administration controlled the electoral process to ensure victory by any means necessary, including fraud. Liberals led a series of demonstrations and military uprisings protesting Conservative party control over the presidency until Liberal candidate Gerardo Machado cobbled together an electoral victory in the 1924 elections.

Machado had promised to lead a government of moral regeneration and clean government. Once in office, however, Machado's administration followed the ongoing practice of using control of the government to enrich oneself. As the Cuban economy struggled amid falling sugar prices, Machado negotiated with all major political parties to lengthen the presidential term to six years. By sharing government resources with his opponents, he also convinced the two major opposition parties to support his reelection campaign in 1928. Faced with only token opposition, Machado won handily, but the public outcry for reform grew louder.

Citizens' frustration grew as Cuba's economic fortunes worsened with the onset of the Great Depression in 1930. Strikes and protests called for Machado's resignation and clean elections. In addition, more and more Cubans publicly criticized the Platt Amendment. As the conflict increased, the U.S. government mediated between representatives of the Machado government and the opposition in May 1933. Those talks continued, but the Cuban military removed Machado from office in August; many officers claimed that they acted to prevent the U.S. government from removing Machado. Nonetheless, the U.S. ambassador played a crucial role in shaping the new interim government led by Carlos Manuel de Céspedes.

The Céspedes government struggled to deal with ongoing discontent. In this troubled context, Cuba's political future hinged on a spontaneous event. In a major military base in Havana, sergeants and enlisted personnel led a protest demanding improved pay and working conditions. The protest culminated in their seizure of the base when officers refused to discuss their demands. As the sergeants contemplated the mutiny charges they potentially faced, civilian opposition leaders convinced them to expand their demands to include an end to the interim government. The so-called sergeants' revolt proclaimed a new provisional government led by reformist politician Ramón Grau.

For the next 100 days, the Grau government worked to live up to longstanding demands for reform. After his inauguration, Grau unilaterally rejected the Platt Amendment. Other reform announcements followed: women's suffrage, an eight-hour workday, a minimum-wage law, redistribution of publicly owned land, and a requirement that Cubans constitute at least half of each firm's workforce. The Grau government angered not just the U.S. government, but also the traditional political parties, landholding interests, and senior military officers who resented the sergeants' movement as the power behind Grau's presidency. The U.S. ambassador and several Cubans began talks with the leader of the sergeants, Fulgencio Batista. By January 1934, the U.S. government convinced Batista to move against Grau and to create a different, less reformist civilian government.

From the Batista Era to Castro's Revolution (1934–1958)

Fulgencio Batista became the central figure in Cuban politics for the next quarter century. Initially, Batista served as the power behind several short-lived civilian governments. In exchange for assurances from Batista that the Cuban government would not harm U.S. economic interests in Cuba, the U.S. and Cuban governments jointly agreed in 1934 to remove all provisions of the Platt Amendment but one: the U.S. would retain rights to military bases in Cuba in perpetuity. In an effort to lessen political discontent, Batista organized a multipartisan constituent assembly to revise the 1901 constitution. The new 1940 constitution contained a wide variety of provisions calling for socioeconomic and political reform. Workers' rights, civil liberties, and social security clauses were now enshrined in the constitution, but it would take a new political will to realize this vision completely. The incomplete fulfillment of the 1940 constitutional ideals would become the major political complaint in Cuba for the next two decades.

After the promulgation of the new constitution, Ramón Grau returned from exile to run for the presidency in the name of reform. In response, Batista ran for office for the first time and won the 1940 presidential elections handily. While propertied Cubans prospered during World War II, the benefits of wartime food sales tended not to trickle down sufficiently to compensate for rising prices on many imported goods. The reform movement concentrated its hopes for power once again in Ramón Grau, who won as the candidate for the *auténtico* ("authentic") faction of the Cuban Revolutionary party in 1944.

The reformist *auténticos* had finally risen to power after two decades of mobilization and protest. Once in office, however, Grau and his associates disappointed those who had dreamt of the arrival of clean government. Corruption reached new levels under the presidencies of Grau and his successor (Carlos Prío) during the years 1944–1952 because many *auténticos* increased preexisting levels of bribery and misuse of public funds. Disillusioned reformists broke away from the party and formed a new *ortodoxo* ("orthodox") reform party. The *ortodoxos* seemed likely to win the upcoming 1952 presidential elections when, on March 10, 1952, Fulgencio Batista led a successful military coup. Few politically active Cubans protested the end to the Prío government, but many *ortodoxos* mourned the cancellation of the 1952 elections.

You might recognize the name of one of those disappointed Cubans: Fidel Castro. In 1952, the twenty-six-year-old law student had a good chance of winning a legislative seat as an *ortodoxo* candidate. Castro did not trust Batista's pledge to hold open elections in 1954. In response, on July 26, 1953, Castro led a band of minimally armed fellow college students in an ill-fated effort to spark a military rebellion in the Moncada barracks in Santiago—the second largest military base in Cuba. Although the rebels dreamed of spontaneously winning over the support of many soldiers, this dream was not fulfilled. Castro and many other rebels were promptly arrested and then tried for sedition. The Moncada revolt failed, but the sedition trial made Castro a national figure who presented a strident and coherent critique of Cuban politics. The 1940 constitution remained an unrealized document: corruption was worse than ever, free elections had not emerged, and the end to the Platt Amendment had not ended Cuba's dependence on the United States. U.S. firms' share of Cuban imports had risen from just over 50 percent in the early 1930s to over 70 percent by the early 1950s.

The Moncada revolt proved to be the first in a series of events that would culminate in the rise to power of a revolutionary movement led by Fidel Castro. Major opposition parties boycotted the 1954 elections as more Cubans began to see Batista not as the young, reformist sergeant but rather as a dictator subservient to the U.S. government. Under pressure from the U.S. government to lessen his use of repressive tactics, Batista released Castro and many other political prisoners in 1955. Fidel Castro, his brother Raúl, and several other Moncada rebels went to Mexico to organize a new rebellion against the Batista government; they called themselves the July 26th movement in commemoration of the failed Moncada revolt. In Mexico, the rebels attempted to raise money from Batista's opponents while they also recruited new members—including a twenty-seven-year-old Argentine called "Che" Guevara (see *Governing Strategies: Ernesto "Che" Guevara* on pages 254–255). In late 1956, nearly 100 rebels returned to Cuba aboard the *Granma* to launch a new rebellion. While most were captured after making landfall, the survivors headed into the Sierra Maestra Mountains of eastern Cuba to form a rural guerrilla movement.

The July 26th Movement became the most visible component of an expanding opposition to the Batista government. The rebels recruited many impoverished rural Cubans and also tried to work with urban opponents of the dictatorship. Batista responded by forcibly relocating many peasant families and by jailing urban critics and other presumed opponents. These measures did not succeed in ending the rebellion. Instead, the repression enabled Batista's opponents to compare his tactics to those used by the colonial government during the wars for independence. As the rebellion continued into 1958, the Batista government lost the support of many citizens and—crucially—of many soldiers. The July 26th Movement expanded its zone of operations across

GOVERNING STRATEGIES
Ernesto "Che" Guevara

The man who would become synonymous with the revolutionary approach to building socialism began his life as an asthmatic youth in Argentina—far removed from the countries in which he would live most of his adult life. Ernesto Guevara studied medicine at the University of Buenos Aires and traveled frequently. In 1954, his travels took him to Guatemala, where he observed a successful U.S.-backed effort to overthrow President Jacobo Arbenz. Guevara wrote home that these events had convinced him of the evils of capitalism.

Perhaps Guevara's belief in the revolutionary power of human will was rooted in his accidental entry into the anti-Batista cause and that movement's triumph in the face of long odds. In mid-1955, he met Raúl Castro on the streets of Mexico City. He later learned of the Castro brothers' plans to overthrow the Batista government; Guevara eventually joined them. He picked up the nickname "Che" because he often used that Argentine interjection to start a sentence. Guevara became a rebel commander and captured Cuba's second largest city, Santa Clara, on December 29, 1958. Two days later, Fulgencio Batista fled into exile.

Che Guevara became a vocal proponent of the rapid adoption of socialism in Cuba and abroad. He supervised many trials in which individuals linked to Batista were found guilty of counterrevolutionary activity and were executed. Guevara then served as minister for industry from 1961 through 1965. He insisted on a full-speed effort to diversify Cuban manufacturing. This policy later became recognized as a disruptive failure that gave way to an effort to industrialize more slowly.

Guevara advocated global revolution. His 1961 guide, *Guerrilla Warfare*, asserted three basic principles. First, victory by revolution was possible. Second, one did not need to wait for favorable conditions; the conditions for revolution could be created. Third, success hinged on the support of the rural population. In 1965, he accused the Soviet Union of collaborating with capitalism by refusing to press for worldwide revolution.

Guevara began to pursue his vision for action. He secretly went to the Congo to assist rebels there. Then, in late 1966, Guevara entered Bolivia under a false identity to launch a rebellion that he claimed would spread from the geographic center of South America across the continent. In April 1967, while his efforts in Bolivia floundered, the Cuban press published his *Message to the Tricontinental*, which urged people in Africa, Asia, and Latin America to rebel to create "two, three, or many Vietnams."

On October 8, 1967, the Bolivian military captured Che Guevara and the tattered remnants of his failed guerrilla movement. They executed him the next day. Guevara's efforts to ignite a continental revolution failed in Bolivia because he did not have the support of the rural population—a point emphasized in his own writings. His movement never gained enough training and forces to conduct operations. Instead, it spent most of its time searching for food while on the run from the Bolivian military. Bolivian peasants found it difficult to support a guerrilla movement dominated by outsiders. Guevara and his Cuban and

Bolivian rebels did not speak Guaraní, the indigenous language prevalent in their zone of operations.

Che Guevara became a symbol of revolutionary idealism. Images of Guevara remain commonplace around the world to this day. Within Cuba itself, Fidel Castro made *El Che* the great martyr of the Cuban Revolution and had a massive portrait created that still looms over one side of the Plaza of the Revolution in Havana.

Cuba, and the urban opposition also grew more assertive. On the evening of December 31, 1958, Fulgencio Batista fled into exile.

From Victory to the Revolutionary Offensive (1959–1970)

After Batista's departure, Fidel Castro led a victorious caravan across Cuba and into Havana during the first week of 1959. Fidel's Rebel Army embodied the triumph over Batista; however, a respected judge from the urban opposition movement, Manuel Urrutia, led the initial interim government. Fidel Castro declared that the revolution would be neither capitalist nor socialist but rather humanist. The Urrutia government's economic program called for the rapid adoption of a state capitalist model: land reform, import-substituting industrialization, and agricultural diversification. Urrutia's cabinet consisted primarily of leaders from outside the July 26th Movement. Castro and the other rebel leaders occupied themselves primarily with a complete reorganization of Cuba's military in which the rebel leaders became the senior officers. Over the weeks and months of 1959, however, it became clear that the July 26th Movement did not see itself as simply the military protectors of a new civilian government dedicated to gradual changes in Cuba's traditionally unequal society. Fidel Castro became cabinet chief in February 1959. One by one, cabinet members resigned in disputes over the speed of change; when they did, leaders allied with Fidel Castro replaced them. When Castro pushed through a more aggressive land reform program in May than Urrutia had favored, the interim president resigned in July. The new president was a lawyer loyal to Castro, Osvaldo Dorticós.

Cabinet changes and military reorganization provided two of several means by which the July 26th Movement consolidated its hold over the Cuban government. Fidel Castro appeared frequently on television and at mass rallies to increase his support among ordinary Cubans. Castro's allies and confidants took control over the urban labor movement, the rural workers federation, and most other major interest groups. To gain and maintain the support of ordinary Cubans, the government organized neighborhood Committees for the Defense of the Revolution (*Comités para la Defensa de la Revolución* [CDRs]) across the country. Amid the dizzying debate over revolutionary change, many figures associated with the Batista government faced televised trials and harsh sentences. The trials dramatized the control of the July 26th Movement over the judiciary and its willingness to demonize its opponents. Subsequently, when more moderate members of the anti-Batista coalition criticized Castro, the so-called maximum leader of the revolution suggested that his critics might also face suspicion of treason along the grim lines experienced by Batista's collaborators. Several wealthy Cubans—both conservative and moderate in their economic views—fled into exile in the United States.

Cuban relations with the U.S. government soured as the revolutionary government continued to delay elections and moved toward increasingly sweeping economic reform. Although U.S. officials treated Castro cordially during his April 1959 visit to the United States, the underlying tension soon became noticeable when the U.S. government criticized the May 1959 land reform program. Relations worsened in early 1960 after Cuba and the Soviet Union signed a five-year economic cooperation agreement in which Cuban sugar exports would be used to underwrite Soviet loans for industrialization assistance. When U.S. petroleum firms in Cuba refused to refine Soviet crude oil, the Cuban government nationalized them. When the U.S. government responded by eliminating Cuba's quota of U.S. sugar imports in August 1960, Cuba retaliated by nationalizing most remaining U.S. firms. The U.S. launched a partial economic **embargo** against Cuba in October and then broke off diplomatic relations in January 1961.

Meanwhile, the U.S. Central Intelligence Agency continued to train a force of Cuban exiles to launch an anti-Castro rebellion. In 1954, a similar strategy had initiated a broader revolt against the Arbenz government in Guatemala when crucial portions of the Guatemalan military and many propertied Guatemalans supported the insurrection. As hindsight would demonstrate, however, conditions in Cuba differed substantially from the prior situation in Guatemala. Castro enjoyed the complete support of the military's officer corps as well as widespread support among Cuban citizens. Cuban forces captured nearly 1,200 of the roughly 1,500 Cuban exiles who landed at the Bay of Pigs on April 17, 1961; over 100 insurgents lost their lives. The Bay of Pigs invasion proved a triumph for Fidel Castro—not for the U.S. government. In the Labor Day celebration on May 1, Castro celebrated Cuba's military victory and reiterated a statement he first made after the initial bombing run prior to the invasion: his government would establish a socialist regime.

This confrontation with the United States erased any remaining speculation that Cuba might ultimately adopt a state capitalist model. The U.S. government launched a complete economic embargo in February 1962. Tensions worsened when U.S. satellite photos depicted Soviet forces placing nuclear missiles on Cuban soil. Cuba prepared for invasion in October 1962 when the U.S. government made its concerns public. Ultimately, the United States launched a naval quarantine of the island to convince the Soviet government to remove the missiles. Then the U.S. government tightened pressure on the Castro government by convincing the Organization of American States (OAS) to join the economic embargo in 1964. In 1965, the U.S. government revised its political asylum policy to grant asylum nearly automatically to almost every Cuban arriving on U.S. soil.

Cut off from its historical trading partners in the Americas, Cuba embraced greater economic relations with the Soviet bloc and moved toward socialism by nationalizing all remaining economic sectors over the course of the 1960s. The Castro government became the first in the Americas to adopt the command economy model in which the government owned all means of production, set production goals, and set most prices (see *Concepts in Action: Command Economics* on pages 258–259). At a time when many people made optimistic forecasts of the benefits of state capitalist economic policies, the young Cuban government steadfastly argued that the command economy would permit Cuba to develop even more quickly. It would reduce inequality while simultaneously reducing a long-running dependence on commodity exports like sugar and nickel. Che Guevara led a group of leaders who argued that a so-called revolutionary offensive could permit Cuba to transform itself at home while spreading the benefits of revolution to people around the world. Guevara's comments at a 1961 international gathering in Uruguay illustrated the optimism prevalent in some quarters: "What does Cuba expect to have in 1980? A per capita income of $3,000, more than the United States has now. And if you don't believe us, that's all right too: we're here to compete. Leave us alone, let us develop, and then we can meet again in twenty years, to see if this siren song came from revolutionary Cuba or from some other source."[3] In 1965, Fidel Castro and other leaders of the July 26th Movement became the key figures in a reorganized Cuban Communist party (*Partido Comunista de Cuba* [PCC]).

Initially the revolutionary government hoped to industrialize quickly to end Cuba's long-standing economic dependence on sugar. Even with Soviet aid, Cuba lacked the financial resources and manufacturing experience to transform the entire economy overnight. By 1964, the government changed course; it resolved to redirect resources to the sugar sector to double production to a record 10 million tons by the 1970 harvest. By maximizing sugar production, the Castro government hoped to generate the export revenues needed to finance a slower diversification of the economy. The sugar campaign also constituted the symbolic heart of the so-called revolutionary offensive because it would demonstrate the power of moral incentives in overcoming economic obstacles. Collaboration with the sugar harvest became a test of political loyalty as billboards and speeches called on all Cubans to help make the dream a reality. In the end, the redirection of most investment and labor into sugar production produced a record harvest of over 8 million tons. However, the single-minded focus on sugar left other agricultural sectors and the manufacturing component of the economy in complete disarray. Cuba began the 1970s more dependent on sugar (and on Soviet trade and aid) than ever before.

Although the Castro government failed to resolve quickly Cuba's age-old problems of economic dependence on a single commodity and on a single

CONCEPTS IN ACTION
Command Economics

In a socialist command economy, private property ceases to exist. The government owns and manages all firms. How does a command economy operate in practice? In the pattern established in the Soviet Union and later adopted in many other socialist systems, governments create five-year plans. A five-year plan sets production targets in each sector of the economy. The planners make decisions about whether or not some sectors will need additional investment resources to meet these targets. Profits earned in one sector can be reinvested to increase production in other sector. For example, profits earned by the sugar sector in Cuba can be used to invest in machinery to increase steel production. To achieve the overall five-year targets, the planners typically set annual and monthly production quotas. Managers of state-owned firms are then evaluated largely on their ability to meet their own annual and monthly targets. Through ownership of all businesses, socialist governments can shift resources from one sector to another and they can instruct firms to help achieve the socialist goals of full employment, income equality, and poverty reduction.

However, the gargantuan task of planning production levels in an entire economy can lead to rigidities that disrupt the day-to-day performance of the system. A command economy is even more vulnerable to supply bottlenecks than is a market economy. For example, the manager of an oven factory depends on the timely delivery of the components that workers will assemble into ovens. In a market economy, if the factory's supplier proves unreliable, it simply changes suppliers. Managers in a command economy often have few or no alternative suppliers. In the more rigid plans, the high-performing state firms have no freedom (and no incentive) to expand production to meet demand from additional customers. Even in flexible plans, firms lack the capability to expand production to drive the unreliable firms out of business.

Incentive problems form another major challenge in a command economy. In a market economy, managers use material incentives to encourage worker productivity and the timely delivery of promised goods and services. Efficient workers receive bonuses and promotions while inefficient workers and firms face the real possibility of unemployment and bankruptcy. In contrast, the socialist call for income equality and full employment makes the use of material incentives troubling. Managers receive pressure to hold wage differentials to a minimum and to employ as many people as possible. In these conditions, worker productivity tends to fall. A 1968 Cuban government study compared worker output to known production norms: it concluded that one-fourth to one-half of the workday was wasted.[1]

During the 1960s, many Cuban revolutionaries—led most vocally by Che Guevara—insisted that the revolution rely on moral incentives rather than material incentives. The new socialist person should shun money as an incentive and simply work for the good of all. Instead of bonuses and raises, productive workers should receive medals and praise that

[1]Carmelo Mesa-Lago, *Cuba in the 1970s*, rev. ed. (Albuquerque: University of New Mexico Press, 1978), p. 38.

would inspire their co-workers to become similarly diligent in carrying out their respective tasks. By the 1970s, the Cuban government adopted limited material incentives (in use in the Soviet Union for years) to try to boost labor productivity. In the mid-1980s, the government went back to moral incentives, only to embrace the more widespread use of material incentives again in the 1990s. This debate over moral and material incentives in Cuba persisted into the twenty-first century.

---

trading partner, the revolutionary government could point to various successes at the end of its first decade in power. The rebels had promised to improve living conditions for ordinary Cubans, and this goal had been largely achieved— particularly in rural Cuba. A massive adult literacy campaign and investment in childhood education increased the literacy rate from below 80 percent to over 90 percent. Improved public health programs and the creation of many free health clinics improved the average life expectancy, from sixty-four to seventy- three years. The command economy reduced the seasonal nature of employ- ment for many rural Cubans; the unemployment rate fell from 12 percent to around 5 percent. Finally, as promised, the regime decreased income inequal- ity. Prior to the revolution, the wealthiest 10 percent of the population earned over sixty times as much as the poorest 10 percent. By 1970, the wealthiest 10 percent earned roughly five times as much as the poorest Cubans.

The Institutionalization of a Soviet-Style System (1971–1985)

Not all the economic news was positive in 1970, however. The chaos of the sugar campaign damaged most other sectors of the economy. A decade of frequently shifting economic strategies had left many planners and managers demoral- ized because objectives shifted from year to year and—at times—from day to day. Although the revolution could highlight several achievements, the Castro government faced demands for economic and political change. In a speech on July 26, 1970, Fidel Castro acknowledged that the revolutionary offensive had failed in several respects. Castro promised to pursue political and economic changes to rectify the problems.

In the political realm, the Castro government embraced the Soviet model. The Communist party held its First Party Congress in 1975 in preparation for the creation of a new constitution. The 1976 constitution imitated many major elements of the Soviet constitution. Article 5 entrenched the PCC as the lone legal political party. As in the Soviet Union, the executive and legislative branches implemented policy decisions made elsewhere: by parallel bodies within the PCC that held the real decision-making power. The 1976 constitution also proclaimed the socialist character of economic life in Cuba.

The Castro government trumpeted the creation of elected local and provin- cial assemblies as a way for people to communicate with their leaders. Never- theless, in practice, the PCC controlled all levels of government and presented a single slate of candidates in each election. Isolated dissident voices criticized the closed nature of the political process but found it difficult to build large organizations capable of challenging the PCC leadership. In April 1980, six dissidents drove a bus through the gates of the Peruvian embassy in Havana in search of political asylum. The Castro government removed its guards from the destroyed embassy gate; within days, over 10,000 Cubans crowded into the facilities. When U.S. President Jimmy Carter announced that the United States would accept 3,500 **political refugees,** Fidel Castro seized the opportunity to open a pressure valve for all dissidents. On April 21, he announced that Cuban-Americans could travel in small crafts to the Cuban port city of Mariel to transport any relatives who wanted to leave. Castro later released common criminals for transport to the United States in an effort to depict the refugees as counter-revolutionary "worms" and criminal "undesirables." Over the next several months, roughly 125,000 Cubans reached U.S. shores in the Mariel boatlift. The Castro government weakened its opposition by permitting many dissidents to leave the country in the boatlift. Castro was willing to permit greater political participation at the local level, but his plans for political reform did not permit frontal criticisms of one-party rule or of socialism.

The economic reforms of the 1970s also adopted key features of the Soviet system. Economic planning in the 1960s had set major targets in certain sectors but frequently initiated new goals in the middle of each planning period. Beginning in 1971, that experimental phase of the revolution gave way to the adoption of a Soviet-style five-year plan that specified all production objectives for all sectors. Foreign advisers from Soviet-bloc countries worked with Cuban technocrats to improve data collection on economic production and on sales to aid in the management of the socialist economy.

As noted earlier in *Concepts in Action: Command Economics,* command economies are prone to low labor productivity. Over decades of experience with command economics, Soviet technocrats developed a system of modest productivity bonuses designed to entice workers to improve their productivity and efficiency. With the launching of the second five-year plan in 1976, Cuban authorities adopted a similar approach called the System of Economic Direction and Planning (*Sistema de Planificación y Dirección Económica* [SPDE]). Later in the decade, the government permitted an increasing number of peasants to sell food grown on small individual plots at farmers' markets and to keep the proceeds. Limited private activity came to be tolerated in some other sectors. These reforms helped to increase the availability of basic consumer goods, and the Cuban economy grew more steadily over the years from 1976 to 1985. In the first half of the 1980s, the economy grew by more than 7 percent annually. Part of the growth could be attributed to Cuba's ability to acquire crude oil at artificially low prices and then resell it at close to market value. The SPDE also helped to improve Cuba's economic performance somewhat.

While the SPDE achieved some of its aims, the political outcomes associated with the renewed use of material incentives fell far short of the government's historical insistence on an end to the profit motive. The creation of a "new Cuban" had been the rallying cry of revolutionary reform in the 1960s. Some party leaders grumbled that the use of material incentives worked against the creation of a truly socialist system and of a people who embraced communist ideals wholeheartedly.

The Rectification Campaign (1986–1990)

This ongoing grumbling came to a boil once changes elsewhere imperiled Cuba's economic situation. When oil and natural gas prices lost half their value on world markets in 1986, Soviet economic fortunes took a turn for the worse. Recently installed Soviet leader Mikhail Gorbachev insisted on Cuba's repayment of outstanding loans as a condition for the extension of new loans. Castro responded by calling on a new generation of Cubans to muster the revolutionary spirit needed to confront the debt crisis. Castro's remarks in a July 1986 address illustrate the themes that dominated his public appearances throughout the year: "Morale, an unselfish spirit of sacrifice, altruism; that was the raw material that made our people, a virtual colony of the United States, a socialist and communist country."[4] By year's end, the government announced an end both to farmers' markets and to the use of material incentives elsewhere in the economy. With a reduction in net Soviet assistance, the Cuban economy slowed down in 1986 and would contract in 1987. At the close of the Third Party Congress in late 1986, the Communist party announced the Campaign for the Rectification of Errors and Negative Tendencies. Moral regeneration and sacrifice would be used to face these new economic challenges.

Fidel Castro had an additional aim during the Rectification Campaign—the extension of his power within the political system. The pursuit of moral regeneration served as a device for rooting out rivals and potential rivals to Castro's leadership of the Communist party. The central political drama of the Rectification Campaign unfolded in the trial of military hero General Arnaldo Ochoa, the leader of Cuban forces active in the Angolan civil war. Ochoa and several other party members faced charges of corruption and drug trafficking; after conviction, they received death sentences. For Castro's supporters, the trial showed the regime's willingness and capacity for renewal. For the regime's opponents, the trial demonstrated the regime's ability to coerce confessions from some of its most powerful and respected members. In addition to trials involving important party members, the Rectification Campaign also served as a vehicle for rooting out dissidents. The Committees for the Defense of the Revolution actively persecuted neighbors suspected of antigovernment thought or action.

As the Cuban government struggled to come to terms with its economic limitations, a beleaguered Soviet government drastically reduced economic assistance to Cuba in 1990. The Soviet Union declared that it would no longer purchase Cuban sugar above market prices while selling crude oil and other key imports to Cuba below prevailing world market prices. All future trade with Cuba would take place at market prices and would be priced in hard currency. Faced with the end of Soviet aid, oil-fueled electricity generators in Cuba slowed to a halt. Buses lacked the spare parts and gasoline needed to function. Many other consumer goods became scarce.

In August 1990, the government declared the Special Period in Peacetime in which nearly all goods became subject to severe **rationing.** The typical family's twenty-one-day ration called for a daily bread roll, twelve eggs, one-quarter pound of chicken or beef, six pounds of sugar, and six pounds of rice; small quantities of other foods could be purchased if they were available. Only small children had access to milk at home; school-age children received one glass of milk with their school lunches. The ration program provided no access to any other dairy products. In many situations in the early 1990s, families found it impossible to acquire even the minimal goods included within the new rationing plan. With the end of Soviet aid, a new chapter in the revolutionary era had begun, and it would serve as the backdrop for the upcoming Fourth Party Congress in 1991.

CONTEMPORARY POLITICAL FRAMEWORK

In contrast to the other political systems we have examined thus far in this book, contemporary Cuba is a one-party state. The Cuban Communist party dominates all political institutions. Article 5 of the constitution entrenches the party, the PCC, as the guiding force in Cuban life. In turn, Fidel Castro has served as the central leader of the PCC since its reorganization in 1965. Because Castro dominates the high-level decision-making of the lone legalized political party, Cuba's formal political institutions are irrelevant in some respects because no genuine separation of power exists across the three branches of government. However, it is useful to study these three branches of government for two reasons. First, despite the minimal separation of power, the organization of authority still helps us understand how major decisions are implemented in the Cuban government. Second, should the aging leader die in office (Fidel Castro turned seventy-seven in August 2003), Cuba's core institutions will become one of several arenas in which the struggle to succeed Castro will take place.

The 1976 constitution organized Cuban politics along Soviet lines. The major executive and legislative bodies have parallel organizations within the PCC. Generally speaking, major decisions are made within the PCC and then implemented by the appropriate government body. To maintain control over the formal levers of government, the PCC leaders control the major posts within the government. Table 8.1 depicts the parallels between the PCC and the government. Fidel Castro serves at the top of both organizations by holding the posts of First Secretary of the PCC and president of Cuba.

TABLE 8.1 Parallel Power in Cuba's One-Party Political System

Cuban communist party (makes key decisions)	Cuban government (implements decisions)
PCC First Secretary	President
Politburo	Council of State
Central Committee	Council of Ministers
Party Congress	National Assembly

The Executive Branch

The chief executive of the Cuban government is the president of the Council of Ministers. The parallel post in the PCC is First Secretary of the Politburo. The PCC's Politburo is the directing board of the party and the focus for major political decisions in Cuba. Fidel's brother, Raúl, has historically served as the Second Secretary on the Politburo. The rest of the Politburo consists of several influential government ministers, provincial PCC leaders, the leaders of major nongovernmental organizations affiliated with the PCC, and senior military officers. The Politburo, like a cabinet, meets frequently on an ongoing basis; usually over half of the Politburo also sits on the Council of State; thus, the PCC leaders also exercise direct control over formal government decisions and policy implementation. In a departure from the Soviet model, the First Secretary of the Politburo and the president of the Council of Ministers have considerable formal powers and are held by a single person: Fidel Castro. In addition, Fidel Castro's position as founder of the revolutionary movement behind the PCC has given him enormous influence over major decisions.

The Council of Ministers directs the governmental agencies charged with carrying out decisions made by the Politburo. In 1994, on the heels of the economic collapse associated with the end of Soviet aid, the Council of Ministers underwent a substantial restructuring: many posts were consolidated into other ministries, and the tourism board gained ministerial status. An eight-member executive committee serves as the working cabinet for coordinating most government policies; all executive committee members also hold seats on the Politburo.

The Legislature

Similarly, the Cuban legislature consists of two major bodies that have parallel organs within the PCC. The National Assembly of People's Power (*Asamblea Nacional de Poder Popular* [ANPP]) serves as the national legislature. However, the 601-seat unicameral body meets for only a few weeks each year. Its members are elected on territorial slates for a five-year term. The National Assembly delegates most of its authority to the thirty-one-member Council of State. When the legislature is not in session, the Council of State can legislate by decree. Fidel Castro serves as president of the Council of State. Formally speaking, the National Assembly elects the Council of State. In practice, however, power flows down from the PCC leaders to the ANPP. Lower-level party members on the National Assembly are extremely unlikely to revoke actions taken by senior PCC leaders, on whom their political futures depend.

The parallel organizations within the PCC are the Central Committee and the Party Congress. Within the PCC's statutes, the Party Congress is the most powerful body in the party. The Party Congress meets every five years to set the path for the party and to elect the Central Committee. The Central Committee consists of 150 party leaders from all geographic regions and professions. The Central Committee meets every few weeks to review major decisions; it is also responsible for selecting party members to the Politburo. In reality, as with the government structures, power flows downward from Castro through the Politburo and down to the Central Committee and the Party Congress. Despite the historical dominance of the party leadership over the delegates to the Party Congress, PCC leaders have often reserved the right to propose and refine major policy changes until the Party Congress can be called to mobilize support for the new initiatives.

The Judiciary

The People's Supreme Court serves as the highest court in Cuba for all but constitutional matters. This large body consists of five distinct chambers dealing with criminal law, civil and administrative law, labor law, national security, and the military. Matters of constitutional law are reserved for the National Assembly; there is no separate constitutional tribunal with the power of judicial review. Supreme Court justices are nominated by the Council of State and approved by the National Assembly.

Under the 1976 constitution, justices are not independent but are deemed subordinate to the legislative authorities who appoint them. In practice, judges adhere to the dictates of the PCC. One would be hard-pressed to name a high-profile case of political importance in which the judiciary ruled against the party's position.

POLITICAL PARTICIPATION

No one can deny that the one-party system of revolutionary government frames all political participation in Cuba. Article 55 of the constitution expressly limits freedom of speech and freedom of the press to expressions in conformance with the ends of a socialist state. All major nongovernmental organizations in Cuba have the formal or informal consent of the PCC. Any organizations operating without the consent of the PCC run the danger of being declared treasonous groups operating outside the law. In this section, we will examine some of the major groups aligned with the Castro regime as well as major elements of the opposition.

Interest Groups and Social Movements

The Committees for the Defense of the Revolution (*Comités para la Defensa de la Revolución* [CDRs]) form perhaps the most important organized movement in support of the Castro government. Since their establishment in 1960, these neighborhood organizations have served as the vanguard of the revolutionary movement. At the outset, the CDRs were quasi-governmental organizations that provided the closest approximation of a local council in revolutionary Cuba. After the establishment of municipal assemblies in the 1970s, the CDRs have constituted the most comprehensive interest group working in support of the government. In a country of just over 8 million adults, over 80,000 CDRs dot the political landscape. The CDRs mobilize support for progovernment rallies. They also organize neighborhood gatherings in which government policies are explained to local residents. Many observers assert that the CDRs serve as the eyes and ears of the regime in its efforts to root out counterrevolutionary thought and action. In many instances, CDR brigades have harangued suspected dissidents and disbanded meetings in which citizens criticize the government.

The largest interest group in Cuban politics is the Cuban Workers' Confederation (*Confederación de Trabajadores de Cuba* [CTC]). The CTC's history predates the revolution. It was founded in 1939 by an ideologically diverse group of labor unions. Communist labor leaders played an important role in establishing the CTC but were expelled from the confederation in a leadership dispute in 1947, at the onset of the Cold War. With the triumph of the anti-Batista rebels in 1959, the major anticommunist labor leaders fled the country and communist labor leaders promptly took control of the CTC leadership. With the establishment of a socialist state, the CTC emerged as the organized expression of the group believed to be at the center of Cuban politics—the workers. During the early 1960s, the CTC leadership weeded out independent labor leaders, and the labor minister repressed unions deemed too aggressive in their efforts to represent their rank-and-file members. The CTC is the lone interest group with the ability to propose laws, and the labor minister is normally a CTC leader. The CTC leadership typically receives around 20 percent of the seats on the PCC Central Committee and a sizable share of seats in the national and subnational legislatures. While the CTC has a central role in the system, it is not independent of the PCC. The CTC has at times expressed (especially privately) perspectives that differed from ideas discussed elsewhere in the government, but to date the CTC has not directly opposed any major governmental initiative since the early 1960s.

Over the years, despite the serious limitations on freedom of expression and the absence of opposition political parties, some Cubans have been able to express dissent with the Castro regime. Often dissidents have worked alone (fearing easier persecution if they were to work with others) or in very small groups. In the early twenty-first century, the most important dissident group has been the Christian Liberation Movement (*Movimiento Cristiano Liberación* [MCL]). Founded in 1988 by Osvaldo Payá in a Catholic parish in Havana, the MCL takes its inspiration from Christian teachings but is expressly a nondenominational movement that is open to Catholics, Protestants, and non-Christians. Twice in the early 1990s, the MCL began to gather signatures to initiate a reform referendum in accord with Article 86 of the constitution (granting citizens the right to initiate a referendum via a petition of 10,000 signatures). Both petition drives faced significant harassment from pro-Castro groups and were shut down before gaining the necessary signatures. Then, along with several other dissidents, Payá called for a reform conference known as the Cuban Council (*Concilio Cubano*) to be held in February 1996. Payá was arrested and the conference was never held. In 1997, the MCL gathered signatures to place Payá on the ballot for the 1998 legislative elections; his request was denied. In 1998, the MCL began circulating a new referendum petition drive in support of a five-point program of civil and political liberties known as the Varela Project (*Proyecto Varela*). This project became the focus of political reform discussions (and government attention), as we shall see later in this chapter.

Given the tight constraints on freedom of association and speech in Cuba, it is perhaps not surprising that one of the most relevant Cuban interest groups was formed by exiles. Most of the nearly 2 million Cubans living in exile reside in the United States and they have formed many nongovernmental organizations during the Castro era. The largest and most influential group has been the Cuban American National Foundation (CANF) founded in 1981 by Jorge Mas Canosa and other wealthy Miami-based exiles. After Mas Canosa died of cancer in 1997, his son Jorge Mas Santos assumed leadership of the organization. The CANF has been the central Cuban interest group engaged in shaping the evolution of U.S. foreign policy toward Cuba. In the 1980s, the group pushed successfully for U.S. government funding for an anti-Castro radio station and later a television station. Radio Martí and TV Martí broadcast various anticommunist and anti-Castro programs, but the Cuban government scrambles their signals so that few Cubans receive the broadcasts. In the 1990s, CANF called for a tightening of the U.S. economic embargo of Cuba (and for heightened legal rights for Cuban exiles). Until then, the embargo had existed via executive order, but the 1992 Cuban Democracy Act entrenched the embargo in law, by establishing strict conditions that must be met before the economic sanctions can be removed. CANF lawyers played a key role in drafting the 1996 Cuban Liberty and Democratic Solidarity Act (frequently called the Helms-Burton Act in reference to its chief sponsors in the U.S. Congress). The Helms-Burton Act further tightened the embargo but also introduced two controversial provisions.

First, the law attempts to pressure other countries into joining the embargo by restricting U.S. visa privileges for employees of foreign companies that operate in Cuba. The law also asserts that those foreign firms could face prosecution in the United States for trafficking in stolen property but thus far, U.S. presidents have exercised their discretion to keep this clause inactive. Several U.S. trading partners, including Canada and the European Union, threatened legal challenges to the provision if it is implemented. Second, the Helms-Burton Act gives those who lost $50,000 or more in property to nationalization by the Castro government the right to sue in U.S. court for damages. At present, this part of the Helms-Burton Act is unused because the Cuban government has no plans to appear in U.S. court. If Cuba moves away from socialism, however, this provision lays the groundwork for considerable legal wrangling over property rights in a postcommunist Cuba.

Parties and Elections

The Cuban Communist party (*Partido Comunista de Cuba* [PCC]) has undergone several transformations since its founding in 1925. In the 1940 elections, the PCC backed the presidential campaign of Fulgencio Batista as the most viable reform-oriented candidate. In 1944, the PCC changed its name to the Popular Socialist party (PSP) in an effort to broaden its appeal. The PSP saw any potential path to power via elections blocked by the creation of the Batista dictatorship in 1952. In response, PSP-affiliated unions pressured for an end to the Batista government, and PSP leaders initially criticized Castro's July 26th Movement. In mid-1958, however, the PSP formally declared its support for the Castro movement, and PSP leaders took several key posts in the revolutionary government established in 1959. In 1961, Castro integrated the PSP, his own July 26th Movement, and the major revolutionary student movement into the Integrated Revolutionary Organizations (*Organizaciónes Revolucionarias Integradas* [ORI]). Over the next four years, this body went through two name changes and various organizational reforms; in 1965, the revolutionary movement reclaimed the original name of the communist party—the PCC. After the name change, the PCC remained a small organization comprised of revolutionary leaders loyal to Castro; less than 2 percent of the population belonged to the party. After passage of the 1976 constitution, however, the PCC took on a structure more commonly observed in the Soviet Union, China, and other communist regimes. The PCC currently consists of around 5 percent of the total population: members must pass a series of loyalty tests and gain the confidence of existing members. Party membership is highly prized because PCC members have the best chance of attaining a major role in government or a high-profile job in the economy.

Elections in a one-party state, by definition, do not involve open competition. Prior to the 1990s, citizens elected municipal assemblies in one-party elections. The municipal assemblies then approved slates of candidates for the

TABLE 8.2 Cuban National Assembly Election Results (1993, 1998, and 2003)*

	Year		
Type of vote	1993	1998	2003
PCC "unity ballot"	88.0	88.2	87.8
Selective votes	4.5	5.6	6.0
Blank or invalid votes	7.0	4.9	3.8
Did not cast a ballot	0.4	1.6	2.4

*All numbers are expressed as a percentage of registered voters. Percentages do not always add up to 100 because of rounding. The unity ballot is one in which the voter supports every candidate presented by the Cuban Communist party (*Partido Comunista de Cuba* [PCC]). Selective votes are those in which the voters supports some PCC candidates, but not all of them.

SOURCE: For the years 1993–1998, data are from the Political Database of the Americas <http://www.georgetown.edu/pdba/Elecdata/Cuba/cuba.html> (accessed on November 14, 2003). For 2003, data are from *Granma* <http://www.granma.cu/ingles/> (accessed on January 21, 2003).

provincial and national legislatures. The 1992 electoral law introduced direct election of all legislators beginning in 1993. Nominating commissions indirectly controlled by the PCC name candidates for the provincial and national legislatures; the commissions nominate a single candidate for each available seat. The PCC views the elections as an opportunity for citizens to demonstrate their loyalty to the regime by dutifully voting for the PCC's slate of candidates. At campaign time, the regime urges citizens to cast the so-called unity ballot— meaning that they turn out to vote and approve every PCC candidate up for election. Dissidents, in contrast, encourage citizens to cast a blank or a soiled (invalid) ballot in protest of the lack of free elections. The most recent elections took place in January 2003 (see Table 8.2). The government presented the low voter abstention and the slight decrease in protest ballots as evidence of stable support for the Castro government. Indeed, the percentage of voters casting the unity ballot has remained stable in the three elections held since the early 1990s economic crisis.

Nevertheless, it remains difficult to interpret voter turnout and the unity ballot as clear expressions of regime support. Many citizens fear the possibility of reprisals from the neighborhood CDR should they choose to cast an invalid ballot or decide not to vote. In addition, no external observers are present for the vote-counting process, which makes it difficult to accept the official results with total confidence. Several dissidents tried to observe the vote count in the 2003 elections but were not permitted to do so (even though the constitution declares the vote count to be public).

THE CONTEMPORARY QUEST FOR DEVELOPMENT, LIBERTY, AND GOVERNANCE

The end of Soviet aid in 1990 marked a watershed in Cuban communism. From that point onward, the existing command economy would need to be restructured to generate sufficient funds to provide education, health care, and other basic services. With the declaration of the "Special Period in Peacetime" in August 1990, the government placed the entire Cuban society on a war footing. The government used the crisis as a justification for considerable infringements on liberty.

In turn, these bleak economic conditions posed a major governance challenge as the government tried to keep economic discontent from bubbling over into public opposition to the continuation of communist rule. Fidel Castro faced a significant potential threat to his ongoing leadership of the revolutionary government. The failure of the 10 million tons of sugar campaign in 1970 proved a major embarrassment for the government, but it had occurred on the heels of many fulfilled promises regarding advances in education, health care, and income equality during the 1960s. In contrast, the Special Period in Peacetime took place on the heels of five years of belt-tightening during the Rectification Campaign.

More important, the 1990s crisis unfolded in a context of generational change. In 1970, most Cuban adults could recall personal hardships during the Batista era and several ways in which their lives had improved under communist rule. In 1990, over half of all Cubans had no memories of life before the revolution. Their reference point for comparison was not the Batista era but rather the decaying economy of the late 1980s. When the economy collapsed in the early 1990s, the Castro government found it increasingly difficult to deflect responsibility for the crisis on the U.S. economic embargo.

The Quest for Development in Cuba

The end of Soviet aid initiated an economic free fall of catastrophic proportions (see Table 8.3 on page 270). During the years 1991–1993, the economy shrank by nearly 35 percent. The end to cheap Soviet petroleum and subsidized spare parts for machines had far-reaching ripple effects across the economy. By many estimates, the agricultural sector produced roughly half of what it had been producing in the late 1980s, before the interruption in Soviet assistance. At times during the early 1990s, even the meager rations (discussed earlier in this chapter) were not available. Some workers on collective farms began to sell food on the black market. Malnutrition became a public health crisis because many adults and children had compromised immune systems. The government-sponsored press tried to put a palatable face on the crisis by stressing that reduced petroleum use made Cuba a model for sustainable development. Even for people interested in

TABLE 8.3 Cuban Economic Indicators (1983–2002)*

Year	GDP growth	Inflation	Unemployment
1983	4.9	—	—
1984	7.2	—	—
1985	4.6	—	—
1986	1.2	—	—
1987	−3.9	—	—
1988	2.2	—	—
1989	0.8	—	—
1990	−3.1	—	—
1991	−10.9	—	7.7
1992	−13.8	—	6.1
1993	−16.0	0	6.2
1994	0.5	0	6.7
1995	2.6	−12	7.9
1996	9.1	−5	7.6
1997	3.4	2	7.0
1998	0.0	3	6.6
1999	5.7	−3	6.0
2000	6.3	−3	5.5
2001	2.9	0	4.1
2002	1.2	7	3.3

*All numbers are percentages.

SOURCE: For the years 1983–1987, data are from United Nations Economic Commission for Latin America and the Caribbean, *Preliminary Overview of the Economies of Latin America and the Caribbean 1989* (Santiago, Chile: United Nations Publications, 1989). For the years 1988–1992, data are from United Nations Economic Commission for Latin America and the Caribbean, *Preliminary Overview of the Economies of Latin America and the Caribbean 1994* (Santiago, Chile: United Nations Publications, 1994). For the years 1993–1997, data are from United Nations Economic Commission for Latin America and the Caribbean, *Preliminary Overview of the Economies of Latin America and the Caribbean 1999* (Santiago, Chile: United Nations Publications, 1999). For the years 1998–2002, data are from United Nations Economic Commission for Latin America and the Caribbean, *Preliminary Overview of the Economies of Latin America and the Caribbean 2003* (Santiago, Chile: United Nations Publications, 2003).

reduced use of fossil fuels, however, the early 1990s constituted one of the darkest development outcomes imaginable. The government's initial response to the end of Soviet aid—rationing and exhortation to work through the problems—did not prevent an economic collapse. It merely attempted to limit some of the suffering associated with economic breakdown.

The horrible conditions heightened pressure for reform from inside and outside the PCC and eventually led to several changes in economic policy during

1993. The initial reform focused on the need to make more food available. Collective farms gained authorization to target a portion of their production for private sale; in other words, they could set their prices and keep the profits. Once a collective farm met its quota under the plan, the farm itself could control any excess production. In addition, several forms of self-employment were legalized, including numerous small restaurants (*paladares* in Cuban slang).

Then, on the fortieth anniversary of the Moncada revolt, Castro announced two major changes on July 26, 1993. First, the U.S. dollar would become legal currency in Cuba. Many Cubans received dollars from friends and relatives living abroad. Those dollars were once used in a thriving black market to buy goods not otherwise available. The legalization of the dollar aimed at redirecting black market activity toward government-run stores that offered scarce goods not sold in the normal stores conducting transactions in Cuban pesos. By legalizing the dollar, the government hoped to reduce illegal transactions and to increase its own hard currency revenues. These dollars could then be used to help restore Cuba's ability to import goods from abroad. Second, Castro announced that foreign investment would be welcomed. This second change represented an effort to invigorate the economy through the creation of mixed enterprises managed by foreign companies. The government initially emphasized joint ventures in tourism, especially in the Varadero sector outside Havana.

In 1996, a third major reform introduced special economic zones (SEZs) in which foreign firms could operate not only joint ventures but also privately controlled enterprises. As with other countries' SEZs, these zones permit duty-free transport of goods into and out of the zone along with other tax concessions. In contrast to SEZs in other countries, however, the Cuban system retains an element of government control: Cuban employees in these firms must be approved by a government-run employment agency that collects wages from the foreign firms and then pays salaries to the workers.

In the wake of these three major economic changes, the government subsequently has referred to the legalization of limited private activity as concessions on the road to socialism and as a mixed socialist economy. From this point onward, Cuba has had a dual economy: most Cubans operate in the command economy, but an increasing portion of the economy operates on market principles. These reforms—along with a reorganization of the command economy's priorities—finally pulled Cuba out of its economic free fall. The economy grew by an average of 4.7 percent annually during 1994–1996. Tourism replaced sugar as Cuba's major source of hard currency. Slowly, the government managed to restore basic services, and food became less scarce (albeit not plentiful for the majority of Cubans who lack access to U.S. dollars).

The Fifth Party Congress in 1997 took place under very different conditions than had prevailed in 1991 at the prior congress. By this time, the economy had been growing for over three years; in 1996, the growth rate reached nearly 9 percent. The U.S. government's 1996 adoption of the Helms-Burton Act had embroiled the U.S. government in a major diplomatic dispute with Canada and with the European Union. The Castro government relished this controversy

GLOBAL PERSPECTIVES
Economic Reform Under Communist Rule

As the Cuban government made decisions in the 1990s regarding the pace and extent of reform, it did so in light of events in the two largest socialist countries—the People's Republic of China and the Soviet Union. Following the 1976 death of Mao Zedong (a founder of the Chinese Communist party), China embarked on a path of economic reform under another veteran leader, Deng Xiaoping. In 1978, the Chinese government implemented what it called the responsibility system. Once state farms met their quota within the command economy, they could produce and sell additional goods freely, setting their own prices and keeping the profits. The success of this reform in boosting agricultural production sparked two additional changes in the 1980s. First, the government permitted many cooperatives in the manufacturing sector to lease government facilities and operate under market principles. Second, the government launched foreign joint ventures in which foreign capitalists could operate in China under market principles in subsidiaries jointly held by the Chinese government.

These reforms ushered in a new era in which an expanding market sector coexisted with the traditional command economy operating under five-year plans. The market mechanisms and foreign investment helped to spawn rapid economic growth. China had the world's fastest growing economy in the 1980s: it grew at an average annual rate of more than 10 percent. These economic changes made many Chinese citizens less dependent on the government. By the late 1980s, a growing dissident movement pushed for political freedoms. In 1989, the movement held a prodemocracy rally in Tiananmen Square in the heart of the Chinese capital, Beijing. Government troops cleared the square, killing many protesters and arresting more. The Chinese Communist party made it clear that it would not tolerate an end to one-party rule.

In 1985, Mikhail Gorbachev became the leader of the Soviet Union. Gorbachev eased some restrictions on the press to mobilize dissident voices in support of economic reform along Chinese lines. In 1987 and 1988, the Soviet Union legalized foreign joint ventures, the responsibility system, and market-oriented cooperatives. In contrast to China, however, the Soviet Union also engaged in considerable political reform beginning in 1988. Soviet citizens elected two-thirds of the reorganized national legislature; there was also competition for some elected offices. The Communist party could field multiple candidates and independents could run for some offices. As the Soviet Union began to put this system into practice, dissidents in socialist countries in eastern Europe began to push for even more extensive political change in their respective countries. In February 1990, the Soviet reforms went even further: Article 6 of the Soviet constitution was revised, thereby ending the Communist party's status as the only legal political party.

The Soviet government was besieged by demands for additional autonomy from all fifteen of its member republics. Gorbachev began a troubled effort to renegotiate the authority of the national and subnational governments in the new Union Treaty that six republics rejected. On the eve of the treaty's signing ceremony in August 1991, opponents of the political opening arrested Gorbachev in a failed coup attempt. By December 1991, the leaders of the fifteen member republics declared their independence. The Soviet Union had ceased to exist.

Fidel Castro stated that he would not follow the Soviet Union's example. While some economic reform might ensue, Cuba would not consider adopting competitive elections. In Castro's view, the gains of the revolution should not be put at risk by engaging in political reform.

---

while it continued to stress Cuba's ability to survive in the face of heightened pressure from the world's most powerful country. While talk of reform had been in the air in the months preceding the 1991 Fourth Party Congress, no one anticipated major changes at the 1997 meeting. Those forecasts proved correct: the regime embraced the controlled dual-economy model adopted in the mid-1990s and ruled out political changes. By pursuing this path, the Cuban government hoped to follow the Chinese Communist party's route to survival while avoiding the regime collapse observed in the Soviet Union (see *Global Perspectives: Economic Reform Under Communist Rule*).

The five-year plan for 1998–2002 called for continued foreign investment and an emphasis on improvements in the command economy. Official government figures had estimated total foreign direct investment (FDI) from 1993 through 1997 at roughly $1.1 billion.[5] During the next five years, additional FDI of just under $1 billion poured into the economy, particularly in the tourist and oil sectors. Although tourist revenue did not double according to the government's goals, it did increase by more than 50 percent. Similarly, although Cuba had a long way to go to reach its goal of self-sufficiency in oil, foreign investment helped to spur a doubling of oil production during this five-year period. Nickel production increased by 50 percent with the help of foreign investment, but the sector's ability to bring in hard currency was limited by low prices on world markets. The tobacco and sugar sectors also suffered from low world prices. As a result, growth in tourism at the turn of the century helped Cuba to avert economic disaster, but tourism alone could not raise the living standards of most Cubans.

The government continued the market-oriented agricultural reforms initiated under the prior five-year plan. By the turn of the century, roughly three-fourths of all land under cultivation operated under market principles. Producers set their own prices and marketed their own products. By 2000, the production of fresh vegetables tripled the level prevailing in 1997. However, many Cubans could not afford to pay the going price for privately grown produce and thus purchased these goods rarely, if at all.

The limited reforms in place since the mid-1990s created a dual economy with diverse winners and losers. Winners include small farmers, successful self-employed people, and workers who receive higher wages in the foreign sector of the economy. Roughly one-third of the Cuban workforce found employment outside the command economy. In addition, thousands of Cubans receive a steady flow of U.S. dollars from relatives living abroad; many estimates pegged the annual value of these remittances at $600 to $800 million in the early twenty-first century. All of these privileged individuals now are less dependent on the government. Their potential support for political change may be voiced more frequently once Fidel Castro is no longer at the helm of the political system.

On the other hand, PCC rank-and-file members and the millions of Cubans within the command economy see themselves losing ground economically since the 1990s. Many of the people most loyal to the regime fall into this category. The future of Cuba's dual economy hinges on the answer to the following question: once Fidel Castro is no longer in charge, will these forces become a voice for a reduction or an increase in market mechanisms in the Cuban economy?

The end to Soviet aid in 1990 posed the most serious threat that the Castro government had faced since it consolidated its control over the government in the first years of the revolution. The subsequent economic collapse proved even more catastrophic than several outside observers had anticipated. In response, the government moved toward the tightly controlled adoption of limited market mechanisms. This new dual economy prevented Cuba from becoming as famine stricken as North Korea has been since 1995.

The economic recovery appeared genuine yet limited in its scope. Heavy investment in the tourist sector fueled a boom as annual tourism revenues expanded from $243 million in 1990 to almost $2 billion by 2000.[6] Despite a stagnation in tourism in the early twenty-first century, the government announced plans to increase hotel capacity by five times over the first decade of the new century. Even if these ambitious plans were to spawn an additional increase in hard currency earnings, the other dollar-earning components of the Cuban economy faced difficult prospects. Nickel, sugar, and tobacco prices remained at low levels on world markets, and Hurricane Michelle did considerable damage to the entire Cuban economy in late 2001. Potential limits to the future expansion of tourist revenues could threaten the Cuban economy, which is what happened when world tourism declined in the wake of the September 11, 2001, terrorist attacks in the United States.

The Cuban economy is no longer in decline, but there is also no expectation of substantial progress toward a more comfortable life for most Cubans. Many Cubans live from day to day, trying to scrape together enough food to provide for themselves and their families. While education and medical care remain nearly free to all Cubans, many schools and hospitals experience supply shortages. Many public schools and hospitals throughout Latin America experience also experience shortages. The difference in the case of Cuba is that improvements in the quality and availability of these two basic services had constituted central triumphs of the first decade of revolutionary rule.

The Quest for Liberty in Cuba

Cuba's economic collapse in the early 1990s created considerable discontent and desperation among most citizens. However, the Rectification Campaign had discouraged calls for more sweeping economic reform or for any political reform whatsoever. The lone increase in human liberty after the 1991 Fourth Party Congress slightly enhanced freedom of religion. The 1976 constitution had a clause outlawing religious expression because it was feared religion would be used as a basis for refusing to defend the revolution. In 1992, a constitutional amendment eliminated that provision, although it retained language permitting the government to regulate the exercise of religion. In addition, the PCC eliminated its historical insistence on atheism as a condition for membership: adherents of organized religion could now join the Communist party.

In addition to continuing formal restrictions on other civil liberties, most citizens depended on resources controlled by the PCC to survive. As a result, most people proved unwilling to express opposition to the government. Instead, during the Special Period in Peacetime, the primary expression of discontent involved rafters (*balseros*) building homemade vessels and sailing to the United States in search of political asylum. The *balsero* option had not been popular historically because the Cuban government often arrested the rafters. If rafters succeeded in clearing Cuba's shoreline, they faced a dangerous journey across ninety miles of open water toward the United States; many rafters have died at sea. Most observers estimate that roughly 100 Cubans sailed annually by homemade raft to the United States during the years 1981–1988.

As economic conditions worsened during the Special Period in Peacetime, the annual number of rafters climbed from a few hundred in 1990 to over 4,000 in 1993. In August 1994, Fidel Castro found himself temporarily surrounded by several angry Cubans in a televised public appearance: the regime's rhetoric of a united people rallying to face the crisis had been contradicted by the day's television images. The Castro government then announced that the Cuban Coast Guard would not apprehend rafters trying to leave the island. In late August and early September, over 30,000 Cubans took to the seas. The U.S. government pressured the Cuban government to retake control of its coastline. In turn, the United States agreed to permit Cubans to apply for an entry visa at the U.S. Interests Section in Havana; 20,000 visas per year would be permitted via a lottery process. As in the Mariel boatlift, the Cuban government responded to dissent by permitting unhappy citizens to leave.

When citizens did choose to express their discontent by speaking out, they encountered various forms of government repression. In late 1995, small dissident groups organized the Cuban Council (*Concilio Cubano*) to discuss political reform in a conference scheduled for February 24, 1996. Many of these dissidents faced so-called acts of repudiation from neighborhood CDRs and other communist activists who labeled them as counterrevolutionary worms via shouting sessions and graffiti written on their residences. Several dissident leaders were

Here are two faces of the Cuban Revolution in its fifth decade. On the top of the page, the Hotel Meliá is a modern, world-class resort catering to foreign tourists. In the second photo, these old cars in a contemporary traffic jam in Havana symbolize economic stagnation during the Castro era.   Top photo: © Langevin Jacques/Corbis Saba; bottom photo: © David G. Hauser/Corbis.

arrested and told that they would be released on the condition that they ask people not to participate in the Cuban Council. After the Council elected new leaders on February 10, the police apprehended the entire governing board in just over one week. Days before the meeting, the Council ceded to this pressure and publicly announced that the meeting would be postponed.

On the planned date of the Cuban Council's meeting (February 24, 1996), the Cuban Air Force shot down two small passenger planes flown by Brothers to the Rescue—a Cuban-American organization that tries to find rafters and secure their passage to the United States. For months, the Cuban government had complained that some of these planes were entering Cuban airspace illegally and dropping anti-Castro leaflets. The government justified shooting down the planes by claiming that they were in Cuban airspace; considerable evidence suggests that the planes were not in Cuban territory at the time they took fire. The murder of unarmed Cuban-American pilots motivated U.S. President Bill Clinton to back away from his planned veto of the Helms-Burton Act. Instead, the president signed the controversial legislation into law—igniting criticism from several U.S. allies. On a day once slated for dissident debate over the future of Cuba in the cancelled *Concilio Cubano*, the Castro government redirected the headlines toward the ongoing conflict between Cuba and its powerful neighbor to the north. In the months that followed, many of the participants in the Cuban Council movement applied for participation in the U.S. visa lottery. In July 1997, four leaders of the Dissident Working Group were arrested for advocating multiparty democracy. They were subsequently convicted and sentenced to prison for three to five years.

The Christian Liberation Movement (MCL) became the most visible dissident force after the Fifth Party Congress. In January 1998, MCL leader Osvaldo Payá launched the Varela Project. This reform proposal called for a referendum designed to legalize five basic liberties in Cuba: freedom of speech, freedom of association, an amnesty for all political prisoners who have not committed violent acts, the right to engage in private enterprise, and a new electoral law that would permit multiple candidates to compete for office. Under Article 88 of the constitution, 10,000 citizens can initiate a referendum via petition; the MCL began to gather signatures. In 1999, the MCL participated in a joint effort with other dissidents, which they called *Todos Unidos* (Everyone Together). In 2001, many of these dissident groups mobilized to gather the required signatures. On May 10, 2002, Payá personally presented over 11,000 signatures to the National Assembly as required under Cuban law. Five days later, former U.S. president Jimmy Carter referred to the Varela Project as a hopeful initiative in his televised address to the Cuban government; it was the first time that most Cubans had heard a specific reference to this petition. The Cuban government shelved the Varela Project, however, and organized its own petition drive, as we will see in the next section of this chapter.

The rejection of the Varela Project constituted the first of several steps taken against dissident thought and action. In early 2003, the Castro government began to arrest dissidents. The authorities blamed the arrests on a meeting between Cuban dissidents and the head of the U.S. Interests Section office in Havana, James Cason. Over seventy dissidents faced trial in early April 2003; many prominent dissidents received sentences ranging from twenty to twenty-eight years. While the trials took place, several Cubans hijacked a ferry in an effort to flee the island. Although Cuban authorities later recaptured the ferry and no hostages were harmed, three of the hijackers received death sentences and were promptly executed (the first executions in Cuba in three years). The Cuban government claimed that the prior dissident meeting and the hijacking constituted part of a larger campaign to destabilize the island. Castro asserted still further that the U.S. military planned to invade Cuba once it completed its operations in Iraq. Castro again insisted on the possibility of a U.S. invasion in May 2004 after the U.S. government tightened existing travel restrictions on Cuban-American visits to relatives living in Cuba.

To limit the potential scope of dissident criticism, the Cuban government has used various tactics to restrict civil liberties. The PCC's control over desirable jobs—in both the command economy and the new foreign sector—can be used to reward public expressions of loyalty and to punish those who refuse to toe the line. When economic pressure fails to prevent dissent, CDRs can hold neighborhood meetings to harass dissidents and to mobilize supporters to isolate the critics. The CDRs and so-called rapid response brigades undertake acts of repudiation that verbally and at times physically abuse critics of PCC policies. Should these tactics fail, the government retains the option of charging dissidents with sedition within a compliant judicial system that is likely to produce a guilty verdict. Faced with an almost certain guilty verdict, Cuban prosecutors pressure defendants to plead guilty and profess regret for their counterrevolutionary thoughts and actions. In exchange, defendants may receive lighter sentences or might avoid reprisals against their relatives.

The Quest for Governance in Cuba

As the economic crisis unfolded, some observers speculated that the PCC would consider political reforms along the lines pursued in the Soviet Union under Mikhail Gorbachev. The Gorbachev government had reduced restrictions on freedom of expression and then opened some legislative seats to competitive elections. The 1991 Fourth Party Congress of the PCC laid that speculation to rest. While Castro's response to economic crisis did not contemplate an end to one-party rule, the PCC did experience considerable leadership turnover. Over two-thirds of the Central Committee chosen at the congress joined the body for the first time. The PCC eased several prominent older revolutionaries out of the Politburo and replaced them with a new generation of leaders. All eleven new appointees to the twenty-five-member Politburo were under fifty years old. In part, the leadership turnover was an attempt to bridge a generation gap in which younger people often saw the veterans of the July 26th

Movement as defenders of a system that had not worked for young Cubans. In addition, the turnover increased Fidel's and Raúl Castro's positions as two of a handful of Rebel Army veterans still prominent in the government; potential rivals for influence had been pushed aside.

Although the government rejected political change, the limited economic reforms created potential political divisions in the revolutionary movement and in the citizenry more generally. The legalization of the dollar made an ongoing distinction in Cuban society more acute than ever before: a privileged minority of Cubans had access to dollars and thus a wider variety of consumer goods, while most citizens could not purchase scarce items at government-run and black-market stores that accepted only U.S. dollars. This change not only frustrated the majority with little or no access to dollars, it also infuriated a cadre of dedicated revolutionaries who claimed that the U.S. dollar created classes in a formerly classless society. The Castro government tried to deal with these concerns by placing increasingly severe limits on certain U.S.-dollar-based earnings. On May 1, 1994, Fidel Castro's Labor Day address attacked profiteering by Cubans. Shortly after the speech, the government closed down several self-employed businesses for failure to comply with government regulations. In turn, the government raised prices in its U.S.-dollar-based stores and then imposed income taxes on the self-employed sector. By criticizing market-based activity and limiting its scope, the PCC hoped to avoid a scenario in which economic reform paved the way for more sweeping political and economic changes of the sort observed in several other communist countries during the 1980s and 1990s. If the Castro government had its way, limited economic reforms would produce new revenues to help maintain both the socialist segment of the economy and Castro's ongoing dominance of the government. In the early twenty-first century, scholars considered why the Cuban government had not yet joined the third wave of democratization in Latin America and beyond (see the *Research Question* on pages 280–281).

At the dawn of a new century, Fidel Castro's major governance task remained the challenge of mobilizing support for the PCC's monopoly on politics and for his ongoing control of the PCC. While many older Cubans shared his antipathy for the United States, Castro's efforts to blame Cuban economic problems on the U.S. embargo often rang hollow with many younger Cubans. Then, in 1999, a human tragedy provided an opportunity for the PCC to mobilize thousands of Cubans in anti-U.S. protests. In late November 1999, then-five-year-old Elián González had been rescued by a fishing boat after the raft he had been traveling on with his mother had capsized; Elián's mother had drowned in the effort to seek political asylum for herself and her son. Elián's arrival on U.S. shores invoked contradictory legal imperatives. On one hand, U.S. immigration law since 1965 had granted political asylum to nearly all Cuban applicants on the grounds that any Cuban citizen faced potential persecution. On the other hand, U.S. and international law gave precedence to the parental rights of biological parents over other blood relatives. Cuban exiles in Miami mobilized to demand

asylum for Elián on the premise that, had his mother lived, Elián would likely
have received asylum on the basis of a petition made by his mother. However,
Elián's father, Juan González, remained in Cuba and requested his son's return.
By early December, thousands of Cubans mobilized in daily rallies in front of
the U.S. Interests Section in Havana, while Cuban exiles rallied in front of the
house of Elián's great-uncle in Miami. The legal wrangling dragged on for
months, as did the demonstrations and counterdemonstrations. Eventually,
the U.S. courts rejected an asylum petition filed by Elián on the grounds that a
six-year-old could not file for asylum and that his Miami-based relatives had no
legal custody to file on his behalf. When Elián's relatives refused to turn over
custody to U.S. immigration officials, the Immigration and Naturalization Service raided the great-uncle's house. After subsequent legal appeals, Elián returned with his father to Cuba in late June 2002. Fidel Castro personally praised
Elián and his father at a massive rally organized to celebrate his return. Juan
González subsequently ran for a seat in the National Assembly in 2003. Like all
other PCC candidates, he won election to a five-year term.

RESEARCH QUESTION

Under What Conditions Are Countries Likely to Develop Democratic
Political Systems?

In a 2001 article, Darren Hawkins applied theories of democratization to Cuba's experiences during the 1990s.[1] Under what conditions would authoritarian political systems be
likely to give way to democratic rule? In light of research on other countries, should one expect Cuba to move toward democracy in the contemporary era?

Hawkins organizes explanations of democratization into two main groups. Structural explanations focus on the socioeconomic and global conditions that frame political life. As discussed in Chapter Two, modernization theory holds that the more economically developed
the society, the more likely democracy will emerge. Another structural factor that can promote
democratization is severe economic crisis. A sharp reversal of economic fortunes can motivate people to challenge the existing authoritarian regime. A third structural hypothesis asserts
that democratization is more likely in countries that are surrounded by other democracies.

Voluntarist theories of democratization focus more on human interaction and on individual choices. In the 1980s, several early analyses of the third wave of democratization
focused on the role played by moderate soft-liners within the authoritarian government.
The more voices favoring modest political reform from within the system, the more likely
democratization will occur. Voluntarist theories also highlight the role of nongovernmental
groups that pressure for change from outside the system.

[1] Darren Hawkins, "Democratization Theory and Nontransitions: Insights from Cuba," *Comparative Politics* 33
(2001): 441–461. For additional research in academic journals regarding democratization, see the appropriate portion of this book's website.

Despite genuine public support for the repatriation of Elian González, the Cuban government still faced an active minority of dissidents attempting to instigate political reform. The MCL used provisions of the Cuban constitution as a potential path for reform; the Varela Project petition constituted a direct challenge to the PCC's ongoing dominance. The PCC responded by trying to demonstrate that it could mobilize more support than the MCL could. On June 12, 2002, Fidel Castro personally led a march of over 1 million Cubans rallying in support of socialism. In the days that followed, the government gathered hundreds of thousands of signatures on behalf of the petition to amend the constitution to make the revolution irrevocable. The official count later reported that 99 percent of all registered voters signed the petition. In June, the National Assembly approved the constitutional amendment. While over 100 speakers took the floor of the legislature in support of the amendment proposal, none of them referred to the prior Varela Project proposal that had triggered the irrevocability amendment drive. The revised constitution now deemed the socialist character of the Cuban state "irrevocable" in Article 3, while changes to Article 137 on amendment

Which hypotheses are most useful for understanding Cuba's failure to move toward democratic rule in the 1990s? Hawkins argues that structural conditions in Cuba largely favored democratization. Cuba was the most literate society in Latin America and performed well in several other development indicators, with its comparatively lengthy life expectancy, low infant mortality, and open access to health care. At the same time, the economic free fall of the early 1990s was more severe than most Latin American crises during the so-called lost decade of the 1980s. International factors generated additional pressure to democratize. During the Cuban economic collapse, the rest of the Americas had already begun to democratize; many countries in the former Soviet bloc also began to adopt democratic political systems. In stark contrast, the voluntarist conditions favoring a democratic transition were in short supply in Cuba. Hawkins notes the nearly total absence of moderate political discourse among the senior and midlevel leaders of the Cuban Communist party. Those few who spoke favorably of more political freedom during the early 1990s were shifted to low-profile jobs. Outside the government, most organized groups remained small and faced constant threats of repression.

Why did so few people push openly for change? Hawkins emphasizes Fidel Castro's leadership skills in outmaneuvering his opponents, tinkering with his rhetoric, and permitting greater religious freedom provided that religious activists (such as Osvaldo Payá of the Varela Project) do not challenge the party's monopoly on political power. Hawkins also asserts that the legitimacy built up during the 1960s and 1970s has not yet completely eroded. Whether political skill could continue to buttress legitimacy and limit prodemocracy forces in the years to come remained an open question.

procedures asserted that Article 3 could not be amended. With these amendments, Fidel Castro tried to close the path to nonsocialist governance to both the MCL dissidents and to future PCC leaders.

Fidel Castro faces two potential governance challenges: mobilization from outside the PCC and competition from within the party. As discussed above, the government proved willing to use all means at its disposal to limit public dissent. Within the PCC, Castro permitted some internal expressions of support for limited economic reform in the weeks prior to the Fourth Party Congress. In and out of the congress, however, Castro made it clear that adoption of widespread market mechanisms did not constitute a potential option. The 1991 Fourth Party Congress provided an opportunity to replace several veteran leaders with PCC activists from a younger generation.

From the 1997 Fifth Party Congress through 2003, however, the regime dug in. Like the Chinese Communist party, it has chosen not to permit any meaningful political reform. The 2003 crackdown has been interpreted as a clear expression of the regime's desire to maintain the existing system.

Future Challenges

In January 2004, Fidel Castro began his forth-sixth consecutive year as the leader of revolutionary Cuba. Although human history has presented many surprises over the centuries (including Castro's own rise to power), few observers in early 2004 believed that Fidel Castro would be motivated to make substantial changes in the current system. As a result, consideration of Cuba's future challenges has focused on talk of what might happen after Castro no longer leads the PCC.

Leadership succession following the death of communist leaders has been unpredictable elsewhere in the world. After Vladimir Lenin's death in 1924, a brutal succession crisis ensued in the Soviet Union in which Joseph Stalin physically eliminated his potential rivals over the course of a decade. Stalin made substantial reforms in the system Lenin had set into motion. When Stalin died in 1953, his successor, Nikita Khrushchev, was selected via standing party procedures; yet he, too, moved away from his predecessor's policies. The founding leader of the Chinese Revolution, Mao Zedong, died in 1976 after leading the government for nearly three decades and the Chinese Communist party for five decades. Mao's initial successor, Hua Guofeng, held most of the reins of the formal political system after Mao died. However, he did not retain power and was marginalized in the late 1970s by veteran party leader Deng Xiaoping. As noted in *Global Perspectives: Economic Reform Under Communist Rule,* Deng injected considerable market-oriented reforms into the Chinese system. When North Korea's founding leader, Kim Il-sung, died in 1994, he was replaced by his son, Kim Jong-il, who generally maintained his father's policies.

Who might succeed Fidel Castro and what would that change imply for Cuba? The above summary of succession patterns in other communist regimes suggests that the death of long-serving leaders may or may not be resolved using the formal rules in place at their departure. In turn, the new leaders may choose to enforce their predecessors' policies, but most have chosen to make considerable changes. The one constant across all these examples is that the successors were all leaders with considerable experience inside their respective communist parties. This pattern may not hold true in Cuba, but it suggests that we should consider major PCC leaders as the most likely successors to Fidel Castro. Should Fidel Castro die in office, his younger brother Raúl is slated to assume Fidel's dual role as leader of the PCC and of the Cuban government. However, Raúl might not outlive his brother, or other leaders might outmaneuver him once Fidel leaves the political scene.

In either scenario, Cuba's next leader inherits an agenda for reform in pursuit of development, liberty, and governance. Some hard-liner communists may push for the elimination of the limited sphere of private activity in the Cuban economy. Other Cubans in the command economy may mobilize in the hope of greater economic opportunity via private enterprise. If the Cuban state were dismantled too rapidly, however, many Cubans might pressure to maintain the minimal security provided by the Cuban government. The debate over liberty will likely be equally divisive. Many PCC activists would have reason to feel threatened by an expansion of electoral competition or other liberties. However, the majority of the Cuban population does not belong to the party and may mobilize with less fear once Fidel Castro leaves power. Finally, as succession crises elsewhere suggest, the governance crisis initially may prove severe. The next leader of Cuba will make a pivotal decision to embrace economic reform, political reform, both, or neither. That decision will shape governing dynamics because some in Cuban society will back the new leader while others could become vehement opponents.

Given the closed nature of the Cuban political system, it remains difficult to determine how much support for political and economic reform exists in the PCC, in the military, and in society more generally. In 2002 and 2003, the Castro government tried to reaffirm the revolutionary system. Once Fidel Castro is no longer in power, we will see whether the 1976 constitution serves as the guiding force of the next Cuban government or becomes a dead letter like the 1940 constitution became after Castro's rise to power.

Activities and Exercises

1. What were Cuba's major development successes and shortcomings during the 1950s? What were the principal economic successes and shortcomings in the 1990s? Which era's economic policies would you consider to be more successful? Why?

2. When criticized about the lack of electoral competition and freedom of expression in Cuba, Fidel Castro often replies that pervasive income inequality makes people in other countries unable to exercise their statutory political freedoms. In contrast, Castro argues, reducing the sphere of political debate to competing paths toward the maintenance of a socialist system helps to prevent Cubans

from falling into a similar circumstance. Compare the liberty of contemporary Cubans to the liberty of contemporary citizens in one of the three countries previously analyzed in this book (Argentina, Brazil, or Chile). On balance, which country's citizens have more freedom? On what do you base your judgment?

3. Recent Cuban governance has centered on the Cuban government's efforts to maintain the PCC's and Fidel Castro's control over all major political decisions. What steps would you take if you were a PCC leader who wanted to preserve the party's monopoly on power when Castro is no longer in charge? What would you do if you were a Cuban dissident who wanted to open up the political system following Castro's departure?

4. *Guantanamera* (*Woman from Guantanamo*) was the last film from the most famous Cuban director of the revolutionary era, Tomás Gutiérrez Alea, before he died of cancer at age seventy-seven in 1996. This 1995 comedy pokes fun at many sides of Cuban life; it also depicts some of the difficult changes in Cuba following the end of Soviet aid. Most of the film's themes remain relevant today. Watch this movie.

5. The continuing U.S. economic embargo remains at the center of the political debate regarding Cuban affairs in the United States. For the U.S. government's perspective on the evolution of the embargo, see the briefing of the Congressional Research Service, which is posted at the website for the U.S. Interests Section: http://usembassy.state.gov/havana/wwwfcrs.pdf. One of the interesting features about the embargo debate is that opponents of Castro in the United States are divided regarding the usefulness of the embargo. For a critical look at the embargo from a decidedly anti-Castro group, see the discussion at the website for the Cato Institute's Center for Trade Policy Studies: http://www.freetrade.org/issues/cuba.html. To see a defense of the embargo, consult the website for the Heritage Foundation at http://www.heritage.org/Research/LatinAmerica/BG1579.cfm. What do you believe would be the best way for the U.S. government to promote an end to one-party rule in Cuba? Why?

Suggested Readings

Azicri, Max. *Cuba Today and Tomorrow: Reinventing Socialism.* Gainesville: University of Florida Press, 2000.

Baloyra, Enrique, and James Morris, eds. *Conflict and Change in Cuba.* Albuquerque: University of New Mexico Press, 1993.

Blight, James, and Peter Kornbluh, eds. *The Politics of Illusion: The Bay of Pigs Invasion Reexamined.* Boulder, Colo.: Lynne Rienner, 1998.

Centeno, Miguel, and Mauricio Font, eds. *Toward a New Cuba? Legacies of a Revolution.* Boulder, Colo.: Lynne Rienner, 1997.

Chomsky, Aviva, Barry Carr, and Pamela María Smorkaloff, eds. *The Cuba Reader: History, Culture, Politics.* Durham, N.C.: Duke University Press, 2004.

De la Fuente, Alejandro. *A Nation for All: Race, Inequality, and Politics in Twentieth-Century Cuba.* Chapel Hill: University of North Carolina Press, 2001.

Eckstein, Susan. *Back from the Future: Cuba Under Castro,* 2d ed. New York: Routledge, 2003.

Erisman, H. Michael. *Cuba's Foreign Relations in a Post-Soviet World.* Gainesville: University of Florida Press, 2000.

Horowitz, Irving, and Jaime Suchliki, eds. *Cuban Communism*, 11th ed. New Brunswick, N.J.: Transaction, 2003.

Jatar-Hausmann, Ana Julia. *The Cuban Way: Capitalism, Communism, and Confrontation*. West Hartford, Conn.: Kumarian, 1999.

López, Juan. *Democracy Delayed: The Case of Castro's Cuba*. Baltimore, Md.: Johns Hopkins University Press, 2002.

Medin, Tzvi. *Cuba: The Shaping of Revolutionary Consciousness*. Boulder, Colo.: Lynne Rienner, 1990.

Mesa-Lago, Carmelo, ed. *Cuba After the Cold War*. Pittsburgh, Pa.: University of Pittsburgh Press, 1993.

Morley, Morris, and Chris McGillion. *Unfinished Business: America and Cuba After the Cold War, 1989–2001*. Cambridge, England: Cambridge University Press, 2002.

Moses, Catherine. *Real Life in Castro's Cuba*. Wilmington, Del.: Scholarly Resources, 2000.

Paterson, Thomas. *The United States and the Triumph of the Cuban Revolution*. New York: Oxford University Press, 1994.

Pérez, Louis. *Cuba and the United States: Ties of Singular Intimacy*, 3d ed. Athens: University of Georgia Press, 2003.

Pérez, Louis. *Cuba: Between Reform and Revolution*, 2d ed. New York: Oxford University Press, 1995.

Pérez-Stable, Marifeli. *The Cuban Revolution: Origins, Course, and Legacy*, 2d ed. New York: Oxford University Press, 1999.

Purcell, Susan, and David Rothkopf, eds. *Cuba: The Contours of Change*. Boulder, Colo.: Lynne Rienner, 2000.

Ritter, Archibald, and John Kirk, eds. *Cuba in the International System: Normalization and Integration*. New York: St. Martin's Press, 1995.

Rosendahl, Mona. *Inside the Revolution: Everyday Life in Socialist Cuba*. Ithaca, N.Y.: Cornell University Press, 1997.

Schwab, Peter. *Cuba: Confronting the Embargo*. New York: St. Martin's Press, 1999.

Smith, Lois, and Alfred Padula. *Sex and Revolution: Women in Socialist Cuba*. New York: Oxford University Press, 1996.

White, Mark. *The Cuban Missile Crisis*. Basingstroke, England: Macmillan, 1996.

Endnotes

1. Louis A. Pérez, Jr., *Cuba: Between Reform and Revolution*, 2d ed. (New York: Oxford University Press, 1995), p. 130.
2. Louis A. Pérez, Jr., *Cuba: Between Reform and Revolution*, 2d ed. (New York: Oxford University Press, 1995), p. 197.
3. As cited and translated in Marifeli Pérez-Stable, *The Cuban Revolution: Origins, Course, and Legacy* (New York: Oxford University Press, 1993), p. 83.
4. Cited in Carollee Bengelsdorf, *The Problem of Democracy in Cuba: Between Vision and Reality* (New York: Oxford University Press, 1994), p. 141.
5. Pablo Spadoni, "Foreign Investment in Cuba," in *Cuba in Transition*, Vol. 12 (Maclean, Va.: Association for the Study of the Cuban Economy, 2002), p. 163.
6. Jorge Pérez-López, "The Cuban Economy in an Unending Special Period," in *Cuba in Transition*, Vol. 12 (Maclean, Va.: Association for the Study of the Cuban Economy, 2002), p. 512.

Guatemala

CHAPTER 9

Guatemala

G UATEMALA HAS THE SECOND LARGEST indigenous population in Latin America. Nearly half the population is officially recognized as indigenous; most are of Mayan descent. In the sixteenth century, Spanish colonization placed the native population at the bottom of the socioeconomic pyramid. In the first few decades after independence from Spain, conditions for indigenous Guatemalans changed little. Most of the change that took place thereafter was for the worse. In the last third of the nineteenth century, the Guatemalan government transferred traditional communal lands to coffee growers and other commercial farmers.

These changes deprived most indigenous peoples of their livelihood and left them subject to the whims of propertied Guatemalans. Many indigenous people fell into a form of indentured servitude known as debt peonage—most landowners manipulated the debts so that workers could not earn enough to repay their debts. In the 1930s, military dictator Jorge Ubico replaced debt peonage with a vagrancy law: those with insufficient land were forced to work 100 days per year. In many cases, landowners refused to certify all of the days worked, thereby extending their access to poorly paid and unpaid laborers. The divisions between light-skinned *ladinos* (all those not classified as indigenous, Asian, or African) and darker-skinned *indígenas* pervaded all aspects of life. In turn, Ubico began to treat all of Guatemala as if it were his own estate.

By the early 1940s, many propertied Guatemalans chafed at Ubico's arrogance and corruption. They pressured him to name a new interim government in 1944, and a subsequent military coup opened the door to ten years of electoral politics known as the decade of spring. The winner of the 1950 presidential elections, Colonel Jacobo Arbenz, launched a serious land-reform program in 1952 that upset domestic and foreign landowners. A U.S.-backed military uprising in 1954 began a long period of military rule that came under increasing nonviolent and violent challenge from many sectors of society.

Between 1960 and 1996, an ongoing civil war cost thousands of Guatemalans their lives. The majority of those deaths involved noncombatants killed by military and paramilitary security forces. By the 1990s, it became increasingly clear to the guerrilla movement's leaders that they were unlikely to overthrow the government by force. At the same time, many members of the civilian and military elite determined that stability would not come to Guatemala without an effort to end the conflict. Peace accords brokered by the United Nations (U.N.) brought an end to open civil war in December 1996.

The peace process raised several issues in Guatemalan politics that had not been seriously discussed since the middle of the twentieth century. First, could Guatemala build an approach to economic development that would bring more citizens out of poverty and reduce income inequality? In particular, could the indigenous population begin to escape its long-standing second-class status in Guatemalan society? Second, could Guatemala begin to develop a fully functioning democracy in which the government would work to guarantee basic civil liberties and the rule of law, in addition to holding elections? As part of that process, what stance would elected officials and the judiciary take toward those accused of committing human rights violations during the long civil war? Third, how would civilian politicians build support for these and other changes without alienating the military and the landed elite?

This human drama unfolds in one of the poorest countries in the Western Hemisphere. The majority of Guatemala's 11 million inhabitants live in poverty. Most of the other countries studied in this book are among the largest and wealthiest in Latin America. Our examination of Guatemala in this chapter serves to remind us that the economic context in which politics unfolds can be more constraining than we have already observed in Argentina, Brazil, Chile, and Cuba.

HISTORICAL BACKGROUND FROM 1871 TO 1996

Guatemala declared its independence from Spain in 1821 along with the rest of Spanish Central America and Mexico. In 1823, Guatemala left the short-lived Mexican Empire and became part of the United Provinces of Central America. In 1838, El Salvador, Costa Rica, Guatemala, Honduras, and Nicaragua each formed separate nation-states as the Central American confederation dissolved amid a dispute between the Liberal leader of Honduras, Francisco Morazán, and the Conservative leader of Guatemala, José Rafael Carrera. Carrera would be the first of several Guatemalan *caudillos* to lead long-term governments. As in much of Latin America, independence opened a series of political conflicts between Liberals and Conservatives. These two political forces—each with its share of military *caudillos*—struggled with each other for power for the next several decades. By the 1860s, coffee had replaced dye as Guatemala's leading export, and the booming world coffee market magnified Liberals' desire to control the government. When Carrera's successor was ousted by a Liberal revolt in

1871, the change in partisan control of the government ushered in a new era in Guatemalan politics—and in society more generally.

The Liberal Revolution and Its Aftermath (1871–1944)

Just as Liberals elsewhere called for an expansion of free trade and a reduction in the role of the Catholic church, so too did the Liberal Revolution in Guatemala. In 1873, another Liberal general, Justo Rufino Barrios, took power and established a dictatorship that would last until 1885. The government confiscated some church land, but the bigger changes were mentioned at the outset of this chapter: the transfer of communal lands held by indigenous peoples to private property held by domestic and foreign landowners with an export orientation. The coffee-growing elite consolidated its position at the center of Guatemalan society. Their power grew under several Liberal *caudillos* that followed Barrios in power.

Wealthy Guatemalans were not the only benefactors of this transfer of wealth. In the decades to come, the U.S.-owned United Fruit Company (UFCo) took full advantage of the government's eagerness to court foreign investment and began growing bananas in Guatemala in 1902, after receiving large subsidies from the Guatemalan government. By the 1920s, UFCo had become the largest landowner in Guatemala, and it developed a major interest in the lone national railroad. UFCo's influence over transportation prices and its control over land extended its ability to gain favorable treatment from the Guatemalan government. In 1930, the government granted UFCo considerable coastal land in the west to build Guatemala's first commercial port on the Pacific. Instead of building this port as promised, UFCo chose to increase its investment in the local railroad in exchange for a reduced freight charge to Guatemala's Atlantic port, Puerto Barrios. Yet the government did not sue UFCo for breach of contract and reclaim the land grant. Instead, it accepted $50,000 in exchange for releasing UFCo from the prior contract and for transferring permanent title of the land originally granted to build the port.

Leaders in the Liberal era in Guatemala spoke the language of liberalism but used the military and the police to quash dissenting voices, similar to Porfirio Díaz's actions in neighboring Mexico. Guatemalan elites attempted to explain away this contradiction by asserting that the indigenous majority was not capable of participating in civilized society. If violent force was used to maintain order and thus promote investment, so be it. As one government official of this era remarked, "For the Indians there is only one law—the lash."[1]

Repression reached new extremes during the Great Depression under the dictatorship of Jorge Ubico, the last of the Liberal *caudillos*. As noted at the start of this chapter, Ubico transformed the rural labor market by replacing debt peonage with a new vagrancy law that forced all landless indigenous men between eighteen and sixty years old to work without pay three months per year (or more if landowners refused to certify compliance on the mandatory work card carried by each rural worker). Ubico stepped up repression in the cities and the countryside. His secret police earned the grim nickname of the Guatemalan Gestapo. In urban areas, the government exaggerated the communist threat in 1932 as a pretext for decimating the labor union movement. In that same year, the government issued a decree that exempted landowners from criminal liability for any actions undertaken to protect their property; this step legalized the ongoing practice of beating (at times, killing) outspoken indigenous peasants.

With the outbreak of World War II, the Allied effort to stop Adolf Hitler catalyzed public demonstrations and other expressions of discontent against several Latin American dictators. In neighboring El Salvador, General Maximiliano Martínez crushed a military revolt in April 1944 only to face a rising tide of labor strikes and public demonstrations calling for an end to his government. When the United States removed its support for his continuation in power, Martínez sought exile in Guatemala. The downfall of the Salvadoran dictator incited many Guatemalan teachers to complain openly about the Ubico dictatorship. Those actions motivated Ubico to suspend all constitutional guarantees. Two days later, on June 24, several hundred Guatemalans signed a petition calling for the restoration of these guarantees. That afternoon bore witness to the first major public protests of the Ubico era. Over the ensuing two days, security forces took control of the streets, but many businesses responded by launching a massive economic shutdown in Guatemala City.

Faced with unprecedented public pressure (and no outward expressions of support from the U.S. government), Ubico resigned on July 1. He retired to one of his many estates in Guatemala. When the subsequent provisional president, General Federico Ponce, called for elections, opposition groups mobilized on behalf of a long-exiled college professor, Juan José Arévalo. In a tense climate, government forces killed the head of a major opposition newspaper; many other opposition figures went into hiding. It appeared that the promised elections (like past elections under Ubico and most other *caudillos*) would be a mere formality. However, a group of junior officers who doubted the government's willingness to hold free elections moved against Ponce on the night of October 19, 1944. By the next day, rebels in the elite Honor Guard unit and other rebel officers in command of armed civilians had control of most of the capital. Ponce resigned and went into exile; four days later, Ubico left for exile in the United States. A new day was dawning in Guatemalan politics.

The Decade of Spring (1944–1954)

Two junior officers central to the coup formed part of a three-person provisional junta. Prior to the coup, Captain Jacobo Arbenz had been an instructor in the army's most important technical academy. In turn, Major Francisco Arana had served as the tank commander in the Honor Guard. The third leader of the provisional government, Jorge Toriello, was a young, wealthy leader of the civilian protests against the Ponce government. After the successful removal of Ponce, armed civilians returned their weapons to the military leaders whose participation had been deemed pivotal to the coup's success. The junta quickly announced that free elections would be held for the presidency and the legislature; in addition, a constituent assembly would be elected to write a new constitution. In the meantime, these elections would be held under the existing suffrage restrictions: only literate men could participate.

Juan José Arévalo campaigned across the country. His promises of a new Guatemala met with a receptive audience. His opponents found it difficult to stem his momentum. Most of the other candidates had held government posts during the Ubico dictatorship (or in prior governments). In contrast, Arévalo had spent most of his adult life in Argentina and none of it in national politics; he was an outsider with no discernible ties to the long-standing Liberal regime. Ultimately, Arévalo won the December election with an overwhelming 85 percent of the vote.

Arévalo's government reshaped the institutional structure of political life. Voting rights expanded to include all citizens except illiterate women. A new labor law regulated work by women and children and instituted a forty-eight-hour workweek; it also guaranteed the right to organize and the right to strike. Most of these rights were not extended to the rural sector, but Arévalo's willingness to support the rights of UFCo workers to unionize and to improve their working conditions earned him the ire of UFCo management in Guatemala and back in the United States. UFCo stridently mischaracterized Arévalo as a communist. Within the Cold War climate of U.S. politics, this approach helped to generate U.S. diplomatic and financial pressure on Guatemala. Although the Arévalo government respected noncommunist political parties' rights to exist, communist parties remained banned in Guatemala.

Arévalo frequently used the term *spiritual socialism* to describe the guiding force of his government. However, his government's approach to economic policy was a slightly modified form of market capitalism that did not contemplate land reform or other potential mechanisms for improving rapidly the living standards of poor rural Guatemalans. Arévalo emphasized the role of education in transforming the countryside in general and the indigenous population in particular. Yet the government did not increase funding enough to provide better-trained and better-motivated teachers in the rural areas.

Notwithstanding the changes under way during Arévalo's six-year term, the reform movement had its limits. Francisco Arana had accepted the outcome of the 1944 elections on the condition that his power would be entrenched in the new constitution. Accordingly, the 1945 constitution created a new post, chief of the armed forces, and the person in that position was not directly accountable to the defense minister and could not be removed unless found guilty of breaking the law. The armed forces chief had ultimate control over all military appointments. In the Arévalo government, Arana served as chief while Arbenz held the post of defense minister.

As more wealthy Guatemalans grew uneasy with the reforms implemented by Arévalo, Arana emerged as the military leader they asked most frequently to overthrow the government. Initially, Arana planned to run for the presidency in the next elections. When his hastily organized political movement did poorly in the 1948 midterm legislative elections, however, he began to consider revolt more seriously. On July 16, 1949, Arana delivered an ultimatum to President Arévalo: he could create a new cabinet (handpicked by Arana) or face a coup. Arévalo asked for two days to implement the changes. In those two days, Arévalo saved his presidency by mobilizing Arbenz and other loyal officers to stop the coup. Their effort to arrest Arana ended in a shootout in which Francisco Arana died. As the news spread, many loyal *aranista* officers rebelled, but Arbenz organized a resistance to put down their uprising. Arévalo issued a public statement blaming Arana's death on frustrated conservatives who could not convince him to launch a coup. Because another injured officer was associated with Arbenz, many people suspected that Arbenz's forces had eliminated Arana as part of an ongoing struggle for power with the military itself. In the weeks that followed, pro-Arana (*aranista*) officers were demoted or retired, while soldiers loyal to Arbenz took over the major command posts.

In the 1950 elections, three of the four major anti-Ubico political parties sponsored Arbenz's presidential candidacy. Unlike the 1944 electoral campaign, most landowners in 1950 supported a military candidate associated with the Ubico era. The labor movement, the student movement, most political parties, and most of the military backed Arbenz. Politicians and leaders of social movements who had spoken privately with Arbenz, believed that he would pursue more substantial economic reform than Arévalo had implemented. Soldiers saw him as a capable and loyal officer who treated his subordinates well. In the end, Arbenz won the presidency with nearly two-thirds of the vote.

At his inauguration, Arbenz pledged "to transform Guatemala from a dependent nation with a semi-colonial economy into a country that is economically independent; to transform Guatemala from a backward country with a semi-feudal economy into a modern capitalist country; to proceed in a way that will ensure the greatest possible improvement in the standard of living of the great masses of our people."[2] In the weeks and months to come, Arbenz worked with a dedicated "kitchen cabinet" of informal advisers culled largely from the Guatemalan communist movement. Their goal for this presidency was to implement a massive land-reform program that would pave the way for economic modernization. In turn, they hoped that Guatemala would industrialize. Then, in the long run, perhaps conditions would permit the creation of a socialist state. Meanwhile, however, they focused on land reform.

One year after taking office, Arbenz presented draft legislation for the most comprehensive land-reform program that Latin America had seen up to that point in its history. All existing government-owned farmland would be redistributed. Any uncultivated land in all private estates of over 672 acres would be expropriated and redistributed. In all estates between 224 and 672 acres, uncultivated land would be expropriated only if less than two-thirds of the estate was under cultivation. Any estate under 224 acres in size would be left untouched. Compensation to landowners was based on the last declared tax value of the property and would be paid out in twenty-five-year bonds with interest. Landowners protested against this form of compensation: both they and the government knew that most people dramatically underreported the value of their property to the tax assessor. Despite these objections, the bill passed in just over one month.

Landowners challenged the legality of a provision asserting that the land-reform program was not subject to judicial redress. An administrative appeals process had been created within the executive branch, but the president was made the ultimate arbiter of any disputes arising from the implementation of the law (a provision inserted precisely to keep the legislation from being blocked in the courts). The court sided with landowners and suspended the land-reform program. Arbenz called a special legislative session in which the Guatemalan Congress impeached the justices and replaced them with judges who reversed the earlier ruling. This move was not the only challenge that Arbenz faced in enacting a land reform that many propertied Guatemalans opposed (see *Governing Strategies: Jacobo Arbenz* on pages 294–295).

While Arbenz fended off a series of domestic challenges to his government and to his land-reform program, he found himself unable to parry the opposition of the U.S. government. In early 1953, the newly elected Eisenhower administration stepped up its criticism of the Arbenz government. The U.S. government also began to search for allies in and out of Guatemala who wanted to end the land-reform program and the Arbenz government. A former *aranista* officer, Carlos Castillo Armas, was recruited to lead a ragtag force of exiles and mercenaries in an invasion of Guatemala from neighboring Honduras. Meanwhile, the U.S. government put considerable financial and diplomatic pressure on Latin American governments to get the vast majority of delegates to the March 1954 Pan-American conference to approve a resolution invoking the Rio Treaty of mutual defense should any hemispheric government fall to communist domination or influence. Guatemala cast the lone dissenting vote—even though its speech in opposition to the resolution had drawn the biggest applause of the entire conference. U.S. officials also pressured the Guatemalan military to withdraw its support from Arbenz. When the U.S. government stopped a secret shipment of Czechoslovakian weapons from breaching its ongoing arms embargo of Guatemala in May 1954, the communist source of the weapons gave the U.S. government the evidence that it needed to rationalize taking action against Arbenz.

On June 17, Castillo Armas led a small force of less than 300 soldiers into Guatemala. Arbenz sent the elite Honor Guard and several other units to defeat the rebels. Over the course of the ensuing week, Arbenz—and Guatemala—learned that the officers had no desire to put down the rebellion and risk the wrath of the U.S. government. Instead, they ultimately asked Arbenz to resign on June 25. When efforts to arm civilian loyalists were thwarted by military opposition and by a lackluster public response, Jacobo Arbenz resigned on June 27, 1954.

GOVERNING STRATEGIES
Jacobo Arbenz

When General Federico Ponce was named provisional president following the resignation of Jorge Ubico, Captain Jacobo Arbenz was the only military officer to resign in protest. Months later he was one of the leaders of the October 1944 coup that led to the election of Juan José Arévalo. After Arbenz prevented Francisco Arana from removing Arévalo in 1949, he emerged as the candidate of the multiparty reformist movement—winning election handily in 1950.

If Arbenz had chosen a path of minimal economic reform, perhaps his term could have proceeded largely without incident. The officers he had selected following the defeat of the *aranistas* dominated the military command. The pro-reform coalition that had supported Arbenz's candidacy controlled the vast majority of the legislature. Landowners had opposed Arbenz's campaign but might have bided their time if the government had largely left them alone.

However, Arbenz came to office committed to land reform. He knew that this policy would be the central act of his presidency and that it would ignite a political firestorm. For this reason, he spent over a year crafting the draft legislation and trying to organize support to ride out the opposition that the law would face. He mobilized the support of the two major labor confederations. He called on a group of informal advisers—taken largely from the Guatemalan communist movement—to help him develop his land-reform program. Amidst all of these preparations, Arbenz also took steps to dampen the extent of opposition.

The central force in Guatemalan politics was the military. As a career officer, Arbenz understood its centrality and tried to ensure its loyalty. Although Arbenz had selected the leading commanders, he knew that many would be subject to pressure from the landed elite to break ranks with his government. Arbenz ensured that officer pay rose faster than salaries elsewhere in the government. He expanded the array of products in military commissaries and controlled their prices. He assigned someone the task of providing gifts to each officer on birthdays and on holidays. Like Juan Perón in Argentina, Arbenz refused to consider arming loyal civilians because he believed a civilian militia would spark opposition from the barracks.

Arbenz worked to design a land-reform bill that would limit the chances for criticism from the diverse coalition that had supported his candidacy. He also considered implementation dynamics. The bill blocked landowners from simply buying back the newly redistributed land by granting many recipients lifetime tenure. The legislation also kept all appeals within the executive branch. When the courts suspended implementation of the law, Arbenz called a special legislative session in early 1953 in which the judges involved were impeached and replaced by judges willing to allow the law to proceed as written.

Over the course of the ensuing year, roughly 100,000 Guatemalan families received title to land—most for the first time in their lives. By focusing on uncultivated land, the reform did not disrupt agricultural production, even though it redistributed one-sixth of all land. Instead, the agricultural sector experienced growth in many respects. Amid the Cold War climate of the time, critics successfully labeled this land reform as a step toward the socialization of agriculture. When the U.S. government expressed its opposition more stridently, Arbenz found it increasingly difficult to fend off his opponents within Guatemala. Once the United States stood behind an insurrection in 1954, it would become clear that Arbenz had lost the support of many senior military officers.

Repression and Civil War (1954–1985)

Over the next eleven days, five provisional governments rose and fell with the active involvement of the U.S. embassy. This process culminated in the interim presidency of Castillo Armas. In October, amid a climate of repression, he held a noncompetitive plebiscite in which over 99 percent of the voters approved a six-year presidential term for the leader of the rebel army. Once in power, Castillo Armas decreed a reversal of the land-reform program. In less than three years, the government stripped nearly all of the reform's recipients of their land. The army forced the communists and labor union activists underground. Basic liberties ceased to exist in practice.

While most of the military appeared unified in its desire to turn back the clock on socioeconomic and political reform, discontent seethed regarding the rise to power of Castillo Armas. His rebel force played a role in the overthrow of Arbenz, but it did not defeat the Guatemalan military on the battlefield. In fact, two different sets of active-duty officers had played a more direct role in pressuring Arbenz to step down. In July 1957, Carlos Castillo Armas was murdered; the case has never been solved.

The death of Castillo Armas did not end military rule; it simply paved the way for a new political process in which a series of soldiers and conservative civilians would run for the presidency in tightly controlled and frequently fraudulent elections. The military dominated politics, but conservative civilians also played an ongoing role in and around the government. This civil-military coalition called for the repression of any voices that might challenge the political, economic, and social order. As the era progressed, the military's economic role expanded via the transfer of enormous tracts of public land to military officers.

Faced with considerable repression and no indication of an eventual democratic opening, increasing numbers of Guatemalans took up arms against the government. In the early 1960s, many poor *ladino* peasants in eastern Guatemala joined the Rebel Armed Forces (*Fuerzas Armadas Rebeldes* [FAR]). The rise of a potential military threat led to a reorganization of the military; U.S. advisers provided training in counterinsurgency techniques. With much fanfare, the military permitted a civilian to win the presidency for the only occasion during this era. Under that civilian façade, the military launched a brutal assault on insurgents and presumed insurgents; thousands of people died. While this temporarily quashed the rebel movement, three new guerrilla movements emerged by the late 1970s. These movements enjoyed greater support from indigenous Guatemalans; half a million Mayans are estimated to have taken part. In early 1982, the guerrilla movement formed a unified front under the banner of the Guatemalan National Revolutionary Unit (*Unidad Revolucionaria Nacional Guatemalteca* [URNG]).

In the early 1980s, the government responded by increasing repression in cities and the countryside. As in Argentina, Brazil, and Chile, the military targeted student and labor activists along with presumed members of the guerrilla movement. Once General Efraín Ríos Montt took power in a coup in March 1982, state violence reached unprecedented levels. Ríos Montt, a born-again Christian, used the language of religion to present a crusade against corruption and insurgency. He removed all elected local civilian officials and replaced them with military officers. In a scorched-earth campaign, security forces massacred hundreds of indigenous communities. Other rural Guatemalans were herded into so-called model villages in which their activities were closely controlled. Throughout the highland region, the government formed civilian self-defense patrols (*Patrullas de Auto-Defensa Civil* [PACs]) in which male villagers were conscripted to prevent dissent and to root out guerrillas. Ríos Montt's evangelical style alienated many of his fellow officers along with much of the civilian elite. In addition, the enormity of the violence endangered the government's ability to obtain military and economic aid from the United States and other wealthy countries. Like much of Latin America, Guatemala experienced economic stagnation and decline in the early 1980s. Demand for its commodity exports declined abroad. The civil war damaged many sectors of the economy— particularly the two main engines of foreign exchange earnings: agriculture and tourism.

In August 1983, a new military coup initiated a transition toward tightly controlled elections in which civilians would be given a greater role. However, the government continued its war on insurgency; it did not disband the PACs and the model villages. In 1984, voters elected delegates to a constituent assembly charged with creating a new constitution. Only centrist and rightist political parties whose leaders met with military approval were permitted to participate. The new constitution created the institutions of representative democracy but also permitted many of the ongoing counterinsurgency activities of the military. The military retained a constitutionally defined role as the defender of internal order. The 1985 constitution embraced the continuation of the PACs, the model village program, and the departmental military commands that had full authority to review all local government activity. In addition, the outgoing military government issued a blanket amnesty by decree prior to leaving power. The decree blocked prosecution for human rights violations alleged prior to the enactment of the constitution.

From Civilian Rule to Peace Negotiations (1986–1996)

Vinicio Cerezo won the 1985 presidential election as the candidate of the most moderate of the four major political parties, the Christian Democratic party (*Democracia Cristiana Guatemalteca* [DCG]). He promised to restore economic growth and to build a functioning democracy. His economic program focused on the promotion of nontraditional exports in the commodity sector (similar to the Chilean economic strategy during the Pinochet dictatorship). Although the economy resumed moderate growth in the late 1980s, poverty, unemployment, and underemployment remained the state of affairs for most Guatemalans. Regarding liberty, Cerezo rejected efforts to convince him to overturn the amnesty decree. Instead, he claimed that his regime would hold the government accountable to new standards from this point onward, and he established a human rights ombudsperson to monitor the government's respect for basic liberties. In 1986, most analysts observed a reduction in the prevalence of political violence by government security forces. From that point onward, however, most nongovernmental organizations asserted that state-sponsored violence increased (despite persistent denials from Cerezo). Although the president claimed that the hallmark of his government would be judicial accountability for human rights violators, in only one case were security forces convicted— and that conviction was overturned on appeal during his term. Electoral politics had resumed, but respect for basic civil and political liberties remained uneven, to put it mildly. Human rights activists and other social movements came under increasing pressure as the years passed.

Amid the rising violence, however, some international dynamics built hope that the civil war might come to an end. Guatemala participated in the regional Central American peace process designed to end open conflicts in El Salvador, Guatemala, and Nicaragua. The 1987 Esquipulas II Accord called for Guatemala to establish a national dialogue across governmental and nongovernmental organizations. Although the guerrilla movement expressed interest in this process, the government refused to permit the participation of the URNG in the ensuing talks. However, the National Reconciliation Commission chair, Bishop Rodolfo Quezada Toruño, agreed to read URNG statements into the record. Toward the end of Cerezo's term, the guerrilla movement gave up on the creation of a socialist state as a central goal. Instead, it put forward four reforms as central to ending the conflict: ending the nearly permanent repression of dissent, changing the constitutionally expansive role of the military, respecting the right to private property (conditional on socioeconomic reforms), and recognizing the rights of the indigenous peoples of Guatemala. The army and the major business confederation continued to boycott the dialogue organized through the National Reconciliation Commission.

The 1990 elections took place amid continuing discontent and ongoing civil war. The troubled climate worsened because of controversy over the proposed presidential candidacy of Efraín Ríos Montt. In theory, Ríos Montt could not run for the presidency because the 1985 constitution expressly forbade anyone who rose to power via military coup to compete for the presidency. Ríos Montt replied that his right to participate in the political process had been unduly limited. When election officials prohibited him from registering as a candidate, he appealed the matter all the way to the constitutional court. As the appeal process wore on, Ríos Montt emerged as the front-runner in preelection polls. In accordance with the constitution, however, the higher courts upheld the decision to block his candidacy. Jorge Serrano, who had worked for Ríos Montt's government in the 1980s and shared his Protestant beliefs, proved to be the principal beneficiary of Ríos Montt's exclusion. Serrano presented himself as a candidate who could bridge the gap in the ongoing conflict. He had conservative credentials, but his service on the National Reconciliation Commission and his criticism of some actions taken by the Ríos Montt government illustrated his willingness to explore a negotiated solution to the conflict.

Serrano put together a coalition cabinet. His weak legislative base motivated his initial search for allies and partners: his party held only 15 percent of the seats in Congress. Serrano opened direct talks with the URNG that produced partial agreement on democratization and demilitarization goals but deadlocked on how human rights violations would be handled after an end to the conflict. Hard-liners in the military and in the business community urged Serrano to focus on obtaining a cease-fire, while the URNG insisted on a broader substantive agenda as a condition for agreeing to one. In January 1993, Serrano gave the guerrillas ninety days to accept a cease-fire. The URNG refused the offer in accordance with its announced position against an unconditional end to the hostilities.

After Serrano's party did well in local elections in early May 1993, an emboldened president tried to break stalemates in the legislature and in the peace talks by declaring a self-coup (*autogolpe*) inspired by Alberto Fujimori's actions in Peru in 1992. Claiming a need for extraordinary powers to fight corruption and drug trafficking, Serrano closed Congress, the Supreme Court, and the Court of Constitutionality. He promised to call elections for a constituent assembly within ninety days. In contrast to Fujimori's self-coup, Serrano's self-coup (the *serranazo*) met with considerable opposition from most of the political spectrum as well as economic sanctions from the United States and the European Union. Faced with this criticism, on May 30, Serrano attempted to convince all organized groups—including the URNG—to participate in writing a new constitution. Guatemalan parties and interest groups rejected this offer; Serrano, under pressure from his own military commanders, resigned and went into exile on June 1, 1993.

Congress then blocked the inauguration of the conservative vice president, Gustavo Adolfo Espina. Two days later, Congress accepted Espina's resignation and held a special vote in which Serrano's human rights ombudsperson, Ramiro de León Carpio, became president. While Carpio's accidental presidency disappointed many who dreamed of a quick end to impunity for human rights violators, it did pave the way for several constitutional reforms and led to more meaningful peace negotiations.

In the name of national renewal, Carpio reorganized the military high command and began exploring a way to promote changes in the legislative and judicial branches. In late August, his request for the resignation of all sitting legislators and Supreme Court justices led to protracted negotiations that culminated in forty-three constitutional amendments passed by Congress in November 1993. In late January 1994, these amendments received 68 percent approval in a hastily organized plebiscite in which a slim 16 percent of the voters cast legitimate votes. Nearly 20 percent of the voters cast null or blank votes in the plebiscite.

Earlier that same month, the government and the URNG reinstated peace talks under U.N. mediation. The United Nations had sent an observer to prior negotiations. Now, both the government and the guerrillas formally requested that the United Nations serve as mediator. In 1994, a framework accord laid out

The establishment of the United Nations (U.N.) Verification Mission in Guatemala (MINUGUA) provided a structure through which U.N. observers could monitor protection of several civil, human, and political rights—including respect for free and fair elections. MINUGUA/DPI, © United Nations.

a more inclusive negotiating process as well as a substantive agenda for talks aimed at ending the hostilities. The process then lurched forward in fits and starts. The March 1994 Human Rights Accord was followed by the assassination of the head of the constitutional court. Human rights violations generally increased from April onward, until the November arrival of the U.N. verification mission (*Misión de Verificación de las Naciones Unidas en Guatemala* [MINUGUA]) mandated by the human rights agreement. By March 1995, other accords had been reached regarding the resettlement of people dislocated by the conflict, the creation of a truth commission, and indigenous rights. Several foreign countries applied economic pressure to try to keep the talks moving forward.

Talks then stalled regarding socioeconomic issues when the peace negotiations became overshadowed by the 1995 presidential election campaign. Álvaro Arzú, the former mayor of Guatemala City, squared off against the candidate sponsored by Ríos Montt, Alfonso Portillo. Ríos Montt's party criticized the existing peace accords and the peace process itself; many believed that the party would scuttle or delay the talks if its candidate were elected. Guatemala appeared to reach a crossroads in which the decades-long civil war would end shortly or continue indefinitely.

In a dramatic runoff election in January 1996, Arzú defeated Portillo by a narrow margin (51 to 49 percent). Early in his presidency, Arzú signaled his willingness to complete the peace process by traveling to Mexico to meet personally with several guerrilla leaders. In the months that followed, accords were reached regarding socioeconomic issues, demilitarization, and political reform. On December 29, 1996, the signing of the Final Peace Accord formally concluded the civil war. The end to internal conflict raised hopes for a new era in Guatemalan society more generally.

CONTEMPORARY POLITICAL FRAMEWORK

The 1985 constitution—as modified in 1993—forms the legal framework for contemporary politics. In line with the 1996 peace accords, several constitutional amendments were developed over the course of 1997 and 1998. Several of these amendments aimed at implementing key portions of the Peace Accords on human rights and on indigenous rights. The military's autonomy and its mission would be reduced via the proposed amendments; indigenous rights would gain constitutional status. In the prolonged negotiations, a host of additional proposals also gained congressional approval. Critics of this process claimed that the multiple issues limited support for the reform package as a whole.

Opponents of the reforms alleged, among other criticisms, that the changes would give indigenous peoples more rights than other citizens, that the amendments involved secret deals designed by and for legislators, and that the plebiscite represented a triumph for the URNG. While the two major political parties' leaders officially endorsed the referendum, neither party campaigned vigorously to promote its passage; opponents publicized their criticisms via broadcast media and street rallies. Although most preliminary tracking polls predicted that the reforms would pass, low voter turnout (less than 19 percent) doomed the May 1999 plebiscite. Among the small minority who voted, 55 percent opposed the amendments. Those who advocated these constitutional changes would have to wait; as of April 2004, these amendments had not been resurrected.

The Executive Branch

Guatemala has a presidential system of government. In 1994, a constitutional amendment shortened the presidential term from five to four years. Reelection is prohibited; in addition, any person who attained the presidency by means of a coup is similarly proscribed from serving as a candidate. The electoral system established by the 1985 constitution was left unchanged by the 1994 reforms. The president is chosen using the ballotage system: if no candidate gains a majority of the votes in first-round presidential elections, a second-round runoff election is held between the two candidates who received the most votes in the first round.

Within the analytical framework developed by Mainwaring and Shugart (review Table 4.6), the Guatemalan presidency can be termed *reactive*. As in much of Latin America, Guatemalan chief executives can name and remove their ministers at will. Congress can remove a minister by majority vote but if the president objects, it takes a two-thirds vote in the legislature to remove the minister. The president has a strong veto that can be overridden by a two-thirds majority in Guatemala's unicameral Congress. The agenda-setting powers of the legislature are limited to the exclusive introduction of the annual budget bill. The emergency decree powers of the president are potentially extensive because the chief executive may take measures deemed necessary to deal with a serious emergency or national disaster. Except for that scenario, however, the president has no legislative decree powers.

The Legislature

Guatemala has a unicameral legislature, the Congress of the Republic (*Congreso de la República*). With each election since the promulgation of the 1985 constitution, the size of Congress has been adjusted. In the 2003 elections, voters elected 140 representatives. All members are chosen by closed-list proportional representation, but there are two different types of legislative constituencies. One-fourth of the seats are elected in a single nationwide list, while the other three-fourths of the members stand for election in districts that have from two to ten seats.

The failed constitutional plebiscite in 1999 would have altered the role of the legislature in two potentially important ways. One amendment mandated the creation of a multipartisan, permanent congressional committee charged with overseeing the government's intelligence activities. The committee would have had constitutionally entrenched power to review intelligence operations, with the express charge of defending the basic liberties and rights of the citizenry. A second amendment would have opened the door for more potential non-government participation in the legislative process. The proposed amendment would have required the legislative committees to provide a minimum of eight days for public input regarding any bill prior to reaching a decision to submit the matter to the full legislature. After the plebiscite failed, neither potential change has yet been revisited as of April 2004.

The Judiciary

Like much of Latin America, the Guatemalan judicial system has a separate Court of Constitutionality that exercises the power of judicial review, but it is not the highest court in Guatemala for other matters. The Court of Constitutionality consists of five members, each of whom is appointed for a five-year term by a different nominating body—the president, the Congress, the Supreme Court, the national bar association, and the board of the University of San Carlos. The post of the chair of the court is held by a different one of the five judges each year. In comparison with constitutional courts in many Latin American countries, the Court of Constitutionality has a more open process of reviewing laws, which permits it to take jurisdiction in disputes over new legislation relatively quickly if existing law in that area calls for immediate judicial review. One can see this process at work most notably in the area of tax law because any new tax is subject to judicial review by the Court of Constitutionality.

The Supreme Court of Justice serves as the highest court in Guatemala on most matters. This court consists of a panel of thirteen judges who are frequently organized into separate chambers. Supreme Court justices must gain the two-thirds approval of a diverse nominating commission comprised of university administrators, lawyers, and sitting judges. In turn, nominees must be confirmed by Congress. Justices serve five-year terms.

A central concern regarding the judiciary has been the de facto impunity of most security forces in the relatively few cases that made it to trial in the first two decades following the enactment of the 1985 constitution. Although the constitutional guarantees offered are considerable, many people question the extent to which the rule of law is evenly applied. A central demand of the peace process was the resolution of various well-known cases of crimes against humanity that had not been granted amnesty. As of early 2004, however, concerns about impunity had not yet crystallized in an attempt to expand the autonomy of the judiciary by expanding the length of judicial terms beyond the current limit of five years.

POLITICAL PARTICIPATION

Political participation is shaped by the context in which it unfolds. Most countries' political evolution during the twentieth century includes one or more periods in which legal restrictions and extralegal acts of intimidation repressed the free expression of ideas by interest groups and political parties. In this book, we have already seen numerous examples during dictatorial periods in Argentina, Brazil, Chile, and Cuba. We have also seen significant constraints on freedom of association and freedom of speech under elected governments. What distinguishes the Guatemalan experience is that severe constraints on political participation were the norm for almost the entire twentieth century.

With the exception of business organizations, all other types of organized interests in Guatemala were frequently forced underground—or out of existence entirely. Political parties tended to express a narrowly conservative stream of policy ideas and were often personalist movements with minimal enduring distinctions from other parties. In the contemporary era, the peace process permitted a flowering of interest groups, social movements, and political parties that advocate various issues—many of them related to realizing different components of the Peace Accords agenda. At the start of the twenty-first century, most of the major political organizations in Guatemala began in the 1980s or later.

Interest Groups and Social Movements

The one major exception to the newness of organized movements in Guatemala can be found in the representation of business interests. For the first half of the twentieth century, business interests in Guatemala (as in many other countries) were divided largely by sector of activity. Those sectoral divisions exist to this day, but since 1957, business interests have also worked together on major national issues in a single business confederation. The Coordinating Committee of Agricultural, Commercial, Industrial, and Financial Associations (*Comité Coordinadora de Asociaciones Agrícolas, Comerciales, Industriales y Financieras* [CACIF]) has voiced its firm opposition to almost every major proposal to redistribute income or wealth in Guatemala since its formation. In the peace process, CACIF initially boycotted the proceedings until it became clear that the process was moving forward and that Guatemala might lose foreign aid if the process failed. At that point, CACIF began to participate more directly in the talks and worked diligently to block many proposals in the negotiations on socioeconomic issues. After the conclusion of the Peace Accords, CACIF has been a vocal critic of efforts to implement the tax target central to the socioeconomic accord.

Given the lack of protection for basic civil liberties during much of the twentieth century, it should come as no surprise that the Guatemalan labor movement found it difficult to build enduring organizations. Freedom of association, freedom of assembly, and the right to strike rarely were respected, and labor activists were frequent targets of counterinsurgency efforts. The urban and rural labor movements had been somewhat influential during the decade of spring, but then lapsed into a long period of disarray during the civil war. Perhaps the most visible labor organization from the 1980s onward has been the Peasant Unity Committee (*Comité de Unidad Campesina* [CUC])—one of the two largest rural workers' associations at the start of the twenty-first century. The CUC formed in 1978 under the leadership of *ladino* and indigenous peasants inspired by the message of hope they found in liberation theology. The initial demands of the CUC centered on an end to the escalation of violence in the countryside and the subsequent possibility of improving conditions for rural workers and small farmers. On January 31, 1980, leaders of the CUC, along with activists from other organizations, launched a nonviolent takeover of the Spanish embassy to demand assistance in reducing the level of violence in the Guatemalan highlands. Guatemalan security forces killed all of the protesters (and some embassy personnel) despite the firm insistence of the Spanish ambassador that the protesters did not threaten him and his staff. Later in 1980, the CUC helped to organize the largest strike in national history and succeeded in raising wages for rural workers. Because the government increased repression in the countryside, however, the CUC was forced underground until the late 1980s. Thereafter, CUC activists slowly began to reinvigorate the organization and eventually played a prominent role in the peace process. Since the signing of the Peace Accords, the organization has advocated greater compliance with the letter and spirit of the Accords. In addition, like the Landless Movement in Brazil, the CUC has begun to make greater use of land seizures to try to speed up the process of clarifying disputed claims to land.

One of the victims of the 1980 Spanish embassy massacre was Vicente Menchú, the father of Rigoberta Menchú, who was twenty-one at the time of her father's death. In the years to come, Rigoberta Menchú would gain acclaim as an advocate for indigenous rights and for basic human rights more generally.[3] She ultimately won the Nobel Peace Prize in 1992. Shortly thereafter, she established the Rigoberta Menchú Tum Foundation, with the goal of promoting human rights and economic development. An older human rights organization in Guatemala is the Mutual Support Group (*Grupo de Apoyo Mutuo* [GAM]). Family members of persons who disappeared during the harsh repression of the early 1980s formed the GAM in 1984. After two founding members were murdered in 1985, the group's directors have traveled with round-the-clock bodyguards. The GAM has worked tirelessly to try to locate the remains of the disappeared and has monitored ongoing human rights violations into the twenty-first century.

With the end to the civil war, preexisting Mayan organizations faced less repression. Additional groups formed to deal with a wide variety of concerns: the preservation of Mayan languages, the protection of long-standing customs, and improvement in living conditions for indigenous peoples. During the peace process, five national indigenous social movements formed an umbrella organization: the Coordination of Mayan Peoples' Organizations of Guatemala (*Coordinación de Organizaciones del Pueblo Maya de Guatemala* [COPMAGUA]). COPMAGUA (also known by the Mayan abbreviation SAQB'ICHIL) worked to articulate indigenous concerns during the peace process and helped to frame portions of the Indigenous Rights Accord.

Parties and Elections

With the exception of the decade of spring, competition among political parties was tightly constrained in the twentieth century until the creation of the 1985 constitution. Political parties existed during the Liberal era and in the post-Arbenz era, but the legal parties embraced a narrow slice of the ideological spectrum, and many elections were widely believed to be fraudulent. Voter abstention and the casting of invalid ballots proved to be a popular means of expressing discontent with the political system and a reflection of prevailing cynicism regarding the importance of the electoral process.

Since 1985, the political party system has been in a continuing state of flux. In the five elections that have been held since the system's promulgation, five different political parties have supported victorious presidential candidates. The one political party from the civil war era that proved successful initially, the DCG, has been in persistent decline since its electoral triumphs in 1985. In the 2003 legislative elections, the DCG got 3 percent of the legislative vote and won no seats in Congress. In the 2003 elections, the two parties of the 1990s that received the most votes shared the stage with two political movements launched in the twenty-first century.

One of the most important and controversial parties in contemporary Guatemala has been the Guatemalan Republican Front (*Frente Republicano Guatemalteco* [FRG]). The FRG formed in 1989 as an electoral vehicle for the presidential aspirations of Efraín Ríos Montt, dictator during the most violent period of the civil war in the early 1980s. Like Ríos Montt himself, this party has voiced a populist appeal emphasizing a mixture of economic and security concerns as reasons to vote for the FRG. As noted earlier, the 1985 constitution expressly prohibits any person who became president via a military coup from running for the presidency. In the 1989 and 1995 elections, Ríos Montt tried in vain to mount a legal challenge that would authorize his candidacy. In 2003, following the successful 1999 campaign of FRG candidate Alfonso Portillo, Ríos Montt tried for a third time to challenge his proscription from the elections on the grounds that the 1985 constitution was written after the action in question (his 1982 coup). This time, although the electoral courts and the Supreme Court again ruled against him, the Court of Constitutionality found his proscription unconstitutional by a narrow margin of four votes to three. While jubilant FRG supporters celebrated the court's decision at the time, Ríos Montt's subsequent third-place finish and advanced age called into question the future of the party he founded. In the meantime, however, the FRG remained the second largest party in Congress when it convened in early 2004.

The other major party of the 1990s, the center-right National Advancement Party (*Partido de Avanzada Nacional* [PAN]), also formed in 1989. Like the FRG, the PAN came together under the leadership of a presidential aspirant: then-mayor of Guatemala City, Álvaro Arzú. Arzú won one-sixth of the presidential vote in 1990 and then narrowly defeated Alfonso Portillo in the January 1996 presidential runoff. Once his presidency ended, Arzú became embroiled in a leadership battle to maintain control of the PAN and subsequently left to form a new political party (with which he was elected mayor of Guatemala City again in late 2003). The PAN's 1999 presidential candidate, Oscar Berger, left to form a new political movement in the aftermath of that election. Although the PAN retained nearly one-tenth of the seats in Congress in the 2003 elections, its future seemed somewhat uncertain.

The winner of those 2003 elections was former PAN candidate, Oscar Berger. Berger left the PAN to stand as the candidate of a new political coalition in 2003, the Grand National Alliance (*Gran Alianza Nacional* [GANA]). As he had done in two previously successful campaigns for mayor of Guatemala City, Berger emphasized national unity, free enterprise, and respect for democracy as central themes in his 2003 campaign. This coalition of three smaller parties—the Patriotic Party, the National Solidarity Party, and the Reformist Party—won just over one-third of the seats in Congress. At the outset of Berger's presidency in January 2004, it was too early to tell how well the GANA coalition would function as a group in its interactions with the legislature.

The second-place finisher in the 2003 presidential elections is the lone major politician with a background outside the center-right and rightist political movements in Guatemala: Álvaro Colom. In 1999, Colom had finished third in the presidential race as the candidate of the center-left New National Alliance (*Alianza Nacional Nueva* [ANN])—a coalition that included the now-legalized URNG, operating as a political party for the first time. Leadership struggles and ideological differences led Colom and several other ANN leaders to form a new political party, National Unity of Hope (*Unidad Nacional de la Esperanza* [UNE]). In both the first-round presidential elections and in Congress, UNE garnered approximately one-fourth of the votes with a reformist message of clean government and economic progress for all Guatemalans. In turn, the URNG ran its own slate of candidates in the 2003 election and received a disappointing 4 percent of the legislative votes and 2 seats in Congress.

The presidential election results for the contemporary era and dating from the beginning of the Peace Accords are presented in Table 9.1. During this period, the winner in each election has been a major candidate in the previous election. In 1995, Álvaro Arzú campaigned successfully as the more moderate of the two major center-right candidates. His apparent willingness to continue the peace process galvanized many of his supporters but also mobilized opposition from many critics of the Peace Accords, which had been signed by that time. In

TABLE 9.1 Guatemalan Presidential Elections (1995, 1999, and 2003): Percentage of Popular Vote in First-Round Elections

Party	1995	1999	2003
FRG	22	48[†]	19
PAN	37*	30	8
GANA	NA	NA	34[‡]
UNE	NA	NA	26
Others	41	22	13

*In 1995, the PAN candidate, Álvaro Arzú, won the presidency with 51 percent of the vote in a runoff election against FRG candidate Alfonso Portillo (49 percent).

[†]In 1999, the FRG candidate Alfonso Portillo won the presidency with 68 percent of the vote in a runoff election against PAN candidate Oscar Berger (32 percent).

[‡]In 2003, the GANA candidate Oscar Berger won the presidency with 54 percent of the vote in a runoff election against UNE candidate Álvaro Colom (46 percent).

SOURCE: Political Database of the Americas <http://www.georgetown.edu/pdba/Elecdata/Guate/guate.html> (accessed on November 14, 2003).

the runoff election, Arzú narrowly defeated Alfonso Portillo, who ran as the FRG candidate after the proscription of Ríos Montt. In 1999, Portillo used his rugged image and discontent over rising street crime to defeat PAN candidate Oscar Berger. As we shall see, however, several corruption scandals during Portillo's presidency tarnished his image and that of the FRG more generally. The surprising constitutional court ruling permitting Ríos Montt's candidacy changed the dynamics of the 2003 presidential election. Nearly 60 percent of the registered voters participated in the first-round elections—the highest voter turnout under the system created by the 1985 constitution. Ríos Montt's low vote total (11 percent) and his advanced age (seventy-seven years old in 2003) suggested that his political career might be coming to an end. In turn, both of the leading candidates, the victorious Oscar Berger and Álvaro Colom, intentionally emphasized clean government as a central campaign theme in a concerted effort to distinguish themselves from the FRG as a whole and from Alfonso Portillo in particular.

Legislative election results largely coincided with outcomes in the presidential vote in 1995 and 1999 (see Table 9.2 on page 308). The PAN's majority showing in the legislative elections in 1995 and the FRG's congressional majority in 1999 foreshadowed their respective candidates' eventual second-round victories in the presidential election. In 2003, however, a more diverse political landscape emerged when four parties won considerable shares of the seats in Congress, while no party received more than 30 percent of the seats. For the first time in nearly a decade, the president's party would not be able to control the legislature without the cooperation of other political parties.

TABLE 9.2 Guatemalan Congress of the Republic (1995, 1999, and 2003): Percentage of Seats Won, by Party

Party	1995	1999	2003
FRG	26	56	27
PAN	54	33	11
GANA	NA	NA	30
UNE	NA	NA	12
Others	20	11	11

SOURCE: For 1995, data are from the Political Database of the Americas <http://www.georgetown.edu/pdba/Elecdata/Guate/guate.html> (accessed on November 14, 2003). For 1999, data are from the Elections Around the World website <http://www.electionworld.org/guatemala.htm> (accessed on November 14, 2003). For 2003, data are from the Elections Around the World website <http://www.electionworld.org/guatemala.htm> (accessed on May 26, 2004).

THE CONTEMPORARY QUEST FOR DEVELOPMENT, LIBERTY, AND GOVERNANCE

As the civil war came to a close, Guatemala faced daunting development challenges. More than three decades of civil war had ravaged much of the countryside. While most of the rural population had traditionally been poor, the conflict drove thousands of Guatemalans into abject poverty. Although the economy recovered from its collapse during the early 1980s, the pattern of economic growth that followed had proven insufficient to begin to pull significant numbers of citizens out of poverty. The economy grew roughly at the same pace as the population—just under 3 percent a year. To reduce poverty, either the economy would need to grow more quickly, poor Guatemalans would need to get a larger share of the stagnant national income, or both.

The peace process also framed the context in which the human rights debate would unfold in the years to come. Families and friends of thousands of victims of repression wanted the end to the civil war to create a new environment in which disappeared loved ones could be found and those guilty of grave crimes against humanity could be held accountable. Guatemalans had many reasons to be concerned about the climate for contemporary liberty. They had already learned following the creation of the 1985 constitution that new constitutional guarantees and more open electoral competition did not put an end to long-standing practices of political intimidation and violence. In many locales, street crime had been on the rise—giving impetus to movements calling for government to protect the safety of the population.

The troubled climate for development and liberty demonstrated the governance challenges that would confront Guatemala's leaders in the wake of the

Peace Accords. The peace process had raised expectations in many parts of Guatemalan society that change would come relatively quickly. At the same time, business interests and many military officers had made it clear during the peace talks that they did not support most demands for socioeconomic change. Guatemalan political leaders would need to display considerable inventiveness to expand the field of debate by incorporating leftist forces into the political debate for the first time in half a century while also expanding government activity in several spheres. These weighty tasks awaited contemporary presidents, while memories of the *serranazo* remained fresh in the minds of many Guatemalans.

The Quest for Development in Guatemala

The outcomes on several major macroeconomic indicators in Guatemala after the conclusion of the Peace Accords seemed sound (see Table 9.3 on page 310). In comparison with widespread price instability in Argentina and Brazil, inflation rates in Guatemala had been relatively low and much more stable. In comparison with Chile, Guatemala's recession in the early 1980s had been far less severe. In contrast with all three of the Southern Cone countries, Guatemala never experienced severe indebtedness as a percentage of its export volume, and official unemployment remained relatively low.

These four major indicators did not tell the whole story, however: official unemployment rates in Guatemala underestimated rural unemployment. Subemployed workers (people who work fewer hours than they would like or who do not earn a living wage despite working full-time) constituted nearly half of all employed persons by some unofficial estimates. Roughly three-fourths of the population was estimated to live in poverty. Meanwhile, two-thirds of all farmland was controlled by 3 percent of the landowners. Guatemala's low national wealth made it difficult to tackle these problems. In the late 1990s, Guatemala was one of five Latin American countries with a gross domestic product (GDP) per capita below $4,000, and it had the lowest average life expectancy in the region.

Poverty in Guatemala remained particularly widespread among its indigenous population. Efforts to reduce their socioeconomic and political exclusion would have to overcome barriers constructed by their rural isolation. Indigenous households were much more likely to lack access to electricity, potable water, adequate sewage, and other basic services than were *ladino* households. Over 60 percent of school-age children (seven to fourteen years old) who had dropped out of school were classified as indigenous. Indigenous citizens formed the largest majority of the one-third of the Guatemalan population estimated to be illiterate. Average life expectancy among indigenous Guatemalans trailed the average for *ladinos* by over eleven years. Given the geographic isolation, limited education, and absolute poverty suffered by many

TABLE 9.3 Guatemalan Economic Indicators (1983–2002)*

Year	GDP growth	Inflation	Unemployment	Debt service ratio[†]
1983	−2.7	15	9.9	9
1984	0.0	5	9.1	12
1985	−0.6	32	12.0	15
1986	0.3	26	14.2	17
1987	3.6	10	12.1	14
1988	4.0	12	9.9	14
1989	3.7	20	6.2	11
1990	2.9	60	6.4	11
1991	3.5	10	6.7	7
1992	4.7	14	6.1	9
1993	1.3	12	2.6	6
1994	4.1	12	3.5	6
1995	5.0	9	3.9	16
1996	3.0	11	5.2	11
1997	4.4	7	5.1	14
1998	5.1	8	3.8	15
1999	3.9	5	—	13
2000	3.4	5	—	9
2001	2.6	9	—	10
2002	2.2	6	3.1	11

*All numbers are percentages.

[†]The debt service ratio expresses interest paid on foreign debts as a percentage of total exports.

SOURCE: For the years 1983–1987, data are from United Nations Economic Commission for Latin America and the Caribbean, *Preliminary Overview of the Economies of Latin America and the Caribbean 1989* (Santiago, Chile: United Nations Publications, 1989). For the years 1988–1992, data are from United Nations Economic Commission for Latin America and the Caribbean, *Preliminary Overview of the Economies of Latin America and the Caribbean 1994* (Santiago, Chile: United Nations Publications, 1994). For the years 1993–1997, data are from United Nations Economic Commission for Latin America and the Caribbean, *Preliminary Overview of the Economies of Latin America and the Caribbean 1999* (Santiago, Chile: United Nations Publications, 1999). For the years 1998–2002, data are from United Nations Economic Commission for Latin America and the Caribbean, *Preliminary Overview of the Economies of Latin America and the Caribbean 2003* (Santiago, Chile: United Nations Publications, 2003).

members of the indigenous population, efforts to improve their conditions constituted a central demand of the peace process. Yet the extent of the problem—and the limited political presence of indigenous groups in the major political parties—made it difficult to forge a ready path toward progress. Mayans in Guatemala were not the only indigenous group facing serious difficulties at the turn of the twenty-first century (see *Global Perspectives: Contemporary Indigenous Movements*).

GLOBAL PERSPECTIVES
Contemporary Indigenous Movements

Indigenous peoples are the presumed descendants of civilizations whose presence in a given territory predates the establishment of written property claims. Indigenous peoples are defined not just by their ancestry but also by their efforts to defend traditional languages, religions, and customs that differ from the contemporary norms in the countries in which they live. Indigenous peoples often constitute nations without states. In many situations, they face discrimination from the dominant ethnic or racial group in their respective countries. In the early twenty-first century, there were nearly 200 nation-states in the world, but estimates of nations with their own distinctive civilizations ranged from 7,000 to 10,000. Of those groups, the United Nations estimates that over 350 million indigenous persons form part of over 5,000 indigenous groups spread across more than seventy states. The marginal socioeconomic and political status of many indigenous peoples threatens their ability to survive as a distinct civilization.

During the twentieth century, more and more indigenous groups organized to preserve their traditions, protect their rights, and improve their economic conditions. In 1977, the World Council of Indigenous Peoples sponsored a nongovernmental conference to bring attention to the plight of many indigenous nations. Many of the principles emphasized at that conference formed the basis of domestic and international political demands in the years to come. Within nation-state boundaries, indigenous movements have worked to raise awareness about their presence, and in many situations they have pressured governments to protect their property and to redress past land seizures. These groups have also attempted to create formal recognition of indigenous languages and cultures into their national legal systems.

In the international sphere, efforts to advance indigenous interests have similarly focused on achieving legal recognition and protection. In 1994, the United Nations completed work on a draft Declaration on the Rights of Indigenous Peoples; the draft was crafted with the participation of well over 100 indigenous nations. The proposed declaration would assert indigenous peoples' rights to the protection of their cultural identity, including the right to language, religion, and education. It would also protect indigenous peoples' cultural and intellectual property (such as traditional medicine and other customs). Specifically, it advocates remuneration for the development of pharmaceuticals. The draft declaration also asserts the right of indigenous peoples to own land collectively according to traditional practices, even if the prevailing legal system asserts different procedures for establishing and holding title to land.

After the creation of the draft declaration, the United Nations established the period from 1995 to 2004 as the International Decade of Indigenous Peoples. To heighten attention to indigenous concerns, during this decade the United Nations established a voluntary development fund to create projects for improving conditions for indigenous peoples and for preserving their cultures. A fellowship program helped to assist indigenous youth leaders in their efforts to work as community activists and educators. A separate program attempted to make journalists in different countries more knowledgeable about indigenous concerns.

In 2004, the United Nations hoped to achieve final passage of the Declaration on the Rights of Indigenous Peoples; it had not yet passed as of April 2004. If passed, the challenge facing indigenous peoples around the world would become similar to the challenge facing indigenous Guatemalans. They would need to find a way to convert political and legal commitments into public and private actions that meet the stated goals.

The gravity of the poverty reduction challenge was also exacerbated by considerable political disagreement over the role of government in the development process. Throughout the twentieth century, propertied Guatemalans used various often brutal means to keep government economic activity to a minimum. The Guatemalan government's economic resources had long been the smallest in Latin America: in the mid-1990s, taxes equaled roughly 8 percent of GDP. The average Latin American country's tax base totaled nearly 20 percent of GDP (review *Global Perspectives: The Size of Government* in Chapter Four).

Increasing governmental resources toward improving public education, health care, and other basic services had been a central demand in the peace process. Opposition to tax increases from CACIF and from conservative political parties deadlocked peace talks regarding socioeconomic issues for over a year—the longest negotiations in the entire peace process. Many observers believe that pressure from many donor governments convinced the government to agree to raise tax revenues by 2000, from 8 to 12 percent of GDP, as part of the Socioeconomic Accord reached in May 1996. In addition, the accord called for more of the tax burden to be shifted toward wealthy citizens. Spending on education and on health care was to rise by 50 percent or more, while the military budget would shrink. Without those commitments, foreign aid pledged to support implementation of the Peace Accords would have been withheld.

Despite that pledge, however, many of the most powerful organized forces in Guatemala favored a continuation (and extension) of the market capitalist economic model after the conclusion of the civil war. Arzú came from a wealthy family and favored market-oriented policies. The FRG spoke in a more populist manner about some economic issues but remained reluctant to make major changes. CACIF remained opposed to any tax increases, especially those that might increase the share of taxes paid by wealthy Guatemalans. Many military officers also supported that view. Ironically, many ordinary Guatemalans were also suspicious of tax increases because they had minimal confidence that government officials would use this money to improve conditions for the general population.

The Arzú government emphasized its allegiance to the market capitalist model by launching a privatization program. During Arzú's term, most of the major state-owned enterprises—including the phone company, the national airline, the postal service, and the railroads—were sold. In addition, reforms to the social security system converted the pay-as-you-go pension program into a private investment system analogous to reforms undertaken in Chile and Argentina. Arzú also participated in efforts to speed up integration among the member states in the Central American Common Market (CACM). In the mid-1990s, CACM made progress in converting itself from a free-trade association toward a customs union (review *Global Perspectives: Regional Economic Integration,* for economic integration terminology, in Chapter Five).

The government proceeded slowly regarding implementation of the tax reforms mandated by the Peace Accords. Although the participants had agreed that the tax base should expand by 1998 (to show progress toward the stipulated goal for 2000), the government waited almost a full year following the Final Peace Accord before submitting a tax reform bill to Congress. In late 1997, the PAN majority in Congress passed a progressive property tax reform that taxed expensive properties at a much higher rate than that levied on smaller properties. The reform ignited considerable opposition from the FRG and from other conservative politicians outside the PAN. Some conservative critics alleged that the new tax would harm lower- and middle-income families. These charges swelled the ranks of the tax's opponents to include figures from across the political spectrum—including Nobel laureate Rigoberta Menchú. Some reform opponents took full advantage of an institutional provision that enables citizens to ask the Court of Constitutionality to review any tax legislation. In response to all this pressure, in February 1998, the Arzú government instructed the PAN legislative majority to repeal the law. Later that year, the government worked through a compromise tax package that slightly raised taxes on businesses; it also reorganized tax collection procedures nationwide. In addition, the government rescheduled the deadline for increasing taxes to 12 percent of GDP from 2000 to 2002.

The experience of the Arzú government disappointed those who had hoped that the Socioeconomic Accord would be the basis of an improvement for poor Guatemalans. This disappointment created an opening for Alfonso Portillo to criticize the privatization program and the role of big business when he campaigned again for the presidency in 1999. Portillo promised to review the privatization decisions of the prior administration and to defend the interests of ordinary Guatemalans. Despite retaining some of this populist campaign rhetoric throughout his term, Portillo maintained the market orientation of prior governments when he was elected in 1999. The privatization decisions were upheld and negotiations continued to reduce trade barriers within the Central American Common Market. In addition, Guatemala worked with other CACM members to develop serious negotiations toward a CACM–U.S. free-trade agreement over the second half of Portillo's term.

The tax issue remained the most contentious economic issue in Guatemalan politics. When Portillo took office, tax revenues remained less than 10 percent of GDP. During his first year as president, Portillo brokered a new tax reform package that would increase business tax rates and would also increase the **value-added tax** rate from 10 to 12 percent on most goods; the value-added tax is charged on the value-added portion of each transaction from the initial production of a good, to its wholesale exchange, and to its final retail price. This tax increase package met with vocal public opposition from both organized business and from representatives of low-income groups, as tax increases had during Arzú's term. For a portion of 2001, Portillo declared a state of emergency to broaden the government's power to break up street demonstrations and roadblocks. The government rescheduled yet again the deadline for reaching the stated revenue target—to 2004. Even with these tax changes, the Guatemalan government would not meet the deadline for enlarging state resources so, in 2002 and 2003, the government increased excise taxes on alcoholic beverages. As a result of these changes, taxes rose to around 11 percent of GDP by the end of Portillo's term in January 2004.

The political controversy and backtracking surrounding tax reform in contemporary Guatemala illustrate two central features of the politics of economic policy. First, in an unequal society with a small government, economically powerful individuals and groups have grown accustomed to a minimal tax burden and to a minimalist government that rarely challenges their privileges. Not surprisingly, wealthy opponents of tax reform worked hard to limit the extent to which new taxes affected their interests. Second, governments cannot count on the political support of potential beneficiaries of proposed policy changes. To cultivate political support, governments need to work diligently at developing a broad-based coalition that sees itself in a position to gain from the tax reform. Both Arzú and Portillo failed to convince most lower-income Guatemalans that the tax increases would likely benefit ordinary Guatemalans. Some critics have gone so far as to allege that the PAN and the FRG intentionally undersold their tax proposals because they did not favor the tax hikes proposed by the Peace Accords.

The Quest for Liberty in Guatemala

As part of the peace negotiations, the guerrilla movement and human rights organizations accepted (after considerable complaint) that many human rights violations of prior years would not be prosecuted. The March 1994 Human Rights Accord itself dealt primarily with a commitment to respect human rights from that point onward—with the observation of a U.N. mission designed to monitor compliance with this accord. The U.N. Mission in Guatemala (*Misión de las Naciones Unidas en Guatemala* [MINUGUA]) began to perform this function in November 1994. It had no enforcement power, but its reports regarding contemporary human rights violations—and its organizational presence more generally—changed the context for liberty in Guatemala. The MINUGUA operation reflected the United Nations' evolving role in attempting to promote peace around the world via **peace-making, peace-keeping,** and **peace-building** (see *Concepts in Action: Peace-Making, Peace-Keeping, and Peace-Building*).

CONCEPTS IN ACTION
Peace-Making, Peace-Keeping, and Peace-Building

Multilateral action to promote peace has been part of the mission of the United Nations (U.N.) since its inception. Although the U.N. Charter does not use the term *peace-making,* Chapter VI of the Charter calls for the United Nations to engage in peace-making by offering to serve as a mediator in the resolution of violent conflicts. This goal of peace-making quickly led to U.N. efforts to deploy peace-keeping military forces to enforce cease-fire agreements and peace agreements between combatants. In 1948, the U.N. Security Council voted to establish the United Nations Truce Supervision Organization (UNTSO) to preserve the truce that ended the first Arab-Israeli war. In the decades that followed, peace-keeping operations would become an increasingly prevalent activity of the United Nations, particularly from the 1980s onward. Blue-helmeted U.N. peace-keeping troops would be deployed in fifty-six missions over the next fifty-five years. In early 2003 alone, approximately 37,000 persons from eighty-nine countries served in fourteen U.N. peace-keeping missions around the world.

The initial vision of the United Nations focused on the promotion of peace among the nation-states of the world—as illustrated by the 1948 effort to restore peace between Israel and neighboring Arab states. It became clear in subsequent years, however, that many violent conflicts took place between intrastate combatants. In these conflicts, socioeconomic and political demands were often central to the dispute. In response, the United Nations developed a new approach to conflict resolution.

In the late twentieth century, the U.N. Security Council authorized the creation of peace-building missions that went beyond the previous scope of peace-keeping efforts. Peace-building missions tried to end conflicts by monitoring the enforcement of component portions of peace agreements, including political reforms, socioeconomic development programs, and human rights protection. The logic of peace-building saw the creation of new societal dynamics as essential for the resolution of long-running conflicts as well as for the prevention of future violence. In 2003, the United Nations carried out thirteen different peace-building missions around the world, including one in Guatemala.

From the late 1980s onward, the United Nations has assumed a multifaceted role in an effort to end the lengthy civil war in Guatemala. In 1990, the Guatemalan government and the URNG guerrilla movement formally requested that the United Nations send an observer to their peace negotiations. In January 1994, both sides signed a framework accord that set a substantive agenda for peace talks aimed at ending the conflict; the accord called for the United Nations to serve as the official mediator of the peace process. When the negotiating parties reached the Human Rights Accord in March 1994, they asked the United Nations to establish a verification mission in Guatemala (MINUGUA).

MINUGUA began operations in November 1994. After the signing of the Final Peace Accord in December 1996, the MINUGUA mandate expanded to include the verification of all of the various Peace Accords signed over the years 1994–1996. In addition, the mission provided technical assistance to Guatemalan authorities in developing government programs to comply with the conditions and goals set out in the Peace Accords. The initial MINUGUA mandate called for it to continue operations until the 2002 deadline set for compliance with all aspects of the Peace Accords. When that compliance deadline shifted to 2004, the MINUGUA mandate was extended through December 2004.

Two additional accords in the peace process set the agenda for how past human rights violations would be handled. First, a June 1994 agreement called for the creation of a truth commission to investigate past human rights violations from 1960 to the present. Both sides in the peace talks came away disappointed with this accord. The government had staunchly opposed any such investigation and yielded only under considerable pressure from forces inside and outside Guatemala. Human rights advocates disliked a provision that prohibited the commission from investigating and documenting which individuals were responsible for the violations in question. The Historical Clarification Commission (*Comisión de Esclarecimiento Histórico* [CEH]) would consist of three members: a U.N. representative and two Guatemalan citizens. The CEH would have a six- to twelve-month period in which to conduct its work once the peace process ended.

The other relevant accord emerged following Arzú's election as the peace process entered its final stages. As part of the accord that legalized the URNG, both sides attempted to walk a fine line in the construction of a national reconciliation policy. Security forces and guerrillas would receive a mutual amnesty for taking part in the civil war, but that legislation would leave open the possibility of prosecution regarding the unjustifiable use of force as well as for crimes against humanity. Shortly after language had been agreed to as part of the final accord, the legislature began to modify the bill so that it would create a blanket amnesty for government security forces. In the end, under pressure again from the international community, the National Reconciliation Law passed on December 18, 1996, left open the possibility of prosecution for acts of genocide and torture, which was in line with Guatemala's treaty obligations. In the give and take over this issue, however, the law included summary executions within the amnesty unless they could be categorized as acts of genocide or torture. Ultimately, it would be up to the judicial system to resolve which violations fell within the amnesty and which violations could be prosecuted.

The CEH began its work in mid-1997 and delivered its report in February 1999. The truth commission talked with nearly 10,000 victims but had difficulty gaining the cooperation of the security forces. The lone military officer who spoke publicly about human rights abuses during this period was placed under military arrest for a month for talking without orders. In the end, the CEH report held that over 200,000 people had been killed or had disappeared during the conflict, with 93 percent of the deaths attributed to security forces. More important, in regard to the National Reconciliation Law, the truth commission asserted that many actions during the early 1980s against indigenous villagers constituted acts of genocide. The CEH called for the creation of a reparations program, a search for the remains of victims, a purging and reorganization of the armed forces, and meaningful civilian control of the security forces.

Over the rest of 1999, in a political context framed by a presidential race between the FRG and the PAN, the Arzú government became an increasingly strident critic of the CEH report and its recommendations. Initially, the government responded by stating that most of the recommendations regarding the reorganization of the security forces had already been implemented. Later, Arzú rejected the finding that many actions constituted genocide and stressed the nonbinding nature of the report. In turn, the FRG's position regarding the CEH report proved even more dismissive once Alfonso Portillo won the 1999 elections. Nonetheless, the final say regarding which violent acts committed prior to the Peace Accords could be prosecuted belonged to the attorney general and to the courts. During the years 1997–2003, relatively few cases made it to trial; those that did tended to be high-profile cases. One such example is the murder of anthropologist Myrna Mack, who was killed by security forces not long after publishing findings regarding the extent of violence in the countryside and its impact on indigenous people. Although her killer was sentenced to twenty-five years in 1993, Mack's family and other human rights groups mobilized to try to bring the killer's superiors to court for ordering her murder. After many delays and much legal wrangling, three officers faced trial in 2002. The court found the junior officer guilty but acquitted his two superior officers. Among the few human rights cases that have gone to trial, most have followed a similar dynamic in which superior officers have been acquitted while the person(s) physically responsible receive a jail sentence (often shorter than those observed in the Mack case).

These investigations and trials unfolded in an environment rife with intimidation and violence. Thousands of human rights activists and witnesses suffered acts of intimidation, and many people involved have died trying to resolve the issues. By far, the most dramatic example was the April 1998 murder of Bishop Juan José Gerardi, head of the Catholic church's human rights office in Guatemala. Gerardi was bludgeoned to death near his home just two days after he submitted the church's report on the extent of human rights violations during the civil war era. For the rest of Arzú's presidency, Gerardi's murder remained unsolved. Alfonso Portillo blamed the incumbent administration for the problems and claimed that the matter could be cleared up during his first year in office. Eventually, in June 2001, three military officers received thirty-year sentences for Gerardi's murder. In October 2002, however, all three convictions were overturned on appeal. In February 2003, a second appeals court reversed that verdict on the grounds that the second court lacked jurisdiction in the matter it decided. This ruling left the matter in the hands of the Court of Constitutionality, which ordered that a lower court issue a new opinion. On the sixth anniversary of Gerardi's death in late April 2004, his murder case remained an open matter pending in the judicial system. Several potential witnesses to Gerardi's murder have suffered violent deaths, which makes a resolution of this case all the more difficult. The investigation of the Gerardi case further illustrates the difficult climate for civil liberties in contemporary Guatemala.

Given concerns about the likelihood of successful domestic prosecution of human rights violators, Rigoberta Menchú formally called for international prosecution. In December 1999, she filed charges against eight government officials—including Efraín Ríos Montt—for genocide and torture. She called on Spain to assert international jurisdiction on the grounds of international conventions against crimes of humanity. Menchú did so in light of Spanish judge Baltazar Garzón's October 1998 arrest warrant for Chilean general Augusto Pinochet (review *Global Perspectives: International Human Rights Trials* in Chapter Seven) and in light of the CEH's assertions that genocide took place. The Spanish courts initially rejected jurisdiction on the grounds that such crimes should be prosecuted in Guatemala. In March 2003, however, the Spanish high court partially reversed that ruling. It found that Spain could investigate and potentially try Guatemalan authorities for any crimes committed against Spaniards, including the Spanish victims of the 1980 embassy massacre.

Problems with intimidation surrounding human rights trials testify to broader problems in protecting the right to person and the right to property in Guatemala. The movement to create civilian control over the national police succeeded formally, but informally the reorganization of the police faced severe limitations. The vast majority of the existing force survived the reorganization. Many of the new members were army personnel shifted to the police as part of an effort to reduce the defense budget, as mandated by the Peace Accords. In addition, operational cooperation between the military and the police remained extensive. Abuse of authority remained difficult to detect and to punish.

An even more prevalent threat to most citizens came in the form of violent crime: kidnapping and armed robbery became more widespread. In 2002, the head of the Central Bank was kidnapped, and many Guatemalans fear this possibility every day. A 2003 MINUGUA report detailed the rise in crime with considerable concern. In several instances, demobilized security forces, former paramilitary members of the PACs, and guerrillas have been charged with violent crime. In two other situations in 2003, former PAC members took hostages to demand compensation for the loss of livelihood associated with the demobilization of the PACs. In that same year, the U.S. government formally criticized the Guatemalan police for insufficient cooperation in countering drug trafficking amid suspicion that several officers may be working with drug traffickers.

In this troubled context regarding contemporary liberty, Arzú and Portillo campaigned under different themes. In 1996, during the peace talks, Arzú emphasized the need for greater liberty to contrast himself with the FRG's skeptical position toward the peace process. In the 1999 campaign, Portillo and the FRG presented themselves as the party of order. In practice, however, both leaders used a minimalist approach to implementing the provisions of the Peace Accords that directly affect human liberty. In dealing with past human rights violations, both presidents worked publicly and privately to speak out against a broader approach to defining crimes outside the amnesty provided by the National Reconciliation Law. Portillo continued the human rights reparations process begun under Arzú, but his government did not increase funding. The military budget remained over 100 times as large as the budget for the presidential agency charged with implementing the peace accords, including the reparations.

In creating policies to prevent contemporary and future human rights violations, these two governments again took minimal steps. Military spending remained considerable, and the elite units most involved in the counterinsurgency campaign were not reorganized in compliance with the Peace Accords. Meanwhile, funding for the police and for the judicial system remained insufficient to cover their needs. Faced with military opposition to reform, both Arzú and Portillo proposed minimal changes in the hope of not losing the support of the security forces.

The Quest for Governance in Guatemala

Álvaro Arzú's presidency began under some propitious circumstances. Although he had won a narrow electoral victory in the runoff election, the PAN gained control of 54 percent of the seats in Congress. Unlike most contemporary presidents in Argentina, Brazil, and Chile, Arzú could conceivably govern without acquiring the support of other parties in the legislature. When Arzú helped to reenergize the stalemated peace talks at the outset of his presidency, his support among many Guatemalans grew. The Guatemalan Peace Accords, along with the prior peace agreement in neighboring El Salvador, raised hopes for a new approach to governance in Central America (see the *Research Question* on pages 320–321 regarding the relationship between civil war and democracy).

Beyond these favorable conditions, however, lurked a host of problems. First, although the PAN potentially controlled Congress, many of its legislators took policy positions closer to those of the FRG than to those of Arzú, particularly concerning the implementation of the Peace Accords. Second, business interests and the military chipped away at aspects of the accords with which they had agreed reluctantly or not at all. Third, when faced with these uncertainties, Arzú tried to sustain the momentum of the peace process by launching a multisectoral roundtable that included all political parties and many interest groups. Within months, this process fizzled out. In part, Arzú's effort to broaden his support failed because of personality differences. In addition, several participants questioned his willingness to build consensus via dialogue and compromise. They became convinced that Arzú simply sought approval for his approach to most issues.

As the years passed, all the initial challenges deepened in the face of two highly publicized events that mobilized public opinion against the Arzú government. First, his 1997 tax reform proposal inspired cross-class protests with leaders and activists from across the political spectrum. This reaction made it difficult for him to mend fences with the more conservative wing of the PAN. It also made it harder for Arzú to try to reach out to more centrist political movements outside his own party. In turn, his government's inability to solve the 1998 murder of Bishop Gerardi further weakened his ability to govern. By early 1999, he was a lame-duck president with few solid bases of support.

Alfonso Portillo's presidency exhibited many of the same features of his predecessor's. Although Portillo did not come to power amid the optimism associated with the peace process, he earned a large majority of the votes in the presidential runoff. His party, the FRG, also controlled a majority in the legislature. In addition, the then-forty-eight-year-old Portillo's cowboy image created hope for many Guatemalans that he could make good on his promises for

---

RESEARCH QUESTION
Under What Conditions Are Civil Wars Likely to End?

Under what conditions is conflict resolution more likely? In particular, how can the international community help to resolve long-standing conflicts? Mark Peceny and William Stanley addressed these issues in a 2001 study.[1]

They argue that many analysts have overemphasized the role of security guarantees in ending civil wars. These earlier studies assumed that combatants are unlikely to stop fighting until a third party steps forward to guarantee their safety. Without a physical peace-keeping presence, combatants keep fighting as a means to self-preservation.

Peceny and Stanley claim that a social reconstruction approach can help to produce an end to civil war even in the absence of international security guarantees. In particular, they emphasize efforts to build support for democratic norms of power-sharing and policy compromise. In this sense, Peceny and Stanley build on the democratic peace theory of interstate war, which notes that democratic countries rarely go to war with one another. By extension, combatants may be willing to end civil war if they believe a democracy can be built.

They assert that this shift from internal violence toward democratization can take place in three phases. First, amid pressure from major world powers and neighboring countries, local elites begin to express support for democracy. Second, the international community

[1] Mark Peceny and William Stanley, "Liberal Social Reconstruction and the Resolution of Civil Wars in Central America," *International Organization* 55 (2001): 149–182. For additional research in academic journals regarding conflict resolution, see the appropriate portion of this book's website.

change. During the campaign, Portillo admitted that he had killed two men in Mexico; he had never been charged and the statute of limitations had expired. The admission paved the way for a new campaign slogan that paradoxically re-inforced his law-and-order emphasis: "A man who can defend his own life can defend yours."

Early in his term, Portillo invited leaders from other political parties to work with his government. Portillo worried that potential divisions within the FRG could also weaken his presidency. Portillo saw his administration's influence hampered by two main issues. First, corruption allegations haunted his govern-ment from the beginning and worsened over time. In June 2000, Congress passed a new tax on alcohol as part of an effort to meet the revenue target set in the Peace Accords. When the law appeared in the official bulletin, however, op-position legislators claimed that the law published had halved the tax rate that had been approved. Since the official bulletin fell under the purview of the leader of Congress, Efraín Ríos Montt, suspicion immediately fell on the two

offers to mediate the conflict; these mediation efforts try to create a framework in which combatants can move toward ending the war. In the third phase, the international com-munity offers to help develop new governing institutions that can support and internalize democratic norms.

Peceny and Stanley examine these ideas via an analysis of El Salvador, Guatemala, and Nicaragua. In Nicaragua, the international community provided armed peacekeepers to protect disarmed antigovernment *contras*. International observers monitored the transition elections but most left shortly thereafter. This structure helped to end the open civil war, but within a few years, forces associated with the military and the *contras* were fighting once again. Conversely, in El Salvador, the United Nations brokered a broader peace agreement that transformed the political system. Rather than providing international peacekeepers, the government and the rebels agreed to share a role in the police force. To help build trust in the new system and to support implementation of the accords, the United Nations estab-lished an ongoing mission that stayed in place for several years. Peceny and Stanley view the Guatemalan situation as an intermediate case. The United Nations pursued a course of action similar to that used in El Salvador and it helped end the war despite an absence of peace-keeping forces. However, despite a similar U.N. mission charged with verifying the implementation of the peace accords (review *Concepts in Action: Peace-Making, Peace-Keeping, and Peace-Building*), progress toward implementation proved slower than it did in El Salvador.

Why was progress slower in Guatemala? Peceny and Stanley argue that the central prob-lem in Guatemala is that the groups that negotiated the peace accords (the PAN and the URNG) were both out of power in just over three years (and even more marginalized by early 2004). Conversely, both the governing party and the Salvadoran rebels remained major political movements long after the peace accords had been signed.

leaders of the FRG, Portillo and Ríos Montt. Several additional scandals followed in which Portillo was accused of improper use of government funds. The
other challenge for the Portillo presidency came from a familiar source: opposition to tax reform. Portillo's proposal to raise the sales tax rates by 2 percent
while also raising business taxes did not meet with much public approval. Opponents of this tax hike proposal seized on Portillo's corrupt image as another
rationale for opposing the tax increase: if the money would not be spent well,
why raise taxes?

Throughout his presidency, Portillo attempted to bolster his support by
using populist rhetoric that portrayed him as a man of the people. His constant
criticism of big business in Guatemala tried to inspire support from ordinary
Guatemalans. Portillo's core problem in implementing this strategy was not
public faith in business but a large part of the population who perceived Portillo
as being just as corrupt as the figures he criticized.

Governance dynamics during these two presidencies also help us to understand why several Latin American countries have been debating the region's
traditional prohibition on reelection. The 1985 constitution in Guatemala has
the harshest version of the prohibition: no possibility of reelection whatsoever.
Most countries in the region either permit presidents to stand again for election
after sitting out one term or they allow presidents a maximum of two consecutive terms. During both the Arzú and the Portillo presidencies, what little momentum each president sustained through the middle of his respective term
faded as attention shifted to the next electoral cycle. One can understand the
role of no-reelection clauses in trying to prevent the emergence of an endur-
ingly dominant president. However, this system calls for every president to face
the lame duck scenario in which they cannot build loyalty on the grounds that
they might become chief executive again.

Future Challenges

As noted at the start of this chapter, the peace process of the 1990s revived several issues that had not been seriously contemplated for decades. Could
Guatemala forge an approach to economic development that would bring
more of its citizens out of poverty and reduce income inequality? In particular,
how might conditions for indigenous peoples be improved? In turn, could
Guatemala forge a more robust democracy in which the government would
guarantee basic civil liberties and the rule of law, in addition to holding elections? Finally, how would Guatemala's elected leaders build support for their
proposed solutions to these problems?

When Oscar Berger took office in January 2004, just over seven years had
passed since the Final Peace Accord was signed. Progress on meeting the above
challenges had been minimal under his predecessors. Relatively few poor
Guatemalans escaped poverty. Despite some efforts to increase government activity as a way to reduce absolute and relative poverty, income inequality

increased by 22 percent from 1996 to 2002. Guatemala remained among the countries with the greatest income inequality in Latin America.

The outlook for liberty that Berger inherited was somewhat more mixed yet still troubling. A few people faced meaningful prosecution for past and contemporary human rights violations. Despite that progress, however, the dominant images remained widespread impunity and a persistent fear of abuse at the hands of government authority. Several constitutional amendments designed to provide more institutional checks on state violence had been defeated in the 1999 plebiscite by a mixture of dedicated opposition and voter apathy among its potential supporters. Street crime and organized crime also posed serious challenges to the enjoyment of human liberty on a day-to-day basis.

To complete a troubled picture, both of Berger's predecessors found it difficult to pursue their respective announced agendas. Their program goals that could be pursued through the use of existing law were achieved relatively quickly, while proposals requiring legislative or judicial support all too frequently failed. It could not be heartening to Berger that his opponents struggled to realize their agendas even though their parties held legislative majorities.

Like Arzú and Portillo, Berger promised in his campaign to make Guatemala a more prosperous, just, and secure society. Unlike the past two presidents, Berger's newly formed political movement held just under one-third of the seats in Congress. In recognition of that limitation, Berger began his presidency by trying to build a multipartisan coalition in support of his government. Early steps included offering a post to Rigoberta Menchú in his government as a special ambassador in charge of promoting the fulfillment of the Peace Accords.

As of May 2004, it is difficult to predict whether Berger can be more successful than his predecessors. Perhaps his greater need to build a legislative coalition will lead his government to work harder to forge a consensus through dialogue and compromise. Will he focus on poverty reduction? Will his government prosecute Ríos Montt for human rights abuses now that the ex-dictator no longer has the immunity from prosecution that he enjoyed as the leader of the Congress from 1996 to 2004? Will Berger or other leaders revive some of the failed constitutional reforms? It is harder still to discern what proposals might emerge with the support needed to carry them through from the idea stage to implemented public policies affecting people's lives. One issue is certain: if more of the hopes raised by the Peace Accords are to become realities, existing political dynamics in Guatemala will need to change.

Activities and Exercises

1. Both the Arzú government and the Portillo government faced public protests against their respective proposals to raise tax rates. Yet raising government revenues was deemed essential in the Socioeconomic Accord for increasing government spending on education, health, and other basic services. If you were

charged with designing a political strategy for raising government revenues in Guatemala in the early twenty-first century, what tax rates would you increase? How would you build sufficient political support for your preferred policies?

2. Rigoberta Menchú has formally requested that the Spanish government assert jurisdiction over past human rights violations in Guatemala. Do you believe foreign countries should assert jurisdiction to punish crimes against humanity committed outside their borders? Why or why not? How would you respond to the principal arguments of those who do not agree with your view?

3. A brief discussion of the pros and cons of an absolute prohibition on presidential reelection was presented toward the end of this chapter. Do you believe that this prohibition solves more problems for Guatemala than it creates? Why or why not?

4. *El silencio de Neto* (*Neto's Silence*) is a 1994 Guatemalan film directed by Luis Argueta. The movie follows a boy growing up against the backdrop of efforts in 1954 to bring down the government of Jacobo Arbenz. This film is available in VHS format with English subtitles, but it is unlikely to be available at local video stores. See if you can find it in a library or in your school's language department.

5. In addition to the struggle to escape poverty, many indigenous peoples in Guatemala and elsewhere are organizing to preserve different core elements of their culture: language, religion, customs, etc. Many indigenous cultures are working in and out of Guatemala to survive in the new century. For a list of online resources related to indigenous peoples across Latin America, see the web page on the Latin American Network Information Center (LANIC) site at http://lanic.utexas.edu/la/region/indigenous/index.html. For links to resources related to indigenous peoples around the world, check the NativeWeb website at http://www.nativeweb.org/.

Suggested Readings

Arias, Arturo, ed. *The Rigoberta Menchú Controversy.* Minneapolis: University of Minnesota, 2001.

Barry, Tom. *Inside Guatemala.* Albuquerque, N.M.: Inter-Hemispheric Education Resource Center, 1992.

Brockett, Charles. *Contentious Political Movements and Political Violence in Central America.* Cambridge, England: Cambridge University Press, 2005.

Burgerman, Susan. *Moral Victories: How Activists Provoke Multilateral Action.* Ithaca, N.Y.: Cornell University Press, 2001.

Chase-Dunn, Christopher, Susanne Jonas, and Nelson Amaro, eds. *Globalization on the Ground: Post-Bellum Guatemalan Development and Democracy.* Lanham, Md.: Rowman and Littlefield, 2001.

Dosal, Paul. *Power in Transition: The Rise of Guatemala's Industrial Oligarchy, 1871–1994.* Westport, Conn.: Praeger, 1995.

Fischer, Edward, and R. McKenna Brown, eds. *Maya Cultural Activism in Guatemala.* Austin: University of Texas Press, 1996.

Garrard-Burnett, Virginia. *Protestantism in Guatemala: Living in the New Jerusalem.* Austin: University of Texas Press, 1998.

Gleijeses, Piero. *Shattered Hope: The Guatemalan Revolution and the U.S.* Princeton, N.J.: Princeton University Press, 1991.

Jonas, Susanne. *Of Centaurs and Doves: Guatemala's Peace Process.* Boulder, Colo.: Westview, 2000.

Landau, Saúl. *The Guerrilla Wars of Central America: Nicaragua, El Salvador, and Guatemala.* New York: St. Martin's Press, 1993.

Levenson-Estrada, Deborah. *Trade Unionists Against Terror: Guatemala City, 1954–1985.* Chapel Hill: University of North Carolina Press, 1994.

Luciak, Ilja. *After the Revolution: Gender and Democracy in El Salvador, Nicaragua, and Guatemala.* Baltimore, Md.: Johns Hopkins University Press, 2001.

May, Rachel. *Terror in the Countryside: Campesino Responses to Political Violence in Guatemala, 1954–1985.* Athens: Ohio University Press, 2001.

McCleary, Rachel. *Dictating Democracy: Guatemala and the End of Violent Revolution.* Gainesville: University of Florida Press, 1999.

Menchú, Rigoberta, with Elisabeth Burgos Debray. *I, Rigoberta Menchú: An Indian Woman in Guatemala.* London: Verso, 1984.

Nelson, Diane. *Finger in the Wound: Body Politics in Quincentennial Guatemala.* Berkeley: University of California Press, 1999.

Perera, Víctor. *Unfinished Conquest: The Guatemalan Tragedy.* Berkeley: University of California Press, 1993.

Sanford, Victoria. *Buried Secrets: Truth and Human Rights in Guatemala.* New York: Palgrave Macmillan, 2003.

Schirmer, Jennifer. *The Guatemalan Military Project: A Violence Called Democracy.* Philadelphia: University of Pennsylvania Press, 1998.

Seider, Rachel, ed. *Guatemala After the Peace Accords.* London: Institute for Latin American Studies, 1998.

Smith, Carol, ed. *Guatemalan Indians and the State: 1540–1988.* Austin: University of Texas Press, 1990.

Stoll, David. *Rigoberta Menchú and the Story of All Poor Guatemalans.* Boulder, Colo.: Westview, 1999.

Trudeau, Robert. *Guatemalan Politics: The Popular Struggle for Democracy.* Boulder, Colo.: Lynne Rienner, 1993.

Yashar, Deborah. *Demanding Democracy: Reform and Reaction in Costa Rica and Guatemala.* Stanford, Calif.: Stanford University Press, 2000.

Endnotes

1. Cited in Susanne Jonas, "Guatemala: Land of Eternal Struggle," in Ronald Chilcote and Joel Edelstein, eds., *Latin America: The Struggle with Dependency and Beyond* (New York: John Wiley, 1974), p. 106.

2. Cited in Piero Gleijeses, *Shattered Hope: The Guatemalan Revolution and the United States, 1944–1954* (Princeton, N.J.: Princeton University Press, 1991), p. 149.

3. Rigoberta Menchú became a much more public figure outside Guatemala with the 1984 publication of *I, Rigoberta Menchú: An Indian Woman in Guatemala.* In the 1990s, a U.S.-based anthropologist, David Stoll, challenged the veracity of several elements of her story in his *Rigoberta Menchú and the Story of All Poor Guatemalans* (1999). Menchú eventually responded that some elements of the book were a composite of the experiences of people she knew, which she presented within a narrative of her own life to personalize the issues. For a discussion of several aspects of this controversy, see an edited volume by Arturo Arias, *The Rigoberta Menchú Controversy* (2001).

Mexico

CHAPTER 10

Mexico

I N MOST OF LATIN AMERICA, the period from 1930 to 1980 was filled with considerable turmoil. The quest for development met with frustration: most countries found it difficult to maintain consistent economic growth and macroeconomic stability. The quest for liberty was all too often put on hold as military governments took power and suspended most (or all) civil and political rights. These two challenges (along with other factors) made it difficult for chief executives to govern; most elected presidents lacked legislative support and many failed to finish their terms of office.

Mexico formed an exception to all three of those regional trends. The economy grew relatively steadily—especially during the 1950s and 1960s. The military played a comparatively small role in politics from the 1940s on, and there were no successful military coups. Elected presidents consistently enjoyed an overwhelming majority in the legislature that made it easier for them to pursue their policy agendas.

How did Mexico's political evolution take such a distinctive path in the twentieth century? Much of the answer lies in the unusual resolution of the Mexican Revolution. In most revolutions around the world, various strong-willed individuals competed for political dominance. This scenario occurred in Mexico during the first three decades following the outbreak of civil war in 1910. From the late 1930s onward, however, Mexico's revolutionary leaders agreed to share power over time: presidents would have tremendous authority for a six-year term, name a successor, and then leave the center of the political stage. The individual leaders were not eternal, but the revolutionary party was.

Mexican political life was by no means free of conflict. Although the economy grew fairly steadily, economic inequality increased and many Mexicans did not escape poverty. Although a military government did not emerge to suspend all civil liberties, the fusion of the party and the government blurred the lines of accountability because no independent forces emerged to control potential abuses of power. Presidents did not face the challenge of double-minority rule, but the government's permanent majority created a different governance problem: the charge that too much power was held by the revolutionary party and, in particular, by the president. From its creation in 1929 until 1988, the Institutional Revolutionary party (*Partido Revolucionario Institucional* [PRI]) won all presidential elections, all gubernatorial elections, and nearly every legislative seat that came up for election. Octavio Paz, Mexico's first Nobel laureate in literature, referred to this state of affairs as "the perfect dictatorship."

Over the years 1988–2000, the PRI's dominance of Mexican politics unraveled. The PRI began to lose some elections for governor. The party lost its majority in the lower house of the legislature in 1997. Finally, on July 2, 2000, the PRI lost the presidential elections to opposition candidate Vicente Fox. That electoral result ended seventy-one years of uninterrupted rule by the PRI.

In light of Mexico's unusual political evolution, consider three main questions while reading this chapter. First, how did Mexico develop and sustain this distinctive political path for so long? Second, what caused the PRI to lose its grip on power during the 1980s and 1990s? Third, now that the political process has changed, how will Vicente Fox (and future Mexican presidents) approach the ongoing quest for development, liberty, and governance? Understanding the dynamics of this country of 105 million inhabitants is important in its own right, but it has taken on added significance for U.S. residents with the ongoing increase in U.S.-Mexican economic relations. By 2002, Mexico was the United States' second-largest trading partner.

HISTORICAL BACKGROUND FROM 1876 TO 1988

Mexican politics in the first decades after independence were characterized by rampant instability. From 1821 to 1861, Mexico had over fifty different governments—none of which lasted more than a year. Instability stemmed from infighting among competing *caudillos* combined with conflict between conservative and liberal principles, particularly regarding the role of the Catholic church. Liberals led by Benito Juárez pushed for the creation of a new constitution in 1857 that motivated conservatives to rebel in the War of the Reform (1858–1861). After the liberals triumphed, some conservatives convinced Napoleon III to install Archduke Maximilian von Hapsburg as monarch of Mexico. French forces managed to take control of a considerable amount of Mexican territory, but they were eventually defeated by military forces led by General Porfirio Díaz during the Wars of the French Intervention (1862–1867). In 1871, Díaz narrowly lost the presidential elections to Benito Juárez. Porfirio Díaz then led a failed rebellion against Juárez; Díaz presented his insurrection as a protest against the repeated reelection of Juárez (who had just won his fourth term). After Juárez died of a heart attack in 1872, Sebastián Lerdo became Mexico's next president, serving until Díaz overthrew him in November 1876.

The *Porfiriato* (1876–1910)

After serving a four-year term as president, Porfirio Díaz supported the candidacy of Manuel González. In 1884, Díaz ran successfully for the presidency again. This time, however, he would not step aside again until 1911. The general who had justified his first insurrection in the name of no reelection became the longest-serving president in Mexican history. Díaz retained power via machine politics combined with violent coercion against his opponents. His more than three decades in power would come to be known as the *Porfiriato*.

During the *Porfiriato*, Mexico established an enduring national government through the authoritarian imposition of order. Many members of the Díaz cabinet considered themselves to be the agents of modernity; these adherents to positivism called themselves *científicos* ("scientists"). When challenged, they argued that the brutality of the federal police was necessary to create a favorable environment for investment and economic growth.

The economy grew quickly during most of this era. Overall, the gross domestic product (GDP) expanded twice as fast as the population. The government aggressively welcomed foreign capital aimed at building an infrastructure in support of the export of primary commodities. The rail network grew from 400 miles of track to over 15,000 miles. Foreign capital came to dominate the mining and petroleum sectors. In agriculture, the 1883 land law paved the way for the rapid concentration of landownership. Many of these larger farms began to produce for export.

However, this aggregate prosperity came with a heavy price tag in two areas. First, the effort to promote agribusinesses pushed thousands of rural Mexicans off communal land that their families had farmed for generations. The Díaz government intentionally gave large tracts of publicly held land to foreigners willing to survey the area: this strategy aimed at further marginalizing indigenous peoples, whom the *científicos* viewed as an obstacle to progress. Toward the end of this era, several hundred families gained control over 134 million acres of fertile land.[1] As a result, many peasants passed from subsistence agriculture to an even more precarious existence as day laborers either in agribusinesses or in the expanding urban areas. In addition, the colonization practices sowed the seeds of political nationalism because lower- and middle-class Mexicans resented the preferential treatment accorded to many propertied foreigners.

Second, the authoritarian rule of Porfirio Díaz angered the middle sectors of Mexican society. White-collar professionals and some wealthy landowners outside the Díaz circle chafed at the ongoing centralization of power. By the early twentieth century, many Mexicans desired change yet felt that elections had become a mere formality in which change would not be possible.

In this troubled context, wealthy landowner Francisco Madero launched his 1910 presidential campaign. Madero's aptly named Anti-Reelectionist party called for clean elections and an end to reelection. The government repressed Madero's campaign, and Madero and many of his party's activists spent the June 1910 election in jail. He was later released on bail and went into exile in the United States. From exile, Madero publicly announced in October that he would launch a revolt against the Díaz government on November 20, 1910.

The Mexican Revolution (1910–1928)

Madero's clarion call constituted the beginning of the twentieth century's first major social revolution. It sparked a civil war in which one out of ten Mexicans would die. For many rural Mexicans, the war marked the first time that they had traveled outside their home states.

The Mexican Revolution was really two revolutions fought simultaneously. On one hand, middle-income Mexicans (particularly in urban areas) rallied around Madero's call for "effective suffrage, no reelection." Madero's troops forced Díaz into exile in May 1911 and installed Madero as provisional president. As war raged on in several areas of the country, Madero organized new elections in November 1911 in which he became Mexico's elected leader. The political reform movement was under way.

Meanwhile, many rural Mexicans were energized by Emiliano Zapata's demand of land for all. When Madero won the November elections, Zapata criticized the new government for its limited agenda for socioeconomic change. In particular, Zapata wanted redress for the rapid concentration of landownership during the *Porfiriato*. Zapata's Ayala Plan called for a return to the communal farms (*ejidos*) that predated the arrival of the Spanish colonizers; he wanted these *ejidos* to be reestablished via land redistribution.

These two revolutionary visions—for political reform and economic reform—would weave their way through a decade of tumultuous civil war filled with enough twists and turns to fill many books. Madero's presidency fell victim to the betrayal of one of his leading generals, Victoriano Huerta. Huerta had Madero arrested and then summarily executed in February 1913. Huerta's actions unleashed a torrent of opposition in various parts of the country; a frustrated Huerta resigned in July 1914 amid pressure from many of Madero's other generals, especially Venustiano Carranza, Álvaro Obregón, and Francisco "Pancho" Villa. Carranza tried to seize the initiative by calling a constitutional convention at Aguascalientes in October 1914. When Carranza and other prosperous revolutionaries found themselves outnumbered by delegates supportive of a more assertive agenda of socioeconomic reform, however, Carranza abandoned the convention and established a provisional government in Veracruz. In hindsight, the last months of 1914 marked the high point of the economic revolutionaries' influence during the civil war. This era is symbolized by the dramatic meeting of Zapata and Villa in Mexico City in December 1914. At that time, it seemed that land reform and other changes would be just around the corner.

Pancho Villa and Emiliano Zapata were at the height of their influence in late 1914.
© Underwood & Underwood/Corbis.

In fact, a kaleidoscope of bickering rebel forces held different portions of Mexican territory. By February 1915, four men simultaneously claimed to be president of Mexico. A mixture of military might and convention engineering would resolve these conflicts. In April 1915, Obregón defeated Villa at the Battle of Celaya. While Villa would fight on for several years, he never again mustered sufficient forces to shape the outcome of the revolution. Zapata's armies were also preoccupied with fighting. In the months ahead, Carranza negotiated alliances with likeminded generals and launched a new constitutional convention at Querétaro in October 1916. This convention culminated in the passage of the 1917 constitution.

The 1917 constitution embodied both ideological strands of the Mexican Revolution: the demands for political reform and the demands for social justice. Madero's call for no reelection echoed beyond the office of the presidency. The prohibition on reelection was extended to executive branch officials at all levels of government and would later be extended to the legislature. Economic demands also found expression in the new constitution. Article 27 enabled the government to engage in land redistribution. Inspired by Zapata's Ayala Plan, the government made the communal *ejido* the vehicle through which landless Mexicans would gain access to redistributed land. The urban labor movement also realized its goal of constitutional protections for the right to organize and the right to strike. The nationalist sentiment underlying both the political and the economic strands of the revolution came together in the government's assertion of ultimate ownership over all subsoil resources.

The Querétaro Convention did not end conflict among the rival generals of the civil war. On the contrary, many leaders would meet violent deaths in the following decade. Emiliano Zapata was betrayed by one of his lieutenants and killed on his way to a meeting in 1919. Venustiano Carranza, who had been elected president in 1917, was hunted down during a military campaign in 1920. Pancho Villa was murdered in 1923. Álvaro Obregón, the general who led the overthrow of Carranza, became the first president to finish his term since Porfirio Díaz. He handed power to another general, Plutarco Calles, in 1924. Obregón later convinced Congress to interpret the 1917 constitution as permitting nonconsecutive terms. Obregón then launched a successful election campaign in 1928 but was assassinated shortly before his inauguration.

The Emergence of the Revolutionary Party (1929–1940)

After the death of Obregón, Plutarco Calles organized a new political movement that tried to stop the cycle of violence by giving the remaining generals a stake in the political system. In 1929, Calles convinced most generals to join the National Revolutionary party (*Partido Nacional Revolucionario* [PNR]). While Calles was genuinely interested in lessening the use of assassination as a political tactic, he also wanted to extend his own political influence. Calles's plan called for him to serve as the central leader of the PNR: he would arbitrate disputes among rivals and play the most important role in selecting the new party's presidential candidates. Because of Calles's role as the *jefe máximo* ("maximum leader") of the PNR, Mexican historians would refer to this system as the *Maximato*.

In the *Maximato*, Calles delegated considerable authority in regional affairs to other leaders but remained the power behind the presidents chosen in this system. Because the PNR elicited the cooperation of major revolutionary figures from across the country, its ability to mobilize voters was unmatched. Calles had created a political party that would govern Mexico without interruption for the next seven decades.

Calles's unquestioned leadership of the PNR did not last nearly as long. In 1934, Calles asked Lázaro Cárdenas to serve as the PNR presidential candidate. Cárdenas had been one of the youngest revolutionary generals and later served as governor of his home state of Michoacán. The thirty-nine-year-old had built a reputation as someone interested in the generally neglected socioeconomic aims of the civil war. Once Cárdenas assumed the presidency, he changed Mexican politics forever.

Lázaro Cárdenas took actions that thrilled many working-class Mexicans. In his six-year term, he redistributed twice as much land as all the presidents since 1917 combined. He also directed substantial sums of money to create an infrastructure to support the *ejidos* created out of this land redistribution. As Juan Perón would do a decade later in Argentina, Cárdenas used executive branch authority to resolve many labor conflicts in favor of the unions—raising their wages and improving their working conditions. Because Cárdenas feared that Calles might lead an effort to unseat him, he asked grateful workers and peasants to form a citizens' militia to protect his government. By the time Calles tried to mobilize opposition, Cárdenas's organizational strength and rising popularity deterred most generals from rising against him. Cárdenas forced a bitter Calles into exile in 1936. Meanwhile, a triumphant Cárdenas went on to dramatize the antiforeign bent of the revolution by nationalizing the oil sector in 1938, thus creating a new government-owned monopoly called *Petróleos Mexicanos* (PEMEX).

While these economic reforms cemented Cárdenas's popularity with ordinary Mexicans, his political reforms had an even more lasting influence. Cárdenas transformed the PNR from an elite party filled with generals into a modern mass political party that organized most of society along state corporatist lines (review *Concepts in Action: Pluralist and Corporatist Interest Group Politics* in Chapter Six). The new party had four main branches representing nearly all sectors of society—the military, peasants, blue-collar workers, and white-collar workers. The core constituency of the PNR, the military, became one of four pillars of the new movement. Peasants were organized into the National Peasant Confederation (*Confederación Nacional Campesina* [CNC]) while blue-collar workers joined the Mexican Workers Confederation (*Confederación de Trabajadores Mexicanos* [CTM]). White-collar workers formed a national confederation that would eventually be called the National Confederation of Popular Organizations (*Confederación Nacional de Organizaciones Populares* [CNOP]). To highlight the changes, the PNR was renamed the Mexican Revolutionary party (*Partido Revolucionario Mexicano* [PRM]) in 1938. This state corporatist structure—buttressed by Cárdenas's popularity and the government's growing role in the economy—formed a massive political machine that could reward its supporters while punishing its opponents.

The last act of Cárdenas's presidency perhaps proved more central to the survival of one-party rule than all of his other decisions. Rather than running for reelection (as Obregón had done) or pursuing indirect rule through other presidents (as Calles had done), Cárdenas surprised many observers by choosing Manuel Ávila Camacho as the party's next presidential candidate. Cárdenas would serve as a living reminder of the no-reelection principle to the generation of politicians that followed. Until his death in 1970, Cárdenas remained a respected leader in the so-called revolutionary family of party elders who were consulted informally. His willingness to walk away from the presidency set the tone for the next six decades: presidents would enjoy tremendous authority in office (including the so-called *dedazo* in which the president had the final word on naming the party's next presidential candidate), but then they would be expected to suppress any remaining presidential ambitions.

The PRI and the Mexican Miracle (1940–1970)

After Cárdenas's many reforms, the instability of the revolutionary era gave way to a period of prolonged political stability. Cárdenas's successor, Manuel Ávila Camacho, would be the last former general to serve as president. In 1946, as open conflict subsided, the PRM abolished its military wing and renamed itself the Institutional Revolutionary party (*Partido Revolucionario Institucional* [PRI]). This institutionalized movement now known as the PRI held power for the next three decades through a largely consistent approach to the pursuit of development, liberty, and governance.

In economic policy, the PRI pursued state capitalism. The government expanded its recently nationalized oil sector and launched state-owned enterprises in public utilities, steel, and several other sectors. The government employed an import-substituting industrialization (ISI) model in which high tariff barriers, controls on foreign investment, and government subsidies all worked toward the expansion of the manufacturing sector. With considerable policy continuity from one president to the next (in comparison with most Latin American countries), the ISI model achieved several of its objectives in Mexico. The PRI took pride in its ability to maintain high growth with low inflation. From 1940 to 1970, the economy grew at an annual average rate of 6 percent; GDP per capita rose by over 3 percent per year. This so-called Mexican miracle had its shortcomings, however. As occurred in Brazil, high growth slightly reduced poverty, but income inequality worsened during these three decades.

In the realm of liberty, the PRI permitted a diversity of ideological expressions provided that one remained loyal to the party itself. To retain the support of the citizenry, the party employed a carrot-and-stick approach. The state corporatist structure of the PRI gave party activists ample opportunity to interact with citizens from all walks of life. People willing to support the PRI could hope to gain access to a small portion of the economic resources directly (or indirectly) managed by government officials. Conversely, those disloyal to the party or openly opposed to the PRI faced potential problems. At a minimum, their chances of getting government to make decisions in their favor were limited. If one openly organized opposition to the regime, one faced the possibility of verbal intimidation and sometimes violent coercion or illegal detention. *Governing Strategies: Adolfo Ruiz Cortines* discusses the diverse governance tactics used by one president during this period.

For most of this period, the growing economy and the government's willingness to dole out economic favors proved sufficient to convince most citizens not to challenge the PRI's continuing dominance of all branches and levels of government. The PRI's use of transactional politics took patron-clientelism to a new level—transforming most of the country into a patchwork of interrelated political machines. The line between the party and the government evaporated. There was no meaningful check on authority because the PRI's control of the

GOVERNING STRATEGIES
Adolfo Ruiz Cortines

The presidency of Adolfo Ruiz Cortines provides a window into the PRI's carrot-and-stick approach to politics. Ruiz Cortines spent his entire adult life within the political movement forged by the Mexican revolution. At age twenty-two he entered the conflict after Francisco Madero's execution in 1913. Ruiz Cortines served in Venustiano Carranza's forces during the civil war. Then he served as a government bureaucrat, rising to become chief administrative officer of Mexico City by 1935. He showed an ability to work with a diverse group of political interests and was recruited to run for state office in 1937. In 1940, he was the treasurer for Manuel Ávila Camacho's presidential campaign. Ruiz Cortines joined the cabinet and remained there until he was named the PRI's candidate for governor of Veracruz in 1944. In 1948, he resigned as governor to join the cabinet of President Miguel Alemán. Then, in 1951, Alemán chose the veteran politician as the PRI's presidential candidate for the 1952 elections.

Adolfo Ruiz Cortines rose to power through his ability to make compromises along the way. He remarked, "[I]n politics, the shortest line between two points is a curve."[1] Ruiz Cortines had an apparently well-earned reputation for personal honesty but proved comfortable working with a wide variety of people and situations. Now that he held the most powerful post in the political system, Ruiz Cortines (like his predecessors) insisted that the diverse forces inside and outside the PRI respect the ultimate authority of the president. In dealing with state governors, he followed the practice used by Miguel Alemán: Ruiz Cortines either imposed his preferred candidates in the next gubernatorial elections or he replaced disobedient governors with appointees more to his liking. In the Mexican Congress, the president similarly had the final word. He approved legislative candidates and tolerated minimal dissent: 95 percent of the Chamber of Deputies voted in favor of every bill proposed by the Ruiz Cortines administration.

Interest group leaders needed to support the president to receive favorable treatment. Members of the PRI-sponsored peasant movement (the CNC) received parcels from several large estates purchased from foreigners. In contrast, the outspoken leader of the sugar workers union, Rubén Jaramillo, faced an arrest order in 1954 and was driven into hiding. When the government devalued the peso in December 1954, the PRI-sponsored labor confederation (the CTM) called for a wage increase (because the devaluation increased the cost of imported goods). Ruiz Cortines kept the CTM unions from striking by having his labor minister (Adolfo López Mateos) agree to wage hikes. Conversely, when unions outside the CTM made demands and threatened strikes, the government responded with repression. Riot police broke up many demonstrations. The leader of the dissident teachers union, Othón Salazar, was periodically kidnapped, kept incommunicado for several days, and then released.

[1]Cited in Enrique Krauze, *Mexico, Biography of Power*, trans. Hank Heifetz (New York: HarperCollins, 1997), p. 619.

For Salazar and all other politically active individuals, the limits to liberty were marked by the PRI through its control of all levels of government. As for Adolfo Ruiz Cortines, he retired after naming Adolfo López Mateos as the PRI's next presidential candidate. The PRI's nearly absolute power continued, but Ruiz Cortines's had come to an end.

---

national government faced only token electoral opposition. In some instances, the government subsidized small opposition parties that were willing to participate in elections without publicly criticizing the PRI's abuses of power.

In its quest for governance, the PRI combined executive centralism within presidencies and systematic power sharing across presidencies. Within each administration, the president was the unquestioned leader of the entire system. The president enjoyed massive majorities in the legislature, a judiciary filled with PRI appointees, and PRI governors who could be removed from office if they strayed too far from the president's policy line. In addition, the president reserved the final word on all PRI candidates for office. This role within the governing party helped presidents avoid the so-called lame duck scenario in which their inability to run for reelection might have caused them to lose authority over the course of their six-year terms. The president's control over PRI nominations kept most party officials in line as they jockeyed for positions during the next electoral cycle.

If outgoing presidents were to nominate leaders with similar views at the end of each administration, the big ideological tent of the PRI probably would have collapsed rather quickly. However, Cárdenas (the most center-left president to date) set the tone by choosing a centrist, Manuel Ávila Camacho, as the next presidential candidate. In turn, Ávila Camacho selected a center-right candidate, who later chose a centrist, who then named another center-leftist, and so forth. Analysts tend to refer to this practice as the pendulum theory of Mexican politics: rival groups stayed in the PRI because they believed that, eventually, each ideological faction would get its chance to lead the executive branch. Table 10.1 illustrates the shift in presidential candidates across the center-left, centrist, and center-right factions of the party from the 1934 election through the 1970 vote.

Despite the PRI's ongoing dominance, the party's leaders praised their political system as the most stable democracy in Latin America. The government trumpeted Mexico's selection as host for the 1968 Olympic Games as proof of its growing stature among the world's democracies. The PRI's self-congratulatory stance infuriated Mexican citizens willing to criticize various limitations on liberty. Despite the PRI's uninterrupted hold on power, some cracks had begun to show in the system during the course of the 1960s.

The government resorted more frequently to arrest and intimidation to repress criticism from activists in the trade union and student movements. Student protests reached new heights in 1968 when university students in Mexico, the United States, France, and elsewhere mobilized in the name of political change. In late August, students organized the largest antigovernment

TABLE 10.1 Pendulum Politics and the PRI's Presidential Candidates (1934–1970)*

Year	Center-left candidates	Centrist candidates	Center-right candidates
1934	Lázaro Cárdenas		
1940		Manuel Ávila Camacho	
1946			Miguel Alemán
1952		Adolfo Ruiz Cortines	
1958	Adolfo López Mateos		
1964			Gustavo Díaz Ordaz
1970	Luis Echeverría		

*The abbreviation PRI stands for the *Partido Revolucionario Institucional* (Institutional Revolutionary party). The PRI won all presidential elections held during this period.

rally in postrevolutionary Mexico; approximately 500,000 protesters assembled in front of the presidential office. With the Olympic Games approaching, the government ordered security forces to occupy the major public university and to arrest most student leaders. In response, around 8,000 protesters launched an anticrackdown protest on October 2 at the Plaza of the Three Cultures in the Tlatelolco district of Mexico City. Military helicopters dropped flares into the crowd of demonstrators and gunshots rang out in the plaza. Many panicked demonstrators ran headlong into security forces equipped with automatic weapons; somewhere between forty and 300 people died in a matter of minutes. The incident dramatized opposition to the PRI's stranglehold on government as well as the PRI's willingness to use violence against its opponents.

Change and Continuity During the Oil Boom Era (1970–1982)

Although Luis Echeverría bore responsibility for the Tlatelolco massacre as the interior minister in charge of security forces, he campaigned extensively in 1970 in the name of political change. He promised to complete the unfinished business of the Mexican miracle by increasing economic activity in rural Mexico and by expanding the role of opposition voices in Mexican political life. He also promised to incorporate the nation's youth into the political system and to free the jailed leaders of the university student movement.

In the final analysis, most of the political changes undertaken by Echeverría and by his successor, José López Portillo, were cosmetic in nature. Echeverría created a mix of new multiparty and nonpartisan consultative bodies at all levels of government; many leftist and student leaders agreed to serve in these posts. In addition, both Echeverría in 1973 and López Portillo in 1977 increased the size of the Chamber of Deputies to provide more seats for opposition voices. By the late 1970s, 100 new seats (chosen by proportional representation) had been added to the preexisting 300 seats (chosen by plurality). While opposition parties had little chance of winning the plurality seats, they seemed certain to win a healthy percentage of the new seats. Although some had hopes that the PRI was relaxing its grip, over time most observers noted that these reforms served mainly as a vehicle for letting off steam. The opposition's role in policy-making had not expanded meaningfully.

The government also tried to limit discontent by subsidizing new economic opportunities. Echeverría relied on deficit spending to fund several rural development projects. In 1976, the rise in deficit spending helped to trigger the first devaluation of the Mexican peso since 1954. The Mexican economic miracle of price stability and economic growth appeared to be ending. Mounting economic problems began to hamper the government's use of clientelist tactics to maintain support and to silence the opposition.

Renewed economic successes during the 1970s distracted many from the continuing constraints on liberty. The first OPEC-led oil price hike in 1973–1974 spawned an increase in oil exploration around the world because the rise in petroleum prices meant that even marginal holdings could generate profits. In Mexico, expanded oil exploration unearthed billions of barrels of proven oil reserves off the Yucatán Peninsula and in Chiapas. The value of Mexico's newly discovered oil reserves rose further during the second OPEC-led price hike of 1978–1979. Between 1973 and 1979, the price of oil increased elevenfold.

The López Portillo administration (1976–1982) welcomed the oil discoveries and the price increases. The government harnessed the oil bonanza by borrowing heavily from foreign banks. Some of the money went to rush new wells into production, thus tripling oil production during López Portillo's term. His government spent lavishly to subsidize basic consumer goods (including milk and tortillas). López Portillo and other government officials also appear to have spent large sums of money on their own conspicuous consumption (as press exposés would eventually reveal). The Mexico City police chief, Arturo Durazo, had a mansion filled with stylish marble statues and his own private zoo—something like a combination of Citizen Kane's fictional Xanadu estate and Michael Jackson's Neverland Ranch.

When oil prices fell in the early 1980s amid a recession in most major economies, the sharp drop in oil revenues prevented Mexico from keeping up with its growing debt payments. On the so-called Black Friday of August 13, 1982, Mexico's finance minister held a press conference in New York to announce that Mexico was suspending all principal payments on loans for ninety days. The debt crisis of the 1980s had begun (see *Global Perspectives: The Debt Crisis of the 1980s*). López Portillo tried to blame banks for the financial crisis; he nationalized Mexican banks in September 1982. The unexpected decision to nationalize the banks worsened the investment climate and failed to generate much political support. A presidency started in newfound oil wealth and high expectations of a new stage in Mexico's economic development ended in a mixture of despair, controversy, and corruption scandals.

GLOBAL PERSPECTIVES
The Debt Crisis of the 1980s

"When you owe $100 that you cannot repay, you're in trouble. When you owe $100 billion that you cannot pay back, your banker is in trouble." The dark humor in this joke points to a central trait of the 1980s debt crisis: its implications went beyond the borders of several heavily indebted economies in Latin America and elsewhere. The origins of the crisis lay in countries' responses to the petroleum price hikes of 1973–1974 and 1978–1979. Oil prices rose from under $3.00 per barrel in 1973 to over $30.00 per barrel by 1980. Oil producers deposited many of their profits in banks headquartered in the United States and Europe. These banks had a difficult time putting those so-called petrodollars to work because most industrialized countries slowed economic activity (to prevent an inflationary spiral). In response, banks began to offer more loans to governments and firms in less developed countries (LDCs).

In the oil-exporting LDCs (including Mexico and Venezuela), governments took out loans for a wide variety of purposes. In the oil-importing LDCs, governments and firms borrowed to reduce the impact of the oil price hike. Petroleum prices began to fall in 1982, and they kept falling—reaching $14.00 per barrel by 1986. The decline in oil prices coincided with a recession in the industrialized economies that reduced demand for nearly all LDC exports. To make matters worse, many loans had adjustable interest rates that rose amid the recession. The combination of high debt, falling export revenues, and rising interest rates motivated many banks to refuse to grant new loans in early 1982. This policy ignited a latent financial crisis that became evident once Mexico announced in August 1982 that it could not meet its debt payments.

The crisis threatened not just the LDCs but also many major banks in the United States, France, and the United Kingdom that had made numerous loans in the Third World. If depositors pulled out of these banks amid worries that these loans would not be repaid, their actions could trigger a global financial panic. To avoid this scenario, the International Monetary Fund (IMF) lent emergency funds to LDCs that agreed to conditions calling for budgetary austerity. The IMF and the U.S. government also pressured private banks to grant new loans that debtors could use to make current interest payments. When this strategy failed to improve most debtors' situations, U.S. Treasury Secretary James Baker announced in 1986 a new program of debt rescheduling under the condition that recipient LDCs undertake market-oriented reforms. The Baker Plan generated minimal progress toward financial solvency in the indebted LDCs.

In 1989, U.S. Treasury Secretary Nicholas Brady spearheaded a revised approach. The Brady Plan retained the Baker Plan's call for market capitalism but added an inventive debt transformation. Private banks could convert existing loans into publicly tradable bonds (backed by the IMF, the World Bank, and the U.S. government); in exchange, those banks had to forgive a portion of the loan. This approach produced over $200 billion in debt reduction. Why did the Brady Plan succeed where the two previous approaches had failed?

First, embattled LDC governments began to agree to market-oriented conditions that they had rejected in the early years of the crisis. The countries most willing to shift toward market capitalism received the most debt reduction; Mexico was one of few countries to cut its debt service ratio in half. Second, the private banks became more willing to renegotiate because the Brady bonds were more liquid assets and because most banks had already written off many of their bad loans (by using bank profits to repay the loans themselves). By the mid-1990s, LDC debt no longer threatened the stability of banks in the industrialized countries. In the LDCs themselves, however, the legacy of the debt contracted in the 1970s can be seen in the market-oriented economic reforms adopted by most countries and in the persistently high debt levels found in many countries to this day.

The Breakup of the PRI's Revolutionary Family (1982–1988)

José López Portillo chose his budget chief, Harvard-trained Miguel de la Madrid, to run as the PRI's presidential candidate in 1982. The De la Madrid government implemented an economic austerity program to close the budget deficit and to try to resume payment on the debt. The swift reduction in government spending deepened the recession. In 1982, the GDP contracted by 0.6 percent, but in 1983, it shrank another 4.2 percent. When growth resumed in 1984 and 1985, several observers in and out of Mexico began to wonder if the crisis was over. A massive earthquake in central Mexico in September 1985 quelled any such optimism. The earthquake killed thousands, left 300,000 people homeless, and caused billions of dollars in property damage. In 1986, the economy contracted again by nearly 4 percent.

The De la Madrid government responded by embarking on a series of market-oriented economic reforms. The government declared that it would unilaterally dismantle most of its tariff barriers. It applied for entry into the General Agreement on Tariffs and Trade (GATT)—a decision designed to signal the PRI's willingness to continue to reduce tariffs in the future. The government also announced plans to sell various state-owned enterprises. This policy swing embraced the Washington Consensus in support of market capitalism in pursuit of new funding from both intergovernmental financial institutions and private investors.

These major economic reforms moved away from the state capitalist model that had characterized the PRI's economic policies for half a century. This willingness to accept policy ideas favorable to foreign capital violated Mexico's postrevolutionary emphasis on economic nationalism. The center-left portion of the PRI did not take these changes lightly. Instead, critics of the changes formed an internal faction that they called the Democratic Current; they tried to harness party discontent into a rank-and-file vote in favor of a state capitalist candidate for the next presidential elections. The internal opposition included several major figures—including a past chair of the PRI, Porfirio Muñoz Ledo, and Lázaro Cárdenas's son, Cuauhtémoc. Miguel de la Madrid rebuffed his opponents by making it clear that he planned to name another market-oriented politician as the PRI's candidate. In mid-1987, the Democratic Current announced that it would break ranks with the PRI. Cuauhtémoc Cárdenas became the presidential candidate of several small center-left political parties hastily organized into a coalition known as the National Democratic Front (*Frente Democrático Nacional* [FDN]). De la Madrid tried to ensure the continuation of his policy shift in October 1987 by naming another Harvard-trained cabinet minister, Carlos Salinas, to run as the PRI candidate.

The PRI now faced the most serious electoral challenge in its history. The 1988 elections also provided an ideological showdown: Cuauhtémoc Cárdenas used his father's legacy to label his campaign a call for a return to the principles of the Mexican Revolution, while Salinas presented himself as the face of a new Mexico in tune with economic globalization. For the first time in recent memory, Mexicans on election night wondered which party's candidate would emerge victorious as rumors circulated that Cárdenas held the lead in early returns. This sense of anticipation quickly turned to bitter disappointment when the interior minister, Manuel Bartlett, declared that unspecified electronic problems had disrupted the vote-tallying process. Mexicans waited a week until the national election commission announced that Salinas had won the elections with 51 percent of the vote (while Cárdenas was credited with 31 percent). The announcement stunned election observers whose informal quick counts and limited exit polls indicated an extremely close race. Most people concluded that the official election results were fraudulent. Salinas's presidency began under a cloud of illegitimacy.

The PRI held on to the presidency, but the 1988 elections signaled the dawn of a new era in Mexican politics. For the first time, an opposition candidate mounted a serious challenge for the presidency, and several opposition candidates won seats in the Senate. The PRI won only 52 percent of the seats in the Chamber of Deputies. The controversy over the presidential election also spawned calls for improvements in the voting process. The PRI had won the elections but now faced increasingly insistent demands for institutional reforms.

CONTEMPORARY POLITICAL FRAMEWORK

Mexico's current political institutions are based on the 1917 constitution. Francisco Madero launched the Mexican Revolution calling for no reelection in an attempt to end the decades-long domination of government by Porfirio Díaz and his circle of friends. The most distinctive element of the Mexican constitution has endured to this day: no candidate for elected office can run for immediate reelection. The no-reelection principle met its goal of generating a continuing change in the individuals serving in government.

Nevertheless, the informal dynamics of one-party dominance kept Madero's vision of no reelection and effective suffrage from being fully realized. The formal separation of powers ingrained in the constitution never came to life during the PRI's long-standing control of all branches and levels of government. The blurred line between the PRI and the government limited legislators' and judges' autonomy from the president (while it also constrained citizens' autonomy outside the PRI). The PRI's electoral defeat in the 1997 legislative elections and the 2000 presidential elections have set into motion a new era in which the branches of government have begun to function less as appendages of the PRI. The give and take of partisan politics has become increasingly prominent in twenty-first-century Mexico.

The Executive Branch

During the PRI's long, uninterrupted rule, many observers noted that the power of the chief executive knew few limits. Most of that power was intimately linked to the president's informal role as the leading figure within the governing party during the six-year term. Unlike the double-minority scenario common in much of Latin America (review *The Peruvian Experience: Toledo's Search for Governance* in Chapter Four), Mexican presidents during most of the twentieth century won election with substantial majorities; the PRI controlled the entire Senate, all governorships, and the overwhelming majority of the Chamber of Deputies. In turn, presidential control over legislative and gubernatorial candidates gave the chief executive considerable influence over these candidates once they won their respective elections. This influence meant that each president's agenda sailed through the legislature with minimal opposition, as did appointments to judgeships. Another informal tradition further expanded the president's power over the judiciary: by custom, all federal judges tendered their resignations at the outset of a new presidential term, thereby giving each president free rein to bring in personally loyal appointees.

The vast informal authority of Mexican presidents masked the fact that their formal authority is more limited than that of many Latin American chief executives. Under the framework developed by Mainwaring and Shugart (review Table 4.6), the Mexican president's formal powers are largely reactive in nature. The president has a strong veto that can only be overridden by a two-thirds majority of the legislature. The agenda-setting authority of the presidency is limited to the exclusive ability to introduce legislation on spending and revenue collection. The arrival of Vicente Fox to the presidency signaled not only a new style based on campaign promises but also a new approach to governance dictated by the end of one-party rule.

The Legislature

Like most Latin American countries, Mexico has a bicameral legislature. The Chamber of Deputies, the lower house, represents states according to their population size. Deputies serve three-year terms, with the entire chamber going up for election each electoral cycle. Originally, all deputies were chosen by plurality elections in single-member districts. However, reforms in the 1970s and 1980s added another 200 seats to the chamber that are chosen by closed-list proportional representation (PR). As a result, the electoral system for the Chamber of Deputies in the contemporary era is a hybrid system, with 300 deputies elected by plurality and another 200 elected via PR.

A 1993 constitutional reform doubled the size of the Senate. Previously, the upper house consisted of two members from each of thirty-one states plus two for the Federal District of the nation's capital. Beginning with the 1994 elections, thirty-two senators are chosen in a nationwide PR election, and three senators for each state are elected via a majority-minority electoral system in which the party receiving the most votes wins two seats while the second-place party wins the other Senate seat.

The Mexican legislature was overshadowed by the president for years because large PRI majorities supported presidential initiatives with minimal opposition. The complexion of the legislative process changed after the 1997 election, when the PRI lost its majority in the Chamber of Deputies. After his historic victory in the 2000 presidential elections, Vicente Fox faced a legislature in which no party held more than two-fifths of the seats. From the mid-1990s onward, the legislature assumed a higher profile. Some legislators began to discuss the desirability of reforming the constitution to permit the reelection of legislators. Advocates of the reform wanted to improve the capacity of the legislature. By pursuing a career in Congress, politicians could enhance their expertise and political visibility.

The Judiciary

The Supreme Court is the highest court of appeal for all cases. Its eleven justices are appointed for fifteen-year terms. All presidential appointees must have at least ten years of legal experience and must be approved by a two-thirds vote in the Senate. A six-person body, the Federal Council of the Judiciary, appoints justices at other levels of the judicial process.

The Mexican Supreme Court has historically been one of the weakest in the Americas. Its members were beholden to the PRI (and to the person of the president more specifically). In addition, the 1917 constitution tightly constrained the court's ability to set binding legal precedents and did not grant the Supreme Court the power of judicial review.

These components of the constitution were amended in the 1990s during the presidency of Ernesto Zedillo. Now the Supreme Court has judicial review: it can rule that legislation is invalid on the grounds that it is unconstitutional. A related reform permits one-third of the legislature to request that the Supreme Court review the constitutionality of newly passed legislation. Contemporary presidents like Ernesto Zedillo and Vicente Fox have faced several instances in which the courts have ruled in cases that have gone against the executive branch.

POLITICAL PARTICIPATION

During the long period of one-party rule, the PRI's control of the government at all levels profoundly influenced all forms of political participation. From the founding of the revolutionary party until 1988, other political parties held no hope of gaining control of state governments, much less the national government. In turn, the PRI's state corporatist structure tied most of the largest interest groups directly to the party. When independent groups emerged, the PRI used clientelist tactics to try to convince independent interest group leaders to work with the government. If those tactics failed, the PRI resorted to repression in several cases.

After the PRI's controversial victory in the 1988 presidential election, Mexican political life began a process of transformation that culminated in the triumph of opposition presidential candidate Vicente Fox in July 2000. With the end of one-party-rule, several political parties now play an important role in the legislative process. Accordingly, interest group leaders and individual citizens no longer assume that cooperation with the PRI constitutes the lone route to gaining access to government resources.

Interest Groups and Social Movements

The most important business associations—the Confederation of National Chambers of Commerce (*Confederación de Cámaras Nacionales de Comercio* [CONCANACO]) and the Confederation of Chambers of Industry (*Confederación de Cámaras de Industria* [CONCAMIN])—were formed in the late 1930s during Cárdenas's presidency and maintained their stature until the 1980s. Although these groups were not formally members of the PRI, they were established and sustained by government intervention because membership was mandatory. Many business leaders worked informally to support the PRI via personal campaign donations. As Mexico's era of high growth stalled in the early 1980s, the stature of additional business associations outside the corporatist confederations increased considerably. The largest rival organization is the Employer Confederation of the Mexican Republic (*Confederación Patronal de la República Mexicana* [COPARMEX]). Over time, COPARMEX became identified with the call for market-oriented reform. It often supported candidates from the National Action Party (*Partido de Acción Nacional* [PAN]); the PAN's 1988 presidential candidate had served earlier as president of COPARMEX. The context in which business associations operate changed substantially in 1996, when the Supreme Court ruled that businesses could no longer be forced to pay dues to the corporatist associations. From that point onward, the importance of COPARMEX (and several of its member associations) increased, while the role of the other groups declined.

The labor movement historically has held close ties to the PRI and to the government more generally. Members of the CTM were members of the PRI. Nearly half of the CTM's affiliates were either government employees or worked in state-owned enterprises. From the 1940s until his death in 1997, Fidel Velásquez served as the leader of the CTM. During his long tenure, Velásquez reinforced the CTM's support of the PRI. In exchange, he worked to increase the confederation's presence in government; by the 1980s, around 20 percent of the PRI's legislative candidates were CTM leaders. Neither the PRI nor Velásquez expected union leaders to advocate positions at odds with the government. One observer wrote in 1984, "The government treats labor as a firm parent would a teenager. When it needs support in family crises and labor quickly provides it, it rewards the action. But when labor strays away from the family fold, it is scolded in a variety of ways. The government, not organized labor, controls the relationship."[2] The government's ability to limit criticism from labor declined in 1997 when the PRI lost its majority in the legislature and Fidel Velásquez died at age ninety-seven. Shortly after Velásquez's death, independent labor unions formed a new rival confederation, the National Workers Union (*Unión Nacional de Trabajadores* [UNT]). The UNT's nearly 2 million workers make it roughly one-third as large as the CTM. These changes—along with the PRI's defeat in the 2000 presidential election—have eroded the CTM's close ties to the government. In turn, the Supreme Court ruled that the country's closed-shop rules (which gave union leaders the ability to discipline uncooperative members) violated constitutional protection of freedom of association. A new era in organized labor had arrived.

The erosion of the PRI's control over the political system expanded citizens' willingness and ability to launch other independent nongovernmental organizations (NGOs). For years, the government either co-opted independent voices by enticing them to work with the government or marginalized them by shutting off access to all levels of government. After the 1988 elections, more and more citizens, particularly in urban areas, began to pressure for change. In the run-up to the 1994 presidential elections, the Civic Alliance (*Alianza Cívica*) formed as an umbrella organization that would coordinate the activities of many smaller NGOs that wanted to ensure a more transparent electoral process. The group managed to send nonpartisan electoral observers to over 5,000 voting precincts. By 2000, the organization mobilized over 7,000 volunteers to look for irregularities in the voting process. The main leader of the Civic Alliance, Sergio Aguayo, has his roots in human rights activism and has called for enhancements of liberty beyond voting rights during the Fox presidency.

The 1990s also saw the emergence of Mexico's first sustained guerrilla uprising since the revolutionary era. In the predawn hours of January 1, 1994, forces of the Zapatista Army of National Liberation (*Ejército Zapatista de Liberación Nacional* [EZLN]) took several communities in the poor southern state of Chiapas. The Zapatistas timed their incursion to coincide with the date that the North American Free Trade Agreement (NAFTA) entered into effect. The EZLN asserted that the PRI had become a new variant on the *Porfiriato* because voting rights and other civil liberties were not respected, foreign capital was welcomed at the expense of national interests, landownership was increasingly concentrated, and the needs of indigenous peoples were not met. Many observers have described the EZLN as a new form of guerrilla organization because of its extensive use of electronic media and because of its eclectic set of demands focused on voting rights, indigenous rights, and sustainable development. Later in this chapter, we will examine the interaction between the government and the Zapatistas during each of the presidencies of the contemporary era.

Parties and Elections

As noted in the background section of this chapter, the PRI constituted the most important political party in twentieth-century Mexico. The party's roots date back to the revolutionary generals organized by Plutarco Calles. One of those generals, Lázaro Cárdenas, transformed the organization into a corporatist political party with a large mass membership across all sectors of society. Over the rest of the century, the PRI used its control of the government in myriad ways to maintain its hold on power. Until the late 1980s, the government held a monopoly on newsprint; it threatened to stop shipments to newspapers deemed too critical of the PRI. For decades, no other party was permitted to use all three colors (red, white, and green) of the Mexican flag in its party symbols. Every election cycle, government funds would be spent lavishly to promote the PRI's candidates. In short, the PRI was a party of winners who maintained party loyalty and voter support on the long-running assumption that the PRI would continue to control all levels of government. As the PRI's electoral invincibility decayed over the course of the 1980s and 1990s, divisions within the party became increasingly visible. The dominance of market-oriented, technocratic politicians that began with Miguel de la Madrid's presidency continued into the next decade at the national level, while more traditional, nonideological politicians dominated the PRI's activity in most states. This division in the PRI between the technocrats and the old-style politicos continues into the twenty-first century. Several analysts predicted after Fox's victory that the so-called free-market "smurfs" and state capitalist "dinosaurs" would break away into separate parties, but this prediction had not come true as of May 2004. Instead, the PRI gained seats in the 2003 legislative elections.

For decades, the most visible electoral opposition to the PRI's continued dominance came from the PAN. The PAN formed in 1939 in reaction to the expansion of state capitalist economic policies undertaken by Lázaro Cárdenas. The party's founders emphasized a greater role for the market but also a more important role for the Catholic church. Initially, the party fielded candidates primarily at the local level. But from 1958 onward (with the notable exception of the watershed 1988 elections), the PAN served as the main electoral opposition to the PRI in federal, state, and local elections. The PRI shifted toward a market orientation in the 1980s, and this policy change robbed the PAN of one of its historical policy demands. From that time onward, the PAN presented itself as the party of clean government that would eliminate electoral fraud and reduce government corruption. The economic ideas within the party became increasingly diverse: some favored an even more radical reduction in government's role; others (led by Fox) called for a general market orientation combined with targeted welfare spending and improvements in education and other government services. After the 2003 midterm legislative elections, it was unclear whether the PAN's next presidential candidate would come from its conservative or its moderate wing.

The third major party in the political system has a much shorter history than the PRI and the PAN. The Democratic Revolutionary Party (*Partido Revolucionario Democrático* [PRD]) was established from several components of the center-left coalition of small parties that supported Cuauhtémoc Cárdenas's candidacy in 1988. When the PRD's share of the vote receded in the 1991 and 1994 elections, party factionalism became a more prominent issue, and two distinct groups emerged to challenge Cárdenas for leadership of the party. After Cárdenas ran and lost as the party's presidential candidate for a third consecutive time in 2000, most observers predicted that it would be nearly impossible for him to run again in 2006.

Table 10.2 presents the presidential elections that took place during the pivotal era from 1988 through 2000. As discussed earlier, many people disputed the official election results for 1988, in which Carlos Salinas was declared the winner after a one-week delay. However, Cuauhtémoc Cárdenas did not maintain the momentum established in 1988. When the PRD's support waned in the 1991 legislative elections, the PAN once again emerged as the strongest challenger to the PRI. PAN candidate Diego Fernández de Cevallos called for "a Mexico without lies." The 1994 campaign took place in a tense atmosphere marked by the outbreak of guerrilla warfare in southern Mexico and the assassination of the PRI candidate, Luis Colosio, during a campaign appearance in Tijuana. After

TABLE 10.2 Mexican Presidential Elections (1988, 1994, and 2000): Percentage of Popular Vote, by Party*

Party	1988	1994	2000
PRI	51	50	36
PAN	17	26	43
PRD	31	17	17
Others	1	7	4

*In 1988, the PRD participated in the elections as the National Democratic Front (*Frente Democrático Nacional* [FDN]); the PRD was formed the following year.

SOURCE: Political Database of the Americas <http://www.georgetown.edu/pdba/Elecdata/Chile/chile.html> (accessed on November 14, 2003).

Colosio's death, the PRI named another soft-spoken, foreign-trained, ex-budget chief—Ernesto Zedillo—as its presidential candidate. He emphasized the PRI's proven ability to govern in tough times while he criticized the other parties' lack of experience. This approach—along with the PRI's traditional use of clientelist voter mobilization—spurred Zedillo to victory. Although nonpartisan electoral observers reported several irregularities, none alleged that the problems were so widespread as to affect the outcome of the presidential race. Zedillo won the presidency with far less controversy than had Salinas. In the 2000 election, the PRI's Francisco Labastida found it difficult to frame a compelling campaign message, while the PAN found a more colorful candidate. Vicente Fox took full advantage of his varied experiences as a state governor, cattle rancher, and business executive (with Coca-Cola's subsidiary in Mexico). Fox peppered his speeches with slang expressions while simultaneously presenting himself as a pragmatist who spoke English and had experience dealing with foreigners. He said that his campaign was in favor of *el cambio* ("the change")—a slogan referring to an end to one-party rule. Many Mexicans voted for the PAN for the first time in their lives in July 2000.

Historically, the PRI enjoyed massive majorities in the legislature. From its founding until 1988, the party always controlled more than two-thirds of both houses, thereby enabling the PRI to amend the constitution without the support of the political opposition. This dominant position ended with the 1988 election, in which the PRI barely retained a majority in the Chamber of Deputies (see Table 10.3). In 1991 and 1994, the PRI regrouped and managed to increase its majority slightly. The 1997 election marked the beginning of the end of one-party rule, however, because the PRI lost its majority in the lower house. The 2000 election also produced a divided legislature in which no party

TABLE 10.3 Mexican Chamber of Deputies (1988–2003): Percentage of Seats Won, by Party*

Party	1988	1991	1994	1997	2000	2003
PRI	52	64	60	48	42	45
PAN	20	18	24	24	41	31
PRD	15	13	14	25	11	19
Others	12	5	2	3	6	6

*In 1988, the PRD participated in the elections as a coalition of parties organized as a coalition known as the National Democratic Front (*Frente Democrático Nacional* [FDN]); the PRD was formed the following year. Percentages do not always add up to 100 percent because of rounding.

SOURCE: For the years 1988–2000, data are from the Political Database of the Americas <http://www.georgetown.edu/pdba/Elecdata/Mexico/mexico.html> (accessed on November 14, 2003). For 2003, data are from the Elections Around the World website <http://www.electionworld.org/mexico.htm> (accessed on November 14, 2003).

controlled the lower house. The PAN enjoyed its best election ever in 2000, but it could not build on that success in the 2003 midterm elections. Instead, amid slow economic growth and frustration with the speed of change during the Fox administration, the PRI rallied to expand its contingent of deputies. While Fox spent the first half of his term hoping to gain a majority in the lower house, he declared after his party's defeat in 2003 that he would redouble his efforts to make policy compromises with opposition parties.

THE CONTEMPORARY QUEST FOR DEVELOPMENT, LIBERTY, AND GOVERNANCE

The presidency of Miguel de la Madrid (1982–1988) marked a turning point in Mexico's pursuit for development, liberty, and governance. Prior to 1982, Mexico's state capitalist path to development had produced high growth (although its success in the 1970s was due mainly to newfound oil wealth). The PRI had a distinctive approach to liberty in which multiple parties and points of view could exist provided that one did not pose an open challenge to the PRI's uninterrupted dominance of the political system. With competition from outside the PRI marginalized, the major potential obstacle to governance lay in the challenge of keeping this big tent political party working together. From Lázaro Cárdenas onward, presidents held their internal opponents at bay with the use of pendulum politics.

During De la Madrid's presidency, all three of these distinctive characteristics of postrevolutionary Mexico were lost. First, the state capitalist model struggled to overcome the burdens posed by the debt crisis and the 1985 earthquake. De la Madrid responded by beginning a shift toward market-oriented economic reform. For the first time in the PRI's history, the gross domestic product was no bigger at the end of a six-year-term than it had been when the president took office. Second, the controversial 1988 election shattered the PRI's claim to electoral invincibility. It seemed that clientelist voter mobilization had proven insufficient and that the party engaged in the most widespread electoral fraud in its history. Bitterness over this outcome sparked greater demands for increased procedural protections for political liberties. Third, the pendulum approach to governance came to a halt when De la Madrid named his budget chief as the next PRI candidate. Like De la Madrid, Carlos Salinas was a foreign-trained, market-oriented technocrat with no experience in elective office prior to becoming a presidential candidate.

The Quest for Development in Mexico

The 1988 electoral controversy did not deter Salinas from his plans to deepen the market-oriented reforms begun under De la Madrid. He supported Mexico's application for entry into the GATT and continued the privatization program.

By pursuing these economic reforms, Salinas hoped to improve his position in ongoing debt negotiations with Mexico's creditors. In July 1989, Mexico became the first country to participate in the Brady Plan (review *Global Perspectives: The Debt Crisis of the 1980s* on pages 339–340). In exchange for its economic liberalization, Mexico renegotiated its foreign debt on more favorable terms, reducing its debt service burden by 14 percent immediately and by 36 percent over the next two years (see Table 10.4).

TABLE 10.4 Mexican Economic Indicators (1983–2002)*

Year	GDP growth	Inflation	Unemployment	Debt service ratio[†]
1983	−4.2	81	6.6	38
1984	3.6	59	5.7	39
1985	2.6	64	4.4	37
1986	−3.8	106	4.3	38
1987	1.9	159	3.9	30
1988	1.2	52	3.5	33
1989	3.3	20	2.9	28
1990	4.4	30	2.9	24
1991	4.2	19	2.7	18
1992	3.7	12	2.8	18
1993	1.8	8	3.4	19
1994	4.4	7	3.7	18
1995	−6.1	52	6.2	15
1996	5.4	28	5.5	13
1997	6.8	16	3.7	11
1998	5.1	19	3.2	10
1999	3.6	12	2.5	9
2000	6.7	9	2.2	8
2001	−0.3	4	2.5	8
2002	0.8	6	2.7	8

*All numbers are percentages.

[†]The debt service ratio expresses interest paid on foreign debts as a percentage of total exports.

SOURCE: For the years 1983–1987, data are from United Nations Economic Commission for Latin America and the Caribbean, *Preliminary Overview of the Economies of Latin America and the Caribbean 1989* (Santiago, Chile: United Nations Publications, 1989). For the years 1988–1992, data are from United Nations Economic Commission for Latin America and the Caribbean, *Preliminary Overview of the Economies of Latin America and the Caribbean 1994* (Santiago, Chile: United Nations Publications, 1994). For the years 1993–1997, data are from United Nations Economic Commission for Latin America and the Caribbean, *Preliminary Overview of the Economies of Latin America and the Caribbean 1999* (Santiago, Chile: United Nations Publications, 1999). For the years 1998–2002, data are from United Nations Economic Commission for Latin America and the Caribbean, *Preliminary Overview of the Economies of Latin America and the Caribbean 2003* (Santiago, Chile: United Nations Publications, 2003).

The biggest changes would come later in Salinas's presidency. In 1990, the Mexican government began negotiating a free-trade agreement (FTA) with its largest trading partner, the United States. Salinas proposed the mutual elimination of all tariff barriers with its economically powerful northern neighbor. As initial talks began, Canada (having recently signed its own FTA with the United States in 1988) pushed for the creation of a trilateral North American Free Trade Agreement (NAFTA). The trade negotiations and treaty ratification process dominated Salinas's presidency. To demonstrate his willingness to open the agricultural sector, Salinas pushed to amend land tenure rights on *ejidos,* thus opening the door to the reconcentration of landownership. Over the course of 1991–1992, the Mexican negotiators made many nontariff concessions (including opening the financial sector to foreign entry and increasing legal protections for foreign patents and trademarks) in pursuit of U.S. approval of NAFTA. The Mexican government also hired a team of Washington-based lobbyists to help persuade the U.S. Congress to ratify the agreement in 1993. After U.S. ratification, Salinas presented himself to fellow Mexicans and to the world as a champion of free trade. Salinas hoped to become the first director-general of the newly created World Trade Organization (WTO) once his presidency ended in late 1994.

Despite the triumphant tone of the Salinas administration, the economic situation in Mexico proved decidedly more fragile than some had believed in 1993. Three major developments in 1994 devastated the Mexican economy. First, the Zapatista uprising raised the prospect of even more widespread rebellion while simultaneously drawing attention to ongoing discontent with market-oriented policies. Second, the assassination of two major PRI leaders—presidential candidate Luis Colosio in March and party chief José Francisco Ruiz Massieu in September—increased the perception of political instability. For example, when the special prosecutor investigating Ruiz Massieu's assassination announced on November 15, 1994, that his work was being obstructed to cover up PRI politicians' involvement, investors pulled over $1.5 billion out of the country in a couple of days. Third, the PRI's victory in the 1994 presidential election was offset by economic problems. Salinas's government sold increasing numbers of dollar-denominated bonds to cover its lavish spending in pursuit of voter support. The rising total of short-term, dollar-denominated bonds constituted a bill that would come due early in the next presidency.

These three factors combined to reduce Mexico's hard currency reserves. Prior to the Colosio assassination, the government held nearly $30 billion in reserves; by October 1994, reserves had fallen below $20 billion. During November, rumors circulated that the government's next report on reserves would place the figure at below $10 billion. With dwindling reserves and a ballooning budget, more and more investors pulled out of Mexico. This chain of events put enormous pressure on the Mexican peso, but a proud Salinas refused to devalue. Thus, Salinas handed the emerging economic crisis to his successor, Ernesto Zedillo, who was inaugurated on December 1, 1994.

CONCEPTS IN ACTION
Exchange Rate Policy

The exchange rate expresses the value of a country's currency relative to another currency. When Ernesto Zedillo took office on December 1, 1994, one U.S. dollar was worth 3.44 Mexican pesos. What makes an exchange rate go up or down? First, an exchange rate is shaped by the demand for goods, services, and capital available in one country relative to that country's demands for foreign goods, services, and capital. In short, a country's exchange rate is tied to its balance of payments. Second, the exchange rate is also linked to cross-national trends in inflation rates. If prices rise faster in Mexico than they do in the United States, then the Mexican peso is likely to lose value relative to the U.S. dollar, all other factors being equal. Third, exchange rates are colored by people's perceptions of the current and future value of different currencies. To maintain confidence in their respective currencies, each government's central bank holds large amounts of foreign currencies (and precious metals) as exchange reserves.

If a government promises to maintain a given exchange rate, it is pursuing a fixed exchange rate policy. This approach can provide a stable economic environment, but it is difficult to maintain over time because of changes in the three aforementioned factors: the balance of payments, inflation rates, and human perceptions. If firms and individuals at home and abroad lose confidence in a currency, fixed rates can come under attack, which is what happened to Argentina's fixed one-to-one exchange rate with the U.S. dollar during 2001. Residents and foreigners sold Argentine pesos in exchange for dollars. The Argentine central bank began to spend its reserves to defend the fixed rate. This policy continued until January 2002, when the government announced that it would no longer defend the fixed exchange rate. Instead, the Argentine government devalued the peso, permitting it to lose value relative to other currencies.

If a government announces that it will let market transactions determine exchange rates, it is implementing a free-float policy. In a free float, the central bank does not sell its reserves to defend the exchange rate. This approach eliminates the loss of reserves associated with speculative runs against a fixed-rate policy. It also implies, however, that government has abandoned the goal of a stable economic environment. Normally, free floats are used to permit devaluation. Sometimes governments devalue because they believe that a run is forthcoming and sometimes because they want to improve their balance of trade. With the devaluation of the Argentine peso in 2002, Argentine exports to Brazil (its major trading partner) became cheaper and Brazilian imports grew more expensive. After the devaluation occurs, governments typically abandon the free float because they are unwilling to accept the continued risk of sharp fluctuations in exchange rates.

From the late 1970s on, most countries have pursued managed-float exchange rate policies. The government allows market transactions to determine exchange rates, but the central bank will be an (often) active participant in that market—buying its own currency to prevent major devaluations and selling its own currency to prevent major revaluations.

Absolute stability is replaced by the goal of relative stability. In addition to avoiding the worst-case scenario of a run against a fixed rate, the managed float can be used to adjust exchange rates gradually (in response to changes in the balance of payments, inflation, and/or market speculation). Nevertheless, managed floats are no panacea. The Mexican government was pursuing a managed-float policy when investors began to sell pesos in larger and larger amounts over the second half of 1994. The Zedillo government initially responded on December 19 by shifting the range of exchange rate values it was willing to defend. When this approach failed to stop the run, the government announced a free float on December 21 that lasted through early 1995. By January 30, 1995, one U.S. dollar was worth 6.37 Mexican pesos.

The rising pressure on the Mexican peso exploded during the first month of Zedillo's term. The government's exchange rate policy was under the microscope (see *Concepts in Action: Exchange Rate Policy*). After taking office, Zedillo and his cabinet spent nearly every day denying rumors that they would devalue the peso. Then, on December 19, premature press reports that the Zapatistas had expanded their territory shook jittery investors into another selloff of peso-denominated assets. In a hastily organized meeting that evening with business and labor leaders, Zedillo's economic team discussed three options: (1) pursue a **fixed exchange rate** policy by continuing to defend the current exchange rate (and likely lose most remaining reserves over the next few weeks), (2) change to a **managed float** to devalue the currency by around 15 percent (to meet market predictions of a devaluation), and (3) shift to a **free float** policy (thus permitting the peso to devalue according to the demand for pesos). The government's economic advisers initially recommended a free float but ultimately sided with business calls for a modest **devaluation** aimed at minimizing the loss of national purchasing power. This initial devaluation went poorly because many Mexican investors sold pesos, thus forcing the government to use precious reserves to defend the new exchange rate. By December 21, another $4 billion left the country and the government announced that it would float the peso. This move caused further panic, and the peso lost nearly half its value by mid-January.

The peso crisis imposed losses on many U.S. investment funds with holdings in Mexico, hurt U.S. exports to Mexico, and began to send shock waves to other Latin American financial markets. The U.S. government cobbled together a $50 billion rescue package of loan guarantees and fresh money for Mexico to stabilize its currency and to make its current debt payments. The U.S. government promised $20 billion in new loans, while the IMF pledged $17.8 billion. In exchange, the Mexican government agreed to budget cuts and took the unprecedented step of providing shares in its oil reserves as collateral for the U.S. loan.

The financial crisis and subsequent budget cuts shook the economy to its core. The economy shrank by 6.1 percent in 1995, consumer prices rose by

52 percent, and unemployment increased by over 67 percent. Businesses went bankrupt, individuals could not make their loan payments, and many Mexicans struggled to survive. Over the rest of Zedillo's term, the economy stabilized, but the memory of the chaos at the outset of his presidency was not erased by the economic growth that followed.

The major poverty reduction initiative during Zedillo's presidency was the launching of the Education, Health, and Nutrition Program (*Programa de Educación, Salud, y Alimentación* [PROGRESA]. The initiative mirrored policy changes under Fernando Henrique Cardoso's presidency in Brazil: the government targeted support to families with school-age children. In exchange for assistance, the children had to remain enrolled in school. By the end of Zedillo's presidency, PROGRESA extended assistance to nearly 3 million families.

Vicente Fox's campaign platform contained an array of ambitious economic goals. He promised to create millions of jobs by promoting economic growth. He wanted to lower the inflation rate to 3 percent by 2003 and to balance the budget by 2004. At the same time, Fox pledged to increase spending on education by 67 percent while also increasing other social spending. Fox planned to combine fiscal responsibility with higher government spending by increasing tax revenues by over 50 percent—from 11 percent of GDP to around 17 percent.

Fox completed the first half of his six-year term on December 1, 2003. His plan to combine balanced budgets with increased social spending was made difficult by two events. First, economic growth in the United States slowed to a trickle during 2001–2003. This economic stagnation in Mexico's largest trading partner reduced the rate of growth in Mexico, thereby making it more difficult to balance the budget while increasing spending. The Mexican economy grew by 1 percent annually during 2001–2003 and unemployment rose. Second, Fox's ambitious tax reform package did not find support in a divided legislature. To make matters worse for Fox, the PAN lost one-fourth of its seats in the Chamber of Deputies after losing the 2003 midterm election. After his party's defeat, Fox promised to improve his efforts to compromise with opposition parties in pursuit of legislative support for his tax reforms.

In its contemporary quest for development, Mexico began the 1980s flush with optimism driven by the oil boom of the 1970s. By 1982, hope had turned to despair because Mexico's economic fortunes took a turn for the worse. The onset of the debt crisis called into question the sustainability and desirability of the state capitalist model that Mexico had pursued since the 1930s. Initially, the De la Madrid government attempted to escape the crisis through fiscal austerity alone, but by the mid-1980s the government embraced market-oriented reform. This reform process continued under Carlos Salinas: the privatization program expanded, tariff levels decreased further, and Mexico entered the North American Free Trade Agreement. Ernesto Zedillo and Vicente

Fox subsequently maintained the central components of the market-oriented model. As a result, compared to the other countries examined in detail in this book, Mexico has applied the market capitalist model longer than every country except Chile.

Has this fairly consistent use of more market-oriented policies helped to achieve economic development? During Salinas's term, several short-term objectives of the move to the market were achieved. By meeting the market-oriented conditions for the Brady Plan, Mexico reduced its debt burden substantially. In turn, economic growth rates rose while the inflation rate fell from 52 percent to 7 percent.

However, these economic policies cannot be considered an unmitigated success story. The peso crisis that erupted when Ernesto Zedillo took office in December 1994 made it clear that Mexico's economic fortunes were vulnerable to swings in the confidence of the domestic and international financial community. The effects of the peso crisis also wiped away the small progress in poverty reduction and income redistribution that had occurred during the first part of the 1990s. Zedillo's government presided over an economic recovery, but the renewed economic growth with low inflation in the late 1990s returned poverty rates to the levels experienced before the debt crisis. During both the Salinas and Zedillo presidencies, income inequality increased slightly. The election of Vicente Fox raised expectations that his presidency would reduce poverty substantially, but these hopes went unfilled during the first half of his term. Instead, the economy stagnated.

The Quest for Liberty in Mexico

The primary issue in the quest for liberty at the outset of Carlos Salinas's term was the electoral process. Protests and formal complaints regarding the 1988 presidential election called for political reforms. In 1989, the Salinas government changed the composition of the Federal Electoral Commission so that the PRI's representatives would no longer automatically constitute a majority. In addition, the PRI recognized its electoral defeat to the PAN in the 1989 gubernatorial election in the state of Baja California Norte, which marked the first time that the PRI lost a governorship. The next year, additional reforms improved oversight procedures for future elections by replacing the Federal Electoral Commission, which reported to the minister of the interior, with a new semiautonomous body called the Federal Electoral Institute (*Instituto Federal Electoral* [IFE]). The new institute was charged with creating a new voter registration list and a photo identification process before the 1994 election. Despite these procedural changes, the government faced protests alleging fraudulent PRI victories in two gubernatorial races in 1991. Salinas stepped in to remove the controversial PRI candidates. In San Luis Potosí, he appointed a different PRI politician; in Guanajuato he installed the PAN candidate. As the

NAFTA negotiations continued, Salinas tried to present himself as a political reformer.

It is important to note the limits to Salinas's initial wave of political reforms. While the newly formed IFE was less overtly controlled by the government than was its predecessor, many of the organizations that appointed people to the IFE governing board were still controlled by PRI loyalists. In addition, the 1990 electoral law that created the IFE also retained the so-called governability clause. The governability clause had been inserted into the electoral rules for the Chamber of Deputies in 1987 to ensure that the PRI would retain its majority. The clause stipulated that if a party earned a majority of the 300 plurality seats, it would have to be assigned enough of the 200 PR seats to control at least a total of 251 seats among the 500 seats in the lower house. Under Salinas, the governability clause was rewritten so that if a party earned 35 percent of the national vote, it would automatically receive a majority in the Chamber of Deputies. By retaining the governability clause, Salinas attempted to preserve the PRI's hold on all branches of government.

Several factors forced the Salinas government to make additional political reforms during his last two years in office. The international attention stemming from the NAFTA talks put electoral reform back on the agenda. In fall 1993, the PRI agreed to eliminate the controversial governability clause. It also took steps to make the IFE board more independent of the government and created the majority-minority electoral system for the Senate, thereby guaranteeing a presence in the upper house for the opposition. The political reform process did not end there. Strident criticism from the EZLN rebels during early 1994, along with the fear of disorder reignited by the assassination of Luis Colosio, increased the pressure for additional reform. The three major political parties agreed to make the IFE into a largely nonpartisan body in which independent appointees unaffiliated with political parties would constitute 55 percent of the IFE's board of directors. The limit for campaign spending was cut by 80 percent. With these changes, the PRI's electoral advantages in 1994 centered on its continuing dominance of media coverage and its ability to mobilize government resources in support of its candidates.

The quest for liberty during Ernesto Zedillo's presidency took place in two principal arenas: the extension of political reform and the ongoing efforts to end the Zapatista rebellion. Zedillo made much more progress in the first arena than he did in the second. In early 1995, the government began to meet with leaders from the PAN and the PRD; the process of electoral reform was completed in 1996. The IFE became completely autonomous because its head would no longer be named by the government. This move minimized remaining fears that the PRI might be able to block unfavorable election results. In addition, the hybrid electoral system was modified so that a party would need to win 42 percent of the plurality seats in the lower house to gain enough of the PR seats to win an overall majority in the Chamber of Deputies. This reform paved the way for the PRI's subsequent loss of its majority in the 1997 midterm elections: had the old rule been in place, the PRI would have retained control of the Chamber of Deputies.

Political reform did not stop there. Zedillo decided to eliminate one of the principal informal powers of the presidency—the *dedazo*. Rather than appointing the PRI's next presidential candidate, Zedillo sanctioned an open primary election in which all citizens could vote. While many observers asserted that Zedillo still used money and organizational resources to back the primary winner, Francisco Labastida, this presidential primary deepened a process of internal party reform that was already under way in some states.

The other major debate over liberty was framed by the Zapatista rebellion in Chiapas. Shortly after Zedillo took office, the military launched a new offensive in February 1995. The campaign failed to dislodge the EZLN from most of its strongholds. The Zedillo government then reopened negotiations with the Zapatistas in which both sides agreed to discuss several subjects sequentially: indigenous rights and culture, democracy and justice, social welfare and development, women's rights, reconciliation in Chiapas, and a cessation of hostilities. After months of talks, the government and the EZLN signed the San Andrés Accords on February 16, 1996. The accords called for constitutional recognition of indigenous peoples, steps to improve the living conditions for indigenous peoples, and a structure for self-government. This agreement marked the high point of optimism regarding a potentially peaceful resolution of the conflict during Zedillo's presidency. Some reports in the U.S. media inaccurately made it seem as if these accords were the last stage (rather than the first stage) in the peace process.

The events that followed destroyed that optimism. Although formal talks began regarding democracy and justice, the EZLN's efforts to discuss national political reform (and to involve national political movements in the negotiations) were rejected by the government. In August, government negotiators declared that they had no intention of meeting the Zapatista proposals for democracy and justice; instead, the government wanted to proceed to the next issue. The EZLN refused to continue the talks under those conditions. In its refusal, the EZLN noted that the government not only made no formal concessions regarding democracy, it also had yet to implement the San Andrés Accords. In late August, the EZLN formally withdrew from the peace talks. The Zapatistas set the following conditions for a return to negotiations: release of imprisoned Zapatistas, a meaningful reopening of the democracy and justice talks, and implementation of the San Andrés Accords on indigenous rights. The congressional committee involved in the peace process tried in vain to restart the talks over the next year. The climate soured further after paramilitary forces linked to the PRI murdered forty-five people (mostly women and children) at the Chiapan village of Acteal in December 1997. From this point onward, no hint of the optimism surrounding the San Andrés Accords returned during Zedillo's term.

Like Zedillo, Vicente Fox began his presidency with a lengthy list of reforms aimed at the enhancement of liberty. The most high-profile efforts again involved the EZLN rebellion. Fox claimed during his campaign that he could resolve the Chiapas crisis in fifteen minutes. During his first month in office, Fox presented an indigenous rights bill based on the Chiapas congressional committee's proposal, which had been languishing without support during the Zedillo administration. In February and March, Subcomandante Marcos and other Zapatista leaders launched a march across Mexico (with the Fox government's approval) to campaign for the indigenous rights bill. In April, however, the approved bill had undergone several key amendments that blocked the realization of indigenous autonomy discussed in the San Andrés Accords. The EZLN left the negotiating table in protest, but their walkout did not transform the legislation under discussion: in July, the new indigenous rights law passed both houses of Congress. Various organizations challenged the constitutionality of the new law, but the Supreme Court ruled in September 2002 that it would not overturn the legislation. The Zapatista movement maintained control of several portions of Chiapas, and the stalemate between the EZLN and the Mexican government continued.

The Fox administration made noticeably more progress in its efforts to improve government transparency on a day-to-day basis. Fox became the first Mexican president to make public the audit of presidential expenditures. With much fanfare, Fox required his cabinet ministers to take an oath expressly rejecting corruption. Some government agencies followed suit at lower levels, while the presidency launched public-service announcements asking citizens to refuse to offer (and to accept) bribes. Over time, Fox built a multipartisan legislative coalition to back his proposed freedom of information law. In 2002, Congress unanimously passed legislation that permits citizens to request access to most government documents, including information on government salaries and on audits. Many observers hoped that this law would help to destroy the veil of secrecy that had surrounded government during the PRI era.

In Mexico, the quest for liberty in the 1980s and 1990s centered on demands for political rights that might bring an end to the PRI's dominance of political life at all levels of government. Just as the economic crisis of the early 1980s put pressure on military governments in many Latin American countries, the PRI faced increasing calls for political change. The debate crystallized in Mexico following the controversial 1988 presidential election. Over the course of the next decade, the Salinas and Zedillo governments made several changes that increased the transparency of the electoral process. These procedural reforms helped make possible a growing role for opposition parties in the political system. The percentage of the Mexican population governed by the PRI at the local level fell from 97 percent in the early 1980s down to 47 percent in 1999. In the 1997 midterm legislative elections, the PRI lost its majority in the Chamber of Deputies. In July 2000, the PRI lost the presidential elections for the first time in its history. Concerted pressure from groups and individuals inside and outside the PRI succeeded in expanding political liberty in Mexico.

The Quest for Governance in Mexico

Carlos Salinas inherited several governance challenges. While the PRI had suffered divisions in the past, the rupture in 1986–1988 had been the largest and most prominent rift in its history. The PRI's narrow majority in the Chamber of Deputies made Salinas the first president in the PRI's history who could not amend the constitution without the support of opposition parties. The controversy surrounding Salinas's election also meant that the PRI might have a harder time mobilizing public support and winning the midterm legislative elections.

Salinas took steps early in his presidency to address these three issues. First, in response to the intraparty conflict between technocratics and machine politicians (respectively, smurfs and dinosaurs in Mexican slang), Salinas appointed prominent dinosaurs to his first cabinet in an effort to mend fences within the party. In addition, he supported Luis Colosio's selection as the new PRI party chief with the goal of reconciling differences and rebuilding the PRI's voting base. Second, Salinas tried to win the PAN's support for several market-oriented constitutional reforms (particularly the aforementioned changes to the *ejido* system). Seen in this light, Salinas's willingness to recognize the PAN's victories in several high-profile local and state-level elections was one part political reform and one part coalition building. Salinas was willing to give the PAN a greater role in subnational government in exchange for its support in the national legislature. Third, Salinas attempted to soften his image by reshaping welfare policy. Disparate agencies were reorganized into the Solidarity Program (*Programa Nacional de Solidaridad* [PRONASOL]). Salinas called on the best public speaker among his political collaborators, Luis Colosio, to lead this showcase initiative. The PRONASOL claimed to spend money more responsibly by targeting welfare spending to the needy. Several subsequent analyses would also demonstrate that the PRI funneled many of the spending changes in PRONASOL into the districts in which it had run poorly in the 1988 election.

These changes enabled Salinas to maintain control of the political agenda for most of his term. He picked Colosio to run for the presidency to head off criticisms from dinosaurs that the PRI had picked inexperienced campaigners as presidential candidates in the recent past. As noted earlier in this chapter, however, Salinas's control over events faltered considerably over the course of 1994.

The outbreak of the EZLN rebellion in Chiapas shattered the image of a rejuvenated PRI government (see the *Research Question* on pages 360–361). When initial attempts to dislodge the rebels by force met with only partial success, the government confronted the possibility of a violent civil war in an election year. On January 12, the government offered a cease-fire as a basis for negotiations; the EZLN accepted the cease-fire a few days later. On January 22, the Zapatistas presented a list of thirty-four demands; the Salinas government made a nonbinding offer to consider thirty-two demands and offered amnesty to all who would lay down their arms. The EZLN negotiators agreed to present the government's offer to their forces. In the meantime, the March assassination of Luis Colosio further disrupted the Salinas government. In July, the EZLN rejected the government's offer and Salinas's negotiator resigned. Ultimately, the Salinas government worked to resolve these governance challenges by a combination of electoral reform (to limit criticism from the opposition) and massive public spending (to get out the vote in the August 1994 election).

More than any of his recent predecessors, Ernesto Zedillo attempted to govern by consensus—both within his party and with other parties. At the start of

RESEARCH QUESTION

Under What Conditions Are Indigenous Rebellions More Likely to Occur?

The act of rebellion constitutes a governance challenge in its rawest form: people who rebel reject the legitimacy of the existing political system and place their lives at risk in the process. Under what conditions are rebellions more likely to emerge? Matthew Cleary examined this issue in a 2000 study that focused on a particular type of revolt: ethnically framed rebellion.[1]

Perhaps the most prevalent theory of ethnic rebellion builds on a straightforward premise: the more discrimination the indigenous population faces in the political and economic spheres, the more likely it will rebel against the prevailing order. Yet Cleary's examination of data on discrimination and ethnic violence around the world from 1950 through 1995 shows that indigenous groups in Latin America rebelled infrequently despite facing comparatively high levels of political and economic discrimination. From 1980 to 1995, only three countries experienced large-scale rebellions framed around indigenous concerns: Mayan participation in the guerrilla uprising in Guatemala during the late 1970s and 1980s, the Miskito revolt against the Sandinista government in Nicaragua during the 1980s, and the 1994 Zapatista uprising in Mexico.

What explains the relative absence of indigenous rebellion in Latin America? Beyond the discrimination theory, Cleary reviews additional hypotheses. The greater the cultural, social,

[1]Matthew Cleary, "Democracy and Indigenous Rebellion in Latin America," *Comparative Political Studies* 33 (2000): 1123–1153. For additional research in academic journals regarding rebellion, see the appropriate portion of this book's website.

his term, Zedillo's biggest challenge came from so-called dinosaurs in the PRI who felt that Zedillo would not be willing and able to maintain the party's control of government. Prior to his inauguration, Zedillo had promised to decrease the links between the president and the PRI and to end the *dedazo* approach to nominating PRI presidential candidates. Many veteran PRI politicians criticized these ideas as a path toward weakness. At the 1996 PRI party convention, the dinosaur faction pushed through a reform that required the party's presidential nominee to have previously held elective office. The internal change in party rules was a frontal assault on the ongoing dominance of the PRI's technocratic wing during the 1980s and 1990s. Despite the criticism, Zedillo maintained his position regarding the *dedazo*. Several observers asserted that Zedillo appeared to limit conflict with the dinosaur faction by retaining the pattern of impunity in corruption allegations. Although Zedillo publicly stressed that the rule of law would apply to all, his administration's

and linguistic separation between the indigenous group and the dominant ethnic group, the more likely rebellion will occur. This ethnic differentiation can serve to alienate the indigenous group from the rest of society, and vice versa. The more geographically concentrated the indigenous population, the more likely a rebel movement will emerge. Geographic concentration makes it easier for the indigenous population to organize politically and militarily. The more readily available are weapons, the more likely rebellion will occur. The capacity to arm oneself makes rebellion more feasible. The wealthier the country, the less likely rebellion will occur because greater affluence increases society's hope for the future while it also increases the capacity of the government to deter potential rebels. The higher the level of political protest, the more likely rebellion will occur. Protests demonstrate both the mobilization capacity of the population and its discontent with the current state of affairs; in this sense, protests are a leading indicator of future rebellions. Finally, the more democratic the political system, the less likely rebellion will occur. In a functioning democracy, the government is more likely to respond (at least partially) to demands for policy change. Democracies are also less likely to repress protest movements, thus minimizing the escalation scenario behind the protest hypothesis.

Cleary examines these hypotheses in two ways: via a narrative analysis of contemporary Ecuador, Mexico, and Nicaragua and via a statistical analysis of nineteen Latin American indigenous groups over the years 1980–1995. In both analyses, Cleary finds democracy (and the relative lack thereof in some situations) to be an important influence on the probability of rebellion. In addition, he finds support for the geographic concentration hypothesis and the protest hypothesis. The other hypotheses found less support in his analysis. In considering the implications of Cleary's work, do you believe that Mexican democracy has improved enough to reduce the probability of future rebellions? Why or why not?

pursuit of corruption allegations was limited to former PRI activists who had left the party. The dinosaur faction did not face serious investigations (much less prosecution).

The 1997 midterm elections introduced an unprecedented challenge to the president's ability to govern: the PRI lost control of the Chamber of Deputies and also lost the mayoral election in Mexico City. Although the PRI remained the largest delegation in the lower house, it would now be forced to seek the support of opposition parties in order to legislate. Zedillo sought the support of the PAN in regard to economic policy issues in which the two parties shared several goals. To cultivate the PAN's support, Zedillo delegated considerable authority to state governors by decentralizing government revenues. Because the PAN controlled several governorships, these reforms extended the party's power within the political system. In the immediate aftermath of the midterm elections, Zedillo's strategy bore fruit because the PAN supported the central elements of Zedillo's budget proposal in December 1997 (even though the PAN had stated its opposition during the campaign). By the end of Zedillo's term, however, his lame duck status and the heat of the 2000 presidential campaign limited his ability to gain the opposition's cooperation. For the first time in recent memory, the president's budgetary proposal underwent some significant changes. The days of the rubber-stamp legislature had come to an end.

Vicente Fox attempted to enhance his pragmatic campaign image by naming a decidedly diverse cabinet. Activists from the PAN formed a minority of his major appointees. His other ministers spanned most of the political spectrum. Fox tried to build a bridge to the PRI by appointing Francisco Díaz Gil as his finance minister. In turn, Fox appointed two prominent figures on the center-left to keep the lines of communication open with the PRD—Jorge Castañeda became foreign minister and Adolfo Aguilar Zinser was named national security adviser. Fox also reached out to the business community with several appointments.

Despite these efforts, the Fox administration found most of its major proposals blocked in the legislature. The PAN and the PRD disagreed on most policy issues. The PRI shared some goals with the PAN on several issues, but the PRI generally refused to work with Fox during his first three years in office. As noted earlier, all three major parties came together in support of a freedom of information act in 2002. Beyond that issue, Fox's proposals in other areas—including tax reform, energy policy, education, electoral reform, and labor law—made no substantive progress during the first half of his term.

Vicente Fox's hopes were pinned on a PAN victory in the 2003 midterm elections. Ultimately, the PAN did not gain a majority in the legislature. Instead, the party's share of the Chamber of Deputies fell from 41 percent to 31 percent (review Table 10.3). In the first state of the union address following the elections, Fox publicly called for all parties—including the PAN—to make compromises in pursuit of new policy reforms during the remainder of his presidency.

The debate over political liberty in the 1980s and the subsequent expansion of political rights during the 1990s changed the nature of governance challenges in Mexico. In the past, the major focus of governance involved maintaining the PRI's unity while limiting opposition through various carrot-and-stick measures. When demands for electoral transparency boiled over in the late 1980s, the Salinas government initially responded within the PRI's historical pattern. His government tried to expand political liberty without seriously compromising the PRI's dominance of national politics. However, the Zapatista rebellion and the assassination of Luis Colosio forced Salinas to make additional changes prior to the 1994 vote. In turn, the subsequent assassination of José Francisco Ruiz Massieu and the peso crisis motivated Zedillo to embrace still greater political reform.

As a result, both Zedillo and Fox have faced a divided legislature—something that had not existed in Mexico since the constitutional conventions during the Mexican Revolution. Once the PRI lost its dominance, the Mexican presidency no longer possessed its centrality to decision-making. This loss of informal authority was crucial because the formal powers of the president are more limited than those prevailing in most Latin American countries. If legislative stalemate continues in the years to come, one wonders whether one or more political parties will call for an expansion of executive authority.

Future Challenges

Mexico began the 1980s with optimism, only to face many disappointments. The start of the twenty-first century has similarly shifted from the hopes unleashed by Fox's victory to a period of economic stagnation and political stalemate. During the second half of his presidency, Vicente Fox and all of Mexico confront some steep challenges.

Fox promised to reduce poverty and to create jobs by modifying slightly the market capitalist economic model adopted by the PRI in the late twentieth century. In particular, Fox planned to expand educational spending without abandoning fiscal discipline. In the first half of his term, however, he could not steer a tax reform package through the legislature. Without the revenue enhancement that would flow from his proposal to curtail exemptions from both sales taxes and income taxes, Fox noted that substantial spending increases would be impossible. Would he be able to convince legislators from opposition parties to support his agenda on this matter? Early evidence from the second half of his term illustrates the difficulties faced by Fox. His efforts to pass a revised version of his tax proposal failed in late 2003. Although Fox gained the support of the leader of the PRI caucus in the Chamber of Deputies, a major portion of the PRI's legislators refused to support this tax reform compromise.

Instead, PRI deputies removed the PRI leader who had worked out the compromise with the Fox administration.

While the debate over liberty previously focused on political rights, the political reforms of the 1990s have shifted attention today to a broader array of topics. Corruption, street crime, drug trafficking, and limited protection for indigenous peoples dominated the headlines during the first half of the Fox presidency. The government forged multipartisan support for its freedom of information law, but progress on other fronts has been limited. Fox's claim that he could solve the Chiapas conflict in fifteen minutes proved unfounded. The EZLN deemed his indigenous rights legislation unsatisfactory. Although Fox raised the possibility of additional legislation regarding indigenous peoples, this issue remains unfinished business as he begins the second half of his presidency. With regard to street crime, many wondered if the national government would contemplate adopting the New York City approach that was adopted in Mexico City. In April 2003, the Mexico City government created a zero tolerance policy toward petty crimes along the lines used by Mayor Rudolph Giuliani in New York City. The possibility of a national get-tough policy worried several human rights organizations in August 2003 when the Fox government fired its undersecretary for human rights and eliminated the position altogether. While the administration claimed that this move represented bureaucratic streamlining, the decision provoked debate over whether the Fox government might reshape the bounds of liberty. Human rights advocates also criticized what they saw as minimal progress in the investigation of human rights abuses during previous presidencies. Although Fox had appointed a special commission to investigate past abuses, many observers argued that the special prosecutor named in 2001 still had insufficient resources to investigate allegations and to identify potential recipients of reparations.

The conditions for governance were redefined by the PAN's defeat in the July 2003 legislative elections. With the PAN's share of the lower house dropping from 40 percent down to 30 percent, Fox will have to work harder than ever before to build majority support for his legislative initiatives. In addition, Vicente Fox will be Mexico's first president in over a century to face the lame duck scenario in its purest form. Prior to the Mexican Revolution, presidents avoided becoming lame ducks by running for reelection. After the revolution, presidents retained their power in the system through their control over presidential succession. Presidents typically waited until less than one year prior to the elections to unveil their selection of the PRI's next candidate. This delay enabled the president to control the political agenda for nearly the entire six-year term.

Fox's lame duck status (emerging in the context of ongoing legislative stalemate from 1997 through 2003) may place the reelection question on the agenda in various forms. Will Fox and the legislature agree to end the prohibition on legislative reelection? Will they decide to permit presidents to run for reelection? If so, will Fox's supporters push for such a change to take effect immediately? As we have seen in previous chapters, sitting presidents in Argentina, Brazil, and Peru have argued that reelection can give presidents more time to pursue complex agendas. Many observers in and out of Mexico have noted that the prohibition on legislative reelection makes it difficult for the legislature to build up expertise and to pursue greater continuity in the exercise of its authority.

As the twenty-first century began, Mexico left behind its distinctive form of one-party government. The so-called imperial presidency has been replaced by a political pattern much more common in Latin America—the double-minority president. In the years to come, we will see whether the government adopts additional reforms to strengthen the presidency, to strengthen the legislature, or perhaps both. Regardless of the outcome of this institutional debate, the central political question in Mexico is now the same one found in all other Latin American democracies: under what conditions will politicians from different political parties come together to support public policies that improve most people's lives?

Activities and Exercises

1. How did the PRI maintain power for so long? What factors led to its defeat in the 2000 elections?

2. On January 1, 2004, the EZLN rebellion began its second decade. Why have past efforts to resolve the conflict failed? If you were president of Mexico, what would you propose as a path toward resolving the conflict?

3. Several observers believe that the debate over the no-reelection clause will become a central issue during the second half of Fox's presidency. Do you believe that the 1917 constitution should be amended to permit presidents to run for reelection? Why or why not? Do you believe that legislators should be able to run for reelection? Why or why not?

4. *Y tu mamá también (And Your Mother, Too)* became one of the most popular Mexican films of the past several years. This 2001 film tracks the sexual exploits of two young Mexican men from different backgrounds alongside a running commentary on the diverse socioeconomic realities of contemporary Mexico. If you have not already seen this film, watch it. If you have already seen the movie, consider watching it again now that you've learned more about Mexico.

5. Persistent poverty and income inequality have plagued Mexico for decades. Are conditions improving? What policies are being debated as possible solutions? One of many excellent online resources for the study of economic development in Latin America can be found at the website maintained by the U.N. Economic Commission for Latin America and the Caribbean (ECLAC) at http://www. eclac.org/default.asp?idioma=IN. The ECLAC site contains a wealth of data and analysis.

Suggested Readings

Babb, Sarah. *Managing Mexico: Economists from Nationalism to Liberalism.* Princeton, N.J.: Princeton University Press, 2001.

Bruhn, Kathleen. *Taking on Goliath: The Emergence of a New Left Party and the Struggle for Democracy in Mexico.* University Park, Pa.: Penn State University Press, 1997.

Cameron, Maxwell, and Brian Tomlin. *The Making of NAFTA: How the Deal Was Done.* Ithaca, N.Y.: Cornell University Press, 2000.

Camp, Roderic. *Politics in Mexico: The Democratic Transformation,* 4th ed. New York: Oxford University Press, 2003.

Castañeda, Jorge. *Perpetuating Power: How Mexican Presidents Were Chosen.* New York: Free Press, 2000.

Domínguez, Jorge, and Rafael Fernández. *The United States and Mexico: Between Partnership and Conflict.* New York: Routledge, 2001.

Domínguez, Jorge, and Chappell Lawson, eds. *Mexico's Pivotal Democratic Election: Candidates, Voters, and the Presidential Campaign of 2000.* Stanford, Calif.: Stanford University Press, 2004.

Gonzales, Michael. *The Mexican Revolution, 1910–1940.* Albuquerque: University of New Mexico Press, 2002.

Hamnett, Brian. *A Concise History of Mexico.* New York: Cambridge University Press, 1999.

Harvey, Neil. *The Chiapas Rebellion: The Struggle for Land and Democracy.* Durham, N.C.: Duke University Press, 1998.

Hodges, Donald, and Daniel Gandy. *Mexico, the End of the Revolution.* Westport, Conn.: Praeger, 2002.

Levy, Daniel, and Kathleen Bruhn. *Mexico: The Struggle for Democratic Development.* Berkeley: University of California Press, 2001.

Lustig, Nora. *Mexico: The Remaking of an Economy,* 2d ed. Washington, D.C.: Brookings Institution Press, 1998.

Middlebrook, Kevin. *The Paradox of Revolution: Labor, Authoritarianism and the State in Mexico.* Baltimore, Md.: Johns Hopkins University Press, 1995.

Oppenheimer, Andrés. *Bordering on Chaos: Guerrillas, Stockbrokers, Politicians, and Mexico's Road to Prosperity.* Boston, Mass.: Little, Brown, 1996.

Preston, Julia, and Sam Dillon. *Opening Mexico: The Making of a Democracy.* New York: Farrar, Straus and Giroux, 2004.

Purcell, Susan Kaufmann, and Luis Rubio-Freidberg, eds. *Mexico Under Zedillo.* Boulder, Colo.: Lynne Rienner, 1998.

Rodríguez, Victoria. *Women in Contemporary Mexican Politics.* Austin: University of Texas Press, 2003.

Rubio-Freidberg, Luis, and Susan Kaufman Purcell, eds. *Mexico Under Fox.* Boulder, Colo.: Lynne Rienner, 2004.

Serrano, Mónica, ed. *Governing Mexico: Political Parties and Elections.* London: Institute of Latin American Studies, 1998.

Tangemann, Michael. *Mexico at the Crossroads: Politics, the Church, and the Poor.* Maryknoll, N.Y.: Orbis, 1995.

Teichman, Judith. *Privatization and Political Change in Mexico.* Pittsburgh, Pa.: University of Pittsburgh Press, 1995.

Tulchin, Joseph, and Andrew Selee, eds. *Mexico's Politics and Society in Transition.* Boulder, Colo.: Lynne Rienner, 2003.

Williams, Heather. *Social Movements and Economic Transition: Markets and Distributive Conflict in Mexico.* Cambridge, England: Cambridge University Press, 2001.

Williams, Mark Eric. *Market Reforms in Mexico: Coalitions, Institutions, and the Politics of Policy Change.* Lanham, Md.: Rowman and Littlefield, 2001.

Endnotes

1. Michael Meyer and William Sherman, *The Course of Mexican History,* 5th ed. (New York: Oxford University Press, 1995), p. 458.

2. Roderic Camp, "Organized Labor and the Mexican State: A Symbiotic Relationship?" *Mexican Forum* 4 (October 1984): 4.

Venezuela

CHAPTER 11

Venezuela

I N 1982, A GROUP OF VENEZUELAN JUNIOR OFFICERS formed an organization within the military called the Bolivarian Revolutionary Movement 200 (*Movimiento Bolivariano Revolucionario 200* [MBR-200]). On the 152nd anniversary of Simón Bolívar's death (just a few months prior to the 200th anniversary of his birth), they took an oath to save the nation from decay, to restore dignity to the armed forces, and to fight corruption. The young officers (many of them from low-income and lower-middle-income families) discussed public affairs in Venezuela and elsewhere in Latin America. As Latin America's lost decade of the 1980s took its toll on the Venezuelan economy, the officers' discontent grew, especially when the government turned toward market capitalism in 1989. When President Carlos Andrés Pérez ordered the military to restore order amid widespread looting in Caracas during late February 1989, some MBR-200 members asked themselves if they had used force against the wrong side.

At around 9 P.M. on the evening of February 3, 1992, many officers in the MBR-200 launched a coup against the Pérez government. Paratroopers surrounded the presidential residence (*La Casona*) in Caracas, but the president had recently returned from Switzerland and had not yet reached his residence. Rebels took control of the state government of Zulia, along with its airport and its oil fields. In several other important cities in northwestern Venezuela, the rebels also controlled strategic positions and facilities. However, they did not achieve their initial objective of arresting the president nor did they seem to have the support of the military high command. From the presidential offices in the Miraflores Palace, Pérez secured the cooperation of most military units. By 9 A.M. on February 4, 1992, one of the leaders of the coup attempt, Lieutenant Colonel Hugo Chávez, surrendered and received television time to ask other rebels to stand down and thus avoid bloodshed. He took full responsibility for the coup. He also characterized his actions as a pursuit of national interests that had failed—for now.

Chávez's 178-word address made him a symbol of many citizens' growing rejection of the prevailing political and socioeconomic order. While he served a prison sentence for sedition, some poor Venezuelans began to wear red paratrooper berets in solidarity. Folk songs, graffiti, and poems praised him. One such tribute revised the Catholic version of the Lord's Prayer as follows:

Our Chávez who art in jail
Blessed be your coup.
Come to (avenge) us your people
Your will be done
That of Venezuela and your army.
Give us our lost confidence
and do not forgive the traitors
Just as we will not forgive those who captured you.
Save us from all the corruption
and deliver us from CAP [Carlos Andrés Pérez].
Amen.[1]

The Venezuelan legislature removed Pérez from office in 1993 via impeachment proceedings pertaining to the misuse of public funds. The winner of the 1993 presidential elections, veteran politician Rafael Caldera, released Chávez from prison. The two major political parties that had governed Venezuela since 1958 suffered their worst election results in a generation in 1993. Hailed as a stable democracy from the 1970s through the 1980s, Venezuela now had a democracy under considerable stress. Chávez organized a political movement that culminated in his triumph in the 1998 presidential elections; he won 56 percent of the vote.

Chávez's victory opened a new era in Venezuelan politics. He used his popularity to spearhead sweeping revisions in Venezuela's political institutions. He spoke constantly of the need to redirect resources from privileged Venezuelans to the impoverished. For many poor Venezuelans, Chávez represented what Evita Perón had meant to an earlier generation of Argentines: a person from a modest background driven to help transform their lives.

Just as Evita cut a controversial figure through her words and actions, so did Hugo Chávez. Many middle- and upper-income citizens criticized him. In April 2002, Chávez appeared to have lost power in a military coup, only to regain the presidency two days later amid large street demonstrations demanding his return to power. Since then, Chávez's opponents have placed considerable economic pressure on the government and have demanded a recall election. In mid-2003, the government rejected the validity of the signatures on the recall petition and forced the organizers to begin a new petition. In early March 2004, the electoral authority required over one-third of the citizens who signed the second recall petition to step forward to reconfirm their signatures. Three months later, the electoral authority announced that sufficient signatures had been confirmed to hold a presidential recall election in August 2004. As of early June 2004, it was not clear whether Chávez would win or lose the recall vote.

Regardless of the outcome of the recall effort, there is no denying that Hugo Chávez tried to transform Venezuelan politics. For some, he constituted the most viable path toward a more inclusive political and economic system. For others, his tactics represented an erosion of democracy. Over the course of this chapter, you will have the opportunity to reach your own conclusions regarding his impact on this oil-rich country of nearly 25 million inhabitants.

HISTORICAL BACKGROUND FROM 1908 TO 1993

Venezuelan post-independence politics began under the leadership of José Antonio Paez. Paez served as a general under Simón Bolívar during the wars for independence, which had forged the state of Gran Colombia with its capital in present-day Bogotá, Colombia. By 1829, however, Paez led Venezuela's separation from Gran Colombia. Paez forged an oligarchic democracy that for sixteen years proved more stable and more tolerant than most other Latin American governments in the mid-nineteenth century. Coffee revenues funded the beginnings of a national infrastructure. When coffee prices dipped in the 1840s, however, support for Paez slipped and he was forced into exile.

The second half of the nineteenth century bore witness to an almost continuous cycle of regional armies fighting for predominance, gaining it for a time, and then being pushed out by a different army. From 1870 to 1888, Antonio Guzmán Blanco presided over an export-oriented dictatorship analogous to the Porfirio Díaz regime in Mexico. Anti-Guzmán rallies launched while the *caudillo* was vacationing in Europe convinced him to retire (as a very wealthy man) in Paris. Regional armies resumed their infighting until a *caudillo* from the Andean state of Tachira, Cipriano Castro, took control. Castro governed until one of his chief lieutenants, Juan Vicente Gómez, led a coup while Castro was undergoing surgery in Europe.

Juan Vicente Gómez and His Legacy (1908–1945)

Gómez became the last and most powerful *caudillo* in a country whose first century after independence had been dominated by military leaders. Gómez took the reins of power from Castro in 1908 and did not relinquish them until his death in 1935. Under his rule, Venezuela entered the twentieth century with an unbalanced push toward state building and economic development.

First, Gómez took steps to end the cycle of regional warfare. He built a truly national military by extending Cipriano Castro's practice of dispatching fellow Andean officers throughout the country. These officers built a hierarchy loyal to the president. Then, to further this process, Gómez established the first national military academy in 1910. These steps ensured the dominance of officers from the Andean region of the country, which would become a factor in political disputes later in Venezuela's history.

With the discovery and exploitation of oil in the Lake Maracaibo area, Venezuela became the world's largest oil producer in the 1920s. Gómez and his entourage grew wealthy because petroleum royalties and taxes provided new revenue flows that could be diverted directly and indirectly into their own pockets. Oil revenues also assisted state building via the creation of a transportation infrastructure. Public works projects linked the country together as never before through the construction of railroads and highways. Gómez employed the widening grasp of state control mainly to maintain his own position rather than to promote economic development. Perhaps the most striking illustration of this point occurred in 1925 when he opposed the construction of a deep-water channel into Maracaibo for fear that the region might secede if given ready access to the sea. Consequently, Shell Oil Company constructed a large refinery on the Dutch island of Curaçao, to which Venezuelan crude was barged for processing.

Political repression remained the most consistent characteristic of the Gómez regime. His forces put down several military rebellions, including some supported by the unseated Cipriano Castro. Unions and political parties were outlawed throughout the period, and the small extralegal organizations that formed met with forceful government repression. Student groups led the most significant protests. An ostensibly tame week of university social and cultural fundraising events scheduled for February 1928 initiated the most noteworthy expressions of anti-Gómez sentiment to date. Student leaders Jóvito Villalba and Rómulo Betancourt delivered bitter denunciations of life under Gómez, as did poet Pío Tamayo. The subsequent arrest of several student leaders triggered unprecedented popular demonstrations in Caracas and Maracaibo that culminated in the release of most of the dissidents. On April 7, 1928, a group of junior officers, cadets, and students led a dawn assault in Caracas that nearly toppled Gómez. They captured the presidential palace before being turned back by government troops led by Eleazar López Contreras. A new round of repression ensued in which almost all dissident leaders were arrested, exiled, or sent into hiding. This group of opposition leaders would become known as the Generation of 1928.

Gómez died at age seventy-eight in December 1935; he was said to be the wealthiest man in South America at that time. Gomez's war minister, Eleazar López Contreras, became provisional president. He relaxed restrictions on civil liberties. Many of the exiled Generation of 1928 returned and began to reestablish opposition groups. The newly formed National Democratic party (*Partido Democrático Nacional* [PDN]) provoked considerable antigovernment activism. López Contreras responded by outlawing the PDN and suspending most civil liberties. Forty-seven opposition leaders (including Betancourt, Villalba, and Raúl Leoni) were given one-year expulsions from the country for communist leanings. To alleviate military discontent, the government created a separate naval academy and a national guard for public works projects. Nonetheless, Andeans continued to dominate the senior officer corps, much to the dismay of the already disgruntled junior officers. López Contreras set the stage for a new era in Venezuelan politics by voluntarily stepping down at the end of his five-year term. He was succeeded by his minister of war, Isaías Medina Angarita.

With the onset of Medina's government, political repression eased considerably. Exiles returned, press censorship slackened, and—most noticeably—opposition parties achieved legal status. In 1941, the organizers of the PDN learned that certification for their new party, Democratic Action (*Acción Democrática* [AD]), had been approved. AD organized doggedly, strengthening its ties with unions and peasants under the banner of social reform and universal direct suffrage. Medina organized his own progovernment party. In 1944, the government legalized the Venezuelan Communist party (*Partido Comunista de Venezuela* [PCV]) and López Contreras announced that he planned to run for office. Politics heated up considerably as the elections grew near. Medina's first choice as the pro-government candidate became ill and could not run. Medina's subsequent choice proved unpopular with both the left and the supporters of López Contreras on the right.

In the midst of considerable political disaffection in many parts of the political spectrum, a group of junior officers began to discuss launching a coup attempt. Frustrated by continuing Andean domination of the military (and of government more generally), the soldiers approached AD leaders with an invitation to form a civil-military junta should their planned coup prove successful. After some soul-searching, AD leaders became convinced that these officers would permit them to run the government and to implement their programs for political and socioeconomic reform. With the success of the coup on October 18, 1945, a junta of two officers, one independent civilian, and four AD leaders took control of the government. AD leader Rómulo Betancourt served as the provisional president of the junta.

The *Trienio* of the Democratic Action Party (1945–1948)

The 1945 coup initiated a three-year period (*trienio* in Spanish) of considerable political and economic reform. Immediately, the civil-military interim government enhanced protection for civil liberties. January 1946 witnessed the formation of a new conservative Christian Democratic party, the *Comité de Organización Política Electoral Independiente* (COPEI). This group organized Christian student and professional groups primarily around a staunchly anti-communist stance and a call for the maintenance of ecclesiastical influence over the educational system. Many *copeyanos* (members of COPEI) viewed AD, which favored the secularization of education, as basically communist in orientation.

Despite the prospects of electoral opposition from COPEI, the PCV, and Jóvito Villalba's newly formed Democratic Republican Union (*Unión Republicana Democrática* [URD]), the promised electoral reform proceeded quickly. In March 1946, Degree 216 established a system of universal direct suffrage for all

Venezuelans eighteen years of age and older to be employed in the election of a constituent assembly. The October 1946 election illustrated AD's organizational dominance as well as its popular appeal. Its delegates received 79 percent of the vote, while COPEI came in a distant second with 13 percent. The subsequent 1947 constitution reflected AD's social reform emphases, with its calls for the creation of an ambitious social security system to include major housing and health-care projects. Labor's right to organize and its right to strike were formally recognized, as were electoral liberties that AD had long championed.

AD's candidates also triumphed handily in the December 1947 presidential and legislative elections. AD presidential candidate Rómulo Gallegos received 74 percent of the vote; COPEI leader Rafael Caldera attracted 22 percent. Congressional elections finished along the same lines, with AD netting 70 percent of the vote to COPEI's 20 percent; the URD and the PCV received a few representatives according to the proportional representation electoral system.

The relative openness that characterized these elections did not mean that Venezuela had become a conflict-free society. On the contrary, AD's programs created an impressive array of enemies. Many Christians hated the educational reforms. The oil companies disliked the government's new, tougher negotiation stances regarding taxation and royalties. Business elites worried about increased labor militancy after the AD-led formation of the Venezuelan Workers Confederation (*Confederación de Trabajadores de Venezuela* [CTV]) in 1947. Landholders feared the advent of land reform efforts promised during the campaign. Finally, all these groups chafed under AD's seemingly invincible electoral machine that kept getting 70 percent of the vote.

To make matters worse, AD gradually lost control of the armed forces. Despite AD's fulfillment of its promise to increase defense spending, grumblings over partisan politicization of the armed forces multiplied. Although the military put down coup attempts in 1946 and 1947, AD leaders grew increasingly anxious over the possibility of military disloyalty; many fears centered on outspoken Major Marcos Pérez Jiménez. Steps to create a partisan civilian militia only fed the activity of an already churning military rumor mill. In November 1948, opposition parties tried to push for a major cabinet reorganization aimed at weakening AD's dominance of the government. This conflict could not be resolved to the satisfaction of both sides, and by November 23, the vast majority of the armed forces no longer supported the Gallegos administration. The next day, a provisional military junta formed after a bloodless coup.

The Pérez Jiménez Dictatorship (1948–1958)

The new junta, comprised of Lieutenant Colonel Carlos Delgado, Major Felipe Llovera Paez, and the aforementioned Marcos Pérez Jiménez, outlawed AD and the CTV. It also announced plans to return quickly to democratic rule. The junta then stalled, however, on the electoral question amid internal divisions and disagreements with civilian politicians. In November 1950, the provisional president Carlos Delgado had his ambitions extinguished by a fatal gunshot. Pérez Jiménez (whose involvement in the Delgado assassination was never proven) quickly assumed de facto control of the junta.

Finally, in 1952, the junta organized elections to select a constituent assembly that would write a new constitution and select a new president. Supporters of Pérez Jiménez ran under the banner of the Independent Electoral Front (*Frente Electoral Independiente* [FEI]). Amid harassment and censorship of the two remaining major political parties (COPEI and the URD), the outlawed AD party initially backed a policy of abstention in protest. As the election approached, though, AD partisans quietly and often spontaneously gave their support to the URD. Preliminary returns for the November 30 elections had the URD leading the FEI; however, the voters did not ultimately decide the matter. The junta relinquished its power to the armed forces, which in turn named Pérez Jiménez interim president. Two weeks later, the official results gave the FEI a majority in the assembly. Villalba, the founder of the URD, protested these actions and proposed to lead a civilian regime with Pérez Jiménez as his minister of war. The military rejected this compromise and instead exiled Villalba and six other URD leaders on December 16. Boycott efforts in the constituent assembly by URD and COPEI delegates failed to prevent a quorum: the assembly gave Pérez Jiménez full decree powers as the newly elected president of Venezuela on April 17, 1953.

The regime grew increasingly unpopular and repressive. By the end of 1953, the COPEI leadership shared the fate of AD and the URD: prison or exile. This circumscription of the heretofore conservative party produced a cleavage that would prove significant later. The party's right wing split to support the dictator; the more moderate remainder joined the opposition to military rule. For a moment, Pérez Jiménez ruled over the bounty of an economic boom fueled by new oil discoveries and the initial exploitation of iron ore reserves. The wealth created did not make its way to government social programs, but rather to the coffers of regime supporters and to several grandiose public works projects.

By 1957, opposition to the regime had spread even among some of its earlier supporters in the Catholic church, the military, and the urban middle class. Archbishop Rafael Arias Blanco of Caracas issued a strident pastoral letter condemning the corruption of the regime as well as its complete disregard for the worsening poverty of the masses. The armed forces resented the infiltration and surveillance of military operations by the security police. The middle class chafed at the suspension of civil liberties. In November, the nature of the announced elections galvanized the opposition: a plebiscite would be held in which voters could register only pro- or antigovernment sentiment. Although the December 15 elections officially claimed that Pérez Jiménez had received 85 percent approval, public protests of the plebiscite proved swift and effective.

On January 1, 1958, loyal forces led by Llovera Paez barely put down a military uprising. The *Junta Patriótica* (Patriotic Junta), a civilian opposition group formed in mid-1957, built a united front composed of nonpartisan independents, clergy, students, and the clandestine leaders of the banned political parties. A call for a general strike on January 21, 1958, in Caracas brought the city to a halt and spread to other cities the following day. This action met with violent repression by loyal security forces. Nonetheless, military pressure led by Rear Admiral Wolfgang Larrazábal convinced Pérez Jiménez to flee the country on January 23, 1958.

The Rise of Two-Party Democracy (1958–1989)

During the years 1958–1964, political parties, especially AD, played a critical role in the formation of a stable democratic regime. The AD leadership wanted to avoid the political polarization of the *trienio* in the 1940s. How did the major political parties achieve consensus?

As the Larrazábal junta honored its pledge to organize national elections, the leadership of the three leading parties—AD, COPEI, and the URD—met to discuss backing a national unity candidate for the presidency. While they could not agree on such a candidate, they did reach a pivotal agreement on the democratic rules of the game. The Pact of Punto Fijo, signed October 31, 1958, pledged that each party would accept the outcome of the elections and that they would work to establish a common minimum program through a coalition cabinet.

The Pact of Punto Fijo represented an about-face for Venezuelan party politics. The shared experience of repression and exile worked to bring together the bitter adversaries of the *trienio*, AD and COPEI. The turmoil of the years 1945–1958 convinced many party leaders that all-or-nothing politics opened the door to would-be dictators. This search for consensus, often referred to as the spirit of January 23, carried over into the coalition cabinet formed by AD founder Rómulo Betancourt (who won the 1958 presidential elections with 49 percent of the vote). Betancourt argued that increasing taxes on foreign-owned oil companies could provide public revenues that would fund increased spending on all major government priorities. He also worked to heal long-standing tensions between AD and several sectors of Venezuelan society (see *Governing Strategies: Rómulo Betancourt*). Although AD's move to the political center prompted several of its more left-leaning leaders to form new political movements, AD retained the support of most voters and used military force to battle new guerrilla movements inspired by the Cuban revolution.

After the end of Betancourt's term, AD and COPEI leaders did not renew their agreement to form a coalition cabinet. When AD candidate Raúl Leoni defeated Rafael Caldera, Leoni did not bring *copeyanos* into his cabinet. Despite the end to high-level power sharing, however, both parties retained the centrist platforms they had developed during the Pact of Punto Fijo. Both backed state capitalist policies calling for the use of oil revenues to finance import-substituting

GOVERNING STRATEGIES
Rómulo Betancourt

When Rómulo Betancourt won the 1958 presidential election, he was beginning his fourth decade in national politics. As a young adult, Betancourt had spent much of his life in exile trying to end a long-running military dictatorship. The founder of the Democratic Action (*Acción Democrática* [AD]) party then supported the 1945 military coup that paved the way for open elections—elections won handily by AD. In 1948, a new military coup sent Betancourt back into exile.

The 1948 coup convinced Betancourt to take a more consensual approach to governance after the reestablishment of democracy in 1958. He tried to heal old rifts with the military, the church, the business community, and the major center-right political party, the Christian Democratic COPEI. Betancourt proposed to increase tax revenues from the foreign oil companies to generate money to assist many different organized interests.

The Betancourt government took steps to shore up its support in the armed forces. From the Gómez era onward, a general staff dominated by Andean army officers had run the military. Betancourt formed a joint chiefs of staff to provide greater branch autonomy and a reduction in the Andean dominance of the armed forces. Betancourt offered amnesty to officers facing suspicion of wrongdoing during the dictatorship. He also dismantled the infamous national security police—to the joy of soldiers and civilians alike. When public revenues from oil increased, military expenditure rose in absolute terms.

To mend fences with business interests, the Betancourt administration tried to negotiate wage hikes while preventing strikes. The government also cultivated business support by launching an import-substituting industrialization (ISI) program. New government revenues funded subsidies for industrial promotion (as well as for education and health spending hikes).

The government also tried to heal wounds in the Catholic church. AD relaxed its former anticlerical education stance. Its willingness to share power in the cabinet with COPEI also went a long way toward bringing the church in support of the democratic regime. Finally, the use of budgetary largesse cannot be overlooked because the Betancourt government tripled the subsidy granted to the church under the Pérez Jiménez regime.

Betancourt forged a centrist, programmatic consensus between AD and its main electoral rival, COPEI. Working together in government, they experienced the fruits and frustrations of policy compromises for the first time. AD did not push for as many socioeconomic reforms as it did in the 1940s, and COPEI did not oppose the more modest reform pursued in the early 1960s.

Betancourt left the presidency in 1964 as one of the architects of a new Venezuelan democracy while democracies crumbled elsewhere. When many Latin American countries returned to democracy in the early 1980s, Betancourt's successful attempt to prevent a quick return to military rule would be discussed as a potential governance model for other countries. However, when Venezuelans began to complain in the 1980s that AD and COPEI held power too tightly, some debated whether Betancourt's emphasis on power-sharing had transformed itself into the enjoyment of power for power's sake.

industrialization (ISI) so that the economy could be diversified to reduce Venezuela's dependence on oil. Both parties supported considerable spending on health and education: by 1968, the Venezuelan government spent more per person on education and health care than did other Latin American governments. COPEI's founder, Rafael Caldera, won a four-candidate race for the presidency in 1968 with 29 percent of the vote. His campaign called for an extension of many of the policies pursued by two prior AD presidents.

As AD and COPEI moved toward the political center, they became the two dominant political parties in the country. In the 1958 elections, Betancourt and Rafael Caldera garnered 64 percent of the vote. By the 1973 elections, the victorious AD candidate, Carlos Andrés Pérez and his COPEI counterpart, Lorenzo Fernández, netted 85 percent of the vote. The legislative elections mirrored this consolidation because the two parties received 75 percent of the vote and even fared well in geographic areas in which they had traditionally performed poorly.

Pérez assumed the presidency in March 1974—six months after the first oil price hike by the Organization of Petroleum Exporting Countries (OPEC). Venezuela's considerable oil reserves had just quadrupled in value. Pérez promised to administer the newfound abundance with an eye toward making every dollar count. In practice, however, the avalanche of new fiscal resources produced a massive increase in spending on nearly all fronts that proved difficult to manage. Government subsidies and price controls reduced the cost of many foodstuffs and other basic consumer goods. The high value of the Venezuelan currency made foreign imports cheaper, thus propelling the purchase of European, Japanese, and U.S. imports by middle- and upper-income citizens. Government spending on education and health care increased. Pérez also created the Venezuelan Investment Fund to share a portion of the Venezuelan windfall with neighboring countries through grants and low-interest loans to Andean, Caribbean, and Central American countries.

While most Latin American countries endured military dictatorships in the 1970s, Venezuela received regional and international praise as a model democracy. The guerrilla movements of the 1960s had faded into the background. Most citizens supported one of the two major parties, AD and COPEI, in public-opinion polls. Some analysts of Latin American politics asked whether Venezuela's democratic exceptionalism during this period contained lessons for other countries. Others countered that Venezuela's success in maintaining democratic rule had been fueled primarily by oil (see *Global Perspectives: Resource Wealth and Democratization*). Despite their disagreements, both sides of this debate saw the Venezuelan political system as enviably stable.

GLOBAL PERSPECTIVES
Resource Wealth and Democratization

Does oil wealth explain Venezuela's ability to build a democratic political system precisely when most Latin American democracies collapsed? Writing in 1975, Franklin Tugwell put forward the oil thesis rather succinctly:

> This [oil] has provided an important cushion, facilitating the institutionalization of conciliatory patterns of conflict resolution. In game-theoretic terms, Venezuelan democracy has been an expanding-sum game; the raw edge of conflict has been softened by a growing total resource base. Compared to most developing nations, Venezuela, with government income (in constant bolivars) growing at an average annual rate of over 7 percent (since 1958), has been able to satisfy more demands and fund more programs while asking fewer sacrifices of her citizens.[1]

Government income rose during the 1960s because AD and COPEI agreed to raise taxes and royalty rates. Oil companies paid the Venezuelan government under two-fifths of their total production in taxes and royalties in 1959 at the start of the new democracy. By 1973, their payments to the government comprised nearly two-thirds of their production. By raising taxes on the oil sector, AD and COPEI could spend considerably more money on nearly all areas of government activity—and did so without raising tax rates on individual Venezuelans.

Yet oil alone cannot explain the emergence of democracy in Venezuela during the 1960s and 1970s. Most oil-rich countries did not have functioning democracies. For example, in 1971, Venezuela stood out as the lone democracy among the eleven members of the Organization of Petroleum Exporting Countries (OPEC). Algeria, Indonesia, Iran, Iraq, Kuwait, Libya, Nigeria, Qatar, Saudi Arabia, and the United Arab Emirates all had nondemocratic political systems.

Many analysts emphasized the role of political learning in Venezuela's democratization. The 1958 Pact of Punto Fijo tried to avoid the titanic conflict of the *trienio* government led by the AD party in the 1940s. This pact built a pattern of moderation, cooperation, and power-sharing among the major center-left party (AD) and the major center-right party (COPEI).

When Latin American countries returned to democracy in the 1980s, some asked whether foundational pacts among the major political parties could be a path toward democratic consolidation elsewhere. Terry Karl's response to this question affirmed the importance of oil, political parties, and the leadership decision to engage in what she called a "pacted democracy." At the same time, Karl also noted several potential limitations of pacted democracy as a path toward democratic consolidation in the medium run. In particular, she emphasized the vulnerability of any oil-rich state to continuing conflict over the distribution of the riches produced by petroleum. The spoils system used for divvying up oil wealth makes political actors focus on increasing and retaining their respective shares of easy money rather than on improving the efficiency of public- and private-sector activity.

[1]Franklin Tugwell, *The Politics of Oil in Venezuela* (Stanford, Calif.: Stanford University Press, 1975), p. 164.

Writing just before oil prices fell by 50 percent in 1986, Karl concluded that "the long-term viability of this form of pacted democracy and its value as a model for other countries may become clear only when the oil money begins to disappear."[2]

[2]Terry Karl, "The Transition to Democracy in Venezuela," in Guillermo O'Donnell, Philippe Schmitter, and Laurence Whitehead, eds., *Transitions from Authoritarian Rule: Latin America* (Baltimore, Md.: Johns Hopkins University Press, 1986), p. 219.

Inside Venezuela, however, some already questioned the sustainability of the approach employed during the mid-1970s. Numerous substantive changes could be seen in the expansion of state capitalist development plans. The government launched many new state-owned manufacturing firms. The government formed the Venezuelan Corporation of Guyana to build and manage ambitious investments in steel, aluminum, and hydroelectric power. The Pérez government also used oil wealth to nationalize several existing firms. In January 1975, the government purchased the two major U.S.-owned iron-ore mines for over $100 million. In August 1975, the government created a publicly owned holding company, Venezuelan Petroleum Incorporated (*Petróleos de Venezuela, S.A.* [PDVSA]), to purchase the fourteen existing foreign-owned oil companies for roughly $1 billion. In both cases, the former owners also received lucrative contracts to provide technical and managerial assistance to the newly nationalized enterprises. By the end of Pérez's term, total public employment had doubled. Amid the rapid expansion, corruption scandals proliferated regarding padded contracts for the construction of public facilities, kickbacks paid to gain public contracts, and ghost employees who were kept on the public payroll while doing little or no work. COPEI candidate Luis Herrera won the 1978 presidential campaign by promising to impose limits on this free-spending approach.

Perez's presidency during the 1970s marked the height of Venezuela's economic ambitions: the economy grew at annual rate of 6 percent. After a short-lived doubling of oil prices in 1979–1980, Venezuela's economic fortunes took a turn for the worse. A world recession in the early 1980s—along with a considerable decline in the price of oil in 1982 and in 1986—sent shock waves throughout the country. Since two-thirds of government revenues (and the pace of economic activity more generally) depended on oil revenues, the Venezuelan economy found itself with a rising foreign debt and falling national income. During Herrera's presidency, the economy stagnated. Amid the crisis, the Herrera administration had the Central Bank seize nearly $5 billion of PDVSA's financial reserves to help the government make its debt payments. The move ended the holding company's traditional managerial autonomy.

In the 1983 presidential election campaign, AD challenger Jaime Lusinchi won the presidency primarily by criticizing the economic collapse under

Herrera. His somewhat successful efforts to reschedule Venezuela's debt and to reactivate the economy ran headlong into a second major drop in oil prices; crude oil prices fell by 50 percent during 1986. Lusinchi decided to spend the government's fiscal reserves and to borrow additional funds in an effort to stimulate an economic recovery; his government spent relatively freely in 1987 and 1988. This approach helped to spark economic growth after the oil price drop but left an empty treasury to his successor. The government deficit in 1988 equaled nearly 10 percent of gross domestic product (GDP).

Carlos Andrés Pérez won the 1988 elections with a nostalgic political campaign in which the veteran politician recalled many events from his presidency in the 1970s, when oil prices were booming. He noted that the country faced great challenges but promised to use his experience to raise wages and to spark an economic recovery. Similar to Carlos Menem's victorious populist campaign in the 1989 presidential elections in Argentina, however, Pérez did not inherit the economic resources necessary to implement the state capitalist economic approach that their respective speeches invoked.

Although AD and COPEI continued to receive between 85 and 90 percent of the vote in the 1978, 1983, and 1988 presidential elections, calls for change among voices outside these two parties had become louder and louder as the 1980s progressed. In addition to a focus on corruption, critics of the two major parties noted that conditions for impoverished Venezuelans had not improved much even during the oil boom. For example, despite the rise in social spending during Pérez's presidency, conditions for the poorest two-fifths of the population had improved minimally and income inequality worsened. The 1988 Venezuelan presidential elections were not nearly as controversial as they had been in Mexico. In hindsight, however, the election marked the beginning of a new era in which long-running economic and political patterns would come under increasing challenge from various political forces. The era of rising incomes driven by the oil boom had come to an end.

CONTEMPORARY POLITICAL FRAMEWORK

In the late 1980s, neither the two major parties nor their critics imagined that the desire for political change eventually would crystallize in the 1998 election of Hugo Chávez. In his inaugural address in February 1999, Chávez asked for temporary decree powers and called for the election of the National Constituent Assembly (*Asamblea Constituyente Nacional* [ANC]) to revise the constitution. On April 25, 1999, a referendum was held regarding the convocation of the ANC: although 92 percent of those voting approved the referendum, Venezuelan law required 50 percent voter turnout, and only 39 percent of the registered voters had participated. Nonetheless, the National Electoral Council validated the referendum vote. In the July 1999 elections for delegates to the ANC, Chávez's coalition, the Patriotic Pole (*Polo Patriótico*) received 120 of the 131 seats.

Chávez's supporters thus controlled the creation of the revised constitution that frames contemporary political life. Chávez achieved his goal of renaming the country the Bolivarian Republic of Venezuela. In considering potential institutional reforms, Chávez blamed Venezuela's problems on a corrupt system in which AD and COPEI shared power but failed to improve conditions for most Venezuelans. In response, he argued that the revised document should reduce the power of political parties while providing new mechanisms for **direct democracy** and advisory roles for nongovernmental organizations (NGOs). One of the most striking revisions in this regard has been the creation of **recall elections** for all elected officials. During the second half of their mandates, the president, governors, legislators, and elected judges can face a recall election if 20 percent of the registered voters request it. For the recall to succeed in removing the official, a larger number of voters must support the recall than had previously voted to elect the official. In addition, at least 25 percent of the registered voters must participate in the recall election. Another clause gave 15 percent of the registered voters the power to convoke a constituent assembly to consider revisions to the constitution.

While these and other aspects of the 1999 constitution purport to enable the people's "protagonism" (*protagonismo*) as claimed by its backers, it should be noted that Chávez requested and received a considerable increase in the power of the presidency. Preliminary Venezuelan evaluations of the impact of these constitutional reforms tended to be colored by one's position on Chávez himself. His supporters argued that he broke up the old parties' monopoly on power and that his own centralization of power will help transform Venezuelan society. His critics replied that he used the language of inclusiveness to make a hyperpresidentialist constitution more palatable.

The Executive Branch

The new constitution extended the presidential term of office from five to six years. It also removed the historical prohibition on immediate reelection. Presidents could now be reelected for a second consecutive term. With this change, Chávez obtained the ability to serve for twelve consecutive years (in contrast to the five-year mandate he received initially under the 1961 constitution). The 1999 constitution retained the traditional plurality electoral system: whichever candidate received the most votes would assume the presidency.

The Venezuelan presidency can be described as potentially dominant using Mainwaring and Shugart's conceptual framework (review Table 4.6). Like many Latin American presidents, the Venezuelan president can name and remove cabinet ministers at will. In addition, the revisions gave the president the authority to name and remove his own vice president at will. As in the 1961 constitution, the president has a weak veto that can be overridden by a majority vote in the legislature. However, the 1999 constitution granted the president five additional powers in executive-legislative relations. First, the president can now ask the legislature to declare a state of emergency in which the chief executive can legislate by decree for up to one year (in the 1961 constitution, the state of emergency provision expressly denied presidents the ability to legislate by decree). Second, the president gained the ability to call new legislative elections if the legislature chose to remove the vice president three times during the first five years of a presidential term. Third, the 1999 constitution reduced the legislature's role in civilian-military relations. Under the prior framework, the Venezuelan Senate made final decisions regarding the designation of senior officers based on a list of nominees presented by the president. Under the 1999 constitution, the president has exclusive control over all promotions, beginning with the rank of colonel in the army and captain in the navy. Fourth, the president can now convoke a constituent assembly unilaterally; it takes a two-thirds vote in the legislature to take the same action. Fifth, although the president's veto remains weak (as in the prior system), the chief executive can now call a public referendum to overturn almost any law—with the exception of international treaties and budgetary, tax, and human rights laws.

The Legislature

In addition to reducing the relative power of the legislature, the 1999 constitution halved the number of legislators and merged them into a unicameral legislature. The prior Chamber of Deputies and Senate became a new National Assembly. Venezuelans now elect 165 legislators using a hybrid electoral system (three-fifths chosen via plurality elections and the rest chosen via closed-list proportional representation). Legislators serve five-year terms, which means that simultaneous legislative and presidential elections will occur only once every thirty years under the new constitution.

As noted earlier, the Chávez movement criticized the role of political parties as problematic under the old system. The 1999 constitution stands out in contrast to most constitutions around the world by its refusal to use the term *political party*. The constitution also ruled out government financing for political parties. Article 201 implicitly criticizes the use of party discipline in legislative affairs by declaring that no legislative vote can be subject to "mandates or instructions." If taken to its logical extreme, this article opens up a potential constitutional black hole in which any vote taken in apparent conformity with a given political party's stated position could conceivably be deemed unconstitutional. Thus far, however, the government has not suppressed the role of political parties in the legislature. The National Assembly's official information refers to legislators by party and lists the coalition of parties mobilized in support of the president.

The Judiciary

The Supreme Tribunal of Justice (*Tribunal Supremo de Justicia* [TSJ]) is the highest court in Venezuela and treats different matters of law in different chambers.

One of its chambers serves as the constitutional court with the power of judicial review. The TSJ underwent considerable reform during the ANC. Under the old system, justices served nine-year renewable terms pending approval in a joint session of the legislature. The 1999 constitution extended the terms to twelve years but eliminated the possibility of reelection. Article 264 leaves the matter of the justices' election up to subsequent legislation but requires candidates to be nominated through a three-step process involving a nonpartisan nominating committee, a committee of public auditors, and the National Assembly. The 1999 constitution also left the precise number of justices up to subsequent legislation.

In 2000, the National Assembly resolved the matter of electing justices. The legislature empowered a twenty-one-person committee to select justices via a simple majority vote. The committee consisted of fifteen legislators and six civic representatives chosen by the National Assembly. In October 2003, the National Assembly contemplated exercising its power over the composition of the TSJ. The Chávez bloc in the legislature proposed to increase the number of justices from twenty to thirty-two and to reform the TSJ's governing statute to permit a simple majority of the legislature to select the justices. While this proposal did not pass during the rest of the 2003 legislative session, pro-Chávez legislators passed the bill in late April 2004. Were this reform to be implemented, the slim majority in support of President Chávez would gain the ability to name all twelve new justices. Opposition legislators pledged to request that the TSJ itself revoke the new law as unconstitutional.

POLITICAL PARTICIPATION

From 1928 through 1998, the central civilian political organizations in Venezuela had been formed by the Generation of 1928, which had opposed the Gómez dictatorship. Two founders of the AD party (Rómulo Betancourt and Raúl Leoni) and the principal founder of the URD (Jóvito Villalba) were high school classmates in Caracas. Along with Rafael Caldera (who led COPEI for nearly half a century), the Generation of 1928 headed the political parties that dominated the legislature from 1958 through 1998. Most major interest groups had personal ties to these leaders and their close associates. The 1999 elections changed all that; now new parties and interest groups compete for influence alongside a few older movements.

Interest Groups and Social Movements

The major business confederation in Venezuela represents nearly all sectors of the economy. The Federation of Chambers and Associations of Commerce and Production (*Federación de Cámaras y Asociaciones de Comercio y Producción* [FEDECAMARAS]) formed in 1944. This major voice for the private sector became a vocal opponent of the AD party during the *trienio* government of the 1940s. When AD moved toward the center after 1958, however, FEDECAMARAS established more cordial relations with the party—beginning with the presidency of Raúl Leoni in the mid-1960s. The association maintained some visibility under AD and COPEI presidents alike from that point onward. However, the emergence of the Chávez government signaled a new era in FEDECAMARAS because many business leaders disliked Chávez's frequent speeches denouncing the negative influence of the economic oligarchy. In the April 2002 coup that briefly removed Chávez from power, the president of FEDECAMARAS, Pedro Carmona, briefly served as interim president of Venezuela. Once Chávez regained the presidency, Carmona went into exile, and several member chambers of FEDECAMARAS backed the prolonged capital strike against the Chávez government in late 2002 and early 2003. When the strike failed to convince Chávez to resign, FEDECAMARAS then began to back the recall election petition drive.

Alejandro Oropeza Castillo and Malave Villalba helped to organize the major labor confederation, the Confederation of Venezuelan Workers (*Confederación de Trabajadores Venezolanos* [CTV]), in 1936 following the death of Juan Vicente Gómez the previous year. Oropeza Castillo, the secretary general of the CTV, later helped to found the AD party in 1941, thus beginning an enduring association between the reformist political party and the largest labor confederation in Venezuela. After the divisive experience of the *trienio*, AD's leaders pressured its affiliates in the CTV to reunify the labor movement. Union leaders of all partisan distinctions gathered in 1958 to form the Unified National Union Committee (*Comité Sindical Unificado Nacional* [CSUN]). The CSUN spearheaded the reorganization of state and local unions according to proportional representation. The CTV congress in November 1959 cemented this process when it chose the executive committee and all functioning boards via proportional representation. The CTV enjoyed considerable participation in many of the state-owned enterprises launched during the 1970s and 1980s. As AD's authority waned in the 1990s, other voices became more audible within the CTV. After the election of Hugo Chávez, the new president successfully backed a referendum asking the CTV leaders to step down. Chávez also pushed for a revision of the CTV's by-laws so that a new leadership vote would have to permit direct participation by all members. Although the government promoted the candidacy of a former mayor of Caracas as the new CTV leader, AD veteran Carlos Ortega won the 2001 election with over 57 percent of the vote. In the months that followed, Ortega and other CTV leaders would become vocal critics of Hugo Chávez. However, a CTV general strike failed to mobilize most workers in early 2002; the Venezuelan labor movement appeared divided between its traditional leadership ties to AD and many individual workers' support for the Chávez movement. When the oil workers' strike of late 2002 and early 2003 failed to force Chávez's resignation, Carlos Ortega (a past leader of the oil workers' union) fled into exile in March 2003 to avoid possible imprisonment as an antigovernment activist.

While these two long-standing economic interest groups fiercely opposed the Chávez government, Hugo Chávez helped to organize a new social movement in defense of his presidency. From his presidential campaign onward, Chávez spoke about his support for the people—whom he often called *el soberano* ("the sovereign"). Chávez blamed common people's daily struggles on the "oligarchy" and on the "squalid ones" who opposed his government. For many poor Venezuelans, Chávez represented the hope of immediate improvements in their material well-being. In June 2001, in the weekly broadcast of his *¡Aló Presidente!* (*Hello President!*) call-in show, Chávez asked his supporters to form lists of people willing to back his self-proclaimed Bolivarian Revolution. During the 1990s, Chávez's MBR-200 movement had organized many such small circles of supporters. Such groups had fallen into disuse, however, after Chávez's triumph in the 1998 elections. Within months of Chávez's mid-2001 request, over 7,000 Bolivarian Circles had formed. By late 2003, over 70,000 circles existed across the country. While this social movement is an NGO, its links to the government go beyond its vocal expressions of support and its willingness to take to the streets in support of Hugo Chávez. Opponents of the Chávez government immediately criticized the use of public resources to mobilize the groups and alleged that such use of public funds might be unconstitutional. The Venezuelan government maintains an online register of the Bolivarian Circles, in which it defines the nature and size of the organizations and asks potential groups to submit an online registration form.[2] Many observers believe that the circles played a crucial role in organizing the street demonstrations after the April 2002 coup that demanded Chávez' return as president.

One of the most active social movements in Venezuela in recent years has been Social Group CESAP (*Grupo Social CESAP*). Founded in 1973 as the Center in the Service of Popular Action (*Centro al Servicio de la Acción Popular* [CESAP]), this NGO links over twenty member organizations into a nationwide framework. Its members strive to promote community-level organizations dedicated to civic activism and economic development, and it supported over 1,000 community groups by the early twenty-first century. Although some of the group's roots are in the Catholic church, Social Group CESAP is a nondenominational organization with ties to secular and religious movements. The group received an award from the United Nations in 1991 for its support of literacy campaigns. In the early 1990s, the movement supported calls for a constituent assembly that ultimately did not find sufficient backing in the Venezuelan legislature. Amid the polarization of Venezuelan politics during 2002 and 2003, Social Group CESAP urged the Chávez government and its principal opponents to reach a compromise and to resolve their differences peacefully.

Parties and Elections

The major political party in the early twenty-first century has been Hugo Chávez's Fifth Republic Movement (*Movimiento Quinta República* [MVR]).

After his release from prison in 1994, Chávez rejoined the MBR-200 military movement he had helped to establish in 1982. After the experience of the failed February 1992 coup (and several conspirators' subsequent celebrity), the MBR-200 began to expand its ties to civilian critics of the Venezuelan political system. Initially many MBR-200 leaders remained skeptical about electoral politics. By 1997, most MBR-200 leaders became convinced that they should participate in the 1998 elections. Because Venezuelan electoral law prohibited the use of Bolívar's name in political parties, the MBR-200 created the MVR because the new abbreviation (formed by using the Roman numeral "V" for fifth) would be pronounced similarly in Venezuelan Spanish to MBR. Initially, most envisioned the MVR as the electoral arm of the MBR-200. However, once Chávez was elected to the presidency and the MVR formed alliances with many other political parties and social movements, the MBR-200 withered away. The eclipse of the MBR-200 would form one of several motivations for many of Chávez's initial comrades-in-arms to join the opposition to the MVR in the 2000 elections.

Without question, the most important political party in twentieth-century Venezuela was the Democratic Action party (*Acción Democrática* [AD]). The party's roots lie in the efforts of the Generation of 1928 to end military rule in Venezuela. Rómulo Betancourt and many other leaders forged a series of organizations in the 1930s and then founded AD in 1941 as a center-left party dedicated to rapid socioeconomic and political reform. As discussed earlier, the collapse of the *trienio* government convinced AD's leadership to pursue a much more muted set of reforms when it returned to power in 1958. From 1958 through 1993, AD and COPEI dominated Venezuelan politics; AD candidates held the presidency for twenty-five of those thirty-five years. The upheaval and economic discontent associated with Pérez's second presidency helped to discredit AD, and it steadily lost voter support from the 1990s onward. In the early twenty-first century, AD opposed the Chávez presidency, but its own path back to the presidency seemed unclear even if Chávez left office.

In 1946, during the *trienio*, Catholic conservatives formed a center-right, Christian Democratic party—Committee of Independent Electoral Political Organization (*Comité de Organización Política Electoral Independiente* [COPEI]). The party termed itself a social Christian movement formed to prevent the emergence of communism in Venezuela. Initially, many COPEI activists feared that AD constituted a potential vehicle for the adoption of socialism. After many COPEI leaders joined AD activists in exile during the Pérez Jiménez dictatorship, however, COPEI and AD formed a loose coalition in opposition to military rule. By signing the Pact of Punto Fijo in 1958, the two former enemies began a process of mutual collaboration that would produce considerable power-sharing once the two parties began to dominate electoral politics in the early 1970s. When COPEI founder Rafael Caldera broke with the party in 1993, his exit ignited a loss of support from which the party had yet to recover by May 2004. The future of this once-major party remained very much in doubt.

Caldera was not the only candidate offering a frontal critique of politics as usual in 1993. The *Causa Radical* (Radical Cause [*Causa R*]) party had formed in the 1980s in opposition to what it saw as political and economic stagnation under AD and COPEI. When voters began to abandon AD and COPEI in 1993, *Causa R* received one-fifth of the vote in both the presidential and legislative elections. The party alleged that electoral boards dominated by AD and COPEI had blocked many of its votes from being counted via fraudulent manipulation of the official electoral returns. MBR-200's reluctance to compete for office motivated another of its founders, Francisco Arias Cárdenas, to leave the movement and run as the successful gubernatorial candidate for the *Causa R* party in Zulia in 1995. In 1997, *Causa R* split into two factions divided by a bitter dispute over economic policy. In the years that followed, however, the party saw its electoral fortunes eclipsed by the rise of the MVR and its Patriotic Pole coalition, which became the primary option for voters displeased with the two major parties. In the 2000 presidential elections, *Causa R* cosponsored Francisco Arias Cárdenas as the major opposition political candidate, but its share of the legislature remained miniscule.

Table 11.1 bears witness to the declining electoral fortunes of COPEI and AD. In the 1988 election, their candidates received 93 percent of the vote. In the 1993 campaign, however, these two parties, which had completely dominated presidential elections from 1973 through 1988, got less than half of the vote. The hastily formed Convergence (*Convergencia*) coalition backed the independent

TABLE 11.1   Venezuelan Presidential Elections (1988, 1993, 1998, 2000): Percentage of Popular Vote, by Party

Party	1988	1993	1998	2000
AD	52.9	23.6	*	—
COPEI	40.4	22.7	*	—
Radical Cause	0.3	22.0	0.1	37.5[†]
Convergence	—	30.5	—	—
Patriotic Pole	—	—	56.2	59.5
Others	6.3	1.3	43.7	3.0

*In the 1998 election, the AD, the COPEI, and several smaller parties ultimately backed the candidate sponsored by Project Venezuela, Henrique Salas Römer, who received 40.0 percent of the vote.

[†]In the 2000 election, most parties opposed to Patriotic Pole candidate Hugo Chávez informally supported the campaign of Francisco Arias Cárdenas, who received 37.5 percent of the vote.

SOURCE: For 1988, data are from Miriam Kornblith and Daniel Levine, "Venezuela: The Life and Times of the Party System" in Scott Mainwaring and Timothy Scully, eds., *Building Democratic Institutions: Party Systems in Latin America* (Stanford, Calif.: Stanford University Press, 1995), p. 49. For the years 1993–2000, data are from the Political Database of the Americas <http://www.georgetown.edu/pdba/Elecdata/Venezuela/ven.html> (accessed on November 14, 2003).

candidacy of past president Rafael Caldera. Caldera had broken ranks with the party he founded, COPEI, and became a stern critic of market-oriented reforms pursued under the Pérez administration. Caldera was the one candidate who could combine political experience and a strident critique of politics as usual. Once in office, however, Caldera himself would adopt several market-oriented reforms, beginning in 1996 with the launch of his Venezuelan Agenda economic program. As a recession unfolded in 1997, voters looked outside the ranks of the two major parties for a new leader. The initial leader in preelection public-opinion polls was Irene Sáez, a former Miss Universe who had served as mayor of a Caracas suburb. Over time, however, her campaign lost support because she found it difficult to forge and maintain a consistent campaign message. At first, relatively few observers took Chávez's candidacy seriously. The MVR candidate pledged to restore the "lost honor of the nation," but few believed his brand-new political party could win the election. When the Saez campaign found it difficult to sustain its initial support, Henrique Salas Römer then became the outsider candidate with momentum. Salas Römer's new Project Venezuela party pro-vided a stark contrast to the MVR. Project Venezuela called for a market-oriented economic policy and focused most campaign appearances in comfortable neighborhoods. At the tail end of the campaign, the desperate leaders of AD and COPEI withdrew their endorsement from their respective candidates and threw their support behind Salas Römer. Several observers argued that their support for Salas Römer probably ruined whatever chance he might have had to win the presidency because it tied him to the political establishment. Chávez swept to victory with a convincing 56 percent of the vote.

Legislative elections similarly demonstrated the end to the dominance of the two traditional parties (see Table 11.2). In these elections, however, COPEI and

TABLE 11.2 Venezuelan Legislative Elections (1988, 1993, 1998, 2000): Percentage of Seats Held, by Party*

Party	1988	1993	1998	2000
AD	48.3	27.1	24.5	18.2
COPEI	33.3	26.1	12.3	4.8
Radical Cause	1.5	19.7	3.0	1.8
Convergence	—	12.8	2.3	0.6
Patriotic Pole	—	—	34.2	62.4
Others	16.9	12.9	23.7	12.2

*The data for 1988, 1993, and 1998 reflect the outcome of the Chamber of Deputies election. The 2000 data reflect the outcome of the unicameral National Assembly election held following the creation of the 1999 constitution.

SOURCE: Political Database of the Americas <http://www.georgetown.edu/pdba/Elecdata/Venezuela/ven.html> (accessed on November 14, 2003).

especially AD managed to retain a role. The most marked trend across these past four legislative elections is the continuing fragmentation of the legislative vote. Although the MVR did the best in the Patriotic Pole coalition, it still earned only a little over 40 percent of the seats in the new National Assembly. All other parties received less than 20 percent of the popular vote.

THE CONTEMPORARY QUEST FOR DEVELOPMENT, LIBERTY, AND GOVERNANCE

After his victory in the 1988 elections, Carlos Andrés Pérez inherited serious economic problems. The Venezuelan government could obtain financing only at exorbitant rates of interest. Foreign exchange reserves were not sufficient to meet existing debt obligations that would come due during Pérez's second presidency. While some saw a shift toward market capitalism as a way to solve these problems, many politicians and ordinary citizens viewed the shift away from state capitalism as undesirable.

The debate over liberty also proved increasingly divisive. For three decades, Venezuela had enjoyed a level of democratic stability in an era characterized by military rule in much of Latin America. Over time, however, concerns emerged that AD and COPEI were maintaining their electoral dominance through a combustible mix of clientelism, corruption, and increasing use of electoral fraud.

This combination of worsening economic conditions and calls for political reform presented Carlos Andrés Pérez with governance challenges that he had not faced during the 1970s oil boom. In his first presidency, AD controlled a majority in the legislature, and Pérez could use rising oil revenues to dampen opposition and to extend his political support. In 1988, AD fell just short of controlling a legislative majority, and Pérez would need to devise new governing strategies that did not rely as heavily on oil profits.

The Quest for Development in Venezuela

Two weeks after his inauguration, Carlos Andrés Pérez announced a market-oriented economic plan that he labeled *el viraje* ("the great turnaround"); most Venezuelans tended to refer to it as "the package." According to a new loan agreement with the International Monetary Fund (IMF), the government announced an end to most price controls and government subsidies, plans to freeze salaries and cut government spending, and a devaluation of the national currency, the *bolívar*. On February 27, 1989, buses in Caracas raised their fares, several in excess of the announced price hike. Some poor Venezuelans (who, like most low-income Latin Americans, tend to bring exact change for traveling to work by bus) reacted angrily. In several situations, people turned buses over and burned them. As police responded to these incidents, hundreds of other people began looting businesses in a wave of violence that spread to many areas of the capital. When Pérez declared a state of siege and called in the military, hundreds

TABLE 11.3 Venezuelan Economic Indicators (1983–2002)*

Year	GDP growth	Inflation	Unemployment	Debt service ratio[†]
1983	−5.5	7	11.2	22
1984	−1.5	18	14.3	24
1985	1.7	7	14.3	25
1986	6.0	13	12.1	31
1987	3.8	40	9.9	26
1988	5.9	36	7.9	29
1989	−7.8	81	9.7	27
1990	6.8	37	10.5	17
1991	10.2	31	8.7	15
1992	6.9	32	7.1	17
1993	−0.4	46	6.6	17
1994	−3.0	71	8.7	17
1995	4.8	57	10.3	16
1996	0.0	103	11.8	11
1997	6.9	38	11.4	14
1998	0.6	30	11.3	15
1999	−5.5	20	15.0	13
2000	3.8	13	13.9	9
2001	3.5	12	13.3	10
2002	−9.0	31	15.8	8

*All numbers are percentages.

[†]The debt service ratio expresses interest paid on foreign debts as a percentage of total exports.

SOURCE: For the years 1983–1987, data are from United Nations Economic Commission for Latin America and the Caribbean, *Preliminary Overview of the Economies of Latin America and the Caribbean 1989* (Santiago, Chile: United Nations Publications, 1989). For the years 1988–1992, data are from United Nations Economic Commission for Latin America and the Caribbean, *Preliminary Overview of the Economies of Latin America and the Caribbean 1994* (Santiago, Chile: United Nations Publications, 1994). For the years 1993–1997, data are from United Nations Economic Commission for Latin America and the Caribbean, *Preliminary Overview of the Economies of Latin America and the Caribbean 1999* (Santiago, Chile: United Nations Publications, 1999). For the years 1998–2002, data are from United Nations Economic Commission for Latin America and the Caribbean, *Preliminary Overview of the Economies of Latin America and the Caribbean 2003* (Santiago, Chile: United Nations Publications, 2003).

of people died. These so-called *caracazo* disturbances dramatized the level of popular frustration with Venezuela's worsening economic conditions in 1989 (see Table 11.3). Pérez's turn to market capitalism and his use of force to restore order cost him considerable support among many poor Venezuelans who had voted for him in December 1988 as a potential national savior.

The Pérez administration held firm, however, to its plans for market-oriented reform. The average tariff dropped by two-thirds, and the government eliminated nontariff barriers on most manufactured goods. Pérez overhauled the tax system by introducing a value-added tax that increased government revenues but also raised the level of taxation on low-income citizens. Restrictions on foreign investment fell by the wayside, and the government announced an ambitious privatization program. By 1991, the government sold the national airline, the telephone company, several public banks, and additional firms. It then announced plans to sell most remaining public utilities and a wide variety of manufacturing firms. These reforms helped to restore economic growth in 1990 and 1991; however, much of the economic recovery could be attributed to the doubling of oil prices associated with the Persian Gulf War. The brief oil boom did little, however, to improve conditions for most low-income citizens. Despite the economic recovery associated with the Persian Gulf War, Pérez continued to find it difficult to build public support for his adoption of market capitalist economic policies.

Rafael Caldera had been one of the few established politicians who sharply criticized the failings of the two major political parties in the early 1990s. He cited their failures as the primary motivator for the February 4, 1992, military coup attempt. In the next legislative session after the incident, he addressed Congress: "It is difficult to ask the people to burn for freedom and democracy while they think that freedom and democracy are not able to feed them and impede the exorbitant increase in the cost of subsistence; when it has not been able to deal effectively with the blight of corruption."[3] Caldera followed this rhetorical break with the two traditional political parties with a more tangible break: he left the COPEI party that he had founded forty-seven years earlier. He ran as the presidential candidate of the Convergence (*Convergencia*) coalition of many small political parties. He also enjoyed the support of the largest party on the political left, the Movement Toward Socialism (*Movimiento al Socialismo* [MAS]). On the campaign trail, Rafael Caldera opposed the move toward market capitalist policies under Pérez's second presidency.

Once in office, he initially attempted to mobilize government authority to restore a favorable economic climate. He halted plans for many privatizations and slowed the pace of tariff reduction. In June 1994, Caldera issued a decree in which he suspended five basic liberties—including the right to private property, the right to receive compensation for property expropriated by the state, and the right to pursue profitable activities. He claimed these powers in the name of an economic emergency. When the Venezuelan Congress overturned the decree, he issued a new decree that addressed the specific issue raised by Congress but reinstituted the suspension of these constitutionally entrenched rights. Caldera used this authority to regulate prices, to control the movement of foreign currencies, and to restructure wobbly banks in the financial system (the country's second largest bank had failed just prior to his inauguration). Although Congress relented in this matter, Caldera could not build majority support for a restructuring of the tax system to put government services on a more secure financial footing. While Caldera's state capitalist efforts initially succeeded in lowering inflation and restoring economic growth, the economy reentered a recession by 1996 and inflation surpassed triple digits for the first time in the modern Venezuelan history.

As Venezuela's economic fortunes worsened, Caldera changed course and approved a traditional, market-oriented stabilization policy in April 1996 as part of a loan agreement signed with the IMF. To make this policy shift more palatable politically, Caldera chose an unusual messenger to serve as his economic minister, Teodoro Petkoff. Petkoff had spent his entire life as a leftist political activist associated with MAS and as a popular journalist. He became the face behind the Venezuelan Agenda of market-oriented reforms: budget cuts, tariff reductions, devaluation, an end to the prior investment and exchange controls, and a promise to earmark revenues for the repayment of outstanding foreign debt.

The economy recovered in 1997, only to stagnate in 1998 as oil prices fell yet again, losing one-third of their value over the course of the year. Prior to Caldera's presidency, the number of households living below the poverty line of $2.00 per day had increased markedly from 1990 through 1994. Erratic economic performance under Caldera's government made progress in poverty reduction difficult; the poverty rate remained at 1994 levels and then rose slightly toward the end of his term. In a decade of stop-and-go attempts at market-oriented economic reform, neither Pérez nor Caldera managed to build broad public support for market capitalism (see the *Research Question* on pages 394–395).

Hugo Chávez's campaign speeches on economic policy had not advocated socialism but rather state capitalism. He called for "as much state as necessary and as much market as possible." Once in power, he initially focused on a review of the legal framework for recently privatized economic sectors and on a call for tax reform that would reduce tax evasion and thus increase funds available for poverty reduction. His Bolívar Plan 2000 called for the armed forces to assist other government agencies to improve the provision of health care, sanitation, transportation, housing, and poverty relief. He also restored the long-running government standard for severance pay that had been eliminated under the Caldera government in 1997. Despite rumors among his opponents that Chávez planned to lead Venezuela toward a socialist economy, the new government employed a mixed-economy approach. Nevertheless, investors reacted cautiously. Catastrophic flooding in December 1999 caused enormous property damage. These problems and low oil prices helped to shrink the economy by 7 percent in 1999.

Chávez turned his attention to reforming the oil sector abroad and at home. The Venezuelan government successfully pushed OPEC for production cutbacks that helped raise oil prices by over 50 percent in 2000. The government then set its sights on reforming the national oil company, PDVSA. From the 1980s onward, PDVSA executives had reduced their tax obligation by their manipulation of the **royalty** formula and through the clever use of their foreign subsidiaries (most notably, their ownership of Citgo in the United States). PDVSA's activity comprised four-fifths of all national exports, two-fifths of government revenues, and one-fourth of the GDP. To increase government revenues, Chávez proposed to revise the formula for royalty and taxation payments.

Business interests in and out of the oil sector criticized the PDVSA reform proposals. Their criticisms became more virulent once Chávez received special economic decree powers for one year beginning in November 2000. During this period, he issued forty-nine decree laws. Many of the decree laws regulated elements of all three economic sectors—agriculture, manufacturing, and services—in ways that gave advantages to small farmers, small fishing interests, small manufacturing firms, and small retail businesses. A new hydrocarbons law doubled royalty payments, although it also conceded a nearly 50 percent reduction in the highest income-tax rate relevant to the sector. A new land-reform program aimed at reducing ownership inequality in an agricultural sector in which 3 percent of the owners controlled 70 percent of all agricultural land. Chávez's program set a maximum farm size that varied according to

RESEARCH QUESTION
Under What Conditions Are Citizens More Likely to Support Market-Oriented Economic Reform?

The shift from state capitalism toward market capitalism changed the economic context for millions of people. Under what conditions were people more likely to support market-oriented economic reform? Kurt Weyland analyzed the political dynamics of economic reform in a 1998 study.[1] Weyland examineds two major explanations of public support for market-oriented reforms. He notes that most research in the early 1990s emphasized the compensation hypothesis. Because both the privatization of state-owned enterprises and the reduction of protection for privately owned firms would initially cost thousands of people their jobs, many researchers argued that market-oriented politicians would need to find ways to compensate those harmed by the reforms. In particular, the compensation hypothesis stresses the role of emergency social spending to assist regions, families, and individuals disrupted by the reforms. While Weyland agrees that social spending can be used to build political support, he notes that the desire to reduce government deficits makes it difficult for reforming governments to provide sufficient compensation to generate mass political support. As an alternative explanation, Weyland puts forward the rescue

[1] Kurt Weyland, "Swallowing the Bitter Pill: Sources of Political Support for Neoliberal Reform in Latin America," *Comparative Political Studies* 31 (1998): 539–568. For additional research in academic journals regarding the politics of economic reform, see the appropriate portion of this book's website.

productivity. Farmers who used less than 80 percent of their land faced fines and, under certain conditions, potential expropriation.

Many propertied Venezuelans criticized Chávez's economic program. In this contentious debate over economic policy, PDVSA executives tried to reverse several reforms, and oil workers went on strike in April 2002. Chávez then fired seven members of the PDVSA board. This conflict spread as FEDECAMARAS and the CTV launched strikes and protests. The protests culminated in Chávez's temporary removal in a military coup later that month.

The events of April 2002 did not mark an end to conflict over economic policy or over oil policy in particular. In early December, oil executives and oil workers went back on strike. Ship captains anchored their tankers at sea, oil well supervisors took their wells offline, and most PDVSA activity ground to a halt. The strikers called for Chávez's immediate resignation. Several business owners in comfortable Caracas neighborhoods launched a sympathy strike, but most employees and managers in the national economy kept working. Nonetheless, given the centrality of oil to the Venezuelan economy, the ten-week strike cost

---

hypothesis. Borrowing from prospect theory in cognitive psychology, Weyland argues that, under normal economic conditions, citizens remain risk-averse. This risk aversion limits their willingness to shift toward market capitalism. If the country confronts a major economic crisis that already imposes serious economic disadvantages, however, people will become more risk-accepting, thereby raising the possibility that they might support major economic reform as a potential path out of the crisis. In particular, Weyland argues that hyperinflation can pave the way for economic reform because it affects the vast majority of the public in a dramatic and negative way.

These two hypotheses are examined via a comparative case study of economic reform in the 1980s and 1990s in six Latin American countries. In the four countries that experienced hyperinflationary crises (Argentina, Bolivia, Brazil, and Peru), public opinion became increasingly receptive to market-oriented reforms. Conversely, in the two countries whose economic crises did not produce hyperinflation (Mexico and Venezuela), popular support for market capitalism remained more limited. While the rescue hypothesis closely matches these countries' experiences, the compensation hypothesis does not provide a consistently useful explanation. Market-oriented governments in Mexico and Venezuela spent the most money by far on targeted social programs, yet they encountered the most opposition to their economic agendas. While Weyland accepts the notion that opposition to economic reform might have been even higher without this social spending, he concludes that the compensation strategy is, at best, a complementary approach. The major break with prior economic policies is most likely to be welcomed when economic conditions are viewed as both bleak and deteriorating.

the Venezuelan government millions of dollars in tax revenues and precipitated a nationwide recession. A bitter Chávez government fired one-third of PDVSA's employees. The oil strike ended in February 2003 when the opposition agreed to pursue a recall election aimed at ending Chávez's presidency. It then took several months to get oil production back to prestrike levels. The GDP shrank by 9 percent in 2003.

Of the seven countries examined in this book, Venezuela stayed closest to the state capitalist model of economic policy in the contemporary era. The Pérez government's attempt to dismantle the state capitalist system did not produce a complete shift because of considerable opposition from people inside and outside his own AD party. Rafael Caldera then campaigned stridently against market capitalism and initially suspended the remaining market reforms that Pérez had proposed. With weak oil prices and continuing pressure from the domestic and international financial community, however, the Caldera government reversed its initial stance and approved several additional market-oriented reforms from 1996 through early 1999. Hugo Chávez received a broader electoral mandate in support of his state capitalist proposals. From 1999 through early 2004, the Chávez government attempted to increase its financial resources in support of a more active state by pushing for higher oil prices and by increasing fiscal pressure on PDVSA.

Venezuela experienced erratic economic performance under all of the presidents serving from 1989 to 2003. In part, this uneven performance stemmed from continuing dependence on oil. In years with increases in oil prices, the economy grew quickly. In down years, the economy struggled. Beyond the role of oil, Venezuela's contemporary economic problems also demonstrated the importance of building political support for the economic policies in place. None of these presidents managed to build a sufficient base of political support to sustain the economic policies they preferred. Without political support, the climate for investment and for economic activity more generally soured considerably. In turn, poverty worsened during the initial implementation of the economic opening and did not drop in the decade that followed. Environmental problems in the Lake Maracaibo region—home to most of Venezuela's oil reserves—remained considerable.

The Quest for Liberty in Venezuela

Prior to Pérez's inauguration, the major debate regarding liberty revolved around rising demands for political reform. His predecessor, Jaime Lusinchi, had organized the Presidential Commission on State Reform. The commission recommended many changes, including the decentralization of government services, electoral reform, and internal reforms within the major political parties' organizational structures. In the first year of his term, Pérez implemented several recommendations regarding subnational government. Prior to this reform, governors and mayors had been elected indirectly under the terms of the 1961 constitution. Beginning in 1989, Venezuela held its first direct elections for state governors and mayors. Several of the major political figures in the years to come would first make a name for themselves in state and local politics.

The Pérez administration moved more slowly, however, on the commission's recommendations regarding new mechanisms aimed at reducing corruption. Most of Pérez's anticorruption efforts centered on the investigation of allegations involving the prior administration led by Jaime Lusinchi. Amid the controversy regarding his market-oriented reforms, Pérez's opponents also criticized his efforts to protect liberty. Some seized on his reputation for corruption and began to investigate new scandals. Others claimed that the state of siege amid the *caracazo* riots led to the improper use of force against Venezuelan citizens. Faced with increasing criticism (and in the wake of two failed coup attempts during 1992), Pérez offered in early 1993 to support the creation of a constitutional convention in which institutional reforms regarding these and other matters could be treated. By that time, however, corruption scandals had reached the boiling point. Pérez's low standing in public-opinion polls made his opponents more interested in removing Pérez than in his constitutional proposals.

The initial liberty issue addressed by Rafael Caldera involved civil-military relations. Specifically, the newly elected president argued in 1994 that national reconciliation demanded the release of soldiers who had participated in the two failed coup attempts in 1992. Hugo Chávez and the rest of the February 1992 coup leaders had their sentences commuted, and Caldera declared an amnesty to exonerate the leaders of the November 1992 coup. It should be noted that the coup organizers accepted Caldera's olive branch: they began to enter electoral politics. The leader of the coup mobilization in the oil-rich state of Zulia, Francisco Arias Cárdenas, ran successfully for governor of Zulia as a candidate for *Causa R* in the 1995 midterm elections. As we know, Chávez and many of his other compatriots organized his successful 1998 presidential campaign.

Caldera's use of discretionary powers created considerable controversy. His June 1994 emergency decree did not just suspend economic rights, it also suspended constitutional protections for freedom of movement and for protection against arbitrary arrest and search without warrant. Over time, human rights lawyers raised concern over what they saw as the arbitrary use of police power in Caracas and in several other cities. In May 1995, their legal challenge to the decree reached the Supreme Court. Caldera publicly denounced this attempt to overturn his decree as an effort to stop his government from "guaranteeing the transformation of the country."[4] Ultimately the Supreme Court upheld the decree, but Caldera subsequently ended the state of emergency in July 1995 amid continuing media pressure and improving economic conditions.

After well over a decade of debate, Hugo Chávez renewed the call for political reform in his inaugural address. He argued that all three branches of government needed a complete overhaul. As discussed earlier in this chapter, he

Hugo Chávez frequently wears a beret as a symbol of his paratrooper background and of his participation in the failed February 1992 coup attempt. AP/Wide World Press.

successfully backed a referendum launching a constituent assembly (the ANC) and then campaigned aggressively on behalf of his supporters—who won an overwhelming majority of the seats in the ANC. As a result, both Chávez's supporters and his detractors tended to see the 1999 constitution as his creation. The new document increased the president's powers and reduced the role of the legislature and of political parties in particular. Chávez argued that AD and COPEI controlled decisions too tightly in the past. In response, he spoke constantly about the need for additional checks on party politicians.

Perhaps the most tangible reflections of Chávez's vision of checks and balances in the 1999 constitution can be seen in two additional major changes: the inclusion of some provisions enabling direct democracy and the reorganization of watchdog agencies into the Citizens' Power and the Electoral Power. Several direct democracy provisions are in place in the Bolivarian Republic. First, 10 percent of the voters can request a nationwide vote to pass a new law. At the state and local levels of government, the same provision holds regarding subnational laws. Second, as discussed earlier, the 1999 constitution permits 20 percent of the voters to request a recall election during the second half of any elected official's term; to pass, the recall must enjoy the support of more voters than had previously elected the official (and a minimum of 25 percent of the voters must participate in the recall election). Third, 10 percent of the voters can request a referendum to overturn an existing law; this procedure does not apply to budgetary legislation, tax law, human rights law, or international treaties. To be a valid revocation referendum, at least 40 percent of the registered voters must participate.

To highlight the new government's stated aim of reducing corruption, watch-dog agencies have been transformed into what the 1999 constitution calls the fourth and fifth branches of government. The Citizens' Power section of the constitution creates a Republican Moral Council consisting of a human rights ombudsperson (*Defensor del Pueblo*), the attorney general, and the general comptroller. In addition to fighting corruption and promoting clean government in their respective spheres, they must act together to recommend sanctions for misconduct. The Electoral Power section of the constitution creates the new five-person National Electoral Council (*Consejo Nacional Electoral* [CNE]) and expressly prohibits people affiliated with political parties from serving on the CNE. The National Assembly must approve the CNE members by a two-thirds vote, with members selected at staggered intervals during a legislative mandate.

Although the 1999 constitution calls for a new morality in government affairs as well as popular checks on presidential authority, many of Chávez's critics argue that the new institutions in practice have infringed on liberty in several ways. For example, when the government organized new presidential and legislative elections in 2000 (following the ratification of the 1999 constitution), many argued that the CNE had failed to produce a trustworthy and accurate voter registration list and that it had not adequately prepared at the precinct level for electoral observers and other safeguards. Faced with public criticism and a legal challenge in the Supreme Tribunal of Justice, the CNE eventually relented and the government shifted the election date from May to July for additional time to improve the process. Following those elections, the new National Assembly (controlled by a pro-Chávez majority) selected new justices for the TSJ and the members of the Citizens' Power. Many groups and individuals, including the outgoing human rights ombudsperson, argued that the selection bypassed various constitutional provisions calling for citizen and NGO participation in the nomination and review process. On this occasion, however, the government did not reverse course nor did the courts side with the critics.

The most prominent ongoing debate over liberty under Chávez involved the freedom of the press. Although freedom of speech and freedom of the press are expressly protected in the 1999 constitution, advocates for freedom of the press remained concerned about a provision that gives citizens a right to "true" information; they feared that this vague standard could be used to suppress stories that judges find untrue when compared to this unclear standard. The more tangible disputes involved new legislation passed under Chávez that gave the president considerable authority to shut down television and radio broadcasts and also made it easier for the chief executive to revoke the licenses of broadcast stations. In October 2003, the government seized remote broadcasting equipment from Globovision, Venezuela's twenty-four-hour news network. This action heightened concern that proposed legislation to reduce freedom of the press (by requiring "respectful" treatment of government officials) might eventually pass.

The primary liberty concerns at the outset of the contemporary era revolved around political reform as a path toward reducing government corruption and opening up the electoral process. Under Pérez and Caldera, the decentralization of several government programs constituted the lone major change implemented in the 1990s. Judicial reform proved limited and electoral oversight reform was nearly nonexistent.

Hugo Chávez charged into office as an outsider motivated to redesign most political institutions. His administration delivered on many of its promises for reform: all branches of government underwent considerable revision. In addition, the Patriotic Pole backed the incorporation of several mechanisms of direct democracy as an extension of political liberty that they argued would make citizens better able to serve as protagonists in the new regime. Whether one supports Chávez or not, the recall provision provided a potential institutional path toward resolving the ongoing crisis of his presidency. However, the electoral authority's March 2004 refusal to recognize over one-third of the signatures on the presidential recall petition rekindled fears that the political forces in power might not respect the rights of their opponents. The subsequent reconfirmation of signatures lessened those concerns, but only slightly. Rumors circulated among Chávez's opponents that the government either would block the recall election in the judicial system or it would conduct a fraudulent election.

On other liberty issues, the Chávez experience has echoed concerns about delegative democracy elsewhere in the hemisphere. While Chávez preached the value of Venezuela's five branches of government, his opponents complained that it does not matter how many separate branches or arms of government exist if the president's supporters control them all. Whether Chávez would be willing to share power eventually regarding the naming of judges, the promotion of military personnel, and other issues remains to be seen.

The Quest for Governance in Venezuela

Carlos Andrés Pérez's about-face in economic strategy presented him with considerable political challenges. On one hand, this move toward market-oriented policies infuriated many poor Venezuelans who had voted for Pérez with the idea that his government would protect their economic interests. On the other hand, Pérez's policy shift unleashed a rebellion within his own AD party. Pérez had anticipated opposition and staffed many key cabinet positions with people from outside his own party. While this approach made it easier for the cabinet to develop these policy reforms, it infuriated the opponents of economic reform within AD. The head of the party organization frequently remarked, "This is not an *adeco* [AD] government; neither its men nor its ideas are *adeco*."[5] By 1991, many AD politicians at the national and subnational levels were criticizing the Pérez government and trying to block its ongoing plans for economic reform.

Within this tense climate, junior officers led by Lieutenant Colonel Hugo Chávez launched a coup attempt on the evening of February 3, 1992. Although the soldiers took up several key positions in a handful of cities, the military's high command mobilized in support of the president. The rebels did not control Caracas nor did they capture the president. As discussed at the start of this chapter, Hugo Chávez became a national figure by forthrightly claiming responsibility for the coup while he simultaneously proclaimed that the struggle would continue. Many Venezuelans sympathized with Chávez's rejection of the Pérez government. On March 10, many Caracas residents participated in a pot-banging march (*cacerolazo*) demanding Pérez's resignation and shouting, "Long live Chávez!"

In the months that followed, Pérez's support continued to decline. In early November 1992, a COPEI proposal to shorten his term was blocked by AD opposition in the Senate. On November 27, 1992, a second coup attempt failed amid considerable fighting among all three branches; a few hundred people died in the rebellion. Not surprisingly, the AD candidates in state and local elections in December did poorly.

Pérez tried to reverse his fortunes and clear the air by proposing a constitutional convention. The legislature rejected this proposal in early March 1993. A few days later, the Supreme Court accepted allegations from the *Causa R* party that charged Pérez with the illegal diversion of government funds into the political campaigns of governing parties in Bolivia, Haiti, and Nicaragua. With Pérez's approval rating in public-opinion polls standing at less than 10 percent, the legislature moved swiftly to investigate the matter and began impeachment proceedings by midyear. Congress removed Pérez from office on August 31 and made veteran AD senator Ramón Velázquez the interim president until Pérez's term expired in February 1994.

Rafael Caldera took office as a double-minority president (review *Governing Strategies: Fernando Belaúnde* in Chapter Four). The Convergence coalition and its allies in the MAS party held just one-fourth of the seats in the legislature. Caldera tried to govern by forging an alliance with *Causa R* and a few COPEI legislators with whom he had a long working relationship. The strategy worked at first but came under increasing stress amid the diverse policy perspectives found across the many member parties in the legislative coalition. MAS partisans pushed for more aggressive use of government authority, while both Convergence and *Causa R* found themselves divided over the debate between government-oriented and market-oriented economic policies.

When Caldera opted to move toward the market in pursuit of IMF financing and foreign investment, the decision forced him to redesign his governing coalition. Most of the MAS party refused to support the adoption of market capitalist strategies; Teodoro Petkoff resigned from a party he had helped lead. *Causa R* broke into two factions—one supporting the Venezuelan Agenda and the larger faction opposing it. Faced with the breakup of his legislative support, Caldera turned to the same AD party he had harshly criticized in the 1993 campaign. He offered AD several cabinet posts and helped pass legislation backed by AD. In exchange, he pulled in AD votes in support of laws central to his reform package. The legislative deal-making helped to keep Caldera's government afloat, but disaffected Venezuelans grew frustrated with the inability of established leaders to resolve pressing economic problems.

In this troubled climate, Hugo Chávez garnered a majority victory in the 1998 presidential elections. In his inaugural address in February 1999, he declared a state of social emergency in the country, asked for special powers to pursue economic reforms, and called for the creation of a constituent assembly to write a new constitution. Chávez's initial strategy for governance focused on the quick creation of new political institutions. In pursuing the convocation of a constituent assembly, he capitalized on high approval ratings in public-opinion polls (which averaged around 80 percent), and he worked to incorporate traditional political parties and interest groups in the consultations leading up to the ANC. The ANC process enhanced Chávez's authority both in the short run and the medium run. The immediate implication of the constitutional reform process proved to be the suspension of the existing legislature by mid-1999. For the rest of the year and part of 2000, a special committee of the ANC (a *Congresillo* ["mini-Congress"] dominated numerically by pro-Chávez delegates) served as an acting legislature. When the Patriotic Pole coalition won ninety-two of the 165 seats in the new unicameral National Assembly, Chávez initially enjoyed a larger majority in the legislature and a new constitution that gave the president more powers. In addition, he asked for and received special decree powers from November 2000 through November 2001 to make changes regarding the economy and crime.

While Chávez had relatively few problems pursuing his legislative agenda during the first three years of his presidency, his biggest governance challenge proved to be the increasingly vehement opposition of many sectors of society, including the wealthy, the oil sector, organized labor, and more and more retired and active-duty military personnel. In the 2000 presidential elections, one of the cofounders of MBR-200, Francisco Arias Cárdenas, ran as the primary opposition to Chávez. Arias Cárdenas had the support of several other MBR-200 members who argued that Chávez had incorporated too many experienced civilian politicians in his government. In early 2000, a retired officers' association accused Chávez of politicizing the military and centralizing too much authority. Shortly before the July 2000 elections, active-duty and retired military personnel formed another anti-Chávez military association. The anti-Chávez strikes and mobilizations of early April 2002 began to involve increasingly provocative actions on both sides. A massive antigovernment protest on April 11 marched right into a counterdemonstration supporting the president. Gunfire broke out and around twenty people died; many more were injured. Military forces announced shortly after midnight on April 12, 2002, that Hugo Chávez had resigned. Before dawn, they named the head of FEDECAMARAS, Pedro Carmona, as interim president of Venezuela.

The veteran business leader promptly announced sweeping measures to reform Venezuela's political system yet again. He declared the 1999 constitution null and void. He dissolved the National Assembly and pledged to hold new legislative elections under the old bicameral format in December 2002. Carmona announced that new presidential elections would be held within one year of the coup. He annulled all forty-nine decree laws issued by Chávez, thereby suspending the agrarian reform process and restoring the old royalty structure for PDVSA. Carmona also returned the dismissed PDVSA president to his former post. In addition, he removed all sitting justices from the Supreme Tribunal of Justice.

The coup and the wholesale changes that followed sparked considerable controversy in and out of Venezuela. Most Latin American governments (even those with leaders on uneasy terms with Chávez) denounced the coup and called for respect for the electoral process. In the Americas, two countries— El Salvador and the United States—refused to denounce the coup and several of their government officials expressed satisfaction with Chávez's ouster. Many of Chávez's supporters took to the streets of Caracas and demanded his release. In clashes with the authorities over the next couple of days, additional civilians died. Behind the scenes, many supporters of the coup criticized some or most of the sweeping changes Carmona decreed as interim president. After around thirty-six hours in office, Carmona resigned and went into exile. The next day, April 14, 2002, Hugo Chávez returned to the presidency. The president had prevailed, yet some observers argued that contemporary Venezuelan politics had become characterized by **praetorianism**, which made the country nearly ungovernable (see *Concepts in Action: Praetorianism* on pages 404–405).

Chávez's ability to reverse the 2002 coup attempt demonstrated that he retained considerable support among ordinary Venezuelans and within the military. In the weeks and months that followed, however, his ability to govern effectively remained under nearly constant challenge. The MAS party had left his governing coalition in the National Assembly, thus leaving him with a slim majority on most issues. More important, as noted earlier in the discussion of oil policy, Chávez's opponents launched a devastating strike against the government in late 2002. After two months, the strikers agreed to pursue an electoral

CONCEPTS IN ACTION
Praetorianism

The concept of praetorianism dates back to ancient Rome. The Roman Senate created a special force to protect itself against potential attack from foreign or domestic enemies. This Praetorian Guard began to use its military power as a political resource. By threatening to stop protecting the Senate (or perhaps to arrest the senators themselves), the Praetorian Guard found that it could influence government decisions including, at times, the selection of the Roman emperor.

Twentieth-century social scientists began to use the term *praetorianism* to refer to political systems in which the armed forces frequently influence government decisions through the use or threat of force. In praetorian political systems, the military's coercive power can motivate governments to bypass their existing formal procedures. Military influence sometimes convinces the executive or judicial branch to refuse to implement laws passed by the legislature. In other situations, military pressure shapes decisions made by all three branches. Perhaps the most visible form of military interference occurs when the armed forces simply refuse to respect electoral outcomes that select government officials whom they do not support.

In the 1960s, Samuel Huntington developed a broader definition of praetorianism. He referred to political systems in which most groups—military and civilian—tend to use some form of coercion rather than accepting decisions produced by formal political processes:

> In all societies specialized social groups engage in politics. What makes such groups seem more "politicized" in a praetorian society is the absence of effective political institutions capable of mediating, refining, and moderating group political action. In a praetorian system social forces confront each other nakedly; no political institutions, no corps of professional political leaders are recognized as legitimate intermediaries to moderate group conflict. Equally important, no agreement exists among the groups as to the legitimate and authoritative methods for resolving conflicts. In an institutionalized polity most political actors agree on the procedures to be used for the resolution of political disputes, that is, for the allocation of office and the determination of policy. . . . In a praetorian society, however, not only are the actors varied but so also are the methods used to decide upon office and policy. Each group employs means which reflect its peculiar nature and capabilities. The wealthy bribe; students riot; workers strike; mobs demonstrate; and the military coup. In the absence of accepted procedures, all these forms of direct action are found on the political scene. The techniques of military intervention are simply more dramatic and effective than the others because, as Hobbes put it, "When nothing else is turned up, clubs are trumps."[1]

[1]Samuel Huntington, *Political Order in Changing Societies* (New Haven, Conn.: Yale University Press, 1968), p. 196.

As you consider political life in Venezuela during the first few years of the twenty-first century, would you describe it as praetorian in a strictly military sense, praetorian in a broader sense (as defined by Huntington), both, or neither? On what grounds do you base your response to this question?

---

solution that Chávez himself constantly referred to during the strike: a recall election. Because the recall provision of the constitution is relevant for the second half of an electoral mandate, Chávez asserted that a recall vote could not be held until August 2003. His opponents presented over 3 million signatures immediately after Chávez completed the third year of his six-year term. The National Electoral Council ruled in September that the petition was invalid, however, because the signatures had been gathered in advance of the midway point of the term.

In response, the opposition began a new petition drive in late 2003 designed to gather the roughly 2.4 million signatures that would constitute 20 percent of the electorate. At the conclusion of the signature collection drive, opposition groups claimed that over 3 million signatures had been gathered. After considerable delay, however, the National Electoral Council ruled in early March 2004 that over one-third of the signatures would need to be revalidated: the authors of the signatures in question would have to come forward individually and reconfirm their signatures. This controversial decision (made via a 3–2 vote within the National Electoral Council) caused outrage among the recall's supporters. The dissenters on the electoral board argued publicly that most of the signatures in question had met the technical standards in place at the start of the recall campaign. Subsequent antigovernment protests turned violent when government security forces fired on demonstrators in an effort to prevent them from reaching an international economic summit being held in Caracas at the time. In May 2004, over 500,000 Venezuelans came forward to confirm their signatures on the recall petition; the CNE announced in early June that a recall election would be held on August 15, 2004. In order for Chávez to be removed from office, at least 3,757,774 voters would need to vote for his recall—one more vote than Chávez had received in the 2000 election. The quest for governance remained elusive during the first half of 2004 as the political stalemate between Chávez and his opponents dragged on into its third year.

The governance resources and strategies of Pérez, Caldera, and Chávez varied. Pérez entered with considerable voter support—but not for the economic program that he chose to pursue. When he announced the great turnaround in economic policy, he lost the support of many voters and legislators. In turn, the *caracazo* provided stark visual images of widespread disorder for the first time in a generation. Although Pérez pushed ahead with several initiatives, the popular support for the two 1992 coup attempts made him decidedly vulnerable to the impeachment he ultimately suffered. Caldera, on the other hand, began his term as a double-minority president. He initially strove to maintain his state capitalist coalition in the legislature. Once he decided to zigzag back toward market capitalism, it took all of his political skill to keep his government afloat in the legislature.

Chávez skillfully mobilized opposition to market-oriented reforms in both the 1998 election campaign and during the initial honeymoon of 1999. As noted earlier, the constitutional reform process provided him with considerable discretionary power during the National Constituent Assembly and in the months that followed. Hugo Chávez often employed confrontational rhetoric—regarding Venezuelan politics *and* world politics—to mobilize support for his presidency and his policies. The events of 2002 and 2003 demonstrate how confrontational rhetoric can form a double-edged sword as a governing strategy. One could argue that Chávez's ability to inspire passion in his opponents and in his supporters helped make him more vulnerable to a coup attempt but also made him better able to resist the coup once it occurred.

Future Challenges

When this book went to press in June 2004, the petition to recall Hugo Chávez framed Venezuela's immediate political future. It remained to be seen whether the August 2004 recall election would resolve the multiyear conflict between the MVR and its opponents. If the recall election were won by Chávez, would the opposition allege fraud and go back into the streets? If Chávez were to lose the recall vote, would his government acknowledge the results and would his supporters respect the outcome? In either scenario, would the armed forces side with Chávez or against him?

Regardless of the outcome of the recall drive, the president and the entire country will confront serious problems. The economic challenges facing Venezuela remain severe. Continuing dependence on the oil sector makes the economy vulnerable to price swings on volatile world petroleum markets. In its attempt to diversify the economy and reduce poverty, can the country unite in support of an economic approach that could be pursued more consistently than recent policies have been? In turn, the growing political polarization from the 1990s onward makes it more difficult to protect basic liberties. By early 2004, the political context had become so polarized that many restaurants and bookstores put up signs prohibiting their customers from talking about politics in the hope of limiting the outbreak of shouting matches that can boil over into fistfights. When each side of the political debate distrusts the motives and tactics of the other (and the impartiality of the judiciary), how can political leaders and citizens reduce the tension and increase confidence in the judicial process? These first two challenges have clear implications for the pursuit of governance. After several years largely dominated by conflict, leaders on all sides of the political debate will have to consider potential bases for future cooperation. A decision will be reached during 2004 regarding the future of the Chávez government, but many hard choices remain.

Activities and Exercises

1. One of the goals of the Chávez administration has been the expansion of government revenues. If Chávez ultimately fails in his attempts to increase government revenues generated by PDVSA, what alternative strategies would you recommend that he pursue to increase the flow of money for social programs?

2. On balance, have the changes implemented during the years 1999–2003 made the Venezuelan political system more democratic or less democratic? On what do you base your assessment?

3. Over the course of this text, you have had the chance to review changes in presidential authority in several Latin American countries. Where would you place the changes in Venezuela under Chávez relative to other countries' experiences?

4. *El camino de las hormigas (The Track of the Ants)* is a fifty-four-minute documentary about life in Caracas in 1993. Director Rafael Marziano Tinoco sets a multifaceted look at the city to music. Unlike most Venezuelan movies, this film has been released on video in the United States, but it is unlikely to be at a video store. See if it is available in your library or can be acquired through another library. A 2003 Irish documentary, *The Revolution Will Not Be Televised*, discusses the Chávez presidency with an emphasis on the turbulent events surrounding the April 2002 coup. Members of both sides of the contemporary political divide in Venezuela have criticized this documentary, but one aspect of the film is beyond debate: it provides an unusual, close-up account of several key events.

5. As noted in this chapter, the 1999 constitution changed many aspects of Venezuela's governing institutions. For a wealth of information on government institutions and political parties in Latin America, consult the Political Database of the Americas, maintained by Georgetown University, at http://www.georgetown.edu/pdba/. In addition to providing current and previous constitutions and links to online materials about Latin American governments, the website provides bibliographical resources for further study.

Suggested Readings

Burgess, Katrina. *Parties and Unions in the New Global Economy.* Pittsburgh, Pa.: University of Pittsburgh Press, 2003.

Buxton, Julia. *The Failure of Political Reform in Venezuela.* Aldershot, England: Ashgate, 2001.

Canache, Damarys. *Venezuela: Public Opinion and Protest in a Fragile Democracy.* Coral Gables, Fla.: North-South Center, 2002.

Canache, Damarys, and Michael Kulisheck, eds. *Reinventing Legitimacy: Democracy and Political Change in Venezuela.* Westport, Conn.: Greenwood, 1998.

Coppedge, Michael. *Strong Parties and Lame Ducks: Presidential Partyarchy and Factionalism in Venezuela.* Stanford, Calif.: Stanford University Press, 1994.

Coronil, Fernando. *The Magical State: Nature, Money, and Modernity in Venezuela.* Chicago, Ill.: University of Chicago Press, 1997.

Corrales, Javier. *Presidents Without Parties: The Politics of Reform in Argentina and Venezuela in the 1990s.* University Park, Pa.: Penn State University Press, 2002.

Crisp, Brian. *Democratic Institutional Design: The Powers and Incentives of Venezuelan Politicians and Interest Groups.* Stanford, Calif.: Stanford University Press, 2000.

Ellner, Steve. *Organized Labor in Venezuela: Behavior and Concerns in a Democratic Setting, 1958–1991.* Wilmington, Del.: Scholarly Resources, 1993.

Ellner, Steve, and Daniel Hellinger, eds. *Venezuelan Politics in the Chávez Era: Class, Polarization, and Conflict.* Boulder, Colo.: Lynne Rienner, 2003.

Enright, Michael, Antonio Francés, and Edith Scott Saavedra. *Venezuela: The Challenge of Competitiveness.* New York: St. Martin's Press, 1996.

Friedman, Elisabeth. *Unfinished Transitions: Women and the Gendered Development of Democracy in Venezuela, 1936–1996.* University Park, Pa.: Penn State University Press, 2000.

Goodman, Louis. *Lessons from the Venezuelan Experience.* Washington, D.C.: Woodrow Wilson Center Press, 1995.

Hellinger, Daniel. *Venezuela: Tarnished Democracy.* Boulder, Colo.: Westview, 1991.

Hillman, Richard. *Democracy for the Privileged: Crisis and Transition in Venezuela.* Boulder, Colo.: Lynne Rienner, 1994.

Karl, Terry. *The Paradox of Plenty: Oil Booms and Petro-States.* Berkeley: University of California Press, 1997.

Kelly de Escobar, Janet, and Carlos Romero. *The United States and Venezuela: Rethinking a Relationship.* New York: Routledge, 2002.

Levine, Daniel. *Popular Voices in Latin American Catholicism.* Princeton, N.J.: Princeton University Press, 1992.

McCaughan, Michael. *Venezuela: Polarising Politics.* London: Latin America Bureau, 2003.

McCoy, Jennifer, ed. *Venezuelan Democracy Under Stress.* Coral Gables, Fla.: North-South Center, 1995.

McCoy, Jennifer, and David Myers, eds. *The Unraveling of Representative Democracy in Venezuela.* Baltimore, Md.: Johns Hopkins University, 2004.

Naím, Moisés. *Paper Tigers and Minotaurs: The Politics of Venezuela's Economic Reforms.* Washington, D.C.: Carnegie Endowment for International Peace, 1993.

Salazar-Carrillo, Jorge, and Bernadette West. *Oil and Development in Venezuela in the 20th Century.* Westport, Conn.: Praeger, 2004.

Tulchin, Joseph, and Gary Bland, eds. *Venezuela in the Wake of Radical Reform.* Boulder, Colo.: Lynne Rienner, 1993.

Wright, Winthrop. *Café con Leche: Race, Class, and National Image in Venezuela.* Austin: University of Texas Press, 1990.

Endnotes

1. Cited in Daniel H. Levine, "Goodbye to Venezuelan Exceptionalism," *Journal of Interamerican Studies and World Affairs,* 36, no. 4 (Winter 1994): 169.

2. The online discussion of the Bolivarian Circles and the necessary registration materials can be found at http://www.venezuela.gov.ve/ns/circulos.asp (accessed on October 25, 2003).

3. Cited in Daniel Hellinger, "Political Overview," in Steve Ellner and Daniel Hellinger, eds., *Venezuelan Politics in the Chávez Era: Class, Polarization and Conflict* (Boulder, Colo.: Lynne Rienner, 2003), p. 32.

4. Cited in Mark Ungar, *Elusive Reform: Democracy and the Rule of Law in Latin America* (Boulder, Colo.: Lynne Rienner, 2002), p. 159.

5. Cited in Javier Corrales, *Presidents Without Parties: The Politics of Economic Reform in Argentina and Venezuela in the 1990s* (University Park, Pa.: Penn State University Press, 2002), p. 114.

Support for Democratic Rule in Latin America (2003)   SOURCE: Latinobarómetro, *SUMMARY REPORT Democracy and Economy LATINOBARÓMETRO 2003* (Santiago, Chile: Corporación Latinobarómetro, 2003).

CHAPTER 12

Challenges and Choices in the Twenty-First Century

IN AUGUST 2003, Honduran President Ricardo Maduro launched an initiative to reduce a crime wave in urban areas. He ordered an elite group of police officers to arrest many youth gang members accused of violent crimes— including armed robbery, kidnapping, and murder. Many of these gangs' founding leaders came from youth gangs on the streets of Los Angeles, California. Two of the largest gangs, *Mara-18* and *Mara Salvatrucha* (*mara* is "gang" in Honduran and Salvadoran slang), responded by unleashing considerable violence on police forces and private citizens alike. The Catholic church called for mediation between the government and the gangs. By October, Honduran police arrested several hundred suspected gang members; many others went into hiding. People wondered how the government would restore long-lasting order in a country with minimal economic opportunities for most young people. In the first four months of 2004, these concerns intensified as several decapitated heads were left in different locations in Honduras with notes to President Maduro taunting him for the lack of personal safety in the country.

In September 2003, thousands of Bolivians participated in roadblocks to call for the resignation of President Gonzalo Sánchez de Lozada. The president's opponents had two principal demands. First, they wanted the reversal of a recently announced decision to export natural gas through a pipeline that would carry the fuel through the portion of northern Chile that was once Bolivian territory (prior to the nineteenth-century War of the Pacific). Critics said that the plan would generate more profits for Chilean and U.S. investors than for Bolivians and their government. Second, they demanded an end to the forced eradication of coca leaf crops. In regard to both demands, protest leaders characterized the Bolivian president (raised in the United States) as beholden to foreign interests and uninterested in promoting the welfare of ordinary Bolivians. The Sánchez de Lozada government initially used force to try to clear the roads. Several people died and hundreds more were injured. After weeks of stalemate, one of the major political parties in his governing coalition withdrew its support for his presidency and Gonzalo Sánchez de Lozada resigned. Many protesters cheered both his resignation and the subsequent inauguration of his vice president, Carlos Mesa. Still, the path to resolving the policy disputes behind those earlier resignation demands was not clear in early 2004.

In November 2003, as we saw in Chapter Nine, Guatemalans voted in record numbers in the second presidential elections held since the Peace Accords. Many people voted for the first time in their lives in a successful effort to prevent former dictator Efraín Ríos Montt from becoming president. Most had not forgiven him for the many atrocities committed under the military government that he led with the support of U.S. foreign aid. In the December 2003 runoff election, Oscar Berger defeated Álvaro Colom with 54 percent of the vote. Ríos Montt had been defeated at the ballot box, but an important question remained: would the Berger government be able to improve the lives of ordinary Guatemalans?

These three paragraphs reflect different slices of contemporary Latin American reality—the fear generated by kidnapping and other violent crimes, the use of roadblocks to press for change, and the use of voting to call for change. All three examples take place amid considerable poverty. Honduras, Bolivia, and Guatemala are three of the poorest countries in Latin America; only Nicaragua is poorer. In addition, all three stories unfold in a context in which U.S. citizens and their government play an important role.

Latin American politics centers on efforts to meet serious human needs. In every country in the region, poverty affects anywhere from a large minority to the vast majority of the population. Past human rights violations and current threats to liberty limit people's sense of security in their daily lives. Historical and contemporary political divisions often make governance more difficult. International forces—particularly trends in the world economy and the actions of the U.S. government—also affect the decisions made by Latin American citizens and their governments. People make choices in Latin America, but their choices are often constrained by circumstances or forces beyond their control.

In this chapter we will take stock of efforts to pursue development, liberty, and governance in contemporary Latin America. We will begin by considering collectively the experiences of the seven countries examined in this book. We will also examine events and conditions elsewhere in the region. After doing so, we will return to the question asked at the end of Chapter Four: what are the prospects for democracy? We will explore the relationship between success in these three quests and the prospects for building enduring and more participatory democracies. Our attempt to understand the future of democracy will take into account three of the above reactions to human distress: violent crime, unlawful forms of protest, and voting.

THE QUEST FOR DEVELOPMENT REVISITED

Over the course of this book, we have seen numerous examples of how a shift in economic policy can initiate or intensify political conflict. Carlos Menem's first term in Argentina faced vocal criticisms, strikes, and demonstrations launched in opposition to many privatization efforts and other market-oriented reforms. Fernando Collor's pursuit of market-oriented reforms in Brazil met with even stiffer opposition inside and outside the halls of the legislature. Attempts by all three Concertation presidents in Chile to expand funding for government social policies were only partially successful in Congress. The introduction of market mechanisms into the Cuban economy in the mid-1990s met with internal opposition from the governing Communist party. Álvaro Arzú's government backtracked on tax reform in 1998 after a diverse coalition of wealthy and poor Guatemalans mobilized protests against the new tax law. Much of the center-left wing of the Institutional Revolutionary party (*Partido Revolucionario Institucional* [PRI]) in Mexico left the governing party in protest over the shift to market-oriented policies during the 1980s. During Carlos Andrés Pérez's second presidency, many Venezuelans reacted angrily to the initial announcement of market-oriented reforms. Continuing opposition to Venezuela's move to the market served as one of several motivations for two military coup attempts in 1992. Hugo Chávez's efforts to restore state capitalist economic policies ignited another firestorm of criticism and protests that culminated in a temporarily successful coup against his government.

The potential for political conflict over economic policy raises two central questions. First, how do political leaders and citizens mobilize support for the policy options that they prefer? To build answer to this question, we will review the experiences of the countries examined in this book. Second, which of the three major approaches to economic policy has been the most successful in the contemporary era? In dealing with this question, we will examine economic outcomes across Latin America as a whole.

The Politics of Development as Seen Through This Book

How have reform-minded leaders tried to build support for their respective economic agendas? The principal reform pattern in late twentieth-century Latin America involved a move away from state capitalism toward more market-oriented policies. Some analysts have argued that political leaders find it easier to build support for market-oriented reform when economic conditions are bad; Kurt Weyland has called this scenario the rescue hypothesis[1] (review the *Research Question* in Chapter Eleven). Because the shift away from state capitalism imposes substantial losses on several sectors of society (private firms in protected sectors and employees of state-owned enterprises in particular), people are likely to oppose policy change unless they feel that the current situation is desperate and getting worse. In this book, we have seen reform-oriented presidents get reelected in several countries after their reform programs helped their countries to escape hyperinflation. Carlos Menem in Argentina and Fernando Henrique Cardoso in Brazil (along with Alberto Fujimori in Peru) ran successful reelection campaigns emphasizing an end to hyperinflation. In contrast, in two countries—Mexico and Venezuela—that experienced high inflation of nearly 100 percent (but not hyperinflation), the move toward more market-oriented policies stimulated widespread antigovernment protests and a loss of voters for the parties associated with the reforming leaders: the PRI in Mexico and the Democratic Action party (*Acción Democrática* [AD]) in Venezuela. The rescue approach has clear limitations as a strategy for promoting reform; not all political leaders inherit an economy in a harrowing free fall.

Another path toward market-oriented reform involves targeting compensatory policies to some sectors of society likely to suffer during the initial opening of the economy.[2] We have seen this approach used widely in the countries examined in this book—albeit not always successfully. Back in the late 1980s, Carlos Salinas spearheaded a major redesign of welfare policies into the means-tested Solidarity program that would attempt to provide assistance to those most in need. The Solidarity program also served as a vehicle for increasing government spending in regions where the PRI's support had been falling. While the Collor government in Brazil had devoted little emphasis to welfare policies, the Cardoso administration increased social spending in a high-profile program aimed at assisting poor families with school-age children. The Caldera administration proposed similar policies when it adopted its market-oriented Venezuelan Agenda in 1996; however, it found it difficult to implement this strategy because low oil prices reduced government revenues. Despite inheriting an economy that was already market oriented, the Concertation governments of the 1990s in Chile used targeted social spending to assist people left behind during the initial move to the market. When overall economic performance has been relatively good and politicians have managed to build support for higher social spending, an emphasis on improved social policies can help to build political support while simultaneously reducing poverty. Brazil, Chile, and Mexico were three of the five Latin American countries that experienced a substantial reduction in the poverty rate between 1996 and 2002.

Both the rescue hypothesis and the compensatory approach provide a direct logic of building support for market-oriented policies. A third prevalent tactic postpones the problem of building support by hiding one's reform intentions during the election campaign.[3] Three political leaders discussed in this book—Alberto Fujimori in Peru, Carlos Menem in Argentina, and Carlos Andrés Pérez in Venezuela—followed this strategy. As candidates in the late 1980s, none of these men detailed their plans for market-oriented reform during the election campaign. Instead, they hinted at state capitalist policies and waited to announce sweeping changes until after the elections were over. Two of the three managed to build and extend their support after this policy about-face. Menem

Argentine roadblock movements disrupt traffic on major highways in Buenos Aires to draw government attention to their demands for unemployment benefits.   AP/Wide World Press.

and Fujimori extended their popularity, reformed their respective constitutions, and ran successfully for reelection. Many Venezuelan citizens rejected Pérez's policy shift initially and momentum against reform grew over time. Proponents of the aforementioned rescue hypothesis note that Menem and Fujimori could build support for change by pointing to obvious hyperinflationary crises, while Pérez faced the more difficult challenge of trying to convince citizens that quick reform would avert a potential outburst of hyperinflation that had not yet occurred. While Menem and Fujimori's bait-and-switch campaign tactics amid economic crisis may have proven politically successful at first, we have also seen how the bitterness generated by their postelection conversions to the market worsened over the course of their presidencies.

Development in Contemporary Latin America

The economic policy trend observed within this book holds across Latin America: most countries moved toward more market-oriented policies over the course of the late 1980s and the early 1990s (see Table 12.1 on page 416). For the six capitalist economies central to this book, the average country became 45 percent more market oriented. The average increase in market orientation among all the other countries in the region proved fairly similar. In addition to illustrating this trend, this book has broadened our ability to understand exceptions to this pattern by examining Cuba—the lone socialist economy in the hemisphere. Cuba adopted more market mechanisms than it had previously used but retained a command economy approach to most economic activity.

While the overall trends are similar across Latin America, we can observe three distinct patterns of market-oriented policy changes among the countries in the region: sweeping reform, considerable reform, and minimal reform. Governments in Bolivia, the Dominican Republic, Paraguay, and Peru engaged in sweeping reforms that nearly doubled or more than doubled the market

TABLE 12.1 Degree of Market Orientation in Latin American Economies (1980, 1985, 1990, and 1995)*

Country	1980	1985	1990	1995	Percentage increase from 1985 to 1995
Argentina	.698	.617	.813	.888	44
Brazil	.493	.492	.724	.805	64
Chile	.748	.671	.768	.843	26
Cuba	NA	NA	NA	NA	NA
Guatemala	.520	.530	.695	.838	58
Mexico	.598	.578	.771	.807	40
Venezuela	.404	.456	.472	.667	46
Subregional average	*.577*	*.551*	*.707*	*.808*	*45*
Bolivia	.551	.445	.779	.816	83
Colombia	.610	.578	.689	.792	37
Costa Rica	.559	.494	.798	.847	71
Dominican Republic	.343	.446	.466	.862	93
Ecuador	.518	.556	.610	.801	44
El Salvador	.504	.540	.689	.872	61
Honduras	.646	.626	.624	.780	25
Nicaragua	NA	NA	NA	NA	NA
Panama	NA	NA	NA	NA	NA
Paraguay	.502	.476	.751	.834	75
Peru	.460	.394	.537	.845	114
Uruguay	.759	.815	.844	.891	9
Subregional average	*.545*	*.537*	*.679*	*.834*	*55*
Latin American average	.557	.551	.683	.825	50

*Market orientation is measured on a scale of 0 to 1, with 1 being the most market oriented.

SOURCE: Samuel Morley, Roberto Machado, and Stefano Pettinato, "Indexes of Structural Reform in Latin America" (Santiago, Chile: Economic Commission for Latin America and the Caribbean, 1999).

orientation of their respective economies. All the other countries in the region (except for Uruguay) implemented considerable market-oriented reform. Uruguay increased the market orientation of its economy, but it did so in the context of a national policy that was already, by far, the most market-oriented in Latin America in 1985.

Was this move to the market associated with gains in economic development? Did the countries that had the most market-oriented economies across this period experience better economic outcomes? Table 12.2 examines economic

TABLE 12.2 Development Outcomes in Latin America (1986–1995)

Country	Average market orientation (1986–1995)	Percentage change in GDP per capita (1986–1995)	Percentage change in poverty rate (1986–1995)	Percentage change in income inequality (1986–1995)
Argentina	.784	12.4	78	8
Brazil	.672	7.1	13	−6
Chile	.779	62.8	−28	−1
Cuba	NA	−39.5	NA	NA
Guatemala	.756	7.6	NA	3
Mexico	.746	−7.7	32	26
Venezuela	.538	9.8	81	1
Subregional average	*.713*	*7.5*	*35.2*	*5.2*
Bolivia	.734	7.2	−2	−10
Colombia	.688	29.0	39	11
Costa Rica	.771	19.1	−8	0
Dominican Republic	.598	8.8	NA	NA
Ecuador	.662	2.5	NA	NA
El Salvador	.705	16.9	NA	NA
Honduras	.678	1.8	10	−6
Nicaragua	NA	−32.4	NA	NA
Panama	NA	0.1	6	5
Paraguay	.706	6.7	−7	−3
Peru	.648	−6.1	NA	NA
Uruguay	.853	33.7	−29	−22
Subregional average	*.704*	*7.3*	*1.3*	*−3.6*
Latin American average	**.707**	**7.4**	**15.4**	**0.5**
Above average market orientation*	.782	21	9	2
Average market orientation	.690	9	11	−3
Below average market orientation*	.599	7	81	1

*The six countries over half a standard deviation above the mean market orientation (Argentina, Chile, Guatemala, Mexico, Costa Rica, and Uruguay) are listed as above average, while the three countries over half a standard deviation below the mean (Venezuela, the Dominican Republic, and Ecuador) are listed as below average.

SOURCE: Based on economic data from the Economic Commission for Latin America and the Caribbean.

outcomes during the decade of reform, which spanned the years 1986–1995. Most of the table lists major indicators for growth, poverty, and income inequality during this period for all Latin American countries. The bottom three rows of the table groups the results according to the degree of market orientation in countries' economic policies.

During this initial phase of the move to the market, the most market-oriented economies outperformed the other economies. They grew faster and they experienced the smallest increase in poverty. All three groups of countries maintained income inequality at their prior levels. The countries with an average level of market orientation grew more slowly but experienced similar outcomes regarding poverty and inequality. Finally, the least market-oriented economies grew the most slowly (less than 1 percent per person annually). They also suffered a substantially greater increase in poverty.

The economic booms in several market-oriented economies in the early 1990s bred optimism that Latin America's shift to more market-oriented policies held the key to better development outcomes. In particular, the booms in the three largest market-oriented economies—Mexico, Argentina, and Chile—made headlines in newspapers and magazines across the hemisphere and in many other corners of the world. Many hailed market capitalism as the wave of the future, and governments across Latin America joined the chorus.

By 1995, only one capitalist Latin American economy had a market orientation substantially below the average for the *most* market-oriented economies of the prior decade. Did the more uniform adoption of market capitalism usher in a new era of economic success? Table 12.3 summarizes development outcomes during the years 1996–2002.

The most market-oriented economies experienced slightly higher growth rates at the turn of the century, but their relative advantage over the rest of Latin America narrowed considerably. The average outcomes for the five most market-oriented economies are weak mostly because Argentina and Uruguay suffered serious economic crises. Economic activity shrank markedly, income inequality rose, and poverty expanded rapidly in both countries.

The central trends of Latin America's move to the market can be seen in the group of eleven countries that pursued an average degree of market orientation during this period. In these countries, economic growth also proved to be slow, but the poverty rate declined substantially, especially in Brazil, Chile, Costa Rica, and Mexico. In all four of these countries, governments expanded programs designed to provide assistance to the most impoverished citizens in the country. As we saw in earlier chapters, Brazil and Mexico adopted programs that targeted aid to families with poor children on the condition that school-age children remain enrolled in school; Chile also increased its use of this strategy.

As in the prior decade, the least market-oriented capitalist economies either stagnated or shrank. The one major distinction in economic growth trends between these two periods can be found in Cuba. During the years 1986–1995, the Cuban economy experienced a devastating collapse. Then, after injecting some

TABLE 12.3   Development Outcomes in Latin America (1996–2002)

Country	Market orientation (1995)	Percentage change in GDP per capita (1996–2002)	Percentage change in poverty rate (1996–2002)	Percentage change in income inequality (1996–2002)
Argentina	.888	−11.8	188	34
Brazil	.805	4.3	−16	25
Chile	.843	16.8	−25	17
Cuba	NA	29.2	NA	NA
Guatemala	.838	5.3	NA	22
Mexico	.807	18.3	−11	27
Venezuela	.667	−12.2	−2	29
Subregional average	*.808*	*7.1*	*26.8*	*25.7*
Bolivia	.816	4.0	3	28
Colombia	.792	−5.4	4	14
Costa Rica	.847	11.5	−13	34
Dominican Republic	.862	36.6	NA	NA
Ecuador	.801	−3.1	−7	15
El Salvador	.872	5.3	−7	2
Honduras	.780	0.8	3	23
Nicaragua	NA	13.1	NA	−1
Panama	NA	7.5	−25	24
Paraguay	.834	−15.2	13	35
Peru	.845	5.4	NA	2
Uruguay	.891	−10.1	50	52
Subregional average	*.834*	*4.2*	*2.3*	*20.7*
Latin American average	**.824**	**5.3**	**11.1**	**22.5**
*Above average market orientation**	.878	5	77	29
Average market orientation	.826	5	−10	25
Below average market orientation	.746	−6	2	22

*The four countries over half a standard deviation above the mean market orientation (Argentina, the Dominican Republic, El Salvador, and Uruguay) are listed as above average; the three countries over half a standard deviation below the mean (Venezuela, Colombia, and Honduras) are listed as below average.

SOURCE: Based on economic data from the Economic Commission for Latin America and the Caribbean.

market mechanisms into its largely socialist economy, Cuba grew more quickly than almost all other countries in Latin America during the years 1996–2002. Living conditions remained difficult for many Cubans, but the policy shift reversed the economic free fall of the early 1990s.

The most telling trend in Table 12.3 is the notable rise in income inequality in almost every country. As Latin American governments settled into more market-oriented policies, the region's already unequal income distribution became even more skewed. Across Latin America, income inequality rose by over 22 percent in seven years. The dislocation caused by opening up the economies—combined with insufficient efforts to redistribute gains from the winners of the move to the market—have caused considerable suffering and tension in every country. Urban unemployment rose in Latin America from an average of 7.5 percent in 1995 to 9.1 percent in 2002. Systematic data are not available for rural areas in most countries, but most of the available evidence points to an even greater rise in unemployment in the rural areas of most countries.

Advocates of market capitalism argued that open economies, over time, would grow more quickly. Competition from other countries should spur improved efficiency that could help Latin American economies to become more successful on world markets. In turn, increased economic activity would begin to reduce unemployment and eventually decrease both absolute and relative poverty. As we saw in Chapters Four, proponents of the Washington Consensus argued that the export orientation of successful Asian economies proved central to their success. To date, the growth of Latin American exports has sped up in some instances, but it has not compensated in most cases for the loss of domestic production due to foreign competition.

Thus far, a rosy scenario of sustained economic growth has not materialized. Instead, as noted earlier, the countries with greater emphasis on social policies managed to make some progress in poverty reduction but no headway in reducing relative poverty. In every country in Latin America, plenty of work must still be done to promote economic growth, reduce poverty and income inequality, and pursue these development aims in a sustainable manner.

THE QUEST FOR LIBERTY REVISITED

With an economic context shaped by continuing poverty, worsening income inequality, and often rising unemployment, the quest for liberty takes place under difficult conditions. Those accused of past human rights violations frequently use bleak economic conditions as a rationale for shifting attention away from past accusations and on to so-called more pressing matters. Economic scarcity also frames efforts to extend and to protect contemporary liberty. Courts, police forces, and prisons have small budgets. Their respective economic limitations hamper the quest for liberty in two ways. First, limited resources make it difficult for the authorities to identify and to sanction those guilty of crimes. Second, the resource crunch can be used as a justification for not protecting the rights of the accused and for not providing humane treatment of prisoners. Several presidents argued at times that civil liberties and judicial due process should be curtailed in the name of meeting a national emergency.

Against this stark backdrop, contemporary Latin American governments confront the two questions we raised at the end of Chapter Four. First, how should governments handle unresolved past human rights violations, especially when those allegations implicate past or present government officials? Second, what steps can governments take to secure liberty in the present?

The Politics of Liberty as Seen Through This Book

Political tension regarding past human rights violations did not subside in the three countries that had suffered the most crimes against humanity—Argentina, Chile, and Guatemala. In these three countries, thousands of people died in political murders, and exponentially more people suffered illegal and inhumane detention that often involved torture and rape. None of the various strategies used (amnesties, limited trials, reparations, and truth commissions) provided a path to the prompt reconciliation sought by all postdictatorship governments. Argentina tried to use a truth commission report as the basis for centering legal responsibility on the high command of the military government of its so-called dirty war. However, the report and the trials fanned the desire to hold accountable those directly responsible for these violations. When the Argentine government ended trials and provided modest reparations, human rights activists rejected impunity and pushed until trials reopened in the late 1990s; trials may expand still further under the Kirchner administration. Operating in the wake of the Argentine military revolts and in the presence of a Chilean Senate and judiciary dominated by officials associated with the Pinochet dictatorship, the Aylwin administration initially rejected trials altogether. Instead, Aylwin's government attempted to pursue reconciliation through a truth commission that identified recipients for more substantial reparations than had been provided in Argentina. This approach also proved unacceptable to most human rights activists, who kept pushing for trials until a reformed Supreme Court paved the way for more trials in 1999. In Guatemala, a U.N.-sponsored peace process called for a truth commission and reparations and avoided declaring a preemptive blanket amnesty. Soldiers killed Bishop Juan José Gerardi in 1998 after the release of the Catholic church's human rights report. In a tense atmosphere, the 1999 government-sponsored truth commission confirmed tens of thousands of deaths. Court proceedings ensued, but many have been thrown out of court and most others have proceeded slowly in an atmosphere rife with intimidation of witnesses. Two high-profile convictions—the 2001 conviction of soldiers guilty of the Gerardi assassination and the 2002 conviction for the murder of U.S. anthropologist Myrna Mack—were subsequently overturned on appeal, which constituted an enormous setback. Legal efforts to uphold the convictions in the Gerardi case were still before an appeals court in early May 2004.

In all three countries, the demand for trials remained substantial in 2004—often a generation after the violations occurred. Note that truth commission reports in all three countries instigated additional demands for trials by publicizing and clarifying the often brutal extent of the violations at issue. The inability of these governments to punish those responsible constituted one of the most visible failures of the rule of law in the democracies established in the wake of these violent dictatorships. Advocates of impunity in the name of reconciliation ran headlong into many citizens' unwillingness to accept that approach.

Controversy over past human rights violations is far from the lone issue in the quest for liberty. Limitations on freedom of expression and on freedom of the press created major scandals in Argentina, Chile, and Venezuela. The Cuban government in 2003 departed from its normal tactic of low-profile suppression of dissent; it jailed several leading dissidents convicted of engaging in unlawful speech and publishing. Widespread allegations of police misconduct have been prevalent in all seven countries; the most prominent scandals have occurred in Argentina, Brazil, and Guatemala.

The reduction of government corruption forms another portion of the unfinished quest for liberty. Latin American citizens have long perceived corruption as a problem, but the contemporary era has been characterized by a greater willingness of the media and the citizenry to press for change. In Cuba, Fidel Castro attempted to focus concerns about corruption on the actions of Arnaldo Ochoa and other military officers in the late 1980s. Nevertheless, frustration over personal enrichment by communist officials remained a central complaint of the opposition to his government at home and in exile. In December 2003, the Cuban government removed the head of the largest state-run tourism firm amid several allegations of corruption and embezzlement. Corruption scandals brought down elected presidents in Brazil and Venezuela and led to the eventual widespread repudiation of past presidents in Argentina (Carlos Menem) and in Mexico (Carlos Salinas). In 2002, the Portillo government in Guatemala and the Lagos government in Chile both faced an expanding series of corruption scandals. Despite the greater public attention on corruption, the next task for civic activists will be the much tougher challenge of instituting viable watchdog procedures. In societies rife with income inequality (or, in Cuba, with political inequality), it remains difficult to constrain the actions of the politically and economically powerful.

Beyond the violations of liberty committed by government officials, daily private threats to liberty expanded from the 1980s onward. Street crime became an increasingly important political issue, not just in the largest urban areas but also in rural environments. Newly elected governments in the three largest countries we have examined—Brazil, Mexico, and Argentina—all promised in the early twenty-first century to combat crime with a mix of more frequent police patrols and efforts to weed out police officers involved in criminal networks. It remains to be seen whether these most recent efforts to improve law enforcement will prove more fruitful than prior attempts have been.

Liberty in Contemporary Latin America

Argentina, Chile, and Guatemala were not the only countries in Latin America that launched truth commissions. Bolivia's presidential truth commission established in 1982 formed the first such body in the region. Limited funds and considerable opposition hampered its work: it never produced a final report. Following the establishment of a truth commission in Argentina, the Uruguayan legislature launched a more limited investigation in the mid-1980s. As a consequence of the publicity received by the Rettig commission in Chile, governments in El Salvador and Honduras conducted investigations in the mid-1990s. As noted earlier in this book, Peru established a truth commission in 2001 after the end of the Fujimori government. In all of these instances, as in the countries discussed earlier, the truth commission report did not provide an easy one-step path to reconciliation. Instead, the reports frequently provided a means to identify potential recipients of reparations and played a role in highlighting abuses and building support for trials.

Human rights trials have proven difficult to conduct throughout Latin America: Argentina, Chile, and Guatemala are not exceptional in this regard. Pursuing trials risks private violence and threats of military upheaval. Governments have tended to emphasize these problems as more important than the rule of law. Perhaps the most striking example occurred in El Salvador, when the government passed a sweeping amnesty law five days after the release of the truth commission report. The Uruguayan legislature also enacted an amnesty in the wake of its human rights investigation. Although Uruguayan human rights groups succeeded in forcing the matter to a plebiscite, the government convinced a slim majority of the voters to uphold the amnesty in 1986. While Uruguay stood out at the time as the lone country in which a majority of voters backed an amnesty, its experience over time further demonstrates that impunity can breed discontent. By the early twenty-first century, human rights abuses returned to the Uruguayan political agenda as groups pressed for reparations and trials. In August 2003, the judicial system authorized the trial of the first president of the dictatorship, Juan Bordaberry. The contradiction between impunity and the rule of law has proven difficult to manage across Latin America.

The struggles to address past infringements on liberty occur amid efforts to expand the scope of human freedom in the present. The return to democratic rule in the Americas held out the potential promise of a new era in which political and civil liberties could form tools in the creation of a more enduring democracy and in time a more equitable society. Table 12.4 on page 424 details the evolution of these basic freedoms as tracked by Freedom House (a nongovernmental organization formed in the United States in the 1940s and dedicated to promoting democracy around the world). The political rights examined by Freedom House focus on the electoral components of democracy: election of the leaders of the executive and legislative branches, procedures to build confidence in the electoral process, the right to organize political parties,

TABLE 12.4 Degree of Political and Civil Liberty in Latin America (1980, 1985, 1990, 1995, and 2000)*

Country	Political rights 1980	Civil rights 1980	Political rights 1985	Civil rights 1985	Political rights 1990	Civil rights 1990	Political rights 1995	Civil rights 1995	Political rights 2000	Civil rights 2000
Argentina	2	3	6	6	7	5	6	5	7	6
Brazil	4	5	5	6	6	5	6	4	5	5
Chile	2	3	2	3	6	6	6	6	6	6
Cuba	1	1	1	1	1	1	1	1	1	1
Guatemala	3	2	4	4	5	4	4	3	5	4
Mexico	5	4	4	4	4	4	4	4	6	5
Venezuela	7	6	7	6	7	5	5	5	5	3
Subregional average	*3.4*	*3.4*	*4.1*	*4.3*	*5.1*	*4.3*	*4.6*	*4.0*	*5.0*	*4.3*
Bolivia	1	3	6	5	6	5	6	4	7	5
Colombia	6	5	6	5	5	4	4	4	4	4
Costa Rica	7	7	7	7	7	7	7	6	7	6
Dominican Republic	6	5	7	5	6	5	4	5	6	6
Ecuador	6	6	6	5	6	6	6	5	5	5
El Salvador	2	3	6	4	5	4	5	5	6	5
Honduras	4	5	6	5	6	5	5	5	5	5
Nicaragua	3	3	3	3	5	5	4	4	5	5
Panama	4	4	2	5	4	6	6	5	7	6
Paraguay	3	3	3	3	4	5	4	5	4	5
Peru	6	5	3	3	4	5	4	5	4	5
Uruguay	3	3	6	6	7	6	6	6	7	7
Subregional average	*4.3*	*4.0*	*4.7*	*4.5*	*5.3*	*4.9*	*4.9*	*4.6*	*5.4*	*4.9*
Latin American average	3.9	4.0	4.7	4.5	5.3	4.9	4.9	4.6	5.4	4.9

*Measured on a scale of 1 to 7, with 7 meaning the most protective of liberty.

SOURCE: Based on Freedom House, *Freedom in the World Country Ratings, 1972–1973 to 2001–2002,* <http://www.freedomhouse.org/research/freeworld/FHSCORES.xls> (accessed on June 24, 2002).

the presence of an important opposition party, and some meaningful opportunities for participation by minority groups. In turn, civil rights include freedom of the press, freedom of religion, freedom to organize interest groups, freedom of assembly, an independent judiciary, protection from arbitrary police power, protection from torture and other crimes against humanity, freedom of expression, and the right to private property. Political liberty and civil liberty are each evaluated on a seven-point scale.

In 1980, many Latin Americans lived under military rule or under repressive civilian-led political regimes. Over the course of the next decade, political liberty expanded in most of the region because many countries returned to democratic rule. Political freedom expanded across Latin America in the 1980s. On Freedom House's seven-point scale, political liberty expanded from an average of 3.9 in 1980 to 5.3 by 1990. At the start of the 1980s, nine countries had political rights scores of less than 4.0; by 1990, only Cuba had a score under 4.0. Civil liberties also improved during the same decade, from 4.0 to 4.9.

After the reestablishment of democratic rule, however, additional progress in securing basic liberties did not occur during the 1990s. In the seven countries at the heart of this book, the average political rights score declined minimally from 1990 to 2000, while the average civil rights score stayed exactly the same. In the rest of Latin America, the political rights and civil rights scores in 2000 also remained at their 1990 levels. Public discontent with the third wave of democratization in the Americas did not stem solely from economic problems; it also emerged from an uneven democratic process that showed few signs of improvement over time.

Perhaps no issue symbolizes the limits to contemporary liberty better than political corruption. Government corruption corrodes liberty in two ways. First, it is itself a crime that infringes on the public's right to fair treatment and to the proper use of government funds. Second, the entrenched nature of corruption in many countries can provide government officials with a motivation to limit citizens' access to information and their ability to mobilize for change. Many people held some hope that prolonged democratic rule would reduce corruption by giving citizens the potential to demand improvement and to vote out corrupt officials.

By 1998, every country but Cuba had conducted two or more competitive national elections. The electoral components of democracy had been restored. Did corruption decline in Latin America once the region returned to electoral politics? Because of its illegal nature, corruption is difficult to measure systematically. Transparency International (TI) is a global nongovernmental organization (NGO) dedicated to the reduction of corrupt activity. TI calculates the Corruption Perceptions Index that measures corruption by compiling various surveys of the public, domestic businesses, international businesses, and expert evaluations. Some might note that TI's index does not always correspond completely with the total amount of corruption because some corruption will go undetected while in some instances perceptions can exaggerate the extent of corruption. Regardless, even if one has such concerns, the *perceived* level of corruption is important in its own right. Perceived corruption is an indirect measure of corrupt behavior but perhaps a more direct measure of its societal relevance. If people believe that corruption is minimal, it helps to build support for the political process. Conversely, if citizens believe that corruption is widespread, that belief shapes their thinking about government. Table 12.5 on page 426 tracks perceived political corruption during the years 1998–2003.

The table shows no progress in Latin America as a whole during this time period. Among the seven countries central to this book, perceived corruption

TABLE 12.5 Political Corruption in Latin America (1998–2003)

Country	Year 1998	1999	2000	2001	2002	2003	Percentage change in corruption (1998–2003)
Argentina	7.0	7.0	6.5	6.5	7.2	7.5	7
Brazil	6.0	5.9	6.1	6.0	6.0	6.1	2
Chile	3.2	3.1	2.6	2.5	2.5	2.6	−19
Cuba	NA	NA	NA	NA	NA	5.4	NA
Guatemala	6.9	6.8	NA	7.1	7.5	7.6	10
Mexico	6.7	6.6	6.7	6.3	6.4	6.4	−4
Venezuela	7.7	7.4	7.3	7.2	7.5	7.6	−1
Subregional average	*6.3*	*6.1*	*5.8*	*5.9*	*6.2*	*6.2*	*−1*
Bolivia	7.2	7.5	7.3	8.0	7.8	7.7	7
Colombia	7.8	7.1	6.8	6.2	6.4	6.3	−19
Costa Rica	4.4	4.9	4.6	5.5	5.5	5.7	30
Dominican Republic	NA	NA	NA	6.9	6.5	6.7	NA
Ecuador	7.7	7.6	7.4	7.7	7.8	7.8	1
El Salvador	6.4	6.1	5.9	6.4	6.6	6.3	−2
Honduras	8.3	8.2	NA	7.3	7.3	7.7	−7
Nicaragua	7.0	6.9	NA	7.6	7.5	7.4	6
Panama	NA	NA	NA	6.3	7.0	6.6	NA
Paraguay	8.5	8.0	NA	NA	8.3	8.4	−1
Peru	5.5	5.5	5.6	5.9	6.0	6.3	15
Uruguay	5.7	5.6	NA	4.9	4.9	4.5	−21
Subregional average	*6.9*	*6.7*	*6.3*	*6.6*	*6.8*	*6.8*	*−1*
Latin American average	**6.6**	**6.5**	**6.1**	**6.4**	**6.6**	**6.6**	**0**

*Measured on a scale of 1 to 10, with 10 meaning the greatest perception of corruption.
SOURCE: Transparency International, *Corruption Perceptions Index, 1998–2003*
<http://www.transparency.org/cpi/#cpi> (accessed on October 15, 2003).

decreased in Chile and increased in Argentina and Guatemala. In the other countries, there was little or no change. Across the rest of the region, corruption declined by 1 percent over this six-year period. In 1998, only two countries—Chile and Costa Rica—were perceived as having unusually low levels of corruption. By 2003, only two countries in the region—Chile and Uruguay—had low levels of corruption. Frustration with continuing government corruption was mounting at the start of the twenty-first century. Street protests called for all veteran politicians to leave office in Argentina in early 2002. Some of the same complaints and demands could be heard more quietly across dinner tables in many houses across Latin America.

THE QUEST FOR GOVERNANCE REVISITED

With a considerable gap between aspirations for development and liberty and current conditions, one can understand why many people urge governments to take bold steps to improve their lives. Dissatisfaction with the quest for development and liberty frames the debate over governance. Some argue for enhancing the power of the president to clear the path toward quick decision-making. Conversely, others respond that excessive centralization of power is counterproductive. Which side of this debate seems more persuasive? We will begin by considering the experiences of the seven countries examined in this book. Then we will extend the debate to consider patterns across Latin America.

The Politics of Governance as Seen Through This Book

Advocates of a strong presidency could find vivid examples of executive-legislative stalemate amid the search for consensus in several contemporary situations. In Argentina, Raúl Alfonsín found it difficult to cultivate legislative support for most of his economic initiatives, as did Fernando de la Rúa. In Brazil, all presidents in the New Republic met with their share of legislative disappointment. Even the most successful consensus-broker in recent years, Fernando Henrique Cardoso, failed to achieve most of the major economic initiatives of his second term. Similarly, a center-right majority in the Chilean Senate blocked many proposals from three Concertation coalition presidents, and it significantly modified others as a condition for enactment. Jorge Serrano grew so frustrated with opposition to his government that he suspended the Guatemalan legislature in May 1993 and tried to emulate Alberto Fujimori's self-coup. Once the PRI lost its ability to control all branches of government, the structural weaknesses of the Mexican presidency became clearer to Ernesto Zedillo and especially to Vicente Fox. The Carlos Andrés Pérez and Rafael Caldera administrations in Venezuela also struggled to gain legislative support for their economic programs.

Amid difficult economic situations, several contemporary presidents tried to extend their own authority in various ways. Carlos Menem began his presidency by stretching his institutional power via extensive use of decree powers and a re-structuring of the judiciary. He then pushed successfully for a new constitution that permitted his reelection, launched ballotage elections, and increased the president's institutional power in some ways (while potentially decreasing it in others). Fernando Collor also began his presidency by implementing his economic policy via the controversial use of decree power. However, his confrontational approach ultimately culminated in his impeachment. The winner of Brazil's next presidential elections, Fernando Henrique Cardoso, bargained his way to an end to the prohibition on immediate reelection, but he did not strengthen substantially the president's other institutional powers. Serrano's attempts to re-create the Fujimori experience fell apart amid massive antigovernment protests and opposition from civilian politicians and military leaders alike. Hugo Chávez executed the most dramatic increase in presidential power after winning the 1999 elections. He immediately presented a referendum that gained majority approval to launch a complete restructuring of Venezuela's executive, legislative, and judicial branches.

While the frequently unsuccessful search for consensus has bred calls for enhanced executive power, the costs of hyperpresidentialist solutions should give one pause before supporting them wholeheartedly. To date, the political careers of the leaders associated with efforts to bypass the legislature have suffered their own set of difficulties. As noted above, Collor and Serrano lacked the public and legislative support sufficient to realize their dreams of centralizing authority in the presidency. Menem and Chávez initially mobilized a majority of public opinion in support of their presidencies. Over time, however, the perception (and the reality) of hyperpresidentialism made them the subject of most of the criticism of government. By the time Menem finished his second term, his public support had diminished while his list of outspoken opponents lengthened. Enmity toward Chávez grew even more quickly. By the fourth and fifth years of his presidency, he faced constant antigovernment protests and a temporarily successful military coup. Both presidents' elimination of checks and balances worked to reduce the legitimacy of their economic programs. Critics of Menem's move to the market argued that many reforms would not have happened without the abuse and extension of presidential power. Opponents of the state capitalist reforms enacted by decree under the Chávez government claimed that these policies were illegitimate and should be annulled. Exiles opposed to Fidel Castro in Cuba reject all of his revolutionary policies as illegitimate on the grounds that they were not put into place through democratic means. The ongoing centralization of authority in the person of the so-called maximum leader (that is, Castro) has angered increasing numbers of Cubans who initially supported his revolutionary movement.

It is important to remember that the search for consensus has not always produced a quagmire. The Concertation coalition in Chile has managed over time to enact several policy reforms that have improved the prospects for development and for liberty. The Aylwin government worked out a compromise tax reform that provided revenues essential to funding the increase in social spending proposed by his government. In turn, the Frei government brokered a multifaceted judicial reform. This reform provided new specialization and resources to the entire criminal justice system by creating a separate prosecutorial power. It also led to a change in personnel in the Supreme Court that culminated in the landmark 1999 ruling, which in turn paved the way for human rights trials in Chile. In 2003, the Lagos government generated multipartisan support for administrative reforms designed to root out and punish government corruption.

These efforts to build consensus have avoided the corrosive effect of hyper-presidentialism by making it more difficult for people to reject the Concertation's policies as illegitimate. By building multipartisan support, the Concertation coalition has made an effort to increase policy continuity from one administration to the next. Many observers would argue that this greater continuity over the years provides the most important explanation for Chile's solid economic performance during the years 1990–2003. The performance of the Chilean economy was not perfect during this period, but it did better than the rest of Latin America in several respects—producing higher growth with meaningful poverty reduction.

Governance in Contemporary Latin America

Is this debate over executive power unique to these seven countries or is it reflective of patterns across Latin America? As noted earlier in this book, the debate over executive power has a long history throughout the Americas. The contemporary push for a strong presidency has its roots in criticisms of the double-minority presidencies that were prevalent in the region during the second wave of democratization in the middle of the twentieth century. With this issue in mind, several countries shifted away from plurality elections and toward ballotage elections for the presidency at the outset of the contemporary third wave of democratization (see Table 12.6 on page 430).

By 1990, eight of the eighteen democracies in the region had established ballotage elections for president. In the decade that followed, Argentina, Colombia, and Uruguay joined this trend. A large majority of Latin American countries now employ ballotage elections; most require a majority victory to avoid a second-round runoff election. In Argentina, Costa Rica, and Nicaragua, it is possible to win the first-round vote with 40 or 45 percent of the popular vote. The ballotage device makes it impossible for a candidate to become president with a small minority of the votes (unless the runoff opponent withdraws, as Carlos Menem did prior to his runoff with Nestor Kirchner in 2003).

Argentina, Brazil, and Venezuela were not the only countries to see calls for the immediate reelection of the president. Peru in 1993 and the Dominican Republic in 2002 also rewrote their constitutions to permit reelection. In early 2004, the Colombian legislature began work on a constitutional reform that, if passed, would permit Colombian President Álvaro Uribe to run for reelection. Nonetheless, this move away from the principle of no-reelection is much more

TABLE 12.6 Presidential Power in Latin American Democracies (1990 Versus 2003)*

Country	Ballotage election 1990	Possibility of immediate reelection 1990	Institutional powers 1990	Ballotage election 2003	Possibility of immediate reelection 2003	Institutional powers 2003
Argentina	No	No	Potentially dominant	*Yes*	*Yes*	Potentially dominant
Brazil	Yes	No	Proactive	Yes	*Yes*	Proactive
Chile	Yes	No	Potentially dominant	Yes	No	Potentially dominant
Guatemala	Yes	No	Reactive	Yes	No	Reactive
Mexico	No	No	Reactive	No	No	Reactive
Venezuela	No	No	Potentially marginal	No	*Yes*	*Potentially dominant*
Bolivia	No[†]	No	Reactive	No	No	Reactive
Colombia	No	No	Potentially dominant	*Yes*	No	*Proactive*
Costa Rica	Yes	No	Reactive	Yes	No	Reactive
Dominican Republic	No	No	Reactive	No	*Yes*	Reactive
Ecuador	Yes	No	Potentially dominant	Yes	No	Potentially dominant
El Salvador	Yes	No	Reactive	Yes	No	Reactive
Honduras	No	No	Reactive	No	No	Reactive
Nicaragua	Yes	No	Potentially marginal	Yes	No	Potentially marginal
Panama	No	No	Reactive	No	No	Reactive
Paraguay	No	No	Reactive	No	No	*Proactive*
Peru	Yes	No	Proactive	Yes	*Yes*	Proactive
Uruguay	No	No	Proactive	*Yes*	No	Proactive

*Italics indicate a change between 1990 and 2003.

[†]Bolivian electoral law requires the president to obtain an absolute majority of the popular votes. If no candidate receives a majority, however, there is no second-round ballotage election. Instead, the legislature votes to determine the outcome. Prior to 1995, the legislature chose among the three candidates who received the most votes; after 1995, the legislature chose between the two candidates who received the most votes in the general election.

limited in scope than the adoption of ballotage elections. Many countries held no serious discussions regarding the change, while other countries considered the change but ultimately retained the prohibition on immediate reelection. Voters in Panama rejected this reform by a substantial majority in 1998, and efforts to insert this clause in the Honduran constitutional reform that same year also failed.

After the restoration of democracy, movement toward a hyperpresidentialist system in which the chief executive could dominate the legislature seemed like a distinct possibility. Ecuador launched the third wave of democratization in Latin America in 1979 with a new constitution that substantially increased the power of the presidency. Argentina and Chile later returned to democracy with constitutions modified under military rule in ways that enhanced presidential power and weakened the legislature.

Over time, however, it became clear that massive institutional authority for the president would not become the new norm quickly in Latin America. Three countries—Brazil, Peru, and Uruguay—returned to democracy with proactive presidential powers that helped presidents to set the agenda but denied them a strong veto. In turn, nine countries maintained the U.S. model of reactive presidential power, which centers on a strong veto. Over the course of the 1990s, Venezuela dramatically increased the power of the chief executive, while Paraguay engaged in more modest reforms. Conversely, Colombia reduced somewhat the president's authority in the 1991 constitution. Most countries did not make constitutional changes that substantially enhanced the power of the president.

Instead, the most important powers of the presidency have remained the three central tools used by Latin American presidents during the middle of the twentieth century. First, they can use their control over employment in the public sector to reward their supporters and to maintain their alliances with politicians from other political parties. Second, they can use their control over the awarding of government contracts for similar purposes. Third, they can use their position as the only nationally elected figure in most countries' political systems to appeal to the general public in an effort to mobilize public pressure.

In contrast with the second wave of democratization, however, presidents' ability to use these tools is much more limited today. The shift toward more market-oriented policies has tended to limit the leeway for using public employment and government spending as methods for building and maintaining political coalitions. Privatization has reduced the number of lucrative public-sector jobs, and a quest for fiscal balance frequently has led to a reduction in government salaries, in the number of government employees, or both.

Governments in contemporary Latin America face greater pressure from an international financial community that prizes low inflation. Many presidents across the region have pushed for increasingly market-oriented policies as the easiest way to gain support from foreign investors. Financial resources from abroad can then be distributed to shore up political support, which is a more traditional approach to governance. The Menem administration in Argentina provided the most prominent (and ultimately disastrous) example of this tactic, but Carlos Menem had plenty of company. The Lacalle government in neighboring Uruguay used a similar set of arguments to justify several privatization proposals in the early 1990s. The Mahuad government in Ecuador restructured the entire economy in pursuit of an International Monetary Fund (IMF) agreement. Jaime Paz Zamora shifted from his role as the foremost critic of market capitalism to a strong advocate once he became president of Bolivia in 1989. Similarly, Rafael Caldera bowed to opposition to his call for state capitalism and reversed course toward the market-oriented Venezuelan Agenda program in the middle of his presidency. More recently, lifelong IMF critic Lula da Silva began his presidency with a pledge to eliminate budget deficits to meet the terms of an IMF agreement; after fulfilling that pledge, the Da Silva government reached a new accord with the IMF in December 2003 that was worth over $14 billion in potential loans.

It is rarely easy to serve as chief executive anywhere in the world, but it has been particularly difficult in Latin America during the contemporary era. Economic globalization has made Latin American governments more vulnerable to increasingly volatile financial markets. Most economies remain dependent on one to three commodity exports whose prices jump up and down on world markets. In turn, the global information revolution has raised expectations in two ways. First, it makes the highest living standards at home and abroad more visible to ordinary citizens. Second, high-speed technology serves as a metaphor for the possibility of a rapid advance toward the material comfort prevalent in the world's industrialized societies. Today's governments face greater demands than ever before, but they often have less fiscal leeway than their predecessors enjoyed.

Under such conditions, one can understand why presidents might want the power to make snap decisions with minimal interference. Nevertheless, the hyperpresidentialist approach carries with it significant risk, as the examples studied in this book make clear. Governance by consensus is by no means easy, but it offers at least the possibility of a governing dynamic that can extend beyond a single president. Latin American politicians make choices in constrained domestic and international environments, but they can choose not to pursue the expedient approach of centralizing too much power in the executive branch.

DEMOCRACY IN LATIN AMERICA

We saw in Chapter Four that the quests for development, liberty, and governance are conceptually linked to efforts to improve and to consolidate democratic rule. Now, at the close of this book, it is time to ponder the future of democracy in Latin America. As we do so, several of the ties between these quests and support for democracy will become even more apparent.

Development, Liberty, Governance, and Support for Democratic Rule

As detailed throughout this book, the third wave of democratization has been characterized by considerable disappointment in Latin America. Economic growth has often been erratic. Poverty has fallen in only a few countries, and income inequality has risen nearly everywhere. Respect for fundamental civil and political liberties has not increased significantly over time. Street crime and government corruption remain prominent, often growing concerns. The quest for governance has seen more than its share of failed presidencies. Among the eighteen Latin American democracies, half of them elected presidents who did not manage to serve out their terms.

Despite the unresolved challenges faced by ordinary citizens and their respective governments, most Latin Americans express the belief that democracy is always their preferred political system. The travails of the contemporary era have taken their toll, however, on Latin Americans' support for democracy. This deterioration can be observed in the *Latinobarómetro* poll taken annually in most countries in the region since 1996 (see Table 12.7 on page 434).

In 1996, just over three-fifths of respondents in seventeen Latin American countries agreed with the statement "Democracy is always preferable." The level of general support for democracy was similar in our subset of six democracies (57 percent) and in the rest of the region (63 percent). Majorities in most Latin American countries embraced democracy; in fact, Honduras, one of the poorest countries in Latin America, was the lone exception to this trend.

By 2003, however, support for democratic rule had eroded in many instances. Six countries lacked a majority in support of democracy (including Brazil and Guatemala). The number of citizens expressing a firm preference for democracy fell by an average of 13 percent across Latin America. It would seem that poor economic performance, unmet expectations for human liberty, and struggles to establish stable patterns of governance all took their toll on support for democracy.

The graphs provided in this section of the chapter depict the relationship between the quest for liberty, development, and governance and citizens' support for democracy. In each graph, support for democracy appears on the vertical axis, and an issue examined in this book appears on the horizontal axis. The trend line in each chart summarizes the pattern observed. Upward-sloping lines indicate that the two issues share a positive relationship. For example, greater national wealth may be associated with higher levels of support for democracy. Conversely, downward-sloping lines indicate negative relationships; for example, the higher the poverty rate, the lower the support for democracy. In each graph, the value for Pearson's r summarizes this trend as a number between -1 and 1. The further that r moves away from zero in either the positive or negative direction, the stronger the relationship between the two dimensions of the graph. If r were equal to 1 or to -1, the factor examined along

TABLE 12.7 Latin American Attitudes Toward Democracy (1996 Versus 2003)*

Country	Democracy is always preferable (1996)	Democracy is always preferable (2003)	Percentage change in support for democracy from 1996 to 2003
Argentina	71%	68%	−4%
Brazil	50%	35%	−30%
Chile	54%	50%	−7%
Cuba	NA†	NA	NA
Guatemala	51%	33%	−35%
Mexico	53%	53%	0%
Venezuela	62%	67%	8%
Subregional average	*57%*	*51%*	*−10%*
Bolivia	64%	50%	−22%
Colombia	60%	46%	−23%
Costa Rica	80%	77%	−4%
Dominican Republic	NA	NA	NA
Ecuador	52%	46%	−12%
El Salvador	56%	45%	−20%
Honduras	42%	55%	31%
Nicaragua	59%	51%	−14%
Panama	75%	51%	−32%
Paraguay	59%	40%	−32%
Peru	63%	52%	−17%
Uruguay	80%	78%	−3%
Subregional average	*63%*	*54%*	*−14%*
Latin American average	61%	53%	−13%

*All figures but those in the last column represent the percentage of the population agreeing with the statement "Democracy is always preferable."

†The *Latinobarómetro* is not conducted in Cuba and the Dominican Republic.

SOURCE: Press releases summarizing the *Latinobarómetro* surveys for 1996 and 2003 <http://www.latinobarometro.org> (accessed on November 4, 2003).

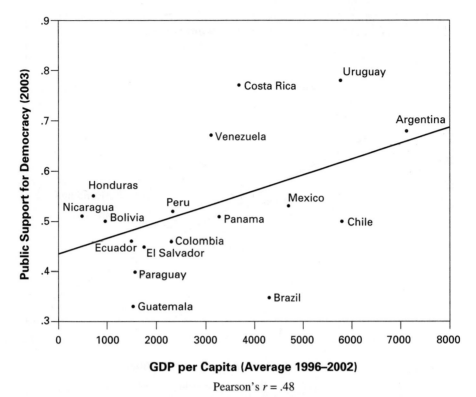

Pearson's $r = .48$

FIGURE 12.1 National Wealth and Public Support for Democracy (2003)

SOURCE: Data on support for democracy are from the 2003 *Latinobarómetro* survey. Data on GDP per capita are from the Economic Commission for Latin America and the Caribbean.

the horizontal axis would perfectly parallel the level of support for democracy. In turn, the sign of r indicates the direction of the trend. Negative values for r indicate downward-sloping trends, while positive values for r indicate upward-sloping trends.

The graph in Figure 12.1 depicts the relationship between national wealth and support for democracy in 2003. The upward-sloping line indicates that citizens in more affluent countries tend to express higher levels of support for democracy. National wealth encourages support for democracy by generating hope. A larger amount of goods and services in circulation per person provides more resources that potentially can be used to improve each citizen's well-being. Conversely, poor economic conditions can foster frustration with democratic governance and a desire for more rapid change via some form of authoritarian rule.

As noted in Chapter Four, aggregate national wealth is not the lone dimension of development. While greater national wealth improves a country's potential for poverty reduction, it does not imply that poverty has been eliminated.

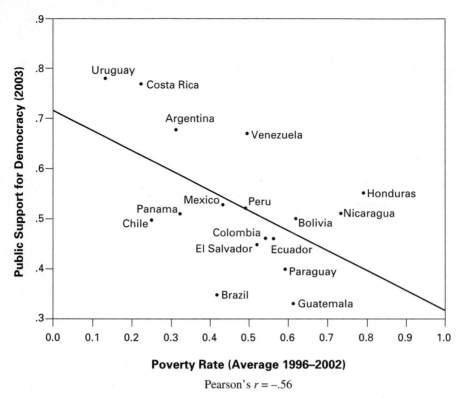

Pearson's $r = -.56$

FIGURE 12.2 Poverty and Public Support for Democracy (2003)

SOURCE: Data on support for democracy are from the 2003 *Latinobarómetro* survey. Data on poverty are from the Economic Commission for Latin America and the Caribbean.

Figure 12.2 compares support for democracy with prevailing poverty rates in Latin America. Generally speaking, the greater the poverty rate, the lower the support for democracy. Societies with more poor citizens find it more difficult to inspire unconditional support for democratic rule. Impoverished people may yearn for a powerful political leader to improve their lives quickly, and the privileged may support authoritarian rule to protect their wealth.

The link between the development and attitudinal support for democracy is stronger still when one examines income inequality (see Figure 12.3). A strong negative relationship exists between the degree of income inequality and support for democracy. Notice that in this figure, countries are grouped much more tightly around the trend line. The value for *r* of −.88 is very close to −1—which indicates that there are only small exceptions to the negative relationship. Income inequality corrodes support for democracy by eating away at the democratic promise of equal rights and equal opportunity. This aspect of the quest for development is the most crucial for contemporary efforts to move from delegative democracy toward a more multifaceted democracy in which civil liberties and the rule of law are widely respected.

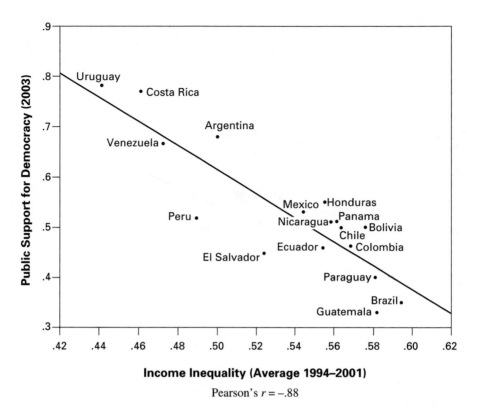

Income Inequality (Average 1994–2001)

Pearson's $r = -.88$

FIGURE 12.3   Income Inequality and Public Support for Democracy (2003)

SOURCE: Data on support for democracy are from the 2003 *Latinobarómetro* survey. Data on income inequality are from the World Bank.

We now turn to the relationship between the quest for liberty and support for democracy. We begin by comparing the prevailing protection of political and civil liberties to citizens' expressed support for democratic rule. In Figure 12.4 on page 438, we can see that Latin American countries that respect fundamental political and civil liberties more consistently are more likely to have higher percentages of citizens who believe that democracy is always their preferred political system. This positive relationship is not as strong as the link between income inequality and democratic support, but it is a palpable trend. Understandably, citizens who see more frequent gaps in the democratic process are less likely to support democracy unconditionally as their preferred political system. Conversely, people who see basic liberties protected are more likely to express strong support for democratic rule.

The reduction of political corruption constitutes another major goal in the pursuit of liberty. Do varying levels of corruption affect support for democracy? Figure 12.5 on page 439 depicts the relationship between these two issues. Higher levels of corruption are associated with lower levels of support for democracy. This trend is the weakest one observed so far, however, in this chapter. The most

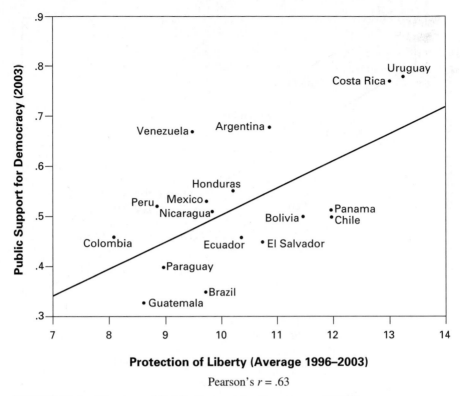

FIGURE 12.4 Liberty and Public Support for Democracy (2003)

SOURCE: Data on support for democracy are from the 2003 *Latinobarómetro* survey. Data on liberty are from Freedom House.

notable exception in the chart is Chile. It has the lowest level of perceived corruption—by a substantial margin—but the expressed unconditional support for democracy (50 percent) is just below the average for Latin America as a whole (53 percent). It seems that factors other than corruption are central to many Chileans' thinking about democracy. For example, corruption has declined in the contemporary era, but income inequality remains high and has risen slightly.

Finally, we turn our attention to the relationship between governance and support for democracy. Chapter One noted that the quest for governance centers on an attempt to balance conflicting imperatives—quick, effective action and adequate inclusion of debate and consensus building. To a certain extent, the development indicators we recently examined provide one important set of results against which citizens judge the effectiveness of government activity. The protection of basic political and civil liberties is one means by which we can assess the inclusiveness of the political process.

However, we do not have precise data with which to gauge citizens' assessments of the balance between quick, effective action and inclusiveness. Perhaps

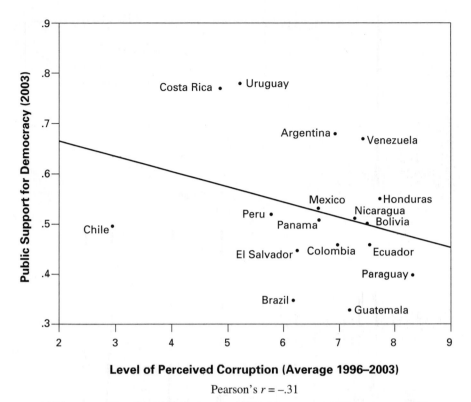

Pearson's $r = -.31$

FIGURE 12.5 Political Corruption and Public Support for Democracy (2003)

SOURCE: Data on support for democracy are from the 2003 *Latinobarómetro* survey. Data on perceived corruption are from Transparency International's Corruption Perceptions Index.

the closest piece of information can be found in the same *Latinobarómetro* public-opinion poll that we have used to measure people's support for democracy. That poll asks citizens to express their degree of satisfaction with how well democracy functions in their country. This question provides an indirect reflection of people's judgments about the balance between action and inclusiveness because people decidedly unhappy with results on either score are unlikely to say that they are satisfied with how democracy works in their respective countries.

Figure 12.6 on page 440 graphs the relationship between satisfaction with democracy and support for democracy. A strong positive link exists between the two: countries with high levels of recent satisfaction with democracy are more likely to express unconditional support for democracy in the present. Conversely, countries with less widespread dissatisfaction with how the democratic process has been functioning are likely to exhibit lower levels of support for democracy. The value for r (.79) shows a consistent trend—second only to the previously examined relationship between income inequality and attitudinal support for democracy.

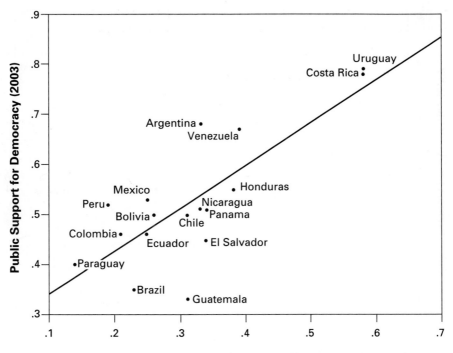

Public Satisfaction with Democracy (Average 1996–2003)

Pearson's $r = .79$

Satisfaction with democracy is measured as the percentage of the population that says it is very satisfied or satisfied with the functioning of democracy in the country.

FIGURE 12.6   Satisfaction with Democracy and Public Support for Democracy (2003)

SOURCE: Data on support for democracy and satisfaction with democracy are from the 2003 *Latinobarómetro* survey.

As you can see by examining the graphs in these six figures, the issues at the heart of this book are central to people's thinking about democratic rule. Where governments succeed in their quests for development, liberty, and governance, support for democratic rule tends to be higher. Where governments have not made nearly as much progress, citizens are less supportive of democracy. Table 12.8 summarizes these relationships by examining each country's relative success in attaining these objectives. Numbers in bold indicate countries ranked in the top half of this distribution of seventeen Latin American countries.

The three countries in Latin America with the highest levels of unconditional support for democracy—Uruguay, Costa Rica, and Argentina—rank in the top half in all six categories. Five of the next six countries with high support for democracy rank in the top half of at least three of the six categories. Nicaragua forms the lone exception in this regard: people express above-normal levels of

TABLE 12.8 Development, Liberty, Governance, and Support for Democracy (2003)*

Country	Support for democracy (2003)	GDP per capita (average for 1996–2002)	Poverty rate (average for 1996–2002)	Income inequality (average for 1996–2002)	Protection of political and civil liberties (average for 1996–2003)	Level of perceived corruption (average for 1998–2003)	Satisfaction with how democracy functions (average for 1996–2003)
Argentina	3	1	4	5	6	9	7
Brazil	16	5	6	17	11	5	14
Chile	10	2	3	12	3	1	9
Guatemala	17	13	14	16	16	11	9
Mexico	6	4	7	7	11	8	12
Venezuela	4	8	8	3	13	13	3
Bolivia	10	15	15	14	5	14	11
Colombia	12	10	11	13	17	10	15
Costa Rica	2	6	2	2	2	2	1
Ecuador	12	14	12	8	8	15	12
El Salvador	14	11	10	6	7	6	5
Honduras	5	16	17	9	9	16	4
Nicaragua	8	17	16	10	10	12	7
Panama	8	7	5	11	3	7	5
Paraguay	15	12	13	15	14	17	17
Peru	7	9	8	4	15	4	16
Uruguay	1	3	1	1	1	3	1

*Each number ranks the country in its success relative to the other countries. Country rankings are inverted for poverty, income inequality, and corruption because success is indicated by low poverty, low inequality, and lower corruption. Numbers in **bold** indicate that the country ranks in the top half of these seventeen countries (at or above the median point in the distribution).
SOURCE: Same as for Figures 12.1–12.6.

satisfaction with democracy and support for democratic rule, yet their country ranks below the median in terms of its success in securing development and liberty.

Table 12.8 also reinforces the relationship we observed earlier between income inequality and support for democracy. The seven countries with the highest unconditional support for democracy all have levels of income inequality below the median for Latin America as a whole. The other two countries with slightly above-average support for democracy, Honduras and Nicaragua, have income inequality levels just above the median. Chile performs well in many respects, but its high income inequality sours the context for democratic thought and action. Among the various issues examined in this text across all countries, income inequality has the greatest impact on the probability of unconditional public support for democratic rule.[4]

The Future of Democracy in Latin America

The previous section paints a rather bleak portrait of the prospects for democracy in Latin America. Public support for democracy has declined considerably in many countries between 1996 and 2003, and it has risen in just two—Honduras and Venezuela. In turn, the factor most closely associated with unconditional support for democratic rule is moving in the wrong direction: income inequality rose between 1996 and 2002 in every country except Nicaragua. These trends illustrate important aspects of the difficult context in which democratic politics unfolds in contemporary Latin America. In this context, one or more presidents failed to finish their terms in nine of the eighteen democracies in the region during the years 1980–2003.

Nevertheless, one could construct a different story out of the same public-opinion trends. What is particularly remarkable about the discussion in the previous section is that support for democracy has not collapsed entirely. Across the region as a whole, a majority of citizens continue to express a clear preference for democracy over authoritarian rule. Continuing public support for democracy helps constrain leaders who might want to launch authoritarian political alternatives. This trend is evident even in the country that has exhibited the lowest unconditional support for democracy in public-opinion polls—Guatemala. In November 2003, Guatemalans voted in record numbers to prevent the potential election of a past military dictator, Efraín Ríos Montt.

Other elements of the context for democratic rule also instill hope for the resilience of democracy. In the situations in which presidents left office early, none of them were replaced by military dictatorships. Instead, the vice president took office or the legislature selected a new president. In this book, we witnessed this type of power transfer in Argentina, Brazil, Guatemala, and Venezuela, as well as in Peru.

The recent resilience of democracy represents an important break from Latin America's past. However, this should by no means inspire complacency among those who wish Latin American countries the best in their respective quests for development, liberty, and governance. The following trends at the turn of the century are sobering:

- National wealth has been declining.
- Income inequality is on the rise.
- Considerable environmental damage continues unchecked in many Latin American countries.
- Improvement in the protection of basic liberties has not occurred since 1990.
- Political corruption remains at constant levels.

- The level of violent crime is stable or rising in most Latin American countries.
- Only a minority of citizens in most Latin American countries express confidence in the executive branch, in the legislature, or in political parties more generally.
- Citizens' satisfaction with how democracy functions in their respective countries is low—and falling lower still in several cases.

This list forms the context in which many citizens went to the polls in the early twenty-first century to elect new leaders who they thought might be committed to reversing these trends. Looking for change, voters in several countries elected candidates associated with the minority center-left faction of major political movements, such as Ricardo Lagos in Chile and Nestor Kirchner in Argentina. In Brazil, they chose Lula da Silva, the leader of the Workers' party, a center-left political party that had never won the presidency before. In other countries, voters chose ex-military officers not associated with the traditional political establishment. Hugo Chávez won in Venezuela, while Lucío Gutiérrez triumphed in Ecuador. In still other countries, people chose politicians with minimal national experience and no ties to governing parties, such as Alejandro Toledo in Peru and Vicente Fox in Mexico.

In years to come, we may view the turn of the twenty-first century as a political watershed. The nontraditional leaders mentioned above inspired optimism in many people whose daily lives are extremely difficult, to put it mildly. If these leaders succeed in reversing some of the trends highlighted in the list above, their successes could lead to a virtuous circle in which one step forward leads to yet another step forward. In turn, progress in the quest for development, liberty, and governance would help to entrench and to enrich democratic rule. In particular, reductions in income inequality would improve people's ability to participate politically and economically. Perhaps fears of delegative democracy would begin to subside. Delegative democracy could evolve into a more multifaceted vision of democracy in which basic liberties and the rule of law are more consistently protected.

Conversely, a failure to respond to basic human goals in the coming years would make the path to a more complete democracy even more difficult than it is now. An inability to generate a working political consensus in favor of change could have dire consequences. In the 1960s, frustration with inequality motivated many young people to take up arms against their governments. In the early twenty-first century, fewer people have chosen this route, but increasing numbers of people have turned to the use of force in two different ways—by blocking highways and by kidnapping.

The roadblock is a form of political coercion: people block roads to coerce the government into changing its policies and/or its leaders. The *piqueteros* began as a movement of unemployed persons in rural Argentina and expanded into a nationwide network capable of disrupting transportation nearly everywhere from 2001 onward. In Mexico, desperate small farmers blocked highways for months in 2001 and 2002 in a successful effort to convince the government to change its plans for building a new airport on their land outside Mexico City. In Peru, protesters shut down the city of Arequipa and access to its airport in 2001 in an effort to stop the planned privatization of the electric company. In Bolivia, roadblocks frequently disrupted the Banzer government by cutting off the highways linking the three largest cities. Then, in 2003, roadblocks and the violence surrounding efforts to dislodge the people responsible for the road-block ultimately forced the resignation of Gonzalo Sánchez de Lozada in October 2003. Hondurans opposed to budget cuts implemented in pursuit of an IMF agreement also blocked major roads in late 2003.

Most contemporary kidnappings have not formed part of a political strategy. In some instances, political groups have captured government officials to demand changes in government policy. Most kidnappers, however, try to extort money from the families of the victims. In nearly every country, one could name several high-profile kidnappings in which relatives of wealthy individuals were held for ransom. The 2002 kidnapping of two sisters of Mexican pop star Thalía provided perhaps the most high-profile illustration of this practice. The more notable change in the contemporary era, however, is the rise in kidnappings of ordinary citizens—many of them of modest means. Citizens' movements have formed in many countries to try to pressure the government into providing more—and more effective—police protection from kidnapping and armed robbery.

The ballot box, the roadblock, and the kidnapping provide very different images for Latin America's future. If democracy is to prevail in a meaningful way, political leaders, business leaders, civic leaders, and ordinary citizens will have to meet a difficult challenge. They must build a more enduring consensus about how to make progress.

Critics of the revolutionary era of the 1960s argued that a wholesale adoption of socialism would not be a viable path to progress. In most countries, they were proven right on political grounds: the opponents of socialism blocked its emergence. In Cuba, the lone country that adopted socialism, the command economy reduced relative and absolute poverty at the expense of nearly all other development goals. The Castro government's limited injection of market mechanisms prevented a complete economic collapse, but it did not solve Cuba's ongoing problems. Frustration with economic stagnation and political repression has mounted in Cuba with each passing decade.

In turn, anticommunists in Latin America cheered the end of the Cold War as the beginning of a new era in which market capitalism and democratic politics would form the path to progress. By 2004, however, market capitalism had not yet produced the desired economic outcomes, as the sobering list of contemporary trends provided above made clear. Just as command economics was dubbed too extreme to be politically and economically successful, advocates of market capitalism could face the same charges.

Instead of choosing between two sides in a dichotomy of state versus market, Latin American countries—like countries around the world—face a much longer list of choices regarding when to let market mechanisms prevail and when to use public authority and resources to improve national welfare. Because of the high level of income inequality in the region, nearly all policies that promise to reduce poverty and lessen inequality can become politicized quickly as an us-versus-them choice. We have seen the politics of the mixed-economy model play out in vivid ways throughout twentieth-century Latin America. Wealthy Mexicans pressured post-Cárdenas governments to limit efforts to redistribute income. Cubans grew increasingly frustrated with a series of reformist governments from the 1920s through the 1940s that used the rhetoric of change but ultimately changed little. The Arbenz government's policy reforms motivated many wealthy Guatemalans to mobilize in support of his downfall. The *trienio* era of Venezuelan politics in the 1940s saw a rapid increase in political polarization that culminated in the 1948 coup. Large landowners in Brazil have mobilized in various ways over the years to prevent land reform. Argentine politics divided into two increasingly separate camps during the Peronist era. An even greater political polarization took place during the Frei government's search for a middle way in Chile during the 1960s.

These and other examples demonstrate the difficulty of pushing for a middle road. Political scientists often refer to this situation as the reformer's dilemma. Move too slowly and people may reject you as unsupportive of change—like the Frei government in Chile during the 1960s, the PRI governments after Cárdenas in Mexico, and nearly every Cuban government prior to 1959. Move too quickly or too heavy-handedly and entrenched interests may brand you as a radical and press for an end to your government—as we have seen in the analysis of the governments of Arbenz, Perón, and several others.

The search for consensus is not easy. However, it is essential to the quest for development, liberty, and governance. Once the transition from one-party dominance is over in Mexico, will Vicente Fox's successor be able to get Mexican voters and legislators to agree on an economic program? Guatemalans turned out to vote in record numbers in late 2003, but will Guatemala's political and economic leaders begin to take steps to improve conditions for ordinary citizens? When Fidel Castro is no longer in power in Cuba, will his successor permit a greater diversity of voices to be heard in Cuban society and in its government? Regardless of the outcome of the 2004 presidential recall process in Venezuela, will the president be able to reduce the level of political conflict and improve the lives of millions of poor Venezuelans? Will Lula da Silva simultaneously meet key demands from the international financial community and from the impoverished half of the Brazilian population? If Joaquín Lavín wins the 2005 Chilean presidential elections, will his center-right coalition extend the reduction in poverty that took place under the Concertation governments and begin to make progress in reducing income inequality? Will Nestor Kirchner's government succeed in restoring ordinary Argentines' faith in their future while simultaneously convincing wealthy Argentines to put their money back into the Argentine economy?

The answers to these questions (and similar ones elsewhere in the Americas) will tell us a lot about the prospects for development, liberty, and governance in the years to come. As the author of this book, I cannot know how you currently feel about the prospects for democracy in Latin America. I can hope that reading this book has improved your ability to make an informed judgment. On a personal level, I also hope that you are motivated to take action—even in some small way—to improve the prospects for development, liberty, and governance in your own country and elsewhere in the world.

Activities and Exercises

1. The reduction of income inequality is important in its own right. In this chapter, we saw that income inequality also plays a crucial role in framing people's attitudes toward democratic rule. If you were the next president of one of the seven countries at the heart of this book, name one policy reform you would recommend as a way to reduce income inequality. Design a strategy for building political support for the reform you propose.

2. Like income inequality, political corruption is a long-standing problem in much of Latin America. For the same country you considered in the first activity, design what you consider to be a set of three useful anticorruption proposals. What steps would you take to prevent your proposed anticorruption watchdogs from succumbing to corruption?

3. Governing a country involves a search for political support; it also requires leaders to choose the major priorities that they will try to achieve during their time in government. For the same country you considered in the first and second activities, write a list of twenty potential goals for your administration. Now rank those goals in terms of their importance. How many do you think you could make progress on during a five-year term as president?

4. U.S. journalist Charles Krause (of the PBS *Newshour with Jim Lehrer*) hosts a one-hour documentary examining a wide variety of major challenges in Latin America. See if *The Americas in the 21st Century* is available in your area. If not, see if your school is willing to purchase or rent it for a single showing.

5. Now that you have acquired considerable working knowledge of the Latin American political landscape, you are in a better position to consider what you would like the U.S. government's foreign policy priorities to be in the region. List your top five priorities. Then go to the U.S. Department of State website, specifically to the section dealing with Western Hemisphere affairs at http://www.state.gov/p/wha/, to see how the U.S. government has been dealing with those issues in its relations with Latin America.

Suggested Readings

Agüero, Felipe, and Jeffrey Stark, eds. *Fault Lines of Democracy in Post-Transition Latin America*. Coral Gables, Fla.: North-South Center Press, 1998.

Chalmers, Douglas, ed. *The New Politics of Inequality in Latin America: Rethinking Participation and Representation.* Oxford, England: Oxford University Press, 1997.

Domínguez, Jorge, and Michael Shifter, eds. *Constructing Democratic Governance in Latin America,* 2d ed. Baltimore, Md.: Johns Hopkins University Press, 2003.

Frühling, Hugo, and Joseph Tulchin, eds. *Crime and Violence in Latin America: Citizen Security, Democracy and the State.* Washington, D.C.: Woodrow Wilson Center Press, 2003.

Garretón, Manuel, and Edward Newman, eds. *Democracy in Latin America: (Re) Constructing Political Society.* New York: United Nations University Press, 2001.

Huber, Evelyne, ed. *Models of Capitalism: Lessons for Latin America.* University Park, Pa.: Pennsylvania State University Press, 2002.

Kumar Saha, Suranjit, and David Parker, eds. *Globalisation and Sustainable Development in Latin America: Perspectives on the New Economic Order.* Northampton, Mass.: Edward Elgar, 2002.

Lievesley, Geraldine. *Democracy in Latin America: Mobilization, Power, and the Search for a New Politics.* Manchester, England: Manchester University Press, 1999.

Mainwaring, Scott, and Timothy Scully, eds. *Christian Democracy in Latin America: Electoral Competition and Regime Conflicts.* Stanford, Calif.: Stanford University Press, 2003.

Mainwaring, Scott, and Christopher Welna, eds. *Democratic Accountability in Latin America.* Oxford, England: Oxford University Press, 2003.

Margheritis, Ana, ed. *Latin American Democracies in the New Global Economy.* Coral Gables, Fla.: North-South Center Press, 2003.

Nun, José. *Democracy: Government of the People or Government of the Politicians?* Lanham, Md.: Rowman and Littlefield, 2003.

Payne, J. Mark, ed. *Democracies in Development: Politics and Reform in Latin America.* Washington, D.C.: Inter-American Development Bank and the International Institute for Democracy and Electoral Assistance, 2003.

Peeler, John. *Building Democracy in Latin America,* 2d ed. Boulder, Colo.: Lynne Rienner, 2004.

Peloso, Vincent, ed. *Work, Protest, and Identity in Twentieth-Century Latin America.* Wilmington, Del.: Scholarly Resources, 2003.

Philip, George. *Democracy in Latin America: Surviving Conflict and Crisis?* Cambridge, England: Polity, 2003.

Rotker, Susana, and Katherine Goldman, eds. *Citizens of Fear: Urban Violence in Latin America.* New Brunswick, N.J.: Rutgers University Press, 2002.

Sieder, Rachel, ed. *Multiculturalism in Latin America: Indigenous Rights, Diversity, and Democracy.* New York: Macmillan, 2002.

Tulchin, Joseph, and Amelia Brown, eds. *Democratic Governance and Social Inequality.* Boulder, Colo.: Lynne Rienner, 2002.

Tulchin, Joseph, and Ralph Espach, eds. *Combatting Corruption in Latin America.* Washington, D.C.: Woodrow Wilson Center Press, 2000.

von Mettenheim, Kurt, and James Malloy, eds. *Deepening Democracy in Latin America.* Pittsburgh, Pa.: University of Pittsburgh Press, 1998.

Walker, Thomas, and Ariel Armony, eds. *Repression, Resistance, and Democratic Transition in Central America.* Wilmington, Del.: Scholarly Resources, 2000.

Wise, Carol, and Riordan Roett, eds. *Post-Stabilization Politics in Latin America: Competition, Transition, Collapse.* Washington, D.C.: Brookings Institution, 2003.

World Bank. *Inequality in Latin America and the Caribbean: Breaking with History?* Washington, D.C.: World Bank, 2004.

Endnotes

1. Kurt Weyland, *The Politics of Market Reform in Fragile Democracies: Argentina, Brazil, Peru, and Venezuela* (Princeton, N.J.: Princeton University Press, 2002).

2. See, for example, Kathleen Bruhn, "Social Spending and Political Support," *Comparative Politics* 27 (1996): 151–77; or Kenneth Roberts, "Neoliberalism and the Transformation of Populism in Latin America: The Peruvian Case," *World Politics* 48 (1995): 82–116.

3. For further discussion of the bait-and-switch approach, as well as a comprehensive analysis of the various political challenges of reform, see Adam Przeworski, *Democracy and the Market: Political and Economic Reforms in Eastern Europe and Latin America* (Cambridge, England: Cambridge University Press, 1991).

4. In a regression analysis using the data from Figures 12.1 to 12.6, the only factor that holds a statistically significant relationship to national levels of support for democracy is income inequality. It is difficult to use regression analysis to evaluate the relationship of all six factors to the support for democracy because of the inter-relationships among these causal influences; this collinearity makes the regression results difficult to interpret by inflating the standard errors of the regression coefficients. If the poverty rate is left out of the regression equation, however, the collinearity diagnostics show that the tolerance statistics for all the coefficients are .25 or greater, which indicates greater stability in the standard errors. In this second analysis, income inequality is still the only factor that has a statistically significant relationship to national support for democracy.

Glossary

absolute poverty: A conceptualization of poverty in which people below a certain material standard are characterized as poor. For example, the World Bank terms people with incomes under $2.00 per day as poor and those earning less than $1.00 per day as indigent.

amnesty: An approach to past human rights violations in which some or all accused persons are legally forgiven by the government and are thereby made immune from prosecution.

ballotage: An electoral system that requires a candidate to get a certain percentage of the vote (often a majority) to win office. If no candidate receives the necessary votes, a second runoff election is held between the two candidates who receive the most votes.

basic needs: A conceptualization of economic development that shifts the focus from growth alone toward efforts to measure progress in human survival and fulfillment across national populations.

binomial electoral system: An electoral system in which each party presents a slate of two candidates in every district. If a single slate wins twice as many votes as the second-place list, then both seats go to the winning party. If no party achieves this goal, then one seat goes to the party receiving the most votes, and the other seat goes to the party receiving the second-most votes.

bureaucratic-authoritarianism: A form of authoritarian rule prevalent during the 1970s in Latin America in which many active-duty officers and civilian bureaucrats rationalized dictatorship by claiming that electoral politics would leave the country vulnerable to communist subversion.

caudillo: A Spanish term for military leader or for a leader more generally.

cleavage: A potential fault line of societal division and political conflict.

clientelism: A political dynamic in which government officials cultivate support by providing material benefits directly to individuals or groups in exchange for their political support.

closed-list proportional representation: An electoral system in which multiple offices are elected in each district. Parties present lists of candidates and voters choose which party's list to support. Seats are allocated roughly according to the percentage of votes received by each list. The party controls the order of the names on the list; for example, if a ten-candidate slate wins five seats, then the first five candidates on the list are elected.

Cold War: An era of international relations in which the United States led a coalition opposed to the extension of communist rule while the Soviet Union headed a bloc of socialist countries with command economies and one-party states. This dynamic shaped much of U.S. policy toward Latin America from 1945 until the fall of the Berlin Wall in 1989 and the disintegration of the Soviet Union in 1992.

command economy: An economic policy in which government owns most or all property. This public ownership establishes a context in which government officials can make most economic decisions regarding the production and pricing of goods and services, employment, etc.

conditionality: A term that frequently refers to the requirements the International Monetary Fund (IMF) places on national governments as conditions that must be met to receive IMF loans. Over time, the typically market-oriented conditions required by the IMF took on importance beyond the disbursal of the loan itself. From the 1970s onward, many private investors and banks have taken governments' compliance with IMF programs as an indicator of an investor-friendly environment and noncompliance as an indicator of greater risk for investors.

conservatives: Citizens and leaders who hold an organic view of society in which individual freedoms were conditioned by traditional ties to church, family, and the land, and who favor a continuing role for the church in education and elsewhere. In nineteenth-century Latin America, many conservatives also supported a greater emphasis on agricultural production for the domestic economy (as opposed to the more export-oriented, free-trade policies favored by liberals).

corporatism: A dynamic in interest group politics in which labor, peasants, and businesses are organized into nationwide groups or confederations that have a formal and informal incorporation into the policy-making process. In societal corporatism, these large confederations emerged largely on their own. In the state corporatism prevalent in several Latin American countries, the government formed these groups and tightly regulated their organizations in an effort to cultivate political support and to limit conflict between labor and management.

criollos: A Spanish term for creoles—the descendants of Spanish colonizers born in the New World.

default: In international finance, this term refers to the suspension of payments due on a debt.

delegative democracy: A term associated with Argentine scholar Guillermo O'Donnell; it describes an electoral democracy that is established for the selection of major government officials, but protection of civil liberties is uneven and respect for the rule of law among government officials is similarly incomplete.

democratic consolidation: A process through which enduring, more completely democratic political systems are built. In several conceptualizations, consolidation is said to have occurred when a country can maintain democratic principles without interruption for a period of thirty or more years.

dependency: A theory of economic development that questions the applicability of neoclassical (market-oriented) economic theory to Latin America and to Third World countries more generally. Although the dependency approach has many variations, nearly all dependency analysts assert that the terms of trade between the industrialized economies at the core (or center) of the world economy and the commodity-exporting economies on the periphery are uneven, thereby making peripheral countries' economic development either difficult or impossible.

devaluation: A foreign exchange rate policy in which the government permits a country's currency to lose value relative to one or more other countries' currencies.

direct democracy: A political dynamic in which laws are passed (or blocked) by a vote of all citizens. Direct democracy contrasts with representative democracy, in which citizens elect legislators with the authority to pass (or block the passage of) laws.

disappearance: A summary execution without formal burial and without notification to the immediate relatives of the person(s) killed.

domestic prosecution: An approach to past human rights violations in which some or all accused persons are tried within their own country's judicial system. This type of prosecution contrasts with the international prosecution approach, in which accused persons face trials in foreign countries' courts or in an international court.

double-minority presidency: A situation in which the president is elected without a majority of the popular vote and in which the political party(ies) supporting the president's candidacy control less than half of the legislature.

embargo: A refusal to conduct economic exchange with another country.

fixed exchange rate: A foreign exchange rate policy in which the government pledges to hold its currency constant (or nearly constant) relative to other currencies.

free float: A foreign exchange rate policy in which the government announces that it will not attempt to influence its currency's value relative to other countries' currencies for a certain period of time.

Good Neighbor Policy: U.S. foreign policy during the years 1929–1945 that formally recognized the principle of nonintervention in hemispheric relations within the Americas. This policy contrasted with U.S. foreign policy toward Latin America during the prior three decades, during which the U.S. government asserted a right to intervene militarily in hemispheric affairs under several circumstances and conducted several military interventions during the years 1904–1928.

gridlock: A situation in executive-legislative relations in which the president's party does not control a majority of seats in the legislature.

growth first: A conceptualization of economic development that focuses on maximizing the amount of goods and services in circulation in a country while placing less priority on how that material wealth is distributed or on other development goals.

hyperpresidentialism: A political dynamic in which the presidency holds considerable formal and informal authority relative to other governmental organs.

import-substituting industrialization: A policy approach to industrialization that focuses on promoting the production of finished goods that had previously been imported from outside the region via the use of tariffs on imports and subsidies for firms that produce the good domestically.

indígenas: A Spanish term for indigenous peoples—the presumed descendants of civilizations whose presence in a given territory predates the establishment of written property claims. In Latin America, the indigenous peoples are the presumed descendants of civilizations that predate the arrival of European colonizers from Spain and Portugal.

intergovernmental organizations: International organizations formed by national governments.

judicial review: The power of the courts to rule that legislation is invalid on the grounds that it is unconstitutional.

land reform: A government policy aimed at redistributing the ownership of arable land.

latifundios: A Spanish term for large, landed estates.

legitimacy: A political concept referring to the extent to which citizens believe that the current officials have a right to govern in the name of the population as a whole. Legitimacy is distinct from political support: a citizen can disagree with the decisions made by government officials, but still believe that the officials have a legitimate authority with which to make those decisions.

liberals: Citizens and leaders who believe in many of the tenets of European liberalism including the rights of the individual, free trade, and a reduction of the power of the church in society.

liberation theology: A theological movement in the Catholic church that emphasized a need to focus the church's energies on the poor and that called for greater involvement of lay parishioners in the church's activities.

living museum: A metaphor associated with U.S. scholar Charles Anderson, which he used to describe the twentieth-century Latin American context as one in which all the forms of political authority of the Western historic experience continue to exist and operate side by side—from landed gentry and brash military officers to business entrepreneurs, labor unions, and political parties of all stripes.

lost decade: A frequently used characterization of the prevailing economic trends in Latin America during the 1980s. Gross domestic product (GDP) per person shrank, consumer prices in Latin America and the Caribbean rose, income distribution worsened, and the percentage of the population living in poverty rose.

machismo: A Spanish term referring to a cultural tradition in which women are assumed to be central to family life and men are central to life outside the home—in the economy, in society, and in politics.

magistrate system: A judicial system in which judges preside over both the investigative and the trial phase of legal proceedings.

majority-minority electoral system: An electoral system in which all parties present three candidates in a three-seat electoral district. Two seats are won by the party slate with the most votes, while the runner-up slate receives the third seat.

managed float: A foreign exchange rate policy in which a government pledges to buy and sell currency in an effort to keep the value of its currency relatively stable in relation to other currencies.

market capitalism: An economic policy in which government intervenes minimally in the economy. Advocates of market capitalism believe that government should stay out of any activity in which market dynamics could conceivably function.

mercantilism: An economic policy that emphasizes the attainment of a positive balance of trade. In the colonial era in the Americas, mercantilist policies focused not only on the overall balance of trade between colonizers and their colonies, but also on the accumulation of precious metals extracted from the colonies.

mestizos: A Spanish term referring to people presumed to be descended from both Spanish and indigenous origins.

middle sectors: A concept in political sociology associated with U.S. scholar John Johnson that referred in Latin America to persons whose socioeconomic standing placed them between the traditional landed elite and the large mass of day laborers in industry and agriculture.

modernization theory: A theory of political development that asserted that the twin socioeconomic changes of urbanization and industrialization would create more viable conditions for the emergence and consolidation of democratic political systems.

Monroe Doctrine: A doctrine in U.S. foreign policy in the Americas first enunciated by President James Monroe in 1823. The policy declares the U.S. government's desire to keep the Western Hemisphere relatively free from overt influence from beyond the Americas. To varying degrees and in varying forms, this doctrine has remained a guiding principle in U.S. foreign policy toward the region from 1823 through the early twenty-first century.

mulattos: A term referring to persons presumed to have Spanish and African roots.

nongovernmental organizations (NGOs): Organizations formed by citizens outside the government; the NGOs can be domestic, international, or a mix of the two.

one-party state: A political system in which only one political party is legally permitted to participate.

open-list proportional representation system: An electoral system in which multiple candidates are elected in each district. Parties present lists of candidates and voters choose which party's list to support. If they choose to do so, voters can also cast one or more preference votes for their favorite candidate(s) from within their chosen party's list. Seats are allocated roughly according to, first, the percentage of votes received by each list and, second, the degree to which candidates received preference votes from their party's supporters. For example, if a ten-candidate slate wins five seats with roughly 50 percent of the vote, then the five candidates who received the most preference votes are elected.

parliamentary system: A system of executive-legislative relations in which the chief executive is selected by a majority vote in the legislature (which can also remove the chief executive by a majority vote).

patria chica: Literally, "little fatherland." A Spanish term that refers to the relative autonomy and isolation of many landed estates in Latin America during the colonial era and for several decades following independence.

peace-building: A multinational approach to the promotion of peace that tries to end conflicts by monitoring the enforcement of component portions of peace agreements—including political reforms, socioeconomic development programs, and human rights protection. The logic of peace-building saw the creation of new societal dynamics as essential for the resolution of long-running conflicts and the prevention of future violence.

peace-keeping: A multinational approach to the promotion of peace that tries to end conflicts by deploying military forces to enforce cease-fire agreements and peace agreements between combatants.

peace-making: A general term used in international relations to refer to various mechanisms and efforts to resolve both international and internal conflicts. In some multinational contexts, people use the term *peace-making* to refer to a narrower concept: the use of multinational military force to get combatants to stop fighting.

pluralism: A dynamic in interest group politics in which groups form independently and compete among one another. The government interacts with these groups but does not intervene dramatically in their activities.

plurality electoral system: An electoral system in which individual candidates compete for a single seat in a single-member district. The candidate that receives the most votes wins even if no candidate receives a majority.

political refugees: Citizens fleeing their country of nationality because of a well-founded fear of persecution due to their political, religious, or other personal beliefs.

populism: A political dynamic in which leaders attempt to build heterogeneous mass support through a diverse series of criticisms of the status quo. In twentieth-century Latin America, populist movements tended to cultivate supporters through a mix of nationalism, developmentalism, and personal appeal.

pork-barrel politics: A political dynamic in which political leaders cultivate legislative (and popular) support by channeling government money into projects in the districts of legislators who support an executive's programs.

praetorianism: A political dynamic in which the armed forces frequently influence government decisions through the use or threat of force. For U.S. scholar Samuel Huntington, the term takes on a broader meaning and includes societies in which most people—civilians or soldiers—pursue their political agendas through the use or threat of coercion.

presidential system: A system of executive-legislative relations in which the chief executive is elected to a fixed term and there is no guarantee that voters will choose a legislative majority that supports the president's agenda.

rationing: A system in which certain goods are distributed by rights granted by an authority (often the government), not by pricing.

recall election: A special election in which citizens have the opportunity to shorten the mandate of elected officials who were originally elected to a fixed term.

relative poverty: A conceptualization of poverty which categorizes people as poor when they lack the resources needed to enjoy the activities and the living standards customary in their own societies.

reparations: An approach to past human rights violations that provides material benefits to the victims of human rights violations and/or to their families.

Roosevelt Corollary: A term referring to a modification to U.S. foreign policy in the Americas during the years 1904–1929. In the 1800s, the Monroe Doctrine declared that the U.S. opposed the reestablishment of foreign controlled colonies in the Americas as well as the undue influence of nonhemispheric powers. Under the Roosevelt Corollary to the Monroe Doctrine, the U.S. proclaimed that it would deploy military force in the hemisphere in response to disputes with European nations and at times in response to internal disputes within Latin American countries.

royalty: A payment made as a percentage of the value of a good or service. For example, in the petroleum sector of an economy, national governments often claim a royalty on the amount of petroleum extracted from the subsoil of the country.

social policy: Government programs designed to improve individual welfare in areas including education, health care, unemployment insurance, and old-age pensions.

special economic zones: Zones in which companies receive special tariff and/or tax treatment for establishing plants within that specific geographic area.

state building: A concept in political development that refers to efforts to increase the capacity of national governments as well as their ability to exercise control over the geographic territory they claim to govern.

state capitalism: A mixed approach to economic policy in which government intervenes in some sectors while leaving others to market dynamics.

sustainable development: An approach to development that focuses on the sustainability of current patterns of economic activity for future generations.

truth commission: An approach to past human rights violations that calls for an official investigation into human rights violations but does not hold those identified as perpetrators criminally responsible.

value-added tax: A common form of indirect taxation in which a tax is charged on the value-added portion of each transaction from the initial production of a good, to its wholesale exchange, and to its final retail price.

Washington Consensus: A term referring to the resurgence of market capitalist economic ideas from the 1970s onward in criticism of state capitalist economic policies. This resurgence was promoted actively by two intergovernmental financial institutions headquartered in Washington, D.C.—the International Monetary Fund (IMF) and the World Bank.

Index